THE SERMON ON THE MOUNT

THE SERMON ON THE MOUNT

A FOUNDATION FOR UNDERSTANDING

ROBERT A. GUELICH

WORD BOOKS
PUBLISHER
4800 WEST WACO DRIVE
WACO, TEXAS
76703

ISBN 0–8499–0110–3
Library of Congress catalog card number: 81–52521
Printed in the United States of America

First Printing   March 1982
Second Printing   December 1983

To
PROFESSOR GEORGE E. LADD
in retirement
PROFESSOR LEONHARD GOPPELT
in memoriam

CONTENTS

In the commentary, I have made reference to various works by author and a key term or phrase from the title given in full in the Bibliography (p. 423). The text also contains abbreviations for the standard reference works: TDNT = Kittel's *Theological Dictionary of the New Testament;* IDB = *The Interpreter's Dictionary of the Bible* (ed. G. Buttrick); RGG = *Religion in Geschichte und Gegenwart* (3rd ed., ed. K. Galling); Str-B = Strack-Billerbeck's *Kommentar zum Neuen Testament aus Talmud und Midrasch;* Bauer = *Bauer's Greek-English Lexicon of the New Testament and Other Early Christian Literature* (ed. Arndt and Gingrich); LSJ = Lidell, Scott, and Jones's *A Greek-English Lexicon;* BDB = Brown, Driver, and Briggs's *A Hebrew and English Lexicon of the Old Testament;* BDF = Blass, Debrunner, and Funk's *A Greek Grammar of the New Testament and Other Early Christian Literature;* and BDR = Blass, Debrunner, and Rehkopf's *Grammatik des neuentestamentlichen Griechisch.* The abbreviations of biblical and extrabiblical works in the commentary correspond to those adopted in the "Instructions for Contributors" by the *Journal of Biblical Literature* 95 (1976): 330–46.

PREFACE

To undertake the writing of a commentary on the Sermon on the Mount may well reflect an act of hubris more than wisdom. Not only has so much been written about such a relatively brief passage, but the volume of literature itself attests to the magnitude and profundity of this discourse in Matthew's Gospel. Yet the absence of an extensive, critical, exegetical commentary in nearly four decades of biblical studies despite the vast literature on the Sermon provides both an opportunity and a need in current New Testament studies. It is hoped, therefore, that this commentary will help fill this rather surprising lacuna.

The commentary began as a project of interpreting the Sermon on the Mount. Yet it soon became evident that a foundational work on the Sermon and its historical context had to precede a more contemporary treatment of the passage. Consequently, the focus turned to the former in the Notes while offering hints of the latter in the Comments. Since the process of exegesis consists first of determining what the text said in its historical context and then interpreting that content for the present audience, the primary objective of this work has been to lay the foundational basis for understanding the Sermon and hearing its message for today in terms of its historical context.

My fascination with the Sermon on the Mount began during student days with the reading of W. D. Davies's *Setting of the Sermon on the Mount* in a seminar led by Professor George Ladd, and it intensified during my doctoral studies under the guidance of Professor Leonhard Goppelt, studies that focused on Jesus and the Law in Matthew's Gospel. Only those whose lives have been immeasurably enriched by academic and spiritual giants can appreciate my gratitude to these two professors. The first and extremely rough draft of the commentary took shape in a series of lectures at King's College, Aberdeen, in the fall of 1973. Since then students at Luther Theological Seminary and Bethel Theological Seminary of Saint Paul, Minnesota, have been the sounding board for what has become the final draft. To these students, not least of whom being my last class at Bethel Seminary, I offer my sincere thanks.

I am also deeply indebted to the Association of Theological Schools for financial assistance and the Alexander von Humboldt Foundation for a grant that permitted me to spend several months at the University of Tübingen at the invitation of Professor Martin Hengel where the commentary was completed. During this time in Tübingen, it was my privilege and benefit to meet Professor Peter Stuhlmacher, whose discussions were most helpful and encouraging. I am deeply indebted to Mrs. Patricia Wienandt, Senior Editor of Word Books, Publisher, for her invaluable help in preparing this manuscript for publication and to Nancy Wiles Holsey, Assistant in Biblical Studies at Northern Baptist Theological Seminary, for her help in the tedious task of constructing the Indices. Last, but far from least, my appreciation and thanks go to Mrs. Carla Dahl Kregness, whose skill in deciphering an almost unintelligible manuscript, whose patience with the "one more things," and whose gift as secretary and typist made order of chaos.

Reformation Day, 1979

I. INTRODUCTION

The Sermon on the Mount represents one of the most familiar sections of the entire New Testament. Containing such well-known units as the Beatitudes, Love Your Enemies, the Lord's Prayer, the reference to the Birds of the Air and the Lilies of the Field, the prohibition on Judging, the Golden Rule, the reference to the Narrow and Wide Gates, and the parable of the Wise and Foolish Builders, the Sermon addresses the Christian's relationship and conduct toward God and others. Consequently, it has received such varied designations as the Christian Magna Charta, the Christian Manifesto, the Design for Life, the Compendium of Rules for Christian Living, or simply Kingdom Ethics. These designations and others indicate the significance generally attributed to this section of Matthew's Gospel in terms of Christian ethics, a significance often found in the popular identification of Christianity with living "according to the Sermon on the Mount."

Despite its familiarity in its own right, the Sermon belongs integrally to Matthew's Gospel where it occurs in chapters 5–7. Read and interpreted within its Gospel context, numerous other issues arise that go beyond or, rather, lie behind the more practical question of whether or how one can really live "according to the Sermon on the Mount" today. Moving from the primarily ethical considerations, the focus turns to literary, historical, and theological concerns that lie at the foundation of the Sermon, its role in the Gospel, and its relationship to Jesus and his ministry. These questions, though more academic in nature, play a vital role in developing our understanding and subsequent interpretation of the Sermon for today. This Introduction broaches some of these underlying issues in summary fashion as the background and setting for the commentary that follows.

A. A History of Interpretation

No passage of Scripture has received the attention of the Sermon on the Mount. So vast is the literature that a detailed history of interpretation has not been written. And just cataloguing the books, articles, and sermons dealing with parts or all of the Sermon would almost be prohibitive in time and energy. Three rather recent works do offer an overview from different perspectives of some of the major works on the Sermon. Harvey McArthur, in chapter 4 of his *Understanding the Sermon on the Mount,* arranges the various Sermon approaches through the centuries under twelve headings, and the author sets his own interpretation of the various issues raised by the Sermon against the background of previous viewpoints. Warren Kissinger's *The Sermon on the Mount* traces the use of the Sermon by briefly sketching various treatments of the Sermon, from the Didache to W. D. Davies' *Setting of the Sermon on the Mount,* including two significant Jewish interpretations, before setting forth Harold Row's extensive—if not exhaustive—bibliography on the Sermon. Ursula Berner's *Die Bergpredigt* focuses on the twentieth-century works divided according to the theological and historical-critical approaches to the Sermon. By offering the very limited sketch that follows, we seek only to gain some historical perspective for the so-called "problem" of the Sermon on the Mount, which consists theologically of how one is to understand the Sermon and practically of how one is to apply the Sermon to everyday living.

1. The Pre-Reformation Period

According to Kissinger (*Sermon,* 6), "Matthew 5–7 [appears] more frequently than any other three chapters in the entire Bible" in the Ante-Nicene writings. From the Didache to Chrysostom, the Sermon offered, on the one hand, a classical expression of Christian ethics, the guide for Christian conduct, with little or no question about how such "impossible" demands could be carried out in an immoral world. On the other hand, the Sermon material, especially 5:17–48, became a major apologetic basis for countering the theological heresy from Marcion to the Manichaeans that interpreted Jesus and the New Testament against a radical break with Judaism and the Old Testament. Thus, the theological problem of how Jesus' teaching related to the Law in particular and the Old Testament in general emerges from the beginning—a question which, as we shall see in the Commentary, has its roots in the tradition underlying 5:17–19.

The first pre-Reformation commentary on the Sermon comes from the pen of *Augustine,* the theological giant of the fourth century. He not only wrote in two volumes what may have been the first complete commentary on the Sermon as such *(De Sermone Domini in Monte),* but he may also have been the first to refer to Matthew 5–7 as the "Sermon on the Mount." As did his predecessors, Augustine viewed the Sermon to be "the perfect measure of the Christian life" and "filled with all the precepts by which the Christian life is formed." For him the Sermon applied to all Christians and was without question applicable to life. But Augustine's treatment also exposes one of the major theological tensions of the Sermon: Jesus' demands as compared to those of the Law. He begins his commentary by noting the significance of the "mountain" in terms of Jesus giving "the greater precepts of righteousness" in contrast to the "lesser" which God had "given to the Jews." Yet in his *Reply to Faustus* (a leading Manichaean), Augustine counters with six different ways in which Jesus "fulfills" the Law and thus demonstrates that the old and new are integrally related. This difference in emphasis within Augustine's writings has led to differences of opinion regarding his understanding of how Jesus' teaching related to the Mosaic Law and once again poses one of the fundamental theological questions of the Sermon itself.

The most significant development in the interpretation of the Sermon in the years between Augustine and the Reformation falls into the more practical category of how the Sermon's demands apply to the believer. *Aquinas* set the tone which is still heard in some circles today by distinguishing between "precepts" and "evangelical counsels." In his *Summa* (part 2.1, quest. 108, art. 4) Aquinas stated unequivocally: "The difference between a counsel and a commandment is that a commandment implies obligation, whereas a counsel is left to the option of the one to whom it is given." He added, "In the New Law, which is the law of liberty, counsels are added to the commandments. . . . We must understand the commandments of the New Law to have been given about matters that are necessary to gain the end of eternal bliss, to which the New Law brings us forthwith: but that the counsels are about matters that render the gaining of this end more assured and expeditious. . . ." This bifurcation between precepts or commandments and evangelical counsels has provided the moral theological basis for applying the Sermon in Roman Catholic theology. Theologically, the demands of the New Law have clearly become "necessary" for gaining the "end of eternal bliss" while the "counsels" only provide optional aids in gaining that end.

2. The Reformation Period

With the dawn of the Reformation, three perspectives emerge, two of which are based on the theological works of Luther and Calvin respectively, and the third on a movement more than on a particular theologian. The emerging "Lutheran," "Calvinist," and "Anabaptist" understandings of the Sermon include crucial theological and practical moments that have influenced the interpretation of the Sermon to the present time.

Martin Luther's primary work on the Sermon consisted of a series of sermons that later became a commentary. Much of his thought took shape in the polemics against the "papists" on the one side and the "enthusiasts" or Anabaptists on the other. In countering the "enthusiasts," Luther dealt with the practical aspects of the Sermon's application to everyday life. He charged the "schismatics" with confusing the "secular" and the "spiritual," the "kingdom of Christ" and the "kingdom of the world," by seeking to implement the Sermon's demands so rigorously that they had to withdraw from worldly affairs. In his "two-kingdom" approach, Luther further distinguished between one's "office" and one's "person." The former represents the God-ordained order for the kingdom of this world, the latter one's "heart" or "spiritual" relationship to God and others. Thus, the Sermon's demands are to be carried out continually within the Christian's "heart" even if the "office" demands conduct to the contrary. For example, as a soldier, lawyer, or businessman, one must carry out the duties commensurate with one's "office"; while not desiring to do anyone harm, one may suffer and grieve for others in one's heart. Furthermore, apart from one's "office," the Christian must follow Jesus' teaching in personal relationships. Thus the Sermon's demands apply to all Christians in all of life.

In his Postscript to the Sermon, Luther addressed the theological question raised by the "papists," who saw the obedience of the Sermon as part of a pattern of "works of righteousness." Since, for Luther, grace and works were antithetical, he insisted that the Sermon addressed those who were already Christians and in whose lives grace was at work producing the fruits of the Sermon. Recognizing the obvious presence of merit-and-reward motifs within the Sermon, he designated these passages as promises intended to "console" the believer in a life of suffering rather than as "the foundation" for one's salvation. Thus, the theological issue for Luther consisted above all in the conflict of the doctrine of works and the doctrine of justification by faith alone. For him the Sermon did not instruct one on becoming a Christian through "works of righteousness" but on being a Christian whose life produced by God's grace the corresponding works and fruit.

For *John Calvin,* whose treatment of the Sermon must be extrapolated from his theological compendium of the *Institutes* and his exegetical *Commentary on a Harmony of the Evangelists, Matthew, Mark and Luke,* the theological question had largely to do with the relationship of Jesus' demands to the Law in particular and the Old Testament in general. In the *Institutes* he went to considerable lengths to deny that Christ was another Moses or even added to the Law. Rather, as the Law's "expounder," Jesus freed it (e.g., Matt 5:21–48) from the falsehoods of the Pharisees "who focused on the external obedience to the Law." For Calvin, the Law—meaning the Old Testament with its commandments and promises—and the Gospel—meaning the New Testament message of salvation and its demands—were integrally bound by an "inviolable . . . sacred tie" seen in the confirmation of the "gospel's authority" by the "fulfillment of the Law."

Consequently, Calvin held no brief for the "schoolmen" of the Roman Catholic interpretations, who distinguished between "optional counsels" and necessary commandments, since all of Christ's demands applied to all believers. But he also took issue with the Anabaptists because of their rigorous application of the Sermon without regard to its larger context of Scripture. Using his hermeneutical method of *analogia fidei,* Calvin argued that the prohibition of all oaths, judging, and nonresistance represented a failure to perceive the intent behind these particular demands as determined by the larger Scriptural context. For example, in his *Commentary* on Matt 5:33–37 he noted that the prohibition of oaths "meant nothing more than this, that all oaths are unlawful, which in any way abuse or profane the sacred name of God. . . ." He then supported his conclusion by the positive use and teaching of Scripture elsewhere regarding oaths. Thus, for Calvin, the applicability of the Sermon's demands involved a hermeneutical concern stemming from the fundamental, theological question regarding Jesus' demand and its relationship to the Law and the Old Testament promise.

The *Anabaptists* represented a complex mixture of various radical groups whose common denominator included, above all, believer's baptism and a rigorous attempt to follow Jesus' teaching, especially as found in the Sermon. This led to the avoidance of the use of oaths, personal or military force, legal justice, and even at times the possession of personal property. Such a posture caused them inevitably to withdraw from political and social life and led to the strict separation of church and state.

The Anabaptists recognized the state as such to be a God-ordained order within the world, but they left its administration to those of this world. For the Christians, the Sermon on the Mount was the Magna Charta.

Thus we have three approaches to the Sermon, with their various theological implications, each seeking in a distinctive manner to apply the Sermon to life. For some, this meant perceiving life as being divided into two compartments, in only one of which could and must one carry out the Sermon's demands. This alternative runs the risk of "compartmentalization" and cultural compromise. For others, the secular and the sacred were continuous, and the Sermon's demands understood against the whole of Scripture applied to all believers and for all areas of life. This alternative runs the risk of casuistry and avoidance of the "impractical." For still others, the secular and the sacred were separate because of the radical nature of discipleship and the evil character of the world, with discipleship meaning the ordering of all life according to the Sermon's demands. This alternative runs the risk of "isolationism" and utopian irrelevancy. All three approaches have left their indelible marks on the Protestant Church's understanding of the Sermon.

3. The Post-Reformation Period

The contemporary scene reflects even more complexity than that of the Reformation. Certainly the prevailing force in the interpretation of the Sermon stems from the Enlightenment and the ensuing critical approach to biblical exegesis. There remain the theological questions about the relationship of Jesus and his demands to the Old Testament and the Law, works and grace, the nature of discipleship, church and state, and the often overlapping practical questions about how these demands were intended to be carried out and by whom. In recent years, historical questions about the background, development, and meaning of the Sermon materials in Matthew's Gospel, the primitive church, and Jesus' ministry have moved to the fore, eventually dominating the current Sermon studies.

During this period, the interpretations of the Sermon have ranged between two extremes. At one extreme are Tolstoi and the Christian Marxists, for whom the Sermon's revolutionary demands are to be lived out within society even more radically than advocated by the Anabaptists. At the other extreme is the earlier American Dispensationalism which relegated the Sermon to the millennial Kingdom, leaving a historical dichotomy between the present and the future more sharply drawn than

Luther's personal dichotomy between the secular and the spiritual. At various points along this spectrum fall the numerous other interpretations such as a *"Gesinnungsethik,"* an "interim ethic," an "ethicized" ideal, a call to repentance, and the "cost of discipleship."

In the midst of the nineteenth-century, Liberal quest for the historical Jesus, the Sermon survived fairly intact as a central part of Jesus' ethical teaching. Yet these demands, while containing the epitome of Christian ethics in the love commandment (Harnack, *What Is Christianity?*), confronted one on the basis of a supposedly outmoded world-view. This situation, according to one of Liberalism's most influential voices, *Wilhelm Herrmann* (*Ethik* and *Essays on the Social Gospel*), left the alternatives of disregarding the demands as being irrelevant, of following them blindly and distorting Jesus' intention, or of understanding them to be a calling for a proper inner "attitude" or "disposition" *(Gesinnung)* in keeping with the "effulgence of Jesus' mind" that frees one to serve rather than binding one to legal maxims. In this way one sought even within the Sermon to remove the "husk" to get at the "kernel."

With the works of *Albert Schweitzer* came not only the demise of the old Liberal quest for the historical Jesus but also a different approach to Gospel studies based on the history of religions. By viewing Jesus through the lenses of the first century rather than the philosophical prism of the nineteenth century, one could see that the Liberal's "husk" of the supposedly outmoded world-view contained part of the "kernel" of Jesus' eschatological perspective of history's imminent apocalyptic end. The Sermon expresses demands for the "new moral conduct" from the disciples during the interim in preparation for and commensurate with the coming of the Kingdom. In other words, the "ethics of the Sermon on the Mount is [*sic*] interim ethics" that "make one meet for the kingdom of God" (*The Mystery of the Kingdom of God*, 97). By confronting them during his ministry with radical moral demands, Jesus sought to lead his disciples to "repentance unto the kingdom of God" and "possession of a character morally renovated." Thus while Schweitzer demonstrated the fallacy of the Liberal interpretation that had ignored the essential eschatological ingredient, he himself was left with an ethic based on Jesus' culturally conditioned misconception of history, "interim ethics" without an "interim."

Martin Dibelius, in a series of lectures at Yale University that were later published as *The Sermon on the Mount,* introduced yet another exegetical method into the study of the Sermon by applying his pioneering work in New Testament form criticism to this material. Recognizing the eschatological element in Jesus' ministry, as Schweitzer and others had noted, Dibelius explained the Sermon's radical demands in terms of Jesus' own disregard for the "circumstances of our life and the conditions of the world" in his anticipation of the "coming world, the Kingdom of Heaven." Jesus set forth in his teaching the "absolute will of God" that intended to transform humanity for the coming of the Kingdom. The Sermon's demands were not intended to become a new law or to offer a new ethic for an "interim" or any other period, but to reveal "God's will" as "signs of the Kingdom of Heaven" in Jesus' earthly ministry.

After Easter, however, the Church collected and shaped Jesus' sayings and made them into a "rule of conduct for the Christian community." The "will of God" thus became "ethicized" through the community's needs for paranetic, or ethical, instruction and its use of the sayings as ethical standards. The "Sermon," never preached as such by Jesus, became the "Sermon" when the various units of tradition stemming from Jesus' ministry were so arranged by the Church as to address their needs as the "law which the heavenly Lord has given." Recognizing that development, one can and must hear the Sermon's demand for what it was in Jesus' ministry, namely, a revelation of God's will for us to "be" rather than to "do." By hearing the will of God and being "transformed," each is then to live responsibly before God and thus be a "sign of the Kingdom" in the world. Thus in Dibelius we discover the tension between Jesus' demand and that of the reworked tradition. This tension becomes even more intense when one adds the redactional input of the evangelist as found in most treatments of Matthew's Sermon today.

Dibelius's work postdated the works of his contemporaries Carl Stange, Gerhard Kittel, and Hans Windisch. Yet significant parallels exist between his work and their quite diverse interpretations. *Carl Stange's* "Zur Ethik der Bergpredigt" (*ZST* 2 [1924–25] 37–74), and *Gerhard Kittel's* "Die Bergpredigt und die Ethik des Judentums" (*ZST* 2 [1924–25] 555–94), concur with Dibelius in perceiving Jesus' demands to set forth God's will that was not expected to be literally fulfilled. In fact, these demands cannot be fulfilled, according to Stange and Kittel. Such absolute and radical demands lie beyond human capabilities, leaving one helpless before the impracticable. Since the commands, however, impose obligation as expressions of God's will and yet remain beyond one's capacity to obey, one responds according to the Sermon's intent by becoming aware of sin and failure and turning to God in repentance and confession (Stange) and thereby experiencing the paradox of God's judgment and acceptance through the cross of Christ (Kittel). In contrast to Dibelius's later work, however, both Stange and Kittel considered the Sermon's demands and Jesus' demands to be one and the same. The Sermon was never intended, therefore, to supply a Christian "ethic" of obedience for the Church post-Easter.

By contrast, *Hans Windisch,* in his pivotal work on *The Meaning of the Sermon on the Mount,* took most of his predecessors, including Stange and Kittel, to task for presupposing a "spiritual orientation" that predetermined the ultimate judgment each passed on the Gospel sayings. He sought to distinguish, therefore, between a "theological exegesis" and a "historical exegesis," with the latter supplying the basis for the former. He then called for a more consistent historical exegesis that recognized the Sermon to be a collection of commandments given by Jesus, the obedience to which was the basis for salvation. In this regard Windisch agreed with Dibelius's later view that the Sermon's commandments, as understood by the Church, were intended and understood to be practicable as conditions for salvation. Thus, while Stange and Kittel stood closer to Dibelius's understanding of the sayings in Jesus' ministry, Windisch concurred with Dibelius's view of the Church's usage of the Sermon. Although Windisch's interpretation has not held for Jesus as much as for the community, his distinction between theological exegesis and historical exegesis has become so complete that, with few exceptions, all subsequent works on the Sermon have fallen into the latter category.

One of the better-known treatments of the Sermon stems from the same period of time as that of Dibelius and Windisch, but it stands apart from them in approach as well as conclusions. Its popularity, and thus significance, doubtless owes much to the character and times of the writer. *Dietrich Bonhoeffer's Cost of Discipleship* contains three works on the nature of discipleship, the second being his exposition on the Sermon on the Mount. Dispensing with the critical discussions that had preoccupied other interpretations, Bonhoeffer approached the Sermon as a concrete expression of discipleship that required "doing" rather than interpreting. Thus, in contrast to his times and since, his primary concern was the "practical" rather than the "theological" dimension of the Sermon studies. His exposition so strongly emphasizes the life and conduct of the Christian as set forth in the Sermon by Jesus that he could, in a manner somewhat related to Windisch's view of Jesus' demands, be accused of surrendering his Lutheran heritage of *sola fide* for salvation by works of obedience. But one can only charge Bonhoeffer with such an understanding by ignoring the underlying christological basis of the Sermon and the balanced tension between faith and works throughout his treatment of the text.

Since the writing of these works—indeed, since the beginning of the 1940s—only two major commentaries have appeared, the lesser-known works *Die Bergpredigt Jesu* by Thaddeus Soiron, and *Die Bergpredigt* by Josef Staudinger, both Catholic scholars. Soiron's study of 1940 represents the last extensive critical exegetical and theological commentary on the Sermon. Meanwhile, numerous articles have appeared in journals on parts or all of the Sermon as well as in various biblical and theological dictionaries and encyclopedias. Several limited treatments of the Sermon have also emerged, such as A. M. Hunter's *A Pattern for Life,* Joachim Jeremias's *The Sermon on the Mount,* Leonhard Goppelt's *Die Bergpredigt und die Wirklichkeit dieser Welt,* and the brief commentaries *Die Auslegung der Bergpredigt* by Georg Eichholz and *Botschaft der Bergpredigt* by Gerhard Schneider. In addition to Hans-Theo Wrege's examination of the history of the tradition in *Die Überlieferungsgeschichte der Bergpredigt,* two major studies on special themes have become standard works, W. D. Davies's *The Setting of the Sermon on the Mount,* a discussion of the background of the Sermon in its various settings, and Jacques Dupont's three-volume work on the literary composition of the Sermon in Matthew and Luke, *Les Béatitudes.*

In the limited survey above, as well as in the commentary that follows, no attempt has been made to deal exhaustively with the literature, a task that lies beyond the confines of this work. Much can be gained in this regard by the use of Kissinger's and Berner's works, cited above. Furthermore, the literature cited in the commentary primarily represents contemporary discussions appearing in the more recent commentaries and articles, since they most generally raise the critical questions under consideration. This procedure in no way intends to pass judgment on the great value or relevance of earlier literature but rather to focus primarily on the current debate in the Sermon studies. The same holds true for the many nontechnical homiletical studies on the Sermon not cited in the commentary, the most popular of which in English have been Martin Lloyd-Jones's *Studies in the Sermon on the Mount,* James Boice's *The Sermon on the Mount,* and Myron Augsburger's *The Expanded Life: The Sermon on the Mount for Today.*

B. A Critical, Historical Commentary

The designation *critical, historical* stands in deliberate contrast to *historical-critical*, since the latter, supposedly denoting a methodology, more often connotes a school of thought. The historical-critical school set out to examine the Scriptures "purely historically" without recognizing that the controlling influence of a nineteenth-century positivistic approach to history had polluted their "pure history" from the outset. The inevitable result was an overly skeptical treatment of the Scriptures, a cul-de-sac in biblical interpretation apart from a theological overlay often foreign to the text, and a denial of the Scriptures' implicit and explicit claim to be the normative revelation of God's word and deeds (see Stuhlmacher, *Historical Criticism*).

While one may repudiate the historical-critical as a "school" of thought, no one who claims that God has chosen to reveal himself in and through history can minimize the contribution of historical criticism to the study of Scripture. If indeed the Scriptures come as God's revelation given to us in history through historical men, circumstances, and means, then one needs all of the critical tools available to discern the content of that Word. Use of the critical tools simply declares that one desires to read and understand the biblical text in terms of its original intent and context, since to fail to understand its intent and to remove it from its historical context only heightens the probability of distortion, despite the best of intentions.

Consequently, this commentary offers a *critical* exegesis in that it makes use of the literary and historical critical tools including text, source, form, tradition, redaction, and structural criticism (see Ladd, *Criticism*). In so doing I recognize first that for many to whom the Scriptures are vital the use of these critical tools has historically been more "destructive" than "constructive." But one need not discard the tool because of its abuse. Like any other "tool," these of literary and historical criticism are basically neutral and often reflect the tendencies of the person using them. Thus one must remain aware both of one's starting point and one's purpose of facilitating the discernment of the intent and context of the biblical text. In using these tools I recognize secondly that they, like all tools, have their limitations. They have been and can still be improved. But they have been refined to the extent that they offer the best instruments to date in exegeting the text.

At the same time, this work represents a *historical* commentary—

historical in the sense that its primary focus falls on the background and meaning of the Sermon for the evangelist and his audience. By historical, I do not mean a history of the Sermon's interpretation, although the impact of the Sermon and its interpretation through the ages *(Wirkungsgeschichte)* has great value for and is an important ingredient in our understanding the text for today. By historical, I do not mean historical in contrast to theological exegesis, since I view these two elements as so integrally related that to remove the one from the other would be like trying to separate Siamese twins who share the same heart. Rather, I have chosen to concentrate my energies primarily on the Sermon in its historical setting of Matthew's Gospel because of my conviction that the written text expressed God's Word that normatively shapes the interpretation and application of the Sermon today. The ultimate objective of the literary and historical questions lies in understanding the Sermon in Matthew's Gospel, not in the pre-Matthean tradition nor in the numerous interpretations in church history except to the degree that these contribute to the primary objective.

C. Matthew and the Sermon on the Mount

In seeking to understand and interpret the Sermon on the Mount in its Matthean setting, one must begin with the Gospel as a literary genre, its author and audience.

1. The Gospels

The Gospels as a literary genre present their own set of questions today. Perhaps an analogy drawn from another medium will illustrate and explain the options. Historically and for a significant number of contemporaries—not least of whom is the majority of lay readers—the Gospels approximate a *snapshot,* an untouched photographlike reproduction of things as they were, with a direct correspondence between what one sees and what actually was. For such, the Gospel in general and the Sermon in particular simply reproduce word for word (thus the red-letter editions of the Gospels) and deed for deed Jesus' ministry. The difference in the multiple accounts merely indicates a difference in location and/or camera angle.

A more radical form of Gospel studies in recent decades offers the opposite alternative. This approach has treated the Gospels as bearing a resemblance to *abstract paintings* that depict the artist's perceptions more than the events themselves and actively involve the reader's or observer's contribution in understanding the final product. The correspondence between the product and the original object depicted remains oblique, making a reconstruction of the underlying object all but impossible historically and illegitimate artistically, in view of the artist's intention. For such writers, the Gospel and the Sermon, consequently, bear little resemblance to Jesus' earthly ministry, since they express and intended to express the more immediate needs and perceptions of the early community and the evangelists.

The common designation of the former as the uncritical and the latter as the critical approach to Gospel studies implies an either/or situation. Fortunately, there is a third option that strikes a medium between the two alternatives and more adequately accounts for the evidence. Rather than providing us a snapshot or an abstract painting, the Gospels as a genre come much closer to serving as a *portrait* of Jesus and his ministry. A portrait can vary between a very precise reproduction that closely corresponds with the object as seen and a very vague reproduction that seeks to convey more an impression than a direct image. Consequently, by designating the Gospels as portraits of Jesus and his ministry, we must seek to determine the degree of correspondence between Jesus' ministry and each Gospel's portrait. This is essentially a historical question.

Matthew's Gospel and the Sermon in particular reflect the portrait artist's freedom to modulate, modify, relocate, rearrange, restructure, and restate as exercised by the community in the traditional process and by the evangelist's redaction. Yet despite the first evangelist's lack of concern for the finer details such as the precise place, time, and verbatim quotation of the tradition, his portrait does closely correspond to Jesus' ministry, particularly as seen in the Sermon. Indeed, as we shall see, the evangelist's primary intention was to portray who Jesus was as seen in his earthly ministry and in his message as expressed in the Sermon. Therefore, the Sermon on the Mount must be understood and interpreted, above all, in terms of its role in Matthew's christological portrait, a theme to which we shall return below.

2. The Author and Audience

Who was or is "Matthew"? Without desiring to enter into the involved discussion about the authorship of the first Gospel, the name *Matthew*

as used in this commentary merely denotes the common traditional designation of the Gospel's author. The Gospel itself, of course, comes to
us as an anonymous document in spite of the early church's assignment
of it to the apostle Matthew, the former tax collector. From the evangelist's writing, we can deduce that he was clearly familiar with Jewish
rabbinic circles and customs, while his use of Greek and especially his
deliberate choice at times to use the Septuagint (LXX) indicates his
familiarity with "hellenistic" Judaism. His theological interests reflect
a keen awareness of the Old Testament Scriptures, a profound understanding of Jesus' ministry, and a deep concern for the current needs
and dangers of his own community. As will be seen, he played a much
more active literary role in writing the Gospel than simply one of compil-
ing an account by using "scissors and paste."

As to the audience, numerous indications within the Sermon point
to a community of believers with a strong Jewish background and setting.
Yet the references to persecution and suffering, the deliberate contrast
with the "scribes and Pharisees" and "hypocrites," and the use of the
Old Testament passages and types suggest an apologetic and polemical
tone commensurate with a community that found itself separated from
and at odds with a Jewish community that now stood under the judgment
of having rejected Jesus Messiah and his followers. This break had left
its wounds that were still open and vulnerable.

A second front also appears within the Sermon that was related to
the first but claiming to be one with Matthew's community. This threat
consisted of a strict Jewish-Christian attempt to maintain the Law of
Moses by using the Jesus tradition as its basis and doubtless raised questions anew regarding the nature of the gospel and the Gentile mission.
This impulse may have resulted from the flight of the Jewish-Christians
from Jerusalem after the fall of that city in A.D. 67–70, a flight that
took the Jerusalem Christians into the surrounding environs of Syria
where their presence in a community such as Matthew's created a renais-
sance of earlier questions not unlike those of the Pauline mission. Their
influence came most of all from their Jesus tradition, and their impact
can be seen in the rigor of the Didache. Matthew saw their presence
as a threat so serious that he reshaped their Jesus tradition (e.g., 5:17–
19) to counter and warn his community about these "false prophets"
(7:15–23). Thus the Sermon must be read within a dual context of Judaism
and a rigorous Jewish-Christianity.

At the same time, no signs of any particularism appear within the
Sermon to indicate a community closed to a Gentile mission. Rather,

the Gospel addresses a community that doubtless consisted of Gentiles as well as of Jews. The Sermon, therefore, could and did address both as the new people of God for whom, since Easter, the distinction of Jew and Gentile had no more relevance (e.g., 28:18–20). The Sermon portrayed Jesus as the Messiah and the presence of the age of salvation when God's will would be revealed to all nations (e.g., 4:12–17).

3. The Sermon in Matthew

The Sermon in Matthew belongs to a series of discourses that form constituent elements of the first Gospel. Each discourse reflects considerable redactional activity by the evangelist and consequently plays an important role in Matthew's portrait of Jesus and his earthly ministry. Yet the immensity and magnificence of the Sermon's content has often led to its isolation and treatment separate from the evangelist's larger setting in his Gospel. For most, therefore, the Sermon has primarily offered a compendium of Christian ethics, sometimes even for those who take the evangelist's role in shaping the material more seriously.

The Sermon, like the Gospel in which it is found, stands as a complex entity. In order to do justice to this complexity in the evangelist's shaping of the material, one can divide the following summary into three interrelated categories of christology, ecclesiology, and eschatology. Above all else, the Sermon on the Mount makes a *christological* statement. Support for such a bald assertion must and will follow in the commentary. But this primary motif stands out first in the general setting of the Sermon within the complex of Matthew 5–9 that sets forth Jesus as the Messiah. The introduction of 4:23–25 and the transitional conclusion of 9:35, each being clearly redactional, enclose Jesus' ministry of word and deed in capsule form. This christological motif stands out secondly in the redactional alignment of the initial Beatitudes with Isaiah 61, the explicit redactional statement regarding Jesus' coming and the Scriptures in Matt 5:17–18, the very nature of the demands in 5:21—7:12 predicated on the person and word of Jesus, and the redactional response by the crowds in the epilogue of 7:28–29 (cf. 9:33). The basic content of the Sermon's christological statement consists in Jesus Messiah as the one whose coming fulfills the Old Testament promise for the coming of the age of salvation, the coming into history of the Kingdom of Heaven. In short, the Sermon's christology corresponds to the Gospel's christology, which is primarily a "fulfillment christology."

Within this christology the question of Jesus and the Law arose inevitably for Matthew's audience, set against Jewish opposition on the outside and faced with a rigorous Jewish-Christian contingent on the inside. From Augustine to the present, this issue has not only dominated the theological discussion of the Sermon but has also divided most interpreters into one of two groups. On the one hand, Jesus stands in continuity with the Mosaic Law as the one who ultimately "fulfills" it by bringing its true meaning to expression through his demands and actions. In other words, in Matthew's christology Jesus comes as the interpreter of the Law, regardless of the various ways this role of interpreter has been depicted in its scholarly representations. On the other hand, Jesus stands in stark discontinuity with the Mosaic Law as the one whose demands transcend and even set aside the Mosaic Law. In other words, in Matthew's christology Jesus comes as the bringer of a new law, a second Moses. Both alternatives stated in these or similar ways fail to perceive the basic thrust of Matthew's christology and consequently distort the evangelist's portrait by emphasizing one part of the Sermon (5:17–19) at the expense of another (5:21–48). Matthew neither viewed Jesus as the New Moses or a lawgiver as such, nor did he view the demands of 5:21–48 as supplying an interpretation of the Mosaic Law.

Rather, seen in terms of Matthew's "fulfillment christology," Jesus came to fulfill the Old Testament prophetic expectations by announcing and effecting the Kingdom of Heaven in history. Thus Jesus' demands reflect the prophetic expectation, for example, of Isa 2:2–4; Micah 4:1–4; Jer 31:31–34, and Ezek 20:35–36 (cf. 40–44); 36:24–28, when God's will would be revealed and his commandments would have a totally different starting point in contrast to those of the Mosaic Law of Sinai. The basis of Jesus' demands lies in the new relationship which God is establishing with his own through Jesus' ministry. Jesus came bringing not a new law but a new covenant through which God was at work forgiving sins (e.g., 26:28; cf. Mark 14:24) and offering reconciliation to and among his own. The conduct, therefore, demanded in the Sermon becomes indicative of one's relationship with the Father, the presence of God's sovereign rule in one's life. Like fruit from a "good tree," this conduct was not optional but inherent to true discipleship because of what God was doing for his own through Jesus Messiah. In other words, the Sermon's imperatives must always be read in terms of the christological indicatives of the Sermon's setting, the Beatitudes, and the explicit prologue to the demands of 5:20—7:12 in 5:17–18.

But what about the so-called Mosaic Law? Matthew does not directly address this subject in a Pauline fashion. The Law offers the counterpart to Jesus' teaching in 5:21–48, 15:1–20, and the divorce pericope of 19:3–9. Yet 5:18 suggests that the Law remains in force until "heaven and earth pass away" and 23:2–3, 23 imply its binding force. Perhaps two observations at the outset will suffice. First, Jesus' demand definitely demonstrates the inadequacy of the Mosaic Law in expressing the will of the Father for the age of salvation. To this extent, Jesus' coming brought an end to the Law as seen in the Antitheses and in 5:18 (cf. "until all things come to pass"). God offers to his own a new starting point in relationship with himself and with others. Second, this expression of the Father's will apart from and even in contrast to the Mosaic Law did not abrogate the Law as such. One was free to keep the Law— indeed, needed to keep the Law—to the extent that it expressed conduct in keeping with the Father's will as revealed through Jesus Messiah. Not only does such a perspective appear in Jesus' own ministry in reference to the Law and in Paul's practice when moving between Jewish and Gentile Christians, but such a perspective permitted an integrated community of Jew and Gentile believers to live together with different life styles until threatened by a legalistic or libertine extreme. In that event, Jesus' ministry and demand became the ultimate criterion.

Since for Matthew Jesus came as the Messiah who fulfilled the prophet's expectation through his ministry, the corresponding gathering of a "messianic community" took shape in the persons of those who responded in faith and followed Jesus. Under *ecclesiology* we include the community that formed the people of God, its signs and conduct. The coming of Jesus Messiah meant reconciliation and salvation for God's people (e.g., Isa 61; Jer 31:31; Ezek 36:24–28). Therefore, the very existence of the community around Jesus and its style of life bore witness to Jesus as the Messiah (5:13–16). In Jesus' earthly ministry, the twelve disciples formed the nucleus of this new people of the end times and included those who came to Jesus recognizing that God was at work in him on their behalf and willing to entrust themselves to him for his acceptance and help. Matthew never "labels" the community of believers as the "new" or "true Israel." Rather, he permits them to gain their profile in contrast to the uncommitted crowds and the self-righteous religious leaders called the "scribes and Pharisees," and "hypocrites."

For the Sermon, the composition of this community lies in the subjects of the Beatitudes. Jesus announces his eschatological blessings to those who stand before God empty-handed and destitute, who seek from him a new relationship with God as well as with others, who come open to God's mercy and forgiveness with integrity, and who desire to experience and establish *shalom* (5:3–9). Such ones stood at odds, as did their Lord, with their contemporaries, and the cost was high (5:10–12). But they had been called out to become "the salt of the earth" (5:13), and through them as the "light of the world" God revealed himself to a world lost in darkness (5:14–15). The promises for Israel's role appropriate to the age of salvation were now being applied to the disciples. Like Zion, they were a "city set on a hill"; like Israel, they were a "light" to the nations through their "good deeds" that brought "glory to the Father" (5:14–16).

But the evangelist warns that true discipleship involved conduct commensurate with the new relationship offered by God to his own. This conduct is simultaneously the "good deeds" that bring glory to the Father (5:16), the "greater righteousness" (5:20), the "good fruit" (7:16–20), and the doing of the "Father's will" (7:21). More specifically, the corresponding conduct finds its illustration in the demands of 5:21—7:12 that point to the narrow gate and constricted way (7:13–14) of Jesus' own teaching (7:24, 26). At this point, the *ethics* of the Sermon on the Mount enter the portrait. If Jesus' demands in the Sermon were indicative of the presence of the age of salvation and represented a new starting point in one's relationship with the Father (6:1—7:12) as well as with one another (5:21–48), how did they pertain to the disciples? Were they understood by the evangelist to be the conditions for discipleship, the minimum requirements for entrance into the Kingdom? Repeatedly, from the Didache to the present, one finds the answer to this question is yes. And this affirmative response gains support by the sharp renunciation of the "righteousness of the scribes and Pharisees" as inadequate and the demand for a "greater righteousness" (5:20) synonymous with entrance through the narrow gate and constricted way (7:13–14) of doing the "Father's will" (7:21) as found in "these words" of the Sermon (7:24). Matthew indeed appears to have moved considerably down the road toward a "Christian rabbinate" in his portrait of Jesus.

Yet the Sermon's demands do not nor did they ever intend to express a new legalism by which one was guaranteed entrance into the Kingdom. This false impression stems from a failure to perceive these demands as part of Matthew's basically christological portrait in the Sermon. To be sure, such conduct is declared necessary for entrance into the Kingdom (e.g., 5:20; 7:13–14, 21–23, 24–27), but its basis lies in the person of Jesus Messiah and the new relationship which God is establishing for his own through Jesus' ministry. This relationship inherent to the age of salvation is offered to those who respond in total surrender to the

Father through response to Jesus Messiah in whom the Father is at work establishing his sovereign rule on earth. The conduct demanded represents the "good fruit" of discipleship, not the basis for or the means to achieving discipleship. Jesus does not pronounce as blessed those who obey his words or do the will of the Father but those who stand as empty-handed, desperate, those hungering and thirsting for a right relationship with the Father and others. Accompanying that blessing comes God's response with the enablement to live accordingly. Therefore, a life devoid of the conduct demanded reveals a life devoid of any evidence of the new age, the presence of the Kingdom, and such a life results in exclusion from the future Kingdom regardless of one's claims and actions (7:21–23).

By setting forth Jesus' demands as prerequisites for the Kingdom, the evangelist accomplished two objectives. First, he used Jesus' demands to show the inadequacy of a "righteousness" measured by the keeping of the Mosaic Law (5:20–48). Such a usage most likely stemmed from Jesus' own ministry to the "righteous" of his day. For Matthew, these demands, addressed to the disciples, warned against any false sense of security before God based on anything less than the new relationship which he demanded and offered through Jesus Messiah (7:13–27). Confronted by the humanly impossible demands of 5:21—7:12, one turns again to God in destitution and with empty hands in search of the right relationship with God and others. The Beatitudes assure such ones of God's acceptance and blessing. Perhaps this sense of God's acceptance and forgiveness underlies the evangelist's strong emphasis on mercy and forgiveness in his Gospel (e.g., 5:7; 6:12, 14–15; 18:23–35; 26:28). Second, he used Jesus' demands as an indication of the presence of the age of salvation, calling the disciples to live commensurately with that reality as the salt of the earth, the light of the world, and warning that failure to do so was like building one's house on the sand. To recognize one's failure is not enough; one must also live and bear fruit in keeping with the presence of the Kingdom.

This dual function of the demands stands in an unresolved tension in Matthew's Sermon. Whereas Paul seems to have resolved the issue with greater emphasis on the former—particularly in view of Jesus' death and resurrection—and James, in terms of the latter, Matthew, perhaps because of the tradition which he faithfully followed and because of his more strongly Jewish-oriented constituency, never resolved the tension that confronts every believer. In any event, for Matthew, apart from the person and ministry of Jesus Messiah who brings about the presence of the age of salvation, the Sermon's demands would be absurd. The latter conditions the former even when left theologically unexplicated.

To a considerable extent this tension relates directly to the evangelist's *eschatology*. As noted under *christology* and *ecclesiology,* Jesus' coming and the implications for his disciples indicate the dawn of the age of salvation, the fulfillment of the "Law and the Prophets" and the "coming to pass of all things" (5:17–18). Thus Jesus could declare, "Blessed *are*" the subjects of the Beatitudes even now, and at the same time he could demand conduct corresponding to the new relationships characteristic of the presence now of the Kingdom of Heaven. In other words, the Sermon expresses a "realized eschatology" that has too often been over-looked in the failure to perceive the evangelist's primary christological focus. Yet the Sermon's thrust extends beyond that of "realized eschatology" to speak explicitly of a future time when the Kingdom of Heaven will be consummated at the accompanying final judgment. Since Schweitzer, this eschatological perspective has dominated the Sermon discussions. The future orientation of the Beatitudes, 5:19–20, 29–30; 6:2–6, 16–18, 10–11, 14–15; 7:1–5, 13–14, 19, 21–23, 24–27, material consisting of both tradition and redaction, without doubt supports a "consistent eschatology." How can these apparently mutually exclusive elements coexist except in the inconsistency of the evangelist?

This tension arises neither from the needs of the community who shaped the tradition nor from the evangelist's inconsistency but from Jesus' own ministry which the evangelist has sought to capture in his portrait. The Sermon's content and function merely underscore this tension between the present and the future. On the one hand, Jesus comes as the fulfillment of the promises for the age of salvation; on the other hand, the consummation of these promises lies in the future manifestation of the Kingdom of Heaven in history. The present directly relates to the future, since one's response to God's activity through Jesus Messiah determines one's "entrance" into the future Kingdom, one's standing at the final judgment. Therefore, the disciple finds himself living in this evil age but called to live a life corresponding with the age of salvation in which evil has been defeated through the person and ministry of Jesus Messiah. The dangers of succumbing to the pressures of this age rather than remaining faithful to Jesus Messiah lead to the warnings of 5:13, 7:6, and 13–27.

That the evangelist perceived this new life to consist in more than human resolve becomes evident in the Beatitudes, but most evident in his use of the Lord's Prayer set in the middle of those radical demands

(5:21—6:18). One brings to bear in one's own life this succinct expression of Jesus' ministry through living out this Prayer as explicated in 6:19—7:6. Yet the Lord's Prayer itself (6:9–13) and its practical explication (6:19—7:6) are couched in the assurance of answered prayer (6:7–8; 7:7–11). Thus the life that one is called to live, the "greater righteousness," itself comes as a part of God's redemptive activity in history (6:33) in the form of answered prayer. In this way, God's name is hallowed, his sovereign rule is established, and his will is done through his own on earth in anticipation of the future consummation. In other words, the Sermon on the Mount with its christological, ecclesiological, ethical, and eschatological focus expresses the "gospel of the Kingdom" of Jesus' ministry.

D. The Sources of the Sermon on the Mount

When one hears the phrase "the Sermon on the Mount," one generally identifies it with Matthew's Gospel and correctly so, not only because of the presence of the Sermon in the first Gospel but because the Sermon on the Mount, as we know it, is ultimately the literary product of the first evangelist. Yet the evangelist himself did not "write" the Sermon as such but composed it by combining various traditional units, the largest of which provided the basic framework and outline of the Sermon in Matthew 5–7 and Luke 6:20–49. Furthermore, as the table below indicates, the majority of the traditional units came from the Q materials common to Matthew and Luke. But combined with this Q material, we also find sayings and units that are distinctive to Matthew and most likely stem from the evangelist's own source. In order to gain a perspective on the Sermon's composition at the outset, a table of parallels and a brief summary is provided here, with a more detailed discussion of the traditional material and the evangelist's use of it to be found in the commentary.

Based on the parallels shown in the table, we can make the following observations regarding the Sermon's composition. First, with the exception of the Woes in Luke 6:24–26, all of Luke's Sermon has a direct parallel in Matthew's. Second, with the exception of the Golden Rule (Luke 6:31, par. Matt 7:12), both Sermons follow the same order of material in their parallels. The difference in order within the Beatitudes (Luke 6:21; cf. Matt 5:4, 6) and the Love Your Enemies section (Luke 6:27–36; cf. Matt 5:38–48) simply reflects the internal rearrangement by the evangelist. Third, the additional Q material in Matthew's Sermon

TABLE OF PARALLELS

for the most part occurs in four blocks of Q tradition in Luke: (1) Luke 11:2–4, 9–13, 33, 34–36, with Luke 11:14–34 appearing in Matt 12:22–42; (2) Luke 12:33–34, 34–36, 57–59 with Luke 12:37–53 divided between Matt 24:43–51 and 10:34–36; (3) Luke 13:23–24, 25–29, with Luke 13:18–21 parallel to Matt 13:31–33, Luke 13:34–35 parallel to Matt 23:37–39; and (4) Luke 14:34–35 with Luke 14:15–24 comparable to Matt 22:1–14. One might also note that the Q materials just cited not occurring in Matthew's Sermon frequently occur in his other discourse settings. Finally, most of the non-Q material appears in 5:17—6:18, a section dealing with Jesus and the Law and traditional Jewish piety.

It has been suggested from time to time that the two Sermons in Matthew and Luke represent Jesus' preaching of the "Sermon" on more than one occasion—a thesis most often supported by homiletical experience—thus resulting in the differences of setting, length, and expression between the two Sermons. But a closer examination demonstrates the common traditional bond underlying the two passages in Matthew and Luke. Furthermore, as Dibelius suggested, even this underlying tradition resulted from the early community's compilation of various traditional units to meet their own catechetical needs. Therefore, while the traditional units themselves most likely stem from Jesus' ministry, as will be seen in the commentary, and reflected his "preaching," the actual "Sermon" as such came into being when the tradition was combined into its present form in the post-Easter community, a process that makes moot the questions of when and where Jesus "preached" the Sermon.

This Q Sermon tradition underlying Matthew and Luke apparently consisted of three major sections: a series of Beatitudes (Luke 6:20–23, par. Matt 5:3–12), a series of admonitions (Luke 6:27–45, par. Matt 5:38–48, 7:1–5, 16–20), and a concluding warning in the form of a parable (Luke 6:46, 47–49, par. Matt 7:21, 24–27). The Beatitudes most likely consisted originally of the three found in Luke 6:20–21 (par. Matt 5:3–4, 6), a unit that may well have come intact from Jesus' ministry. Then a fourth Beatitude (Luke 6:22–23, par. Matt 5:11–12), most likely a separate traditional saying, differing in form and focus from the other three, supplied the transition in form to the previous Beatitudes and in content to the following unit on Love Your Enemies. These four Beatitudes underwent further modification in the tradition with the change of person, with the expansion in number to eight in Matt 5:5, 7–9, the first relating to the Beatitude of 5:3 and the other three corresponding in content to the three admonitions that followed in the tradition, and with the formulation of the antithetically parallel Woes in Luke 6:24–

26, either in the tradition or by Luke. Therefore, Matthew found eight Beatitudes in his Sermon tradition which he then adapted redactionally for his own purposes.

The series of admonitions grew out of the combination of three separate traditional units consisting of Love Your Enemies (Luke 6:27–35, cf. Matt 5:38–48), the heart of which stems from Jesus' ministry, a unit on mercy or not judging one another (Luke 6:36–42, cf. Matt 7:1–5) and a unit on recognizing one's fruits (Luke 6:43–45; cf. Matt 7:16–20), two units which also have their roots in Jesus' ministry. The first evangelist's expansion and modification of this section in the traditional material becomes most obvious simply by comparing the references. Matt 5:13–37 appears between 5:11–12, the final Beatitude, and 5:38–48, the first of the three traditional admonitions. The whole of Matthew 6 appears between 5:48 and 7:1–5, the second admonition. And 7:6–15 appears between the second and third admonitions of 7:1–5 and 7:16–20.

The final section of the underlying Sermon tradition opened with a warning in the form of a rhetorical question (Luke 6:46; cf. Matt 7:21) that led to the concluding parable (Luke 6:47–49, par. Matt. 7:24–27). Yet in this section as in the previous one, the evangelist has also expanded the material—even if not as extensively—by adding an additional warning at the outset (7:13–14) followed by a particular warning against false prophets (7:15) that pertains directly to the third admonition of the tradition (7:16–20; cf. Luke 6:43–45). He has also expanded the original warning in 7:21 with a clarification in 7:22–23.

In this brief summary, one can see that Matthew has considerably changed the extent and profile of the Sermon tradition. He did so, however, by the use of other tradition as well as his own shaping of the material, as can be seen in the table above and will be seen in particular in the commentary to follow. With this extensive modification of the underlying Sermon tradition arises the natural question about Matthew's organizing principle or principles, if any. Does the Sermon become a rather randomly collected series of traditional units with the one leading to the other and having little or no organization, or does the Sermon reflect a basic outline that gives contours to the composition? This question leads to the search for an outline in or behind Matthew's Sermon.

E. An Outline of the Sermon on the Mount

In seeking to discover and delineate the evangelist's own "outline" for the Sermon rather than to impose one somewhat arbitrarily upon the material, one must look for the pivotal concepts and phrases, the thematically related material, and the underlying framework of the Sermon tradition. The consistent sequential parallels between Matt 5:3—7:27 and Luke 6:20–49, in spite of the considerable difference in amount and use of the traditional material, clearly demonstrate that the evangelist chose to follow the order of the tradition. His own redaction consisted in supplementing and reshaping the tradition by drawing from the Q tradition and his own source. Consequently, the basic division of the Sermon tradition into the Beatitudes (5:3–12, par. Luke 6:20–23), Admonitions (5:21—7:12, par. Luke 6:27–42; cf. 43–45), and Warnings (7:13–27, par. Luke 6:[43–45] 46–49) still obtains for Matthew's Sermon.

Yet within the Matthean Sermon several clues as to further groupings occur. The Beatitudes stand out as a unit in 5:3–12; the "greater righteousness" of 5:20 introduces the Antitheses of 5:21–48; "doing righteousness" in 6:1 continues the theme through 6:1–18; the location and ending of the Golden Rule in 7:12 appears to have a structural function, and the series of warnings in 7:13–23 corresponds to the thrust of the concluding parable in 7:24–27. These rather obvious indicators, however, leave 5:13–19 and 6:19—7:11 as somewhat extraneous, at worst, or loosely related, at best, to the other Sermon elements. This rather awkward situation stems from a paradox in the evangelist's manner in dealing with the tradition. On the one hand, Matthew reveals a certain constraint to follow the Sermon tradition rather than an arbitrary disregard for its order and content. On the other hand, he displays a freedom to take the tradition as a point of departure for the development of specific themes through the appropriation of other traditional materials. Consequently, it is difficult to find clear-cut divisions within his final product. Rather, the material moves or flows from one theme into another. Therefore, the major components of Matthew's Sermon such as the Beatitudes (5:3–12), Admonitions (5:20—6:18), and Warnings (7:13–27) stand out, with the transitional elements of 5:13–19 and the additional admonitions of 6:19—7:12 appearing to be parenthetical and miscellaneous respectively. But even these apparently parenthetical and miscellaneous materials belong integrally to the evangelist's theological shaping of the Sermon.

First, the Beatitudes of 5:3–12 set forth the theological basis for the Sermon materials of 5:17—7:27. Beginning with the Beatitudes as found in the tradition, the evangelist has heightened their christological and eschatological focus by aligning them with the Old Testament promise, particularly that of Isaiah 61, rather than "ethicizing" or "spiritualizing"

them, as often suggested. The Beatitudes stand as foundational for the
Sermon because they depict Jesus Messiah as the fulfillment of the Old
Testament promise of the one bringing about the age of salvation, God's
sovereign rule in history, through his ministry. But concomitant with
the coming of the new age comes the establishment of a new relationship
by God with his own and among his own (e.g., Jer 31:31–34). This
"ecclesiological" element also belongs to the "good news of the Kingdom"
and finds its expression in the address of the Beatitude, "Blessed
are. . . ."

It is precisely this second element that the evangelist underscores by
introducing in 5:13–16 the eschatological figures of "light" and a "city
on a hill" for Israel in the world. Together the christology and ecclesiology
of 5:3–16 announce the eschatological moment of the "gospel of the
Kingdom," Jesus by means of his ministry and the disciples by means
of their "good deeds" that bring "glory to the Father in heaven." Furthermore, the reference to the "good deeds" in 5:16 sets the stage for the
demands that follow in 5:21—7:12 pertaining to the "greater righteousness." This call for conduct inherent to discipleship in 5:14–16 begins
with a warning in 5:13 that the disciples take their calling as the "salt
of the earth" seriously, especially in view of the persecution and rejection
noted in 5:10 (cf. 5:3 and 5:12). The threat of judgment—"be cast out"—
for apostasy sounds a note that rings loud and clear in the warnings
of 7:13–27. Thus, 5:3–16 forms the introductory section of the Sermon
by setting forth the blessings of the Kingdom christologically and ecclesiologically. What follows presents an explication of the "good deeds" of
the Kingdom.

Second, drawn from the language of 5:20, the "greater righteousness"
stands as the heading for the heart of Matthew's Sermon, which begins
with a preface in 5:17–18 and closes with the Golden Rule in 7:12.
The preface of 5:17–18 again lays the christological basis for the demands
that follow. By reworking the tradition of 5:17–19, the evangelist declares
explicitly the implicit christology of 5:3–12, namely, Jesus came to "fulfill" the Old Testament Scriptures, and with his earthly ministry "all
things have come to pass" (5:17–18). Therefore, God has acted to establish
a new relationship between himself and his own and offers the basis
for a new relationship among his own that expresses itself in the conduct
demanded in 5:21—7:12, the "greater righteousness." This conduct stems
from a "wholeness" (5:48) in one's relationship to God and others, a
"wholeness" that bespeaks the total commitment of the whole person
to God through Jesus Messiah (cf. 19:16–22).

In the demands that follow, those of 5:21–48 center on one's relationship towards others, while those of 6:1—7:11 center on one's relationship towards God. This latter relationship finds its essential expression in the Lord's Prayer of 6:9–13, which the evangelist explicates and develops by the use of other traditions in 6:19—7:11 depicting a life of prayer. The evangelist's use of the tradition on answered prayer in 7:7–11, along with his pointed christological preface in 5:17–18, indicates that the conduct demanded between 5:21 and 7:6 stems from this new relationship of the disciples as "sons" of the Father, a relationship offered by Jesus Messiah and inherent to the presence of the Kingdom. Thus the conduct itself becomes a pointer to the Father in heaven (e.g., 5:16) rather than to one's own personal achievement, the "righteousness" of the "scribes and Pharisees" in 5:20, the "hypocrites" in 6:1, and the "false prophets" in 7:21–23.

Third, the evangelist, following the order of the tradition, concludes with a series of warnings setting forth the alternatives of responding positively or negatively to Jesus' ministry, in particular, to his "words" (7:24, 26) of the Sermon that set forth the "Father's will" (7:21) for his own. The danger of apostasy appears again in the danger of the false prophets who threaten to undermine Jesus' ministry by short-circuiting the radical implications of Jesus Messiah for a life of discipleship. The "gospel of the Kingdom" stands as the great alternative, but the gate is narrow and the way is constricted (7:13–14) even for those claiming his lordship and power (7:21–23).

Thus one can outline the Sermon as follows:

A. The Blessings of the Kingdom: 5:3–16
   1. The Beatitudes: 5:3–12
   2. Discipleship: 5:13–16
B. The Greater Righteousness: 5:17—7:12
   1. Jesus and the Law: 5:17–20
   2. Righteousness with Reference to Others: 5:21–48
   3. Righteousness with Reference to God: 6:1—7:11
      a. Worship: 6:1–18
      b. A Life of Prayer: 6:19—7:11
   4. Conclusion: The Golden Rule: 7:12
C. The Alternatives: 7:13–27
   1. The Two Ways: 7:13–14
   2. False Prophets: 7:15–23
   3. The Two Builders: 7:24–27

F. Arrangement of the Commentary

Choosing a suitable format presents one of the first hurdles when writing a commentary. A straightforward verse-by-verse approach represents the most common approach and is generally the least complicated to use. One seldom needs or finds a table of contents in such an arrangement. Because of the complexity of exegetical discussion, the trend in more recent works has been toward multiple sections for each unit under discussion in order to divide the material according to the interest of the reader. This arrangement, however, may facilitate the use of the commentary for one while only making it more difficult for another who seeks to obtain the total picture of the passage under consideration. Furthermore, this approach of necessity results at times in repetition and a certain amount of redundancy. Recognizing these limitations, this latter format has been chosen with the desire to make the commentary more accessible for a larger spectrum of readers. Those seeking a translation and general summary of the passage in question and those with more technical interests in the literary and theological issues can each find the appropriate discussion.

The commentary has been divided into chapters that follow the sections rather than the outline of the Sermon. Each chapter consists of a translation, literary analysis, notes, and comments. The translation seeks primarily to reflect the conclusions growing out of the discussion in the notes. Occasionally, the more "traditional" rendering, such as in "Blessed" of the Beatitudes, appears for lack of an appropriate synonym. The literary analysis offers in summary a designation of the source, form, and function of the constituent elements of the section, with the more detailed discussion of these questions coming in the corresponding notes and at times in the history of the tradition in the comments. The notes give the most detailed discussion of the various exegetical facets on a word, phrase, or clause in a verse-by-verse order. Finally, the comments offer a more general commentary as a summary of the notes and often additional comments on issues related to the section.

II. THE SETTING OF THE SERMON ON THE MOUNT
Matthew 4:23—5:2

Translation

4 ²³Jesus began to move throughout all Galilee—teaching in their synagogues, preaching the gospel of the Kingdom and healing every illness and frailty among the people. ²⁴His fame spread throughout all Syria. They brought to him all the sick—those suffering from various illnesses and severe pain, demoniacs, epileptics and paralytics—and he healed them. ²⁵Large crowds from Galilee and the Decapolis, from Jerusalem, Judea, and Perea, followed him.

5 ¹When Jesus saw the crowds, he went up the mountain. After he had sat down, his disciples came to him ²and he began to teach them.

Literary Analysis

The setting of the Sermon on the Mount arises from a summary (4:23–25) and an introductory statement (5:1–2). The use of summaries as a literary device has long been a topic of discussion in Mark's Gospel (most recently, Egger, *Frohbotschaft*) and in the Book of Acts (Cadbury, "Summaries," 392–402, and more recently, Benoit, "sommaires," 1–10). The traditional character of the summaries—to what extent did they exist as independent traditional units—and their historical value—how reliably do they reflect Jesus' ministry—have been the major issues for some time. These questions are somewhat moot for our particular concerns, since the summary of 4:23–25 doubtless reflects Jesus' ministry that included teaching, preaching, and healing in Galilee, even if Matthew shaped the material to serve his immediate purposes of depicting Jesus and his ministry in Galilee.

Matthew himself used summaries in various ways. His most common summary—"When Jesus had finished . . ." (7:28; 11:1; 13:53; 19:1; 26:1)—functions formally as the conclusion for each of the five major discourse sections in his Gospel. The more extended summaries of 4:23–25, 9:35, and 15:29–31 function materially to set Jesus' ministry in capsule form.

Matt 4:23–25, redactionally composed from two Marcan summaries (4:23, cf. Mark 1:39; 4:25, cf. Mark 3:7), serves a dual purpose. First, it summarizes Jesus' ministry in Galilee that eschatologically represented the fulfillment of Isa 8:23—9:1 (Matt 4:13–16). Second, the summary introduces Jesus' public ministry in Galilee by focusing on his teaching, preaching, and healing. Consequently, 4:23–25 offers a general setting for the Sermon of Matthew 5–7, which develops the theme of Jesus' teaching, and for the miracles of Matthew 8–9, which develops the theme of Jesus' healing. This larger section (Matt 5–9) then concludes with the summary of 9:35, an almost verbatim counterpart to 4:23 that also serves to bridge to the sending of the disciples in Matthew 10. Therefore, 4:23 and 9:35 form an inclusion around Jesus' ministry as depicted in Matthew 5–9.

The introductory statement of the Sermon (5:1–2), giving the location and audience for the Sermon, offers the immediate setting in a manner frequently found at the beginning of a traditional unit. The unit probably stems redactionally from Matthew's use of Mark and Q tradition (see Notes on 5:1–2).

Notes

4:23. *began to move throughout all Galilee.* In contrast to ἦλθεν of Mark 1:39, Matthew uses the less common περιῆγεν (9:35, par. Mark 6:6 and 23:15) in the imperfect tense. This verb, with the following phrase, *throughout all Galilee,* underlines at the outset the scope and itinerant character of Jesus' ministry. Yet one should avoid overemphasizing the itinerant nature of Jesus' ministry. The stress in 4:23–24 on the crowd's movement to Jesus suggests that the evangelist used the imperfect inceptively to emphasize the beginning of Jesus' eschatological ministry in

Galilee (cf. 4:13–17). Three subsequent participles describe the nature of this Galilean ministry, and the aorist tenses of 4:24–25 express its impact.

teaching. Matthew replaces the κηρύσσων of Mark 1:39 with διδάσκων (cf. 9:35, par. Mark 6:6), quite probably because of the setting, *in the synagogues.* For the first Gospel a formal parallel clearly exists between Jesus' teaching and the teaching of first-century Judaism. Of the twelve relevant usages of διδάσκω, five have directly to do with the synagogue (4:23, cf. Mark 1:39; 9:35, cf. Mark 6:6; 13:54, par. Mark 6:2) or the Temple (21:23, cf. Mark 11:27; 26:55, cf. Mark 14:49); four have to do with the rabbis' concern for the Law (5:19, 2x; 15:9, par. Mark 7:7; 22:16, par. Mark 12:14); and two have to do with the teaching style of the rabbis (5:1–2; 7:29). To this extent, Matthew's usage of διδάσκω reflects a halachic character (Bornkamm, "End-expectation," 38, n. 1). Consistent with this formal perspective in Matthew, "teacher" is the common term of address used by those who fail to recognize Jesus in faith (Bornkamm, "End-expectation," 41; see 8:19, cf. Luke 9:57; 9:11, cf. Mark 2:16; 12:38, cf. Mark 8:11; 17:24; 19:16, par. Mark 10:17; 22:16, par. Mark 12:14; 22:24, par. Mark 12:19; 22:36, cf. Mark 12:28). In other words, Matthew's Gospel underscores the point that Jesus fit into the scenery of his day as a teacher, at least on the surface. Jesus appeared to be like other rabbis.

Yet this formal similarity between Jesus and the rabbis also offers the point of greatest contrast between Jesus and the rabbis for Matthew. Not only does the crowds' response—". . . He was teaching as one having authority and not as their scribes" (7:28, par. Mark 1:22)—signal this great difference, but so does Matthew's own redactional combination of "teaching" with "preaching" as parallel activities (4:23, cf. Mark 1:39; 9:35, cf. Mark 6:6; and 11:1) as well as the actual content of Jesus' teaching (e.g., 5:2—7:29) and that of his disciples (28:20). To this extent, Matthew has filled *teaching* with a christological content that is anything but halachic in character. Consequently, although Jesus appeared to be but another rabbi to many, Matthew has so reworked his tradition that those who followed Jesus (e.g. Judas in 26:25, 49) or came in faith seeking his help never used the designation "rabbi" or "teacher" with reference to Jesus (Bornkamm, "End-expectation," 41; see Mark 4:38, cf. Matt 8:25; Mark 9:5, cf. Matt 17:4; Mark 10:35, cf. Matt 20:20; Mark 10:51, cf. Matt 20:33; Mark 11:21, cf. Matt 21:20).

Jesus' teaching, therefore, plays a double role for Matthew. On the one hand, the *formal* aspect places Jesus appropriately within the context of Judaism as more or less a first-century rabbi, thus the corresponding designation of "teacher" by those who do not respond in faith. The roots of this perspective doubtless stem from Jesus' actual ministry as well as from Matthew's sensitivities for Jewish customs. On the other hand, the *content* of Jesus' teaching sets forth the nature and demands of the Kingdom (e.g., especially the discourse sections of 5–7; 10; 13; 18; 23–25). To those who have the "eyes" and "ears" of faith, who have been given "understanding" (13:10–17), Jesus' teaching actually reveals who he is, namely, the one in and through whom the Kingdom has both come and is yet to come (see Note on 5:3, *Kingdom of Heaven*). For those who "see" and "understand," the corresponding address to Jesus is "lord" (κύριε) rather than "teacher" (διδάσκαλε). As Kingsbury (*Matthew*, 20–21) has noted, even the structure of Matthew's Gospel supports this dual usage. Jesus' teaching appears in a "positive light" in 4:17—11:1 when he presents himself and his teaching of the Kingdom to Israel. After 11:1, however, his teaching continues to be positive only for his own (13; 18; 24–25). A note of conflict appears when his teaching is given in the context of Israel (15:1–9; 16:12; 23:23–28 and 22:15–40).

in their synagogues. The synagogue worship service often included a reading of the prophets followed by a didactic or expositional "sermon" whenever a qualified person was present (Str-B 4:171–88; cf. Luke 4:17–21; Acts 9:20; 13:5,15). Matthew maintains *their synagogues* (cf. Mark 1:39), which sets a tone of distance that may well reflect the situation in his church, removed from the Jewish life of the synagogue (also 9:35; 10:17; 12:9, cf. Mark 3:1; 13:54, cf. Mark 6:2; 23:34, cf. Luke 11:49). Kilpatrick (*Origins*, 110–11) attributed this situation of Matthew's church to the consequences of the *Birkath ha-minim,* a curse formula introduced into the liturgical prayer, the Eighteen Benedictions, during the time of Jamnia (ca. A.D. 85). Davies (*Setting*, 297) has disputed such a basis, suggesting rather that local pressures lay behind the separation. Regardless of the basis, this expression is one of several that reflect the conflict between Matthew's congregation and its Jewish context (see Note on 5:11, *persecute*).

preaching. Matthew found this verb at hand in Mark 1:39 and adds it later to form a similar parallel with *teaching* in 9:35 (cf. Mark 6:6). As noted above, however, instead of leaving κηρύσσω within the context of Jesus' ministry *in their synagogues* (Mark 1:39, par. Luke 4:44, also Acts 9:20), he substitutes διδάσκω there and builds a parallelism by setting κηρύσσω in the context of the *gospel of the Kingdom.* This redactional rearrangement of *preaching* from Mark's more didactic setting of the synagogue and the alignment in close association with *the gospel* clearly demonstrate a special usage for this verb in Matthew. κηρύσσω is reserved exclusively for the announcement of the concept and content of the gospel (4:23; 9:35; 24:14; 26:13 par Mark 14:9). Although Matthew may have been influenced by an earlier association (cf. Mark 14:9), the parallel usage in Isa 61:1-2, an influential text for Matthew (see Notes on 5:3–12), lies closer at hand. *Preaching,* therefore, for the first evangelist is the special proclamation, the "heralding," of the coming Kingdom, whether by Jesus (4:17, par. Mark 1:14b; 4:23, cf. Mark 1:39; 9:35, cf. Mark 6:6), by the Baptist (3:1, cf. Mark 1:4) or by the disciples (10:7; 24:14; 26:13, par. Mark 14:9). The only absolute usage of the verb occurs in the summary of 11:1. Such a coupling of *preaching* with *gospel* reflects the synonymous relationship of the verbs κηρύσσω and εὐαγγελίζομαι, the roots of which are found in the Aramaic usage (Friedrich, *TDNT* 3:711–12).

As Stuhlmacher (*Evangelium,* 109–53) has documented, the New Testament roots of *preaching the gospel* lie in the Old Testament and Aramaic-speaking Judaism. The hope for one who would proclaim the "good news" (εὐαγγελίζομαι) of peace, God's rule, deliverance, and healing finds its distinctive basis in the passages from Isaiah (e.g., 41:27; 52:7; 61:1–2). Whereas these promises were variously applied in the intertestamental period to God, angels, the eschatological prophet Elijah, and the Messiah, Jesus is the one who distinctively fulfills this promise in Matthew, not only by his preaching but by his work as well (4:23; 9:35; cf. 11:2–6). Both his work and his preaching/teaching come together for Matthew in 24:14 and 26:13 (cf. Mark 14:9) where *this gospel* refers to the content of the Church's mission proclamation.

Since the focus of the Baptist (3:1) and the disciples' preaching (24:14; "this gospel" in 26:13) is ultimately Jesus' ministry, Jesus is more than just another preacher of the good news for Matthew. The gospel has to do with Jesus himself together with his preaching. The word κηρύσσω, therefore, connotes a christological affirmation in Matthew. In and through Jesus' ministry of preaching and mighty works, the Kingdom (see Note on 5:3, *Kingdom of Heaven*) comes to those who receive it in faith. As was the case with *teaching* above, the structure of Matthew's Gospel offers supporting evidence. Jesus' own preaching is limited to the section of 4:17—11:1 in which he presents himself and the Kingdom to Israel. Corresponding with his rejection in 11:2—16:20, the verb is found only within the context of the Church's mission (24:14; 26:13, par. Mark 14:9) in the rest of the Gospel (Kingsbury, *Matthew*, 20).

the gospel of the Kingdom. Although the phrase is rather infrequent in Matthew, it expresses the basic theme of his Gospel. Matthew uses the noun *gospel* (εὐαγγέλιον) four times (7x in Mark, none in Luke or John), and he always combines it with the verb κηρύσσω and adds the phrase *of the Kingdom* (4:23; 9:35; 24:14) and/or *this* (24:14 and 26:13, cf. Mark 14:9). Since the evangelist has consistently combined κηρύσσω with εὐαγγέλιον, it is not surprising that the synonymous verb form εὐαγγελίζομαι is found only in the quotation of Isa 61:1 in 11:5 (par. Luke 7:22). The *gospel*, therefore, is the "good news" that is proclaimed or preached. In 3:1 the Baptist and in 4:17, par. Mark 1:14, Jesus *preached* repentance and the coming (ἤγγικεν) of the Kingdom; in 10:7 the disciples *preach* the coming of the Kingdom (ἤγγικεν). Obviously these expressions are synonymous with and explanations of the Matthean phrase, *the gospel of the Kingdom* (4:23; 9:35; 24:14).

Yet Matthew can also speak more generally of *this gospel* in 26:13, cf. Mark 14:9. Is the content of *this gospel* the Gospel document itself? Does Matthew make the equation found in Mark's usage (Marxsen, *Mark*, 126–38)? The answer is a clear negative. Matthew's reference to the Baptist's preaching (3:1), to Jesus' preaching, as well as to the Church's preaching of the gospel, precludes a simple identification of *this gospel* (26:13) with his Gospel (Strecker, *Weg*, 128; Stuhlmacher, *Evangelium*, 242; and Kingsbury, *Matthew*, 130). Yet *this gospel*, found as it is within the context of the passion narrative in reference to the anointing at Bethany (26:13), does point to the "subject matter of the entire document" (Kingsbury, *Matthew*, 131). Since Jesus is the one who fulfills the Old Testament expectation for Matthew by his preaching and work, Kingsbury can correctly define *the gospel of the Kingdom*, the "capsule-summary" of the first Gospel, as "the news, which saves or condemns, that is revealed in and through Jesus Messiah, the Son of God, and is proclaimed to Israel and the nations alike to the effect that in him the Rule of God has drawn near to humankind" (*Matthew*, 136–37).

healing. The third member of the parallelism—*preaching, teaching, and healing*—is no less significant for Matthew, who uses θεραπεύω sixteen times (5x in Mark, 14x in Luke), only four of which have parallels in Mark (8:16, par. Mark 1:34; 12:10, par. Mark 3:2; 12:15, par. Mark 3:10) or Q (10:1, par. Luke 9:1). The evangelist actually inserts this verb seven times into the Marcan parallel (4:23, 24; 9:35; 14:14; 17:16, 18; 19:2). As with διδάσκω and κηρύσσω, Matthew also used θεραπεύω in the summaries of Jesus' ministry (4:23–25; 9:35; 15:29–31; 19:2, cf.

21:14). He has also deliberately combined *healing* with Jesus' *teaching/ preaching* (4:23, cf. Mark 1:39; 9:35, cf. Mark 6:6), arranged chapters 5–9 to illustrate both the *teaching* (5–7) and the *healing* (8–9) ministry, and has Jesus giving power to his disciples for *teaching* and *healing* (10:1, 8). Furthermore, *healing* has a christological thrust similar to *preaching the gospel of the Kingdom.* In 8:17 the evangelist explicitly interprets Jesus' healing of 8:16 by the formula-citation of Isa 53:4, 11: "He has taken our infirmities and carried our illnesses." A similar fulfill-ment motif with general reference to Isaiah's promises occurs in 11:2– 6, par. Luke 7:22 (Q), which Matthew introduces as "the works of the Messiah" (11:2, cf. Luke 7:21–22). Since exorcisms are also a part of the healing ministry in the first Gospel (4:24; 10:1, 8, par. Luke 9:1, 2; 17:16–18, par. Luke 9:42), the Q saying of 12:28, par. Luke 11:20, is also relevant, ". . . Then the Kingdom of God has come upon you." *Healing,* therefore, is an integral part of Jesus' ministry as the Messiah who fulfills the Old Testament promises.

Although Jesus' *preaching* is limited to the period of his presentation of himself and the Kingdom to Israel (4:17—11:1) and his *teaching* contin-ues after that in both a positive and negative manner (see above), Jesus' *healing* continues unchanged throughout the Gospel (Kingsbury, *Mat-thew,* 21). This is consistent with Matthew's portrait of Jesus' ministry. His *preaching* was the proclamation, the "heralding," of the Kingdom. His *teaching* continued even after his rejection (11:2—16:20). To those who had "ears to hear" and "eyes to see," especially the disciples, this was positively received; to those whose "hearts were hardened" this was negatively received, a basis for conflict. Jesus' *healing* was available to all who would accept it (as was his *preaching* and his *teaching*). In that regard his *healing* parallels the positive thrust of his *teaching.* Jesus does not cease *teaching* or *working* as the Messiah at the point of his rejection. The *gospel of the Kingdom* both "saves and condemns" (Kingsbury, *Mat-thew,* 136), as seen by the *healing* of the sick as well as the response to the healings (e.g., 12:14, par. Mark 3:6; 12:24, par. Mark 3:22; 21:14– 15).

every frailty. The adjective *every* is to be taken in the general tone of hyperbole which runs through this summary (cf. *all* Galilee, *every* illness, 4:23; *all* Syria, *all* of the sick, 4:24). Matthew alone in the New Testament uses the rather rare Greek expression μαλακία (cf. Deut 7:15 LXX; *T Jos* 17) and always in combination with illness (νόσος, cf. 9:35 and 10:1).

among the people. Matthew uses *the people* in its more specialized

Old Testament sense in 1:21, "He shall save *his people* . . ."; in the
Old Testament quotations of 4:16, 13:15, and 15:8; and in the formula,
"high priests and elders/scribes of *the people*" (21:23; 26:3, 47; 27:1
and 2:4). These occurrences clearly point in one way or another to *the
people of God,* namely, Israel. It is not so clear, however, to what extent
this specific meaning controls the absolute usage of *the people* (λαός) in
4:23; 26:5; 27:25, 64. In 4:23, at least, the same overtones would seem
unavoidable, since its content relates so closely to 4:16. If *the people*
does, then, refer to "the people of God," it would mean that for Matthew,
Jesus' ministry as summarized in 4:23–25 was directed to Israel. The
location and nature of his ministry rather than its Gentile audience would
be the focal point (con. Jeremias, *Promise,* 34) not only in 4:13–16 but
also in 4:23–25.

4:24. *his fame.* Similarly in 14:1.

throughout all Syria. The structure of 4:24a may have come from
Mark 1:28, but the evangelist is responsible for its content. Syria has
two meanings. In the rest of the New Testament, Syria refers to the
Roman province which included Palestine (Luke 2:2; Acts 15:23, 41;
18:18; 20:3; 21:3; and Gal 1:21). Yet the common Jewish usage denoted
the area adjacent to Palestine to the north-northeast, as seen in the
Mishnah's several references to Syria, all of which have this narrower
meaning (e.g., *Demai* 2:2, Syria is the "country beyond Chezib"). It is
also of interest to note that rabbis of the first century (e.g., Gamaliel,
Eliezer, and Akiba) set regulations for a variety of concerns pertaining
to Jews living in Syria. In fact, those living in Syria had a different
status from those in Israel, but they also had a special status in contrast
to the Jews living in more remote countries ("He that owns [land] in
Syria is as one who owns [land] in the outskirts of Jerusalem," *Hallah*
4:11). These references in the Mishnah to first-century conditions for
those living in Syria indicate not only the narrower geographical meaning
of Syria but also the presence of Jews there. Which meaning did Matthew
intend?

Syntactically, the *all Syria* of 4:24 could be a heading for the places
of 4:25 which are specific examples of the regions within the Roman
province of Syria. Furthermore, if Matthew's Gospel was written in Syria,
as most think today, then the Roman province of Syria would tie his
church quite closely with Palestine, the area of Jesus' ministry. By contrast, however, *all Syria* may stand as the counterpart of *all Galilee* in
4:23. This would mean that 4:24 stands more closely with 4:23. Matt

4:25 would then be a summary of the results of both 4:23 and 4:24 and would move toward 5:1-2. The geographical areas of 4:25 sketch an outline of Palestine from the north—Galilee and Decapolis—to the south—Jerusalem, Judea, and Perea. The reference to Syria in 4:24, consequently, might reflect the geographical context of Matthew's church by expanding the boundaries of the overall impact of 4:23. Although it is impossible to know with certainty which alternative Matthew intended, the latter seems much more probable, since the evangelist frequently uses concepts in keeping with the normal Jewish customs (cf. *teaching*, 4:23; *sat down*, 5:1, within this context).

severe pain. The term βάσανος with medical overtones occurs only here in the New Testament. It generally refers to torment, pain afflicted on another, torture.

he healed them. Matt 4:24 expands and specifies Jesus' healing of 4:23. It sets the stage for Matt 8-9 where a number of miracles illustrate this aspect of Jesus' ministry. The list of the sick included various forms of illness—disease, demon possession, epilepsy, and lameness—and indicated the scope of Jesus' healing ministry.

4:25. *large crowds.* This verse states the results of Jesus' ministry as summarized in 4:23-24. The *large crowds* which emerge in 4:25 serve as the backdrop for 5:1 and the response to the Sermon in 7:28. The *crowds* (ὄχλοι) is characteristically Matthean (Van Tilborg, *Leaders,* 142-65). He uses the noun forty-nine times, of which nineteen have parallels in the Mark or Q tradition, and generally in the plural (31x, changing Marcan parallels 7x, e.g., 9:36, cf. Mark 6:34). The *crowds* have little theological significance as such in contrast to the evangelist's use of the *people* (see Note on 4:23), the *scribes and Pharisees* (see Note on 5:20), and the *disciples* (see Note on 5:1). They are a large and necessary part of the landscape for Matthew's portrait of Jesus' ministry. The *crowds* "follow" him (4:25); they "hear" his teaching (7:28); they bring their sick to him (15:30); but they eventually cry, "Crucify him" (27:22). Their response to Jesus is quite varied. They are "amazed" at his teaching (7:28), exorcisms (9:33), and healing (15:31). Indeed, they "glorify" God because of him (9:8 and 15:31), call him the "prophet" (21:11), "Son of David" (12:23), and shout "Hosanna to the Son of David" (21:9) while spreading palm branches before him (21:8). Eventually, they are orchestrated by the high priests and elders to call for his death (27:20). Basically, the *crowds* in Matthew function neutrally, like a Greek chorus, for Jesus' ministry (Suhl, "Davidssohn," 57-81) in contrast to the role of the disciples and the religious leaders of the Jews (cf. 23:1 with 13:36; 27:20).

followed him. Matthew uses the verb *to follow* (ἀκολουθέω) twenty-four times in his Gospel (18x in Mark, 17x in Luke) meaning more technically "discipleship" (e.g., 4:22, cf. Mark 1:20) as well as more literally "to follow" (e.g., 9:27, cf. Mark 10:46). The *crowds follow* Jesus eight times, half of which are redactional (4:25; 8:1; 14:13; 19:2). In view of the rather neutral role of the *crowds,* it seems unlikely that the verb should mean any more than that the *crowds* accompanied Jesus in the style of that day (con. Strecker, *Weg,* 230). In other words, the actual meaning of ἀκολουθέω is determined more by the subject's response in the context to Jesus than by the verb or subject itself.

from Galilee and the Decapolis, from Jerusalem, Judea, and Perea. This summary verse has a parallel in Mark 3:7–8, but the geographical listing is somewhat different. Mark does not mention *the Decapolis* in his context (cf. Mark 5:20; 7:31, without parallel) and has additionally Idumea, Tyre, and Sidon. Matthew clearly abbreviates the list and in so doing gives the outline of the borders of Palestine from north-northeast to south-southeast. Idumea, consequently, has little interest for him, while Tyre and Sidon have their own special role to play later in the Gospel (11:21, par. Luke 10:13; 15:21, par. Mark 7:24).

The *Decapolis* became a part of the province of Syria after Pompey's conquest in 65 B.C. It consisted of a league of ten cities, nine of which lay east of the Jordan. Some of the names found in the New Testament are Damascus, Gadara, and Gerasa. *Perea,* the area of the Trans-Jordan, was to the south what the *Decapolis* was to the north. Together both may cast a glance back at πέραν τοῦ Ἰορδάνου in the prophecy of Isa 8:23— 9:1, used in Matt. 4:15. The *large crowds* attracted by Jesus' ministry from all over Palestine serve now to set the stage for the first example of Jesus' actual teaching which follows.

5:1 *When Jesus saw the crowds.* With this verse Matthew begins his introduction to the Sermon on the Mount. *The crowds* appears to be a Matthean bridge between the summary of 4:23–25 and the setting of 5:1–2. They recur redactionally at the end of the Sermon as somewhat of a surprise (7:28, cf. Mark 1:22), since Jesus seems to be withdrawing from them in 5:1 and the focus clearly turns to the disciples who approach him on the mountain. A similar change in the audience is even more explicit, for example, in 13:10–11, 36; 17:14,19, par. Mark 9:14, 28. Yet the construction in 5:1 does not exclude the presence of *the crowds* from the Sermon. Their presence, which goes unnoticed at the beginning of the Sermon, places them in the outer circle, so to speak, with the disciples forming an inner circle (see Comment C).

he went up the mountain. The familiar title Sermon on the Mount comes from this brief statement. Since Mark has no Sermon and Luke has the Sermon on a "level place," the Sermon on the Mount has had a distinctively Matthean character. This mountain setting, however, may well result from the use of pre-Matthean tradition. Mark 3:13 has the same expression preceding the call of the disciples (Mark 3:13–19), and Luke also has a similar phrase in 6:12 where Jesus goes up the mountain to spend the night in prayer prior to his calling of the Twelve (6:13–16). Jesus then descends to minister to the crowd on a "level place" (6:17–19, par. Mark 3:7–12), where he gives the Sermon to the disciples (6:20). Schürmann has convincingly argued that we have two separate traditions at work in Luke 6:12–20a (*Untersuchungen*, 281–82; *Lukasevangelium*, 318–19; see also Jeremias, *Abba*, 94–96). Behind the Lucan material stands the Q tradition that includes a reference to Jesus going up the mountain to select his twelve disciples (6:12–16), followed by the Sermon as instruction for the disciples (6:20b–49). In 6:17–19 Luke has inserted the section about the crowds and Jesus' healing from Mark 3:7–12. This section (Mark 3:7–12) is one of the two in the complex of Mark 3:7–35 without a Q parallel (the other, Mark 3:31–35, is inserted later in Luke 8:19–21). Luke's use of Mark 3:7–12 in the present context hints at the post-Easter situation of Jesus' ministry with his disciples in the church (Schürmann, *Lukasevangelium*, 320–21).

Matthew most likely found the same basic content in Q of Jesus going up the mountain to call his disciples, followed by the Sermon. Contrary to Luke, Matthew interweaves the Marcan and Q material in his own style to make use of both Mark 3:7–19 and Q. Using Mark 3:7–8 for the summary in 4:25, Matthew relocates the actual calling of the Twelve from the context of both Mark (3:13–19) and Q (Luke 6:13–16) to follow his redactional complex of chapters 5–9 where he then introduces the calling of the disciples in the mission setting of 10:1–4. The evangelist, however, does draw from both the Q and Marcan material for his location (Mark 3:13, cf. Luke 6:12) and his audience (Luke 6:20; see *disciples* below).

The definite article in *the mountain* has led some to look for a particular mountain. Various possibilities such as Mount Tabor and, since the thirteenth century, the Mount of Beatitudes *(Karn Hittim)* have been suggested. Yet, the definite article is probably no more definite here than

in the same phrase in Mark 3:13 and Luke 6:12. In fact, many have
noted that the area in question is so hilly that "hill country" or "the
hills" would be a more accurate translation of τὸ ὄρος (Dalman, *Orte,*
166).

Of even greater interest has been the related question about the theological significance of "mountain" in Matthew. One of the more frequent
answers is found in the Moses and Sinai parallel with Jesus on the mountain (classic expressions: A. Loisy, *Evangiles* 1:535, and B. W. Bacon,
Studies, 165–86). Yet Davies (*Setting,* 93, 99) has demonstrated that
such a parallel is more apparent than real and lacks any explicit supporting evidence in Matthew.

Others have suggested that the mountain in 5:1, 15:29, and 28:16
connotes a particular place of revelation, a *topos* for the presentation
of an "eschatological event" (most recently, Strecker, *Weg,* 98). This
concept of mountain is hardly distinctive to Matthew but rather was
common to Judaism as well as the New Testament writings (Foerster,
TDNT 5:484–85, and Strobel, "Berg," 133–46). Whereas the events accompanying 5:1, 15:29, and 28:16 might point to such a special meaning
for Matthew, this conclusion must be tempered by the fact that he uses
mountain thirteen other times, most of which have a parallel in the
Marcan tradition, as well may 5:1. Furthermore, Jesus' healing and teaching, the "eschatological events" of 5:1 and 15:29, are in no way exclusively
characteristic of a mountain (cf. 4:23–24; 11:1; 13; 18). Therefore, such
a special meaning appears to be no more characteristic of Matthew than
of his tradition.

after he had sat down. Matthew twice introduces this phrase (5:1;
26:55, cf. Mark 14:49) to align Jesus with the Jewish custom of teaching
from a seated position (cf. 23:2 and Luke 4:20). It sets the tone for *he
taught them* in 5:2.

came to him. The verb προσῆλθεν is one of Matthew's favorite expressions (52x; 6x in Mark; 11x in Luke; 1 in John).

his disciples. Here we have the first of nearly sixty-five occurrences
of Jesus' *disciples* in Matthew. Not only does the frequency of this term
(ca. 45x in Mark; 38x in Luke) reflect Matthew's special interest in
the designation but also the fact that he has it forty-five times without
parallel in Mark or Luke. The presence of μαθηταί in Luke 6:20 suggests
that it may well have been a part of the setting in the Q tradition (see
Note on *mountain* above). Its presence in Q would explain the focus
on the *disciples* at this point in apparent contrast to the *crowds* in 5:1
who appear on the scene again in 7:28 (see Note on 7:28).

Who are the *disciples* for Matthew? In the view of some scholars, Matthew has limited the noun to the twelve disciples as part of his "tendency to historicize" (so Strecker, *Weg,* 191). Such identification was already at hand in the Marcan tradition. Matthew simply makes it more explicit, as seen in his use of Mark (10:1, cf. Mark 6:7; 11:1; 20:17, cf. Mark 10:32; 26:20, cf. Mark 14:17; cf. 28:16, the "eleven disciples"). Indeed, in contrast to Luke, there is no basis for seeing Matthew's circle of disciples as being any larger than the Twelve (e.g., Luke 6:13, 17). For others, the "church is embodied in the μαϑηταί" (Barth, "Understanding," 100, n. 2); the disciples are the "Christians" (Davies, *Setting,* 94–97); they are "idealized" as "paradigms" of disciples (Trilling, *Israel,* 50). Support for this view is the redactional use of the verb μαϑητεύω as the ultimate missionary goal (28:19, cf. 27:57). If "to make disciples" is the missionary goal, then the *disciples* become models for disciples per se.

Rather than choosing either alternative, there is a moment of truth in both. Matthew does, as the evidence suggests, limit his focus to the Twelve in the context of Jesus' ministry. Yet, like other elements in his Gospel (cf. *scribes and Pharisees*), the *disciples* serve a dual purpose. He uses the "historical context" of Jesus' ministry to typify the concerns of his community (Frankemölle, *Jahwebund,* 143). Consequently, the evangelist's genuine interest in the past, as seen by his consistent use of the *disciples* as the Twelve, has a present application. The past tradition is not merely preserved; rather, it is used in terms of the context and concerns of his present situation.

The *disciples* stand in stark contrast to the *people* and the *crowds* (see Notes on 4:23, 25). For Matthew, the *disciple* is one who does the will of the Father (12:49–50, cf. 7:21); discipling means baptizing and teaching what Jesus commanded (28:19–20). Perhaps the clearest difference is seen in the response to Jesus' ministry. Whereas the *crowds* together with the *disciples* are audience to Jesus' teaching and healing (see Note on 4:23, *teaching*), only the *disciples* are "given" to understand (cf. Mark 6:52; 8:17, 21, without parallel) what God was doing and to respond to Jesus' ministry (e.g., 13:10–17). Yet this gift of understanding is not the cognitive advantage of an enlightened, esoteric group. Consequently, the *disciples,* in contrast to the *crowds,* call him *Lord* (κύριε), thereby expressing their allegiance to him. In spite of this very positive picture, Matthew also preserves the more negative side found in the tradition as well. The *disciples'* faith is often weak, at best. Thus the charge of "little faith" (6:30, par. Luke 12:28; 8:26; 14:31; 16:8) and the exhortation to have "mountain-moving faith" (17:20, par. Luke 17:6; 21:21, par. Mark 11:22–23) is still pertinent.

5:2. *he opened his mouth.* Omitted in the translation because of its redundancy, this phrase gives a somewhat formal tone to the setting (cf. 13:35, from Ps 78:2; Job 3:1; Dan 10:16; Acts 8:35; 10:34).

he began to teach them. Although Jesus repeatedly teaches in Matthew, the imperfect tense most probably reflects the beginning of this teaching (cf. ἤρχατο λέγειν in Syˢ). Matthew has set the stage for this moment with the summary of 4:23. What follows in Matthew 5–7, is a concrete example of Jesus' teaching, the content of which points to Jesus' person for Matthew (cf. 7:28). *Them* (αὐτούς) has for its antecedent the *disciples* (see Comment C for the question of audience). *Stop*

Comments

In the comments that follow, we shall discuss first the setting of the Sermon within the structure of the Gospel and then its place and audience. In the last section, we shall raise the question to what extent Matthew 5–7, is indeed a "Sermon" on the Mount.

A. The Setting of the Sermon in Matthew's Gospel

Taken out of context, the Sermon, like any other passage, can be greatly misunderstood. If we truly desire to hear what was said, we must first of all hear it in context. Unfortunately, even when we seek to do justice to Matthew's context, we encounter multiple views of what the context might be, views ranging from topical outlines superimposed on a Gospel to theological constructs of Matthew's view of redemptive history. (See Kingsbury, *Matthew,* 1–4, for a thorough survey of the literature dealing with the structure of the Gospel.)

1. By far the most prevailing view of Matthew's structure has been the impressive work of Bacon (*Studies,* 81–82), who saw the key to Matthew in the five major discourses concluded by the repeated formula: "When Jesus had finished . . ." (7:28; 11:1; 13:53; 19:1; 26:1). These five discourses, according to Bacon, constitute a pentateuchal motif comparable to the Five Books of Moses. Furthermore, his additional literary analysis of the extended narrative materials between the discourses proved

them to be analogous to the extended narratives of Yahweh's role in Israel's history. Add a preamble and an epilogue and you have the Gospel as it now stands. Interpreted within this framework, the Sermon furnishes its own supporting evidence. Matthew, a "converted rabbi," actually portrayed Jesus as the giver of the New Law, the Sermon on the Mount being the New Torah. The Sermon, therefore, represented the New Torah for Matthew's community.

The strength of Bacon's hypothesis lies in its attempt to take the internal structure of the Gospel seriously. The Sermon finds its place within the Gospel interpreted accordingly. The weakness of the hypothesis is fundamental, however, since it breaks down from both a literary and theological standpoint.

From the literary side, the ascription of "preamble" and "epilogue" is totally inadequate for such integral structural elements as the infancy and passion narratives (on the infancy narratives, see Brown, *Birth*, 48–50; on the passion narrative, see Kingsbury, *Matthew*, 21–25). As to the discourses themselves, the weight of the pentateuchal thesis rests on the five concluding formulas, since there are clearly six discourses when we separate Matthew 23 and 24–25, passages whose audience, location, and content are so different. Furthermore, it is highly dubious that these concluding formulas can serve as the substructure for the entire Gospel. Their function is much less grand. They are primarily concluding formulas that summarize and focus on Jesus' role as teacher while offering a transition to the following material.

From the theological side, any content similarity between the five discourses and the Five Books of Moses is forced at best. In fact, the most "obvious" parallel between Jesus and Moses, offered by the Sermon itself, totally lacks any explicit support. The most that can be said is that Matthew presents Jesus as the one who transcends the "mosaic categories" of the Law, Sinai, and Moses rather than offering the Christian counterpart of same (see Davies, *Setting*, 17–108). Consequently, there are neither literary nor theological bases for understanding the Sermon as set within the context of a pentateuchal theme in Matthew.

2. The safest way to answer the question of the setting is to go again to the Gospel itself. All other suggestions must take seriously Matthew's own work in giving the Sermon a setting. The evangelist has very deliberately given the Sermon an immediate context. The summary (4:23–25) and introduction (5:1–2) which precede the Sermon are basically his redactional products, and he has intentionally placed these verses with view to what follows. Matt. 4:23 opens the summary by detailing three

aspects of Jesus' ministry throughout Galilee—teaching, preaching, and healing. Through his teaching and preaching, the former being essentially a stylistic difference in the elaboration of the latter (see Note on 4:23, *teaching* and *preaching*), Jesus presents the message of the Kingdom, and shows himself to be the fulfillment of the Old Testament promise (see 4:15-16 from Isa 8:23—9:1, cf. Isa 61:1-2). Through his healing, Jesus effects the presence of the Kingdom and shows himself to be the Messiah in whom the Kingdom has come (cf. 11:2-6; 12:28). Matt. 4:24 briefly sets forth this healing ministry and sets the stage for Matthew 8-9, where the evangelist has gathered ten illustrations of Jesus' mighty works. Matt 4:25 notes the impact of Jesus' ministry in Galilee as drawing large crowds from all of Palestine, from the north to the south, including the areas east of the Jordan. These crowds then become the backdrop for the Sermon itself (5:1; 7:28). Matt 5:1-2 next introduces the Sermon as a concrete example of Jesus' teaching (5:2; 7:28). Together the five chapters (5-9) form specific demonstrations of Jesus as being the "Messiah of Word" (5-7) and the "Messiah of Deed" (8-9). The inclusion formed by the identical summaries of 4:23 and 9:35 reflects the evangelist's intention that the Sermon be understood as an integral part of the larger complex, Matt 4:23—9:35.

This setting drawn from the immediate context of the Sermon concurs with the overall structure of Matthew as suggested by Stonehouse (*Witness*, 129-31) and developed by Kingsbury (*Matthew*, 12-25). Matthew's Gospel is divided into three major sections by the phrase: "From that time on, Jesus began . . ." (4:17; 16:21). This expression serves as an introduction to parts two (4:17—16:20) and three (16:21—28:20). The first division 1:1—4:16) focuses on the person of Jesus Messiah; the second (4:17—16:20) on the presentation of Jesus Messiah himself and the summons to the Kingdom; and finally, the third division (16:21—28:20) encompasses the suffering, death, and resurrection of Jesus Messiah. The strength of this alternative lies in its recognition of the literary and the theological structure of the Gospel.

In this understanding of Matthew's structure, the Sermon would be an integral part of Jesus' presentation of himself and his summons to the Kingdom. Therefore, the setting in Matthew, in view of both the immediate as well as the overall context, highlights the christological concerns of the evangelist. These christological concerns must not be minimized nor ignored in an attempt to understand the Sermon on the Mount. Indeed, it is in light of this christological center that the ecclesiological and redemptive historical perspectives must be read.

B. Sermon on the Mount/Plain

In the Lucan parallel (6:12–49) Jesus, who had gone up the mountain to pray and to choose the twelve disciples (6:12–16), descended to "a level place," where he was met by crowds of people with their sick, whom he healed (6:17–19). He then "lifted up his eyes on his disciples and said . . ." (6:20). On the basis of this apparently different setting, Luke's Sermon has sometimes been called the "Sermon on the Plain" in contrast to Matthew's "Sermon on the Mount." Several explanations have been offered for this difference in location.

1. Some answers reflect what might be called a *historical* concern. Since, as is assumed, the Gospels intend primarily to give precise statements of history, statements about the when and where of past events, we must either "harmonize" these differences of location or accept them as reflecting two different Sermons. In view of the other differences between the Sermons in Matthew and Luke, the latter alternative removes any further tension between the two accounts. This position is plausibly supported by the claim that Jesus, during his three-year ministry, may well have preached essentially the same sermon at more than one location. Yet one can also harmonize the two locations (most recently, Marshall, *Luke*, 241–42). Since Jesus was in the hill country of Galilee, he could have descended from the top of a mountain to a plateau where the multitudes were gathered (Luke 6:17) and still be on the mountain (Matt 5:1, the general heading). Presumably the difficulty of bringing the sick to such an area could be overcome by their earnest desire to reach Jesus for healing at any cost. The issue is not whether Matt 5:1–2 and Luke 6:17–19 can be aligned but whether the rest of the Sermon (or for that matter the Gospels themselves) reflects in any way such a precise historical interest by the use of such introductory statements.

2. Other answers reflect what might be called a *theological* concern. In this case the Gospels, it is assumed, are concerned primarily with theological rather than historical issues. Luke accordingly has a developed Sinai motif in 6:12–20. Just as Moses, Aaron, Nadab, Abihu, and the seventy elders of Israel were called up Sinai apart from the rest of the nation (Exod 24:2, 9), so Jesus went up the mountain to spend the night in prayer and to call apart his twelve disciples (6:12–16). And just as Moses descended from the mountain to address the people (Exod 32:7,15; 34:29), so Jesus descended from the mountain (6:17) to address the people (Schürmann, *Lukasevangelium*, 313, 320). A similar suggestion has often been made regarding the mountain in Matt 5:1. If in Luke the focus is

on ascending and descending the mountain, the focus in Matthew has been more on Jesus, the New Moses, who gives the New Law on the New Sinai (Loisy, *Evangiles* 1:535, and, recently, Grundmann, *Matthäus*, 114). The support for this view is the programmatic character of the Sermon itself.

Both solutions lack concrete evidence within the texts themselves. In the first case, one must ignore the sharp differences between Exodus 24 and Luke 6:12–17. Furthermore, Luke does not stress the descent of Jesus but the "level place" which has no parallel in the Exodus account. In Matthew's case, the apparent parallel between Jesus and Moses breaks down, if the Sermon is not taken as a New Law and Jesus is not viewed elsewhere in Matthew as the New Moses. Others who explain the mountain in more general terms as a place of revelation do have supporting evidence for such a usage in that day (see Note on 5:1, *mountain*). But the lack of solid evidence that *mountain* consistently functioned so specifically elsewhere in Matthew makes it questionable whether it had that primary meaning for Matthew.

3. A much more prosaic alternative suggests that the intention of both evangelists in this instance was neither primarily historical nor primarily theological but *literary* in character. Each evangelist was influenced by his own context and the context of his tradition. Matthew had the tradition of Jesus on the mountain in both Q (cf. Luke 6:12) and Mark (3:13). He simply followed his tradition for this setting. The situation is not a lot different in Luke, who apparently introduced a "level place" into his material in view of his insertion of the crowds and their sick from Mark 3:7–12, par. 6:17–19, into his Q material. The large crowds and their obvious physical limitations would condition Jesus' descending to meet them on a "level place" to heal and address them, whereas a typological concern needs only a descent. Consequently, the difference between Matthew and Luke's location of the Sermon is ultimately the result of Luke's redactional insertion of Mark 3:7–12 into the Q context. Any theological tendencies are secondary, if at all. According to the tradition, therefore, Jesus gave the Sermon on a mountain.

This solution simply moves the question back one stage to the tradition itself. To what extent does the tradition reflect a theological tendency to localize events such as the calling of the Twelve, the Sermon, the Transfiguration, and the Olivet Discourse on a mountain, and to what extent was this a historically accurate description of the location of the events; or was it both? The ultimate answer to this question lies beyond our historical control. For example, the dual tradition (Mark and Q) about the calling of the Twelve on a mountain may support the historical probability of such a locale. But the combination of the Sermon tradition with the traditional mountain setting for the calling for the Twelve may have resulted merely from the Church's catechetical interest in the Q Sermon material for new "disciples" in the early church.

C. The Question of Audience: Then and Now

For whom was the Sermon on the Mount intended? For whom is it intended today? Naturally, the ultimate answer to that question is closely related to the content and intent of the Sermon itself. Yet one may gain insight into the evangelists' understanding by a closer look at the texts. Our answer to the question must at least start there.

1. The underlying Sermon tradition (5:1–2, par. Luke 6:20) clearly had the disciples as the audience for the Sermon (see Note on 5:1, *disciples*). Both Matthew and Luke, however, have the crowd(s) in the larger context (5:1; 7:28; Luke 6:17–19). Does this not imply that the Sermon was spoken indiscriminately to both groups—the crowds and the disciples? The answer is a definite affirmative. Why then the distinction?

In Luke the crowds are deliberately introduced into the setting from Mark 3:7–12. They interrupt the Q tradition between the call of the disciples (6:12–16) and the giving of the Sermon (6:20–49). In 6:17 they are "the people" in contrast to the disciples. Yet they have come to hear and to be healed (6:18–19). The crowd of the people represents the masses who respond to the Church's mission, a prefiguring of the new People of God (cf. Acts 15:14; 18:10) who stand in continuity with the "People of God," Israel. Luke has intentionally introduced Mark 3:7–12 into the context of Jesus and his disciples to foreshadow Jesus' ministry through the disciples to the Church (see Schürmann, *Lukasevangelium*, 321–22; more remotely, Flender, *Heil*, 120–21). For Matthew, the crowds are a neutral chorus with little or no theological significance (see Note on 4:25, *crowds*). They often form Jesus' audience alongside the disciples (e.g., 13:2, 10; 15:10, 12; 23:1). Although both are part of the audience, only the disciples have been given "ears" to "hear" (13:10–16). The disciples are the ones who respond, who do the will of the Father (12:49–50, cf. 12:46). They stand in stark contrast to the crowds.

In Luke 6:17–20, the crowd and the disciples form concentric circles, with the disciples being the closer (6:20a); in Matthew, however, this relationship is not as clear. The tension between the crowds' role which stands in contrast to that of the disciples in 5:1 and their somewhat unexpected appearance in 7:28 is again more literary than theological. In 7:28 the crowds play their role as a "chorus" by responding with astonishment at Jesus' authority. The crowds in 5:1 are the redactional bridge between 4:23–25 and the Sermon. Matthew's Q tradition specified the disciples as the actual audience. Consequently, the resultant tension between 5:1 and 7:28 is characteristic of Matthew's style of leaving loose ends when using tradition and his own redaction, as we shall see. Recognizing this tension to be a literary product, we should not push Matthew beyond his own limits.

2. But what about the audience today? In view of the discussion above, we cannot take the Sermon in either Luke or Matthew as being directed primarily towards humanity in general. It was never intended to be a general statement which could be readily heard and practiced by everyone. Neither is it to be understood as an esoteric body of material intelligible only to a select few. Both Matthew and Luke, each in his own way, have two elements, the crowd(s) and the disciples, in order to reflect the impact of the Sermon. For Luke, it is for all who will hear and respond to Jesus' ministry; for Matthew, the Sermon distinguishes the disciples from the crowds—the one element "hears" and responds by doing (7:21; 12:49–50, 46), while the other is "astonished" (7:28). The Sermon becomes the dividing line. Both Luke and Matthew agree that the actual audience, the ones who do "hear," has to do with how one relates to Jesus. Accordingly, the Sermon is available to all today, but not all will "hear." The ultimate question today, as then, is not to whom does Jesus speak, but who "hears" him.

D. Sermon or Instruction?

Using the familiar biblical theological distinction, is Matthew 5–7 kerygma or didache? Or, to change the nomenclature to that of systematics, is it Law or Gospel? For a great part of the church, if not its vast majority, and certainly for the average person who seeks to "live according to the Sermon on the Mount," these chapters are ethical instruction or paranesis, the Law, the Magna Charta, the Constitution, the ethical essence of Christianity. Even Matthew seems to support this perspective by introducing and concluding the "Sermon" as Jesus' "teaching." To what extent can we then call it a "Sermon"? Was it kerygma or didache for Matthew?

It is much too early to answer this basic question, since the final answer must come after we have sought to hear what the evangelist was saying. Only then can we ask, on the one hand, the historical question of how the Sermon correlates with what Jesus said and, on the other hand, the ultimate question of what it says to us today. It is at that point that the question of the Sermon's essential character becomes acute. Suffice it to say for the present that Matthew himself would probably be unaware of the sharp distinction between kerygma and didache as seen by his tandem use of teaching and preaching (see Note on 4:23, *teaching, preaching*) as well as his understanding of Jesus' ministry per se as being the *gospel* (see Note on 4:23, *gospel*). His christology has, in fact, not been eclipsed by his ecclesiology.

III. THE GOSPEL OF THE KINGDOM
Matthew 5:3–12

Translation

5 ³Blessed are the poor in spirit,
    for theirs is the Kingdom of Heaven.
⁴Blessed are those who mourn,
    for they shall be comforted.
⁵Blessed are the meek,
    for they shall inherit the earth.
⁶Blessed are those who hunger and thirst for righteousness,
    for they shall be satisfied.

⁷Blessed are the merciful,
    for they shall receive mercy.
⁸Blessed are the pure in heart,
    for they shall see God.
⁹Blessed are the peacemakers,
    for they shall be called sons of God.
¹⁰Blessed are those who are persecuted for righteousness' sake,
    for theirs is the Kingdom of Heaven.

¹¹Blessed are you whenever people ridicule you, persecute you,
    and falsely say all kinds of evil things about you for my sake.
¹²Rejoice and be glad for your heavenly reward will be great,
    for in similar manner they persecuted the prophets before you.

Literary Analysis

A. Form

The Beatitudes of the Sermon have a distinctive literary form called a beatitude (Latin, *beatitudo*) or a makarism (Greek, μακάριος). There are forty-four such beatitudes in the New Testament: twenty-eight in Matthew and Luke (Matt 5:5, 7, 8, 9, 10; 16:17; Luke 1:45; 11:27, 28; 12:37, 38; 14:14, 15; 23:29; counted together, Matt 5:3, 4, 6, 11–12, par. Luke 6:20, 21, 22; 11:6, par. Luke 7:23; 13:16, par. Luke 10:23; 24:46, par. Luke 12:43), two in John (13:17; 20:29), three in Paul (Rom 4:7, 8; 14:22), two in James (1:12, 25), two in 1 Peter (3:14; 4:14), and seven in Revelation (1:3; 14:13; 16:15; 19:9; 20:6; 22:7, 14). Yet these beatitudes lack uniformity in form and content. This diversity corresponds to the variety in Hellenism and Judaism.

In classical Greek, the form usually began with a μακαρ-formula (sometimes with the earlier ὄλβιος) followed by a relative clause (ὅς, ὅστις) and a finite verb generally in the third person plural. The content generally reflected the Greek philosophy of life by referring to internal and external conditions, such as material wealth or honor, that assured one of happiness. In the Hellenistic period, the same form and content persisted, but its frequency faded significantly except in the LXX. Although its influence is occasionally felt in the biblical literature, Judaism offers the more immediate background for the New Testament.

In Judaism, the actual form is quite varied. Beginning with the forty-five occurrences in the Hebrew Old Testament, each is introduced by the plural construct *'šry* generally followed by a participle or a noun/pronoun with a participle that identifies the subject (see Keller, " 'béatitude,' " 90–91, for various Old Testament forms). These beatitudes are almost all in the third person (cf. Gen 30:13). The content consists of the blessing and a description of the recipient, usually identified by an attitude or conduct befitting the blessing. The details of the blessing or its promise are inherent in the pronouncement or the immediate context and correspond to Israel's understanding of "well-being": life (Prov 8:34); security (Ps 40:4); deliverance (Ps 2:11); military success (Deut 33:29); prosperity (Ps 1:2); posterity (Ps 127:5); help, justice, and abundance of food (Ps 146:5–7). Any hint of an eschatological hope is rare (e.g., Isa 30:18; 32:20; Dan 12:12).

With the greatest concentration of the beatitudes occurring in the Psalms and Wisdom literature, the original setting for the beatitude in Israel's history is much debated. Some have viewed the beatitude as a derivative of the blessing-formulas and at home in the cult (Pedersen, *Israel* 1:140–64; Mowinckel, *Psalms* 2:44–52; Brun, *Segen,* 39–48). Its function in such a setting would be almost sacramental, a dynamic pronouncement that conveys a blessing to the recipient. Others, following Gunkel's lead, have placed it originally within a Wisdom context where its function would be more paranetic, "a classic form of religious and moral exhortation" (George, " 'Form,' " 400; Gunkel, *Psalmen,* 55, 296; Bertram, *TDNT* 4:365; Koch, *Tradition,* 7; Kiefer, "Seligpreisungen," 36–43). Still others have posited neither a cultic nor a Wisdom setting but the more common formulas of greeting and congratulations as the background for the beatitude. Its function then would neither convey a blessing nor exhort one morally or religiously but recognize and declare what is already the case for the group or individual (Schmidt, "Grüsse," 141–50; Kraus, *Psalmen* 1:2; Lipinski, "macarismes," 321–23; Janzen, "*Ašrê,*" 224–26; Dupont, *Béatitudes* 3:317–18). Ultimately the question of original setting and function becomes rather moot, since the Wisdom motif of "living in keeping with principles prescribed by God and the wise" (Koch, *Tradition,* 7) eventually predominates in these expressions. The declarative sentence gradually becomes an exhortation, as illustrated by the beatitudes' numerous occurrences in the Wisdom writing of the later period.

In the intertestamental literature (including the apocalypses of the early Christian era), the beatitude reflects two very different usages. The first stands in continuity with the majority of the Old Testament beatitudes and appears within the Wisdom-oriented literature of the period (Wis 3:13–14; Sir 14:1–2, 20; 25:8, 9; 26:1; 28:19; 31:8; 34:15; 48:11; Tob 13:15–16; 2 *Bar* 4:4; *Pss Sol* 4:23; 5:16; 6:1; 10:1; 17:44; 18:6). Formally, the only change is the introduction of an extended explanation of the promise (2 *Bar* 4:4; Tob 13:13–16; Wis 3:13–14). Materially, the content also remains quite similar to the beatitudes of the Old Testament, with the one notable exception being the eschatological character of Tob 13:13–16. The second usage, however, is completely future-oriented and differs significantly from the Old Testament usages. It is found primarily in the apocalyptic writings. The form remains basically unchanged, but a tendency to group beatitudes in greater numbers and at times with antithetical woes does appear (e.g., 1 *Enoch* 103:5; 2 *Bar* 10:6–7; cf. 1 *Enoch* 99:10–15). The content, by contrast, has undergone considerable change. First, the ones pronounced blessed are people in distress, under severe pressure and all but hopeless. Second, the promise is otherworldly with no hope of well-being offered for this life. The content is clearly eschatological and reflects a pessimistic view towards this age and the apocalyptic hope for the age to come. The roots of this strictly eschatological usage may extend back to Isa 30:18; 32:20; and Dan 12:12. The effect of the content change underlines the declarative aspect of the beatitude. Therefore, it comes as consolation, assurance, and encouragement rather than ethical paranesis.

Consequently, in the Jewish literature of the Old Testament and intertestamental period we find a certain variety in the beatitude form but always including a pronouncement of blessing upon a recipient whose identity reflects a certain conduct or attitude. The content of these beatitudes points to two very different contexts within Judaism (Koch, *Tradition*, 7). In the Wisdom-cultic setting, the beatitude is a declarative statement whose implications border on a paranetic exhortation. The statement of blessing becomes in turn a model to be emulated or a goal to be attained. An ethical tone prevails. In the prophetic-apocalyptic setting, the beatitude is a declarative statement of future vindication and reward. It comes as assurance and encouragement in the face of trouble. The eschatological tone prevails. How do the Beatitudes of Matt 5:3–12, par. Luke 6:20–23 compare against these backgrounds?

The Beatitudes are similar in construction to those of the LXX: μακάρισμοι followed by a substantival participle or adjective. Even the difference between Matthew's third person and Luke's second person has a correspondence in Jewish (and Greek) literature. Yet there is one significant formal difference. The promise is consistently explained with a ὅτι-clause. In terms of content, the explicit promise with reference to the future aligns the Beatitudes with the prophetic-apocalyptic settings. But the difference between the condition, in Luke, of being poor, weeping, being hungry, and being hated and the apparent attitudes, in Matthew, of being poor in spirit, hungry and thirsting for righteousness, of being meek, merciful, pure in heart, and peaceable, seem to place the Matthean Beatitudes in line with the Wisdom-cultic setting. Consequently, Luke's Beatitudes have been taken as eschatological blessings, whereas Matthew's appear more like entrance requirements for the Kingdom. Ethics have been placed over eschatology. This difference between Matthew and Luke is further accentuated by the use of the more aphoristic third person in contrast to Luke's direct address of the second person. Apart from the question of the source for this difference, one should remember that such a distinction is more apparent than real. By far the majority of beatitudes in the Hebrew and Greek literature were in the third person, even in acute situations like the apocalyptic literature.

On the basis of form criticism, therefore, we are left with the crucial question: are Matthew's Beatitudes blessings of the new age (eschatological) or are they new principles for living (ethical)? To what extent have ethics swallowed up eschatology in Matthew? The answer can first come after the content of the Beatitudes has been more closely examined (see Comment, B).

B. Source

A comparison of the Matthean and Lucan accounts shows that they share four Beatitudes in common (5:3, 4, 6, 11–12, par. Luke 6:20–23). The consensus of scholarship has assigned these to the Q tradition. Yet there are significant differences in the four parallels: Matthew's third person plural in contrast to Luke's second person plural, Luke's Woes, and Matthew's five additional Beatitudes. Furthermore, Matthew and Luke differ in the wording of each parallel and in the order of the second and third parallels (5:4, 6, cf. Luke 6:21). Most have attributed these differences to the redactional interests of the respective evangelists. But there are sufficient differences to raise seriously the question of whether they indeed shared a common tradition (Wrege, *Überlieferungsgeschichte*, 5–27). These differences will need to be discussed in their appropriate places (see Notes on 5:3–12), after which we shall return to the question of source and the history of the tradition (see Comment, C).

Notes

5:3. *Blessed are.* The word μακάριοι (Hebrew, ʾšry) introduces a literary form called a *makarismen* or, more commonly, a beatitude (see Literary Analysis). In addition to the nine Beatitudes of 5:3–12, Matthew has four others (11:6, par. Luke 7:23; 13:16, par. Luke 10:23; 16:17; 24:46, par. Luke 12:43). The difficulty of expressing the meaning of the Greek term in English is apparent in the diverse translations: "Blessed"— KJV, RSV, ASV: "how blest"—NEB; "how happy"—JB, PHILLIPS; "Happy" —TEV; "fortunate"—LB.

The question of translation is integral to the beatitude's function. For those who consider a beatitude against a cultic setting to be a type of blessing, a sacramental or cultic expression, with its inherent, dynamic role of effecting what it announces (Brun, *Segen,* 39; cf. Schweizer, "Formgeschichtliches," 126), the more precise translation would be "blessed." Since, however, the correlation between the beatitude and the blessing is very dubious (Janzen, "*ʾAšrê,*" 218–24) and since it definitely loses its sacramental character in the Wisdom setting, this function is highly suspect. For those who consider a beatitude against a Wisdom background to be an exhortation for one to exhibit a particular attitude or conduct (George, " 'Form,' " 400; cf. Strecker, "Makarismen," 261–66, 273–75), the word "happy" or "fortunate" is more appropriate. In other words, "happy" or "fortunate" are those who become "poor in spirit," for the promise of the Kingdom of Heaven is theirs. Somewhat related to the first view but less sacramental is the function of the beatitude as a formula of greeting or congratulations (Lipinski, "Macarismes," 321–67; Dupont, *Béatitudes* 2:332–84). "Congratulations to" conveys the dynamic character of μακάριοι in the English idiom.

By the congratulatory statement, the subject is recognized and directly affected by the content of the declaration. The primary difference between the paranetic and the congratulatory perspectives lies in the point of focus. The former emphasizes the subject's attitude and behavior; the latter stresses the declaration of μακάριοι and its explication in the promise. The question of translation ultimately depends on whether Matthew has "ethicized" the Beatitudes to become "entrance requirements" for the Kingdom or whether they are eschatological promises announced to the unsuspecting or undeserving. By using *blessed* in the translation, we have maintained the familiar—even if ambiguous—term.

the poor in spirit. Matthew's *poor in spirit* stands in contrast to *the poor* of Luke 6:20b. Whereas Matt 5:3 apparently refers to an attitude, Luke 6:20b apparently refers to a socioeconomic status, especially when set in antithetical parallelism with the Woe to *the rich* of 6:24. In order to see more clearly the similarity and dissimilarity between the two forms of this Beatitude, we need to examine the Lucan form in detail.

Excursus: Blessed Are the Poor

Who were *the poor* in (1) the Greek setting, (2) the Jewish setting, (3) the pre-Lucan traditional setting and the Lucan setting, and (4) in the setting of Jesus' ministry?

(1) In Greek literature πτωχός has an exclusively socioeconomic meaning (Hauck, *TDNT* 2:886–87). The antithetical Woe to *the rich* in 6:24, the hunger and weeping of the other Beatitudes as well as the Greek concept of περιπετεία—the great reversal of conditions—evident in the Beatitudes and Woes (Dodd, "Beatitudes," 5–6) all appear to point to a "Hellenistic" understanding of *the poor* as the economically deprived. The key element, however, in the first Beatitude is the promise of the Kingdom of God. This promise not only breaks the neat περιπετεία pattern *(poor/rich)*, but it is hardly a Greek concept. Therefore, *the poor* of this Beatitude must first be understood in terms of its Jewish background.

2) In the Old Testament, πτωχός occurs nearly one hundred times as the translation for six Hebrew terms (Bammel, *TDNT* 6:888–89). The most common of these words, ʿny and its later relative, ʿnw have a much broader scope than simply to denote a socioeconomic status. A close look at these terms leads to some general observations. First, ʿny has both a socio-economic as well as a religious connotation. The basic meaning refers to one's dependency upon another to whom one is answerable. The ʿny refers to one so powerless and dependent as to be vulnerable to exploitation by those who have the power base. Thus the accent falls on a socioeconomic *relationship* rather than on material possessions as such (Bammel, *TDNT* 6:888). Yet this powerless and dependent relationship caused one to rely upon God for one's needs and vindication. This humble posture of *the poor* devoid of pretention before God reflects the religious dimension and comes out frequently in the Psalms (e.g., Pss 14:6; 22:24; 25:16; 34:6; 40:17; 69:29; 82:3; 86:1; 88:15). But the religious dimension is never exclusive of the socioeconomic. Both elements are integral to ʿny (Percy, *Botschaft*, 40–81).

Second, the reliance upon God results from the consistent Old Testament portrait of God as being the protector and vindicator of *the poor* (2 Sam 22:28; Ps 72:2, 4, 12; Isa 26:6; 49:13; 66:2; Zeph 3:12). His concern for the plight of *the poor* is also reflected in the Law (Exod 22:25–27; 23:10–11; Lev 19:9–10; 23:22; Deut 15:7–11) and his vindication of *the poor* means that justice will be done and judgment will be the lot of the rich and powerful who abuse *the poor* by misuse of the Law (e.g., Pss 7; 10; 35:10; 37:14–15). Third, the prophets echo the theme of vindication and judgment. They charge the rich and powerful of the nation with abusing *the poor* and helpless and announce God's coming judgment accordingly (Amos 8:4; Isa 3:14, 15; 10:2; 32:7; Ezek 16:49; 18:12; 22:29; cf. Jer 22:16; Zech 7:10). Furthermore, two significant modifications occur in Isaiah. On the one hand, *the poor* becomes more or less synonymous with the exiled People of God (26:6; 49:13; 51:21; 54:11; cf. 29:19; 61:1). On the other hand, the promise of God's vindication of *the poor* in the future emerges in full view as an eschatological hope (cf. Isa 49; 51; 54; 61).

Fourth, the term ʿnwm begins to appear in the later Old Testament writings.

It overlaps in meaning with the dual focus of ʿny (cf. Pss 6; 10:9–12; 22:24, 26; 34:2 and Isa 51:21; 54:11; 61:1), but the accent is clearly on the religious element of the dependent relationship between *the poor* and God. Consequently, whereas the LXX only rarely translated ʿny with πραΰς (Zeph 3:12; Zech 9:9; Isa 26:6), the LXX commonly translates ʿnwm with πραΰς in the Psalms (25[24]:9; 34[33]:2; 37[36]:11; 76[75]:9; 147[146]:6; 149:4). Both ʿny and ʿnwm with their dual socioeconomical and religious connotations continue in usage into Qumran (ʿnyym: 1QH 1:36; 2:34; 5:13, 14; 1Q45 1:1; 3:2; CD 6:16, 21; 14:14; 19:9; ʿnwm: 1QM 14:7; 1QH 5:21; 14:3; 18:14; 1QSb 5:22; 4QpIsᵃ). Rabbinic usage, by contrast, relegated ʿnyym to a label of opprobrium for those too poor to keep the Law (Bammel, *TDNT* 6:901–2; Str-B 1:191–94, 197–200), while ʿnwm was preserved strictly as a virtue meaning "humble."

Fifth, there is no solid basis for positing the existence of a particular group within Judaism known as *the poor* (Percy, *Botschaft*, 40–81, con. Wrege, *Überlieferungsgeschichte*, 6–7). Qumran's use of ʿnyym, ʿnwm, and even ʾbnm (1QpHab 12:3, 6, 10; 4QpPs 37 1:9; 2:10) merely indicates that they used several designations rather than a single term to describe themselves in the language of the Old Testament and its promise (Schubert, "Sermon," 122; Légasse, "Pauvres," 336–45). Furthermore, the New Testament offers little support for the existence of such a group either inside or outside the church (Keck, "The Poor," 100–129).

In summary, *the poor* in Judaism referred to those in desperate need (socioeconomic element) whose helplessness drove them to a dependent relationship with God (religious element) for the supplying of their needs and vindication. Both elements are consistently present, although ʿnwm does place more stress on the latter. Only in rabbinic thought do the two Hebrew terms mean strictly poverty or piety. How does Luke's Beatitude to *the poor* fit into this background?

3) In Luke 6:20b πτωχοί appears to stand in conflict with this Jewish background by referring strictly to the socioeconomic status of *the poor*. The antithesis between the Beatitude to *the poor* and the Woe to *the rich* is also characteristic of Luke's Gospel, which contrasts elsewhere the rich and the poor (e.g., 1:48–53; 6:20–24; 12:13–21; 14:7–14, 15–24; 16:19–31; 19:1–10). It would be easy to conclude, therefore, that any understanding of *the poor* apart from a socioeconomic aspect is far from Luke's interest and intention and that the Beatitude reflects his redactional modification of the tradition (cf. Matt 5:3–4, 6).

Such a conclusion, however, is premature for several reasons, not least of which is the fact that each of the supporting illustrations noted above belongs to the pre-Lucan tradition. The theme of judgment of *the rich* and the vindication of *the poor* has its basis in Old Testament Judaism. Yet it is important to note that *the rich* in none of these illustrations is judged because of his exploiting or abusing *the poor*. Rather, the terms *rich* and *poor* demonstrate primarily differing attitudes towards God which express themselves secondarily in one's relationship to others and their needs. Whereas *the rich* were culpable for their sense of self-security, their having taken God for granted (1:51–53; 12:15, 19, 21; 14:15–20; 16:25, 29, 31), *the poor* found their only hope in God (1:48, 53; 14:21–23; 16:25). Consequently, even in the pre-Lucan tradition, the concepts *poor* and *rich* maintain their religious as well as their socioeconomic points of reference.

Luke clearly chooses to use the traditional pericopes that stress the difference between *the rich* and *the poor*. He does so quite possibly because they correspond in a general way to the socioeconomic realities of the church's situation. *The poor* and social rejects have in fact responded to the message of the Kingdom. *The rich* and powerful, on the contrary, have generally rejected the message. To say that poverty itself was either an ideal of or a prerequisite for the gospel in Luke would be going too far. Poverty was more of a reality than an ideal for his church. By using these traditional pericopes, Luke both clarified the situation within the church and its mission and also offered the church encouragement. The promise of the future is indeed theirs already. In this light, *the poor* of 6:20b refers to the church for Luke as the socioeconomically deprived, comparable to the tax collectors and sinners (Luke 15:1–2) who have responded to God's offer on their behalf in the present and future (Degenhardt, *Lukas,* 50–51; Schürmann, *Lukasevangelium,* 328; cf. Dupont, *Béatitudes* 3:28). The "rich" and the "righteous" will ultimately be judged (6:24) because of their self-righteousness and self-sufficiency (Dupont, *Béatitudes* 3:56–64; Schürmann, *Lukasevangelium,* 337–39). The pre-Lucan tradition and Luke's application of this Beatitude, therefore, are not so far removed from the Old Testament perspective after all.

(4) The basic question remains: what did *the poor* mean in the original setting of the Beatitude? When we move to the underlying Hebrew term behind πτωχοί, we are most certainly at home in Isaiah's promises directed to the ʿnyym and ʿnwm (26:6; 29:19; 49:13; 51:21; 54:11; 61:1–2). In fact, the pronouncement of *the poor* as *blessed* because the *Kingdom of God* is theirs is unavoidably similar to Isa 61:1. This relationship between the Beatitude and Isa 61:1 seems all but confirmed by the fact that πτωχοί = "poor" is the LXX translation for ʿnwm which is usually translated by πραεῖς = "meek" (also Isa 29:19). When we add to this Beatitude the ones to the *hungry* and *weeping* of 6:21, we have a vivid portrait of the oppressed poor of both the Psalms and Isaiah.

Since these Beatitudes are then analogous to the prophetic/apocalyptic beatitudes that console and encourage the faithful in view of the future deliverance, some have suggested that they had their original setting in the sayings of the early Christian prophets (Käsemann, "Beginnings," 100–101; cf. also Schulz, *Spruchquelle,* 78). This approach, however, overlooks the distinctive tension between the present fulfillment and the future consummation of the promises in 6:20b, 21, a tension that is totally uncharacteristic of apocalyptic eschatology. It also is influenced more by the form than by the content of the Beatitudes, since it leaves unanswered the question of how those within the Church came to be called *the poor.*

The Gospel tradition clearly identified Jesus' ministry with the fulfillment of Isa 61:1–2 (Luke 4:16–21; Matt. 11:5, par. Luke 7:22). This association was not made because the Church understood Isa 61:1 as referring to the eschatological prophet expected by Judaism (Stuhlmacher, *Evangelium,* 222–25) and applied it to Jesus. Rather, they saw him as "more than a prophet," and his ministry bore witness to that. He came declaring the good news and effecting the rule of God in the lives of those who followed him (Matt. 12:46–50), who sat at table with him (Mark 2:16; Matt 11:16–19, par. Luke 7:31–35), and who were in need of physical wholeness (Mark 2:1–12; Matt 12:28, par. Luke 11:20). If *the poor* applied to any in Jesus' ministry, it applied to those who responded to him, those to whom the Kingdom was announced and in whose lives it was effected (see Note below on *Kingdom of Heaven*). It is among the people gathered around Jesus that we find the clue to *the poor* and the original setting of the Beatitude.

Nevertheless, the people whom Jesus called and attracted to himself were neither particularly poor, oppressed—although doubtless numbered among the ʿm hʾrṣ—nor were they devout in the rabbinic sence of the ʿnwm. From a Jewish perspective they obviously did not qualify as *the poor* of Judaism. Yet Jesus' ministry is twice described in the tradition in terms of Isa 61:1 in which the "good news" is preached to *the poor* (Luke 4:16–21; Matt. 11:5, par. Luke 7:22). Since there was such obvious discontinuity between the people who responded to Jesus' ministry and *the poor* of Judaism, is it not most probable that Isa 61:1 came to describe Jesus' ministry in the tradition of the early church precisely because he himself used it in his own unique way?

Indeed, there is a sense in which *the poor* of Jesus' ministry did stand in continuity with the Old Testament concept. Those attracted by his ministry were the social and religious outcasts of Jewish religious society. They had no claim upon God but his mercy (Luke 18:9–14). Recognizing in various, admittedly limited, ways that God was somehow at work in Jesus, the sick turned to him out of desperation and the disciples left their families and professions to follow him. In so doing, they showed themselves to be *the poor,* namely, those who stood empty-handed, without a power base and pretense, before God.

In view of this continuity and discontinuity between the use of *the poor* in Jesus' ministry and the Old Testament, the Beatitude to *the poor* and the theme of Isa 61:1 are part and parcel of Jesus' earthly ministry which, although a part of, stands over against Judaism. Both the Beatitude and the application of Isa 61:1 to Jesus have their most natural *Sitz im Leben* in his ministry to *the poor* rather than in early Christian prophecy (so Percy, *Botschaft*, 108).

In summary, the Beatitude *Blessed are the poor* has the Old Testament concept of *the poor* as its frame of reference. The roots of the Beatitude go back to Jesus' ministry which fulfilled the promise of Isaiah directed to *the poor*. Recognizing the dire need and helplessness of the social and religious rejects of that day who responded to his ministry of the Kingdom, Jesus, using the language of Isa 61:1, declared such *poor* as *blessed,* for theirs was indeed *the Kingdom of God.* In so doing, he was announcing the day of fulfillment, the age of salvation in and through his work and teaching.

Later this and the other Beatitudes were set in an antithetical context with the Woes in a manner reminiscent of the Old Testament concept of God's vindication of the poor and needy by judging the rich and powerful. Luke, who may have simply taken this antithesis from the tradition along with other similar reversal motifs (Schürmann, *Lukasevangelium*, 339–40) addressed a church that was composed largely of the socioeconomically poor and Gentile. By reiterating Jesus' teaching of promise and hope that God has indeed acted on behalf of those in need, he encouraged his own community and explained the situation of the church's mission. The basis for the Beatitude in Jesus' ministry emerges in Luke's introduction of Jesus and his public ministry in 4:16–21, namely, Isa 61:1–2.

The interpretations of *the poor in spirit* range from "voluntarily poor" (Ps Clem, *Recog* 2:28; Lohmeyer, *Matthäus*, 82–83; Schubert, "Sermon," 122) to "spiritually poor" or "humble" (Zahn, *Matthäus*, 181–82; Dupont, *Béatitudes* 3:462–65, 470–71). Between these alternatives lie various combinations of the socioeconomic and religious dimensions, the one being more prominent than the other (Schlatter, *Matthäus*, 133; Percy, *Botschaft*, 41–43; Schniewind, *Matthäus*, 41; Hill, *Matthew*, 110–11; Schweizer, *Matthew*, 86–87; Légasse, "Pauvres," 341–45). The phrase has also been interpreted outside the socioeconomic and religious context as referring to the Spirit of God (e.g., "the poor enriched by the Holy Spirit," Flusser, "Blessed," 6) and as the equivalent of "faint-hearted" (Best, "Matthew," 256–57). See Dupont, *Béatitudes* 3:385–471, for a general survey of the history of interpretation.

1. The ambiguous dative of reference πτωχοὶ τῷ πνεύματι (BDR §197, n. 3) translates the Hebrew/Aramaic construct position of *poor* with *spirit.* What this construction actually means must be determined by parallel expressions and similar constructions: e.g., "crushed in spirit," Ps 34(33):18(19); "proud in spirit," Eccl 7:8; cf. "upright in heart," Pss 11(10):2; 32(31):11 and "pure in heart," Ps 24(23):4. Two of these

expressions appear in Matthew (5:8, "pure in heart," and 11:29, "meek and lowly in heart"). Each phrase refers to the "heart" and "spirit" as the seat of one's feelings, spiritual and rational functions, and volition (Baumgärtel, *TDNT* 6:361–62). The focus is on the noun rather than the adjective itself. From this analogy one can conclude that *poor in spirit* means the "spirit" is qualified as being "poor." External or material poverty seems to be transferred to an internal "poverty of spirit" (so Dupont, *Béatitudes* 3:386–99).

2. The Hebrew equivalent, ʿnwy rwḥ, actually occurs in the War Scroll of Qumran (1QM 14:7) and offers the first direct parallel in Jewish literature to Matt 5:3. But even here in Qumran the meaning is not unequivocal. According to Schubert ("Sermon," 122), the members of the Qumran community called themselves the "voluntarily poor" since they had voluntarily abandoned their material possessions. (A similar understanding of "voluntarily poor" can be found as early as Ps Clem, *Recog* 2:28 and as recent as Lohmeyer, *Matthäus*, 82–83.) Yet it is very doubtful whether such an understanding captures the full force of the construction "poor in spirit" or whether the Qumran usage explains that of Matt 5:3.

Best, noting the apparent similarity between 5:3 and 5:5, has suggested that 1QM 14:7 connotes lack of courage and that the translation "fainthearted" is more appropriate for 1QM 14:7 as well as for Matt 5:3 ("Matthew," 256–58). Apart from the dubious need to distinguish between 5:3 and 5:5 (see Note on 5:5), Légasse ("Pauvres," 340) has pointed out that the *poor in spirit* of 1QM 14:7 stands in parallelism with the "perfect of way" and in antithesis to the "hardened heart" and "wicked nations." The overtone, consequently, is hardly one of "faint-heartedness."

By contrast, Légasse and Dupont have taken the phrase in Qumran in a more religious sense (as has Wrege, *Überlieferungsgeschichte*, 6–7). For Légasse, the *poor in spirit* moves from the question of poverty as such to the external conditions of stress and persecution found in the Psalms and the Qumran Hymns by which the community justified the use of the term as a self-designation for religious perfection ("Pauvres," 443–45). For Dupont, however, the transferral of meaning from external to internal poverty is total. *Poor in spirit* has been totally spiritualized in both Qumran and Matthew. Rather than referring to a "spirit of poverty," it expresses a "poverty of spirit," an attitude of "humility" ("Matthieu 5:3," 53–64; *Béatitudes* 3:385–471, esp. 457, 470–71). 1QM 14:7 does give us a Semitic parallel to Matt 5:3 (Davies, *Setting*, 251), but the question still remains whether it has any direct bearing on Matthew's usage.

3. Matthew's usage is best determined by examining it in its present context of the Beatitudes. Apart from those like Butler (*Originality*, 31–32), who hold to the priority of Matthew in general, the vast majority of scholars accept the phrase τῷ πνεύματι to be a secondary modification of the *poor* (recent exceptions, Schubert, "Sermon," 122, and Flusser, "Blessed," 1–13, with Dodd, "Beatitudes," 8–10, and Best, "Matthew," 256, noncommittal). Furthermore, almost all assign this addition to the evangelist (see Dupont, *Béatitudes* 1:211, n. 1; Wrege, *Überlieferungsgeschichte*, 7, sees it modified in the pre-Matthean tradition).

The Matthean character of the qualification, *poor in spirit*, stands out when viewed alongside of the distinctively Matthean elements in the parallel Beatitudes of 5:4, 6, par. Luke 6:21 (see Notes on 5:4, 6 and Comment C). The common denominator in the differences found in these three Beatitudes lies in Isaiah's prophecy, in particular Isaiah 61 (Flusser, "Blessed," 4, 10–13; Frankemölle, "Makarismen," 69–71; Schürmann, *Lukasevangelium*, 336, n. 84; Guelich, "Beatitudes," 426–28).

Viewed in this manner the first Beatitude displays a dual redactional intention characteristic of the evangelist rather than the tradition itself. On the one hand, by aligning the Beatitudes more closely with Isaiah 61, Matthew follows his basic christological interest of demonstrating who Jesus is by his fulfillment of the Old Testament promise (cf. the twelve "fulfillment-citations"). Matthew opens Jesus' teaching ministry with this deliberate allusion to Isaiah 61 in the Beatitudes (cf. Luke 4:16–21). By proclaiming the gospel of the Kingdom in terms of Isaiah 61, Jesus simultaneously fulfills its promise. On the other hand, Matthew ecclesiologically defines his community in light of these promises, and he prevents the Beatitudes from being misconstrued as general maxims for all who are economically destitute (Schweizer, *Matthew*, 88; Guelich, "Beatitudes," 426–31) by his modification of each in terms of Isaiah (see Notes on 5:4, 5, 6, 10).

In its present context, therefore, "poor in spirit" is Matthew's equivalent of the ʿnwm in Isa 61:1. The addition τῷ πνεύματι modified the rare use of πτωχοί = "poor" in the LXX for the Hebrew ʿnwm rather than the more usual πραεῖς = "meek." (Of the nearly twenty occurrences of ʿnwm in the Old Testament, πτωχοί is only used here and in Isa 29:19.) Furthermore, this interpretation of ʿnwm by Matthew is consistent with its usage in the Old Testament, the LXX, Qumran, and Judaism in general. While maintaining the socioeconomic element, ʿnwm (πραεῖς) places greater stress on the relationship of *the poor* to God (Bammel, *TDNT* 6:888). Ultimately, the *poor in spirit* of 5:3, viewed as an explication of Isa 61:1, is no different from Luke's *poor*, since each refers to those who stand without pretense before God as their only hope.

4. Although Matthew underlines one's relationship to God by his *poor in spirit* in contrast to *the poor*, which might be understood more socioeconomically, he has not entirely "spiritualized" or "ethicized" the Beatitudes as such (con. Strecker, "Makarismen," 262; Dupont, *Béatitudes* 3:469–71). By deliberately placing the Beatitude in the Old Testament setting of Isa 61:1, where the physical needs and pressures were an integral, although not primary, part of the life of the ᶜnwm, Matthew has maintained the "external" as well as the "internal," the "physical" as well as the "spiritual" connotations. Whereas Luke appears to have used the Beatitude with reference to the socioeconomic status of the Church and the nature of its mission, Matthew places it within Isaiah's context of *the poor* as the oppressed and abused. That this "external" element is not lost in Matthew's redaction is seen by the redactional addition of the eighth Beatitude (5:10), which forms a synonymous parallelism between the *poor in spirit* and those *persecuted for righteousness' sake* and thus an inclusion for all eight Beatitudes. Suffering for *righteousness' sake* and being *poor in spirit*, therefore, are basically conditions, not attitudes. For Matthew, the *poor in spirit* are those who find themselves waiting, empty-handed, upon God alone for their hope and deliverance while beset with abuse and rejection by their own social and religious context (see Note on 5:11–12).

for. This clause beginning with the causal ὅτι is very rare in beatitudes outside the New Testament. Whereas the content of the promise is normally inherent in the beatitude's declaration itself (see Literary Analysis), the ὅτι-clause in these Beatitudes explicitly states it.

theirs. This pronoun points to one of the major differences between the Beatitudes of Matt 5:3–10 and Luke 6:20b–21, the difference between the third person "theirs" (αὐτῶν) and the second person "yours" (ὑμετέρα). It appears to be more than a question of syntax, since Matthew's Beatitudes in the form of a statement appear more aphoristic, while Luke's in the form of direct address make a pronouncement to a specific audience. Because of this difference in form, some have taken Luke's to be the earlier, with Matthew's being the more developed gnomic and "ethicized" form of the Beatitude (Dibelius, *Tradition*, 247–48; Percy, *Botschaft*, 40–45; Walter, "Seligpreisungen," 250–53; Schweizer, "Formgeschichtliches," 123–24). Since this argument depends to an extent on Matthew's "ethical" intention to remold the Beatitudes, it loses weight if his interest is indeed "eschatological" after all.

Two factors weigh in favor of the Matthean form. First, the vast majority of beatitudes in the Jewish, Greek, and New Testament literature are in the third person. The second person format is easily explained in terms of the specific application of the Beatitudes to a given context. Second, Luke's parallel Beatitudes open with a rather general statement in the form of a substantival adjective or participle and only become specific in the ensuing explanatory clause (Dupont, *Béatitudes* 1:272–98). For the first Beatitude, that meant merely substituting pronouns, and in the second and third, only the change in verb endings (6:20b–21). The Lucan Woes, however, are consistently placed in the second person throughout ("Woe to you . . . you . . . ," 6:24–26).

These differences in person and form, however, have been proven more apparent than real, since both forms occur in Greek and Jewish literature without connoting any significant difference in *Sitz im Leben* (Dupont, *Béatitudes* 1:274–80; cf. Schweizer, *"Formgeschichtliches,"* 123–24). It is primarily a question of style rather than content. Either form could have been used without detracting from the force of the Beatitudes for their audience. Therefore, the question of person is ultimately academic. The actual audience of these Beatitudes is determined by the Beatitudes' subject rather than person.

is. The present tense verb (ἐστιν) here and in the parallel promise of 5:10 stands in contrast to the future tenses of the following promises. Although the Hebrew/Aramaic construction would have omitted the copulative verb, both Matthew and Luke and their tradition were working with the Greek in which the verb is very explicit. What then is the significance of this present tense? Although the present is most commonly read as a future in alignment with the other promises (e.g., Allen, *Matthew,* 40; Klostermann, *Matthäusevangelium,* 34; Eichholz, *Bergpredigt,* 28; Hill, *Matthew,* 111), the choice of ἐστιν rather than ἔσται may correlate with the specific promise—*the Kingdom of Heaven/God.* Whereas the other Beatitudes combine the present (the declarations; cf. Luke's *now* in 6:21) and the future (the promises), the Kingdom in Jesus' ministry (see below) involved both the present ("already") and the future ("not yet"). Jesus came to announce and effect the Kingdom, God's redemptive reign, now. The fulfillment of Isa 61:1 includes the present. The good news of Jesus' proclamation was that God has acted in time and space; the Kingdom has come. The Beatitude announces that God is entering now into a new relationship of blessing, one anticipated in the

Old Testament promise, with those turning to him in desperation. *the Kingdom of Heaven.* This phrase appears thirty-two times in Matthew and nowhere else in the New Testament. The evangelist also uses simply *the Kingdom* with the same meaning (4:23; 6:33, par. Luke 12:31; 9:35; 13:19, 41, 43; 24:14) and the more common *Kingdom of God* (12:28, par. Luke 11:20; 19:24, par. Mark 10:25; 21:31; 21:43). Since he uses *Kingdom of Heaven* and *Kingdom of God* interchangeably in 19:23, 24, the difference is more indicative of the evangelist's inconsistency of style than of his theology (con. Kretzer, *Herrschaft,* 21, 167–72).

Although most have explained the Matthean phrase in terms of the rabbinic practice of circumventing the divine name with a metonym (Dalman, *Worte,* 1:178–79; Str-B 1:172), Matthew does not exhibit any predilection for avoiding the divine name otherwise (cf. the traditional character of most of Klostermann's examples in *Matthäusevangelium,* 10). *Heaven* (οὐρανός) has a much broader function in his Gospel than simply as a metonym for God (e.g., *Father in heaven*). It stands in continuity with the Old Testament concept of *heaven* as being God's realm where, enthroned, he rules over all the world (von Rad, *TDNT* 6:505). Therefore, *heaven* is another symbol for God in his sovereign activity (Kretzer, *Herrschaft,* 26–31). When we add the biblical understanding of βασιλεία as referring primarily to a dynamic rule or reign in contrast to a static concept of a realm (Ladd, *Presence,* 118–44), *Kingdom of Heaven* is a double reference to the sovereign rule or reign of God whose heavenly designation has great import for Matthew.

The many facets of Matthew's understanding of the Kingdom have been summarized under three categories: (1) the redemptive historical element involving the relation of the *Kingdom of Heaven* to history; (2) the personal and ethical implications of the *Kingdom of Heaven* in Jesus' ministry, and (3) the cosmological-universal focus of the *Kingdom of Heaven* (see Kretzer, *Herrschaft,* 261–64, and especially Kingsbury, *Matthew,* 137–49).

1. Of these three aspects, the relation of the *Kingdom of Heaven* to history is by far the most prominent. The roots quite probably go back to the ministry of Jesus (Kümmel, *Promise,* 141–55; Schnackenburg, *God's Rule,* 77–113). The Kingdom is exclusively an eschatological concept in that it expresses God's sovereign activity in Jesus Messiah for Israel and the nations as anticipated for the last times. God's activity in Jesus' ministry is confirmed above all in Matthew's formula-citations by which he demonstrates that God's promise for the future is now being fulfilled in Jesus' person and ministry. Yet there remains an obvious

tension between the present and the future, the already but the not-yet, the fulfillment and the consummation, as expressed in the ambiguous verb "the Kingdom has come near" (ἤγγικεν in the perfect tense: 3:2; 4:17, par. Mark 1:15; 10:7, cf. Luke 10:9). On the one hand, God's sovereign rule has arrived in this age in the person of his Son and is recognized by the community of "understanding believers" (Barth, "Understanding," 105–16). On the other hand, it has not yet arrived in all its visible power and glory as anticipated when the Son of Man appears at the end of this age (24:3, cf. Mark 13:4; 25:31).

The *Kingdom of Heaven* is present as God's sovereign rule from heaven in his Son, Jesus Messiah (1:23; 11:27; 21:23–37). It is evident in Jesus' ministry of healing of the sick (Matt 8–9; 11:2–5), of sharing the table with sinners (9:10; 11:19; 22:1–10), and of defeating Satan and the forces of evil (12:28, par. Luke 11:20). It is evident in Jesus' preaching/teaching, which announces that the Kingdom has come (11:12, par. Luke 16:16; 21:43; cf. 5:3, par. Luke 6:20), reveals the mystery of the Kingdom through parables to those who have ears to hear (13:9, 16–17, 43), and sets forth God's will as a righteousness that exceeds the demand of the Law (5—7; 23; 28:19–20).

The *Kingdom of Heaven* is also future as the ultimate consummation through the appearance of the Son of Man to effect vindication and judgment. The "righteous" will then "enter the Kingdom," their "inheritance" (5:20; 7:21; 13:41, 43; 25:34), and their present condition will be reversed in terms of their reward (5:4–9; 6:1–6, 16–18; 10:39; 19:30; 20:16; 23:12). Those who fail to hear and respond to the gospel of the Kingdom face the final judgment (13:40–43; 16:27; 24:29–31, 50–51). Therefore, present and future are not two separate realities but rather are continuous aspects of God's sovereign rule in history. The relationship between the present and the future is the "mystery of the Kingdom" (Ladd, *Presence*, 217–25). "From the unprecedented activity of God in the person of Jesus in the present there will issue in the future the consummated Kingdom of Heaven" (Kingsbury, *Matthew*, 146).

2. The cosmic universal character of the Kingdom also reflects the redemptive historical aspect and takes an unexpected turn. The Kingdom of Heaven has already invaded history spatially and temporally in the person and work of the Son, Jesus Messiah. Yet instead of the grand finale when God would apocalyptically and triumphantly manifest his sovereign rule in and through his people Israel, with the accompanying cosmic consequences for all peoples, Jesus, his ministry, and that of his followers were vulnerable to abuse and rejection. Israel, the "sons

of the Kingdom" (8:12), rejected God's rule offered in his Son (11–12; 13:13–15; 23:13 and the consistent adversary posture of the "scribes and Pharisees") and ultimately put him to death (16:21, par. Mark 8:31; 20:18, par. Mark 10:33; 27:25). Consequently, the true "sons of the Kingdom" (13:38) are seen to be the tax collectors and sinners (21:28–32; 22:1–14) and the Gentiles (21:43; 24:14; 28:19–20) to whom the Kingdom is now offered. Parabolically, the Kingdom comes as a mustard seed (13:31–32) and leaven (13:33); the wheat and tares grow together until the harvest (13:24–30, 36–43); and the seed is vulnerable to the forces of this age (13:3–9, 18–23). Yet at the future consummation, God's sovereign rule will be visibly established by the appearance of the Son of Man in all his power and glory to effect vindication and judgment. The cosmic-universal aspect will be completed. The mustard seed will be a fully grown tree in which the birds of heaven build their nests, the leaven will have leavened the whole lump, and the harvest will bring the separation of the wheat and the tares. All the nations will be brought to judgment (25:31–46) and the Son of Man will be revealed as the ruler of the world (κόσμος, 13:36–43). Therefore, Matthew's phrase, *the Kingdom of Heaven,* appropriately depicts God's sovereign heavenly rule as it invades history from above both temporally and spatially in the person and work of Jesus Messiah as Son of God and Son of Man (Kingsbury, *Matthew,* 143–46).

3. The personal-ethical dimension of the Kingdom is seen in the confrontation between Jesus, his ministry, and the individual. His person and ministry created a moment of decision to respond in repentance and faith (4:17, par. Mark 1:15), to hear and understand (13:19, 23), and to do the will of the Father (7:21–23; 12:50). Such are those who enter the narrow gate (7:13), seek first the Kingdom of God's righteousness (6:33), hear and do Jesus' words (7:24), and produce the corresponding fruit (7:16–20; 12:33–35; 21:43). The opposite is also true. Those who do not respond and repent (11:20–24, par. Luke 10:12–15), who choose the broad way (7:13–14), who produce bad fruit (7:16–20; 12:33–35, cf. 7:22), who do not hear and understand (13:13–16), will experience the exclusion and judgment of the wedding guest (22:13; 7:19; 13:30, 42, 50; 25:30, 46). The corollary of the Kingdom of Heaven for Matthew, therefore, is "righteousness" (see Note on 5:6).

5:4. *who mourn.* This Beatitude differs in vocabulary and order from Luke 6:21 (cf. Matt 5:6, 4) and in some manuscripts it follows as the third Beatitude in Matthew (see Note on 5:5). Luke's Beatitude is addressed to those *who weep* (κλαίω) for they shall *laugh* (γελάω). Generally, laughter in the Old Testament pejoratively connotes an expression of the individual's autonomous status by denying God's role in one's life (so Luke 6:25; Rengstorf, *TDNT* 1:659). Weeping, by contrast, connotes the realization of one's dependency upon God for better or for worse (Rengstorf, *TDNT*, 3:722–23). The Hebrew text of Ps 126:2–6 is the one exception in the Old Testament where weeping and laughing are used in a complementary fashion. The "weeping" (126:5–6), like "the poor" of Isa 61:1, describes the rejected and scorned; the shouts of joy and laughter (126:2, cf. LXX, χαρά) describe those vindicated on whose behalf God has intervened. Therefore, Luke's Beatitude quite probably reflects the setting of Ps 126:2–6 (Rengstorf, *TDNT* 1:661–62; Schürmann, *Lukasevangelium*, 331–32) and refers to those whose tears come from the anguish of this age, who, knowing the pain of rejection and ridicule, stand dependent upon God for acceptance. Whereas for Luke the first Beatitude (6:20) placed more emphasis on one's economic status, this Beatitude stresses one's social status, but both have their distant roots in Jesus' ministry to the needy of his day. In the Lucan order this Beatitude stands in appropriate proximity to the fourth Beatitude (6:22–23) which elucidates the plight of those who are "weeping."

By comparison, Matthew appears to have continued his adaptation of the initial Beatitudes to the language and order of Isaiah 61 (Guelich, "Beatitudes," 427). Rather than Luke's "weeping" (κλαίω) and "laughing" (γελάω), 5:4 has "mourning" (πενθέω) and "comfort" (παρακαλέω) that correspond to the LXX of Isa 61:2. Furthermore, the order of the first Beatitudes (5:3, 4) follows that of Isa 61:1–2. By aligning the first four Beatitudes with Isaiah 61, the evangelist would not only be responsible for rearranging the order of the parallel Lucan Beatitudes (6:20–21, par. Matt 5:3, 4, 6) but also for placing the second Beatitude (5:4) in its present location and separating the synonymous parallelism of 5:3, 5 (see Note on 5:5).

Since Isa 61:2 played an influential role in shaping this Beatitude, the meaning of *those who mourn* would at least partially be conditioned by the Isaiah context (Eichholz, *Bergpredigt*, 38–39) where the parallelism describes the mourners in the language of bereavement (Isa 61:3, "a garland instead of ashes, oil of gladness instead of *mourning*, a mantle of praise instead of a faint spirit"; cf. Dupont, *Béatitudes* 2:36). The bereavement of the mourners in Zion stems from their national loss resulting from their sin and God's judgment. Consequently, *mourning* cannot be limited exclusively to expressing sorrow for one's sin (Huber,

Bergpredigt, 29–31) or grief surrounding death (Schlatter, *Matthäus,* 134). Rather, *those who mourn* has the more comprehensive sense of Isa 61:2–3, an inclusive grief that refers to the disenfranchised, contrite, and bereaved. It is an expression of the intense sense of loss, helplessness, and despair. To this extent the content of 5:4 is not unlike that of Luke 6:21b. There is little basis, therefore, for concluding that Matthew's primary intention involved a paranetic interest (con. Strecker, "Makarismen," 263–64; Dupont, *Béatitudes* 3:545–47, 550–54).

shall be comforted. The passive form and the future tense (παρα-κληθήσονται) express the divine comfort integral to the promise for Israel's future (Isa 49:13; 51:12; 66:13; Jer 31:13). The concept was so closely related to the messianic age that the Messiah was known as the *Menachem,* the "Comforter," in rabbinic circles (Str-B 1:66, 83). The comfort promised in this Beatitude is the ultimate consolation and encouragement that God alone can effect for those whose mourning expresses their sense of total loss and helplessness. It is a part of the future consummation when God will destroy sin and death and "wipe away all tears" (Rev 21:4, par. Isa 25:8). The promise of 5:4 for Matthew, however, is not simply a repetition of Isa 61:2–3. The fulfillment motif in Jesus' ministry sets the promise of the Beatitude in another dimension. The mourner is pronounced *blessed* by Jesus, in whom God is already at work fulfilling Isaiah 61 and through whom the consummation will be accomplished. In Jesus Messiah, one not only has the promise but the assurance of God's comfort.

5:5. *the meek.* This Beatitude is the first of five that are distinctively Matthean. The subject, *the meek,* and the promise, *inherit the earth,* are identical to Ps 37(36):11. In Greek the *meek* (πραεῖς) of 5:5 apparently differs from the *poor* (πτωχοί) of 5:3, but the underlying Hebrew term ʿnwm of Ps 37:11 is either synonymous with ʿnyym, if it lay behind 5:3, or identical with ʿnwm, if, as is more likely, 5:3 reflects Isa 61:1 (see Note on 5:3). This synonymity between the subjects of 5:3 and 5:5 raises the question about the original *Sitz im Leben* of the Beatitude. Text-critically, we have no manuscript evidence indicating its being a gloss (con. Manson, *Sayings,* 152), but we do find two different locations attested. Whereas the vast majority of manuscripts place it third, several have it second (Alexandrian—33, Δ, Clement; Western—D, pc lat, Vulgate, Syrᶜᵘʳ; Caesarean—700, 28, 544, 543; see Dupont, *Béatitudes* 1:252). This variation in location most likely resulted from differing degrees of recognition of the synonymous parallelism between 5:3 and 5:5 (Dupont, *Béatitudes* 1:253). Yet this alternate order (5:3, 5, 4) may have come from the tradition. Assuming that the original Beatitude was addressed to the *poor* ($\pi\tau\omega\chi o\acute{\iota} = {}^{c}nyym/{}^{c}nwm$), the synonymous parallelism of 5:5 drawn from Ps 37(36):11 (${}^{c}nwm = \pi\rho\alpha\epsilon\tilde{\iota}\varsigma$) would have formed a couplet (Black, *Aramaic*, 156; rather than a doublet, Dupont, *Béatitudes* 1:252, 254–55) and maintained the lexical balance between the socioeconomic and the religious inherent in both Hebrew terms ${}^{c}nyym/{}^{c}nwm$ (see Note on 5:3). The two Beatitudes would then have been transmitted together in the tradition until Matthew in his desire to align the initial Beatitudes (see Notes on 5:3, 4) more closely to the language and order of Isa 61:1–2 rearranged them. The evangelist, consequently, would have been responsible for the relocation but not the actual creation of the Beatitude ($\pi\rho\alpha\acute{\upsilon}\varsigma$ in 21:5 comes from Zech 9:9 and was probably traditional in 11:29).

Such a background also clarifies the meaning of the *meek* ($\pi\rho\alpha\epsilon\tilde{\iota}\varsigma$). Even assuming the different Hebrew terms ${}^{c}nyym$ and ${}^{c}nwm$ behind 5:3 and 5:5, there is little or no difference between the *poor* (${}^{c}nyym$) and the *meek* (${}^{c}nwm$) in the Psalms or Isaiah (see Note on 5:3). The only possible difference in these terms would be one of emphasis with the latter (${}^{c}nwm = \pi\rho\alpha\epsilon\tilde{\iota}\varsigma$) focusing on one's dependent relationship to God, whereas the former (${}^{c}nyym = \pi\tau\omega\chi o\acute{\iota}$) focuses more on one's socioeconomic status. But these emphases were not exclusive, since the terms were used interchangeably in Qumran (see Excursus on 5:3). It is clear that ${}^{c}nyym$ came to have exclusively socioeconomic and ${}^{c}nwm$ religious overtones in rabbinic writings. But it is no longer possible to determine at what point. The question in any event is moot, since there is no evidence that the Beatitude to the poor, regardless of the underlying Hebrew term, was ever intended in an exclusively socioeconomic manner even in Luke (see Note on 5:3). Yet it might have been so misconstrued on the basis of the exclusive socioeconomic force of $\pi\tau\omega\chi o\acute{\iota}$ in the Hellenistic mission. In such a context, the addition of this Beatitude as a synonymous parallel to the first would have protected the broader LXX meaning of the *poor* ($\pi\tau\omega\chi o\acute{\iota}$). Therefore, *the meek*, like *the poor*, refers to those who stand empty-handed before God in total dependence upon him. The term in no way connotes weakness or softness, an attitude rather than a condition.

shall inherit the earth. This promise also stands as a parallel to *the Kingdom of Heaven* in 5:3. The inheritance of the land was part of Israel's prerogative as the People of God (Deut 4:1; 16:20). It came to be an expression of God's intervention on their behalf in the future as seen, for example, in Isa 61:7 (Str-B 1:199–200). The disenfranchised who were totally dependent upon God for help would be vindicated when God's rule became visible on earth. Therefore, the only difference between 5:3 and 5:5 is the temporal perspective of the promise. The language of the promise drawn from Ps 37(36):11 fortuitously corresponds to the promise of Isa 61:7. The only redactional modification of the tradition would have been the evangelist's rearrangement of the order of the second and third Beatitudes in order to correlate the Beatitudes with Isaiah 61.

5:6. *who hunger.* With this subject the Beatitudes of 5:6 and Luke 6:21a converge, but only momentarily, since Matthew modifies this verb by adding another, *to thirst,* and a direct object, *righteousness.* In Luke 6:20b, 21a *the hungry* and *the poor* stand in a parallelism familiar to the Old Testament (Isa 32:6, 7; 58:7, 10; Ps 107:36, 41; Job 24:4, 10) where both concepts have a socioeconomic and a religious sense by referring to those whose destitution leaves them only one recourse, namely, God's intervention on their behalf (Dupont, *Béatitudes* 3:46). Like the first Beatitude, this one also has a double reference for Luke. First, his insertion of *now* (νῦν) intensifies the realism appropriate to his own context, where the poverty of the believing community extends to the basic necessities of life. Second, his use of the contrasting Woe to those who *have been filled* points to the religious as well as the socioeconomic situation of the Church's mission. The *full* is but another designation for the *rich* expressed in terms of abundance of food as seen in the parables of the rich fool (12:16–21), the rich man and Lazarus (16:19–31), and the great feast (14:15–24, cf. 14:12–14). As with the Woe to the *rich*, the *full* contrasted with the *hungry* reflects the mission context of the rejection of the gospel in lieu of the *poor* who respond.

and thirst. In adding this verb, Matthew underscores the element of need by combining the ultimate human needs for food and drink. The combination is also reminiscent of God's provision of food and drink during the Exodus (Ps 107:6; Isa 48:21; Neh 9:15, cf. Exod 17:6 and Deut 8:15), which is typologically applied to the promised eschaton (cf. Isa 25:6; 41:17–18; 43:20; 44:3; 49:9–10; 55:1–3; Wrege, *Überlieferungsgeschichte,* 17). Therefore, the theological moment behind the verbs "hungering" and "thirsting" of 5:6 already had its own history in the Old Testament expectation.

for righteousness. With this word Matthew appears to transfer the Beatitude's focus from the material, physical needs of the oppressed poor in the original setting (Luke 6:20b–21) to a spiritual, ethical level (Strecker, *Weg,* 151; *idem,* "Makarismen," 265; Dupont, *Béatitudes* 3:383–84). It is evident from its distribution that *righteousness* (δικαιοσύνη) is both Matthean and one of his key concepts in the Sermon. In the four Gospels, except for Luke 1:75, this word occurs only in Matthew, and five of his seven usages are in the Sermon. The other two have to do with the Baptist (3:15; 21:32). This focus on *righteousness* in the fourth Beatitude has its parallel in the eighth Beatitude (5:10), where it rounds off a second group of four Beatitudes and forms an inclusion with the first (see Note on 5:10). But what does *righteousness* signify in this context? What does it mean to *hunger and thirst for righteousness?* The answer lies in the broader setting of *righteousness* in the Sermon.

Excursus: Righteousness in Matthew 5–7

Various interpretations of Matthew's usage of *righteousness* have emerged (see Dupont, *Béatitudes* 3:355–65). (1) Some have interpreted *righteousness* as being God's vindication of the righteous desired by Psalmists and anticipated in Isaiah's eschatological promise. This understanding corresponds to the Old Testament context of the promises behind the Beatitudes to the poor and mourning/weeping (Schniewind, *Matthäus,* 44; Wrege, *Überlieferungsgeschichte,* 19; Grundmann, *Matthäus,* 126–27; Eichholz, *Bergpredigt,* 43–44; Hunter, *Design,* 34). (2) Others have taken *righteousness* in the sense of an eschatological gift for the individual incapable of ever achieving it and based purely on divine grace (Schlenk, *TDNT* 2:198–99; Soiron, *Bergpredigt,* 171–72; cf. Lohmeyer, *Matthäus,* 87–88; Barth, "Understanding," 123–24, but cf. 139–40). (3) The position most commonly held views *righteousness* as referring to one's life and conduct lived in keeping with the will of God. Whereas the second alternative accentuates the divine aspect, the third stresses human responsibility to live in keeping with the will of God as taught by Jesus (most recently, Bornkamm, "End-expectation," 31; Strecker, *Weg,* 156–58; "Makarismen," 264–66; Hill, *Matthew,* 112; Dupont, *Béatitudes* 3:361–84). (4) A fourth alternative seeks to combine certain elements of the first three by maintaining the Old Testament background as well as the gift and demand elements in Matthew (Schlatter, *Matthäus,* 235; cf. Ladd, *Presence,* 211; Descamps, *Justes,* 213–20, 235–36; Kretzer, *Herrschaft,* 265–71, cf. Stuhlmacher, "Biblische Theologie," 48–51).

The last alternative recognizes that *righteousness* involves both a gift and a demand. That *righteousness* involves conduct in keeping with the will of God is most clear in the usage of 5:10, 20; 6:1, the contrast in 13:41, 43 (cf. 25:34–46) between the "evildoers" (ἀνομία) and the "righteous" (δίκαιοι), and in the material similarity between the entrance-sayings of 5:20 and 7:21. That *righteousness* stands integral with the Kingdom is explicit in 5:10, 20; 6:33, and that it comes as a gift with the Kingdom seems clear enough from 5:6 and 6:33. Yet the dilemma arises from whether Matthew's usage focused more on the gift-character of the Old Testament promise for the age of salvation or on an apparently first-century Jewish understanding of righteousness referring primarily to conduct. The confusion grows from the reference to the "doing of the will of God" and the material similarity between the entrance-sayings of 5:20 and 7:21.

On the surface, to do the will of God appears formally like that of Judaism, but Matthew's usage differs significantly in the content of the will of God. Whereas Judaism conceives of the will of God in terms of the Law, Matt 5:20 serves as the preamble to the Antitheses of 5:21–48 that define the *what* of *righteousness* in bold contrast to the Law (cf. "But I say to you . . ."). Furthermore, Matt 6:1 redactionally introduces a section (6:2–18) describing the *how* this *righteousness* differs in expression from that of the scribes and Pharisees.

The similarity of the entrance-sayings found in 5:20 and 7:21 has led some to label *righteousness* as the "entrance-requirement" for the Kingdom (e.g., Barth, "Understanding," 139; Strecker, *Weg,* 155). Yet to label *righteousness* as the entrance-requirement for the Kingdom risks two dangers. First, it tends wrongly to assume that Matthew has exchanged the declaration of the gospel of the Kingdom in Jesus' ministry for a paranetic demand for conduct as a prerequisite to entering the Kingdom. Second, it tends to overlook the tension between the present and future dimensions of the Kingdom in Matthew (see Note on 5:3). Consequently, this label can short-circuit Matthew's usage of *righteousness* if righteousness is taken solely as the entrance-requirement for the Kingdom in the future.

For Matthew, however, the Kingdom also has a present tense in Jesus' ministry as God's redemptive activity in history bringing the promised blessings of the age of salvation to those who respond to him. This response, like the Kingdom, involves both gift (5:3; 13:11) and demand (4:17). God's sovereign rule is offered as good news to the poor—those whose helpless, socioeconomic, and religious condition has left them empty-handed before God. But it also demands a yielding response of acceptance and obedience. Fulfillment of the demand is not the prerequisite for receiving the gift; it is concomitant with the gift itself. The recognition and acceptance of the gift enable one to respond accordingly. In other words, one is accepted into a new relationship with God by means of God's gracious intervention in one's life through Jesus Messiah (gift). Yet inherent to this new relationship (gift) with God as sovereign is a life lived (demand) in keeping with that new relationship to God (6:1–18) and others (5:21–48). Doing the will of God, *righteousness,* is a sign ("fruit," 7:16–20) of God's sovereign rule in one's life in the present. It is this *righteousness* which "qualifies" one for the Kingdom in the future (5:20; 7:21).

Therefore, the presence of the Kingdom brings a new relationship now between God and his creation (5:6; 6:33), a relationship that issues in corresponding conduct in keeping with God's will (5:10). This conduct will distinguish the wheat from the tares (13:41–43), the disciple from the scribe and Pharisee (5:20), the true from the false disciple (7:21–23) at the consummation of the Kingdom in the future. Only in this very limited way can one speak of *righteousness* as the "entrance-requirement" for the Kingdom. It is also the accompanying gift of the present Kingdom.

This "gift"-character of *righteousness* for Matthew stands out most clearly in 5:6 and 6:33 as well as in the evangelist's interest in Isaiah 61. Matt 6:33 stands in contrast to 6:32. Whereas the Gentiles seek food, drink, and clothing, Jesus' followers are to "seek first the Kingdom and his righteousness." *Righteousness,* parallel with Kingdom and qualified by "his" (αὐτοῦ), referring to the Father of 6:32 (see Note, 6:33), forms the direct object of the verb "to seek." "To seek" in no way implies what is often misunderstood, namely, that one is to seek the Kingdom by producing the righteousness pleasing to God. According to 6:33, both the Kingdom and God's righteousness are to be the primary objects of one's search. One is to "seek" to obtain the Kingdom and God's righteousness rather than the food, drink, and clothing of 6:32. By seeking the Kingdom and God's righteousness, those very items of food, drink, and clothing "will be added [by God]." This divine passive (προστεθήσεται) implies that "the Kingdom and his righteousness" come from God as well as the "all these things" added over and above. Therefore, the Kingdom and God's righteousness must be seen along with "all these things" as gifts which one can enjoy in this world (see Note on 6:33).

The same emphasis is found in 5:6, where hunger and thirst describe one in dire need. Instead of softening this Beatitude to the hungry, Matthew has intensified it by adding "thirsting." To take these metaphors in any way other than passive (con. Strecker, *Weg,* 156–58; *idem,* "Makarismen," 265) ignores the context of 5:3–6 and the divine passive of the promise, *they shall be satisfied [by God].* The "gift"-character of *righteousness* in 5:6, consequently, is doubly attested by the metaphors in the subject and the divine passive of the verb. Furthermore, this understanding of *righteousness* in 5:6 corresponds to the evangelist's redactional desire to align the traditional Beatitudes with Isaiah 61, as noted in 5:3, 4. In 61:10 God initiates the action by "covering" one with the "robe of righteousness"; in 61:11 he causes "righteousness" to "spring forth before the nations"; and in 61:3 those whom God comforts will be called "oaks of righteousness, the planting of the Lord."

In summary, Matthew's use of *righteousness* in the Sermon must be read against the background of the Old Testament usage and promise. Consequently, *righteousness* in the Sermon is soteriological. *Righteousness* connotes the "gift" of a new relationship between God and the individual (5:6; 6:33). Matthew's use of *righteousness* in the Sermon is ethical. *Righteousness* connotes the demand for conduct in keeping with the will of God seen in relationship to others (5:20, 21–48) and to God (6:1–18), a conduct of concomitant with the "gift." Finally and most importantly, Matthew's use of *righteousness* in the Sermon is eschatological or, more accurately, christological. *Righteousness* expresses the new relationship that one has with God and with others in view of Jesus' ministry; it expresses the commensurate conduct growing out of this relationship and demanded by Jesus. Such relationships and such conduct are characteristic of the age of salvation and are part of Jesus' coming as the fulfillment of the Old Testament promise, the Messiah Son of God who comes declaring and effecting the Kingdom present and future.

To *hunger and thirst for righteousness* describes the dire need of a right relationship with God and others. Aware of the estrangement in person and life, the *hungry* ones gladly respond to the good news of God's activity on their behalf in and through Jesus and his ministry. These are the desperate ones of the previous Beatitudes who stand before God without pretense or power base in material goods or spiritual riches. Their hunger and thirst stand in fundamental contrast to those who are full (Luke 6:25). The evangelist's redactional additions merely intensify the need (hunger *and thirst*) and align the subject with the promise of Isa 61:10–11; cf. 61:3 *(righteousness)*.

These modifications do not "spiritualize" the original Beatitude of *the hungry* (cf. Luke 6:21) by moving from the material to the spiritual level. Such a suggestion fails on two counts. First, the Beatitudes in Luke 6:20–21 involve more than the physical state of poverty, weeping, and hunger. Poverty, tears, and hunger per se do not mean blessedness. Rather, these physical conditions also express, as noted above in Old Testament terminology, the posture of one before God and with others. Second, the language of Matthew's Beatitudes set against Isaiah 61 has not abandoned the physical dimension but has underscored this posture by use of the words and promises of Isaiah 61 (*poor in spirit, mourning,* and now *righteousness*). In effect, the Beatitude to those *hungering and thirsting for righteousness* cuts to the heart of all three Beatitudes, namely, the dire need for a right relationship with God and with others. For Matthew, as for Jesus, this relationship with God involves one's total person—physical and spiritual—including one's daily sustenance (cf. 6:11, 33).

shall be satisfied. This verb χορτασθήσονται is the counterpart to *hun-*

gering in the subject. It means to eat until one is filled. Such expression of abundant provision was a part of the Old Testament future expectation (Isa 49:10; 65:21–22; Pss 132:15; 146:7). This promise is no less applicable in light of the new focus of the declaration. The satiation of one's hunger was indicative of God's action on behalf of his own who stood in dire need. The new age promises a time of plenty, when one's deepest needs are met by God's redemptive activity. Therefore, the promise of this Beatitude, like the three previous, points ultimately to the future consummation. But the future conditions the present, as 6:33 indicates. God is even now at work in Christ establishing the new relationship with himself and enabling those who follow him to live accordingly.

5:7.   the merciful.   With this Beatitude we move to a series of four distinctively Matthean Beatitudes. Most scholars have assigned the introduction of these, if not their actual development, to the evangelist (e.g., Dupont, *Béatitudes* 1:250–57, 260, 264; 3:557; Walter, "Seligpreisungen," 249; Frankemölle, "Makarismen," 214–15). Yet the language and context speak for a pre-Matthean development (Strecker, "Makarismen," 259). The Beatitudes of 5:7, 8, 9 are each directly related to the three following blocks of the Sermon tradition (Guelich, "Beatitudes," 421–26).

Merciful (ἐλεήμων) occurs thirty times in the LXX, twenty-five of which clearly describe God (Ps 112:4 uncertain) and four of which refer to human beings (Prov 11:17; 19:11; 20:6; 28:22). In the New Testament, *merciful* occurs elsewhere only in Heb 2:17, in reference to Jesus' role as high priest. The biblical concept of mercy (ἔλεος, ἐλέω, ἐλεήμων) points in two directions: (a) the pardon accorded one in the wrong (Exod 34:6–7; Isa 55:7; Matt 18:32–34), and (b) the kindness shown one in need (Ps 86:15–16; Isa 30:18; Ezek 39:25; Mark 10:47). This latter usage becomes an "act of mercy" or "alms" (ἐλεημοσύνη; see Note on 6:2–4).

The meaning and background for *merciful* in 5:7 is best understood by its relation to the Sermon section on Judging (Luke 6:36–42, cf. Matt 5:48; 7:1–5). The *merciful* (ἐλεήμονες) of the Beatitude (5:7) stands as a material parallel to the *merciful* (οἰκτίρμονες) of Luke 6:36 (cf. Pss 86 [85]:15; 103[102]:8; 111[110]:4; 112[111]:4; 116[114]:5; 145[144]:8) which forms a transition between the section on Love for One's Enemies (6:27–35) and the section on Judging (6:37–42). Matthew's parallel (5:48, cf. Luke 6:36), by contrast, has the adjective *perfect* (τέλειοι) and appears at the conclusion of the Antitheses (see Note on 5:48). Therefore, the Beatitude would have most likely been introduced into the pre-Matthean tradition where the ἐλεήμων of the Beatitude was either reminiscent of an earlier Q form (Harnack, *Sayings,* 63) or, as in the Psalms, it stood in tandem with οἰκτίρμων (Lührmann, "Feinde," 415). There is no solid evidence that Matthew has introduced the Beatitude as a commentary on the οἰκτίρμων (Schürmann, *Lukasevangelium,* 336, n. 43). Matthew not only changes the latter in 5:48, but the other occurrences of the various forms of the "mercy"-complex lack any characteristic unity (con. Dupont, *Béatitudes* 3:619–23; Matt 6:2–4 and 23:23 are different in kind and pre-Matthean; 9:13 and 12:7 quote Hos 6:6 in yet a different usage).

Against this broader setting in the pre-Matthean Sermon tradition, *merciful* refers to the act of judging rather than to the acts of kindness. One is declared *blessed* who exercises mercy towards those who are in the wrong (Dupont, *Béatitudes* 3:632–33). Such conduct appears on the surface to be the same as that frequently taught by the rabbis (Montefiore, *Literature,* 23, and Str-B 1:203–5) and paralleled in Jesus' teaching in the context of the Lord's Prayer (6:12, par. Luke 11:4; 6:14). James 2:13 and a traditional logion of 1 *Clem* 13:2 ("Be merciful in order that you might receive mercy") underscore the paranetic force of the Beatitude's theme. Nevertheless, one must not overlook, first, that 5:7 was set in the form of a Beatitude, not a command. Jesus is declaring, not exhorting, the *merciful* to be *blessed.* And second, the mercy being demonstrated is predicated on the experience of divine mercy already. This understanding of the divine basis for mercy is distinctively Christian as seen in the parable of the Unforgiving Servant in Matt 18:21–35. That such an understanding also underlies this Beatitude is seen by its relation to Luke 6:36: "Be merciful as your Father is merciful." In other words, one's "forgiveness is to be the natural result of what one has already experienced" (Schniewind, *Matthäus,* 46; also Soiron, *Bergpredigt,* 179–80). To the extent that we have experienced God's mercy and respond in kind towards others, God's mercy is at work in us affecting others. There is a sense, consequently, in which our ability to show mercy is proportionate to our having experienced mercy. The Beatitude declares such a demonstration of mercy to others in the wrong as *blessed.*

for they shall receive mercy. The promise clearly looks to the final judgment when God will show mercy to the merciful. Yet in this Beatitude God's mercy to be experienced at the final judgment belongs already to the merciful and furnishes the basis for their behavior towards others. Therefore, the difference between this Beatitude and the understanding of Old Testament and Judaism is not in the *mercy* of the promise but in the *merciful* of the subject. One does not earn the reward; one simply receives in full what one has already freely experienced through Jesus

Messiah, namely, the pardoning acceptance of God. Thus the declaration of the Beatitude: "Blessed are the merciful, for they shall receive mercy." It is on the grounds of this declaration that the paranetic demands of the section on Judging (Luke 6:36–42, par. Matt 7:1–5) emerge.

5:8. *pure in heart.* The language of this Beatitude was taken most likely from Ps 24(23):4, 6. The setting is cultic with the question: "Who shall ascend to the hill of the Lord . . . [to] stand in his holy place?" (Ps 24:3). The answer follows in a parallelism: "He who has clean hands and a 'pure heart,' who does not lift his soul to what is false and does not swear deceitfully" (24:4). The first element of the parallelism is a general statement explicated by the second. In other words, "clean hands and a pure heart" describe the whole person standing in total honesty and integrity before God. The *purity of heart* means an attitude of perfect sincerity, loyalty before God (Dupont, *Béatitudes* 3:603).

This meaning of the *pure in heart* corresponds to the section of the Sermon tradition involving behavior consistent with one's character (Luke 6:43–45, par. Matt. 7:16–20). As was the case with the fifth Beatitude (5:7), this Beatitude is also close to the Lucan form of the tradition. The material occurs with differences in two places in Matthew (Luke 6:43–45, par. Matt 7:16–20; Luke 6:43–44, cf. Matt 12:33; Luke 6:45, par. Matt 12:35, 34b, cf. 34a). Consequently, this Beatitude also reflects a pre-Matthean stage in the Sermon tradition where *heart* (καρδία) in 5:8 is reminiscent of the καρδία in Luke 6:45 (cf. Matt 12:34–35). The paranetic section of the Sermon states that "fruits" are indicative of the nature of the tree (6:43–44, par. Matt 7:16–20) or, in other words, a "good person" and a "bad person" produce according to the "treasure of their heart" (6:45, cf. Matt 12:35).

Therefore, the *pure in heart* viewed against the background of Ps 24(23):4 and the Sermon tradition of Luke 6:43–45 cannot be narrowly defined in terms of thoughts and intentions. Rather, the designation refers to the complete integrity and sincerity of one's existence before God (cf. James 4:8, "Draw near to God . . . cleanse your hands and *purify your hearts,* you men of *double mind*"). These *pure in heart* are distinguished by their "fruits" or product according to Luke 6:43–45 (cf. Matt 7:16–20; 12:33–35).

shall see God. In Ps 24(23):6 the subjects are described as seeking "the face of the God of Jacob" (LXX). The uncertainty of this reading attests to one of two different aspects in the Old Testament use of "seeing God." On the one hand, in keeping with God's holiness and majesty

(Michaelis, *TDNT* 5:332) and in contrast to human failure and unworthiness, no one could "see God and live" (Exod 33:20; 19:21; 3:6). On the other hand, in keeping with God's gracious self-revelation, God appeared to Abraham (Genesis 33), met Moses "face to face" (Deut 34:10, cf. Exod 24:10–11), and overwhelmed Isaiah in a vision with his presence (Isa 6:1, 5).

Ps 24:3–6, in its cultic setting of worship, expresses the hope of "seeing God" found in similar contexts (Pss 17:15; 63:2; Job 19:26, cf. Isa 38:11). The cultic setting of being accepted into the presence of God becomes the basis for the eschatological hope of "seeing God" found in apocalyptic and rabbinic Judaism (Str-B 1:206–215) and in the New Testament (Heb 12:14; 1 John 3:2; Rev 22:4). Therefore, the promise of 5:8 is that the *pure in heart* will stand before God, in his very presence, accepted by him at the last judgment. The focal point of one's life, the singleness of purpose, the object of one's loyalty and commitment—namely, God himself and his claim upon the individual—reach their ultimate fulfillment by the ultimate acceptance into God's presence.

5:9. *the peacemakers.* The adjective *peacemakers* (εἰρηνοποιοί) only occurs here in the New Testament. The verb form "to make peace" (εἰρηνοποιέω) does, however, occur in Prov 10:10 (LXX) and Col 1:20, and the phrase εἰρήνην ποιέω appears in Eph 2:15 and James 3:18. Consequently, we should take the adjective in its more literal, active sense of one who makes peace, who brings reconciliation between opposing parties rather than one who patiently endures in a passive posture of nonresistance for the sake of peace (Dupont, *Béatitudes* 3:635–40). In the Old Testament God is the primary source for "peace," *shalom,* an inclusive expression of wholeness and well-being (cf. Judg 6:23–24; von Rad, *TDNT* 2:402–3). But in Isa 9:5–6 and Zech 9:9–10, the Messiah, the Prince of Peace, is described as the one who will effect peace on earth. The *peacemaker* occurs frequently in rabbinic writings in reference to God, the Messiah, and the individual (Str-B 1:215–18; Fiebig, *Bergpredigt,* 44). The actual adjective εἰρηνοποιός was current in the Hellenistic world, as noted by Windisch, "Friedensbringer," 240–41, as a description of Greek and Roman rulers who by force had established peace, security, and the socioeconomic welfare of their peoples.

Within the larger Sermon context, the Beatitude of 5:9 corresponds to the section on Love Your Enemies (Luke 6:27–35, cf. Matt 5:38–48; Lührmann, "Feinde," 214–15, cf. Dupont, *Béatitudes* 3:665–66). The subject of the Beatitude has its direct counterpart in the paranesis (εἰρήνη/ἔχθρα, Luke 6:27–28, par. Matt 5:44) and both have the same promise of sonship ("sons of God" = "sons of the Most High/Heavenly Father," Luke 6:35, par. Matt 5:45). Furthermore, this combination of conduct with sonship is found only here in the New Testament (Lührmann, "Feinde," 415). As was the case with 5:7, 8, the pre-Matthean character of 5:9 and its specific content become clearer in this correlation with the Sermon tradition. Whereas the Beatitude would have set the stage for the next section of the Sermon tradition in Q (cf. Luke's order without the Woes), Matthew has separated the two elements by the intervening sections of 5:13–37 and the antithetical format of 5:43–48. In light of Luke 6:27–35, par. Matt, the *peacemakers* are those who demonstrate love and concern for their enemies. This act of love is nothing less than the redeeming love exhibited and demanded in Jesus' ministry (see Note on 5:44).

Peacemaking, therefore, is much more than a passive suffering to maintain peace or even "bridge-building" or reconciling alienated parties. It is the demonstration of God's love through Christ in all its profundity (John 3:16; Rom 5:1, 6–11). The *peacemakers* of 5:9 refers to those who, experiencing the *shalom* of God, become his agents establishing his peace in the world (Schniewind, *Matthäus,* 48).

shall be called sons of God. The future of the promise looks toward the final judgment at the consummation. The verb *to be called* (κληθήσονται) in the passive voice denotes the divine act by which one becomes a son of God. As 5:45 (par. Luke 6:35) notes, it is more than a label one receives; rather, it is an actual becoming a son of God (Dupont, *Béatitudes* 3:654–55). The name reveals and identifies a person's nature (McNeile, *Matthew,* 53). Therefore, the promise speaks of what the *peacemakers* will be or become at the consummation, namely, *sons of God.*

In the Old Testament the designation *son of God* generally referred to Israel in reference to the people's special relationship with God who had chosen them and made his covenant with them (Exod 4:22; Deut 14:1; Hos 1:10 [2:1]; Jer 31:9). In rabbinic materials, however, the phrase was used with increasing frequency of the individual, especially the one who concerned himself with the Law and its fulfillment (Str-B 1:219–20). The *son of God* in 5:9 and 5:45, however, is an expression of the future intimate relationship with God as Father, as well as of the similarity of character between Father and Son (Schweizer, *TDNT* 8:390). By exhibiting conduct corresponding to that of the Father (5:9, 45), they show themselves indeed to be *sons of God.* The ultimate status of sonship declared at the consummation expresses the complete acceptance by God.

5:10. *persecuted for righteousness' sake.* Both the language and context of this Beatitude suggest a Matthean product. If it existed as an independent logion in the catachetical tradition, as might be suggested by 1 Pet 3:14 and Pol *Phil* 2:3 (Wrege, *Überlieferungsgeschichte,* 26–27), Matthew would at least be responsible for adapting it to its present context. The subject consists of the motif of persecution (δεδιωγμένοι) drawn from 5:11–12 (cf. Luke 6:22–23) and the typically Matthean concept of "righteousness" (see Note on 5:6). By introducing this Beatitude involving righteousness, the evangelist concludes the second group of four Beatitudes (5:7–10) with the same concept found at the end of the first group of four (5:3–6). In this manner, he forms two groups of four Beatitudes each. Furthermore, this subject, *those having been persecuted for righteousness' sake,* also picks up the synonymous *poor in spirit* (ʿnwm) of 5:3 (cf. Isa 61:1). Consequently, the eighth Beatitude offers not only a formal parallel to the fourth (5:6) but also a content parallel to the first (5:3) and thus forms a deliberate inclusion.

The rather unexpected perfect participle, δεδιωγμένοι, makes the subject quite concrete, focusing on the community's actual experience rather than on a more general, indefinite possibility (cf. 1 Pet 3:14 in the optative mood). *For righteousness' sake* in the Matthean context states the grounds for the persecution. It comes to those who live according to the will of God. But, as noted in the fourth Beatitude (see Excursus on 5:6), such conduct for Matthew must be seen as that based on and growing out of the new relationship offered by God to humankind in the gospel of Jesus' ministry. Such conduct led inevitably to conflict with the standards of that day, Jewish and Greek, for the disciple just as certainly as it did for Jesus' own ministry (5:11–12). Living in that new relationship was an expression of the reality of God's sovereign rule in one's life. Therefore, those living in this way are indeed *blessed* because the redemptive rule of God, *the Kingdom of Heaven,* was already at work in their lives (cf. 5:3). This promise concludes the series of eight Beatitudes but the subject bridges to the final Beatitude of 5:11–12.

5:11. *Blessed are you whenever.* This Beatitude with its parallel in Luke 6:22–23 stands in bold contrast to the previous eight. Apart from the address form of the second person plural, the Beatitude's structure is much more complex in its subject as well as its promise. Since Matthew and Luke agree in the structure in this Beatitude (5:11–12, par. Luke 6:22–23) and since they also agreed in the very different structure of the other common Beatitudes (5:3, 4, 6, par. Luke 6:20a, 21), we have very compelling evidence that these common Beatitudes had been brought together in the pre-Matthean and Lucan tradition. Further support for this tradition is found in the corresponding lexical similarity between the final Beatitude of each Sermon and the subsequent material on loving one's enemies (Schürmann, *Lukasevangelium,* 356–57; Lührmann, "Feinde," 214–15). In Luke 6:22–23 "hatred" (μισέω) and behavior by one's enemies has its counterpart in 6:27, whereas Matt 5:11–12 speaks of persecution (διώκω) and behavior by one's enemies with its lexical counterpart in 5:44. Consequently, this rather complex Beatitude had once formed a transition between the other three Beatitudes and the following section addressed in the second person plural (5:44, par. Luke 6:27) in the Sermon tradition. The intervening materials (5:13–43; Luke 6:24–26) of the present Sermons reflect a later development.

ridicule you.   Matthew and Luke have ὀνειδίζω in common, and it also appears in the form of a Beatitude in 1 Pet 4:14. It refers to verbal abuse directed at one personally (cf. Matt 27:44).

persecute you.   Matthew differs from Luke at this point. Whereas Luke's temporal clause (6:22) opens with the verb *to hate* (μισέω), Matthew does not employ it. The same difference occurs in the description of the *enemy* in Luke 6:27, cf. Matt 5:44. Many have attributed both instances to Matthew's redaction (e.g., Kilpatrick, *Origins,* 16; Trilling, *Israel,* 80; Strecker, *Weg,* 151; Dupont, *Béatitudes* 1:232; Schürmann, *Lukasevangelium,* 333, n. 49). Yet this difference may well have emerged in the pre-Matthean tradition (Lührmann, "Feinde," 416), since διώκω is pre-Matthean in 10:23 (M) and 23:34, par. Luke 11:49 (Q). Both logia share a similar mission context with 5:11–12. Consequently, only 5:10 influenced by 5:11–12, 44 and the parallel motif of the ʿnwm behind 5:3 would have been redactional. Matt 5:11–12, 44, therefore, would be transmissional variations of Luke 6:22–23, 27. The differences between Matthew and Luke reflect different settings in the Church's mission. Persecution is a more general expression for the antagonistic behavior experienced by the Church in mission, while exclusion (ἀφορίζω, Luke 6:22) may well refer to the earlier, more specific mission within the synagogue setting (Schürmann, *Lukasevangelium,* 333).

falsely say all kinds of evil things about you.   Luke has the more complicated structure of *throw out your name as evil,* whose precise meaning is unclear. It may refer to part of the synagogue ban process alluded to in John 16:2 (Str-B 4:329–33; Schürmann, *Lukasevangelium,* 333, cf. Marshall, *Luke,* 253). The difference between Matthew's and Luke's expressions most likely goes back to the tradition, since neither expression is characteristic of the respective evangelist. But both phrases refer essentially to the defamation of one's person. This is not only obvious in Matthew but also clear from the Lucan Woe of 6:26. As with Matthew's first example (ὀνειδίζω), verbal abuse was involved. *Falsely* is rather awkwardly introduced and redundant in view of the *for my sake.* It is probably a redactional qualification (cf. 26:59, cf. Mark 14:55; 15:19, cf. Mark 7:22) added by Matthew (Dupont, *Béatitudes* 1:236–38).

for my sake. Luke has *for the Son of Man's sake.* The meaning is the same, since Son of Man is understood as a self-designation of Jesus. The difference may reflect a Matthean tendency to accentuate the person of Jesus (Strecker, *Weg,* 124, n. 11; see 10:32–33, cf. Luke 12:8–9; 16:21, cf. Mark 8:31; 23:34, cf. Luke 11:49). Furthermore, Luke never adds the title Son of Man, as far as we can tell (Schürmann, *Lukasevangelium,* 334, n. 62).

5:12. *Rejoice and be glad.* The Beatitude is now expressed as a present imperative. Luke has the aorist imperatives with the more specific *in that day* analogous to his *now* of 6:21, 25. It most likely refers to the judgment day in the setting of the synagogue ban (Schürmann, *Lukas-evangelium,* 334, n. 63) when one is to celebrate the occasion with "jumping for joy" (σκιρτήσατε, cf. 1:41, 44). Matthew shares the call to rejoice (χαίρω) but has the more usual verb *be glad* (ἀγαλλιάζω, cf. 1 Pet 1:6, 8; 4:13; Rev 19:7 and Isa 61:10). One is to celebrate with joy in light of the persecution, not in spite of it. The reason is twofold.

for your heavenly reward will be great. The theme of reward (μισθός) appears elsewhere in Jesus' teaching (5:46, par. Luke 6:35; 6:1, 2, 5, 16; 10:41, 42, par. Mark 9:41; Luke 10:7, cf. Matt 10:10; 20:8) and seems to approximate the prominent teaching of rewards in Judaism (Str-B 1:231–32; Moore, *Judaism* 2:89–97, cf. Sanders, *Paul,* 117–25, and see Note on 6:1). This impression is reinforced by the parables on employer-employee and master-slave (20:1–16; 24:45–51, cf. Luke 12:41–46) as well as by the distinction in status and quantity (5:19; 18:1–4; Luke 19:17, 19, cf. Matt 25:20–23) and the punishment by loss of reward (Luke 12:47–48; Matt 25:28–29, cf. Luke 19:24). In 5:12, par. Luke 6:23, and 5:46, par. Luke 6:35, the promise appears to come as an assurance rather than an expected "reward."

Yet this accent on reward actually distinguishes Jesus from Judaism. Even though in Judaism the divine reward may far exceed the merit (Montefiore, *Literature,* 34), the focus still remains on the obedience. Jesus' teaching, stated in concepts current within Judaism, ultimately breaks through the stress on human response. The very opportunity to serve or respond is itself a gift (25:14–15, par. Luke 19:13). The reward is ultimately an unmerited bonus depicted beyond all proportion to one's actions (19:29, par. Mark 10:30; 20:1–16; 24:47, par. Luke 12:44; 25:31; Luke 17:7–10). The promise is ultimately the Kingdom of Heaven (cf. 5:3–10) which is given to those for whom it has been promised (20:23, par. Mark 10:40; 25:34). It is the eschatological context of salvation which must be read behind Jesus' teaching on rewards in 5:12, 46. In 5:12 this focus is expressed by the phrase *in heaven*. The persecution and defamation that one experiences now (5:11, par. Luke 6:22) does not *earn* the "heavenly reward." Rather, the "heavenly reward" is a promise affirming that God is indeed in control and concerned about his own. The promise leads to the declaration of such as *blessed* and calls for celebration even in the midst of suffering.

for in similar manner they persecuted the prophets. The second basis for rejoicing, introduced with a different conjunction from the previous explanation clauses (γάρ rather than ὅτι), rests in redemptive history. Those under duress stand in line with the *prophets,* God's agents in the past. This reference to the fate of the prophets is a recurring theme in early Christian tradition (Matt 23:29–35, par. Luke 11:47–50; 23:37, par. Luke 13:34; Mark 12:1–12, par. Matt 21:33–46, Luke 20:9–19; cf. Matt 22:6; Acts 7:51–52; Rom 11:3; 1 Thess 2:14–16; Heb 11:35–38). While Old Testament references to this theme are rather infrequent (1 Kgs 19:10, 14; 2 Chr 24:20–21; Jer 2:30; 26:20–24; Neh 9:26), the major context appears to have been in the intertestamental literature (Schoeps, "Prophetenmorde," 126–43; Steck, *Geschick,* 110–264). In the New Testament the theme is most used either polemically against Israel (e.g., Acts 7:51–52; 1 Thess 2:14–16) or as an expression of judgment upon Israel (Matt 23:29–35, par. Luke 11:47–50; Mark 12:1–12, par. Matt 21:33–46, Luke 20:9–19, cf. Matt 22:6). In this Beatitude, however, the prophets' fate becomes a paradigm for the disciple (cf. Heb. 11:35–38).

before you. Luke has "their fathers" as the subject for this clause. The reference to the fathers in connection with the persecution of the *prophets* appears elsewhere in the early Christian tradition (Matt 23:29–30, 32, par. Luke 11:47, 48; Acts 7:51, 52). Yet stylistically Luke tends to avoid impersonal subjects (Dupont, *Béatitudes* 1:248) and the emphasis on the *their* (αὐτῶν) reflects a strong break with Judaism (cf. Luke 11:47, 48; James 5:10). Furthermore, there is no particular reason for Matthew to have dropped the subject from his source.

Matthew's phrase may only intend to state, as does Luke, that the followers of Jesus have cause for rejoicing since their experience parallels that of the prophets of old. If, however, the evangelist's *before you* is to imply that the disciples were also prophets, it is only in the broadest sense of that term. Just as the prophets were God's agents of salvation, his messengers, so are Jesus' followers (10:40–41; 23:34; 28:18–20). Consequently, they are blessed and are to *rejoice* and *be glad* in view of who they are in God's redemptive plan.

Comments

A. The Beatitudes: Then and Now

1. Poor in Spirit: Matt 5:3

The first Beatitude pronounces the "poor in spirit" blessed and announces that "theirs is the Kingdom of Heaven." What is "poor in spirit"? This question has led to various answers, including voluntary poverty, an attitude of poverty, spiritual poverty, and humility. The phrase, however, stems from Matthew's desire to align the initial Beatitude to "the poor" (cf. Luke 6:20b) more closely with Isa 61:1 (see Note on 5:3). By modifying the Beatitude in this manner, the evangelist makes a christological and an ecclesiological statement. Christologically, Jesus' pronouncement of blessing to the "poor in spirit" set in the language of Isa 61:1 at the beginning of his teaching ministry demonstrates that Jesus was the fulfillment of God's promise to Israel. Jesus fulfilled God's promise of Isaiah 61 in this and the following Beatitudes by effecting God's sovereign rule, the Kingdom, in history through his Word. The age of fulfillment, the day of promised salvation, had come in Jesus' ministry.

Ecclesiologically, those accepting God's initiative on their behalf through Jesus Christ were then identified as the ʿnwm, "the poor in spirit," of Isa 61:1. The Old Testament concept of the poor included a dual reference to the socioeconomic condition of the individual as well as the religious dimension of resultant dependency upon God for help and vindication (see Excursus on 5:3). In Isa 61:1 the term ʿnwm was applied specifically to God's People who had remained faithful to him and his Law in spite of their predicament and affliction in exile. To these poor God had promised the message of good news, 'the message that he did care for them and would act to deliver them. This promise eventually became the hope of the righteous faithful in Israel. Jesus, however, clearly broke with the contemporary usage of the term in his day. He came "not to call the righteous but sinners" (Mark 2:17, par. Matt 9:13, Luke 5:32) to whom he announced the accomplishment of God's promise and to whom he offered the healing, forgiving fellowship with God through his person. "The poor" of Isa 61:1 was the designation applied, most likely in Jesus' own ministry, to the collection of disciples, the sick, sinners, and possessed who responded to God's work through his person and ministry on their behalf (cf. Luke 4:16-21; 6:20b; Matt 11:5, par. Luke 7:22; see Note on 5:3).

By expressly aligning the Beatitude with Isa 61:1, Matthew maintains Jesus' usage of Isaiah 61 with reference to his own ministry (see Excursus on 5:3) as well as the basic meaning of the traditional Beatitude (Luke 6:20b). "The poor" referred to the social and religious outcasts, the rejects of the rich and righteous of Jesus' day, who out of desperation turned empty-handed to God by responding positively to Jesus' ministry. Yet Matthew was not merely preserving tradition from Jesus' ministry. He applied the tradition to his own community's situation as seen by his redactionally parallel Beatitude in 5:10. Just as the poor in spirit of Isa 61:1 were under severe duress (cf. Isa 61:1-4), so Matthew's church was also acquainted with "persecution for righteousness' sake" (5:10-12). Therefore, Jesus' message, anchored in his own ministry as the fulfillment of Isaiah's promise, declares anew that the poor in spirit, the afflicted, are blessed because theirs is the Kingdom of Heaven.

Our situation today differs in many ways from that of Jesus and Matthew's day. Perhaps the most appropriate synonym for the "poor in spirit" is "desperate." The desperate are not defined today, nor were they in Jesus' day, primarily in socioeconomic terms. Yet inevitably the ultimate bankruptcy of the socioeconomic context—life as we know it in relationship with others—can cause us out of desperation to stand open before God. Or it may be that an unexpected experience with God as he confronts us through Jesus Christ leaves us with the sense of the emptiness of our socioeconomic or even our religious resources. In any case, "the poor in spirit," now as then, are ultimately those standing without pretense before God, stripped of all self-sufficiency, self-security, and self-righteousness. To that degree the "poor in spirit" of today are analogous to those of Jesus' ministry.

What did the Kingdom of Heaven connote for Matthew's audience?

The Kingdom of Heaven is Matthew's own equivalent for the parallel Kingdom of God in the rest of the New Testament (see Note on 5:3). With this expression the evangelist makes a double reference to the sovereign rule of God. The term *Kingdom* is more accurately rendered by the concept of "reign" rather than "realm" in most instances, and *Heaven* is an Old Testament equivalent for the realm of God's sovereign rule over all creation. Consequently, the focus is on the dynamic aspect of God's sovereignty. This dynamic activity is underlined by the integral association of the Kingdom of Heaven with Jesus' ministry, basically encapsulated by the phrase "the gospel of the Kingdom" (see Note on 4:23). In Jesus' person and ministry the good news about God's promise-fulfilling, redemptive activity is announced. Jesus has come to fulfill the Old Testament promises by effecting God's sovereign rule in history.

Yet for Matthew, as for the gospel tradition, a dual feature of the Kingdom emerges in Jesus' ministry. On the one hand, the Kingdom is already present spatially and temporally as God's sovereign rule from heaven in Jesus' ministry as the Son. Evidence of this redemptive rule is the healing of the sick (Matthew 8–9), the acceptance of sinners into a restored relationship (9:10; 22:1–10), the defeat of Satan and his forces (12:28), Jesus' preaching/teaching of the "good news to the poor" (4:23; 5:3–12; 11:5), and his parables of the Kingdom (Matthew 13). If the Kingdom comes as God's deliverance for his people, it also comes as judgment (Matthew 23). On the other hand, the sovereign rule of God is also future. Jesus as the Son of Man will return to consummate the fulfillment begun in history during his earthly ministry and continued through the mission of his own (28:16–20). In the consummation, the mustard seed will be a fully grown tree (13:31–32), the wheat and the tares will be separated (13:24–30), and the righteous will enter the Kingdom (5:20; 13:41, 43) while the wicked will be judged and punished (13:40–43; 24:29–31).

In the Beatitudes of 5:3 and 5:10, the promise of the Kingdom of Heaven is given to the "poor in spirit" and those who have been "persecuted for righteousness' sake." In both cases it is the announcement of the good news that God is sovereign and his sovereign rule has entered history even though the consummation and ultimate vindication is still to come. In the first-century context, this message came indeed as good news, the "gospel of the Kingdom."

The concept of the Kingdom of Heaven is quite removed from our context today. Its meaning is certainly not self-evident, particularly when the very term *Kingdom* connotes realm rather than reign. Furthermore, the religious heritage of Old Testament and intertestamental Judaism that gave meaning to the phrase is foreign to most today. Consequently, we must both philologically and theologically define the phrase. Furthermore, since we lack an equivalent phrase in our experience, we must paraphrase its meaning. As a theological symbol, the coming of the Kingdom of Heaven is one way of expressing God's initiative in history through Jesus Christ to restore humankind to a proper relationship with himself. It connotes God's desire to stand at the center of our lives, to be our sovereign, and to accept us into a reconciled relationship with himself. This relationship is one of support, healing, and forgiveness. Such an overture, however, does not come by force but by invitation to those willing to yield to God, to recognize God as God. The Kingdom in the future points to God's ultimate expression of his authority made visible in history by the consummation of what was begun in Jesus' ministry. It will be a time of complete healing, restoration of fellowship between God and his creation, and the total demise of death and evil. Consequently, it will be a time of judgment, a separation, for those who do or do not recognize him as God in their lives.

The first Beatitude, therefore, declares that any who in desperation turn without pretense to God through the person and ministry of Jesus Christ are "blessed." They have received God's promised redemptive acceptance and intervention for their lives. They stand in a new relationship with him and with others, a relationship made possible through Jesus Christ. Such a posture is life-changing: "Blessed are the poor in spirit, for theirs is the Kingdom of Heaven."

2. Those Who Mourn: Matt 5:4

The second Beatitude addressed to those "who mourn" also reflects Matthew's redactional interest in Isa 61:1–2 (see Note on 5:4). Whereas Luke's Beatitude and the traditional wording whose roots lie in Jesus' ministry may have the weeping/laughing of Ps 126:2–6 in view, Matthew's Beatitude corresponds to the language and order of Isa 61:2. The meaning of the two Beatitudes, however, is the same. "Those who mourn" expresses the bereavement that is part and parcel of this age. Based on the context of the Exile in Isaiah 61, mourning connotes an intense sense of loss and helplessness. It includes the grief of disenfranchisement and contrition resulting from the recognition of Israel's sin and failure before God. Therefore, the term contains the dual element of remorse and grief over one's loss. Like the poor in spirit, the mourners stand before God stripped of any recourse, totally dependent on him for better or worse.

The promise "they shall be comforted" is the announcement of divine intervention. Implicit to the divine comfort is the removal of the cause for mourning. The time of remorse, disenfranchisement, loss, or bereavement is over, since God will act on behalf of those who turn to him in order to restore that lost relationship. One's confidence in God's future intervention is based on the fact that he is now at work in Jesus, bringing his promises to fruition. Therefore, while our hope for the future does not remove the reality of our present mourning, it places our context in a totally different light (1 Thess 4:13–18).

There is little in our experience today that reveals more our ultimate lack of control, our insufficiency, our ultimate dependency on Someone greater than ourselves, than the experience of mourning. Regardless of whether our mourning takes the shape of anger, grief, or remorse, it betrays our vulnerability and sense of helplessness. Our only hope lies beyond our own capacities. The restoration that brings true comfort must come from the Comforter himself. Therefore, this Beatitude announces the good news of "comfort" to those who are in despair and open before God.

3. The Meek: Matt 5:5

The third Beatitude, with its verbal parallel in Ps 37(36):11, means essentially the same thing as the first (see Note on 5:5). Any attempt to draw a line of distinction between the parallel subjects, the poor in spirit and the meek, breaks down on the basis of the Old Testament background of the two Beatitudes. The first, with its reference to Isa 61:1, and the third, with its reference to Ps 37:11, ultimately go back to the same Hebrew term for "the poor" (*ᶜnwm*). The same is true for the promises. The hope of inheriting the earth is but another Old Testament expression for the initiative of God's sovereign rule in history on behalf of his own (e.g., Isa 61:7). The only difference is the future aspect of the promise in 5:5 in contrast to the present reality of the Kingdom of Heaven in 5:3. But even the presence of the Kingdom in Jesus' ministry anticipates the coming visible consummation (see Note on 5:3).

This Beatitude most probably arose as a parallel to the first in order to maintain the dual Old Testament force of the socioeconomic and

religious connotations of the concept "the poor." The "meek" offered
a balance in the Greek for the strictly socioeconomic understanding of
the "poor" at a time in the Church's mission when the first Beatitude
was in danger of being misconstrued in an exclusively materialistic sense.
Ironically, Matthew's own redactional alignment of the first Beatitude
with Isa 61:1, and this parallel reference to the meek, when divorced
from their Old Testament background, leave us with two Beatitudes
that can easily be misunderstood in a strictly spiritual sense. Both Beatitudes refer to an attitude of total dependence upon God, an attitude
arising out of our helpless condition.

4. Those Who Hunger: Matt 5:6

Matthew's fourth Beatitude has an expanded subject, "those who hunger and thirst for righteousness," in contrast to Luke's simpler "you
that hunger" (6:21a) which is closely related to the Beatitude to the
poor of 6:20b in a manner reminiscent of the Old Testament (e.g., Isa
58:7, 10). Both subjects refer to the same people who turn in their destitution to God for his help. Matthew has intensified his subject by adding
"to thirst" in order to include both necessities of life, namely, food and
drink. This dual emphasis is reminiscent of God's provision for Israel
in the Exodus (Exod 17:3; Deut 8:15) which became a typological basis
for the promise of God's future blessing for his people (e.g., Isa 25:6;
41:17-18; 55:1-3). Furthermore, the evangelist apparently "spiritualizes"
the Beatitude by introducing "righteousness" as the object of one's hunger
and thirst. By adding "righteousness," Matthew changes the verbs to
metaphors and moves the focus from the verbs (cf. Luke 6:21) to the
direct object, "righteousness," whose meaning becomes crucial to that
of the Beatitude.

"Righteousness," a distinctively Matthean concept in the Gospels (see
Excursus on 5:6), has a dual aspect: (a) conduct in keeping with the
will of God (5:10, 20; 6:1), and (b) the eschatological gift of the new
relationship with God brought about by the presence of God's redemptive
work in the Kingdom (6:33). In light of the metaphorical use of the
verbs "to hunger" and "to thirst" that express dire need, the divine
passive of the promise, and the Old Testament context of the Beatitudes
in general (Isaiah 61), the second aspect of righteousness takes precedence
in this Beatitude. With the extended subject of 5:6, the evangelist summarizes the first four Beatitudes by describing the poor, mourning, meek,
and hungry and thirsty as those who, conscious of their own inabilities

and dependency upon God alone, turn to him for his acceptance and help. To this extent, the evangelist has not "ethicized" or "spiritualized" this Beatitude but rather has underlined the Old Testament promise characteristic of the age of salvation, which includes both the material and spiritual dimensions of God's activity (cf. Isaiah 61 and Matt 6:32–33).

Who are those who "hunger and thirst for righteousness" today? In view of Matthew's usage, one cannot limit this Beatitude to a context of political justice. It is much broader than the question of human rights. But in that human rights and injustice are part of the plight of the human predicament, as indeed they were in the Old Testament context, these issues are certainly involved. Like the poor and mourning, this subject refers ultimately to a posture before God. The theological element is primary. But this posture is not devoid of external circumstances. The social-anthropological element has not been eclipsed. The subject denotes those who, aware of their inadequacies and personal need of God's transforming activity in their lives, turn to him for his acceptance and help. The actual nature of our "hunger and thirst" may take various forms in our experience. But it always pertains to the basic necessities for living life as God has intended.

The promise also comes in language familiar to the Old Testament for the age of salvation. God promises to meet our needs, to "satiate" our "hunger." The promise declares the good news that God does hear and will respond to meet the needs of those who turn in faith to him. This promise, however, is much more than a mere repetition of the Old Testament prophecy. The one who announces the Beatitude is himself a sign, an assurance of God's concern for his own, since his very person and ministry is establishing the new personal relationship between God and humanity which was integral to the Old Testament promise itself. Furthermore, as 6:33 implies, God is already at work not only in accepting us into a new relationship with himself but also in supplying our needs (6:33).

5. The Merciful: Matt 5:7

The fifth Beatitude, addressed to "the merciful," and the seventh, addressed to "the peacemakers," appear to break with the declarative context of the Beatitudes in favor of a more ethical, paranetic tone. Divorced from their context, they appear to praise or reward specific conduct rather than a condition or posture before God as found in the other Beatitudes. Read in context, however, one must considerably modify such an impression.

The family of terms for "mercy" (verb, nouns, and adjectives) has two connotations in the Scriptures. At times these terms refer to the act of pardoning one in the wrong (Exod 34:6–7; Matt 18:32–34). At other times they refer to kindness shown one in need (Ps 86:15–16; Mark 10:46). Since this Beatitude and the two subsequent Beatitudes (5:8, 9) are closely related to the three major sections of the Sermon tradition which follow (see Notes on 5:7, 8, 9), the meaning of "merciful" in 5:7 is determined by its correlation with the "merciful" of Luke 6:36 (cf. Matt 5:48) that introduces the Sermon tradition on Judging (Luke 6:36–42, par. Matt 7:1–2). "The merciful," then, are those who forego judgment and offer forgiveness and pardon.

The Beatitude receives an even sharper profile when we realize that mercy as an act of pardon is applied exclusively to God in the Old Testament. Furthermore, the corollary in Luke 6:36 exhorts us to be "merciful as [our] Father is merciful." In other words, the merciful are those who demonstrate the Godlike conduct of offering pardon to those in the wrong. The basis for such Godlike conduct in Jesus' ministry was not human graciousness but one's own experience of God's mercy as seen in the parable of the Unforgiving Servant (Matt 18:32–34). Thus, this Beatitude is addressed to those who have recognized their failure before God, have experienced his forgiving mercy and reflect it in their relationship toward others in the wrong (cf. 6:12–15). Rather than being merely a paranetic ideal for conduct, this Beatitude involves, as do the others, the basic posture of the individual before God.

The promise of receiving mercy in the future obviously refers to the Last Judgment. This future reference would appear at first glance to dispute our previous observations about having already experienced God's mercy in our lives. The demonstration of mercy that is declared blessed in the Beatitude seems to have its own self-fulfilling reward as in Prov 11:17. One receives according to what one has done. Such a conclusion, however, overlooks the tension between the present fulfillment and future consummation in Jesus' ministry and in all of the Beatitudes.

In contrast to Judaism, the present does not condition the future as much as the future conditions the present. The display of mercy shown by the merciful is already the mercy that will be expressed ultimately in the consummation. What God has done and is doing for one through the accepting and forgiving ministry of Jesus Christ and the presence of the Kingdom now will be expressed openly and with clarity at the consummation of the Kingdom, the last judgment. In other words, those who *will* receive mercy are those who *now* have experienced it and practice it in view of God's work through Jesus Christ.

The "merciful" for us today in light of the Beatitude does not refer to those who practice deeds of kindness or who respond graciously to charitable causes. Rather, the merciful are those who reflect God's acceptance of the unworthy, the guilty, and the ones in the wrong, because the merciful themselves, conscious of their own unworthiness, guilt, and wrong, have experienced God's forgiving and restoring acceptance through the message of Jesus Christ. There is often a unique feeling of understanding, a healing rapport, between those sharing a common trauma. This common bond can serve as a basis for conduct. Yet, as the parable of the Unforgiving Servant illustrates (Matt 18:32–34), it is only a basis, and the paranesis of Luke 6:36–42 exhorts us to live accordingly. Our life is indicative of our true posture before God.

6. The Pure in Heart: Matt 5:8

The sixth Beatitude, announced to "the pure in heart," doubtless reflects the language of Ps 24(23):4–6 describing those qualified to enter the sanctuary. The parallelism of Ps 24:4—"does not lift up his soul to what is false, and does not swear deceitfully"—denotes the meaning of integrity, singleness of devotion, undivided loyalty. This meaning is further supported by the relationship of this Beatitude to the Sermon tradition on conduct consistent with one's true nature (Luke 6:43–45, par. Matt 7:3–4; 16–20). In fact, the Lucan tradition actually concludes this paranetic section with a reference to one's heart as the source of one's conduct and speech (Luke 6:45, cf. Matt 12:34–35). Therefore, this Beatitude addresses a much deeper level than purity of thought or behavior. It speaks of standing with total integrity, without dissimulation, totally committed to God (cf. Matt 6:24, par. Luke 16:13), a posture not unlike that connoted in the previous Beatitudes.

The thematic similarity of this Beatitude to the previous ones becomes even clearer in the content of the promise, "they shall see God" (cf. Ps 24[23]:6, LXX). This promise stands in direct line with the Old Testament references to the hope of "seeing God" (Pss 17:15; 63:2; Job 19:26, cf. Isa 38:11), a privilege accorded to Abraham (Genesis 10), Moses

(Deut 34:10), and Isaiah (Isa 6:1, 5). This expression stands in tension with the statements that no one can see God and live (Exod 33:20; 19:21). Yet this difference is simply one of perspective. The one expression focuses on God's gracious self-revelation; the other, on his transcendent holiness and human unworthiness. To see God in terms of the Beatitude's promise is to be able to stand before him, accepted into his presence at the Last Judgment. The intervening verse of Ps 24:5 explicates that experience—"He will receive *blessing* from the Lord and *vindication* from the God of his salvation." Therefore, the promise to see God corresponds to the future perspective of the previous promises that focus on God's redemptive activity at the consummation.

For us today, this Beatitude to the "pure in heart" has frequently been understood with reference to moral purity. Thus it has become an exhortation, an ethical ideal, pertaining to morality. But "pure in heart" is even more basic than the question of moral purity. It deals with the very nature of our relationship with God. Perhaps the more appropriate term for us today would be "integrity," integrity in our entire person before God. Such honesty or transparency before God is not self-generated. As with the subjects of the other Beatitudes, it is a posture that comes with being confronted by God in Jesus Christ and called to an allegiance and loyalty to him. Because of his mercy (5:7) and acceptance of us, we can stand and live without pretense before God and others. With the Beatitude as the basis, the paranesis of 7:16–20 (par. Luke 6:43–45) can follow.

7. The Peacemakers: Matt 5:10–12

The seventh Beatitude is addressed to "the peacemakers," an adjective that occurs only here in the Scriptures. Whereas Hellenistic and Roman literature use the term to describe the conquering ruler, its conceptual background in basically Jewish (cf. Prov 10:10, James 3:18, and the rabbinic parallels in Str-B 1:215–18). The peace intended is not merely that of political and economic stability as in the Greco-Roman world but peace in the Old Testament inclusive sense of wholeness, all that constitutes well-being. The subject also has its eschatological moment in Isa 9:5–6 and Zech 9:9–10 where the Messiah, the Prince of Peace, is described as the one who will effect peace on earth. It is this dynamic aspect that predominates in the term *peacemaker,* as seen by the corresponding section of the Sermon tradition on Love Your Enemies (Luke

6:27–38, cf. Matt 5:38–48). The "peacemakers," therefore, are not simply those who bring peace between two conflicting parties, but those actively at work making peace, bringing about wholeness and well-being, among the alienated. The paranesis clarifies the procedure as being love for one's enemies, of "doing good" to the undeserving. It is nothing short of the love commandment itself which takes a new focus in Jesus' ministry (see Notes on 5:44–47). The peacemakers, as the merciful, are engaged in expressing to others what they themselves have come to experience in Jesus' ministry.

The promise states the climax of a series of promises that began with "receiving mercy" (5:7), "to see God" (5:8), and now to be called "the sons of God." The divine passive connotes God's action in naming one, giving one the very nature of sonship. Nothing could express the intimacy of the promised relationship with God more than to be called "sons of God." At the same time, the peacemaker is recognized at the Last Judgment as God's son because as a son he exhibits the work of the Father (5:45, par. Luke 6:35). Again we see the promise as being the culmination, the consummation of what is already a reality in one's life—another example of the tension between the present fulfillment through Jesus' ministry and the future consummation of all things.

This Beatitude is far more profound than simply offering a social or political ideal of pacifism or passive restraint to avoid conflict. Pacifism is nowhere in sight. Yet one is not to spiritualize this Beatitude so that making peace is "evangelism" narrowly defined as reconciling another's "spiritual" alienation from God (cf. 5:13–16). To make peace is to engage actively in bringing God's redemptive purposes to bear in all of our broken society. The process may be diverse, even involving conflict at times (cf. 5:10, 11–12 and Jesus' own ministry), but it is concomitant with sonship for each individual.

8. Persecuted for Righteousness' Sake: Matt 5:10–12

The eighth Beatitude is addressed to those "who have been persecuted for righteousness' sake" and most likely reflects the redactional hand of the evangelist (see Note on 5:10). Not only is the subject of persecution drawn from the following Beatitude (5:11–12) but, combined with the concept of righteousness, it forms a parallel to the first Beatitude where the poor in spirit refers to the poor, the afflicted, of Isa 61:1. This inclusion formed by the first and eighth Beatitudes indicates how Matthew understood and applied the Beatitudes to his own situation. Each Beatitude addressed those who recognized that God's promised redemptive work and will were effective in Jesus' ministry.

This recognition was not a mere intellectual assent but an "understanding" that had changed the focal point of their lives. Their lives, now possible because of Jesus' person and ministry, and lived in keeping with God's will as expressed in Jesus' ministry ("righteousness"), had led to conflict ("persecution"). The perfect tense denotes the integral relationship between the past and the present. Such ones were indeed "the poor," but precisely because of Jesus' ministry by which they had already become the eschatological people of God (Isa 61:1; theirs was *already* the Kingdom of Heaven) and for which they suffered affliction awaiting the deliverance and vindication of "the poor" at the consummation. In Matthew, therefore, Jesus' message of the Beatitudes comes again as "good news" both by affirming Jesus' role as the fulfillment of the Old Testament promise (his person) and by his declaring God's ultimate salvation for those who now respond to God's redemptive work through him (his message).

In brief, Matthew's Beatitudes are a declaration of the present and future aspects of the Kingdom of Heaven in Jesus' ministry. To use the evangelist's own words, they are nothing less than the "gospel of the Kingdom." They are the eschatological blessings of the Old Testament promise seen in the redemptive historical tension between the already but not yet. This tension becomes most evident in the final Beatitude of 5:11–12.

The final Beatitude differs considerably in form from the preceding eight. Apart from its second person form, the subject and promise are much more complex. This difference is most likely explained in terms of the pre-Matthean tradition, since Matthew and Luke stand in closer agreement in this Beatitude than in their previous three parallels.

Matthew's subject (5:11) specifies three forms of abuse experienced for Jesus' sake: ridicule, persecution, and slander. Luke's subject probably reflects a proximity to the synagogue ban (6:22). Such behavior serves as a fitting transition to the section on loving one's enemies (Luke 6:27–35, par. Matt 5:38–48) which may well have followed. The promise is declared in two causal clauses. The one looks forward to the reward in heaven; the other looks back to the pattern of suffering by the prophets in redemptive history (5:12, par. Luke 6:23). Therefore, the suffering is an occasion for rejoicing even now. Here we see a clear example of how the past, present, and future correlate when viewed in light of God's redemptive purposes. This Beatitude now sets the stage for the examples of 5:13–16 that illustrate the disciples' role in the world, a role that is similar to that of the prophets.

B. The Beatitudes: "Entrance Requirements" or "Eschatological Blessings"?

The Beatitudes belong to the category of the most familiar portions of the Scriptures. They, along with the Ten Commandments, represent for many the essence of the Judeo-Christian religion. In one sense, understood in their total context, this viewpoint contains a large element of truth. Yet, in another sense, divorced from their intention and context, such a view represents a great distortion. This difference in perspective becomes clearer when we consider the Beatitude's primary purposes in terms of either "entrance requirements" for the Kingdom or "eschatological blessings" inherent to the coming of the Kingdom into history. The Matthean Beatitudes in particular have generally been taken in the more ethical sense on both the academic and practical levels.

On the academic level, an examination of Matthew's Beatitudes supposedly demonstrates an "ethicizing" or "spiritualizing" tendency on the part of the evangelist's modification of the tradition. This apparently stems from the obvious reworking of the parallel Beatitudes of 5:3, 4, 6 (cf. Luke 6:20, 21) and his five additional "ethical" Beatitudes that deal with attitudes and conduct (5:5, 7–10). Furthermore, the context of 5:17–20 and the ensuing Antitheses of 5:21–48 heighten this apparent paranetic tendency. The prelude of 5:20 and the epilogue of 5:48 remove any vestige of doubt about Matthew's intention of listing the Beatitudes as "entrance requirements" for the Kingdom (Dibelius, "Bergpredigt," 120, cf. 93; Strecker, "Makarismen," 262–63; Dupont, *Béatitudes* 3:382–83, 665–67).

On the practical level, one frequently hears comments to the effect of trying to "live according to the Sermon on the Mount." This generally means orienting one's attitudes and conduct by the various Beatitudes, such as the "meek," "pure in heart," "merciful," "peacemakers." The Beatitudes have become an ideal for human conduct, a goal to be pursued. The classic example, of course, is the use of the "peacemakers" as a model for conscientious objection. Yet even within the Church one generally hears the Beatitudes preached as exhortations for Christian conduct. Rare is the occasion when one hears any of the Beatitudes without being left with a sense of guilt or inadequacy. In fact, some circles of the

Church view these Beatitudes as impossible demands along with the Antitheses of 5:21–48 and relegate them to the future Kingdom as Kingdom ethics, when they will characterize the Christian's life in the millennium.

Both the academic and practical levels of understanding the Beatitudes fail to grasp correctly the meaning and intention of the Matthean Beatitudes. The academic approach fails by misconstruing the intention of Matthew's redaction. First, rather than "spiritualizing" or "ethicizing" the parallel Beatitudes, Matthew's redaction (see Notes on 5:3, 4, 5, 6, 10) was basically christological, an attempt by aligning the Beatitudes *expressis verbis* with the Old Testament promise, especially with Isaiah 61, to demonstrate that God was at work in Jesus Messiah accomplishing his redemptive purposes for humankind. The initiative in this fulfillment process of Jesus' ministry is clearly divine, and the Beatitudes must be understood from that perspective or the human component is completely distorted in terms of the doctrine of merit and reward. The Beatitudes are viewed by Matthew as Jesus' declaration, an announcement of congratulations, in the sense of Isa 61:1 rather than a demand for conduct.

Second, rather than being primarily responsible for the nonparallel Beatitudes (5:5, 7–9; 5:10 is Matthean but synonymous with 5:3), either by having constructed them or having introduced them from his special tradition, Matthew used them as being an integral part of his tradition (see Comment C). But even should these Beatitudes be more "ethical in tone than those with parallels," their presence in Matt 5:3–12 does not imply more than the evangelist's faithfulness to his tradition, since his own redaction in 5:3–6, 10 points in a very different direction (con. Strecker, "Makarismen," 256, n. 2).

It is, however, at the point of their ethical character that one should proceed very cautiously before assigning primarily an ethical intent to these Beatitudes. This material drawn from the Psalms and the paranetic sections of the Sermon tradition (see Notes on 5:7, 8, 9 and Comment C) was deliberately placed in the form of a beatitude as an introduction to and in contrast with the corresponding paranetic sections. As Beatitudes they announce congratulations for attitudes and conduct commensurate with one's experience of a commitment to God's redemptive work in Jesus Messiah. It is on the basis of one's present experience of mercy, integrity, and peace through God's work in Jesus' ministry (5:7–9) that the future promises of the Beatitudes are announced, and it is on this basis that the following paranetic sections become intelligible.

The failure on the practical level stems from the misunderstanding of the Beatitudes as a literary form. Although beatitudes in a Wisdom context may have a more exhortative or paranetic function (see Literary Analysis), the Beatitudes of 5:3–12 do not promise well-being and success. They are much closer to the function of the beatitude in prophetic/ apocalyptic writings. They address those who already *are* what they are identified as being. The identity of the Beatitudes' subjects first comes into being in the encounter with God through Jesus' ministry in which God's redemptive initiative in history confronts the individual and calls for a decision to surrender, to yield one's all to God. To those who so respond out of desperation, the subjects of the Beatitudes, the various promises of the future are given. These promises are given as assurance rather than as reward.

At this point, however, the Beatitudes of 5:3–12 break with the apocalyptic genre. The promise is future but not exclusively. The future consummation of God's reign is still to come but it also has made its impact in the present. Not only is God's redemptive rule declared to be the present lot of the "poor in spirit" (5:3) and of those who have been "persecuted for righteousness' sake" (5:10), but the conduct of the subjects, such as showing mercy, having integrity, and making peace, reflects the experience of God's role in one's life in the present. The "eschatological blessings" of the promises are both present and future.

Therefore, the Beatitudes of Matt 5:3–12 are no less eschatological blessings than those of Luke 6:20–23. They are to be read and heard in the dynamic context of proclamation and response as statements of congratulations that effect what they announce. With the announcement the recipient's identity is changed. Put another way, the blessing of salvation "is so announced to the hearer in Jesus' word of authority that the hearer becomes a new person through Jesus' summons, a person called by God and therefore blessed" (Schweizer, *"Formgeschichtliches,"* 126).

For Matthew, as for the tradition, these Beatitudes were not intended to be benedictions that pronounce one blessed in a sacral rite, nor did they intend to express popular wisdom or ethical teaching of that day. Rather, these are to be heard and understood as having been spoken by the one who came to fulfill the Law and the Prophets (5:17). Instead of ethics swallowing up eschatology in Matthew, we have just the reverse. The implicit attitudes and conduct of the Beatitudes as well as the demands of 5:20–48 are only intelligible in light of that new eschatological moment between God and humanity established by Jesus' person and ministry.

C. History of the Tradition

On the basis of our detailed analysis of the Matthean Beatitudes (see Notes on 5:3–12) we can now draw some general conclusions about the history and development of the tradition. The history and development reflects three major stages: (1) Jesus' own ministry, (2) the pre-evangelists' tradition, and (3) the evangelists' modifications and applications of the tradition.

1. Jesus' Ministry

The Beatitudes to "the poor" (Luke 6:20, par. 5:3), the "hungry" (Luke 6:21a, par. 5:6), and the "weeping" (Luke 6:21b, par. 5:4) have their original setting in Jesus' ministry. First, these three Beatitudes express in various ways the plight of the Old Testament poor who in their desperation depended upon God rather than their own inadequate resources. Yet the poor of Jesus' ministry, those who heard and responded to him, hardly fit either the Old Testament or rabbinic understanding of this term (see Excursus on 5:3). Since the identity of those around Jesus as the poor stands in bold discontinuity with either contemporary Jewish or Hellenistic thought, this usage of "the poor" must have its roots in Jesus' ministry. Second, the tension between the present experience of being "blessed" and the future experience of the promises (6:21, par. Matt 5:6, 4) corresponds to the eschatological perspective in Jesus' ministry. Jesus preached and taught that God's future initiatives on behalf of his own not only conditioned the present by providing hope to the poor (as in apocalyptic Judaism), but God's future reign was already present in history for the poor (5:3, cf. 5:4, 6, par. Luke 6:20, 21). Third, the Old Testament Scriptures contained all the Beatitudes' ingredients of form, subjects, and promises. Yet Jesus, commensurate with his use of the Old Testament, uniquely combined these elements and addressed them as an expression of the "gospel of the Kingdom" to those who responded to him.

The fourth parallel Beatitude (5:11–12, par. Luke 6:22–23) exhibits several secondary characteristics simply by comparison with the two accounts. The original structure and content lie beyond our grasp. But numerous levels and various sources of the Church's tradition attest that the Beatitude's concern with suffering was a part of Jesus' teaching to his disciples (e.g., Mark 13:9–13, par. Matt. 10:17–22; Matt 10:34–36, par. Luke 12:51–53; John 15:18–25; 16:1–14; 1 Pet 3:13–17). Furthermore, the motif of suffering and vindication stands clearly allied with the Old Testament concept of the poor as being the afflicted and oppressed.

2. Pre-evangelists' Tradition

a. The first stage in the development of the tradition involved the combining of traditional sayings, or logia, to form the basic Sermon material. The first three Beatitudes doubtless constituted a traditional unit, whereas the fourth most likely existed in the tradition as an independent saying or logion. These elements were brought together to form an opening statement (6:20–21, par. Matt) and a transition (6:22–23, par. Matt) to the next traditional section on the Love Your Enemies (6:27–35, par. Matt). The chances of three Beatitudes similar in structure and content (5:3, 4, 6, par. Luke 6:20–21) being coincidentally combined in a similar manner with a fourth Beatitude (5:11–12, par. Luke 6:22–23) so different in structure and content by two different accounts is too random to be credible. Therefore, the similarity still evident between Matthew's and Luke's parallel Beatitudes (5:3, 4, 6, 11–12, par. Luke 6:20–23) presents almost irrefutable evidence for the existence of a common tradition at an early stage of the Sermon's development. Most scholars would call this material Q and place its setting and function in the catechetical context of the early church.

In spite of these basic parallels between Matthew's and Luke's present accounts, the obvious differences indicate a significant development in the tradition. Many, like Dupont (*Béatitudes* 1:250–64, 265–98), have attributed these changes in the Beatitude tradition to the respective evangelist. Whereas this solution may well explain Luke's distinctive features, it overlooks the integral character of Matthew's additional Beatitudes with the pre-Matthean Sermon tradition.

Before turning to Matthew's additional Beatitudes, the lexical differences in the subject and promise of the fourth parallel Beatitude (5:11–12, par. Luke 6:22–23) demonstrate the flexibility of the tradition in light of its various contexts. Whereas Luke's subject (6:22) apparently referred to conflict situations within the synagogue that led to expulsion, Matthew's subject (5:12) spoke of persecution in general and verbal abuse in particular. This difference also carried over to the section on Love for One's Enemies which immediately followed this Beatitude in the early Sermon tradition (cf. "persecute," Matt 5:12, 44; "hate," Luke 6:22, 27). Luke's form of the tradition would then reflect the earlier setting of the church's struggles within the synagogue. The secondary Woe (6:26) shows that the Beatitude's primary thrust at the time of the Woe was on verbal abuse. Matthew's Beatitude may be a later generalization of suffering. To be sure, redactional elements also occur in this Beatitude (e.g., Matthew's "falsely," "for my sake" in 5:12, and Luke's "leap for joy," "their fathers" in 6:23; see Note on 5:11–12), but the basic difference in the setting of the subject has its roots in the tradition.

b. Of Matthew's five additional Beatitudes, only one (5:10) stands on his account. Beginning with the Beatitude to the *meek* (5:5), drawn almost verbatim from Ps 37(36):11, the redundant synonymity in Greek between the *poor in spirit*, Matthew's modification of 5:3, and the *meek* of 5:5 strongly mitigates against its being a redactional addition. Furthermore, the Hebrew subject (ʿnwm, LXX = πραεῖς) of Ps 37(36):11 is the same as the subject of 5:3 (ʿnwm, LXX = πτωχοί) of Isa 61:1. Therefore, a Hellenistic-Jewish context, in which the distinction between πραεῖς and πτωχοί as variants for ʿnwm would be at home, offers the most likely setting for this Beatitude. It would then have formed a synonymous parallelism and couplet with 5:3 in order to protect the πτωχοί of 5:3 from being misconstrued strictly socioeconomically in a Hellenistic context. The location of this Beatitude as second in some early manuscripts (see Note on 5:5) may reflect the earlier tradition. The present location of the Beatitude as third resulted from Matthew's desire to align the initial Beatitudes expressly with Isaiah 61.

The Beatitudes of 5:7–9 also reflect a pre-Matthean stage in the tradition. Each correlates with one of the following three major sections of the Sermon tradition, in particular with the tradition as it now stands in Luke. The first, "Blessed are the merciful," addresses those who have their counterpart in Luke 6:36–42. The two terms for "merciful," ἐλεήμων (5:7) and οἰκτίρμων (Luke 6:36), frequently stand in tandem in the Psalms (see Note on 5:7). In this relationship, the Beatitude to the merciful sets the indicative for the paranetic section on Judging that follows in Luke (see Note on 5:7). Matthew, by contrast, has not only relocated the context of Luke 6:36, par. 5:48 (cf. Note on 5:48), but he has also changed the parallel "merciful" (οἰκτίρμονες) to "perfect" (τέλειοι).

A similar phenomenon occurs with the Beatitude to the "pure in heart" of 5:8. The Psalm motif appears again with a verbatim subject drawn from Ps 24(23):4. According to the Psalm context, the "pure in heart" demonstrate integrity and honesty. This theme is developed paranetically in the Sermon tradition on "fruits" consistent with one's character (Luke 6:43–45, cf. Matt 7:15–20; 12:33–35). The reference to the "heart" actually occurs in Luke 6:45 (cf. Matt 12:35). Finally, the Beatitude to the "peacemakers" (5:9) has its corollary in the section on Love Your Enemies (Luke 6:27–35, par. Matt 5:38–41). Not only is the "making of peace" synonymous with "loving one's enemies," but the promise of the Beatitude and that of the paranesis is identical, namely, they shall be "sons of God." The intervening materials between 5:9 and 5:44 in Matthew conceal this earlier literary relationship.

Therefore, four Beatitudes, based to a great extent on language taken from the Psalms and closely related to the three subsequent sections of the Sermon tradition, expand the original number of the Beatitudes. The function of these additional Beatitudes appears to be primarily introductory to the following sections. No specifically theological tendency emerges that would enable us to assign these Beatitudes to a particular community. The greater affinity of these Beatitudes with the Lucan Sermon tradition rather than the redactionally modified Matthean material demonstrates their pre-Matthean character. Therefore, Matthew's traditional source for the Beatitudes displays considerable expansion of the four found in the Q tradition. The symbol Q^{mt} would then more accurately designate the particularly Matthean form of the Q Beatitude tradition.

3. The Evangelists' Redaction

Three features are apparent in the Lucan Beatitudes: the consistent use of the second person plural address form, the Woes built as antithetical parallels to the Beatitudes, and the use of "now" in 6:21, 25. Apart from the characteristic use of "now" (νῦν) in Luke (25x in Acts; 12x in Luke; cf. 4x in Matt; 3x in Mark; 11:39, cf. Matt 23:25; 22:18, cf. Matt 26:29; 22:69, cf. Matt 26:64), it is quite difficult to determine whether the second person form or the Woes reflect the evangelist's hand or pre-Lucan changes in the tradition. Matthew's redaction, by comparison, stands out in bold relief.

Without doubt, Matthew has deliberately aligned the first through fourth Beatitudes with the promises of Isaiah, in particular with Isaiah 61, and introduced the eighth accordingly. In 5:3 the qualification of "the poor" as "the poor in spirit" corresponds to the Greek and Hebrew lexical content of Isa 61:1. First, the LXX renders the Hebrew ʿnwm with πτωχοί and offers the contextual background for the Beatitude in Luke as well as in Jesus' ministry (see Note on 5:3). Yet the usage of πτωχοί in Isa 61:1 presents a bit of an oddity, since πραΰς rather than πτωχός is the common translation for ʿnwm (the only other exception,

Isa 29:19). Second, πτωχοί removed from its Old Testament background would have had a strictly socioeconomic connotation for a Hellenistic audience. This danger, as noted above, probably contributed to the pre-Matthean construction of the Beatitude to the "meek" drawn from Ps 37(36):11. Third, since πραεῖς, the expected LXX term for ʿnwm, was already a part of a Beatitude relating directly to Ps 37(36):11, Matthew chose the synonymous paraphrase "poor in spirit" to bind the first Beatitude more closely to the ʿnwm of Isa 61:1.

The second Beatitude (5:4) exhibits the same Matthean interest in Isaiah 61. Whereas Luke's Beatitude to the "weeping" who "shall laugh" is set against the background of Ps 126:2–6, Matthew has the "mourners" who "shall be comforted" corresponding verbatim with the LXX of Isa 61:2. Furthermore, the evangelist has changed the order of the Beatitudes by placing this one second according to the sequence of Isa 61:1–2. By changing the order to comply with Isaiah 61, Matthew no longer maintains the familiar Old Testament association of "the poor" and "the hungry" (e.g., Isa 32:6–7; 58:7, 10; Ps 107:36, 41; Job 24:4, 10) as found in Luke 6:20–21a, nor does he preserve the previous parallelism of 5:3 and 5:5 that was most likely present in his own source.

The relation of the third Beatitude (5:5) to Isaiah 61 was more fortuitous than redactional. Apart from the relocation of this Beatitude from second to third, Matthew made no further changes. But the promise, to "inherit the earth," drawn from Ps 37(36):11, agrees verbatim with the promise of Isa 61:7 LXX. The fourth Beatitude (5:6), by contrast, has both an additional verb, "to thirst," and a direct object, "for righteousness," rather than simply Luke's "to hunger" (Luke 6:21a). Matthew's insertion of "to thirst" intensifies the subjects' dire need by including both elements of food and drink necessary to human existence. The concept of hungering and thirsting does not stem from Isaiah 61 (cf. Isa 55), but it definitely belongs to the metaphors of God's eschatological blessings for his people drawn from Isaiah (e.g., Isa 55:1–4; see Note on 5:6). By adding "righteousness" the evangelist moves the focus from the physical hunger and thirst to the more comprehensive relationship with God in which one's entire person—physical and spiritual—is involved (cf. 6:33, "and all these things [i.e., food and clothing] will be given additionally by God"). Matthew takes this focal point from Isaiah 61, where three times the prophet refers to God's effecting righteousness (61:3, 10, 11; cf. 8), and he uses this Beatitude to round off the first group of four Beatitudes in summary fashion.

The eighth Beatitude (5:10) has Matthean redactional elements in both

content and location. Whether the evangelist formed the Beatitude from
5:11–12 with view to the "poor in spirit" in 5:3 or whether he adapted
traditional material (cf. 1 Pet 3:14) is relatively moot. In either case he
added the Beatitude and set the subject in the perfect tense to reflect
the situation of his community. As "the persecuted for righteousness'
sake," the Matthean community corresponds to "the poor in spirit" of
5:3 and the ʿnwm of Isa 61:1 to whom Jesus announces the good news
of "the Kingdom of Heaven." By adding this Beatitude, the evangelist
(a) interprets and applies Isa 61:1 with reference to his own community,
(b) forms a conclusion to the second group of four Beatitudes with the
same focus as his conclusion to the first group of four (5:6), and (c) he
builds an inclusion around all the Beatitudes with the parallelism of
5:10 and 5:3.

The literary correspondence between Matthew's redaction and Isaiah
61 gains further support from the theological tendency of the evangelist.
By aligning the Beatitude with Isaiah 61, Matthew follows consistently
his *christological* concern to demonstrate that Jesus is the fulfillment of
the Old Testament. Jesus not only uses Isaiah's language, he actually
fulfills Isaiah's promise of the age of salvation by doing so. The Beatitudes
are the "gospel of the Kingdom" in terms of Isaiah 61 for Matthew.
Furthermore, the evangelist also *ecclesiologically* defines his community
in terms of Isaiah 61 as "the poor in spirit," "the afflicted for righteousness' sake" who have been brought into a new relationship with God
through Jesus the Christ (5:3, 10). They have become the people of
the promise who look with anticipation to the consummation promised
in the Beatitudes.

In summary, the Beatitudes of Matt 5:3–12 indicate several stages of
development. First, the core (5:3, 4, 6 par. Luke 6:20–21) had roots
extending to Jesus' ministry to the desperate ones of his day. Using
language familiar to the Old Testament promise and the paradox motif,
Jesus declared the good news of the Kingdom in beatitude form. The
fourth Beatitude (5:11–12, par. Luke 6:22–23) depicts the continuing
struggle in this age for God's people, caught in the tension between
what God was effecting now in Jesus and the future consummation.
Second, these four Beatitudes, brought together to make a clear declarative statement as the opening of the Sermon tradition, were later expanded
by the use of the Psalms and Jesus' sayings to form four additional
Beatitudes (5:5, 7–9) commensurate with Jesus' teaching and preaching
as found in the tradition. Third, Matthew expressly adapted these Beatitudes (5:3, 4, 5, 6, 10) to Isaiah 61 in order to underline Jesus' person

and work as the fulfillment of the Old Testament and to identify Jesus' followers as the new people of the promise whose life lived in this new relationship with God corresponded to his will and led to conflict with those of his age. Throughout the entire process of development, these nine Beatitudes remain consistent with the Jesus of the tradition. The process serves to clarify and amplify the tradition rather than to distort it in either Matthew or Luke.

IV. THE ROLE OF DISCIPLESHIP
Matthew 5:13–16

Translation

5 ¹³You are the salt of the earth. But if salt becomes worthless, what can restore its value? It has no value except, being thrown out, to be walked on by people.

¹⁴You are the light of the world. A city situated on a hill cannot be hidden. ¹⁵Nor does one keep a lamp burning only to set it under a basket. Rather one sets it on a lampstand to give light for all in the house.

¹⁶Let your light shine for others in such a manner that they will see your good deeds and give the glory to your Heavenly Father.

Literary Analysis

The unit of 5:13–16 consists of two metaphors (5:13a, 14a), two parables (5:13b, 15), and a paranetic conclusion (5:16). The first metaphor, "You are the salt of the earth" (5:13a), is developed by a parable on salt (5:13b). The second metaphor, "You are the light of the world" (5:14a), is developed by a proverbial reference to a city on a hill (5:14b) and a parable on the appropriate use of a lamp (5:15). The paranetic conclusion, "Let your light shine . . ." (5:16), focuses on the light motif of the second metaphor and applies it to one's good works, resulting in a literary tension between the metaphors that refer to one's person ("you are . . .") and the paranesis that singles out one's conduct ("your good works").

119

The source(s) behind this unit are not at all clear. Whereas some have taken this to be a pre-Matthean unit (Wrege, *Überlieferungsge-schichte*, 27–34), most view it as being the redactional work of the evangelist. The metaphors (5:13a, 14a) and the paranesis (5:16a) have no parallels in the tradition and may well be redactional emerging from the traditional material brought together by the evangelist (cf. 5:10 and 5:11–12 above). The parable of the salt appears in Mark 9:50 and Luke 14:34–35. Since Matthew and Luke demonstrate closer affinities with each other than either does with Mark (see Note on 5:13), it is probable that their saying comes from the Q tradition. The differences would then be transmissional variations and redactional modifications. The reference to a city on a hill (5:14b) has no parallel in the New Testament, but its appearance in a more developed form in *Gos Thom* 32 and Pap Oxy 1:7 demonstrates its traditional character. The parable of the lamp also has a parallel in Mark 4:21 and Luke 8:16; 11:33. Yet Luke 11:33 offers the closer traditional parallel leading to the conclusion that this saying, like the parable of the salt, was also found in Q (see Note on 5:15). Each of these traditional sayings was quite likely an independent unit at one point in the tradition, since neither the parable of the salt nor the lamp has the same context or function in any two of the three Gospels. Finally, the conclusion of the paranesis in 5:16b may well reflect an underlying traditional saying that appears in a similar context in 1 Pet 2:12.

Notes

5:13. *You are.* The subject is clearly the same as that of the transitional Beatitude in 5:11–12. For Matthew, the *you* suffering for Christ's sake of 5:11 are the *poor in spirit* of 5:3, *the persecuted for righteousness' sake* of 5:10. Having applied the Beatitudes to his own community of *disciples* (see Note on 5:2), the evangelist takes the occasion to bring together several sayings (5:13–16) to address his community concerning their role in the world, a role not unlike that of *the prophets before you* (5:12). Therefore, the theme of 5:12 most likely triggered Matthew's expansion of the Sermon material with this section on the disciple's role in the world (Dupont, *Béatitudes* 3:315–29).

the salt. Both Mark 9:50 and Luke 14:34 begin with "Salt is good." But Matthew's introduction makes that statement redundant. *Salt* had several functions in the ancient world. Apart from its cultic use in sacrifices (Lev 2:13), it functioned as a seasoning (Job 6:6), a preservative, and a means of purification (Str-B 1:235). Yet the present metaphor, *salt of the earth,* betrays the influence of the following parable, since, taken literally, salt has no positive significance for *the earth.* In other words, the sense of the metaphor comes from the ensuing parable. The disciples are to the earth what salt is to everyday life.

of the earth. Earth ($\gamma\tilde{\eta}$) parallels *world* ($\kappa\acute{o}\sigma\mu\sigma\varsigma$) in the second metaphor (5:14a) and refers to the realm of human existence that stands under God's sovereign rule through the coming of the person and work of Christ (cf. 28:18). It sets the universal scope of the Church's mission (28:19–20; see Kretzer, *Herrschaft,* 139, 280). Although the evangelist does not explain how the disciple's role parallels that of salt, the metaphor, by using such a common, necessary ingredient from everyday living, speaks for itself.

becomes worthless. Literally means to become *foolish* ($\mu\omega\rho\acute{\alpha}\nu\vartheta\eta$). Both Matthew and Luke 11:34 have this unusual verb, whereas Mark 9:50 has the more appropriate "saltless" ($\acute{\alpha}\nu\alpha\lambda\sigma\nu$). The Hebrew verb *tpl* has a double meaning, "to become unsavory," "insipid" and a "fool" (Black, *Aramaic,* 166; Jeremias, *Parables,* 168). The Greek rendering *to become foolish* might then reflect an early interpretation of the parable as a warning for the disciples to take their role seriously rather than to waste it foolishly (Jeremias, *Parables,* 168). Since salt cannot lose its chemical properties and remain salt, the literal meaning of the phrase is no longer certain. It doubtless referred to the adulteration of salt in some fashion. Rabbi Josua b. Chananja (ca. 90) noted the nonsense of this saying by comparing salt's losing its savor to a mule's giving birth. This rabbinic reference may have arisen as part of Jewish apologetic against the use of the parable to explain Israel's rejection of God's salvation (Str-B 1:236).

restore its value. Literally, *to be salted* ($\acute{\alpha}\lambda\iota\sigma\vartheta\acute{\eta}\sigma\epsilon\tau\alpha\iota$). If salt has lost its saltiness, what can make it salty? Mark 9:50 ends with the question whose answer is obvious. Nothing! Matthew and Luke have a concluding statement.

It has no value. Matthew has, *It is capable of doing nothing more* ($\epsilon\dot{\iota}\varsigma$ $o\dot{\upsilon}\delta\grave{\epsilon}\nu$ $\iota\sigma\chi\acute{\upsilon}\epsilon\iota$ $\acute{\epsilon}\tau\iota$). Luke uses a different construction: "It is not suitable" ($\epsilon\ddot{\upsilon}\vartheta\epsilon\tau\sigma\nu$) for either the soil ($\gamma\tilde{\eta}\nu$) or the dunghill ($\kappa\sigma\pi\rho\acute{\iota}\alpha\nu$).

except being thrown out. This phrase expresses the common practice of discarding one's trash by throwing it out. But the verb ($\beta\lambda\eta\vartheta\acute{\epsilon}\nu$) has an eschatological ring to it in Matthew (cf. 8:12; 22:13; 25:30).

to be walked on by people. Luke 14:35 does not have this phrase.

Matthew completes the context by noting the consequence. *To be walked on* (καταπατέω) connotes disdain and judgment (cf. Hos 5:11, LXX).

5:14. *You are the light.* This metaphor introduces the theme of the following traditional units (5:14b, 15). It stresses in a positive manner the mission of the disciples. In the Old Testament, light used as a metaphor applies to God (Ps 18:28; Mic 7:8), the servant (Isa 42:6; 49:6), and Zion/Israel (Isa 60:1–3). In Judaism, Israel, the Law, the Temple, and Jerusalem are the light (Str-B 1:237). In the New Testament Paul notes that the Jews considered themselves to be the light to those in darkness (Rom 2:19). But Paul also reminds the Christians to shine as lights in the world (Rom 13:12), and John 8:12 and 13:35 refer to Jesus as the "light of the world." Furthermore, Matthew has just introduced Jesus' public ministry in Galilee (4:15–16) as the fulfillment of Isa 9: 1–2, the great light for those who sit in darkness. Although these metaphors have various referents, each points to God's revealing light, the light that illumines the way for those in darkness.

of the world. The *world* (κόσμος) has three points of reference for Matthew (Kretzer, *Herrschaft*, 32–33): (1) in distinction to heaven, the spatial element where people live (5:14; 13:38; 4:8); (2) a personal element as the sphere where human events, good (26:13) and bad (18:7), take place (cf. ἄνθρωποι in 5:13, 16); and (3) a temporal element comparable to "this age" whose beginning is the "foundation" of this world (13:35; 24:21, cf. 24:3). In this context, *world* refers to the global scope of the mission both spatially and personally. It is reminiscent of the great commission to "disciple all nations" (28:19, cf. 5:13).

A city situated on a hill. This saying, without parallel in the New Testament, has a more developed form in Pap Oxy 1:7 and *Gos Thom* 32, "A city built on a high mountain [and] fortified cannot fall nor can it be hidden." This saying may have been an allusion to the Old Testament role of Jerusalem. For example, Isa 2:2–4 and Mic 4:1–3 speak of the "mountain of the house of the Lord," the city of Jerusalem, towering above all others and depicting God's redemptive work for the nations in the day of salvation. Furthermore, the prophet in Isa 60:1 addresses Zion with the command, "Arise and shine, for your light has come and the glory of the Lord has risen upon you." By introducing the saying into this context, the evangelist has combined two symbols for Israel, the concept of light (5:14a) and the city on a hill (5:14b), and applied them to the disciple's mission in the world (cf. von Rad, "Stadt," 439–47).

cannot be hidden. This verb expresses a note of assurance reinforced in the expanded parallel of Pap Oxy 1:7 and *Gos Thom* 32, ". . . fortified cannot fall. . . ." This note of confidence rings through the commission of Matt 28:18, "All authority has been given to me. . . ."

5:15. *Nor does one keep a lamp burning.* *Nor does one* (οὐδέ) is Matthew's redactional bridge to this parable. This saying occurs in Mark 4:21, par. Luke 8:16 and Luke 11:33 (Q), each of which have secondary features compared to Matt 5:15. An indication of the earlier character of Matthew's form is the impersonal third person plural of the verbs καίουσιν and τιθέασιν, an Aramaism for the passive voice (Black, *Aramaic,* 126–27). The verb καίουσιν stresses the action of keeping something burning (Bauer, *s.v.*) more than the act of lighting (cf. ἅπτω in Luke 11:33 and 8:16) a lamp or fire (Schneider, "Bildwort," 192).

place it under a basket. The word for basket (μόδιον, Mark 4:21, cf. Luke 8:16) is a Latin term for a measure that contained about one peck. This peck-measure, found as a loan word in Aramaic and Greek, was a common utensil in the average farm household (Jeremias, "Lampe," 100–101). Both Luke and Mark have additional elements. Luke 11:33 refers to placing the lamp in a "cellar," indicating a different architectural setting from the one-room Palestinian farmhouse. Mark 4:21, par. Luke 8:16, also has the phrase, "under a bed." But beds were unusual in the simple Palestinian house where one slept on the floor in winter and the roof (cf. Mark 13:15) in summer (Jeremias, "Lampe," 99, n. 1). These additional elements in Mark and Luke help determine the original point of the parable. Rather than contrasting lighting and extinguishing (by covering with a basket) the lamp (as does Jeremias, "Lampe,"102), the focus is on the appropriate use or purpose of the lamp (Schneider, "Bildwort," 192). By contrast, one places the lamp on a "lampstand" to enhance its efficiency.

to give light for all in the house. Matthew has the paratactic construction of *and* (καί), another Aramaism (Jeremias, "Lampe," 100), rather than the purpose clause (ἵνα) of Mark 4:21, par. Luke 8:16 and 11:33. *Light for all in the house* implies a one-room house, whereas Luke's "so that those entering can see the light" (8:16; 11:33) suggests a house with a vestibule.

5:16. *in such a manner.* With this characteristic expression (32x, as compared to 10x in Mark and 21x in Luke), Matthew moves into the paranesis that summarizes and applies the previous metaphors. Although this adverb can be taken grammatically with the result clause that follows, Matthew frequently uses it to draw an application from a previous parable or illustration (e.g., 13:40; 17:12; 18:14, 35; so Dupont, *Béatitudes* 3:322).

let your light shine. The application of the metaphors leads the evangelist from the second person indicatives of 5:13a, 14a to the paranetic imperative. The integral relationship between the paranesis (5:16) and the second metaphor (5:14–15) is apparent in the common vocabulary: *light* (φῶς), *your* (ὑμεῖς), *shine* (λάμπω).

for others. The characteristically Matthean usage of *before* (ἔμπροσθεν, 18x, cf. 2x in Mark and 10x in Luke) with *men* (ἀνθρώπων, cf. 5:13) denotes the personal focus of the disciple's mission in the *world* (see Note on 5:14).

your good deeds. The same phrase and motif behind the context of 5:16 also underlies 1 Pet 2:12b. Apart from the verbal similarity between 5:16b and 1 Pet 2:12b, 1 Pet 2:11–12 expresses a paranesis for the mission situation that sets the believers in contrast to the world (2:11, 12a), a contrast that leads to false accusations (2:12a, cf. Matt 5:11–12), and calls for conduct that not only counters the false accusations but also leads the one who "observes" to "glorify God" (2:12, cf. 3:1–2). This proximity of setting and language most likely indicates a common tradition reworked appropriately by the evangelist and by the writer of 1 Peter to fit their respective contexts and purpose (Best, "1 Peter," 103–11; Goppelt, *Petrusbrief,* 162, n. 28). Behind this tradition may lie a *verbum Christi* (Selwyn, *Peter,* 170, 363; cf. Gundry, "Verba," 336–50). The evangelist refers to *deeds* (ἔργα) five other times (11:2, 19; 23:3, 5; 26:10), only one of which has a parallel (26:10, par. Mark 14:6). In 11:2, 19 (both redactional—11:2, cf. Luke 7:18; 11:19, cf. Luke 7:35) *deeds* are the distinguishing marks of Jesus Messiah and Wisdom and are comparable to fruit indicative of one's true nature (3:10, par. Luke 3:9; 7:16–20, cf. 12:33–35, par. Luke 6:43–45). Matt 23:3, 5 warns against emulating the exhibitionist tendencies in the *deeds* of the scribes and Pharisees. This comparison with the scribes and Pharisees parallels Matthew's use of δικαιοσύνη in 5:20 and 6:1. In other words, *good deeds, fruits,* and *righteousness* are all interrelated for Matthew. Therefore, *good deeds,* like righteousness, are the *life* lived consistent with the new relationship established by Jesus' ministry between God and humankind (5:6; 6:33). It is provokingly different from the life lived by others (cf. 5:10, 11–12) with a totally different starting point and appearance (5:21–48; 6:1–18). Such a life bears witness to the transforming power of God in the human experience (cf. 5:16b).

Yet to limit *good deeds* merely to one's actions would hardly be fair to Matthew. The redactional setting of 5:16 is the world mission (5:13a, 14a) and the disciple's mission, no less than Jesus', included both the word and the deed (11:1–(5)–6; 28:18–20; cf. 10:6–8). The disciples were the salt of the earth and the light of the world through their words and deeds. Without doubt Matthew intends to make a strong ethical statement in the paranesis, as indeed he does in 7:21–23. But he does so precisely in order to combat the dichotomy between one's words and one's actions, not to replace the one with the other. Therefore, *good deeds* connotes basically a life of dicipleship that includes both word and deed.

give the glory to your Heavenly Father. The visibility of one's *good deeds* of 5:16 stands in stark contrast to the warning of 23:3, 5 and the admonitions of 6:1–18. The significance lies in the focus of the audience's attention. God, *your Heavenly Father* (see Note on 6:9), receives the glory, not the individual himself. But how is it possible for an unbelieving observer *to give the glory to God?* To *glorify God* in the mission setting of 5:13–16 implies that the disciple becomes the agent *(light)* through whom others come to recognize and acknowledge God as Father. Like Jesus in 4:16, the disciple becomes the "light to those who sit in darkness." One's *good deeds,* like a light in the darkness, stand in such bold contrast from one's context that others either recognize and acknowledge the transforming presence of God's role in the disciple's life or they strongly reject it with the negative consequences of 5:10–12 (cf. Jesus' ministry). Both elements are inherent to Christian ministry, to discipleship. The evangelist, recognizing the negative results in the Beatitudes of 5:10–12, stresses nonetheless the positive impact of the mission in 5:13–16. Suffering and rejection (cf. 5:10, 11–12, and 5:3) do not diminish the imperative of discipleship's role to be the *salt of the earth* and the *light of the world.*

Comments

Three comments follow. The first reviews in a general manner the themes of the section. The second deals with the function of 5:13–16 within the structure of the Sermon, and the third focuses on the implications for the nature of mission.

A. Discipleship

The unit of 5:13–16 takes up the subject ("you") and the focus (the disciple in the world) of the transitional Beatitude (5:11–12). Whereas that Beatitude's content dealt with the negative consequences of life lived "on account of me" (5:11), a life of discipleship, this section develops the positive aspect of the disciple's role in mission (5:16a). Therefore, we might properly call this section the disciple's mission in the world.

1. Salt of the Earth: Matt 5:13

The evangelist opens with the metaphor of salt. The strength of the metaphor lies in its being a common household ingredient and in its vital role in everyday life. Salt not only served as seasoning for bland food (Job 6:6) but also as a purifying agent and as a preservative. Relying on the inherent significance of salt in the life of his audience, Matthew does not attempt to delineate more precisely how the disciple was like salt. The disciple is to the earth what salt is to food. Both ingredients are necessities.

The evangelist does elaborate on his choice of the salt metaphor for the disciple by adding a parable on salt. This parable, with its differing contexts in Matthew, Mark 9:50, and Luke 14:34–35, evidently had its own independent existence in the tradition. The only common denominator in the three Gospels is the parable's application to discipleship. The point of the parable, in spite of the variations in all three sayings, remains constant. Salt that has lost its "savor" cannot be reconstituted. Matthew and Luke note further that it is to be discarded. Without attempting to explain how, this statement simply asserts that salt can lose its value as salt. To venture an explanation goes beyond the purpose and limits of the parable itself. That both Matthew and Luke have used as the underlying verb the Aramaic with the unexpected meaning "to become foolish" (see Note on 5:13) merely indicates the application of the parable in the tradition of Q. A disciple who ceases to function as a disciple has indeed become "foolish," has lost his "meaning" as a disciple.

By using the metaphor and parable of salt, Matthew underscores the radical demand for discipleship. On the one hand, the metaphor focuses on discipleship as an integral part of God's purposes for "the earth" (5:13a), the sphere of human existence now under the sovereign rule of God through Jesus' ministry (28:18). The scope of discipleship extends far beyond one's own personal interests. The disciple stands before God with a mission, a responsibility for "the earth." Discipleship and mission are integral, not optional elements for Matthew. On the other hand, the parable also warns of the responsibility accompanying discipleship, since discipleship and mission are inseparable. One becomes "useless" for the mission when one fails to take the role of discipleship seriously.

Indeed, one ceases being a disciple and stands under judgment ("cast out and walked on"). Matthew, for whom the judgment motif is very prominent (see Bornkamm, "End-expectation," 15–24), sets the warning here in the context of mission. To fail in mission is to fail in discipleship. Therefore, the evangelist opens the section with a somewhat negative emphasis and moves to the more positive admonition in what follows.

2. Light of the World: Matt 5:14–15

This metaphor (5:14a) stands in synonymous parallelism with the salt metaphor (5:13a). It, too, focuses on the role of the disciple ("light") and the parameter of the disciple's mission ("world"). Whereas the Jewish background variously compared Israel, the Servant, and the blessings of Israel such as the Law, Temple, and Jerusalem with the light, Matthew is most likely alluding to the comparison of Jesus' ministry with the "light" of Isa 9:1–2 found in Matt 4:16. In 10:6–8 Jesus charged his disciples with this ministry and commissioned them for this ministry in 28:18–20. With the designation of "light," the disciple, as did Jesus, fulfills the various eschatological expectations symbolized by light in the Old Testament. The disciple's role is to illuminate those who "sit in darkness" in the world. The goal of the disciple's mission is the "world," the arena of God's sovereign activity in Jesus Christ (cf. 28:18, "all authority in heaven and on earth"). It is the world of people (28:19, "make disciples of all nations"). The mission has no boundaries, neither geographical nor ethnic.

Matthew first explicates the metaphor by using another Old Testament motif of the city on a hill. The parable sounds a note of inevitability and thus assurance. To stand out, to be obvious, belongs to the very nature of such a city. By combining this image with the metaphor of light, the evangelist may well have intended an additional Old Testament application of this saying to the disciples. The city may well be an allusion to Jerusalem situated on the "mount of the house of God," that was to have a particular role among the nations according to Old Testament prophecy (cf. Isa 2:2–5; Mic 4:1–3). Isa 60:1–3 also applies the light metaphor to Zion, "Arise and shine, for your light has come. . . . And nations shall come to your light. . . ." If this application is correct, then Matthew has deliberately placed the disciples in the light of Israel's future role for the nations. The disciples in their mission fulfill the Old Testament promises for Israel in a way not unlike Jesus' ministry as seen in the preceding Beatitudes.

In 5:15 the evangelist adds a second explication of the light metaphor by way of the parable of a lamp. This parable, found in Mark's tradition (4:21, par. Luke 8:16) and in Q (5:15, par. Luke 11:33), refers to the common oil lamp made of clay and used to light the interior of the windowless, one-room houses of Palestine. The point of comparison lies in the contrast between covering a burning lamp and setting it on a lampstand. Mark 4:21, par. Luke 8:16, has the parable following the explanation of the parable of the Sower. The context applies the use or misuse of the lamp to the reception of the gospel. By contrast, Luke 11:33 has the parable in a context referring to one's response to Jesus. Matthew, who has the earlier form of the tradition (see Note on 5:15), has applied it to the disciple's role in the world. Consequently, as with the salt parable, the different contexts within the Gospels indicate an independent traditional saying with its various usages by the respective evangelists.

Whereas the salt metaphor warns the disciple to take one's calling seriously, the light metaphor describes positively one's role as a disciple in the world. The disciple is an integral part of God's design to bring light into the world of darkness as promised for the day of salvation. The task, like the visibility of a city set on a hill, is inherent to the nature of discipleship. Furthermore, Jesus has given to his disciples the divine authority by which he accomplished his task in the world in order that they might reach the people of the world in his name (28:18–20). Therefore, as a city on a hill cannot be concealed, one's light as Jesus' disciple cannot be hidden. Matthew then brings a second parable (5:15) showing that the function of a lamp is to let its light shine unhindered in order that its full value might be utilized. What that light is, the evangelist develops in the paranesis of 5:16.

3. Let Your Light Shine: Matt 5:16

Perhaps the location of this section on mission at the outset of Jesus' teaching ministry (5:13–16) is more than coincidentally related to his final instructions for his disciples in 28:18–20. This material on the missionary nature of discipleship immediately follows the declaration in the Beatitudes of the "good news" set in the context of Isaiah 61. Disciples are not only those who hear and respond to the good news but become by the very nature of discipleship messengers of this good news. This role, which was once Israel's, is integral to being a part of the age of salvation. The recipients of the good news become themselves messengers of the good news. Thus we have the indicatives of the metaphors: "You are the salt of the earth"; "You are the light of the world." With the imperative, "Let your light shine," Matthew summarizes the force of these metaphors in the language of 5:14–15.

The paranesis grows out of and is based on the indicatives of the proclamation. Like salt to everyday living, like a city on a hill, like a lamp shining on a lampstand, the disciple is to function according to the very nature of discipleship. The evangelist moves from the metaphor to the more concrete language of *good deeds*. In other words, the disciple "shines" by means of corresponding life and conduct. Mission for Matthew clearly involved the words of proclamation (cf. 10:7; 28:19–20). But mission involved much more than words. It included one's life in its entirety. As fruit betrays the nature of the tree (7:16–20), so one's actions are indications of one's commitment (7:21–23). The life of the disciple does not stand out by a greater obedience to the Law (cf. 19:16–23; 23:3, 5)—either the Mosaic Law or Jesus' "new law"—but by a conduct that reflects the new relationship between the individual and God (6:1–18; 22:37). This relationship (5:6; 6:33) and its corresponding conduct (5:10, 20) are "righteousness" for Matthew.

Since this life and conduct or *good deeds* are characteristic of life in the new age of salvation (cf. Jer 31:31), they bear witness to God's eschatological activity on behalf of humanity. Just as Jesus' life and preaching/teaching bore witness to God's redemptive activity to those who had eyes to see and ears to hear, so the disciple's *good deeds* lead others to recognize the presence of God's transforming power in the world. Discipleship itself thus becomes a witness to God's salvation. This "light" seen by those in darkness leads them to "glorify" God, to acknowledge God as God and yield to him as their "Heavenly Father." This role of mission is how the Kingdom, God's sovereign rule, becomes a reality in the world of people (28:19–20).

B. Matt 5:13–16: Parenthesis or Pivot?

It is easy to read past this section as though it were a parenthesis between the Beatitudes and the section on Jesus and the Law (5:17–48). Yet structurally 5:13–16 plays a much larger role within the Sermon than such a parenthesis would allow. First, the close interweaving of christology and ecclesiology between the Beatitudes of 5:3–12 and the passage of 5:13–16 reminds us of the larger structure of Matthew 5–9, which presents Jesus as Messiah of word and deed, and Matthew 10, which presents the disciples as carrying out that ministry in mission.

The same pattern concludes the Gospel, as the resurrected, vindicated, and exalted Lord (28:16–18) again commissions the disciples for mission (28:19–20). Therefore, the redactional shaping of the Beatitudes to set Jesus as the fulfillment of Isaiah 61 is followed by the stress on the disciples' corresponding role in mission.

Second, this interrelationship of christology and ecclesiology has its redemptive historical roots in the Old Testament promise. With the coming of Messiah as fulfillment (christology) comes the focus on the People of God (ecclesiology), the fulfillment of God's redemptive promises for his own. One must beware of focusing primarily on ecclesiology, an important strain in Matthew (cf. Bornkamm, "End-expectation") or on christology, the dominant strain in Matthew (cf. Kingsbury, *Matthew*), at the expense of ecclesiology, since there could be no Matthean "fullfill-ment" christology without the accompanying "fulfillment" ecclesiology. The use of the metaphor of light and the parable of the visible city on a hill and a lamp that illuminates applies to the disciples (Church) the promised role of Israel to the nations (cf. *earth*, 5:13; *world*, 5:14; 28:18–20), a role which the disciples receive from their Master, the Church from her Lord (cf. 4:16 and 5:14–16; 28:19–20). Therefore, 5:13–16 with 5:3–12 illustrates the tandem relationship of christology and ecclesiology for Matthew.

Third, 5:13–16 plays a pivotal role in the structure of the Sermon by bridging between the Beatitudes and the demands of 5:17—7:12. On the one hand, the final Beatitude (5:11–12, cf. 5:10 and 5:3) strikes the chord of rejection and suffering inherent to the mission for Matthew (cf. 10:17–39 with Mark and Luke), a rejection that was not only the fate of the prophets (5:12) but also of Jesus' own mission (11:2—16:20; 16:21—27:66). Thus the warning of 5:13 cautions the disciples, the *salt of the earth*, about losing their effectiveness as disciples in mission. Whereas the Beatitudes of 5:3, 10, 11–12 assure the "afflicted" of God's blessing, 5:13 admonishes one to beware of capitulating to the pressures of discipleship (cf. Matthew 10).

On the other hand, the nature of that mission (5:14–16) introduces the theme of 5:17—7:12 (Burchard, "Theme," 62–64). The *light* that shines (mission) is the *good deeds* that bring *glory to the Father* (5:16). The *good deeds* are synonymous with the "greater righteousness" (5:20) and are defined in 5:21—7:12. These *good deeds*, as will be seen, bring glory to the Father because of their very nature as life and conduct commensurate with the restored relationship *(your Father)* between the disciple and others (5:21–48) and between the disciple and God (6:1—7:12). Such a life inherent to discipleship is indicative of the presence of the age of salvation and bears witness to what God has done and is doing in human history for his People through Jesus Messiah.

Thus, rather than an interlude or parenthesis, the ecclesiology of 5:13–16 represents a necessary counterpart to the christology of 5:3–12 and offers the discipleship-mission context for what follows in the Sermon.

C. Matt 5:13–16 and the Nature of Mission

Mission has often been considered as part of discipleship but not necessarily identical with it. Being only one of many constituent elements of discipleship, mission becomes somewhat optional for the Christian. Consequently, for many the task of mission belongs to certain identifiable individuals or organizations. It is often something extraneous to our own experience. Such a perception is circularly related to our definition of mission itself. Rather than defining mission in terms of discipleship, we have partially defined discipleship in terms of mission. This definition has taken two very different turns. Indeed, mission has long suffered under the dichotomy of word and deed.

The "gospel," on the one hand, connotes the proclamation of the good news about what God has done for us in Jesus Christ. Mission means "bearing witness" by verbal expression of the biblical message to those in "darkness." The "light" of the world is the "word." Jesus, the Living Word, and Scripture, the Written Word, have supplied the biblical character for such an understanding of mission. Life and conduct are also very important but in a negative sort of way. The disciple must avoid anything or anyone that would bring a reproach on this gospel or the Lord he serves. This concern to avoid reproach often relates both to vices as well as virtues. Not only is one to forego vices (often explicitly taught) but one is to distance oneself (often implicitly taught) from "righteous causes" or "social action" whose Band-aid approach might dilute the potency of the Word.

The "gospel," on the other hand, connotes change for the improvement of another's lot or station in life. Mission means "bearing silent witness," the "cup of cold water" for those in darkness. The "light" of the world is one's actions and deeds by which the less fortunate are benefited. Jesus' ministry to the poor, the sick, and the sinners supplies the biblical model. The verbal expression of the gospel appears to be mere theological rhetoric with little value. Rather than avoiding reproach, this view of mission frequently identifies reproach with righteousness. As Jesus attacked the injustices of his day, the power establishment, and championed the rights of the disenfranchised, paying the natural consequences, so mission without suffering is hardly worthy of the name.

In Matt 5:13, 14 the evangelist shatters these illusions about discipleship. First, mission belongs to the essence of discipleship; discipleship means mission. The disciple is the salt of the earth, the light of the world. As the salt metaphor and parable demonstrate, being "salty" is not optional. Either one is or one is not. If not, then one is not worthy of the name. The only recourse is to be discarded with disdain (5:13). The light metaphor and parable of the city on a hill also indicate that mission is inherent to discipleship. Mission is the inevitable consequence of discipleship, since discipleship means the authorization and the carrying out of Jesus' commission (28:18–20).

Second, Matthew clearly identifies one's life and conduct with mission in the paranesis of 5:16. Discipleship means living one's life in relationship to God and to others so that God's life-changing role might become evident to others. The nature of such a life creates two different responses. In 5:10–12 life lived for "righteousness' sake" or for "my sake" stands out in stark contrast to life as usual. This difference is very unsettling for the advocates of the status quo. This life leads to rejection and persecution, the fate of the prophets as well as Jesus Messiah. In 5:16 the life of discipleship, called *good deeds*, leads others, however, to "glorify" God, to come into a new relationship with God. In one sense, therefore, what others see in this life of the disciple leads them to God. The emphasis is clearly on one's life as a disciple (5:20–48; 6:1–18; 7:21–23).

Third, it would be most unfair to Matthew to limit his understanding of mission even within this context to *good deeds*. These verses give little support for a "silent witness." The paranesis of 5:16 concludes the broader context of mission in 5:13–16. The role of the disciple to the world is the role of the disciple's Master to the world. The evangelist portrays Jesus' instruction about the missionary character of discipleship (5:13a, 14a) in this opening discourse in parallel with his concluding words to the disciples of 28:18–20. Matthew's accent on Jesus' preaching and teaching about the Kingdom, his understanding of the "verbal" proclamation of the mission (10:6; 26:13; 28:19–20) and the similarity between the disciples' role and that of the prophets (5:12) remove all doubt about the integral part of the word in mission. The evangelist saw no dichotomy between word and deed. Both were essential ingredients in the gospel. Proclamation belongs to the *good deeds* (11:1–6, cf. 11:1, 5), to the life of the disciple.

This brief section growing out of the indicative mood of the Beatitudes and based on it (e.g., "you *are* the salt/the light") sets the implications in the imperative for those who hear and respond. To become one of the People of God is to become a part of God's redemptive plan for creation, the world. The nature of these implications is spelled out more specifically in the sections that follow pertaining to one's relationship to others (5:21–48) and to God (6:1—7:12). The focus now turns to the life one is to live before others and God which illuminates those who sit in darkness.

V. JESUS AND THE LAW
Matthew 5:17–20

Translation

5 ¹⁷Do not think that I have come to annul the Law; I have not come to set aside the Scriptures but rather to fulfill them. ¹⁸I assure you, until heaven and earth pass away, not even the slightest detail of the Law will ever become passé, until all things come to pass. ¹⁹Consequently, whoever breaks the least of these commandments and teaches others to do the same shall be called least in the Kingdom of Heaven. But whoever keeps the least of these commandments and teaches others to do the same shall be called the greatest in the Kingdom of Heaven. ²⁰For I tell you, if your righteousness does not greatly exceed that of the scribes and Pharisees, you will never enter the Kingdom of Heaven.

Literary Analysis

Matt 5:17–20 consists of four different kinds of sayings: an ἦλθον-saying (5:17), a legal saying (5:18), a sentence of holy law (5:19), and an entrance-saying (5:20). Matthew has four ἦλθον-sayings (5:17; 9:13, par. Mark 2:17; 10:34, 35, cf. Luke 12:51); Mark has one (2:17, par. Matt); Luke has one (12:49, cf. 5:32 [ἐλήλυθα], par. Mark 2:17); John has three (12:27, 47; 15:22; cf. 5:43; 16:28 with ἐλήλυθα). Matthew also has three similar constructions with Son of Man as the subject (10:23; 11:19, cf. Luke 7:34, 20:28, par. Mark 10:45); Mark has one (10:45, par. Matt) and Luke one (19:10 [par. Matt 18:11 *v.l.*]; cf. 7:34 with ἐλήλυθεν, par. Matt). The second saying reflects a distinctive syntactical pattern consisting of (a) an introductory formula, (b) a main clause stating a subjunctive of emphatic negation (οὐ μή plus subjunctive), and (c) a limiting temporal clause (ἕως plus subjunctive). This form occurs seven times in Matthew (3x from Mark—16:28, par. Mark 9:1; 24:34, par. Mark 13:30; 26:29, par. Mark 14:25; 2x from Q—5:26, par. Luke 12:59; 23:39, par. Luke 13:35; and 10:23; 5:18). According to Käsemann ("Beginnings," 93, cf. 85–86) Matthew has an "unmistakable love" for the form of the third saying, a sentence of holy law, and the unit concludes with an entrance-saying, a motif that Matthew uses nearly ten times elsewhere (7:21; 18:3, cf. Mark 10:15; 19:23, 24, par. Mark 10:23, 25; 23:13; cf. 18:8, 9, par. Mark 9:43, 45, 47).

Form-critically, each saying apparently has its original setting in the life of the early church. But a final judgment must ultimately be qualified by the sayings' contents. All too frequently form criticism has failed to give the material parallels the same weight as the formal parallels. Consequently, we shall return to the question of the history of tradition in the Comments after completing a more detailed exegesis.

As to the source or sources underlying this unit, one can find a complete spectrum of suggestions running from one traditional saying (5:18, par. Luke 16:17) to all four sayings having been found by the evangelist in his tradition. Only 5:18 has any sort of synoptic parallel. Differing in form, this saying shares a material parallel with Luke 16:17 which suggests the possibility of a transmissional variation within the tradition. This conclusion gains support from the absence of any redactional tendencies on either Matthew's or Luke's part to favor their respective form (con. Harnack, *Sayings,* 42, Schulz, *Spruchquelle,* 114, and Meier, *Law,* 57–65). Furthermore, it is quite possible that 5:17, closely related in content to 5:18, and 5:19, apparently an explication of 5:18, circulated as a pre-Matthean unit (e.g., Bultmann, *Tradition,* 146–47; Streeter, *Four Gospels,* 256–57). This suggestion leaves 5:20 as a Matthean addition, possibly a redactional summary of 5:17–19 and an introduction for 5:21–48. Support for these possibilities can only develop out of the detailed exegesis of the respective sayings.

In no other section of the Sermon does the meaning of the passage depend so much on the use of tradition and redaction. The complexity of this material has led to many different interpretations resulting from a failure to distinguish between the meaning of the tradition and its usage by the evangelist. Consequently, the primary focus of the exegesis of 5:17–20 centers on the literary questions of form, source, and redaction.

In this way, one can attempt to delineate the various stages in the development of this unit with its differing, at times conflicting, meanings.

Notes

5:17. *Do not think.* This saying has a structural parallel in 10:34. Yet Luke 12:51, the parallel to Matt 10:34, has a different structure with the rhetorical question, "Do you suppose (δοκεῖτε) . . . ?" (cf. Luke 13:3-4, 5-6 for same formula). In spite of the opinion of several scholars (e.g., Trilling, *Israel,* 171; Barth, "Understanding," 66-67; Hummel, *Auseinandersetzung,* 66; Strecker, *Weg,* 144), one finds little concrete evidence suggesting that the similarity of the two sayings in 5:17 and 10:34 points to Matthean redaction. The first evangelist's use elsewhere of a similar rhetorical question with δοκέω (17:25; 18:12, cf. Luke 15:4; 21:28; 22:17, cf. Mark 12:14; 22:42, cf. Mark 12:35; 26:66, cf. Mark 14:64), his use of δοκέω rather than νομίζω in 3:9, cf. Luke 3:8 (see also 6:7; 24:44, par. Luke 12:40; 26:53), and the absence of any Matthean preference for νομίζω otherwise all support the pre-Matthean formulation of these two sayings. Furthermore, the fact that Luke has this rhetorical question only in the following traditional material (13:3-4, 5-6) may indicate Luke's choice to modify the Q saying of 12:51 in terms of 13:3-4, 5-6 or more likely that 12:51 represents a pre-Lucan transmissional variation of the saying. Of the two forms, Matthew's μὴ νομίσητε is clearly the stronger and appears to counter false assumptions or misunderstandings about Jesus' coming in 5:17 and 10:34 rather than to accentuate as a rhetorical device the positive element of the saying (cf. Trilling, *Israel,* 171; Arens, Ηλθον-*sayings,* 67-68, 98-102).

I have come. Matthew appears to have particular interest in verbs relating to Jesus' coming and sending (Trilling, *Israel,* 171-72), an interest consistent with his christological concerns. Yet the evangelist may well have found these sayings in his tradition (9:13, par. Mark 2:17; 10:34, 35, cf. Luke 12:51; see also the Son of Man sayings in the Literary Analysis). Luke's παρεγενόμην for ἦλθον in 12:51, par. 10:34, 35 is redactional (8x in Luke, 20x in Acts, compared to 3x in Matt, 1x in Mark; also note change from ἦλθον to ἐλήλυθα in 5:32, par. Mark; 7:34, par. Matt).

to annul/to set aside. Behind both verbs stands the Greek καταλύω. The most frequent meaning of καταλύω in the New Testament is "to

destroy by tearing down" (Ljungmann, *Gesetz*, 17, 59–60). But this meaning arises from the context, particularly with reference to the Temple
(Mark 13:2, par. Matt; Mark 14:58, par. Matt; Mark 15:29, par. Matt;
Acts 6:14; 2 Cor 5:1; Gal 2:18). Luke uses it twice with the sense of
"to lodge" (9:12; 19:7). In classical and Hellenistic Greek καταλύω has
the more technical meaning "to annul" when law is the object (LSJ
s.v. Bauer, *s.v.*). From these various connotations one can see that the
context ultimately determines the meaning of καταλύω. Since this verb
stands in antithesis to πληρόω with *Law and Prophets* as its object in
5:17, we need to examine these expressions more closely before returning
to the contextual usage here.

the Scriptures. Behind this translation stands the rather unusual phrase
the Law or the Prophets. Apart from 5:17, Matthew has introduced the
phrase *the law and the prophets* into a Marcan (22:40, cf. Mark 12:31)
and a Q (7:12, cf. Luke 6:31) context. In 11:13 the evangelist followed
with significant modifications Luke 16:16, another Q passage. The phrase
Law and Prophets was current in Judaism and referred to *the Scriptures*,
particularly those used in worship services (Gutbrod, *TDNT* 4:1059;
Moore, *Judaism*, 1:236–40, and Sand, *Gesetz*, 33–45, 183–93). In the
two instances where Matthew has introduced this expression, he has
placed it in a legal context. In 7:12 (cf. Luke 6:31) the "Golden Rule,"
though not explicitly found in either the Law or the Prophets, does
summarize their ethical thrust. In 22:40 (cf. Mark 12:31) the love commandment represents the "hinges" on which the "whole Law hangs
and the Prophets." Therefore, *the Scriptures, the Law and the Prophets*,
definitely contained a normative, ethical moment for Matthew (Trilling,
Israel, 173). Yet his modification of the Q saying in 11:13 (cf. Luke
16:16), a context perhaps not unrelated to 5:17 (Luke 16:17, par. 5:18),
highlights the prophetic moment of Scripture as well. When we add
the twelve so-called fulfillment-citations found in Matthew, each referring
explicitly to the Old Testament's prophetic fulfillment in Jesus' ministry,
the evangelist's stress on this prophetic moment becomes quite obvious.
The question, of course, is which emphasis *the Law or the Prophets* has
in 5:17.

A partial clue may lie in the disjunctive *or* (ἤ) in *the Law or the
Prophets*. Since there is apparently no grammatical basis for the *or* rather
than the more usual *and* (καί) in this phrase (Zahn, *Matthäus*, 210–11;
Banks, *Jesus*, 206), this disjunctive becomes all the more significant. A
closer look at the first Gospel reveals thirteen similar uses of *or* (cf. 5x
in Mark; 9x in Luke, four being with verbs). Of these thirteen other

occurrences, four come from Mark (15:4, 5, 6, par. Mark 7:10, 11, 12; 13:21, par. Mark 4:17) and the other nine were added by the evangelist (12:25; 16:14; 18:8 in Mark; 5:18; 6:25; 10:11, 14; 17:25). In each case, with the exception of 6:25, the evangelist has consistently added a *noun* related or supplementary to another noun *already* present in his tradition. Therefore, the presence of *or* in 5:17 betrays a Matthean redactional trait and implies (1) that 5:17 was indeed a pre-Matthean saying referring originally to the *Law* and (2) that Matthew inserted *or the Prophets* to complete his preferable phrase, *the Law and the Prophets*. But why?

Generally, the evangelist added the companion noun on the basis of "an unconscious association of ideas" with little or no theological basis (Banks, *Jesus,* 206–7). But the present modification appears much more deliberate. First, Matthew does not add *the Prophets* unconsciously in 5:18; 12:5; 22:36, or 23:23, where it would have been particularly pertinent (cf. the Prophets' insistence on "justice," "mercy," and "faithfulness"). Second, had the evangelist wanted to maintain the accent on the *normative* moment of *the Scriptures* (cf. 7:12), he would have found the *Law* already present in the tradition together with καταλύω and πληρόω as the more specific expression. Third, the redactional use of the verbs in 11:13 and 22:40 is most important, since the verbs determine the evangelist's normative or prophetic emphasis on Scripture. Fourth, since twelve of the sixteen occurrences of "to fulfill" (πληρόω) refer specifically to the prophetic fulfillment of the Scriptures, and since eleven of these references are redactional, the presence of πληρόω in 5:17 appears clearly to have influenced Matthew's redactional introduction of *the Prophets* into this context. By adding *or the Prophets* to this context, the evangelist alters the saying from being a reference to Jesus' coming related specifically to the Law to being a reference to Jesus' coming related generally to the Scriptures. This modification has resulted in the blurring of the antithesis between the verbs καταλύω and πληρόω.

to fulfill. This verb holds not only the key to this verse but also to the crucial question of Jesus' relationship to the Law. Let us take a closer look at its background and usage in this context.

Excursus: To Fulfill the Law and the Prophets

If our analysis of *the Law and the Prophets* correctly reflects the tradition and redaction behind this saying, then we must first distinguish between two possible usages of *to fulfill,* the one pre-Matthean—*to fulfill the Law*—and the other Matthean—*to fulfill the Scriptures.*

1. The earlier, pre-Matthean tradition had simply *the Law* as the object of *to fulfill.* This leaves us with the question of how Jesus' coming *fulfilled the Law.*

a. The most common answer to this question is that Jesus "brought the Law to its full expression," "established the Law's true meaning," "set forth its ultimate intention," and thus "completed the Law" generally through his own teaching about the Law (e.g. McNeile, *Matthew*, 58; Klostermann, *Matthäusevangelium*, 41; Kümmel, "Traditionsgedanken," 127–30; Windisch, *Sermon*, 66–67; Filson, *Matthew*, 83; Dupont, *Béatitudes* 1:143–44; McConnell, *Prophecy*, 25–30; cf. Strecker, *Weg*, 147).

Apart from its vagueness, this solution has two very serious weaknesses. First, it begins with a false understanding of the Law by assuming an "inner-outer" distinction of attitudes rather than actions uncharacteristic of the Law in Judaism and Jesus' teaching (Banks, *Jesus*, 208). Jesus' charge of hypocrisy against the Pharisees (6:2, 5, 16; 23), his statement about that which defiles (Mark 7:18–23, par. Matt), and his demands in the following Antitheses (5:21–48) go much deeper than mere concerns with intentions and attitudes (see Notes on 5:21–48). Second, this view of Jesus' fulfillment of the Law begins with a faulty christological basis conditioned too much by the immediate context of Matt 5:17–48. This position considers Jesus to be either a New Moses or a giver of a new and final interpretation of the Law as seen by the examples in 5:21–48. Such a starting point may be appropriate for the present context of 5:17 but fails to recognize that 5:17 most likely existed originally independently of 5:21–48.

b. A second answer to the question of how Jesus fulfilled the Law also has a long history in scholarship, namely, that Jesus came "to establish" or "to validate" the Law (e.g., Dalman, *Worte*, 52–57; Fiebig, *Bergpredigt*, 27; Percy, *Botschaft*, 120; Daube, *Rabbinic Judaism*, 60–61; Hill, *Matthew*, 117). The strength of this view is the precise statement of the antithesis between *to annul* (καταλῦσαι) and "to validate, establish" (πληρῶσαι) the Law. Its weakness, however, lies in its basis in the use of *qyym* in the Aramaic Targums for the Hebrew *mlʾ*. This Aramaic usage of *qyym* for *mlʾ* runs counter to the LXX usage of πληρόω. On the one hand, the LXX generally renders *qyym* either ἵστημι or βεβαιόω but never πληρόω. On the other hand, πληρόω consistently translates *mlʾ* in the LXX (Ljungman, *Gesetz*, 17, 29–31; Delling, *TDNT* 6:287–88, 293–94; Moule, "Fulfilment-Words," 314). Therefore, this alternative fails to take the Old Testament background seriously enough.

c. A third approach begins with the biblical use of πληρόω and attempts to do justice to the *mlʾ*/πληρόω complex (Ljungman, *Gesetz*, 53–65; Moule, "Fulfilment-Words," 293–320; Banks, *Jesus*, 209–12; cf. Luz, "Erfüllung," 416–17). Ljungman's extensive study of the terms led him to conclude the *mlʾ*/πληρόω complex maintains its root meaning "to fill up" and connotes the "completeness" of the Law, adding that it means "to bring to its final conclusion all that the Law stood for." Moule, recognizing the moment of *Heilsgeschichte* inherent in πληρόω ("Fulfilment-Words," 297–99), has written, "In so far as the Law bears witness to the will of God as an ideal yet to be achieved, and the Prophets held out hope of a time coming when it shall be fulfilled, one who perfectly fulfills the will of God confirms also the predictions of prophecy" ("Fulfilment-Words," 316, cf. IDB, "Fulfil," 2:327–28). In other words, Jesus' ministry fulfills the Law by fulfilling the "covenant-promise" of the total realization of the right relationship between God and his people (Moule, "Fulfilment-Words," 294).

Coming from a different direction, namely, from the meaning of Law in the Old Testament, but supporting such a dynamic redemptive-historical meaning of πληρόω, Gese has called attention to a development of an eschatological dimension of the Law long overlooked in New Testament studies ("Gesetz," 56–84). In the prophets Isaiah, Jeremiah, and Ezekiel, a redemptive-historical contrast emerges between the old covenant with its "Sinai-Torah" and the new covenant with its "Zion-Torah" ("Gesetz," 74–77). With these exilic prophets comes the promise expressed in Jer 31:31–34 as the "new covenant," the self-revelation of God and the Law "written on the heart," and in Ezek 36:25–27 expressed as the cleansing forgiveness, a "new heart" and "spirit" connoting a new relationship between God and his people and their obedience of his will. This motif of God's redemptive activity, often associated with Zion, runs through Isaiah (cf. 2:2–6; Mic 4:1–5) and reaches its culmination with Isa 56:1, "keep justice and do righteousness, for my salvation comes and my 'righteousness' *(ṣdqh)* will be revealed."

Such an understanding of the "Zion-Torah" included the nations and the ability to walk according to God's will that would come as a gift, the product of the divine initiative of the end times. Consequently, the "Zion-Torah" of the Old Testament prophets stood in contrast to the "Sinai-Torah" but did not annul it. The "Zion-Torah" superseded the "Sinai-Torah." The promise of this "Zion-Torah" comes to full expression in Jesus' coming, according to Matt 5:17. Jesus' coming "fulfills," "brings to completion," the full realization of the personal relationship, involving an ethical and moral "fulfillment of God's will" (Moule, "Fulfilment-Words," 317).

This third alternative has the support of the lexical usage of *mlʾ*/πληρόω and is not rooted in the present context of 5:17 within Matthew 5. Furthermore, such a use of the Old Testament is certainly commensurate with Jesus' understanding of his own ministry. One need only compare this with the reference to Isaiah 61 as discussed in terms of the first Beatitude (see Excursus on 5:3). In fact, Moule has even suggested that this fulfillment saying has its ultimate roots in Jesus' ministry ("Fulfilment-Words," 317–18, also Banks, *Jesus,* 210–12). Like 10:34, this saying would then have counteracted a false conception of Jesus' mission. The Gospel tradition gives ample witness that Jesus was in trouble with the Jewish leaders over the question of his actions and teachings regarding the Law. Indeed, some might well have accused him of annulling the Law, or his disciples might well have mistaken his intentions regarding the Law. Such a pregnant use of *ml³/πληρόω* by Jesus with reference to the Law would have countered any misunderstanding about his intention to set the Law aside.

But it also left open the specifics of how his "fulfillment of the Law" as a part of redemptive history related to the question of the enduring validity of the Law. Consequently, 5:17, within a strict Jewish-Christian wing of the early church, might easily have served a very different purpose. By placing the accent on the negative, *I did not come to annul the Law,* the more legalistic wing of the Church could have interpreted the verse as an affirmation of the Law's validity. The verb *πληρόω* would in such a context express Jesus' intention to "complete" or "fill up" the Law by his teaching and actions. This usage appears all but certain when 5:17 is read in conjunction with 5:18 and 19. The deeper perspective of his fulfillment of the "covenant-obligation" in redemptive history would thus have been filtered out or understood differently.

This verse, along with 5:18–19, might then have offered a basis drawn from Jesus' ministry for insisting on the observance of the *whole* Law. Such a *Sitz im Leben* in legalistic Jewish-Christianity might also explain the absence of this or similar logia in the debates over the question of the Law in Acts as well as in Paul's own teaching. Yet Paul's reference to the "fulfillment" of the Law in Rom 13:9–10 and Gal 5:14 stands closer to the earlier meaning of 5:17 within the context of Jesus' ministry than to that of Jewish-Christianity. Furthermore, 5:17, reflecting the influence of a Jewish-Christian *Sitz im Leben* in the early church, gives greater significance to Matthew's modification of *the Law* to *the Law and the Prophets.*

2. The Matthean understanding of *to fulfill* must begin with his sixteen usages of *πληρόω* (cf. 2x in Mark; 9x in Luke) that indicate a definite interest in this verb. Twelve of the sixteen deal directly with the fulfillment of Scripture, and eleven of these are distinctively Matthean, the so-called "formula-citations" (1:22; 2:15, 17, 23; 4:14; 8:17; 12:17; 13:35; 21:4; 26:54; 26:56, par. Mark 14:49; 27:9). Two references have the root meaning of "to fill up" (13:48; 23:23), leaving only 3:15 and 5:17 somewhat ambiguous. Since Matthew's characteristic usage obviously refers to the fulfillment of Scripture and since he has added *the Prophets* to refer to the Scriptures as *the Law and the Prophets* in 5:17, it is most logical to understand *fulfill* in the typically Matthean manner (Meier, *Law,* 80). But what did *to fulfill the Scriptures* mean for Matthew?

Contrary to Moule, who relegates Matthew's use of the fulfillment motif to "a shallow sense of prediction-fulfillment" ("Fulfilment-Words," 297–98, 216–17), Matthew uses the formula-citations and the Old Testament concepts as such in a more profound manner than as mere "proof-texts" that demonstrate Jesus' fulfillment of Old Testament predictions (cf. Rothfuchs, *Erfüllungszitate*, 113–17; R. E. Brown, *Messiah*, 104). Matthew's use of the Old Testament is foundational for his christology that perceives Jesus to be the Messiah Son of God who comes as the fulfillment of God's promise to his people for the end times. The evangelist is most concerned to demonstrate that Jesus stands in line with the prophetic promise of Scripture, but only as the ultimate fulfillment of that promise—the new, final chapter in God's redemptive plan for history.

The redemptive historical motif so characteristic of Matthew is doubtless at work in 5:17 as well. By expanding the tradition that referred to Jesus' coming with specific reference to the Law to state now that his coming related to the fulfillment of the Scriptures, the evangelist refocused the redemptive historical moment of πληρόω that had been lost in the legalistic context of strict Jewish-Christianity. The question of the Law's continuing validity now becomes a part of the larger context of Jesus' coming as the one who brings that new relationship between God and humankind promised in the Scriptures. The normative character of the Law remains in the picture (5:18, 19) but set within the broader panorama of Jesus' coming as the Bringer of the age of salvation to fulfill the Scriptures (cf. 5:18).

Whereas the tradition behind 5:17 spoke of Jesus' coming *to fulfill the Law,* Matthew has deliberately rephrased the saying to emphasize Jesus' coming *to fulfill the Scriptures.* Not only is this *Heilsgeschichte* theme explicit in the evangelist's formula-citations, but we have also found it in his editorial aligning of the Beatitudes with Isaiah 61 and in his use of Old Testament images characteristic of the age of salvation for the disciples in 5:14–16. By modifying the tradition, the evangelist has interpreted 5:17 much more in keeping with the intention of Jesus' ministry, while denying simultaneously a Jewish-Christian misuse of the saying for their purposes.

not to annul but to fulfill. The antithetical construction consisting of negative and positive counterstatements has its roots in the tradition (13x in Mark—2:17, 22; 5:39; 7:15, 19; 8:33; 9:37; 10:8, 40, 45; 12:27; 14:36). Matthew preserves all but two of Mark's with an additional ten of his own (4:4; 5:17, 39; 6:13; 7:21; 10:20, 34; 16:12, 17; 17:12). Each statement expresses a sharp antithesis. The verbs καταλύω and πληρόω offer similar antitheses: "to annul" or "to fulfill" and "to destroy" or "to complete." Yet the antithesis of 5:17 as it now stands has lost its sharpness since καταλύω and πληρόω no longer express a clear antithesis with reference to the object *Scriptures.* Whereas Jesus' coming *to fulfill the Scriptures* makes good sense, *to annul* or *to destroy* is awkward at best both lexically and materially. Jesus was hardly viewed as *annulling* or *destroying the Scriptures* in general.

The differentiation between the pre-Matthean and Matthean forms of 5:17 helps to explain this difficulty. The antithesis comes through very clearly in the pre-Matthean tradition. Jesus came *not to annul the Law but to fulfill the Law*, even if the meaning of πληρόω remains ambiguous. Matthew's changing of the verb's object from *the Law* to *the Law and the Prophets* has created the tension between καταλύω and πληρόω. This unresolved tension in the antithesis of 5:17 further demonstrates the evangelist's primary focus to be on the coming of Jesus to fulfill the Scriptures rather than on the issue of the Law's validity as found in the tradition.

5:18. This verse has a content parallel in Luke 16:17 but set in a different format (εὐκοπώτερον δέ ἐστίν . . . ἤ . . ."; cf. Mark 10:25, par. Luke 18:25, par. Matt). Matt 5:18 consists of (a) an introductory formula (ἀμὴν λέγω ὑμῖν), (b) a subjunctive, and (c) a temporal clause (ἕως ἄν plus subjunctive). The difference in format has often been assigned to Matthew's account (e.g., Schürmann, *Untersuchungen*, 128). But there is convincing evidence for the existence of each saying in its present structure within the tradition (Hübner, *Gesetz*, 21–22). First, Matthew has his pattern six other times, each traditional (3x in Mark—16:28, par. Mark 9:1, par. Luke; 24:34, par. Mark 13:30, par. Luke; 26:29, par. Mark 14:25, par. Luke; 2x in Q—5:26, par. Luke 12:59; 23:39, par. Luke 13:35 and 10:23 [M]). Second, whereas one might ascribe either format to the work of the respective evangelist, there is no evidence that either had a tendency to introduce his format except when found in the tradition nor is there evidence that either evangelist dropped the other's format elsewhere. Both formats occur in all three Gospels and are clearly traditional. Third, the awkward presence of two temporal clauses suggests that one was added to a previously formulated saying. Most important, the content of 5:18 and Luke 16:17 points to different settings, as will be seen below. It seems evident, therefore, that Matt 5:18, like the Beatitudes above, comes to Matthew as a transmissional variant of the Q material found in Luke 16:17.

I assure you. This introductory formula, ἀμὴν λέγω ὑμῖν, occurs fifty times in the Synoptic Gospels (cf. John's ἀμὴν ἀμὴν λέγω ὑμῖν), of which Matthew has the most with thirty-one and Luke the least with six. Jeremias has traced the original setting of this usage of ἀμὴν back to Jesus' own ministry ("Characteristics," 12–15). But others, after a detailed analysis of the synoptic passages, have assigned the original *Sitz im Leben* to the early Christian prophets in a Hellenistic setting (e.g., Hasler, *Amen,* 181; cf. Berger, *Amen-Worte,* 4–28). Ultimately the question is moot for our passage. Without doubt the introductory formula in 5:18 was part of the traditional pattern noted above and thus pre-Matthean (con. Meier, *Law,* 58). It should be noted in passing, however, that the strict Jewish-Christian character of the tradition behind 5:18 as well as the imminent end-expectation of several of the parallel sayings (e.g., Mark 9:1; 13:30; 14:25) makes an original Hellenistic setting for the formula at least dubious. In any case, the function of the formula is to introduce the saying with a note of authority comparable to the prophetic "Thus says the Lord."

until heaven and earth pass away. This phrase is the first of two temporal clauses in 5:18: *before heaven and earth pass away* and *before all things come to pass.* The presence of two ἕως-clauses doubtless explains why the first occurs out of the normal order noted above. Since the vocabulary of this clause is also that of Luke 16:17, this phrase was the earlier traditional ἕως-clause relocated by the evangelist when he added the second (*con.* Luz, "Erfüllung," 418). By modifying the tradition in this manner, Matthew breaks the traditional pattern, a trait rather characteristic of his editorial work (Filson, "Patterns," 227–31).

Although the phrase *until heaven and earth pass away* can be simply a colorful way of saying "never" in Judaism (Allen, *Matthew,* 46; Klostermann, *Matthäusevangelium,* 41; Montefiore, *Synoptic Gospels* 2:51), such a phrase in Jesus' ministry or in the early church clearly pointed to the apocalyptic consummation of this age (cf. Mark 13:31–32 and the terminal references in all the other similar constructions except 5:26, par. Luke 12:59). Therefore, this statement declares that the Law's validity extends only to the end of this age (e.g., Schlatter, *Matthäus,* 156; Lohmeyer, *Matthäus,* 109; Schniewind, *Matthäus,* 54; Barth, "Understanding," 65, 70; Schweizer, *Matthew,* 107).

not even the slightest detail of the Law. Literally, *not one iota or one hook of the Law.* Luke 16:17 simply has *one hook.* Matthew's addition of *one iota,* accompanied by his characteristic disjunctive use of *or* (see Note on 5:17), heightens the statement by combining two familiar rabbinic expressions. The *iota,* representing the smallest Hebrew letter *yod,* and *hook,* representing the ornamental touches added to some Hebrew consonants, occur in rabbinic literature—though never combined as in 5:18— to represent the indestructible character of even the smallest detail of the written Law (Str-B 1:247–49). The repetition of the numeral *one* in *not* ONE *iota nor* ONE *hook* accents the quantitative wholeness of the Law that extends to the slightest detail (BDF, §247 n. 2; Schulz, *Spruchquelle*, 115–16). The reference is clearly to the Mosaic Law, in particular the written Law, as the terminology from rabbinic circles indicates (Str-B 1:246, the Pentateuch as such was considered eternal). The Lucan parallel only further confirms that the saying's focus was on the Law and its total validity.

will ever become passé. The main clause consists of a subjunctive of emphatic negation stating that under no circumstances will even the slightest detail of the Law pass away or become invalid or lost (παρέλθῃ). This statement most likely reflects the view of the strict Jewish-Christian community that insisted on the keeping of the whole Law (cf. Acts 15:1–21; Gal 3). It definitely stands in contrast to Jesus' own ministry on the Sabbath, the question of things clean and unclean (Mark 7:1–23, par. Matt 15:1–20), and especially the Antitheses of 5:38–48 and most likely 5:31–32, cf. Mark 10:10–12, par. Matt 19:9. In contrast to the ironic statement of Luke 16:17 whose *Sitz im Leben* might well have been Jesus' ministry, 5:18 together with the pre-Matthean tradition behind 5:17 claimed the continuing validity of the Law based on Jesus' teaching. Such a tradition most likely stemmed from the influence of the strict Jewish-Christian community that molded and preserved the material. The evangelist, however, has modified 5:18 just as he did 5:17 in order to express more accurately Jesus' teaching regarding himself and the Law as well as to counter the strict Jewish-Christian influence felt within his own community. The evangelist modifies this statement by reworking it in terms of 5:18c[2].

until all things come to pass. This second ἑως-clause is redactional, as demonstrated by the broken pattern of the verse's structure (a, c[1], b, c[2]) and by the Matthean use of the phrase πάντα γένηται. The apparent vagueness of this clause leaves us with two related but complicated questions: what does ἑως ἂν πάντα γένηται mean for Matthew, and how does this temporal clause relate to the first?

1. One approach is to take both clauses as being synonymous either in terms of the first or the second. In the first case, both clauses would refer to the final apocalyptic consummation of this age (e.g., McNeile, *Matthew*, 59; Klostermann, *Matthäusevangelium*, 41; Manson, *Sayings*, 154; Filson, *Matthew*, 84). Support for this position appears in 24:34, par. Mark 13:30, where *all these things* clearly connotes the consummation of the events specified in the context (Kümmel, *Promise*, 60). This position, however, breaks down at two points. The similarity between

5:18c[2] and 24:34, par. Mark, is more apparent than real, as will be seen below, and the evangelist would hardly have gone to such length to add a second ἕως-clause in order to repeat the same idea found in the first clause. This objection remains valid, even if one assigns 5:18c[2] to the status of a later gloss.

Davies also views these clauses as synonymous but in terms of the latter, which refers to the culmination of this age (5:18c[1]) in the *coming to pass of all things* (5:18c[2]) through the events of Jesus' death and resurrection ("Matthew 5:17, 18," 61, Meier, *Law,* 30–35). Hammerton-Kelly has sought further support for this thesis in the use of ἅπαντα τὰ γενόμενα of 28:11 (cf. 5:18c[2]) to refer to the resurrection events and the reference to "heaven and earth" in 28:18 (cf. 5:18c[1]). According to this solution, 5:18 connotes the culmination of Jesus' messianic ministry and the inauguration of the Messianic Torah *(halacha)* as found in 5:21–48 by Jesus' death and resurrection. In other words, 5:18 as it now stands declares that the Law has been superseded by the Messianic Torah coming into effect with the dawn of the New Age in Jesus' ministry climaxed by his resurrection ("Attitudes," 19–32).

Apart from the serious question of whether the teaching of 5:21–48 supersedes the Law as the Messianic Torah, the obvious weakness in this position lies in the absence of any concrete evidence that *all these things* refers pregnantly to the coming of the new age in Jesus' death and resurrection for Matthew. Even the apparently similar ἅπαντα τὰ γενόμενα of 28:11 has a specific, literal reference to the complex of events surrounding the resurrection which the guard "reported" to the scribes and Pharisees. For Matthew, the death and resurrection of Jesus Messiah was integral to his ministry, not the all-encompassing event that inaugurated the Kingdom. Such a view unduly restricts the first evangelist's understanding of the "fulfillment" character of Jesus' entire ministry to the cross and resurrection.

2. A second approach to this temporal clause takes the second subordinate to the first in an explanatory or modal relationship (Ljungman, *Gesetz,* 45, 47; Honeyman, "Matthew V. 18," 142; Schweizer, "Matt 5:17–20," 402–4; *idem,* "Noch einmal," 72–73; *idem,* "Matthew," 108; Banks, *Jesus,* 217–18). The second explains how the Law remains valid until the end (5:18bc[1]) either by the Law's having been fulfilled or by the will of God having been fulfilled (5:18bc[2]). For Schweizer, Jesus *fulfilled the Law* (5:17) by bringing the "new commandment" which contains "the whole Law." As the "Bringer of a New Torah," Jesus fulfilled the goal of the Law ("Matt 5:17–20," 402–4; *idem, Matthew,*

108). Banks prefers to see the πάντα as the demands of the Law in its "pointing forward to that ideal which was becoming a reality in the teaching of Jesus." The Law is validated in "the demands of the Kingdom," in "the teaching of Jesus," rather than in its own existence (Banks, *Jesus*, 218; cf. Luke 16:16b, par. Matt 11:12; Luke 16:18, par. Matt 5:21–48).

In other words, the evangelist maintains the thrust of the traditional saying, namely, that the Law continues to remain valid *until heaven and earth pass away*, but he has drastically altered the meaning of the *Law*. The *Law* now means the *Law* as taught by Jesus (Schweizer, "the new commandment"; Davies and Hammerton-Kelly, "the Messianic Torah"; Banks, "the demands of the Kingdom in Jesus' teaching"). The strength of this solution lies in the resolution of the tension between the apparently permanent nature of the Law expressed in 5:18 and the following Antitheses. Matthew's work represents a *via media* between the strict Jewish-Christians behind the tradition and any antinomians who would abuse the freedom from the Law.

This understanding of Matthew, placing him halfway between the strict Jewish-Christian and "Pauline" views of the Law, has emerged as the consensus among recent works on Matthew. Yet this view has two integrally related weaknesses. First, this solution overlooks the clue to the redactional use of πάντα γένηται and limits its referent too narrowly to Jesus' relationship with the Law. Second, this view operates with a christology that interprets Jesus as the Bringer of the New Law, the Messianic Torah, or a Messianic interpretation *(halacha)* that supersedes all others. Such an understanding of Jesus' ministry is relatively foreign to the rest of Matthew's Gospel and misconstrues the christological focus in Matthew 5.

In a variation on this theme, Meier has argued that the second ἕως-clause modifies the first, but in reference to time rather than the Law. For Meier, the "turning point of the ages" occurs in the death-resurrection event *(Law,* 30–35). Thus, "until all things come to pass" refers to Jesus' death and resurrection. The first and second ἕως-clauses, therefore, now refer to the same event, at which time the Law comes to its end *(Law,* 59–65). The strength of this reading lies in the parallelism between the second ἕως-clause and the fulfillment-motif of 5:17. The weakness, however, lies in the identification of Matthew's fulfillment-motif with Jesus' death-resurrection rather than with his coming and ministry as the fulfillment citations indicate.

3. A third alternative takes the second ἕως-clause as a deliberate count-

erpart of the first. This view recognizes the strengths of the second but is more comprehensive in its christology and closer to the Matthean redactional pattern in this immediate context as well as in the broader context of the Gospel at large. As Ljungman (*Gesetz*, 54–56) has noted, γίνομαι expresses a semitechnical meaning at times in the New Testament when pertaining to events previously announced. It means that certain events have "come to pass." Matthew uses γίνομαι in this manner in 1:22; 21:4; 26:54, 56 (Schweizer, *Matthew*, 68). More important, in these passages the evangelist has introduced the verb into the same context with πληρόω in order to declare that Scripture is being fulfilled by the event that "has come to pass" (τοῦτο/ὅλον γέγονεν). By introducing the eschatologically pregnant phrase *until all things come to pass* into the context of the reworked saying of 5:17, we have a similar phenomenon of the πληρόω/γίνομαι combination here. In 5:17 Jesus comes to fulfill the Scripture; in 5:18 the entire Law continues in force *until all things come to pass* (Jesus fulfills the Scriptures). The *all things* (πάντα) is indefinite because of the general statement about Jesus' role as the fulfillment of Scripture in 5:17 (cf. the contextual focus of πάντα ταῦτα in 13:51; 19:20; 23:36; 24:2; 24:34). Furthermore, this broader understanding of Jesus' coming in 5:17–18 to fulfill the Scriptures includes Jesus' fulfillment of the Law and is much more representative of the evangelist's christology. Matthew has neither a New Moses christology nor a "rabbinic" tendency to view Jesus as the Messianic interpreter of the Law any more than did Paul (cf. Rom 13:8–10; Gal 5:14).

Understood in this way, 5:18 expresses a deliberate tension between Jesus' coming and the continuing validity of the Law. On the one hand, the Law in its totality (i.e., *one iota or one hook*) remains in force *until heaven and earth pass away* (5:18bc[1]) at the consummation. On the other hand, the Law remains valid only *until all things come to pass* in Jesus' coming and ministry. The Law continues to be in force; but the Law ceases to be in force. Such an apparently contradictory statement in 5:18 makes little sense except when set against a background of Judaism and extreme Jewish-Christianity that insisted upon the keeping of the whole Law. The evangelist recognizes the claim of the continuing validity of the Law for those who seek to live according to the Law, those who live under the Law as a part of this age, and counters this claim by pointing to the new situation for those who recognize that God is at work in Jesus Messiah fulfilling his promise to his people and establishing a new relationship between himself and his own, no longer based on the keeping of the whole Law (cf. the "righteousness" of 5:6; 6:33).

Yet this new relationship implying the presence of God's sovereign rule in one's life does have its ethical corollary with reference to others, as illustrated by 5:21–48, and with reference to God, as illustrated by 6:1—7:12. This ethical corollary stands over against any Pharisaic understanding of the Law in Jewish-Christianity to be a sum of commandments and prohibitions which one is to keep in view of the coming Kingdom.

Furthermore, the demands of the Kingdom found in 5:21–48 and 6:1—7:12 are not limited to this age, as would be the case with the second alternative above that interprets 5:18c^1 in terms of 5:18c^2. Rather, these demands of the Kingdom call for conduct commensurate with the new relationship established between God and his people, a conduct that far exceeds at times and counters at other times the demands of the Law (5:21–48). In many ways, 5:18c^2 approximates Paul's own expression of Rom 10:4, "Christ is the end of the Law." Matthew does not view 5:21–48 and 6:1—7:12 as the exposition of how Jesus "fulfills the Law" (cf. 5:17–18) by means of his giving a New Law or a final interpretation of the Law (New Torah); rather, the content of these verses points to the new relationships and conduct indicative of the day of salvation, the fulfillment of God's promise for a new day in Jesus' ministry and declared in 5:17.

5:19. This saying has the form and content of what Käsemann has called "sentences of holy law" ("Sentences," 78–89). The form consists of a legal ordinance with its conditional ("if") or indefinite ("whoever") clause or protasis giving the attitude or behavior in question followed by the statement of consequences, or apodosis. The content specifically declares that one's present conduct will receive its corresponding reward or punishment *(jus talionis)* at the impending eschatological judgment. Thus, if anyone abrogates *the least of these commandments,* that one will be *the least in the Kingdom.* Käsemann went on to locate these sayings within the apocalyptic milieu of early Christian prophecy ("Sentences," 76–81). By contrast, Lohmeyer *(Matthäus,* 111) and especially Berger ("Sätzen," 19–25, 38–40) have pointed to a Wisdom background for form and content of such constructions.

Therefore. Matthew characteristically uses the conjunction οὖν to connect two separate traditional units (cf. 5:23, 48; 6:2, 8, 9, 31; 7:24 within the Sermon; Lohmeyer, *Matthäus,* 110; Trilling, *Israel,* 180). Yet the presence of οὖν does not necessarily indicate Matthean redactional activity, since οὖν also occurs within the Q tradition used by Matthew in the Sermon (6:23, par. Luke 11:35; 7:11, par. Luke 11:13). Editorial or redactional, οὖν as an inferential particle combines 5:19 logically to the thought of 5:18.

breaks and teaches . . . does and teaches. To break (λύω) renders the root of καταλύω found in 5:17, and it also means *to annul* with reference to the Law. Annulment is the end effect, if one *breaks* a commandment and then *teaches* another to do the same. *To do* (ποιέω) in a legal context offers the antithesis to λύω and connotes carrying out the Law's demands by doing them. This saying, if it was traditionally related to 5:17–18, might well reflect the early church's (mis)understanding of 5:17. Since Jesus did not come *to annul* (καταλύω/λύω) but *to fulfill by doing* (πληρόω/ποιέω) the Law, anyone abrogating the Law stands in contrast to Jesus and anyone doing the Law stands in line with Jesus' ministry.

The verb *teach* (διδάξῃ), occurring in each member of the parallelism, has been frequently assigned to Matthew (e.g., Schürmann, *Untersuchungen*, 130). Yet this saying, apart from 28:20, offers the only occurrence of διδάσκω in Matthew without Jesus as the subject. Thus, if Matthew has a tendency to add it, it is with reference to Jesus' own ministry rather than that of his disciples. Matt 23:3 offers a similar combination of *do* and *teach*, but the emphasis is very different. In 23:3 the contrast focuses on the great disparity between the teaching and actions of the scribes and Pharisees, whereas here the difference is between breaking/annulling the Law and doing/not doing it. The two sayings represent two different settings. The form and content of 5:19 point to a setting involving one's attitude and conduct regarding the keeping of the entire Law.

one of the least of these commandments. Several different explanations for this phrase have appeared in the literature. Some have taken the dual usage of *least* in 5:19 to be a word-play on Paul's self-designation of 1 Cor 15:9 as the "least of the Apostles" and thus to contain an anti-Pauline focus (Weiss, *Primitive Christianity* 2:753; Manson, *Sayings*, 24). Others have interpreted the "least of the commandments" to refer to the "shortest" of the ten commandments (F. Dibelius, "Zwei Worte," 188; Schlatter, *Matthäus*, 157–58), while still others understand the phrase to point to Jesus' teachings that follow (Lohmeyer, *Matthäus*, 111–12; Carlston, "Defile," 79; Banks, *Jesus*, 223; Schweizer, *Matthew*, 108–9; cf. Kilpatrick, *Origins*, 25–26). Each solution fails to take seriously enough the relationship of 5:19 to 5:18, a relationship that has its roots deep in the tradition, as will be seen below.

Much more compatible with the context is the suggestion that the terminology of 5:19 reflects the debates of contemporary Judaism between the "heavier" and "lighter" commandments of the Law, a distinction based on severity of demand rather than on length (Str-B 1:901–2, and Eichholz, *Bergpredigt,* 63). The only difficulty is in the disparity of language between "heavy"/"light" and "greatest"/"least." The simplest explanation is to view 5:19 as but the practical explication of the principle laid out in 5:18. The *least of these commandments* then would be but a corollary of the figurative *one hook* referring to the smallest detail of the Law. But can this understanding be supported by the history of the tradition and its present context?

The *least of these commandments* contains not only the focal point of 5:19 but also holds the clue to the saying's original *Sitz im Leben.* At first glance, the phrase appears to stand apart from 5:17–18, since these two logia deal with the continuing validity of the *Law,* while 5:19 refers to one of *these commandments.* Furthermore, the lack of a direct grammatical antecedent for *these commandments* has led several to conclude that the saying either had an independent status or belonged to another setting before the evangelist introduced it into the present context (cf. Lohmeyer, *Matthäus,* 110; Kilpatrick, *Origins,* 17, 25–26; Strecker, *Weg,* 145; Banks, *Jesus,* 222–23; Schweizer, *Matthew,* 108; Luz, "Erfüllung," 108–9).

Such a view implying Matthew's redactional addition of 5:19, however, breaks down at three points. First, the thrust of 5:19 is not even close to the thrust of Matthew's redactional work in 5:17–18. Whereas his work in 5:17–18 focused on Jesus' coming and the *fulfillment of the Scriptures,* the *coming to pass of all things,* 5:19 is concerned with the keeping of the *least of the commandments.* Matt 5:20, introduced by the evangelist, also stands in contrast to and qualified the thrust of 5:19 by calling for a *righteousness* exceeding that of *the scribes and Pharisees* (e.g., 5:19!) as necessary for the Kingdom (see Note on 5:20). Second, the question of *doing and teaching the least of the commandments* is materially related to the concern for the continued validity of the whole Law found in the pre-Matthean focus in the tradition of 5:17–18 (Schürmann, *Untersuchungen,* 128–29). Third, the very construction *these commandments* necessarily implies the presence of an antecedent and precludes any independent existence for the saying. What was that antecedent?

That the phrase *(one iota or) one hook* cannot serve as the direct grammatical antecedent is obvious for syntactical reasons. Furthermore, the phrase cannot offer a direct material parallel because of the difference in the literal meanings. Whereas *these* (τούτων) refers to the *command-*

ments, iota and *hook* refer to the smallest calligraphic elements of the written Law. Yet the evangelist's use of the demonstrative pronoun in two other passages may well offer the key to the usage in this context. In Matt 3:9, par. Luke 3:8, the broader context and in 25:40, 45 the logical context supply the antecedents for the demonstrative *these,* whose function in such instances is more adjectival than pronominal. The same function fits 5:18–19, since *one hook of the Law* could easily be the *indirect* antecedent for *one of the least of these commandments* (Ljungman, *Gesetz,* 48). The *figurative* import of *one hook of the Law* is the same as *one of the least of these commandments* (Schürmann, *Untersuchungen,* 129, n. 16), since both phrases represent the details of the Law. Therefore, 5:19 stands as the explication of 5:18 and most likely betrays the original *Sitz im Leben* of 5:19. Whereas 5:17, 18 may have distant roots in Jesus' ministry, 5:19 reflects the nomistic nuance of a strict Jewish-Christian community who may well have shaped the tradition of 5:17, 18 and added 5:19 as a commentary. This commentary would then round out the unit of 5:17, 18 by setting forth the practical implications regarding the keeping and teaching of the Law.

shall be called least/great in the Kingdom. Such mention of rank occurs elsewhere in Jesus' teachings (18:4; 20:16, par. Mark 10:31, par. Luke; 20:21, 23, par. Mark 10:37, 40; 20:26, par. Mark 10:43; Mark 9:35 and Luke 9:48b). In each of these instances the way to being "first" is by being "last," to being "great" by being a "servant," to being "greater" in being like a "child." Yet none of the preconditions for a given rank was ever intended to be a motivation. One was not to attempt to become a "child," a "servant," or "last" in order to receive the corresponding ranking. Rather, each declaration set forth the same basic principle, namely, rank comes as the reverse of what might have been expected. The fact that one's "reward" or "punishment" in 5:19, in contrast to the examples just noted, corresponds directly to one's conduct and was intended as a motivation for certain conduct, underscores the secondary character of the saying. Matt 5:19 is much closer to Jewish teaching on rewards than to Jesus' teaching on the same subject (see Note on 6:1).

The reference to rank may also suggest the original setting in the Church for the formulation of 5:17–19. Obviously, 5:19 with its reference to *the least of these commandments* points to that part of the early church that saw themselves obligated to keep the whole Law. This question about the extent of one's obligation to the Mosaic Law preceded the question of whether circumcision was necessary for salvation (Acts 15:1, cf. Galatians). The circumcision question comes subsequent to that of

5:19 and arose first when Gentiles came into the picture. Consequently, 5:19 had its original setting in the Jewish-Christian struggles at the outset within the Church for whom circumcision was a foregone conclusion. By contrast, the "Judaizers" in Acts 15:1 and Paul's Jewish-Christian opponents viewed keeping the Law as a necessary condition for entering the Kingdom; they doubtless reflect another development of strict Jewish-Christianity when confronted by the question of the Gentile mission. The later question, however, stems from the former. It goes without saying that one demanding the full observance of the Law would also have the most questions about the Gentile mission.

Therefore, the tradition behind 5:17–19 most likely stemming from the early Palestinian church was preserved by strict Jewish-Christianity long after the Gentile mission had been recognized by the leaders of Jerusalem. Matthew himself may well have felt the impact of this tradition and these Jewish-Christians after the fall of Jerusalem. Matt 5:20 may also have them in mind, as did his reworking of 5:17–18.

Excursus: Matthew's Use of 5:19

What about Matthew's use of 5:19? We have seen where Matthew has consistently modified the nomistic force of 5:17, 18 in terms of the *heilsgeschichtliches* moment in Jesus' coming. Consequently, it would appear incongruous that the evangelist would even permit such a nomistic saying to go unchallenged, let alone add such a nomistic saying to the material. Banks has recently explained the demonstrative function of *these* similarly to that above. But rather than 5:18b—*one hook of the Law*—Banks has found 5:18c²—*until all things come to pass*—to be the logical antecedent that refers ahead to Jesus' teaching through which *all things come to pass* (*Jesus,* 222–23, also Lohmeyer, *Matthäus,* 111–12). Matthew, accordingly, would be stressing Jesus' commandments (cf. 28:20) as binding for the community and subject to the distinction between greater and lesser commandments. This view, however, not only has the dubious task of demonstrating that 5:18c² refers to Jesus' teaching (see 5:18c²) but also that 5:18c² offered a clear contextual antecedent for *these commandments.* Furthermore, since it is doubtful that Jesus or the early church differentiated between "lesser and greater" commandments within his own teaching, this understanding of 5:19 also appears to lack an appropriate *Sitz im Leben* in the tradition.

Thus the question still remains: how did Matthew understand the positive reference to the Law in 5:19? First, the very presence of 5:19 in the context of the redactionally modified 5:17–18 demonstrates the evangelist's loyalty to his tradition. Matthew does not replace the tradition (cf. 5:18c[1]); he modifies the tradition through his adaptation and qualification of it (cf. Notes on the Beatitudes). Second, Matthew does interpret 5:19 indirectly by his overall modification of the context 5:17–18, 21–48, and by directly adding 5:20. Whereas 5:19 speaks of one's *rank* in the Kingdom, 5:20 addresses the prior question of *entrance* into the Kingdom.

A similar pair of sayings occurs in 18:3–4, but the order is reversed. Entrance into the Kingdom comes through the conversion demanded in 18:3; one's rank follows in 18:4. Consequently, Matthew used οὖν in 18:4 to express its inferential relationship to 18:3, while he used γάρ in 5:20 to express the basis for the concerns of 5:19. One's rank (5:19) presupposed one's entrance into the Kingdom (5:20). Yet the "entrance-requirement" of exceeding *righteousness* (5:20) was not synonymous with keeping the *least of these commandments* (5:19) as the difference in conjunctions indicates.

Third, whereas the tradition behind 5:19 doubtless focused on the contrast between breaking and keeping the commandments, Matthew, by adding 5:20, as 18:3–4 suggests, focused more on the question of rank and entrance into the Kingdom, motifs found elsewhere in the tradition (see below and Note on 5:20). Yet the question of the Law is not totally missing in 5:18, 19. By simply substituting 5:18c[2] for 5:18c[1] and by eliminating 5:19, Matthew could have dropped the obvious concern for the Law found in his tradition. Why did the evangelist choose not to do so? For many the answer lies in Käsemann's words, Matthew was "well on the way to a Christian rabbinate" ("Beginnings," 93). This answer, however, neither fits with the redactional motifs of 5:17–18 nor with the subsequent Antitheses (see Notes on 5:21–48). Indeed, in his explication of the impact of Jesus' coming on the Law, Matthew may well stand much closer to Paul than to any other New Testament figure.

It is not unrealistic to assume that Matthew's community was indeed integrated, with a mix of Gentiles on the one side and strict Jewish-Christians who perhaps had moved from Jerusalem to Syria after the fall of Jerusalem on the other side and various shades of Jewish-Christians in the middle. Matthew's Gospel, then, of necessity would reflect various interests within the tradition, as well as the evangelist's own varied concerns to apply the tradition appropriately to the needs of his own community. The evangelist's usage of the tradition behind 5:17–19 could easily have had two fronts: first, against the strict Jewish-Christian misuse of the tradition (cf. Matthew's reworking of 5:17–18) and, second, against the "antinomian" overreaction by those "free from the Law," both problems quite familiar to Paul. The significant difference between Matthew and Paul, apart from literary genres, was their audience. Whereas Paul most likely wrote to predominantly Gentile audiences, Matthew's community was more than likely strongly Jewish-Christian, if not in number, certainly in voice. This factor alone could have meant that Matthew had to deal more specifically than Paul with the practical consequences of Jesus' coming in terms of the Law's demands.

To say that Jesus came *to fulfill the Scriptures* (5:17) and that the Law's validity was superseded by the *coming to pass of all things* in 5:18 might result in an antinomian libertinism, leading one to conclude that the Law was no longer binding in any way. Yet throughout his Gospel Matthew carefully guarded against such an extreme by maintaining the necessity to do the "will of the Father" (7:12) found in Jesus' "words" (7:24, cf. 28:20) which repeatedly involved the Law's demands (e.g., 7:12; 15:3, 19; 19:18–19; 22:40; 23:23). Even the Antitheses of 5:21–48 either transcend (5:21–22, 27–28, 33–37) or supersede the Law (5:31–32, cf. Luke 16:18, 38–42, 43–48) as an expression of God's will for this age with a greater demand for conduct, not less. Indeed, failure to do the will of the Father excludes one from the Kingdom (7:21), although keeping the Law does not guarantee one entrance into eternal life (19:18–20, cf. the righteousness of the scribes and Pharisees in 5:20). Precisely this apparent ambiguity regarding the Law creates the confusion in understanding Matthew's perception of the Law.

Matthew actually uses the Law in two different ways without explicitly distinguishing between them (see Note on 5:17). On the one hand, the Law connotes the sum of the commandments and prohibitions, the Law of Moses, "Sinai-Torah," viewed as God's will regulating human conduct. The "righteous" are those who seek to keep the Law as a necessary condition for the coming of the Kingdom. This conception of the Law was current among the Jews, especially the Pharisees, and was doubtless maintained by the strict Jewish-Christians. One the other hand, the Law has an eschatological dimension, "Zion-Torah," found in the prophets' promises of the realization of the will of God in the lives of those to whom God comes bringing a new relationship with himself. In 5:18 the evangelist underscored the Law in the first sense of "Sinai-Torah" by his introduction of *one iota,* but he also added that the Law's validity ended with the *coming to pass of all things* in $5:18c^2$. In 5:19 the evangelist let stand *the least of these commandments,* referring to the Law's commandments, but he qualified the phrase by the demand for a greater righteousness in 5:20. The "greater righteousness" includes the second sense of the Law, "Zion-Torah," as God's will done by those who stand in a new relationship with him. One keeps the "Law" in the second sense (5:20–48) in light of Jesus' coming (5:17–18), not in spite of it. Therefore, 5:20 changes the traditional focus of 5:19 from "Sinai-Torah," referring to the sum of the Law's legal demands, to "Zion-Torah" as viewed in light of Jesus' ministry.

5:20. This verse, using the structure of a future condition with ἐάν and resuming the second person plural of 5:17, 18, sets forth one of eleven "entrance-sayings" found in Matthew. (Six refer to the Kingdom: 5:20; 7:21; 18:3, cf. Mark 10:15, par. Luke 18:17; 19:23, 24, par. Mark

10:23, 24 and 23:13, par. Luke 11:52. Three refer to life: 18:8, par. Mark 9:43; 18:9, cf. Mark 9:47; 19:17, cf. Mark 10:17. Two refer to the joy of the Lord: 25:21, 23.) The traditional parallels to some of these sayings demonstrate the pre-Matthean existence of "entrance-sayings," and some scholars have suggested that the evangelist found 5:20 either at hand or in a different traditional setting (e.g., Soiron, *Bergpredigt*, 243–44; Schniewind, *Matthäus*, 53, 57; Banks, *Jesus*, 224–25).

Yet, apart from the relatively large number of entrance-sayings in Matthew, considerable evidence suggests that this verse is redactional (e.g., Dupont, *Béatitudes* 3:251, n. 2; cf. 1:133). In addition to his redactional modification of 18:9, cf. Mark 9:47 ("enter" for "inherit"), and 19:17, cf. Mark 10:17 ("enter" for "inherit"), there is also the probability that he reworked the indefinite relative construction of Mark 10:15, par. Luke 18:17, into the future condition of 18:3 parallel in structure to 5:20. All these suggest that 5:20 could also have been a redactional product drawing on the traditional entrance motif (cf. Mark 10:15, par. Luke 18:17; 19:23, 24, par. Mark 10:23, 24, par. Luke 18:24, 25). This possibility becomes all but a certainty in view of the characteristic Matthean terms that constitute the verse's content. If we removed *righteousness* (δικαιοσύνη), *exceeds* (περισσεύσῃ), *scribes and Pharisees* (γραμματέων καὶ Φαρισαίων), and *Kingdom of Heaven* (βασιλείαν τῶν οὐρανῶν), we would have nothing left of the saying but the structure.

As a redactional saying, the verse serves as the pivot between 5:17–19, a block of tradition originally pertaining to the Law, and 21–48, a series of sayings expressing Jesus' own demands.

For. The use of this conjunction (γάρ) by Matthew frequently denotes a connecting link between preceding material and material being introduced into the context. For some scholars, however, the conjunction has lost most of its force in 5:20 so that this verse begins a new section of the Sermon by introducing the Antitheses of 5:21–48 (Trilling, *Israel*, 183–84; Strecker, *Weg*, 181; Sand, *Gesetz*, 203; Luz, "Erfüllung," 412). Unfortunately, the use of 5:20 exclusively to introduce the Antitheses without simultaneously relating to 5:19 overlooks the deliberate connection of 5:19 and 20. This connection becomes evident when viewed alongside of the redactional combination of similar themes in 18:3–4 (see Note on οὖν in 5:19).

In 18:3–4 the evangelist, in contrast to Mark and Luke, has Jesus respond to the question about *rank* in the Kingdom (18:1, par. Mark 9:34, par. Luke) by first dealing with *entrance* into the Kingdom (18:3). Furthermore, Matthew has redactionally molded the entrance-saying

(18:3) in the style of 5:20 and introduced it into its present context after taking the saying from Mark 10:15, par. Luke 18:17. Then the evangelist (οὖν) returned to the initial question of rank (18:4) with the more developed response, referring to childlike humility as the basis of greatness in the Kingdom (18:4, cf. Mark 9:37, par. Luke 9:48).

Since the motif of rank was a part of the tradition in both 5:19 and 18:1, 4, and since the evangelist introduces the entrance motif with similar format into the two contexts, 5:20 must be understood as relating to 5:19 in particular and 5:17–19 in general. The inferential particle (γάρ) serves here in the manner of a clamp combining 5:20 with 5:19 and places the accent on 5:20 by shifting one's attention primarily to the question of entrance into rather than rank within the Kingdom.

Whereas the strict Jewish–Christian emphasis behind 5:17–19 stressed the keeping of the whole Law, Matthew by using γάρ stressed the anterior demand for "a greater righteousness" in order to enter the Kingdom. The nature of this "greater righteousness" is defined not as the keeping of the *least of these commandments* in 5:19 but by the demands of the Antitheses that follow in 5:21–48. Thus 5:20 has a dual function of summarizing the Matthean understanding of 5:17–19 while simultaneously introducing the theme of 5:21–48. It offers the redactional introduction to what 5:48 forms the redactional conclusion. Both verses exhibiting redactional traits (see Note on 5:48) stand in material relationship with each other.

righteousness. Matthew's usage of *righteousness* (δικαιοσύνη) in the Sermon includes soteriological, ethical, and eschatological moments (see Excursus on 5:6). All three elements are present in 5:20. The soteriological perspective is inherent in the entrance motif that requires the "greater righteousness." The ethical element is implicit in the comparison with the scribes and Pharisees and is explicit in the evangelist's deliberate pairing of 5:20 with 5:19 as well as by his use of 5:20 to set the stage for the demands of 5:21–48. The *scribes and Pharisees* were called the "righteous" in their day because of their concern to know, teach, and practice the Law. Consequently, any comparison with them would naturally contain an ethical element. Yet 5:19 states that such a *righteousness,* namely, doing and teaching the *least of these commandments,* pertains to rank in the Kingdom. But ethical conduct understood as the keeping of the details of the Law was an inadequate basis for entering the Kingdom. An even "greater righteousness" was necessary. The following section of 5:21–48 indicates what the *righteousness that exceeds* is by giving concrete examples of how that conduct in keeping with the will of God expresses itself. Apart from the third element, the eschatological aspect, however, one not only misses the heart of Matthew's understanding of *righteousness* here, as in 5:6 and 6:33, but fails to grasp the basis of the Antitheses.

Matt 5:20 must be viewed in the context of 5:17–19 as well as 5:21–48. The evangelist has clearly reworked his tradition behind 5:17–18 from an eschatological/christological perspective that underscores Jesus' coming to fulfill the Old Testament promises of God's redemptive activity for his people (5:17), the coming to pass of all things in Jesus' ministry (5:18). The presence of the age of salvation in and through Jesus' person and teaching implies a radically new dimension in one's relationship to God (6:1–18) and to others (5:21–48). It is Jesus' eschatological ministry, a ministry that fulfills God's promises for the new age, that brings the soteriological element of new relationships both now and in the future (5:3–12), as well as the demands for a concomitant ethical response (5:21–5:48).

By introducing the concept of a *righteousness exceeding that of the scribes and Pharisees* in 5:20, Matthew completes his reworking of the strict Jewish-Christian thrust of the tradition found in 5:17–19 in light of Jesus' coming and the implications of his coming for a "Pharisaic" understanding of the Law. Matthew does not merely pass on and thus implicitly endorse the strict Jewish-Christian view of the continued, binding character of the Law, even the *least of the commandments.* Rather, he counters this view and qualifies the tradition by stressing the eschatological/christological import of Jesus' coming and ministry, the central aspect of his use of *righteousness.* In other words, *righteousness* contains an eschatological understanding of one's relationship before God and others as well as one's corresponding conduct. By so interpreting the tradition in 5:17–19, the evangelist realigns the underlying tradition with Jesus' own ministry implicit in the Antitheses of 5:21–48 that demand a conduct befitting the new age of salvation or "Kingdom ethics."

greatly exceeds. This verbal comparison (περισσεύσῃ) gives evidence of being redactional. Of the verb's four other occurrences in Matthew, two refer to the leftovers in the feeding of the multitudes (14:20, par. Luke 9:17, cf. Mark 6:43: 15:37, par. Mark 8:8), and two are clearly redactional additions to the Marcan (13:12, cf. Mark 4:25) and Q (25:29, cf. Luke 19:26) tradition. Furthermore, the evangelist is most likely responsible for the use of περισσόν in 5:37 and 5:47 within the Sermon context.

Lexically, the construction of a double comparative (περισσεύσῃ

... πλεῖον with genitive) can only express a quantitative (Luz, "Erfüllung," 422; con. Strecker, *Weg*, 151–52, and Hubner, *Gesetz*, 37–38) and not a qualitative comparison (cf. 2 Cor 3:9; Phil 1:9; 1 Thess 4:1). But one might legitimately ask how one could ever *exceed the righteousness of the scribes and Pharisees* when the Apostle Paul himself wrote, "As to the law a Pharisee . . . as to righteousness under the law blameless" (Phil 3:5–6, RSV). The answer lies in the use of *righteousness* by Matthew. Contrary to the opinion of some, 5:20 does not demand a more rigorous keeping of the Law or a keeping of a more rigorous Law or interpretation of the Law. Rather, Jesus, according to Matthew, demands a *righteousness* congruent with his coming. *Righteousness* necessary for entrance into the Kingdom connotes the conduct in keeping with the will of the Father, conduct that stems from the new relationships and possibilities inherent in the presence of the age of salvation and implicit in the demands of 5:21—7:12. The *righteousness of the scribes and Pharisees* was inadequate because it did not stem from the eschatological moment of God's redemptive activity in Jesus' Messianic ministry, restoring the broken relationships between himself and his people as well as among his people, enabling them to live in keeping with his will (see further below). Whereas Paul distinguished qualitatively between a "righteousness of my own, based on the Law" and "that which is through faith in Christ" (Phil 3:9), Matthew used a quantitative comparison to express the ultimate inadequacy of "Pharisaic righteousness" for entrance into the Kingdom in view of Jesus' coming and ministry (5:17, 18, 21–48; 6:1–18).

that of the scribes and Pharisees. The phrase *scribes and Pharisees,* implying two separate groups within Judaism, lacks precision since they were not two distinct groups. Yet the phrase, occurring in all three Synoptic Gospels (e.g., Mark 7:1, 5; Luke 5:21), does maintain the dual concern of the Jewish religious leaders for the Law. The *scribes,* in particular, were the interpreters and instructors of the Law (teaching); the *Pharisees,* a broader category referring to one of the Jewish religious groups and often including the former (cf. Mark 2:16; Luke 5:30), were zealous to keep the Law (doing). Apart from the Woes of Matthew 23, the first evangelist uses this phrase here, in 12:28, 15:1, par. Mark 7:1, and in 23:2.

The *righteousness of the scribes and Pharisees* is inadequate from two standpoints, according to Matthew's redaction. From the standpoint of 5:20–48, their *righteousness* meant the fulfillment of the Law's legal demands (cf. Paul's "righteousness under the Law") as expressed in the six premises countered by Jesus' demand in the Antitheses (5:21, 27, 31, 33, 38, 43); in their concern about the Law reflected in the Sabbath controversies (12:1–14); and in their concern for ceremonial cleanliness with reference to Jesus (9:9–13) and his disciples (15:1–9). From the standpoint of 6:1–18, it was a *righteousness* done for the wrong motives, for show or personal reward (6:1; 23:5) on the "surface" (23:25–26, 27–28). Such *righteousness* was ultimately *hypocrisy* (for discussion, see Note on 6:2).

Many have interpreted the *righteousness of the scribes and Pharisees* of 5:20 in terms of the charges found in 23:2–4 and 23:23. Accordingly, their righteousness was judged inadequate because they were more concerned with form than content, with show than substance, with teaching than doing. When, however, one reads Matthew 23 in terms of Matthew's use of *righteousness* in the Sermon and the demands of 5:21—6:18, rather than reading 5:20 and 6:1 in light of Matthew 23, the perspective changes considerably. Instead of viewing the Pharisees as failures at their task of interpreting and keeping the Law with integrity as they understood it, their failure was much more subtle. They did not fail in keeping the Law (cf. Paul the Pharisee in Phil 3:6, 9) but in doing the will of God, the "weightier matters of the Law" (23:23–24) in terms of Jesus' coming. The Matthean redactional portrait of the so-called rich young ruler corresponds to the Pharisees' predicament (19:16–22, cf. Mark 10:17–22). Having kept the Law, they were still far from the Kingdom, from eternal life (19:16–17), since they lacked the "wholeness" (19:20–21; cf. 5:48) that comes with discipleship (19:21). Discipleship implies a new relationship with God through Jesus' ministry as well as the concomitant conduct in keeping with God's will (19:21, 22, cf. 28:19–20). Their concern for the minutiae of the Law, like the rich man's concern for his wealth, had actually blinded them from seeing and doing the will of the Father in light of Jesus' coming (23:25–26).

the Kingdom of Heaven. Once again, *righteousness* and the *Kingdom of Heaven* are brought together (cf. 5:10; 6:33, cf. 7:21). The relationship of *righteousness* in the present to the entrance into the *Kingdom* in the future is not merely a *do et des* (a reward for meritorious behavior), even though the entrance into the future Kingdom will be based on one's *righteousness that greatly exceeds that of the scribes and Pharisees.* To read 5:20 in such fashion is to fail to recognize the deliberate tension between the presence of the *Kingdom* and the future consummation of the *Kingdom* in Matthew (see Note on 5:3). The *righteousness* necessary for the future entrance into the consummated *Kingdom* is both gift and demand which accompanied Jesus' own ministry that effected and effects the presence of the *Kingdom* now (5:3, 10; 6:33). The new relationships and the ability to live in keeping with God's will, that is, to exhibit the *righteousness* demanded in 5:20–6:18, are part and parcel of the presence of God's redemptive, sovereign rule that becomes a part of time and history in Jesus' coming (5:17, 18, cf. 5:3–12).

Comments

Judging by the number and diversity of treatments, Matt 5:17–20 poses one of the most perplexing passages in the first Gospel. Yet these four verses offer one of the pivotal treatments of the subject of Jesus' ministry and its implications for the Law. In addition to the more general question about the meaning and intent of 5:17–20, three specific questions have arisen in the discussion. First, just how does Jesus' person and ministry effect the Law? or what does it mean to say that Jesus came "to fulfill the Law"? Second, how can a passage that repeatedly affirms the continuing validity of the entire Law introduce a series of statements set in clear antithesis to the Law (5:21–48)? Third, and even more basic, where does such unqualified support for the Law (cf. 5:18, 19) have its place in the teaching of one who was accused of breaking the Sabbath (12:1–14) and failing to observe the ceremonial laws of cleanliness (9:9–13) and whose teaching countered that of the Law (5:21–48; Mark 10:11 and Luke 16:18) and cut at the very basis of "things clean and unclean" (Matt 15:1–20)?

Each of these questions is very complex. But part of their resolution lies in the recognition that 5:17–20 is a composite unit of tradition(s) and redaction. One must first distinguish between the tradition and redaction in order to see the distinctive features of Matthew's message more clearly. Only then can one turn to the primary task of what the evangelist actually intended to say by his selection and modification of the traditional sayings focusing on the Law. Consequently, we will examine each of the four verses from the standpoint of tradition and redaction, remembering that our ultimate concern is the latter. In dividing the material into tradition and redaction, we by necessity will also cover the questions of source and history of the tradition.

A. To Fulfill the Law and the Prophets: Matt 5:17

One of the major obstacles in understanding 5:17 has been the rather common misreading of the verse in terms of Jesus' coming to "fulfill the Law" rather than "the Law and the Prophets." Such a misreading is more or less natural in view of the context whose subject is the Law and the commandments (5:18-19, cf. 5:21-48) and the apparent antithesis between "to annul" and "to fulfill" within 5:17 itself. Yet the "Law" was the focus of the tradition that was deliberately modified by Matthew to "the Law and the Prophets" (see Note on 5:17). It is primarily this distinction that separates the tradition from the redaction.

1. Matt 5:17 existed as a traditional saying dealing with Jesus and the Law (see Note on 5:17). The opening warning, "Do not think . . . ," suggests that what follows was meant to correct or to avoid a misconception of Jesus' coming, namely, that Jesus came not to annul the Law but to fulfill it (see Note on 5:17). Such a saying might well reflect a setting either of controversy or of instruction, a response to a charge or a clarification of Jesus' ministry. Depending on the given context, 5:17 could serve various functions. Consequently, the question of *Sitz im Leben* is vital to the saying's meaning and intent.

If our analysis of 5:17-19 is correct (see Notes on 5:17-19), a strict Jewish-Christian wing of the Church brought these verses together and gave 5:17 its present context. Together these sayings set forth the continuing validity of the entire Law (5:18) and the importance of keeping even the least of the commandments (5:19) contrary to what others "think" (5:17a) or "teach" (5:19). In such a setting 5:17 would be primarily a negative statement that Jesus' coming did not annul the Law. The antithetical, positive statement that Jesus fulfilled the Law would then be an affirmation of the Law in the sense of "to fulfill" the Law's legal demands (see Note on 5:17). This viewpoint behind 5:17-19—most likely reflecting the struggles in the early church over the role of the Law— was not only contrary to the ultimate direction of the Church but was also a misunderstanding and distortion of Jesus' own ministry.

Although many have assigned the roots of 5:17 to the Church instead of Jesus, a statement similar to 5:17 about his ministry in relation to the Law would have been most apropos in view of his frequent confrontations with the Jewish religious leaders for whom the keeping of the legal demands of the Law was so vital. Indeed, 5:17 might well have had a very different meaning from that seen by strict Jewish-Christianity and also quite consistent with Jesus' teaching regarding the Kingdom.

Rather than Law referring to the sum of legal commandments and prohibitions which the Pharisees in particular sought to "fulfill" as a necessary prelude to the coming of the Kingdom and entrance into it, the Law was also a part of the Old Testament promise for the age of salvation (see Note on 5:17).

In the promises of Isaiah, Jeremiah, and Ezekiel, an eschatological dimension of the Law emerges in keeping with God's redemptive activity for his people. For example, in Jer 31:31–34 God promises to write the Law upon one's heart within the context of the new covenant. Ezek 36:25–27 promises a new heart and a new spirit that enables one to walk obediently according to God's "statutes" and "ordinances." Such good news is integral to God's revelation of himself and his Law through Zion in Isa 2:2–4, cf. Mic 4:1–3; cf. Isa 51:4–5. Jesus was the one who came to do the will of the Father, to announce the presence of God's redemptive reign in history that establishes a new relationship between God and his people, and thus to enable one to live obediently. By bringing this eschatological dimension of the Law as the dynamic expression of God's will within the context of the age of salvation to its ultimate completion, Jesus "fulfilled the Law."

That Jesus understood his ministry as establishing this new relationship is evident from his ministry to the sick and the sinners to whom he offered the *shalom* of God's healing, forgiving presence. This is evident as well in his rejection of the "righteous" whose very concern for the Law had itself blinded them to God's redemptive activity on their behalf. Such an eschatological understanding of the Law in contrast to that of the Pharisees underlies the Sabbath controversies, the demands of the Antitheses of 5:21–48, the love commandment, and the call to love one's enemies. Devoid of the eschatological framework of Jesus' ministry, these examples could readily lead to the conclusion that Jesus came to annul rather than to fulfill the Law, a charge that doubtless had its place among his Jewish opponents. Even the strict Jewish-Christians failed to grasp accurately the implications of Jesus' ministry, and 5:17–19 represents their own understanding of the continued validity of the Law as the sum of commandments and prohibitions. Matthew, by contrast, having received this traditional material from such a background, modified it to counter such a misconception of Jesus' ministry.

2. Matthew actually did very little to modify the tradition. He simply added "or the Prophets." Since the disjunctive "or" is characteristic of the evangelist's redactional style of adding a supplementary noun (see Note on 5:17), it should not be viewed as separating "the Law" and

"the Prophets" into two categories and can accurately be translated in this case as "the Law and the Prophets."

But by adding the phrase, Matthew considerably alters the force of the saying. Instead of dealing more narrowly with Jesus' coming and the Law as such, the verse now refers to Jesus' coming with reference to the Scriptures. Consequently, the neat antithesis in the tradition between annulling/fulfilling the Law loses some of its sharpness. Whereas the primary thrust of 5:17 in the Jewish-Christian use of the tradition was to stress that Jesus had *not* come to annul the Law, Matthew's primary concern was to stress that Jesus *had* come to fulfill the Scriptures (see Note on 5:17). Such an emphasis in 5:17 concurs with one of the main traits of Matthew's christology as illustrated both by his distinctive use of the eleven redactional fulfillment-citations and by his alignment of Jesus with Isaiah 61 in the Beatitudes above.

For Matthew, to say that Jesus is the fulfillment of the Scriptures had much more significance than merely an apologetic desire to amass Old Testament proof-texts or to underscore the predictive character of Old Testament prophecy. Matthew clearly understood Jesus to be the redemptive historical fulfillment or completion of God's redemptive activity, witnessed to by the Old Testament and promised for the age of salvation. Jesus was the Messiah Son of God who came to announce and effect the Kingdom, the sovereign rule of God, in history. Only when one begins with this broader starting point can one then understand the eschatological character of the "greater righteousness" demanded in 5:20 and illustrated in 5:21—7:12. Such relationships and conduct both implicit and explicit to the larger context of 5:17–20 are characteristic of the presence of the Kingdom, the fulfillment of the Old Testament promises.

Matthew's modification of the tradition behind 5:17, then, not only counters the narrow "legalism" of the strict Jewish-Christianity but it also realigns the sayings with Jesus' own ministry. To say that Jesus' coming fulfills the Scriptures is but another way of declaring the gospel that God has acted in history through Jesus and his ministry to effect what he had promised. What was implicit to Jesus' announcements in the Beatitudes of 5:3–12 stands explicit in 5:17.

B. Until All Things Come to Pass: Matt 5:18

As did 5:17, Matt 5:18 bears some distinctively Matthean editorial traits. Apart from his adding "one iota" with his characteristic "or," the evangelist has also typically broken a traditional pattern by adding a second temporal clause and placing the traditional "until heaven and earth pass away" between the introductory formula and the main clause (see Note on 5:18). Taking these changes into consideration, we find the saying pointing in two very different directions.

1. Matt 5:18 has a material parallel in Luke 16:17. Since the vocabulary of these two sayings is quite similar, many have assigned 5:18 to the Q tradition and have explained the structural differences as either redactional modifications (usually by Matthew) or transmissional variations (see Note on 5:18). The tension between the two "until" clauses in 5:18 and the fact that neither Matthew nor Luke gives indication of a preference for or a bias against the structure used by the other argues strongly for the existence of these two forms of the saying in the tradition (see Note on 5:18). Furthermore, the different structure has critical bearing on the intent of the two sayings. Whereas Luke 16:17 speaks of the difficulty of the Law passing away, Matthew 5:18 clearly declares that the Law will continue in force in its entirety until this age is consummated. This difference in structure may supply the clue for the saying's original setting.

Beginning with Luke's form of the saying, we have a parallel construction in Mark 10:25 where Jesus refers to the difficulty of the rich entering the Kingdom. On the surface, the comparison appears to be exclusive. Even the disciples respond in kind with "Who indeed is able to be saved?" (Mark 10:26). Yet it becomes evident that the comparison does not refer to an ultimate impossibility but to one humanly inconceivable apart from God's redemptive intervention (Mark 10:27, par. Matt, par. Luke). If we interpret Luke 16:17 accordingly, the comparison would imply that while the entire Law was as permanent as heaven and earth, it was subject to God's own redemptive intervention. Such an understanding of Luke 16:17 concurs with its present, though secondary, setting in Luke 16:16–18, since it is surrounded by two sayings that explicitly refer to the "end" of the Law in view of God's redemptive activity.

Furthermore, understood in this manner, Luke 16:17 might well have its roots ultimately in Jesus' confrontation with the religious leaders of his day and their concept of the Law. The recalcitrance of the "righteous" based on their concern for the Law fundamentally paralleled the reluctance of the "rich" based on their concern for wealth. Consequently, Jesus' response to both would be the same. The zeal of Jesus' "righteous" opponents for the Law made it easier for "heaven and earth to pass away" than for even a calligraphic detail to disappear from the Law.

Only God's intervention could alter the humanly impossible situation of the "rich" and the "righteous" and their entrance into the Kingdom ("For all things are possible with God," Mark 10:27).

Matthew's form of the traditional saying points to a very different setting. Beginning with an ἀμήν-formula expressing an authoritative introduction, the main clause emphatically denies that even the slightest detail of the Law will perish until heaven and earth pass away, the consummation of history. The intention of the saying, particularly when taken together with the pre-Matthean tradition of 5:17 and 5:19, is most explicit. The *entire* Mosaic Law remains in force until the consummation. Such an explicit assertion could hardly have had a firm place in Jesus' own ministry in view of the Church's own practice and Jesus' teaching and actions regarding the Law found elsewhere in the Gospel tradition.

Had such an unequivocal statement about the Law's continuing validity been traceable to Jesus in the early tradition, one would expect it to have surfaced more prominently in the early church's struggles over this very question. In fact, the Church from its earliest stages—even in Jerusalem (cf. Acts 6–7, 11)—failed to live accordingly, and certainly the Church, once it left the influence of a rigorous Jewish-Christianity, has never attempted to keep nor to teach the necessity of keeping the entire written Law of Moses. Jesus' own ministry became the basis for a different understanding of the Law, not only in Paul's theology, but in the Gospel tradition itself (e.g., the Sabbath controversies, 12:1–14; things clean and unclean, Mark 7:1–23; the divorce sayings, Mark 10:2–11, cf. Luke 16:18; and the love commandment, Mark 12:28–34). It appears safe to conclude that this saying as formulated in Matthew's tradition did not have its original setting in Jesus' ministry.

The one setting where the saying fits most naturally points again to a strict Jewish-Christianity that sought to observe the Mosaic Law and insisted that others do the same (cf. Acts 15:10–11; 21:20–24). In addition to the present context of 5:17–19, we find a similar motif in the tradition of 23:2–3, which Matthew also reworked by the redactional "balancing" of the traditions in 23:4–12, as well as in the fragments of the Jewish-Christian apocryphal gospels (cf. *Gos Heb*). Consequently, the present formulation of the saying and its context are most likely the products of the reinterpretation or misunderstanding of Jesus' teaching regarding the Law, an interpretation that gave dominical support for a strict Jewish-Christian understanding of the Law. The evangelist, however, having found the traditional material *en bloc*, modified 5:18 in a fashion similar to his reworking of 5:17.

2. Matthew, finding the saying with the traditional structure of introductory statement, main clause followed by a temporal clause, made two additions (see Note on 5:18). First, he added "not one iota" and thus combined two rather common rabbinic expressions symbolizing the integrity of the Law. Second, he added another temporal clause and relocated the first (see Note on 5:18). In so doing, the evangelist opened the saying by underscoring the "Jewish" understanding of the Law's validity but then added a qualifying "until" clause at the end. This "until all things come to pass" holds the key to the meaning of 5:18 as it now stands in the context of 5:17–19 (see Note on 5:18).

Devoid of context, "until all things come to pass" most naturally connotes the final consummation of God's redemptive purposes. This meaning occurs at the conclusion of the Olivet Discourse (cf. Mark 13:24–27, par. Matt, par. Luke). But it is most unlikely that the evangelist would have made such an adjustment by redundantly adding a synonymous "until" clause simply to repeat himself. Consequently, one needs to look for a "Matthean" rather than traditional usage of the second "until" clause. For many, this "until" clause refers narrowly to Jesus' teaching that "fulfills" or "brings to pass" the Law's demands through his final interpretation of the Law (see Note on 5:18). The ensuing Antitheses of 5:21–48 and the centrality of the love commandment serve as supporting evidence.

Yet this interpretation of "until all things come to pass" reflects a narrow conception of Jesus' ministry as the teacher or interpreter of the Law. Doubtless Jesus' relation to the Law was vitally important for Matthew, but only as part of the broader concept of Jesus' role in redemptive history. For Matthew, Jesus was not the New Moses or the Bringer of the Messianic Torah, analogous, for example, to the Qumran Teacher of Righteousness. Rather, Jesus was the Messiah Son of God who came to announce the presence of God's redemptive activity in terms of the Kingdom. Jesus' relationship to the Law and its demands was a concomitant of the ministry. It is the larger theme that we find behind the second "until" clause in 5:18.

We have noted on several occasions Matthew's concern to show that Jesus came to fulfill God's promise for the age of salvation. Matt 5:17 makes such a statement explicitly, whereas the alignment of the Beatitudes with the promises of Isaiah 61 and the application of Old Testament motifs for the day of salvation to the disciples in 5:14–16 make such a statement implicitly. On three occasions, Matthew used the phrase "came to pass" in conjunction with his distinctive fulfillment-citations (1:22;

21:4; 26:54, 56). In doing so, the evangelist has indicated that certain events "came to pass" as part of God's plan that was fulfilled by Jesus' ministry. This same usage is very appropriate to 5:18. "Until all things come to pass" would thus refer in general to Jesus' entire ministry that brings to fruition God's redemptive purposes (fulfills the Scriptures, 5:17) and not simply to his teaching regarding the Law and/or the love commandment.

Understood in this manner, 5:18 would have two apparently contradictory elements. On the one hand, the Law remains valid in its entirety "until heaven and earth pass away," the final consummation. On the other hand, the Law's validity ends with the "coming to pass of all things" in Jesus' ministry. Why this contradictory element when the evangelist could have merely substituted his own "until" clause for that of the tradition? Apart from the fact that the presence of both elements points to Matthew's faithfulness in preserving his tradition, the two "until" clauses set in sharp relief the "Jewish" understanding of the Law and Jesus' own ministry. Matthew, not unlike Paul, maintained that the Law does remain valid in its entirety as part of this age for those who seek to live accordingly. Yet the Law is no longer binding for those for whom all things have come to pass in Jesus' ministry (cf. Rom 10:4).

By modifying the saying in this manner, Matthew accomplishes two goals. First, he positively states that the "coming to pass of all things" in Jesus' coming as the fulfillment of the Scriptures (5:17–18) has definite negative implications for the Law's binding character and sets the stage for the Antitheses of 5:21–48 (cf. 5:20 below). Second, Matthew apologetically counters both the Jewish opponents of his congregation as well as the strict Jewish-Christian element behind the tradition. The Law must now be viewed in light of Jesus' coming as the fulfillment of the Old Testament promise of the age of salvation.

C. The Least of These Commandments: Matt 5:19

Apart from the typically Matthean "Kingdom of Heaven," 5:19 reflects little redactional modification. Some have suggested that the evangelist inserted "to teach" as indicative of the role of the disciple (cf. 28:20 and 13:52). But the additional verb has little consequence for the meaning of the saying, since the contrast lies in one's behavior regarding the details of the Law. Matthew's own qualification of 5:19 comes from the addition of 5:20 (see Note on *for* in 5:20).

1. If the tradition behind 5:18 stood in tension with Jesus' ministry in general and 5:21–48 in particular, 5:19 stands even more so. This saying takes up where the tradition behind 5:18 left off. Whereas 5:18 asserted principally that the Law in its entirety would last until heaven and earth passed away, 5:19, by relating one's rank in the Kingdom directly to one's doing even "the least of the commandments," specifies that one must therefore keep the commandments without exception. Taken literally, this view of the binding character of all the Law's legal demands conflicts with Jesus' ministry (e.g., Sabbath conflicts) and teaching (e.g., 5:21–48; Mark 10:2–11) and the practice of the early church as seen in Acts and Paul's writings. It seems, therefore, that 5:19 most likely had its origin in a strict Jewish-Christian setting that shaped the pre-Matthean tradition of 5:17–18.

This conclusion finds further support in the focus of 5:19 on the question of rank rather than entrance into the Kingdom. The setting of 5:17–19 antedates the questions of the Gentile mission and reflects a Jewish-Christianity in which the issue was the extent of the Law's validity rather than its necessity for salvation. The larger question of circumcision and the keeping of the Law emerged when the Gentile mission raised not only dietary questions (Acts 10) but the basic question of salvation apart from the Law (Acts 15 and Galatians). In other words, the "legalism" of 5:19 was more ethical than soteriological. Such tradition as 5:17–19 could only have been "practiced" within a rigorous Jewish-Christian sector of the Church that sought to keep the entire Law. Such a group may have brought this tradition with them to the Matthean community after the fall of Jerusalem.

Together with 5:17–18, 5:19 presented a strong case for the continued validity of the whole Law. Matt 5:18 declared that the smallest detail of the Law would remain in force until the end of time; 5:19 spelled out the ramifications of the previous verses in terms of one's behavior and rank in the Kingdom. We have seen how Matthew handled the tradition in 5:17–18; what did he do with 5:19?

2. Perhaps the most significant element in Matthew's redaction is not that he made no major modifications to the tradition itself, as he did in 5:17, 18, but that he included the saying at all. This observation becomes all the more surprising when, as will be seen in the Antitheses below, the evangelist not only set the Antitheses in the immediate context of 5:19 but even formulated three of them, the three that most set Jesus' teaching against that of Moses (5:31–32; 38–42; 43–48). As with 5:18,

so with 5:19, the presence of the tradition reflects Matthew's faithfulness in preserving his tradition even when he qualified it by drastically altering it.

Matthew does indeed qualify 5:19 but by adding 5:20 and the following Antitheses of 5:21–48. Whereas the tradition focused on keeping "the least of the Law's commandments," Matthew stressed the "greater righteousness" necessary for entering the Kingdom. Ultimately the question of keeping the Law's legal demands becomes moot, since a "righteousness" that comes through the keeping of the Law is inadequate for entering the Kingdom (e.g., the "righteousness" of the scribes and Pharisees of 5:20 and 19:18–20). Matthew points to the eschatological dimension in Jesus' ministry that sets the "greater righteousness" demanded by God apart from that which keeps the Law (5:20). Yet the "greater righteousness" also includes doing the "will of the Father," the "words" of Jesus (7:21, 24; 5:21–48), and begins with discipleship (19:20–22; 11:28–30). Qualified by the demands of 5:20 and 5:21–48 and read in terms of Jesus' coming in 5:17–18, 5:19 must therefore refer to the Law now as seen in light of the ministry of Jesus (e.g., 5:21–48; 7:12; 11:28–30; 15:3–4, 19–20; 19:7–9, 18–20; 22:36–40; 28:20).

By modifying the tradition in 5:17–18 in terms of Jesus' coming (5:17) and the coming to pass of all things (5:18), Matthew cuts across an ethical legalism incompatible with the gospel of the Kingdom. To be a disciple of Jesus cuts one free from the obligation to the Law as a sum of commandments and prohibitions for life in this age (5:18). By maintaining 5:19 modified by the following verses, Matthew addresses the other extreme that would set one "free," without ethical restraints—the so-called antinomian tendency. Jesus' coming to effect the fulfillment of God's promise for the age of salvation brings not only a new relationship between God and his people but a concomitant demand for corresponding conduct. This relationship reflects itself in conduct toward others (5:21–48) as well as toward God (6:1–18) and is known as the "greater righteousness."

D. The Greater Righteousness: Matt 5:20

Matt 5:20 serves as the hub for 5:17–19 and 5:21–48. By adding this saying and connecting it with "for," the evangelist qualifies 5:19 in terms of the prior question of entrance into rather than rank within the Kingdom (see Notes on 5:20). The righteousness required in 5:20 stands in contrast to that of the scribes and Pharisees, whose righteousness consisted of keeping the details of the Law, not unlike the demand underlying 5:19. At the same time, this "greater righteousness" of 5:20 looks forward to Jesus' demands of 5:21–48. Indeed, 5:20 and 5:48 introduce and conclude this section with a similar demand (see Note on 5:48). Therefore, 5:20 is pivotal to Matthew's understanding of Jesus' coming and its implications for the Law.

Matt 5:19, as noted above, stands more or less untouched as found by Matthew in the tradition. By contrast, 5:20 exhibits almost totally Matthean redactional traits. The evangelist's familiar use of the traditional entrance-motif as well as his characteristic use of "righteousness," "exceed," and the negative reference to "the scribes and Pharisees," and "the Kingdom of Heaven," all betray his editorial activity (see Note on 5:20). Nevertheless, the content of 5:20 is very consistent with Jesus' manner of pointing out the inadequacies of the "righteous" of his day. It is plain that Matthew, using traditional motifs, has formulated in his own language one of the major thrusts of Jesus' ministry.

The meaning of 5:20 clearly hinges on the term "righteousness" (see Excursus on 5:6 for full discussion), since "righteousness" in 5:20 sets the verse as the basis ("for") for 5:19 and the heading for 5:21–48. In fact, it is precisely the comparison with the righteousness of the scribes and Pharisees (cf. 5:19) as well as the meaning of the Antitheses that helps to clarify Matthew's usage. Since the unit of 5:17–18 was christologically qualified by Matthew's pointing to Jesus' coming as the fulfillment of the Scriptures (cf. 5:17, 18) and since Matthew set the Beatitudes in a similar framework by aligning Jesus' ministry with Isaiah 61, the "greater righteousness" must relate in some way to Jesus' coming. The two Beatitudes concerning righteousness (5:6, 10) give added evidence, as does the association of righteousness and the Kingdom in 6:33. In other words, the "righteousness" integral to the Old Testament promise for the day of salvation, found especially in Isaiah's work, is now a reality through Jesus' ministry that effected God's redemptive activity in history for his people (5:17, 18). Such "righteousness" connotes a new relationship established by God with his people and among his people, a relationship that issues in conduct that is in keeping with the Father's will set forth in Jesus' teaching and ministry.

This righteousness integral to the coming of the Kingdom in Jesus' ministry stands in stark contrast to the righteousness of the scribes and Pharisees, a righteousness achieved through the keeping of the details of the Law's legal demands. Such "righteousness" is inadequate because it blinds one to the presence of God's redemptive activity in Jesus Messiah and thus does not stem from the heart (cf. Jer 31:31; Ezek 36:25–27; Matt 19:7–8, par. Mark 10:5–7). To this extent, the righteousness of the scribes and Pharisees is superficial (6:1–18; 23:23–28); it does not stem from the new relationship between God and his people and among his people. By contrast, the "righteousness that exceeds" reflects a change in one's relationship with God (6:1–18) and with others (5:21–48). It is the "good fruit" produced by the "good tree" (7:16–20); it is doing the will of the Father (7:21–24). Put another way, the "righteousness that exceeds" is the concomitant of true discipleship, the life-changing acknowledgment of Jesus as the one in whom God is at work. This acknowledgment includes the obedient doing of the Father's will that comes to its final expression in Jesus' ministry (cf. 5:20 with 7:21–24; 11:28–30; 19:18–22; 28:19–20).

The righteousness necessary to enter the Kingdom, then, is not simply conduct in keeping with the Father's will as set forth by Jesus. Such an understanding would be but another form expressing the "righteousness of the scribes and Pharisees." Such "righteousness" is important for rank in the Kingdom (cf. 5:19) but is not the entrance requirement of the Kingdom (5:20). Yet the righteousness demanded by 5:20 is not merely a new status given one by God. Such a "Pauline" understanding is fair to neither Paul nor Matthew.

Righteousness for Matthew includes both the elements of status and conduct. It is the gift of God's redemptive activity (6:33) establishing new relationships with his people and granting the basis for the corresponding conduct that gives expression of this new relationship (see Note on 5:6). Effecting this "righteousness that exceeds" is part of the christological emphasis behind Matthew's redaction of 5:17–18. Jesus is indeed the one who fulfills the Scriptures (5:17). In him and his ministry as the Messiah Son of God all things promised by God for the day of salvation come to pass (5:18) and the Law and "Pharisaic" righteousness is superseded (5:21–48). Since the Kingdom future is but the consummation of the Kingdom present (see Note on 5:3), one's righteousness now is the basis for one's entrance into the future Kingdom. Understood in this manner and only in this manner, the "righteousness that exceeds" is the entrance requirement for the Kingdom.

By concluding 5:17–20 in this fashion, Matthew accomplishes two important tasks for his church as well as for the Church of the ages. On the one hand, Matthew sets forth in a positive manner the gospel of the Kingdom, focusing on Jesus' ministry as integrally related to God's promise and purpose in redemptive history. Jesus Messiah Son of God came to declare and effect God's sovereign rule among his people. One must not overlook this redactional christological emphasis in the reworking of the Beatitudes, in the application to the disciples of the eschatological Zion motif in 5:14–16, and especially in the modification of 5:17 and 18. All point to the presence of God's redemptive activity in history through Jesus' ministry. Without doubt this christological focus at the outset becomes the basis for all that follows in the Sermon. One cannot overemphasize its importance for Matthew. The rest of the Sermon develops the rather radical implications that the gospel of the Kingdom has for those who respond, who become the new People of God. Apart from this christological/eschatological basis, that which follows is utopian at best.

On the other hand, Matthew confronts in 5:17–20 distortions that doubtless were found in his own congregation and certainly have been part of the Church's history from the beginning, namely, the tendency toward legalism or toward antinomianism. Failing to take Jesus' ministry seriously enough leads to an incompatible legalism that threatens to replace God's proffered acceptance of us on the basis of his work for us in Jesus' coming. For at least part of Matthew's church, the "legalism" took the form of keeping the details of the Mosaic legislation (5:17–19). For the Church through the ages, different forms of "legalism" have appeared to be just as legitimate and subtle, usually growing out of the contemporary cultural understanding of ethical and religious behavior. Matthew's christological concern (5:17, 18) repeatedly summons the Church to examine her priorities and starting point from the standpoint of the heart of the gospel. The demands of the Kingdom often supersede those of the "Law" and often stand in antithesis to the "Law," regardless of how right and secure the latter appears.

Failing to take Jesus' ministry seriously, including the demand for a life lived in keeping with the gospel, can also result in an antinomian attitude in which "everything goes." Ethical conduct becomes relativized or rationalized into nonexistence. Matthew's stress on righteousness involving both relationships and conduct commensurate with the new age, his emphasis on the necessity of doing the will of the Father as being a concomitant element of righteousness, reminds the Church that the gospel of the Kingdom includes inherently the "ethics of the Kingdom." Matthew warns the Church that righteousness including conduct befitting one's new relationship with God and others is the entrance requirement of the Kingdom.

The nature of this righteousness is set forth in the Sermon materials that follow with reference to others (5:21–48) and to God (6:1–18). It is here that the practical implications of 5:17–20 are drawn out. Yet the christological/eschatological motif implicit in the Beatitudes and explicit in 5:17–20 remains the controlling factor even in the subsequent sections.

VI. THE GREATER RIGHTEOUSNESS
Matthew 5:21–48

Translation

5 ²¹You have heard that God said to the generation of old, "You shall not kill. Whoever kills shall be liable to trial."

²²But I say to you, "Everyone who is angry with his brother shall be liable to the same court proceeding; whoever calls his brother 'idiot' shall be liable to the Sanhedrin for a trial; and whoever says 'fool' shall be liable to the final judgment of hell fire."

²³Therefore, if you are in the process of making your offering and remember that your brother holds a grudge against you, ²⁴leave your offering in front of the altar and go first, be reconciled with your brother, and then after returning make your offering.

²⁵Make friends quickly with your legal adversary while you are still on the road with him, least your adversary turn you over to the judge and the judge turn you over to his assistant and you be put in prison. ²⁶I assure you, you shall in no way get out of there until you have paid the last penny.

²⁷You have heard that God said, "You shall not commit adultery."

²⁸But I say to you, "Every man who looks at another's wife as an object of his lust has already committed adultery with her in his heart."

²⁹If your right eye causes you to sin, remove it and discard it. For it is to your advantage that one of your members be destroyed rather than your whole body be cast into hell. ³⁰If your right hand causes you to sin, cut it off and discard it. For it is to your advantage that one of your members be destroyed rather than your whole body ending in hell.

³¹God said, "Whoever divorces his wife must give her a certificate of divorce."

³²But I say to you, "Every man who divorces his wife, except on the grounds of an incestuous marriage, causes her to commit adultery. And whoever marries a divorced woman, commits adultery."

³³Again, you have heard that God said to the generation of old, "You shall not swear an oath falsely and you shall pay to the Lord your oaths."

³⁴But I say to you, "You shall not swear at all—neither by heaven since it is the throne of God, ³⁵nor by earth since it is his footstool, nor by Jerusalem since it is the city of the Great King, ³⁶and do not swear by your head since you are incapable of making one hair white or black. ³⁷But let your word be an emphatic 'yes' or 'no.' Anything more than these is of the Evil One."

³⁸You have heard that God said, "An eye for an eye and a tooth for a tooth."

³⁹But I say to you, "You shall not seek legal vindication against an evil person. Rather turn the other cheek to the one who slaps your right cheek ⁴⁰and give your coat as well to the one who desires to take you to court to get your body shirt. ⁴¹Go two miles with the one who commandeers you to go one mile. ⁴²Give to the one who begs and do not refuse to lend to the one desiring to borrow from you."

⁴³You have heard that God said, "You shall love your neighbor and hate your enemy."

⁴⁴But I say to you, "Love your enemies and pray for those who persecute you ⁴⁵that you might become sons of your Father in heaven, since he causes the sun to rise for the evil and the good and he causes the rain to fall on the just and the unjust. ⁴⁶For if you love those who love you, what reward will you have? Do not even the tax-collectors do the same thing? ⁴⁷If you greet only your brothers, what more do you do? Do not the Gentiles do the same thing? ⁴⁸Therefore, be whole as your Father in heaven is whole."

Literary Analysis

Matt 5:21–48 contains the so-called "Antitheses" of the Sermon on the Mount. In this section, six times Jesus' demands stand in contrast to a requirement of the Old Testament Law. Each Antithesis consists of a premise introduced by the formula, "You have heard that it was said (to those of old)," and an antithetical response introduced by, "But I say to you." While the full introductory phrase of the premise only occurs in 5:21 and 5:33, forming two divisions of three Antitheses each, and an abbreviated, "it was said," begins 5:31, the meaning of the longer phrase is implicit in all six premises. The contrasting "But I say to you" consistently introduces each counterstatement (5:22, 28, 32, 34, 39, 44).

Yet there is a sense in which the term "antitheses" is more appropriate for some of these constructions than for others. Three of the so-called Antitheses actually lack a direct antithetical character. In these units the counterstatement transcends or surpasses the premise rather than opposing it. In 5:22 anger and name-calling are set in contrast to murder in 5:21; in 5:28 lust is set in contrast to adultery in 5:27; and in 5:34, 37 a prohibition of all oaths stands in contrast to swearing false oaths in 5:33. The other three Antitheses live up to their name by clearly setting aside their corresponding premises: no divorce in 5:32 is set against divorce in 5:31; no retaliation in 5:39a is set against the *lex talionis* of 5:38; and love for one's enemy in 5:44 is set against hatred for same in 5:43. In light of this content difference in the nature of the Antitheses, one cannot explain the meaning or background for the introductory formulas simply in terms of the Jewish parallels isolated from the content of their accompanying statements (see Notes on 5:21, 22).

Form-critically, the nature of the six statements breaks down into the two categories of apodictic commands and legal ordinances. On the one hand, three of the Antitheses have the form of legal ordinances that state the ruling and the consequences in the third person (e.g., 5:21–22; 5:27 together with 5:28; and 5:31–32). On the other hand, three of the Antitheses have the form of an apodictic command or prohibition, an absolute demand without qualifications or consequences, set forth in the second person (e.g., 5:33–34, 37; 5:38–39 and 5:43–44). In other words, whereas the first three are set in the form of legal ordinances that are definable and enforceable, the second three Antitheses simply set forth absolute commandments or prohibitions.

All six Antitheses include more than a simple premise and antithesis with the exception of the third (5:31–32), which comes the closest to being the most straightforward. Each of the other five includes an explication either in the form of parables (5:21–22, cf. 23–26), other concrete illustrations (5:33–34, 37a, cf. 5:34b–36; 5:38–39a, cf. 5:39b–42), a hyperbolic warning of judgment (5:27–28, cf. 29–30) or further expansion by rhetorical questions and imperatives (5:43–44, cf. 45–48). Even the Antitheses themselves vary in construction from the simple (5:27–28; 5:38–39a; 5:43–44) to the complex (5:21–22; 5:31–32; 5:33–37). Consequently, the background and development of 5:21–48 itself is quite complex and requires a detailed examination of each of the six antithetical units (see Comment C).

The complexity of the subject extends to the question of sources behind the material in 5:21–48. On the surface, it appears to exhibit a quiltlike pattern of materials drawn from Mark (5:29–30, par. Mark 9:43–48), Q (5:25–26, par. Luke 12:57–59; 5:32, par. Luke 16:18; 5:39–48, par. Luke 6:27–36), M (5:21–24, 27–28, 33–37), and Matthew's redaction. Indeed, even the antithetical format, which is unique to Matthew, raises the question about the ultimate source of the Antitheses.

A survey of the literature would reveal that it covers the spectrum from the view that all six Antitheses are pre-Matthean to the view that all six are the redactional products of Matthew. In spite of the disparity in viewpoints, three major positions have emerged in the critical discussion. One of the dominant positions, that of Bultmann and others, assigns the three Antitheses without content parallel in Luke (5:21–22, 27–28, 33–37) to pre-Matthean tradition and the three with Lucan parallels (5:31–32, 38–48) to Matthew's redaction, since these Q parallels lack the antithetical form (Bultmann, *Tradition*, 135–36; Kümmel, "Traditionsgedanke," 125, n. 75; Klostermann, *Matthäusevangelium*, 42; Strecker, *Weg*, 38; Eichholz, *Bergpredigt*, 70; Strecker, "Antitheses," 39–47). But two recent trends have emerged in the literature. One of these trends has two variations, with the first more characteristic of Anglo-American scholars, namely, that five of the Antitheses are pre-Matthean, with only the third from Matthew (Branscomb, *Jesus and the Law*, 234; Kilpatrick, *Origins*, 26; Bacon, *Studies*, 181; Manson, *Sayings*, 23–24; Davies, *Setting*, 387–88). In the second variation all six Antitheses have been assigned to the pre-Matthean tradition and most generally to Matthew's community as the original *Sitz im Leben* (Wrege, *Überlieferingsgeschichte*, 66–70; Jeremias, *Theology* 1:251–53; Sand, *Gesetz*, 48; Dietzfelbinger, *Antithesen*, 9). By contrast, a second trend has arisen for different reasons in the work of Suggs, who attributes the format of all six Antitheses to Matthew (Suggs, *Wisdom*, 110–15; *idem*, "Antitheses," 432–44; Lührmann, "Feinde," 413, n. 4; Broer, "Antithesen," 50–63).

The question obviously requires a detailed analysis of the individual units as well as a look at the total complex of 5:21–48. Even after such an analysis, the reconstruction of the history of the tradition sails the perilous course steered by possibilities and probabilities. Since the question is vital to our understanding of the text, we cannot avoid it. We shall return specifically to the question in Comment C and argue for the redactional character of three Antitheses (5:31–32, 38–39a, 43–44) and the traditional character of three (5:21–22, 27–28, 33–37) whose roots extend to Jesus' own ministry.

Notes

5:21. *You have heard that God said to the generation of old.* This same introductory formula occurs again in 5:33 accompanied by *again* (πάλιν) and serves to divide the Antitheses into two groups of three each. Three of the six introductory formulas omit the reference to *the generation of old,* and 5:31 simply has *God has said.* The longer introduction consists of three elements: *You have heard, God has said* and *to the generation of old.*

to the generation of old. The phrase τοῖς ἀρχαίοις occurs only in this context in Matthew and means literally "the ancients." Removed from the context, the phrase offers different alternatives for case and usage as well as for meaning. One might translate τοῖς ἀαρχαίοις as a dative of agency, *by those of old* (Str-B 1:254). Such an understanding would then introduce what the "fathers" rather than God had said. The formula would align the content of the premise with the "tradition of the elders" rather than the Old Testament Law.

While such a usage of the dative is conceivable in classical Greek, the dative never has that particular function with the passive verbs in Matthew and only once in the rest of the New Testament (Luke 23:15, cf. BDF §191). In fact, the dative used with verbs of speaking in the passive voice always expresses the dative of indirect object, the ones addressed (Lohmeyer, *Matthäus,* 117). This use of the indirect object in 5:21, 33 gains further support, and the specific referent behind *those of old* clearly emerges from the context, since what has been said *to those of old* is the Mosaic Law. As will be seen below, the Decalogue itself stands behind the premises of 5:21, 27, 33.

Therefore, *to those of old* refers to the generation at Sinai and all following generations who have received the Law spoken by God through Moses (Lohse, "Aber ich sage euch," 198, n. 34) It also may be legitimate to see a deliberate contrast between the giving of the Law *to the generation of old*—namely, God's people Israel—and Jesus' address *to you* in the present eschatological moment of his audience.

that God said. Literally, ἐρρέθη means *it was said.* Rabbinic parallels suggest that a comparable Hebrew/Aramaic expression connotes technically "it has been taught as tradition" (Str-B 1:253–54; Barth, "Understanding," 93–94). Whereas this reading is possible, it suffers on two counts. First, it conflicts with the use of the dative of indirect object accompanying verbs of speaking in the passive voice, if one should take the phrase to refer to what had been taught as tradition by those of old. One could avoid that syntactical difficulty by maintaining the indirect object; but then one would be left with the highly questionable phrase "taught as tradition to those of old," a rather awkward way of alluding to the tradition. The second difficulty pertains to the content of the premises. Matt 5:21, 27, 38 directly quote the Old Testament and 5:31 and 33 have close material parallels drawn from specific Old Testament passages. Only 5:43b lacks a direct Old Testament reference (see Note on 5:43). To suggest, as Barth, that the "Torah was thus received as a part of the tradition and in its traditional meaning" ("Understanding," 93–94; cf. Kümmel, "Traditionsgedanke," 125) ignores the fact that Jesus elsewhere explicitly differentiated between the Law and its "traditional meaning" (cf. 15:3, par. Mark 7:5). Furthermore, while tradition might be confused with Torah by some, the Torah could hardly be confused with the tradition (cf. the Sadducees and Essenes). The one was written; the other was oral.

The translation, *God has said,* reflects another semitechnical practice in Judaism. First, Bacher has noted that the passive *n'mr (it was said)* corresponding to ἐρρέθη was the "most frequently used formula for citing Scripture passages" (Bacher, *Terminologie,* 6). Second, by using the passive voice to refer to the Scriptures as God's word, the force of the passive is to circumlocute the name of God (Dalman, *Jesus,* 66, and Schlatter, *Matthäus,* 165). This meaning not only syntactically concurs with the use of the aorist passive but it fits with the dative τοῖς ἀρχαίοις and the Old Testament content of the premises that follow. Furthermore, ἐρρέθη is the pivotal element in the introductory formula; at least it was seen as such by its earliest readers, since it alone remains in 5:31 to begin the reference to the Law regarding divorce in Deut 24:1. By contrasting *You have heard* with *But I say* to you, one not only misplaces the focus of the formula but also misses the force of the contrast between ἐρρέθη = *God said* and λέγω = *I say,* a contrast that is startling, to say the least. Read in this manner, the introductory formulas could hardly be a preface for differing interpretations of the Law in the manner commonly found in the rabbinic discussions (see Note 5:22).

You have heard. The aorist ἠκούσατε could also have a technical rabbinic usage behind it. On the one hand, there is evidence that *you have heard* connotes the traditional character of what follows. Therefore, one might accurately translate the phrase, *You have heard [received] as tradition* (Str-B 1:253; Klostermann, *Matthäusevangelium,* 42; Dalman, *Jesus,* 65–66; Kümmel, "Traditionsgedanke," 125; Barth, "Understanding," 93). On the other hand, Jewish scholars in particular have long noted a slightly different connotation drawn from rabbinic parallels. In similar contexts of contrasting viewpoints, the *You have heard* means *You have understood,* implying that there is more than one "understanding" and that what follows corrects the former (Schechter, "Rabbinic Parallels," 427–28; Montefiore, *Synoptic Gospels* 2:56, and esp. Daube, *Rabbinic Judaism,* 55–58, followed by Davies, *Setting,* 101–2).

Although both usages of *You have heard* can indeed be attested in rabbinic literature, neither is appropriate to the context of the Antitheses. In the first instance one would have the questionable introduction, *You have heard [received] as tradition what God said to those of old.* Such a phrase would only be intelligible if one posits that what follows in the premise was tradition and that the intent of the formula was to ascribe the origin of the tradition to God. As already noted, the content of the premises is hardly to be described as tradition. In the event that one chose to read ἐρρέθη to mean *It was taught as tradition* (see above), one would then have the highly redundant *You have received as tradition that it was taught as tradition* (Lohmeyer, *Matthäus,* 117). In another variation, others have taken ἠκούσατε more technically referring to tradition but have suggested that ἐρρέθη refers to God's having spoken to those of old: *You have received as tradition that God said to Moses and those of old . . .* (Howard, *Das Ego Jesu,* 192–93; Lohse, "Aber ich sage euch," 198). By avoiding one problem, this solution creates a larger one, since God's giving of the Law was hardly a matter of "tradition," in view of its explicit biblical basis.

In the second instance, should one with Daube take *You have heard* to refer to a different "understanding" of the Law, one would need to overlook the content of both the premises and the Antitheses in which the content of the former is not a misunderstanding of the Law but is the Law itself (Lohse, "Aber ich sage euch," 192) that is not only transcended at times but at other times set aside by the latter. The content of the Antitheses gives no indication of a "correction" aimed at the premises. Yet the most serious weakness in this position is the misplaced emphasis that it places on ἠκούσατε *(You have heard)* when the real focal point of the formula is on *(God said)* as seen in the abbreviated formula in 5:31 and the contrast between ἐρρέθη and λέγω in the Antitheses. By placing too much weight on the ἠκούσατε/λέγω parallels in the rabbinic sources, Daube and others have gone astray in their understanding of the nature of the Antitheses.

Thus, instead of a technical usage behind *You have heard* paralleled in rabbinic sources, we have simply an expression of the common Jewish experience of "hearing" the Law read and expounded in the synagogue and Temple worship context (Lohmeyer, *Matthäus,* 117; Manson, *Sayings,* 153). In other words, the introductory formula reminds the audience that they *have heard*—the normal way of learning—*that God said to those of old* regarding his will, the Law. The formula pointedly draws attention to God's act of giving Israel the Law that was orally read and expounded in the worship settings. It is precisely this Law and not its traditional interpretation or understanding that is countered in the Antitheses.

You shall not kill. This premise contains two statements. The first is the straightforward apodictic prohibition, οὐ φονεύσεις; the second is a legal ordinance, ὅς δ᾽ ἂν φονεύσῃ. The first is clearly a direct quotation of the sixth commandment prohibiting murder (Exod 20:13; Deut 5:17). The future (οὐ φονεύσεις) corresponds directly to the LXX and represents the Old Testament use of the future indicative rather than the imperative in the apodictic commands and prohibitions (BDF §362).

Whoever kills shall be. The second part of the premise appears in the form of a legal ordinance composed of a conditional relative sentence beginning with *whoever* (ὅς δ᾽ ἂν) in the protasis that states the crime, followed by a future apodosis that states the penalty (cf. 5:19, 22bc). Such a form occurs on occasion in the LXX, e.g., Exod 21:17, although the most common form has ἐάν and the aorist subjunctive in the protasis followed by the future indicative in the apodosis. Since this part of the premise (5:21b) lacks a direct Old Testament parallel, some have ascribed the clause to scribal tradition against which Jesus sets his own "understanding" of the Law (e.g., McNeile, *Matthew,* 60–61; Dalman, *Jesus,* 67–68; Stonehouse, *Witness of Matthew,* 201; Barth, "Understanding," 89, 94). Yet the content of 5:21b is no different from the Old Testament teaching of the legal consequences of breaking the sixth commandment (Exod 21:12; Lev 24:17; Num 35:16–17). Together with 5:21a, 5:21b expresses the understanding of the Law common in Jesus' day, namely, as being an integral combination of apodictic commands and legal ordinances. One measured one's relationship to the apodictic or moral demands in terms of the legal ordinances. In other words, one had met the Law's demands to the extent that one had not been convicted of breaking the Law.

liable to trial. This phrase includes two rather difficult problems: the background and usage of *liable* (ἔνοχος), and the meaning of *trial* (κρίσει). Both terms are repeated in 5:22, which conditions their usage in 5:21b at least in terms of the understanding of them by the community behind 5:22, if not by Jesus himself. The first concept, ἔνοχος, occurs rarely in the Old Testament LXX and the New Testament (cf. Mark 3:29, 1 Cor 11:27, James 2:10, Gen 26:11, which all have the genitive; Jos 2:19, which has a dative construction for the absolute usage of ἔνοχος in Lev 20:9; Num 35:27). Its common usage with the dative in extrabiblical Greek occurs primarily in a legal context (LSJ, *s.v.*).

Berger, in an analysis of ἔνοχος in the New Testament and later Greek inscriptions, has assigned the New Testament usages to a Hellenistic context ("Sätzen," 36–38). One serious weakness in Berger's viewpoint, however, is his failure to take into account the Aramaic or "Palestinian" character of 5:22 with ῥακά, μωρέ, *Sanhedrin,* and *lake of fire* (Jeremias, *TDNT,* 6:976). Dalman and Jeremias, by contrast, have predicated an underlying Aramaic ᵓ*thyb* behind the ἔνοχος constructions (Dalman, *Jesus* 67; Jeremias, *TDNT* 6:975). In either case, ἔνοχος/ᵓ*thyb* never has a specific court of justice, as such, for its object. Each refers either specifically to the actual sentence imposed or more generally to the court proceeding or a *trial.* Yet 5:22bc appears to offer conflicting evidence, since *Sanhedrin* is indeed a court, and when the sentence is stated explicitly in 5:22c it appears without the dative case. In other words, ἔνοχος in 5:21–22 does not seem to fit the rules.

A partial solution to the dilemma lies with the other problem in 5:21b, namely, the meaning of κρίσει. The common translation of κρίσει in 5:21b, 22a has been either *local court* (under the influence of *Sanhedrin* in 5:22b) or, apart from the influence of *Sanhedrin* when taken as secondary, *the judgment,* containing a pregnant reference to the final judgment. We can eliminate the first option of *local court,* since ἔνοχος never takes "court" as its object, and *local court* is lexically foreign to the classical and Koiné use of κρίσις as well as its Hebrew/Aramaic *(dyn/dynᵓ)* counterparts *(LSJ, Bauer, BDB s.v.).* We can also eliminate the second option, *the last judgment,* since the context offers little support for this alternative.

Both the Greek κρίσις and the Hebrew/Aramaic *dyn/dynᵓ* mean either a judicial sentence or a court-proceeding, a trial. The first alternative fits 5:21b grammatically and contextually. *Liable* with the dative often expresses the dative of penalty in Greek (as does its Hebrew/Aramaic form *hyb/ʾthyb*). The sentence of the death penalty was prescribed by the Law for murderers (Exod 21:12; Lev 24:17; Num 35:16–17). Therefore, one could accurately translate 5:21b as a legal ordinance: "Whoever kills shall be liable to the sentence of the death penalty."

Unfortunately, such an understanding of 5:21b fails to do justice to 5:22bc. Even if 5:22b and c are secondary expansions of 5:21b and 22a (e.g., Wrege, *Überlieferungsgeschichte,* 59–61), they represent the earliest interpretation of 5:21b, 22a. This leaves us, therefore, with a second alternative. Since ἔνοχος can refer more generally to a *trial* or court proceeding (Xenophon, *Memor,* 1.2.64, "liable to a criminal proceeding"; Taylor, *Mark,* 243, calls it a "dative of tribunal") and since *trial* is also a meaning for κρίσις and *dyn/dynʾ,* one could also accurately translate 5:21b, "Whoever kills shall be liable to a trial." This would mean that *Sanhedrin* in 5:22b implied a court proceeding before that judicial body (see Note on 5:22). Furthermore, the "dative of tribunal" is missing in 5:22c where *hell-fire* is the sentence rather than the process of a *court proceeding* at the final judgment. The penalty in all three instances is ultimately the same, namely, death. The difference lies in the various levels of *court proceedings* (see Note on 5:22).

Therefore, if 5:21 means *Whoever kills will be liable to a trial,* the premise expresses both the Old Testament Law against murder and one's perceived relationship to that Law. The legal ordinance of 5:21 based on the Old Testament was not representative of scribal tradition or casuistry, nor was it an explicit statement of the Old Testament sentence of the death penalty itself (cf. Exod 21:12). Rather, the legal ordinance expressed the contemporary judicial or casuistic understanding of the apodictic Law forbidding murder. One's ultimate standing before the Law was determined by the judgment of a court proceeding in general and God's sentence at the last judgment based on the Law in particular. Jesus' antithetical statement counters the Old Testament Law and the contemporary legal perspective of his day in 5:22 and 28.

5:22. *But I say to you.* This formula (ἐγὼ δὲ λέγω ὑμῖν) consistently introduces all six Antitheses (5:22, 28, 32, 34, 39, 44) and occurs in this form only within the Antitheses (Lohse, "Ich aber sage euch," 190, n. 3). Like the introductory formula of the premises, this expression has apparent parallels in rabbinic literature, and Lohse has concluded that this introduction rather than that of the premises offers the closest parallel between the Antitheses and Jewish sources ("Ich aber sage euch," 193–96; cf. also Smith, *Parallels,* 27–30). In the rabbinic sources *w*'*ny* '*mr* introduced a predominant viewpoint or the opinion of a learned man (Lohse, "Ich aber sage euch," 193–95; Dalman, *Jesus,* 68–69; Smith, *Parallels,* 27–30). To the extent that *But I say to you* sets Jesus' demand in contrast to the common understanding of the Law, this formula does indeed parallel that of Judaism. In fact, the content of several of the antithetical statements also has parallels in Judaism, including Qumran (Str-B 1, *ad loc;* Braun, *Radikalismus* 2:5, n. 2; 85, n. 2). Consequently, in view of the apparent parallels in Judaism between the introductory formulas and even much of the content, one might conclude that the Antitheses of the Sermon do indeed have their parallels in Judaism. They, in fact, do not.

In order to grasp the full significance of the Antitheses, one cannot isolate either the premises or the Antitheses in search of parallels. Rather, one must respect their format and view both elements together in terms of the form and content of each antithesis. Neither Qumran nor the rabbis set their teaching over against that spoken to those of old, the generation at Sinai. Qumran and the rabbis could and did set different understandings and interpretations of the Law's meaning against each other, with each buttressed by use of supporting Scripture and/or tradition. But one never finds a parallel in Judaism for authoritatively setting a demand against the immutable Law. As will be seen by what follows, Jesus' demand does not merely "hedge" one from transgressing the Law (rabbis) nor does it offer the true meaning of the Law (Qumran). Rather, Jesus' demand actually transcends that of the Law. It is this uniqueness that sets Jesus' demand apart and speaks most forcibly for the authenticity of the antithetical format (Lohse, "Ich aber sage euch," 198–99). Furthermore, one must not shy away from the startling antithesis between *God has said to those of old/But I say to you,* since here lies not only the key to the Antitheses but to Jesus' ministry.

Everyone who is angry with his brother shall be liable to a court proceeding. A number of manuscripts have the variant reading εἰκῇ *(without cause)* which is clearly a secondary addition in an attempt to qualify the sweeping character of the statement. The antithetical statement of 5:22 consists of three elements: a statement on anger (5:22a) followed by two on the use of invectives (5:22b, c). The balance of New Testament scholarship leans toward the composite character of this antithesis (e.g., Bultmann, *Tradition,* 134; Manson, *Sayings,* 155; Moule, "Angry Word,"

12; Strecker, "Antithesen," 40; and recent commentaries). But the question of integrity is intertwined with the primary question of the intent of the Antithesis (Guelich, "Mt 5²¹," 49–52).

The first element on anger was without doubt a part of the original Antithesis regardless of the original *Sitz im Leben.* This statement set in the form of a legal ordinance has the common traditional form of πᾶς plus the participle in the condition, or protasis (cf. 5:28, 32a; 7:21), and the future indicative in the result, or apodosis. The presence of the two forms, the conditional relative construction in 5:21b, 22bc and πᾶς plus the participle in 5:22a (cf. 5:32a, b), attests to their interchangeable character, at least in Matthew, if not in the tradition. In content, Jesus counters in a casuistic manner the Old Testament Law's prohibition of murder by himself prohibiting anger. Literally, whereas God has said to those of old that whoever killed would be liable to a trial (implying judgment), Jesus said to his hearers that everyone who was angry with his brother would be liable to the same court proceeding (implying judgment). God through the Law had outlawed murder; Jesus outlawed anger.

And whoever calls his brother "idiot" shall be liable to the Sanhedrin for trial. The second statement moves from an inner attitude *(anger)* to external conduct (name-calling) and has caused many to take this and the following element (5:22c) as secondary halachic applications of 5:22a. But a quick look at the other antitheses demonstrates that the attitude/conduct or intent/action dichotomy is simplistic and untenable (cf. 5:28 with 5:32; 5:34, 37; 5:39; 5:44—all of which involve actions).

The word *idiot* (ῥακά) occurs nowhere else in extant Greek literature. It is generally understood (Jeremias, *TDNT* 6:973–74; Guelich, "Mt 5²²," 39–40) as the Greek transliteration of the Aramaic invective ryq'/κενός ("emptyhead"). Its presence in the Greek text as a transliteration betrays the Aramaic background of the verse and is most likely explained by the lack of an equivalent Greek invective for ryq' (κενός is not used as an invective in Greek) or perhaps by the presence of the Aramaic loanword in a bilingual setting (Guelich, "Mt 5²²," 42).

Sanhedrin, the highest governing body of the Jews in Jerusalem that also occasionally functioned as a judicial court, has been the most common translation of συνεδρίῳ. But recently some have sought a different background and meaning for συνεδρίῳ in terms of an early church disciplinary rite (*Übergaberitus,* "expulsion rite") similar to that found in Qumran (Weise, "Mt 5²¹," 117; Wrege, *Überlieferungsgeschichte,* 59–60; Dietzfelbinger, *Bergpredigt,* 16–17; Hill, *Matthew,* 121). This view is based on Ignatius' use of συνέδριον exclusively for the apostles and the presbyters, the Syriac and Didascalia's use of συναγωγή = ἐκκλησία in 5:22b, as well as the practice of a disciplinary "council of the community" in Qumran. Accordingly, 5:22 reflects the disciplinary action of the Church in dismissing or excommunicating one who calls a brother *idiot*.

There are at least three critical weaknesses in this view. First, even if the Syrian Church understood 5:22 in this way (not at all certain; see Guelich, "Mt 5²²," 43), there is no evidence that such was inherent in 5:22b rather than the Syrian Church's attempt to put 5:22b into practice according to Matt 18:18. Second, there is no trace of a parallel between the "council of the community" in Qumran and the church discipline of the New Testament. Either the church as a whole (18:18; 1 Cor 5:1–2) or a particular apostle (16:19; 1 Tim 1:20) is attested with no mention elsewhere of a "council." Third, and most importantly, this suggestion ignores the New Testament usage of συνέδριον. Occurring twenty-two times, with only two exceptions (10:17, par. Mark 13:9) it always refers to the *Sanhedrin* in Jerusalem. Even in 10:17, par. Mark 13:9, συνέδρια refers to local courts of the Diaspora (Luke omits this reference; cf. 21:12 and 12:11). Therefore, rather than reflecting the practice of church discipline, 5:22b stands parallel with 5:22a expressing the judicial consequences of calling a brother an *idiot*.

In view of the use of ἔνοχος in 5:21b, 22abc and of κρίσει in 5:21b, 22a, ἔνοχος τῷ συνεδρίῳ connotes *liable to the Sanhedrin for a trial* (implying judgment). The penalty would be no greater than that for murder or anger, since the death penalty was not the exclusive prerogative of the Sanhedrin among Jewish judiciaries (Str-B 1:257) and was implied in 5:21b, 22a. But set in parallel with 5:22a, συνεδρίῳ of 5:22b forms a step parallelism with κρίσει in 5:22a. Whereas συνεδρίῳ represented trial by the "supreme court," κρίσει would then represent trial by the "local courts" of the land. We have then an escalation in tribunals.

Whoever says "fool" shall be liable to the final judgment of hell-fire. This final element of the antithesis is clearly parallel to the previous one, the difference being in the offense and the consequence. One of the major difficulties has come in attempting to distinguish between ῥακά *(idiot)* and μωρέ *(fool)*. Three alternatives have emerged in the literature: (a) μωρέ was originally a translation of ῥακά (Köhler, "Mt 5²²," 91–94; cf. Moule, "Angry Word," 12–13); (b) μωρέ is the Greek translation of a Semitic invective (e.g., šty², Dalman, *Jesus,* 76–77; Schlatter, *Matthäus,* 169; Jeremias, *TDNT* 6:975); and (c) μωρέ is the transliteration of the Aramaic mrṣ (Zahn, *Matthäus,* 229, n. 96) or the Hebrew mrh (Allen, *Matthew,* 49; Manson, *Sayings,* 155–56). Since μορός never translates *ryq⁾* ("empty") elsewhere and since the Hebrew *mrh* ("rebel," cf. Num 20:10) takes its invective usage in rabbinic literature from the Greek loan word *mrṣ/mr⁾* (μορός) rather than vice versa (see Guelich, "Mt 5²²," 40–42), the Greek loan words *mrṣ* or its Aramaic synonym *šty⁾* most likely stood behind 5:22c. Furthermore, *mrṣ* only appears in rabbinic texts in word plays on the Hebrew *mrh* ("rebel") with *šty⁾*, a common invective, usually appearing in the immediate context as the explanatory synonym (Guelich, "Mt 5²²," 42). Therefore, one can safely conclude that μωρέ *(fool)* is the Greek translation of the Aramaic *šty⁾* *(fool)* and parallel to the Aramaic *ryq⁾* *(idiot)* behind 5:22bc. More important, however, neither ῥακά *(idiot)* nor μωρέ *(fool)* represents a significant difference in meaning or culpability (con. Strecker, "Antithesen," 48, n. 29). All attempts at distinguishing between the two terms used in name-calling has proven futile in light of the evidence. There simply is little or no difference in nuance between "You idiot!" and "You fool!"

The *lake of fire* (γέενναν τοῦ πυρός), graphically referring to the ravine south of Jerusalem where the city's garbage was burned, was a familiar Jewish symbol for the final judgment (Str-B, 4/2:1029–30). This sentence (εἰς τὴν γέενναν) represents the final judgment by God himself and sets the climax on the ascending tribunals in 5:22abc.

Apart from the absurdity of prosecuting such charges in human society, one can hardly ignore the disproportionate relationship between the offense and the consequence. It helps little to ascribe the verse's difficulties to a radicalizing halachic tendency in the community, since there is little evidence of such rigor in the New Testament Church (cf. *v.l.* εἰκῇ = "without cause" that points in the opposite direction). Rather, the pointed "absurdity" of the antithetical statement offers the clue to its ultimate intention. Not only does Jesus counter the Law's prohibition of murder with his own prohibition of anger and the use of invectives, but by using the casuistic perspective of the Law in his day and setting his demand in the form of a legal ordinance, Jesus demonstrates simultaneously the total inadequacy of measuring one's status before God and others by means of the Law or a court proceeding.

Instead of intending that one should understand his demand casuistically or legalistically (one should not forget that Jesus himself, according to 23:17, 19, called the Pharisees "fools"), Jesus was seeking to penetrate the casuistry of his day by the deliberate use of irony in 5:22 (Zahn, *Mätthaus,* 229) to get at the underlying relationship between individuals. Whereas the Law had prohibited murder arising from broken relationships which presupposed the reality of evil, Jesus ultimately demands a relationship between individuals in which there is no alienation. This is underscored by the use of *brother,* a designation for the new relationship established by Jesus among his followers, and the theme of the following parables (5:23–24, 25–26) that add the earliest interpretation of this antithesis.

5:23. Two parables follow to illustrate paranetically the content of the antithesis. The first of the two focuses on making an offering to God while being at odds with a *brother.* The theme of reconciliation between individuals concurs with the thrust of the antithesis and *brother* (ἀδελφός) offers the verbal connection. The cultic setting obviously points to a time when sacrifices were being offered in the Temple by those following Jesus. Indeed, the material parallel with the antithesis, the material on prayer in Mark 11:25, par. Matt 6:14–15, and the forgiveness request of the Lord's Prayer (Matt 6:12, par. Luke 11:4) suggest that the roots of the material extend to Jesus' ministry. Although *Did* 14:2 has the parable in a different context, the absence of characteristic Matthean terms may suggest that the evangelist found the parable already combined with the Antithesis in the tradition (Strecker, "Antithesen," 49; cf. 5:25–26 below).

Therefore, if you are in the process of offering your sacrifice. Therefore (οὖν) makes the logical connection between the Antithesis and the parable. *In the process of offering your sacrifice* expresses three Greek concepts which when translated literally sound repetitious: "If you should be offering your sacrifice (gift) on the altar." Jeremias has noted that although προσφέρω can mean "to bring," its usage in the context of sacrifices in the New Testament connotes "to offer" (Matt 8:4, par. Mark 1:44, Luke 5:14; Acts 7:42; 21:26; Heb 5:1, 3; 8:3, 4; cf. Matt 5:25), and its usage with ἐπὶ τὸ θυσιαστήριον has similar parallels in the Mishnah, all of which mean "to offer" rather than "to bring" (Jeremias, "Gabe," 103–4). The nature of the sacrifice (δῶρόν = "gift") is not mentioned, but since it involved an individual rather than the community, it could have been either an animal or a meal offering. The latter generally accompanied animal offerings or were brought more commonly by women (Jeremias, "Gabe," 103). Consequently, an animal sacrifice is the more likely.

and you remember. Obviously, the sacrifice did not involve the problem between the two individuals.

your brother holds a grudge against you. The use of *brother* (ἀδελφός) verbally ties the parable with the use of *brother* in 5:22ab and designates the special relationship shared, on the one hand, among Jews in Judaism, and, on the other hand, among Jesus' followers (cf. Mark 3:31–35, par. Matt 12:46–50; cf. 23:8). The question of who is at fault is rather ambiguous in the phrase, *something against you* (τι κατὰ σοῦ). Although one might attribute the ill feelings to the one offering the sacrifice and thus the need for reconciliation prior to making the offering (cf. Mark 11:25), the imperatives that follow suggest that the *brother* holds the grudge.

5:24. The staccatolike imperatives prescribe the necessary actions.

Go. First be reconciled. Interrupting one's offering and leaving the sacrifice at the altar, one is to seek reconciliation. The adverb *first* could go with either imperative, but the contrast between *first* (πρῶτον) and *then* (τότε) sets off the heart of the parable. Reconciliation must precede sacrifice. The aorist passive imperative *be reconciled* (διαλλάγηθι) has a more or less active force of seeking to placate one's adversary (Buchsel, *TDNT* 1:253–54; Marshall, " 'Reconciliation,' " 118–19). This verb does not occur elsewhere in the New Testament, but 1 Sam 29:4 offers a parallel usage where David was to take the initiative *to be reconciled* with an angry Saul.

Then continue your sacrifice. This rendering reflects the force of the present imperative. In one sense this parable offers no advance over the teaching of the rabbis who saw reconciliation to be necessary for sacrifice (Str-B 1:287–88; Montefiore, *Rabbinic Literature,* 40–41). Sacrifice was no substitute for reconciliation, nor was it a device with any virtue in itself for bringing reconciliation about. Such a specific understanding would be to read the parable in isolation from the Antithesis, which spoke of anger and name-calling rather than of the conditions necessary for valid sacrifice. Within the context of the first Antithesis, the parable, by focusing primarily on the need for reconciliation and restored relationships, has gone beneath the surface of the specifics in 5:22 and interpreted the demand for what it was, namely, a demand for restored relationships in which anger and invectives have no place. Both the Antithesis and the parable focus primarily on relationships between individuals.

5:25. The action of the one offering sacrifice to gain reconciliation from his offending brother in 5:23–24 may have been the catalyst for the introduction of the second parable into this context. Yet the judicial setting of the Antithesis (5:21b, 22) and this parable may also have played a role. Matt 5:25–26, par. Luke 12:57–59, involves one's need to make amends with a legal adversary before going to court and has three scenes:

(a) 5:25a, on the way to court, (b) 5:25b, at court, and (c) 5:26, prison. Luke 12:57–59 offers a traditional parallel that agrees almost verbally in the final scene (5:25, par. Luke 12:59) and materially in the middle scene, but that differs considerably in the opening scene (5:25a, cf. Luke 12:58a). This difference may well reflect the difference in setting, with 5:25 being materially related to the basic theme of 5:23–24.

Make peace with your legal adversary. Make peace (ἴσθι εὐνοῶν) literally means "be well disposed" and occurs only here in the New Testament. By contrast, Luke 12:58 opens with the temporal clause and follows with the exhortation: "Make an effort to settle" (δὸς ἐργασίαν ἀπηλλάχθαι). It is of interest to note that the root of Luke's "to settle" (ἀπηλλάχθαι) is the same as the imperative *be reconciled* (διαλλάγηθι) in 5:24. Such a "reminiscence" might have offered another point of contact between the two parables. Yet the admonition of Luke becomes *be well disposed* (ἴσθι εὐνοῶν) in Matthew, with the emphasis more on the nature of the relationship than the act of reconciliation. Furthermore, if Matthew was responsible for this change, the opening command might also pick up the note of the Beatitude to the *peacemakers* (5:9) that precedes and the demand to love one's enemy that follows. *Your adversary* (ἀντιδίκῳ) can mean either accuser or defendant in a court proceeding, but the context (cf. 5:26) determines the former. To go beyond the obvious in search of an allegorical meaning behind *adversary* outruns the evidence of the text.

quickly while on the way. In contrast to Luke's "When (ὡς) you go . . . , make an effort on the way . . . ," Matthew's initial scene opens with a sense of urgency created by the addition of *quickly* (ταχύ; cf. 28:7, 8) and *while* (ἕως ὅτου). *On the way,* common to both Matthew and Luke, sets the opening scene in Matthew, whereas Luke has opened by referring to the trip to the magistrate. The difference hardly reflects a "spiritualizing" tendency in Matthew (Strecker, *Weg,* 159), since *the way* in Matthew is traditional as seen by *the way* in Luke. The defendant and the accuser are simply *on the way* to court. The trial setting is also reminiscent of the judicial tone in the antithesis (5:22).

hand you over. The scene now shifts to the court. Matthew has the legal term (παραδῷ) for "turning one in," whereas Luke 12:58 has the more aggressive "to drag away by force" (κατασύρῃ; cf. Acts 8:3; 17:6, where Luke has σύρω).

to the judge, the judge to his assistant. Both Matthew and Luke note the judge (κριτής) as the one before whom the case opens. Luke 12:58 uses the more technical Roman judicial language (cf. ἄρχοντα = "magistrate" in 12:58a) with "bailiff" (πράκτορι) rather than the less precise *assistant* (ὑπηρέτῃ) of Matthew. Similar Greek usage of *assistant* in a court setting (Bauer, *s.v.*) makes an allegorical usage (Strecker, *Weg,* 159, n. 6) in Matthew quite untenable. Luke, rather than Matthew, has most likely made the modification in any case.

you be put into prison. Luke has the stylistically smoother active construction in contrast to Matthew's somewhat more awkward future passive (βληϑήσῃ).

5:26. This verse has the traditional structure (cf. Note on 5:18) of (a) introductory formula, (b) subjunctive of strong denial, and (c) temporal clause. But this particular saying has the distinction of being the only one of its kind in the Gospels without an explicit eschatological orientation. It is possible that the eschatological moment existed in the original setting of the parable in Jesus' ministry. Jeremias has placed the parable among the "crisis-parables" in which the eschatological moment for decision confronts one now in Jesus' ministry (*Parables,* 43–44, 96) and thus the tone of finality in 5:26, par. Luke 12:59.

I assure you. Luke does not have the introductory ἀμήν. Whereas many assign it to Matthew's account, evidence of Luke's having avoided it elsewhere (e.g., 9:27, cf. Mark 9:1; 21:3, cf. Mark 12:43; 22:34, cf. Mark 14:30) and the absence of concrete evidence that Matthew ever added simply ἀμήν to a formula should caution one about hasty conclusions. Indeed, the ἀμήν-formula in this case could also suggest that the parable's roots extend to Jesus' ministry (see Note on 5:18).

the last penny. Whereas Matthew has κοδράντην, a Latin loan word *(quadrans),* worth less than a penny, Luke has λεπτόν (cf. also Luke 21:2), a small copper coin, worth about half a κοδράντην. The point of each account is obvious, namely, full payment will be required.

To read this parable as primarily admonishing one to avoid a trial—assuming of course that one is guilty and would lose the verdict (cf. 5:25b, 26)—by settling out of court is to remove the parable from its present context in Matthew (cf. Luke 12:57). Such counsel is hardly more than common sense with frequent parallels in everyday life. The primary point of contact lies in the paranetic focus on relationships. It could not be expressed more clearly than by the initial *be well disposed* or *make friends* with your *adversary* and do so *quickly.* As in the previous parable, the responsibility in 5:25–26 falls to the individual not only to have a right relationship with one's brother from one's own standpoint (so 5:22abc) but also to take the initiative to restore broken relationships as seen from the perspective of one's adversary. Together the Antithesis and the parables of 5:21–26 consistently set forth Jesus' demand for behavior commensurate with whole relationships rather than the broken relationships that characterize human experience as negatively illustrated in 5:21b–26.

5:27. *You shall not commit adultery.* The second Antithesis, like the first, cites a commandment from the Decalogue, the seventh commandment. By contrast to the first, this Antithesis simply quotes the apodictic commandment of Exod 20:14, LXX, with no ensuing legal ordinance indicating the legal consequences. The penalty for adultery was death for both parties (Lev 20:10; Deut 22:22).

5:28. *Every man who looks at another's wife.* The antithesis of 5:28, however, does have the form of a legal ordiance with πᾶς and the present participle in the protasis and the aorist indicative in the apodosis. By countering the apodictic command of the premise with the legal ordinance of the antithesis, the former is set in the perspective of the latter. In other words, *You shall not commit adultery* becomes *You shall not be guilty of adultery.*

The content of the antithesis involving the *eye* and *heart* has so many parallels in Jewish literature (Str-B 1:299–300; Montefiore, *Rabbinic Literature*, 41–43) that several have denied its basis in Jesus' ministry and attributed it to the Church's drawing on Jewish teaching (e.g., Percy, *Botschaft*, 143–44; Braun, *Radikalismus* 2:5, n. 2). For example, two passages in particular deal with the specifics of 5:28: "Whoever looks at a woman with a lustful intent is the same as one who has lived with her" (*Kalla* 1 in Str-B 1:299), and ". . . one must not commit adultery . . . not even with the eyes and not in one's heart . . . ," based on Num 15:39 (*Mek der Shimon* iii in Str-B 1:299). These parallels, despite their date from the third and fourth centuries, doubtless reflect the Jew's concern to keep the Law regarding adultery.

The meaning of *to look* at a woman is qualified by what follows in the antithesis. The Greek noun *woman* (γυνή) can refer to a married or single woman. Since adultery in Jesus' day and in the Old Testament always involved a married woman, *woman* (γυνή) more precisely should read *another's wife.*

as the object of his lust. The phrase πρὸς τὸ ἐπιθυμῆσαι αὐτήν means literally "in order to desire having her (sexually)." The same very *to desire to have* (ἐπιθυμέω) appears in the tenth commandment for "to covet" (Exod 20:17, LXX, and Deut 5:21, LXX). "To lust" in English connotes accurately the sensual overtones but lacks the accompanying thought of possession inherent in ἐπιθυμῆσαι.

has already committed adultery personally with her in his heart. In his heart has an apparent parallel in rabbinic sources as noted above. Yet a slight but crucial difference emerges between *heart* as used in the Jewish sources and in 5:28. In the former, *heart* is best translated as "mind" or "intent" (Moore, *Judaism* 2:268). In 5:28 Jesus' statement refers to the *heart* not as one's "mind" or basic "intent," which is expressed by the explicit *to desire her* (ἐπιθυμῆσαι), but as the central focus of the individual's inner life, the center of one's very person (Behm, *TDNT* 3:611–13). Whereas the rabbis warn against committing adultery by means of a lustful look, "the eye," as well as in their "mind," i.e., the "heart" as the center of one's desires and actions, Jesus categorically declares that the lustful desire to have another's wife incriminates one's very person (ἐν τῇ καρδίᾳ).

The force of the aorist indicative *has already committed adultery* (ἐμοίχευσεν) in the apodosis instead of the more common future indicative construction (cf. 5:21b, 22) supports the judicial character of the statement. By setting the antithesis of 5:28 counter to the apodictic *You shall not commit adultery* of 5:27 in the form of a legal ordinance, Jesus not only countered the Old Testament Law with its definition of adultery as an overt physical act between a man and a married woman but he also countered the casuistic, judicial way in which one perceived the Law. In other words, the Law prohibited adultery, i.e., a sexual affair with another's wife, but one was not "guilty" of adultery as long as one had kept that Law. But Jesus set his demand in contrast to this understanding by declaring that having a lustful desire for another's wife made one personally guilty of adultery.

In 5:28 as in 5:22, Jesus' demand is set in the legal format familiar to his day in order to demonstrate the inadequacy of that perspective and to convey his demand for attitudes and conduct reflecting totally new relationships between individuals. Therefore, the demand completely transcends the Law's demands. Jesus' demand implies a vastly different starting point.

5:29. In 5:29–30 there occur two of the most startling sentences in the Gospels. Focusing first on the eye and then on the hand as instruments through which evil attacks the individual, 5:29–30 graphically prescribe drastic measures to avoid total annihilation. Matt 18:8–9, par. Mark

9:43–47, offers another parallel, with the foot being the third member. While Matthew clearly follows Mark in 18:8–9, the background of 5:29–30 remains far from certain. Kilpatrick, in a thorough analysis (*Origins,* 18–19), has assigned the material to Matthew's reworking of Mark 9:43–47. Others have concluded that it betrays a doublette taken from Matthew's special source (e.g., Klostermann, *Matthäusevangelium,* 45; Dupont, *Béatitudes* 1:121–23). Still others have argued that this expansion of the Antithesis took place prior to the evangelist's use of the material (e.g., Manson, *Sayings,* 157; Lohmeyer, *Matthäus,* 101; Wrege, *Überlieferungsgeschichte,* 65–66; Hübner, *Gesetz,* 68–71; Strecker, "Antithesen," 52).

The only clue, and admittedly a small one, is a possible pattern in the other Antitheses. It is quite probable that 5:23–24 was a pre-Matthean application of 5:22, and 5:33–37 contains, as will be seen, pre-Matthean expansions of the third "traditional" Antithesis. Then 5:29–30 would be the pre-Matthean extension of the second Antithesis. The evangelist, by contrast, would himself have added 5:25–26 from Q to the first, the divorce Antithesis of 5:31–32 from Q to the second, and an additional element (5:37b) to the third. Thus both tradition and redaction were at work in the further development of the respective Antitheses. Ultimately, the question contributes little to the basic question about the meaning of the passage.

If your right eye causes you to sin. The unit opens with a reference to the *eye* in contrast to 18:8–9, par. Mark 9:43, that begins with the *hand.* The inversion may well stem from the accommodation of this traditional unit to the Antithesis with its focus on *everyone who looks* . . . (βλέπων). The *right* (δεξιός) *eye* (cf. *right* hand in 5:30) places the accent on one's better side. The *right* side represents one's more valuable and honorable side (cf. 20:23, par. Mark 10:40; 22:44, par. Mark 12:36; 25:33–34; 26:64, par. Mark 14:62; for Old Testament references, cf. Lev 14:14–17, 25:28; 1 Sam 11:2; Zech 11:17, etc.). Matthew may have added it here and in 5:30 (cf. 5:39 against Luke 6:29). If so, he does not follow through with this theme in 18:8–9. The *right eye* or *hand,* of course, implies nothing about the vulnerability of the left. It merely heightens the hyperbole of the action involved.

The verb translated *cause to sin* has the more innocuous meaning of *to cause one to stumble* (σκανδαλίζω). But it most generally has a moral connotation including culpability. The older translation "to offend" is much too mild in this context.

take it out and discard it.   The action prescribed here and later regarding amputating one's hand could hardly be more pointed. It clearly intends to convey drastic measures.

it is to your advantage.   This construction (συμφέρει . . . ἵνα . . . μή) and the clause that follows differs from 18:8–9, par. Mark 9:43, 45, which uses *it is better to . . . than to . . .* (καλόν . . . ἤ). The present clause is stylistically better Greek, with Mark 9:43, 45 the closer to the Semitic style (Black, *Aramaic,* 117). Matthew changes Mark's construction in 18:6, cf. Mark 9:42, in another context with σκανδαλίζω and has the phrase again in 19:10 without parallel.

in order that one of your members be destroyed.   The conjunction ἵνα controls two purpose clauses, the one positive, the other negative. *One of your bodily members* stands in contrast to *your whole body* that follows. *Be destroyed* (ἀπόληται) as well as *be thrown* (βληθῇ) both connote judgment (e.g., 10:28; 22:7; and in the Sermon 5:13, 25; 7:19).

lest your whole body be cast into hell.   The phrase *whole body* (ὅλον tù s⁸ma) plays a dual role. First, it stands in contrast to the one member that is destroyed as referring to one's physical body (cf. 18:8–9). Second, it bears the additional meaning of one's person (Schweizer, *TDNT* 7:1058, 1064–66). So that the prescription calls for one to destroy the debilitating member in lieu of one's person being thrown into *hell* (γέενναν, see Note on 5:22).

5:30.   A few manuscripts (D, 59, 238, 243, Syrˢ, boh, sah) omit this section, most likely because of the more remote focus on the *hand* in the context. The construction of this verse follows closely that of 5:29, with the exception of *hand* and the corresponding verb *to cut off* and the final verb *to enter* rather than *to be thrown,* a change found as well in the tradition of 18:8–9, par. Mark.

One can hardly take this gruesome extreme literally for obvious reasons. What purpose does it then serve in this context? At face value, it appears to continue the direction of the Antithesis. If the lustful look condemns one, then one must take the necessary measures by dealing with the "instrument" of sin. Such consistency, although absurd, should not be ignored. It helps little to interpret these verses as teaching us to what extent we must ultimately go to avoid death without attempting to define these extremes. Perhaps the very absurdity of the hyperbole again expresses the nature of the unit's commentary on 5:27–28. Self-mutilation does not help one to avoid sin any more than outlawing lust as adultery. The issue goes much deeper. It involves our very person which our thoughts and actions represent. Therefore, this hyperbolic section under-scores the totally new starting point of Jesus' demand in the Antithesis, the need for completely new relationships between individuals in which evil no longer is the dominant given.

5:31. *God said.* The one-word introductory formula (ἐρρέθη) stands in bold contrast to the longer introduction of 5:21, 33. Consequently, some have suggested that the third Antithesis was intended originally to be but a "subsection" of the second (e.g., Filson, "Patterns," 229; Grund-mann, *Matthäus,* 158–59). To be sure, 5:31–32 appears in close proximity to the second Antithesis and is related through the common verb *to commit adultery* (μοιχεύω, 5:27–28, 32). But numerous reasons support the full status of the Antithesis. First, the common verb μοιχεύω denotes a secondary theme to that of divorce in 5:31–32 and simply betrays Matthew's redactional tendency to use catch-words as a device for bring-ing together different traditional units (e.g., Filson, "Patterns," 229; Bornkamm, "End-expectation," 30, 54). Second, 5:29–30 sufficiently sep-arates 5:31–32 from 5:27–28 to make it a dangling Antithesis at best. Third, the full introductory formula of the next Antithesis (5:33) appar-ently divides the six Antitheses into two groups of three each. Finally, the abbreviated formula most likely reflects another Matthean stylistic trait of inconsistently using formulas and patterns. A similar modification appears in the series of Woes in Matthew 23. Having doubtless been at least in part responsible for the seven (eight) introductory Woe-formu-las, the evangelist suddenly disrupts with "Woe to you, blind leaders" (23:16) the other "Woe to you, scribes and Pharisees, hypocrites" (23:13, [14], 15, 22, 25, 27, 29). The shortened formula, therefore, represents the absolute minimum of the introduction but simultaneously reflects the evangelist's understanding of the heart of the traditional formula (cf. 15:4, "*God* said" with Mark 7:10, "*Moses* said").

Whoever divorces his wife. This premise, in contrast to the previous two (5:21, 27), has no exact verbal parallel in the Old Testament. It represents a summary of Deut 24:1 expressed in the form of a legal ordinance beginning with the conditional relative clause (5:21b, 22bc, 32b). The same Deuteronomic passage occurs in the controversy narrative on divorce in 19:3–9, par. Mark 10:2–9. In that context the evangelist has moved the divorce logion in the Marcan tradition from the teaching scene with the disciples "in a house" (Mark 10:10) into the controversy scene itself (Mark 10:2–9, cf. Matt 19:3–9). By so doing Matthew has set the divorce saying (19:9, par. Mark 10:11) in sharper contrast to

Moses' command (ἐνετείλατο, 19:7–8) which has also been rearranged (19:7, cf. Mark 10:4) in order to express the antithesis between Jesus' *But I say to you* (λέγω δὲ ὑμῖν) and Moses. Therefore, one may conclude that Matthew has repeated the same process here in the context of the Antitheses by introducing Deut 24:1 in the legal format of the premises. Both style (catch-word redaction and broken formulas) and content (Jesus against Moses) support the thesis that the third Antithesis is a Matthean redactional product.

let him give her a bill of divorce. Let him give (δότω) and *bill of divorce* (ἀποστάσιον) pick up the language of Deut 24:1. *Bill of divorce* (ἀποστάσιον, cf. βιβλίον ἀποστασίου in 19:7, par. Mark 10:4, verbatim with Deut 24:1, LXX) has a technical meaning in Greek expressing the "relinquishing of property" (Bauer, *s.v.*). The connotation of the wife's status is hardly coincidental.

Deut 24:1 in context dealt with the question of remarriage and in particular with the question of a wife remarrying her former husband (24:4). The passage assumed the right to divorce as a given without question and also the wife's right to remarry. In fact, the latter is clearly the point of receiving the bill of divorce that frees her to remarry (24:2). The legal focus based on these assumptions (24:1–3) comes in 24:4 when the wife twice divorced is forbidden to remarry her first husband. That Deut 24:1 later became the Old Testament basis for divorce is seen both in the New Testament pericope of Mark 10:2–9, par. Matt 19:3–9, and in the numerous references to it in the rabbinic sources (Str-B 1:313–14). Furthermore, the issue in 5:31–32 and 19:3–9, par. Mark, is primarily the question of divorce rather than remarriage (see Note on 5:32).

The procedure for granting a divorce was almost as straightforward as the premise suggests. Rabbinic sources give closer details that included the necessity of two witnesses to the writing of the bill, the content of the bill, the manner of delivering it, and the possibility of withdrawing it (Str-B 1:303). The rabbinic teaching concurs with the Old Testament materials that the right to divorce belonged exclusively to the man, although a woman could under certain conditions require her husband to divorce her (Str-B 1:318–19; Montefiore, *Rabbinic Literature*, 47; Moore, *Judaism* 2:125). Consequently, most commentators view the additional element of Mark 10:12 (dropped by Matt 19:9) to be a consistent extension of the divorce logion in terms of Roman law (e.g., Taylor, *Mark*, 420–21; Lane, *Mark*, 358; Pesch, *Markusevangelium* 2:126). Since the Law obviously permitted divorce, the primary question in rabbinic debates (there is no evidence that the possibility as such was ever questioned) centered on the grounds for divorce (see Note on 5:32, cf. 19:3, which differs from Mark 10:2).

The premise, therefore, represents the legal understanding of Deut 24:1. It expressed the Old Testament legal basis and conditions for granting a divorce. Jesus' demand of 5:32 is set in antithesis to this premise.

5:32. *Every man who divorces his wife.* The Gospels contain four divorce sayings in two different forms: the one in Mark 9:11–12, par. Matt 19:9; the other in Luke 16:18 and Matt 5:32. Whereas Mark 9:11, par. Matt 19:9, uses the conditional relative construction and speaks only of him who divorces his wife, Matt 5:32 and Luke 16:18 use the πᾶς plus the participle construction and have a parallel element regarding one who marries a divorcee. Consequently, most scholars have assigned Matt 9:9 to the Marcan and 5:32 to the Q tradition. Both the Marcan and Q sayings circulated early in the tradition as isolated sayings (Greeven, "Ehe," 376). Mark 10:10–12 now occurs in the larger context of the related controversy narrative between Jesus and the Pharisees (19:2–9) through the redactional setting of "in a house" (cf. 9:33); Luke has three formerly isolated sayings grouped together (16:16, par. Matt 11:13; 16:17, par. Matt 5:18; 16:18, par. Matt 5:32; Hübner, *Gesetz,* 15–30; cf. Schürmann, *Untersuchungen,* 132–36).

causes her to commit adultery. Matthew has the aorist passive of the verb μοιχεύω with a causative meaning (Bauer, *s.v.*), but the verb *to commit adultery* varies in 5:32 and in the tradition. Matt 5:32b, Mark 10:11, and Matt 19:9 use the related verb μοιχάομαι, while Luke 16:18a, b agrees with the μοιχεύω of Matt 5:32a. The meaning of the two Greek verbs is synonymous. But the difference in their usage may well offer a significant clue to the traditional background of the divorce saying. The more common of the two verbs is μοιχεύω, with ten occurrences in the New Testament, of which all but one (Rev 2:22) refer to the use of μοιχεύω in the seventh commandment (Exod 20:14, LXX). Furthermore, μοιχεύω generally translated the Hebrew n'p ("to commit adultery") in the LXX. By contrast, μοιχάομαι appears a total of only seven times in Jeremiah and Ezekiel (e.g., Jer 3:8; 5:7; Ezek 16:32; 23:37).

The presence of the more common μοιχεύω in Luke 16:18 comes as little surprise, but the presence in 5:32 of both μοιχεύω and μοιχάομαι seems a bit out of the ordinary. The Koine tradition has the more consistent μοιχάομαι in 5:32a, doubtless a secondary influence of 5:32b, but the divorce saying may well have been formulated in Greek with μοιχάομαι in both 5:32a and b. Luke 16:18a, b and Matt 5:32a would then reflect later modifications by the respective evangelists. Luke's exchange of the verbs concurs with his stylistic desire to use the more common Greek verb. Matthew's modification might well have stemmed from his redactional desire to align the divorce saying with the context of 5:27–28 through the catch-word μοιχεύω. The influence of 5:27–28 might well extend to the choice of the aorist infinitive, since Luke and Mark have the present (see also 5:32b). Such a development would explain the different verbs in 5:32a and 5:32b, in 5:32b and Luke 16:18b, and between Luke 16:18 and Mark 10:11, par. Matt 19:9. To suggest that 5:32b reflects the influence of Mark 10:11, par. Matt 19:9, overlooks the absence of such verbal "influence" on the different expressions of the "except-clause" in 5:32a and 19:9.

Although 5:32a agrees with Luke 16:18a in the verb μοιχεύω, each uses the verb quite differently. Whereas Matt 5:32 has *causes her to commit adultery* (ποιεῖ αὐτὴν μοιχευθῆναι), Luke 16:18 (also Matt 19:9, par. Mark 10:11) has *he commits adultery* (μοιχεύει) on the basis of his *marrying another* (γαμῶν ἑτέραν). In other words, Luke 16:18 and Mark 10:11, par. Matt 19:9, state that a man who divorces his wife and marries another woman commits adultery. By contrast, 5:32a states that a man who divorces his wife bears the responsibility for her committing adultery, *he causes her to commit adultery.* Her adultery consists in her remarrying (cf. Deut 24:1–3 and the contents of the divorce bill, ". . . in order that you may marry when you desire . . . ," Str-B 1:311).

Matt 5:32a reflects a more "Jewish" perspective. Luke 16:18a and Mark 10:11, par. Matt 19:9, offer a form of the saying that would be nonsensical according to the Jewish understanding based on the Old Testament law of marriage and adultery (cf. Str-B 1:303–5). First, in a polygamous society, as found in the Old Testament and, though not frequently practiced, still a possibility in first-century Judaism (Moore, *Judaism* 2:122), a man could marry other women, whether or not he was divorced, without committing adultery. Second, in Jewish law the woman was never the object of adultery, only the husband (Manson, *Sayings,* 136). A man might have more than one wife, concubines, and even relations with a prostitute without his or her partner's being guilty of adultery. But a wife who has sexual relations with any other man, married or single, committed adultery against her husband. Consequently, Luke 16:18 and Mark 10:11, par. Matt 19:9, give a legal status to the wife and presuppose a monogamous situation. Matt 5:32a, on the contrary, concurs with the wife's legal status in Judaism by making the wife instead of the husband the one explicitly guilty of adultery, although the assignment of the responsibility for her action to the husband was foreign to Jewish law. In other words, Matt 5:32a reflects the legal status of the wife's role in Judaism; Luke 16:18a and Mark 10:11, par. Matt 19:9, refer to a status foreign to the Old Testament and Judaism.

But where did the change in focus enter the tradition? A number of exegetes have ascribed priority to either Mark (e.g., Delling, "Mk X.11," 270–74; Schaller, "Ehescheidung," 231–38) or Luke (e.g., Bultmann, *Tradition*, 132; Baltensweiler, *Ehe*, 60–61; Schnackenburg, *Ehe*, 11). Others have ascribed priority to 5:32a (e.g., Greeven, "Ehe," 382–83; Hübner, *Gesetz*, 44–47; Schulz, *Spruchquelle*, 116–17) primarily on the basis of the more compatible *Sitz im Leben* of 5:32a with a Jewish setting and Luke 16:18a, Mark 10:11 with a later Hellenistic setting in the Church. In either case, the fact that Matthew does not repeat the change of the tradition in 19:9, par. Mark 10:11, strongly suggests his finding the content of 5:32a in his tradition. One must then view 5:32 as a transmissional variation of Luke 16:18. Left with the choice of the priority of 5:32a or the double tradition of Luke 16:18a and Mark 10:11, one might look again at the primary evidence.

Without doubt the strongest argument for the priority of Luke 16:18a and Mark 10:11 is the witness of the two separate traditions of Mark and Q. Those holding the second alternative must generally beg the question by suggesting that Luke has modified his tradition in view of Mark (cf. Hübner, *Gesetz*, 44; Schulz, *Spruchquelle*, 117). The strongest argument on the other side for the priority of 5:32a is the compatibility of 5:32a with a Jewish setting and Luke 16:18a and Mark 10:11 with a Hellenistic setting. This view, however, leaves some unanswered questions. First, assuming that Luke was influenced by Mark's tradition, one needs to ask why. The content of 5:32a would hardly have been more foreign to a Hellenistic audience than to a Jewish audience. Second, if one uses the criterion of *Sitz im Leben*, does not the alternative of the priority of 5:32a offer the argument of dissimilarity in reverse? Neither of the sayings would have a suitable *Sitz im Leben*, if pressed. Matt 5:32a was hardly "Jewish"; Luke 16:18a and Mark 10:11 were hardly "Hellenistic." The question is one of degree of difference, since Jesus' statement alters both the Jewish and Hellenistic understanding of the role of the husband and wife in marriage as well as marriage itself. Finally, using the same concern for the appropriateness of the saying for its context, might not such a legally "foreign" saying have been adapted by a community moving towards a more "traditional" understanding of the Law? Evidence for just that kind of movement also appears in the "except-clause" of 5:32a (see below). Furthermore, "Jewish" interpretation of the Q material used by Matthew has already been noted in 5:18, cf. Luke 16:17, and in the following commentary of 5:19.

The evidence of priority would seem to tilt towards Luke 16:18a and Mark 10:11, par. Matt 19:9. These sayings concur that Jesus' teaching involved marriage/divorce as well as the role of women. Jesus not only set marriage in a new perspective, but he also viewed women in the same perspective as men. Matt 5:32a, however, by aligning the concept of the wife's adultery with the Law's teaching, removes the startling change in the woman's legal status and sets a different tone for the saying. The modification clouds the fact that Jesus' statement transcending the Law addressed the basic area of husband-wife, man-woman relationships by means of the divorce question of his day. Consequently, the interpretation of 5:32a in terms of the Law most likely reflects the Jewish-Christian concern for strictly following the Law, a concern found in the underlying tradition of 5:17–19 and in 23:2–3.

Yet even 5:32a, set within the context of the Law, maintains the "new" element of Jesus' teaching on divorce in comparison with Judaism. First, although 5:32a does not redefine adultery as do Luke 16:18a and Mark 10:11, it does maintain the focus on the man's role in the act of adultery by assigning to him the responsibility for the wife's adultery. This assignment of guilt to the husband does not contradict or set aside the Law, but it goes beyond the Law in its extension of responsibility to the husband. This view stands without parallel in Judaism and doubtless stems from the modification of Jesus' even stronger statement as it now stands in Luke 16:18 and Mark 10:11. Second, since adultery in Judaism meant extramarital sexual relations by a married woman and if her remarriage is considered to be adultery, the implications are clear. The bill of divorce does not dissolve the first marriage. In other words, the original couple are still married in spite of a "legal" bill of divorce.

Ultimately, this statement, left unqualified, totally eliminates the possibility of divorce, a conclusion that concurs exactly with Jesus' summary of the divine intention for marriage in the controversy narrative of Mark 10:9, par. Matt 19:6: "What God has joined together let no man put asunder." By setting his demand for marriage in the familiar context of divorce proceedings, Jesus does not merely "radicalize" or extend the Law's demand; he actually sets aside the letter of the Law in Deut 24:1 that explicitly, though vaguely, gives a ground for divorce (ʿrwt dbr/ἀσχῆμον πρᾶγμα). Consequently, a strict Jewish-Christian community desiring to align Jesus' teaching with the Law would have had every reason to add a qualifying "except-clause" to such an unqualified demand. Such a conclusion would gain support, if the "except-clause" maintained a "radicalization" of the Law but avoided setting the Law aside.

except for adultery. Matt 5:32 also differs from Luke 16:18 by the inclusion of the so-called "except-clause." The same holds true for 19:9, cf. Mark 10:11. Furthermore, Paul's reference to Jesus' teaching in 1 Cor 7:10–11 speaks of no such exception. Consequently, Matthew's divorce sayings that apparently give a ground for divorce stand alone against the tradition as found in Luke, Mark, or Paul. But even Matthew's own phrases lack verbal consistency. Although both give πορνεία as the ground, 5:32a has παρεκτὸς λόγου πορνείας *(except the matter of* πορνεία*)* while 19:9 has the simpler μὴ ἐπὶ πορνείᾳ (literally, *not for* πορνεία*).* The preposition *except (*παρεκτός*)* only occurs here in Matthew and the μή of 19:9 most likely represents the abbreviated (εἰ) μή and accompanies the subjunctive construction of *whoever divorces (*ἀπολύσῃ*).* Some scholars, primarily Catholic, have taken παρεκτός *(besides)* and μή *(not even)* in an *inclusive* sense that suggests the prohibition even includes πορνεία (e.g., Staab, "Unauflöslichkeit," 435–52). But παρεκτός has the exclusive meaning in Acts 26:29, its only other usage in the New Testament, and Greek distinguishes between μή ("not") and μηδέ ("not even") as clearly as does English (Delling, "Mark X.11," 269).

The question of the legitimacy of divorce itself never arose as a major question in the rabbinic literature. Not only was divorce integral to the Jewish understanding of the Law based on Deut 24:1, the Law allowing divorce on occasion was even referred to as God's special gift to Israel by interpreting Mal 2:(14)16, "I hate divorce," to pertain only to the Gentiles to whom God has not given the Law (Str-B 1:312). The primary issue in these discussions revolved around the meaning of the rather obscure ʿrwt dbr ("some indecency") of Deut 24:1.

The rabbinic viewpoints tended to break down into two schools of thought. On the one side, Rabbi Hillel and followers took the phrase in a broader sense concentrating on the *dbr* (a "matter," a "case"). This larger umbrella covered such diverse actions as speaking disrespectfully of one's husband and of burning his food (Str-B 1:314–17). On the other side, Rabbi Shammai and followers took the phrase in a narrower sense, concentrating on the term ʿrwh ("indecency"). This smaller umbrella covered primarily behavior contrary to the moral customs of that day, including not only adultery but appearing on the street with hair down, uncovered arms, or a slit in the sides of a skirt (Str-B 1:315). Doubtless the most literal view of all was expressed by Rabbi Akiba, who, focusing on the earlier phrase of Deut 24:1, ". . . finds no favor in his eyes . . . ," allowed divorce when a wife lost her attraction to her husband (Str-B 1:315–16).

Unfortunately, Matthew's "except-clause" leaves us with almost as much ambiguity. The Greek πορνεία offers various possibilities of meaning, most of which have been applied at one time or another to the verses in question. Yet three basic alternatives appear to have emerged from the vast literature on the subject: "fornication," "incestuous marriages," and "adultery." In order to determine which of these alternatives best fits the tradition and context, we must look in closer detail at the possible background and meanings of the "except-clause."

Excursus: The "Except-Clauses" in Matt 5:32; 19:9

1. As to the suggested meaning of πορνεία, the least common of the three alternatives seeks to take πορνεία in its narrower Greek meaning of "fornication," namely, premarital sexual relations by one's wife (e.g., Fridrichsen, *"fornicationis,"* 54–58). Joseph's intended "divorce" of Mary after discovering her pregnancy (1:19) offers a related example of such circumstances. The weakness of this alternative surfaces at two points. First, πορνεία by New Testament times was in no way limited to denoting "fornication," since it had broadened to connote "every kind of unlawful intercourse," including adultery (Bauer, *s.v.;* Schulz-Hauck, *TDNT* 6:590–95). Second, to suggest that the "except-clause" permits divorce in the case of discovering one's wife's premarital fornication but does not include extramarital adultery appears arbitrary, to say the least.

The second alternative referring to "incestuous marriages" has a much stronger case. Its strength lies in the apparent parallel usage of πορνεία in the New Testament within the Apostle's Decree of Acts 15:28–29, cf. 21:25. Baltensweiler offers one of the more developed treatments of this view and sets πορνεία in the context of Jewish proselyte practices ("Ehebruchsklausel," 340–56, and *idem, Ehe,* 87–102; see *Ehe,* 98–99, n. 65, for further literature, especially among Catholic scholars). His argument runs as follows. The underlying basis of the Apostles' Decree stems from Leviticus 17–18 (Waitz, "Aposteldekrets," 227–63; Haenchen, *Acts,* 449, and Conzelmann, *Apostelgeschichte,* 85; Bruce, *Acts,* 300). Consequently, in Acts 15:29 πορνεία corresponds to and connotes the catalogue of forbidden marriages listed in Lev 16:18. Such interfamily marriages, unacceptable in Judaism and Roman law, were legal in the Hellenistic world (see *Ehe,* 95–96, for examples).

The actual context for Matthew's "except-clause" lies in the special problem created by the Jewish view of proselytes coming from this Hellenistic background. Since the Jews viewed the proselyte at the time of conversion as having begun life all over again and having severed all contact and relationships with the past, the rabbis had to struggle with the implications for "family" marriages, entered before and after conversion (Str-B 3:353–58; Fitzmeyer, "Divorce," 218–21, supplements this later material by tracing this issue to the Qumran community in the so-called "Missionary Document" of CD 4:12b–5:14a that addressed first century B.C. and A.D. conditions in Palestinian Judaism). Since the rabbis frequently made "concessions" regarding Lev 18:6–18 consistent with their view of the proselytes having begun a new life, the "except-clauses" of Matthew were directed at such concessions by the rabbis. Therefore, using the term πορνεία in the sense of the Apostles' Decree, Matthew was more rigorously applying Lev 18:6–18 to the "proselyte" question of incestuous marriages as they applied to the Gentile mission in contrast to the rabbis' "laxity" in this matter (*Ehe,* 98–100). The "except-clause" intensified the divorce sayings by *requiring* divorce on the grounds of πορνεία according to Lev 18:6–18, cf. Act 15:29, rather than softened their demand by means of an escape clause (Baltensweiler, *Ehe,* 101).

Lexically, this alternative has solid support regardless of whether Lev 18:6–18 furnishes the background for πορνεία in Acts 15:29 since Paul refers to an incestuous relationships as πορνεία in 1 Cor 5:1. But πορνεία has much too broad a range of usages in the New Testament times to permit the singling out of one particular meaning without strong contextual support. Contextually, Baltensweiler's thesis offers a possible but somewhat remote option. First, granting that Acts 15:29 refers to Lev 18:6–18, Paul in 1 Cor 5:1 makes no allusion to it and registers near incredulity that the Church should arrogantly tolerate more than even that by the "Gentiles." By contrast, he deals at great length with the problem of "food offered to idols" (1 Cor 8, cf. Acts 15:29). Thus one has reason to question the extensiveness of the incestuous marriages as a problem for the Church.

Second, since πορνεία also connoted adultery, how could a community or an evangelist pursuing a more rigorous intensification of the Old Testament Law than found among the rabbis require divorce in the case of the forbidden marriages of Lev 18:6–18 but exclude adultery that brought the death penalty in the Old Testament (Lev 20:10; Deut 22:22) and required divorce according to the rabbis (Moore, *Judaism* 2:125; Str-B 2:520–21; Hauck-Schulz, *TDNT* 6:592; Schaller, "Ehescheidung," 234, n. 28). One could avoid this latter problem by simply assigning the clause to Matthew as stemming from his desire to synthesize the ruling of the Apostles' Decree with Jesus' absolute demand. The motivation would then have resulted from the practical dilemma of the mission situation (cf. Acts 15:27–29) rather than from a rigorous intensification of the Law. Consequently, the validity of the second alternative of πορνεία = "incestuous marriages" depends ultimately on the original setting of the clause, a question to which we shall return below.

The third alternative offers by far the most common interpretation of πορνεία in the "except-clauses," namely, πορνεία = "adultery." Lexically, the broadening of πορνεία by New Testament times to include the more specific μοιχεία= "adultery" has been amply attested (Bauer, *s.v.;* Hauck-Schulz, *TDNT* 6:587–89). But one must not forget that πορνεία also remained broader in scope than μοιχεία, as seen above. Consequently, the specific meaning of "fornication," "adultery," "incest," or any other unlawful sexual immorality must come from the context.

Two sometimes converging trains of thought have led to the meaning of *adultery* in 5:32a, 19:9. The first begins with the premise that Matthew intended to align Jesus' teaching with that of the rabbinic debates of the times (19:3, cf. Mark 10:2). Drawing on the teachings of Shammai's school, the evangelist chose supposedly the conservative grounds of *adultery* as one of the ways in which Deut 24:1 had been interpreted (e.g., Allen, *Matthew,* 20; Klostermann, *Matthäusevangelium,* 46; Dupont, *Béatitudes* 1:120, n.1; Montefiore, *Synoptic Gospels* 1:229, 2:66; cf. Hübner, *Gesetz,* 52–53). The second explanation begins with the inherent implications of the sayings themselves. Since the sayings assume a marriage relationship and since by definition a married woman would be guilty of πορνεία = "adultery" rather than πορνεία = "fornication," πορνεία = "adultery" is the only logical alternative (Hübner, *Gesetz,* 47, n. 31). Furthermore, the wife's *adultery,* understood as the breaking of the marriage bonds, leaves the husband little choice but to recognize what is in fact the case, namely, the broken marriage (e.g., Hauck-Schulz, *TDNT* 6:592; Schaller, "Ehescheidung," 234–36; Hübner, *Gesetz,* 53–61; similarly, Lohmeyer, *Matthäus,* 282). In other words, the logic of the situation leads to the conclusion that πορνεία = "adultery" alone best fits the context.

This widely accepted alternative is vulnerable because it makes four crucial assumptions. First, many who hold this view have assumed that Matthew or his community reflects the rabbinic struggles of the day. As Hübner has pointed out (*Gesetz,* 51–54), the "except-clauses" understood as referring to adultery go beyond even the school of Shammai's "immorality" (cf. Greeven, "Ehe," 38). Second, this alternative implicitly assumes that πορνεία offers only the two choices of "fornication" or "adultery" and overlooks the more specific use of πορνεία in Acts 15:29 and 1 Cor 5:1. Third, this alternative assumes that adultery not only breaks the marriage vows but also cancels them. This assumption has little biblical or legal basis in Judaism, since death or divorce rather than adultery itself actually ended the marriage. Divorce was essentially a legal matter in the Law and Judaism. Finally, the internal logic of the sayings leading to the conclusion that adultery rather than divorce cancels a marriage assumes that these divorce sayings were meant as legal ordinances. We shall return to the third and fourth assumptions below.

2. Was the "except-clause" a part of the saying from the beginning, or did Matthew or the pre-Matthean tradition add it? For some, the very question

conflicts in principle with their understanding of the reliability of the Gospel tradition in preserving Jesus' teaching. Thus the differences between 5:32, 19:9, and their parallels in Luke and Mark must be harmonized either by positing two different sayings, both stemming from Jesus, or by viewing Mark and Luke as an abbreviation implying the "except-clauses" of Matthew. Therefore, Matthew's sayings are primary and offer the normative interpretation of the other sayings. Unfortunately, what appears to be a simple solution obscures the obvious, namely, a contradiction rather than an abbreviation is involved. Matthew permits divorce; Mark and Luke do not. Harmonization of the text distorts the meaning of the text. Furthermore, the presence of the clause in 5:32 contrary to Luke 16:18 and in 19:9 contrary to Mark 10:11 as well as the absence of any trace of the clause in 1 Cor 7:10–11 set the three separate traditions of the divorce sayings in Luke, Mark, and Paul against one evangelist, Matthew, who apparently used two of these traditions (Q and Mark). This evidence argues most forcefully for the secondary character of the "except-clauses."

This occurrence of the "except-clause" in both 5:32 and 19:9 in contrast to two traditions has led most scholars to assign the clauses to Matthew's redaction. This view finds further material support for those who see Matthew to be portraying Jesus in terms of the rabbinic debates familiar to a Jewish-Christian community, since the "except-clauses" supposedly correspond to the school of Shammai's views that were opposed by the school of Hillel (e.g., Klostermann, *Matthäusevangelium,* 46; Montefiore, *Synoptic Gospels* 1:225–28, 2:67; Dupont, *Béatitudes* 1:100, n. 1; Hummel, *Auseinandersetzung,* 50–51). By contrast, Baltensweiler (*Ehe,* 87–108) and Hübner (*Gesetz,* 47–54) view the clauses as an intensification of the Law's demand as understood in Judaism. Since a tendency to intensify rather than to relax the Law corresponds to Matthew's desire to depict Jesus as the one who brings the final interpretation of the Law, the "except-clauses" correspond to the evangelist's redactional designs. In either case, source-critical and redaction-critical evidence would point to Matthew's redaction.

In spite of the rather strong case for Matthean redaction, some surds remain. First, one can hardly ignore the differences between the Semitic παρεκτὸς λόγου πορνείας of 5:32 and the straightforward μὴ ἐπὶ πορνείᾳ of 19:9. As already noted in the introductory formulas of the Antitheses, inconsistency does reflect a Matthean trait. But the differences in this case may point in another direction as well. Second, one cannot ignore the obvious, namely, the evangelist's deliberate redactional activity to set Jesus' sayings in antithesis with the Law in 5:32 and 19:9; indeed, in antithesis to Deut 24:1. In 5:31 the evangelist has actually introduced Deut 24:1 with the formula, *God said;* in 19:9 he rearranged Mark's tradition to set Deut 24:1 with its *Moses said* against Jesus' *But I say.* Matthew's unquestionable redaction thus gives no hint of the evangelist's perceiving Jesus' teachings to be opposing those of the rabbis but rather the Old Testament Law itself. To add then a qualifying phrase drawn from Deut 24:1 resulting in the aligning of the content of the antithesis in 5:32 with the premise of 5:31 would certainly be counterproductive of the antithetical format and highly inconsistent. Third, in 19:3 (cf. Mark 10:2 to the contrary) Matthew gives little evidence of his further placing Jesus within the context of the rabbinic debate or of intensifying the Law's demands in an halachic fashion. The insertion of "for just any cause" may simply indicate Matthew's sensitivities to the rabbinic context of the controversy narrative in which Mark's question ("Is it lawful . . . ?") was inappropriate (note the similar stylistic modification of the young ruler's question in terms of Jewish practice in 19:16, cf. Mark 10:17). In other words, such "rabbinic" tendencies may well have been stylistic as the content of the ensuing material would indicate.

The assigning of the "except-clause" to the pre-Matthean tradition accounts for the source-critical evidence and resolves some of the conflicting redaction-critical evidence (e.g., Delling, "Mark X.11," 268–70; Greeven, "Ehe," 380; Wrege, *Überlieferungsgeschichte,* 68; Schaller, "Ehescheidung," 230). First, we noted above that 5:32a betrays a strict Jewish-Christian interest in maintaining Jesus' teaching consistent with that of the Old Testament Law regarding marriage and adultery. The same motivation could have led to the addition of παρεκτὸς λόγου πορνείας which obviously stems from the Hebrew ʿrwt dbr of Deut 24:1 (e.g., McNeile, *Matthew,* 66; Dupont, *Béatitudes* 1:120, n. 1; Hauck-Schulz, *TDNT* 6:591; Wrege, *Überlieferungsgeschichte,* 68–69; Hill, *Matthew,* 124; Schaller, "Ehescheidung," 235). Whereas the evangelist's redactional premise uses Deut 24:1, LXX, the "except-clause" of 5:32a is closer to the Hebrew than the clause in 19:9 or the LXX ἀσχῆμον πρᾶγμα of Deut 24:1. In other words, the return to the Law of Deut 24:1 for the "except-clause" exhibits the same tendency to set 5:32a in terms of the Jewish Law and corresponds with the same tendency to depict Jesus as supporting the Law in 5:18, cf. Luke 16:17. Matt 5:32a, therefore, represents a transmissional variation of Luke 16:18, as does 5:18, cf. Luke 16:17; and the difference can be attributed to a strict Jewish-Christian community who understood Jesus' teaching to affirm the validity of the Law (cf. pre-Matthean tradition behind 5:17–19).

Second, the "except-clause" of 19:9 differing in style and source from 5:32 stems from Matthew's redaction. No longer concerned to preserve the Deuteronomic context, as seen by his using Deut 24:1 in an antithetical function, and characteristically inconsistent in maintaining uniformity, the evangelist adds μὴ ἐπὶ πορνείᾳ drawn from the tradition of 5:32 to suit his own purposes, which are quite different from those of his strict Jewish-Christian tradition (cf. Notes on 5:17–20). Third, Matthew, as in 5:17–19, faithfully preserves the tradition but again, as in 5:17–19, he radically modifies its basic thrust by his redactional modification of it. In this case, by setting

Jesus' saying in clear antithesis to the Law as given by God (5:31) through Moses (19:7), the evangelist declares that Jesus' divorce saying expresses neither the teaching of the Law nor of the rabbis. We are left with the same juxtaposition of Jesus and the Law in 5:31–32 and in 19:7–9 as found in the controversy narrative of Mark 10:2–9 between the Pharisees, representatives of the Law, and Jesus. What then does *except for* πορνεία mean?

For the tradition behind 5:32, one finds a clue to the meaning and function of the "except-clause" in the strict Jewish-Christians' reworking of 5:32a. In order to soften the more radical statement concerning the woman's role in adultery (Luke 16:18a; Mark 10:11), the Jewish-Christian community modified 5:32a to align it with the Old Testament Law and Jewish custom (see above). Should one take Jesus' absolute rejection of divorce in a similar legalistic fashion and thus deny divorce for any reason, the prohibition would include adultery and incestuous marriages, to name but two such extremes. This prohibition would have been contradictory to the Law and socially "crude and absurd" (Schlatter, *Matthäus*, 180) for Jewish ears at worst and offensive at best (cf. Acts 15:29). Consequently, the strict Jewish-Christian community turned, perhaps for more apologetic than casuistic reasons, to the Old Testament Law and formulated the "except-clause" from Deut 24:1. By expressing the ambiguous ʿrwh with πορνεία, they maintained the distinctiveness of Jesus' teaching, since it was narrower than taught by even Shammai, as well as the continued validity of the Old Testament Law. Since πορνεία = "adultery" and πορνεία = "incestuous marriages" were lexically and contextually possible for this community, one must leave πορνεία open for one or both meanings in the tradition.

Matthew, having found the "except-clause" in his tradition, preserved it in 5:32 and added it in 19:9, even though both sayings were placed by him in contrast to Deut 24:1. Obviously, the evangelist, contrary to the Jewish-Christian tradition, was no longer concerned to maintain that Jesus' teaching on divorce stood in line with the Old Testament Law. To the contrary, Jesus' teaching on divorce, according to Matthew, actually countered the Law. Consequently, the only way for Matthew to have modified the tradition as he did and yet avoided being self-contradictory was for him to have understood πορνεία in terms of the mission situation among the Gentiles and incestuous marriages rather than in terms of Deut 24:1. His motivation for preserving the tradition in 5:32a and for inserting the clause in 19:9 would thus have been in confronting the more practical concerns of the Gentile mission and its consequences for a mixed community of Jewish and Gentile Christians, a context not unlike that of the Apostolic Decree in Acts 15. There is no trace here of a more rigorous interpretation of the Law. Indeed, the "except-clause" may be an important clue to the mixed constituency of the evangelist's community. A Gospel that included strict Jewish-Christian tradition and a strong emphasis on the Gentile mission doubtless paralleled in many ways the mission setting of Acts 15. For Matthew, then, the "except-clause" most likely referred to the Hellenistic interfamily marriages of Acts 15:29 and 1 Cor 5:1 confronted by the Church in its wider mission.

whoever marries a divorced woman commits adultery. This sentence uses the conditional relative construction of the premise, whereas the Lucan parallel has the participial construction analogous to 5:32a, par. Luke 16:18a. The differences here as in 5:22 are essentially stylistic and the origins indeterminable. Luke has additionally "from her husband" (ἀπὸ ἀνδρός) that simply explicates the perfect participle ἀπολελυμένην *(having been divorced).* On the use of μοιχᾶται compared to μοιχεύει in Luke 16:18b, see above. Since 19:9, par. Mark 10:11, consists of only one sentence and 5:32, par. Luke 16:18, has two, it remains uncertain whether the original form was a single or double saying (Schaller, "Ehescheidung," 236–38). The question does not affect the meaning of the verse.

This sentence makes essentially the same statement as the first in 5:32a, namely, divorce does not cancel the marriage. Whereas the wife committed the adultery by remarrying in 5:32a (cf. Luke 16:18a) and the responsibility lies on her husband's shoulders for divorcing her, in 5:32b the man who marries a divorced woman commits the adultery. In this graphic use of the concept of adultery, Jesus declares that the bill of divorce given for the purpose of freeing the woman in order to remarry (Deut 24:1) does not in fact cancel the marriage after all.

By setting 5:32 in antithesis to 5:31, Matthew presents Jesus' teaching on divorce for what it is—a setting aside of the Law's provision for divorce and thus remarriage. The "except-clause" does not soften this antithesis for Matthew, since the evangelist did not use *except for πορνεία* as the casuistic application of *for some indecency (ʿrwt dbr)* of Deut 24:1. Rather, the *except for incestuous marriages* arose in the Church's mission context and was not prohibited because the Law had forbidden it but because the Church had decided to forego it and other practices especially offensive and disruptive to the fellowship and worship among Jewish and Gentile Christians. Thus the "except-clause" was based on accepted Christian practice rather than on the Law.

As was the case with the first and second Antitheses, one could take the third in its form as a legal ordinance forbidding divorce and/or remarriage. The history of the Church's interpretation attests to such an understanding. But does not such a legalistic understanding of this particular Antithesis of the six distort the intention of the antithetical format in general and the function of the legal ordinance in particular?

In the previous examples, the antithetical format demonstrates the inadequacy of the Law's demands in expressing God's will for his creatures. Jesus' demands call for attitudes and actions befitting totally new relationships between human beings. That same dimension of a different starting point for marriage occurs in the materially related controversy narrative where Jesus counters the Law of Moses in Deut 24:1 based on the "hardness of one's heart" (Mark 10:2–9). Therefore, the third Antithesis, as its previous parallels, calls for a relationship between husband and wife in which the divorce Law of Deut 24:1 is redundant, namely, for the "two shall be one flesh" (Mark 10:8–9).

The form of the legal ordinance, common to the first three Antitheses, would then be merely the vehicle used to express in graphic fashion Jesus' ultimate demand. One could hardly expect to prosecute on the basis of 5:22 and 5:28. Nor was 5:32 and parallels ever so intended (note the disciples' reaction in 19:10!). In fact, by focusing on the illegality of anger, name-calling, and lust, and by seeking to eliminate such attitudes and behavior, one misses the underlying thrust of the demand for new relationships. The same has happened particularly in the case of the third Antithesis. But such a legalistic focus also is to be found at times in the Church's understanding of the fourth and fifth Antitheses that follow.

5:33. The fourth Antithesis presents us with the best evidence for the traditional rather than redactional character of the antithetical format. The presence of parallels without the antithetical form to traditional elements in the third (5:32, par. Luke 16:18), fifth (5:39b–43, par. Luke 6:29–30), and sixth (5:44–48, par. Luke 6:27–28, 33–36) Antitheses suggests Matthean redaction. The absence of traditional parallels to the first (5:21–22) and second (5:27–28) Antitheses precludes our drawing firm conclusions. But the material in James 5:12 parallel to the fourth Antithesis offers evidence for the priority of the Matthean format (Guelich, "Antitheses," 450–54).

Again you have heard that God said to the generation of old. The addition of *again* (πάλιν) calls attention to the resumption of the complete introductory formula, especially after the very abbreviated *God said* in 5:31. By using the full formula in the first (5:21) and fourth (5:33)

Antitheses, the evangelist divides the six into two groups of three each.

You shall not swear a false oath. The Greek verb ἐπιορκέω can mean either *to swear falsely* or *to break one's oath* (Bauer, *s.v.*). The second meaning fits the context of 5:33b, *to keep your oaths,* but the first meaning fits the context of the antithesis in 5:34a, 37a—a demand for total honesty. Furthermore, the first meaning has a close parallel in Lev 19:12. The words οὐκ ἐπιορκήσεις as such do not appear in the Old Testament. But Lev 19:12, in the context of dealing honestly with another (19:11), warns, "You shall not swear (ὀμεῖσθε) by my name falsely (ἐπ᾽ ἀδίκῳ)." The basis for the prohibition lies in the third commandment (Exod 20:7) against taking the Lord's name in vain (Lev 19:12b).

Although 5:33a only speaks of swearing falsely, no distinction existed between swearing falsely in God's name and swearing falsely. By definition, a valid oath included the invocation of God's name or an acceptable substitute that clearly referred to God's name (Str-B 1:230). Philo gives contemporary testimony to this effect by cautioning, "One must consider in no careless fashion all that an oath involves. . . . For an oath is an appeal to God as a witness on matters in dispute . . ." (*Decal* 84–86). This very issue arises in 5:34b–36 and 23:16–22 and has ample parallels in the Mishnaic tractate on oaths, *Šebuʿot.* Therefore, 5:33a using the apodictic form of the decalogue, οὐκ ἐπιορκήσεις (so 5:21a, 27) expresses the Law's prohibition of swearing a false oath.

you shall keep your oaths with the Lord. The conjunction δέ generally connotes the adversative meaning *but.* Translated in this way, the second part of the premise stands in contrast to the first. Yet such an understanding of the two commands would not make any sense. Whereas the first prohibits swearing a false oath and assumes the involvement of at least two parties, the second commands the faithful rendering of one's oath to God, an action involving the individual and God. Therefore, δέ in this context merely connotes transition as a continuative particle (BDF, §447, 1, cf. Matt 5:21, 31, 37b) to the related matter of oaths made with God. *To keep* (ἀποδώσεις), the future indicative used as an apodictic command, literally means *to give out* in the sense of *to make payment.* Thus *to keep* one's oaths means to follow through in performing and observing what has been sworn to the Lord.

This commandment has an almost verbatim parallel in Ps 50:14 (49:14, LXX): "Pay (ἀπόδος) your vows (εὐχάς) to the Most High (ὑψίστῳ)." The only difference, but a significant one for the background of this Antithesis, appears in the key word *vows* (εὐχάς)/*oaths* (ὅρκους). Some scholars have ignored the difference and handled 5:33b as though it read or meant *vows* (e.g., Allen, *Matthew,* 53; Manson, *Sayings,* 158; Davies, *Setting,* 240). Such an understanding of 5:33b means that the premise consists of two different commands, the first referring to *oaths* sworn between individuals and the second to *vows* made before God. Since the latter has no further contact with the antithesis that follows (5:34–37), some have explained its presence as a later addition in an abortive attempt to explicate 5:33 (e.g., Manson, *Sayings,* 158, and Davies, *Setting,* 240). To treat ὅρκους *(oaths),* however, as the equivalent for εὐχάς *(vows)* is to ignore the deliberate choice of ὅρκους over εὐχάς (cf. Ps 49:14, LXX) and thus the distinction between the two terms (cf. Kilpatrick, *Origins,* 19–20).

The distinction between *oaths* and *vows,* though not always clear in the first century (Davies, *Setting,* 240), was nonetheless real. The Mishnah has a separate tractate on oaths *(Šebuʿot)* and vows *(Nedarim).* Danby, on the basis of the usage in the Mishnah, suggested, "The vow is different from the oath, in that a vow forbids a certain thing to be used . . . , while an oath forbids the swearer to do a certain thing although it is not forbidden in itself" *(Mishnah,* 264; similarly, Fiebig, *Bergpredigt,* 66, 171). The difference between oath and vows gains further support in the fact that a given formula may be valid for an oath but not a vow (Lieberman, *Greek,* 128–30). Therefore, one must respect the choice of ὅρκους over εὐχάς in 5:33b. Nevertheless, one should not exaggerate the difference, since oaths and vows in Judaism did share considerable common ground, to the point of confusion at times (Lieberman, *Greek,* 117, and Davies, *Setting,* 242). The basis for the confusion may well stem from the dual character of oaths in Judaism.

Oaths belong in two categories (Danby, *Mishnah,* 411 [*Šebuʿot,* 3:1], and Fiebig, *Bergpredigt,* 63). On the one hand, we have the category of "assertive oaths" (positive or negative), e.g., "I swear that I have/ have not done something." On the other hand, we have the category of "promissory oaths" (positive or negative), e.g., "I swear that I will/ will not do something." It becomes obvious that the promissory oath approximates a vow. The specific character of each lies in the focus of the statement. A vow pertains to an object and its usage; an oath pertains to one's future actions (Danby, *Mishnah,* 264, n. 1; Fiebig, *Bergpredigt,* 66; Lieberman, *Greek,* 117).

The *generic* character of a vow and a promissory oath is essentially the same. Both bind one in terms of one's formulaic expression with reference to objects and actions. To this extent the terms could be interchanged in 5:33b without affecting the basic thrust of the Old Testament passages (Ps 49:11, LXX; cf Deut 23:22 and Num 30:3). *Oaths* rather than *vows*, however, fits the particular context of 5:33–37 (see Notes on 5:34–36) which determined the choice of ὅρκους in 5:33b instead of εὐχάς. Therefore, we have the dual focus of oaths in the premise of 5:33 with 5:33a referring to "assertive oaths" and 5:33b referring to "promissory oaths."

5:34. *You shall not swear at all.* The fourth antithesis represents the first in the form of an apodictic command consisting here of the negative infinitive (μὴ ὀμόσαι). James 5:12, in a paranetic setting, parallels this antithesis with the present imperative construction, μὴ ὀμνύετε. The adverb ὅλως in the negative construction means *not at all.* Together the antithesis forbids swearing of any kind. Such an absolute prohibition comes without parallel in Jewish sources. The rabbis warn against false and unnecessary swearing (Str-B 1:328–30; Montefiore, *Rabbinic Literature,* 48), and Philo, influenced by Greek philosophers who spoke against swearing, recommended avoiding the use of oaths except when absolutely necessary (*Spec Laws,* 2:2f; *Decal* 84–86). Even the Essenes who shied away from using oaths apparently took an oath when entering the community (1QS 5:8; CD 15:1–3; see Davies, *Setting,* 241–44). This command stood in bold contrast to Judaism.

The antithesis at this point displays a certain tension with the premise. Whereas *You shall not swear at all* logically counters 5:33a, when set against 5:33b—*You shall keep your oaths*—the antithesis sounds awkward at best. Furthermore, the absolute prohibition of swearing displays a tension with the detailing of specific oaths that follows (5:34b–36). In other words, the antithesis of 5:34a fits with the premise of 5:33a but stands in tension with the second half of the premise in 5:33b and with the following elements of the antithesis itself in 5:34b–36. A clue to the nature and cause of this tension lies in the remaining parts of the antithesis (5:34b–36).

neither by heaven . . . nor by earth . . . nor by Jerusalem. What follows is a list of items, including one's own head (5:36), by which oaths were sworn. James 5:12 has the first two and concludes with a general "nor any other oath." Yet James 5:12 exhibits several stylistic changes over 5:34b–35. Apart from dropping the explanatory clauses in each case, James replaces the awkward μή . . . ὅλως *(not at all)* followed redundantly by a series of *neither . . . nors* with simply μή . . . μήτε . . . μήτε ("do not . . . neither . . ."). James also has the more common Greek construction of the accusative with verbs of swearing, while Matthew has the more Semitic construction with ἐν/εἰς and the dative/accusative. Therefore, Matthew's saying represents grammatically the less polished Semitic influence in contrast to James's more developed syntax.

Each of the oaths noted in 5:34–36 has a counterpart in Jewish literature and each is explicitly rejected as a binding oath (e.g., "heaven and earth," *Šebuʿot* 4:13, Str-B 1:333; "Jerusalem," *Nedarim* 1:3, cf. *t. Nedarim* 1.2.3, Fiebig, *Bergpredigt,* 65; "your head," *Sanhedrin* 3:2). Even the form of εἰς with Jerusalem may reflect the rabbinic distinction of swearing "towards Jerusalem." Consequently, these examples reflect the common Jewish practice of swearing by spurious oaths that had no binding power (cf. 23:16–22). This concern for valid oaths was so extensive that one complete tractate, *Šebuʿot,* of the Mishnah deals with the casuistic use of oaths.

In each instance 5:34b–36 counters such usage by using the Old Testament (*heaven* and *earth,* Isa 66:1; *Jerusalem,* Ps 48:2) to affirm their status as genuine oaths since each was a valid substitute for God's name (cf. the rabbinic test for valid oath formulas, *Šebuʿot* 4:13). Therefore, 5:34b–36 specifically elaborated the implications for 5:34a to block any casuistic use of spurious oaths as found in Judaism. The better rendering of μήτε . . . μήτε in this case would then be *not even* (like μηδέ, . . . μηδέ, BDR, §445, 2; Str-B 1:328–29) rather than the more common *neither . . . nor.* This specific application of 5:34a to scribal casuistry doubtless reflects the situation of a strict Jewish-Christian community. Whereas 5:34a prohibited swearing altogether, 5:34b–36 thus extended the prohibition to include even spurious oaths by demonstrating from the Old Testament that these formulas were indeed oaths.

These elaborations of 5:34a not only reflect an extension of the prohibition to cover spurious oaths, but since each of these "oaths" occurred in the rabbinic discussion involving "promissory oaths," they also reflect a close relationship with the oaths in the premise of 5:33b. This correspondence between the promissory oaths in 5:33b and the formulas of promissory oaths in the antithesis helps explain the tension noted above between the two elements of the premise in 5:33a, b, as well as the tension between the absolute prohibition against swearing (5:34a) followed by specific examples in the antithesis (5:34b–36). While 5:33a and 34a could exist as a unit independently, 5:33b and 5:34b–36 could not, nor could 5:33b exist without 5:34b–36 and vice versa. Thus in terms of content, 5:33b, 34b–36 are clearly of secondary importance to both the premise and antithesis.

By removing the promissory elements, we have an antithesis dealing with assertive oaths based on Lev 19:12: *You shall not swear a false oath,* countered by *You shall not swear at all.* Therefore, 5:33b, 34b–36 reflect a secondary extension of the antithesis introduced to include promissory oaths. Such an expansion presupposes the existence of the antithesis and had to take place within the pre-Matthean antithetically formulated tradition, since the remnants of this expansion are present in James 5:12.

Furthermore, since the content of 5:33b, 34b–36 corresponds to the Woe of 23:16–22 (cf. 15:5–6, par. Mark 7:10–12) involving the use of spurious promissory oaths, this expansion has its material parallel in Jesus' ministry directed at the "righteous." The context of 23:16–22 conveys the note of judgment and was likely preserved in the Jewish-Christian community's struggles with Judaism. The presence of this theme involving the casuistic use of oaths within the Antithesis of 5:33–37 may reflect this polemical setting of the tradition. James 5:12 clearly preserves the more paranetic form and function of the "antithesis" of Matt 5:34–37.

5:36. *by your head.* This verse contrasts with the preceeding series of oaths grammatically and materially. Grammatically, μήτε connects the entire clause rather than the object with the main verb of 5:34a. The clause itself, instead of continuing the negative infinitive construction, has the subjunctive of prohibition (ὀμόσῃς) in the second person singular (cf. plural in 5:34, 37). Materially, the basis for the oath's validity indirectly stems from one's incapacity to do what God alone could do rather than from its being a direct appeal through the use of the Old Testament. These differences from 5:34b–35 indicate the later addition of 5:36 as another example of such oaths.

5:37a. *But let your word be an emphatic yes or no.* Doubtless this clause went together with 5:34a to form the original antithesis. Whereas 5:34a expressed the negative prohibition against swearing altogether, 5:37 countered with the positive demand, *Let your word be yes yes and no no.* James 5:12 has the articular construction, "Let your yes (τὸ ναί) be yes and your no (τὸ οὐ) be no." The differences appear slight, depending on how one interprets Matthew's rather unusual *yes yes* and *no no.*

Two alternative explanations have emerged in the literature. On the one hand, some have interpreted the phrase in terms of the Semitic doubled construction to intensify the words involved (Zahn, *Matthäus,* 248; Allen, *Matthew,* 54; McNeile, *Matthew,* 68; Percy, *Botschaft,* 147; Stählin, "Beteurungsformeln," 119; Mussner, *Jakobusbrief,* 215–16). On the other hand, many have understood the expression to be a formula used in lieu of the forbidden oaths, a surrogate oath formula, with a parallel in rabbinic usage (Str-B 1:336; Dibelius, *James,* 250–51, n. 55; Klostermann, *Matthäusevangelium,* 47; Manson, *Sayings,* 159; Lohmeyer, *Matthäus,* 134; Braun, *Radikalismus* 2:80, n. 6; Strecker, *Weg,* 133–34; *idem,* "Antithesen" 62–63; Wrege, *Überlieferungsgeschichte,* 73). Kutch has offered a variation on the formula approach based on an inscription from Nebuchadnezzar's time ("Rede," 206–218). The formula demands a correspondence of *yes—yes* rather then *yes—no* and thus demands honesty and integrity. Unfortunately, the temporal distance of the nearest such example and especially the incompatibility of this function of the formula with the *anything more than these* of 5:37b renders this suggestion most unlikely.

Those taking the expression as a formulaic *yes yes/no no* base their conclusion on a rabbinic parallel (Str-B 1:336) and the Church's tendency to apply Jesus' demands casuistically (e.g., Strecker, *Weg,* 133–34). Both starting points have serious weaknesses. First, granted that the formulaic usage has rabbinic parallels as an oath, the doubling of words to express emphasis also has its parallels in Semitic usage (e.g., Stählin, "Beteuerungsformeln," 119–20; GHG, §123e). Consequently, both renderings are equally plausible. Second, granting that the Church was concerned about applying Jesus' teaching, would such motivation have blurred the obvious inconsistency inherent in this application of the original demand (Eichholz, *Bergpredigt,* 90–91)? The fine distinction between a "formulaic assertion" *(Beteuerungsformel)* and an oath formula (e.g., Strecker, *Weg,* 133–34, and Wrege, *Überlieferungsgeschichte,* 73) does little to remove the inconsistency. Rather, the suggested difference contains its own inconsistency, since it assumes that to counter the use of oaths the Church used a recognized oath formula from Jewish tradition as a substitute "non-oath" formula.

By contrast, the priority of 5:37a fits with the Semitic construction of doubled words, the Semitic character of 5:34–36, and is no less "practical" than James 5:12. Furthermore, of the two sayings, James 5:12 has by far the more paranetic style and context. It is precisely the antithetical format of 5:33a, 34a, 37a that supplies the meaning of 5:37a explicit in James 5:12. By countering the Old Testament prohibition of swearing false oaths (5:33a) 5:34a, 37a, with its prohibition of swearing altogether accompanied by the demand for a simple, straightforward *yes* or *no,* outlaws false statements of any kind. In other words, the fourth Antithesis demands total honesty just as James 5:12 now does although the latter is removed from the antithetical setting. Therefore, James rather than Matthew reflects the Church's paranetic modification subsequent to but consistent with the Antithesis. The same phenomenon at work between Matthew and James appears in Justin (*Apol.* 1.16.5), Clement of Alexander (*Strom* 5.99.1, cf. 7.50.1–5) and Pseudo-Clement (*Hom* 3.55.1; 19.2.4), each of whom paranetically uses the saying removed from its antithetical context, although each has knowledge of the Matthean context as seen in their references to 5:37b, a Matthean redactional addition.

Therefore, 5:37a uses a Semitic idiom to express the demand, *Let your word be an emphatic yes or no.* Together 5:34a and 37a formed an antithesis to the Law's prohibition of swearing false oaths by prohibiting the use of all oaths and demanding simply a straightforward *yes* or *no*.

5:37b. *Anything more than this is from the Evil One.* This clause contains essentially Matthean terms and is missing from James 5:12. Consequently, one can safely assign it to Matthew's redaction (Strecker, *Weg,* 133). The correlative use of δέ (cf. 5:33b) and the demonstrative pronoun *these* referring to *yes yes* and *no no* of 5:37a connect the clause with 5:34a. *More than* (περισσόν) appears again in 5:47 in contrast to Luke 6:33. The *evil one* (τοῦ πονηροῦ) appears five other times in Matthew (5:39; 6:13, cf. Luke 11:4; 13:19, cf. Mark 4:15; 13:38; 5:44, with the plural), all in either the Sermon or the Parable Discourse. Two of the five usages clearly refer to the *Evil One,* an allusion to Satan as the adversary to the Kingdom (13:19, 38). The same thrust corresponds to the use in 6:13, cf. Luke 11:4 (Lohmeyer, *Our Father,* 215–17). In 5:44 and 39 the term applies to the "children of the Evil One" who stand in opposition to the "children of the Kingdom" (cf. 13:38). In 5:37b, then, attributing anything more than a straightforward *yes* or *no* to the *Evil One* demonstrates Matthew's concern to underscore the contrast between Jesus' demand and life as dominated by the *Evil One.*

The fourth Antithesis, therefore, focuses specifically on swearing, indeed, on the assertive oaths, a necessary part of life in the Old Testament, Judaism, and today. Jesus counters the Old Testament prohibition of swearing a false oath by forbidding swearing at all in lieu of a straightforward *yes* or *no* statement. Taken legalistically, Jesus simply outlawed the use of oaths. Yet, as in the previous Antitheses, the intent is much more radical than merely dispensing with the use of oaths.

In a society built around the use of oaths to guarantee one's honesty, setting them aside would be as impossible as prosecuting anger or lust.

Rather, this Antithesis, consistent with the previous ones, uses a legal concern drawn from everyday life to express Jesus' demand for conduct consistent with completely new human relationships, a context of total honesty. As the evangelist summarized, anything other than this is of the Evil One. Jesus' demand implied the overcoming of the Evil One, a new starting point for the individual, one characteristic of the presence of the day of salvation.

5:38. *An eye for an eye and a tooth for a tooth.* This premise consists of a formulaic expression, the so-called *lex talionis,* that appears in more detail three times in the Law (Exod 21:24; Lev 24:20b; Deut 19:21, LXX). This particular reference, as will be seen in 5:39, comes from the setting of Deut 19:21, LXX. The *lex talionis,* occurring as far back in history as the Code of Hammurabi, originially set the limits for the extent of retaliation and protected individuals and their families from incommensurate revenge. It became the keynote of criminal justice for the Jewish law, as seen in the Old Testament. The extent to which this principle was symbolically or literally followed in Jesus' day remains unclear, although there is evidence in the Mishnah indicating that financial adjustments were acceptable at times (*Baba Qamma* 8:1, cf. Str-B 1:337–41; Daube, *Rabbinic Judaism,* 255–59). In either case, it guaranteed the injured person legal justice while protecting the offender from undue penalty.

5:39. *You shall not seek legal vindication against an evil person.* This antithesis formulated like 5:34a as an apodictic command by use of the negative aorist infinitive contains two rather ambiguous terms, ἀντιστῆναι (*to oppose*) and τῷ πονηρῷ (*evil*). *To oppose* or *to resist* translates the root meaning of the verb. Taken in a general way, the command and its following illustrations (5:39b–41) have become the basis for advocating a "Christian" view of nonresistance. Yet to understand this verb in this manner is to separate it from its antithetical context, a context which requires a much more specific interpretation. One's view of *to oppose* also conditions to an extent whether πονηρῷ is a neuter substantive meaning *evil* in general (e.g., McNeile, *Matthew,* 69; Lohmeyer, *Matthäus,* 136–37) or a masculine substantive meaning an *evil person* (Schlatter, *Matthäus,* 187; Klostermann, *Matthäusevangelium,* 58; Hill, *Matthew,* 127). Set in antithesis to the judicial principle of the *lex talionis, to oppose* connotes legal opposition quite specifically in a judicial sense. Consequently, the personal use of πονηρῷ would be the more natural, although one could also maintain the somewhat awkward abstract meaning. Paraphrased, then, 5:39a would read, *You shall not oppose an evil person in court.*

This understanding becomes most obvious when one examines the Old Testament background of the premise. Of the three Old Testament parallels, Deut 19:21, LXX, fits 5:38–39a as though tailormade. First, the setting of Deut 19:16 involved the hypothetical trial of a false witness, a most appropriate and hardly coincidental sequel to the previous Antithesis. Second, the false witness had *accused* (ἀντῆστε) his brother in court (19:18). Third, the penalty was based on the *lex talionis* principle by assigning to the false accuser the same penalty that would have been incurred by the accused. And fourth, the reason given for such action was to remove the *evil one* (τὸν πονηρόν) from the community. All four elements found in Deut 19:16–21 constitute the premise and antithesis of 5:38, 39a. Furthermore, the judicial setting extends to the next two commands of 5:39b, 40 (cf. Luke 6:29).

The verbal and contextual parallels between 5:38, 39a and Deut 19:16–21 determine the specific usage of ἀντιστῆναι *(to oppose)* and τῷ πονηρῷ (an *evil person*). To oppose connotes legal opposition in court; an *evil person* refers to one's adversary who is in the wrong. This usage of πονηρός also concurs with Matthew's redactional use of πονηρός in the masculine to refer to the Evil One as the adversary of the Kingdom (see Note on 5:37b). Here the "adversary," as the plural "evil ones" in 5:44, represents those who opposes God and his own or, to use Matthew's term, the "sons of the Kingdom" (cf 13:38). Therefore, 5:39a forbids the opposing of an *evil person* in court. As an apodictic command, the antithesis categorically prohibits legal retaliation against an offending party.

who slaps your right cheek. This clause begins a series of examples mostly with Lucan parallels (Luke 6:29–30). Yet Matthew and Luke differ in the immediate context, in the stylistic and grammatical structure, and in content. First, in the immediate context, Matthew has the Antithesis at the outset (5:38–39b) and the sixth Antithesis involving the Love Your Enemies complex afterwards (5:43–48). Luke, by contrast, has no sign of the Antithesis and encloses the unit within the Love Your Enemy complex (Luke 6:27–36). Furthermore, the second person singular of this unit betrays the unit's earlier existence separate from either 5:38–39a or Luke 6:27–36, since both passages use the second person plural otherwise. Yet the appearance of this unit in the larger context of the Love Your Enemy complex in both Matthew and Luke strongly suggests that the two traditional units had been brought together in the tradition.

The possibility of Matthew and Luke individually but coincidentally bringing these two separate units together in the same context seems most remote. Therefore, three options exist: (1) the two units existed side by side in the tradition, with Matthew then adding the Antitheses and Luke integrating them (e.g., Bultmann, *Tradition,* 135; Schulz, *Spruchquelle,* 120–21); (2) the two units existed as Antitheses now found in Matthew, with Luke having dropped the antithetical format and having combined the traditions (e.g., Dupont, *Béatitudes* 1:191); and (3) the units existed combined in the tradition as now found in Luke, with Matthew separating them and adding the Antitheses (e.g., Schürmann, *Lukasevangelium,* 345–47, 357; cf. Manson, *Sayings,* 161, and Wrege, *Überlieferungsgeschichte,* 81–82, who assigns this process to pre-Matthean tradition). The contextual question has a crucial bearing on the traditional or redactional character of the antithetical format. As will be seen below, the material relationship between this unit and its immediate context and the use of δανίσασθαι in 5:41 support the third option which automatically excludes the other two.

Second, stylistically and grammatically Luke's 6:29–30 consists of two double sayings, each beginning with a dative participial construction (6:29a, 30a) followed by an ἀπό plus the participle (6:29b, 30b). Matthew's unit lacks the symmetry with one double and one triple saying. Each begins with the indefinite relative pronoun (5:39b, 41a) followed by a dative participial construction (5:40, 42a) with the last element introduced by an accusative participle construction (5:42b). These stylistic differences doubtless stem from Matthew's preference for the indefinite relative and his inclination, noted in 5:18, to break traditional patterns. Third, in his content Matthew has an additional element focusing on the practice of commandeering people for service (5:41) as well as numerous verbal dissimilarities that will be handled below.

Whoever (ὅστις) indicates Matthean redaction (Matthew adds it 14x; see Schulz, *Spruchquelle,* 121, n. 203). *Slaps* (ῥαπίζει) differs from Luke's *hits* (τύπτοντι) and may point, along with *turn* (στρέψον; cf. Luke, πάρεχε = *offer*), to an alignment of the saying with Isa 50:6, LXX (added in 26:67, cf. Mark 14:65). *Right cheek* (δεξιὰν σιαγόνα), in contrast to Luke's *cheek,* quite likely holds the clue to this illustration. Whereas Luke focuses on the act of being struck on the cheek, an act of violence, Matthew focuses on the degrading nature of the act. The specific reference to the *right* cheek implies that one is slapped with the back of the hand, an action that was particularly degrading to a Jew (Str-B 1:337). One's recourse in Luke's case would be self-defense and retaliation; in Matthew's case of insult more than injury, one would need to take legal action to gain recompense and vindication (Daube, *Rabbinic Judaism,* 260–63). According to the Mishnah (*Baba Qamma* 8:6) the penalty for such damage was twice as severe. Therefore, in Matthew the one on the receiving end foregoes his right to legal action, while in Luke one foregoes personal retaliation. The change to the indefinite relative, the alignment of the verbs with Isa 50:6, and the abusive character of the back-handed slap that sets the stage for legal action all point to Matthew's redaction.

5:40. *To the one who desires to take you to court.* The second example opens with an explicit reference to a judicial process (κριθῆναι = *to be judged*). Luke 6:29b continues the scene of violence by implying a robbery. The difference may well go to Matthew's account, since the change continues the court scene set by the Antithesis and implicit to 5:39b. Furthermore, the evangelist redactionally adds θέλω *(to want)* twelve times into his sources (10x to Mark, 2x to Q besides 5:40, 42).

to get your body shirt, give him also your coat. The *shirt* (χιτῶνα) represents one's basic, form-fitting garment. The *coat* (ἱμάτιον) was a loose wrap, more like a small blanket or an afghan worn as an outer garment during the day and used as bedding during the night. Luke 6:29b (*Did* 1:4) has the reverse order, which would have been more logical in the case of a robbery. The *coat,* according to the Old Testament Law, belonged inalienably to an individual and could not be held even as a deposit overnight (Exod 22:25–26; Deut 24:12–13). Therefore, commensurate with the abdication of one's rights to retaliation in 5:39a, 5:40 demands that one forego even the Law's provision for the poor by voluntarily offering one's adversary the one item that the Law forbids another from taking by legal recourse.

The saying of 5:39b–40 demanded the foregoing of one's legal rights to redress and protection appropriate to the antithesis of 5:39a prohibiting the opposing of one's adversary in court. The next sayings of 5:41–42 no longer fit the judicial scene but represent a descending order of obligatory requests.

5:41. *Who commandeers you to go one mile.* This example introduced by the Matthean indefinite relative construction (cf. 5:39b) does not appear in Luke 6:29–30 (cf. *Did* 1:4). *Commandeer* (ἀγγαρεύσει) represents an old custom stemming from Persian origins (Manson, *Sayings,* 160) that required one to perform or to grant services according to another's wish. The Roman soldiers apparently maintained the detested practice in using Jewish civilians for their purposes. For example, the Romans commandeered Simon to bear Jesus' cross (Mark 15:21). *Mile* (μίλιον) was a Roman measurement of about 1000 paces, just less than a mile. This request was legally binding, but one was to go beyond even the requested limits, to go the "extra mile."

5:42. *to him who begs of you.* Luke 6:30a has the same verb. This request, most likely stemming from a beggar, does not carry the legal obligation, but it does have a religious obligation, since almsgiving was integral to Jewish piety (see Note on 6:2).

do not refuse to lend to the one desiring to borrow from you. The final request has a somewhat different parallel in Luke 6:30b. Instead of *to borrow* (δανίσασθαι) Luke has the more general *to take* (αἴροντος; cf. 6:29b). This difference holds the key to the pre-Lucan combination in Q of the two traditional units, Luke 6:27–36. *To borrow* (δανίζω) only occurs in the New Testament here and in the related section of the rhetorical questions in Luke 6:34–35 (cf. Justin, *Apol* 1.15.10). Consequently, Schürmann has suggested that 5:42b is reminiscent of the earlier term behind Luke 6:30b (*Lukasevangelium,* 348, 354). In other words, δανίσητε in Luke 6:34–35 refers back to the same verb (δανίζω) underlying Luke's αἴροντός of 6:30b (see Note on 5:46), the verb that Matthew found in the Q tradition and has now preserved in 5:42b. Since the occurrence of δανίσητε in Luke 6:34–35 depends on the verb's presence in Luke 6:30 (see Note on 5:46), the unit of Luke 6:29–30 with δανίζω appeared within the larger context of Luke 6:27–36 in the pre-Lucan tradition. Therefore, Matthew, having found them together, has separated the units and set each in an antithesis.

Matthew concludes the series of requests with the command not to refuse the request for a loan (ἀποστραφῆς). This request carried little or no obligation with it. Luke's "do not demand its return" (ἀπαίτει) most likely reflects his stylistic alignment of the verbs in 6:30 (αἰτοῦντι, αἴροντος, and ἀπαίτει). With regard to content, 5:42 and Luke 6:30b are basically the same, namely, one is to grant the request voluntarily. This voluntary granting of the requests in 5:42 corresponds with the voluntary going of the "extra mile" in 5:41. Since these requests in no way relate directly to the judicial context of 5:38–40, their presence here is again indicative of Matthew's faithful use of tradition even when only tangentially related to his primary redactional intention.

The fifth Antithesis strikes at the very basis of legal justice. The Law's explicit basis for such justice, the *lex talionis,* stands over against Jesus' demand of not seeking legal vindication from the evil one in court. In other words, the implications of this Antithesis, like the third (5:31–32), set aside rather than supersede the Old Testament Law. Taken legalistically, such a demand would lead to anarchy. Taken in keeping with the other Antitheses, however, this one also calls for behavior commensurate with a totally different starting point in human relationships. Rather than perceiving these relationships as controlled by legal justice and thus presupposing the presence of evil and the need for such justice, Jesus called for relationships in which evil was no longer the controlling factor.

The Antithesis consisting of the redactional use of Deut 18:16–21 and material drawn from the tradition captures the heart of Jesus' demand. The evangelist uses the same principle of drawing from the framework of concrete human experience to set off the stark contrast between life lived in the everyday and life lived as God desires and enables within the Kingdom. Consequently, the fifth Antithesis stands together with the previous four to set forth Jesus' demand in terms of the Kingdom.

5:43. The Love Your Enemy complex found more or less intact in Luke 6:27–35 and divided into the fifth and sixth Antitheses by Matthew originally followed the Beatitudes in Q (Schürmann, *Lukasevangelium,* 346; Luhrmann, "Feinde," 413–16). This pre-Matthean sequence, still present in Luke with the intervening Woes, is reflected in the lexical and material similarity of the fifth (5:7), seventh (5:9), and especially the ninth (5:11–12) Beatitudes to this section of 5:38–48 (see Notes on 5:7, 9, 11). Consequently, we return in 5:43–48 (cf. 5:39–42) to the sequence of the Sermon tradition as found in Q, which the previous Antitheses have interrupted.

Luke's opening statement, "But I say to you who hear," looks surprisingly familiar (Luke 6:27a). Some have argued that the clause represents the remnants of the original antithetical formula underlying the Q tradition of the Sermon (e.g., Dupont, *Béatitudes* 1:189–91; Manson, *Sayings,* 161; Davies, *Setting,* 388). Yet Dupont himself (Béatitudes 1:189, n. 2) has traced the strong adversative ἀλλά (but cf. Matthew's δέ in "But I say . . .") to Luke's redactional counter to the πλήν of 6:24 introducing the Woes. The contrast resumes the audience of the Beatitudes in 6:18–20 (Furnish, *Love Command,* 55). Furthermore, the frequent use by Q sections of opening statements referring to Jesus' speaking (Lührmann,

"Feinde," 417, n. 22) and the reference to hearing Jesus' words at the conclusion of the Sermon (6:47, 49, par. Matt 7:24, 26) indicate that the "I say to you who hear" belonged to the Q tradition (e.g., Schürmann, *Lukasevangelium*, 345–36; Schulz, *Spruchquelle*, 127; Lührmann, "Feinde," 417). In fact, rather than being the vestigial remains of the antithetical format, this phrase found by Matthew in the Q tradition may well have served as the catalyst for his introducing the Antitheses whose introductory formulas reflect a certain catch-word similarity.

You shall love your neighbor. The premise consists of two apodictically formulated commands using the future indicative. This half of the premise corresponds verbatim with Lev 19:18, LXX, but stops short of the complete command by omitting ὡς σεαυτόν. This omission doubtless resulted from the conjunction of the two commands in 5:43a, b, and does not affect the import of the commandment. Apart from the Marcan context of the question concerning the Great Commandment in 22:39, par. Mark 12:31, the evangelist inserts Lev 19:18, LXX, into the list of commandments of 19:19, cf. Mark 10:19. This usage of the love commandment in 19:19 has particular significance since it, like 5:43, represents the Old Testament Law that proves to be inadequate for the rich young ruler, in view of Jesus' demand for discipleship that follows (cf. 19:20–22).

The first-century use of *neighbor* (πλῆσιον) had narrowed in its reference from that of Lev 19:18. Whereas *neighbor* meant a fellow member of the convenant community, an "Israelite," in the Old Testament context in contrast to the non-Israelite (Fichtner, *TDNT* 6:313–15; Montefiore, *Rabbinic Literature*, 60), the rabbinic discussions contain many examples of the struggles with the casuistic implications of *neighbor* (Str-B 1:353–56). Qumran had clearly limited the designation to members of their community (1QS 1:3–4, 9), and the parable of the Good Samaritan offers the classic example of the question about who is my neighbor (Luke 10:29–37). Yet in the final analysis, it is rather moot whether *neighbor* meant fellow Israelite, fellow sectarian, fellow student of the Law, or simply one's friend or one's "own kind." The focus sharpens with the contrasting element, namely, one's *enemy.*

and hate your enemy. This half of the premise corresponds in form and structure with the first half (5:43a) but without a verbatim Old Testament parallel. Since the premise consists of two commands and since only the first half has a direct Old Testament parallel, many have attributed the premise to the scribal interpretation of the Law (e.g., McNeile, *Matthew*, 71; Smith, "Enemy," 71–73; Stonehouse, *Witness,*

199–200; Lohmeyer, *Matthäus,* 142; Percy, *Botschaft,* 155–56; Barth, "Understanding," 94). More recently, the discovery of the documents of Qumran and an apparent parallel to 5:43b (cf. 1QS 1:4, 10; 9:21–23) has led others to posit an Essene background (Wildberger, " 'Sekten-rolle,' " 37–38; Schubert, "Sermon," 120–21; Braun, *Radikalismus* 2:57, n. 1; Cross, *Library,* 209, n. 23; Davies, *Setting,* 252; Grundmann, *Matthäus,* 176–77; Hübner, *Gesetz,* 97–103). Yet the weakness in these various attempts to find a counterpart for 5:43 lies in the failure to take seriously the redactional character of the premises and the thrust of the previous premises. Therefore, in spite of the apparent verbal parallels to the teaching of the Essenes, one can hardly envision such a context for Matthew's own community. Nor do the previous premises reflect either verbally or in caricature the rabbinic interpretation of the Law as such.

Nevertheless, the rabbinic and Essenic teaching share a material parallel with the premise, a parallel that has its roots in the Old Testament itself. The dual nature of this parallel emerges most clearly in the Qumran writings, since they state explicitly what lies implicitly in the teachings of the rabbis and the Old Testament. First, the Qumran writings distinguished sharply between two groups of people, those chosen by God and called the "sons of light" (1QS 1:3–4, 9) and those despised by God, called the "sons of darkness" (1QS 1:10). The distinction of people into two categories based on one's relationship to God runs from the love command to love one's *neighbor,* meaning a fellow Israelite, to the attempt to define more precisely one's *neighbor* in the rabbinic discussions (Nissen, *Nächste,* 318–29). Second, this distinction in Qumran derives from the Old Testament portrayal of God's redemptive activity past and future involving the righteous and the wicked (Sutcliff, "Qumran," 349–52; Stendahl, "Hate," 344). This same criterion for distinguishing between the groups remains consistently theological, namely, in terms of one's response to God's redemptive activity in history, from Lev 19:18 through the rabbis (Nissen, *Nächste,* 322–28). The different definitions of God's redemptive activity led to the various views of *neighbor* behind the rabbis, Jesus, and Qumran. Therefore, Matt 5:43 in one sense stands in continuity with the teaching of the Old Testament, the rabbis, and Qumran. One's attitude and behavior toward another was conditioned to an extent by who the other person was.

Most likely the actual source and background of 5:43b stems at least indirectly from 5:44a. Just as the Q material of 5:32 conditioned the premise of 5:31, so the Q material on Love Your Enemy triggered for Matthew a reference to the love commandment in Lev 19:18. We have already noted that the evangelist redactionally inserted this command-ment into a Marcan context in 19:19, a context in which keeping of the Law was also superseded by Jesus' demand (19:20–22). Furthermore, since the previous premises set forth the Old Testament Law from the perspective of its legal implications, it only follows that the love com-mandment be expressed in terms of its casuistic consequences. If one is to *love one's neighbor,* then the converse is also true, namely, one is to *hate one's enemy.* The actual wording for 5:43b stems from the Q material of 5:44a. Just as the use of Lev 19:18 conditioned the choice of language in 5:43a, so the command to love one's enemies (5:44a) conditioned the choice of its antithetical expression in 5:43b. The antithe-sis of the *love one's enemy* was to *hate one's enemy.* Thus, 5:43b does not intend to express an additional command but to offer the consequences of the love commandment casuistically stated in terms of 5:44a. Matt 5:43b is epexegetic to 5:43a.

By forming the premise in this matter, Matthew again focuses on the Old Testament Law in its casuistic setting, a focus that remains constant throughout the premises. At the same time, the evangelist ex-presses through the antithetical format the real antithesis between Jesus' teaching in his demand to love one's enemy and the limits generally applied to the Old Testament Law in Lev 19:18, by the Psalmist (e.g., Ps 138:21–22), by the rabbis (Str-B 1:353–54; Seitz, "Enemy," 43–54) and in the Qumran (1QS 1:3–4), despite the absence of *enemy expressis verbis* in these writings. The format also accounts for the tension between the corporate reference to *neighbor* and *enemy* in 5:43 based on Lev 19:18 and the obvious personal reference to *enemies* in 5:44–47.

As formulated by Matthew, the premise of 5:43 sets forth the common understanding of the Law in the Old Testament and contemproary Juda-ism without further attempting to define *neighbor* or *enemy.* One may thus conclude that the distinction in Matthew designating collectively those who did *(neighbor)* and did not *(enemy)* share in a common accep-tance of God's redemption activity in history remained essentially a reli-gious and moral distinction rather than personal, just as it had been in the Old Testament and Judaism.

5:44. *Love your enemies.* This antithesis consists of a double apodictic command to *love one's enemies* and to *pray for one's persecutors.* A positive (5:45) and negative (5:46–47) basis follow, with 5:48 rounding off this and the other five Antitheses. Luke 6:27–36 without 6:29–30, par. Matt 5:39b–42, offers the Q parallel containing several differences in arrangement and wording (Schürmann, *Lukasevangelium,* 345–46, 354–59; Lührmann, "Feinde," 416–22; Schulz, *Spruchquelle,* 126–31; Wrege, *Überlieferungsgeschichte,* 83–94; Guelich, "Antitheses," 447–50).

Whereas Matthew has a double command (5:44), Luke has a fourfold command divided into two synonymous parallelisms. In the first, love and doing that which is good responds to the enemy and to hatred (6:27a, b). The reference to those who *hate you* (μισοῦσιν) picks up the distinctive theme from the last Beatitude (Luke 6:22, cf. Matt 5:11) and indicates the original conjunction of the final Beatitude (6:22) with this section (6:27–35) in the pre-Lucan tradition (Lührmann, "Feinde," 414–15). The second parallelism underscores the ultimate nature of one's concern for those who curse (cf. Rom 12:14; *Did* 1:3) and abuse (cf. 1 Pet 3:16) by calling for blessing and intercession. This expanded form of the command (cf. *Did* 1:3) most likely existed in the pre-Lucan tradition (Bultmann, *Tradition,* 79; Manson, *Teachings,* 52; Schürmann, *Lukasevangelium,* 346; Seitz, "Enemies," 52, cf. Lührmann, "Feinde," 416).

The first half of the premise (5:44a) states the familiar command to *love one's enemies,* a command that occurs in this context only in the New Testament and early Christian literature. The numerous treatments of the Greek verb ἀγαπάω have repeatedly underscored the dynamic character of the term in contrast to a mere feeling or emotion. That love in 5:44a implies action finds its nearest support in the immediate context focusing on what one does in relationship to another (5:45–47, cf. especially ἀγαθοποιέω = "to do good" in Luke 6:33, cf. 6:27b).

Enemies appears in the plural in 5:44a in contrast to the singular of 5:43b. This change in number suggests one's personal *enemies* rather than the collective, religious designation of the counterpart to *neighbor.* Indeed, the personal overtones surface in the parallel *those who persecute you* (5:44b, cf. Luke 6:27b, 28a), and in one's actions of 5:46–47. Yet traces of the collective context remain evident in the contrast between *brothers* and the *Gentiles* of 5:47. The distinction between personal *enemies* and the *enemy* as a corporate, religious term for those who are not *neighbors* ultimately breaks down for Matthew since the expression of personal enmity is "persecution," a religiously based opposition (5:44b, cf. 5:11–12). In other words, *love your enemy* set in antithesis to 5:43 not only demands that one loves one's personal enemies but also those whose enmity reflects a basic enmity with God as well. It is precisely this teaching that sets off Jesus' love command from the Old Testament Law and its usage in Judaism (Seitz, "Enemies," 44).

pray for those who persecute you. The second half of the double command demonstrates the nature of one's concerned action or love for one's enemies. One is to respond with intercessory *prayer* (προσεύχεσθε), a demand illustrated by Jesus and Stephen in Luke 23:34 and Acts 7:60. *Those who persecute you* (διωκόντων) differs from Luke's "those who abuse you" (ἐπηρεαζόντων; cf. 1 Pet 3:16). Although many have assigned διώκω to Matthew's redaction (Kilpatrick, *Origins,* 16; Dupont, *Béatitudes* 1:155, n. 1: Trilling, *Israel,* 80; Hare, *Persecution,* 114–15; Schulz, *Spruchquelle,* 128), the presence of the concept in Matthew's final Beatitude may well suggest that the change goes back to a Q variation and reflect the Church's struggle in the mission situation (Lührmann, "Feinde," 415–16). In any event, *those who persecute you* sets the enmity within the context of one's life of faith, a theme which Matthew developed in his Beatitude of 5:10 (see Note on 5:10).

By setting the command to love one's enemies over against the Old Testament love command, Matthew highlights the distinctiveness of Jesus' demand. This contrast, however, was not created by the evangelist, since it was implicit to the contextual alignment of the final Beatitude and this section in the Q tradition as found by the respective evangelist (5:11–12, 44, cf. Luke 6:22, 27). Matthew has merely followed the precedent of the previous Antitheses and in so doing has provided the stark contrast between Jesus and Judasim—indeed, between Jesus' announcement of the gospel and the Old Testament Law. Such limitless love corresponds to God's redemptive activity on behalf of all the nations as found in the promise of Isaiah and as used by the evangelist to preface Jesus' ministry in 4:14–17 and to conclude it in 28:18–20. Yet the practical focus on one's response to persecution within the mission setting prevents the command from being merely an abstract ideal.

5:45. *in order that you might be sons of your Father in heaven.* This verse in the form of a purpose clause gives the first of two grounds for the commandment. Luke offers a similar ground, but expressed in the form of a promise and occurring at the end of the section (Luke 6:35). The difference in the form and arrangement stems from Matthew's reworking of the tradition after separating 5:39–42 from this context. In Luke the rhetorical questions of 6:32–34 that precede the promise and that are summarized in 6:35a presuppose the presence of 6:29–30, since the questions provide the pre-Lucan ties combining 6:29–30 into the larger context of 6:27–28, 35 (6:29 = 6:33, 35a; 6:30 [pre-Lucan] = 6:34, 35a; cf. Guelich, "Antitheses," 447–48). Matthew's rearrangement of the material removes the need for the imperatives of Luke 6:35a and focuses on the premise of sonship by the redactional use of ὅπως (*in order that*, 17x in Matt; 1x in Mark; 7x in Luke) in place of Luke's paratactic καί to connect the two clauses of reward and sonship. By use of the purpose clause, Matthew subsumes the promise of Luke 6:35 under the reward motif to which he returns in 5:46.

Sonship in both 5:45 and Luke 6:35 appears as a reward. Like 6:1, 4, 6, 18, these verses belong to a group of sayings in Jesus' ministry that apparently teach an ethic of merit. Yet these two sayings, as well as those of Matthew 6, stand within the larger scope of Jesus' ministry in which rewards were seen to be gifts of grace rather than merit (see Note on 6:1). The "goal" or "reward" of sonship in both Matthew and Luke lies not so much in the status as sons but in the characteristic of sonship, namely, conduct becoming the Father (Schürmann, *Lukas-evangelium*, 356). In other words, the thrust of Matt 5:45 and Luke 6:35 was not so much on how to become a son but how a son acts. This emphasis emerges from the accompanying clauses describing the Father's conduct.

Father in heaven. Luke 6:35 has his own designation, "Most High" (ὕψιστος; cf. 1:32, 35, 76; Acts 7:48), whereas the related Beatitude of 5:9 with *sons of God* may be reminiscent of *"God"* (θεός) in the Q tradition (Schürmann, *Lukasevangelium*, 355). Matthew clearly prefers the term *Father* (cf. 5:16; 6:1, 7; see Note on 6:9) and may have drawn it here from 5:48, par. Luke 6:36. For the qualification *in heaven* see Note on 6:9.

he causes the sun to rise . . . the rain to fall. Luke 6:35 has simply the adjective "gracious" (χρηστός; cf. Eph 4:32, a frequent designation for God in the LXX) in place of Matthew's more graphic explanation. Luke's more literary style using the same root in χάρις ("grace," "benefit"), χρηστός ("gracious"), and ἀχάριστος ("ungrateful") may suggest a deliberate, secondary alignment of the terms (Schürmann, *Lukasevangelium*, 356, n. 101; Schulz, *Spruchquelle*, 128).

good and evil. . . just and unjust. These designations (cf. Luke 23:50) correspond to the *neighbor/enemy* distinction of 5:43 as well as the implied difference in the objects of one's behavior mentioned in 5:46–47. Luke 6:35, however, focuses only on the "evil" and the "ungrateful," the latter a possible stylistic alignment with the context as noted above.

With 5:45 Matthew gives the love command of 5:44 its eschatological dimension and furnishes a concrete expression of what the Beatitude to the "peacemaker" (5:9) implied. One's love for the enemy ("peacemaking") corresponds to the Father's indiscriminate goodness and is indicative of sonship, since conduct in keeping with that of the Father belongs to the nature of sonship. Therefore, sonship is not the result so much as the positive basis of the command. The tension between the promise of *future* sonship (5:9b, 45) and yet the demand for and recognition of conduct in the *present* issuing from sonship itself (5:10a, 44) is characteristic of the tension between the future and the present in Matthew's eschatology. The future promise pertains to the ultimate recognition of sonship at the final judgment, but sonship is already a present reality in view of God's redemptive activity through Christ in the present (cf. 5:48; cf. 19:20–22). The future tense expresses the final culmination of what already has begun in the present.

5:46. *if you love.* Matthew follows the positive basis in 5:45 for the love command with a negative basis consisting of two rhetorical questions (5:46–47). Luke 6:32–34 by contrast has three pointed questions, only the first of which has a parallel in Matthew. Each question begins with, "What credit is it to you?" (ποία ὑμῖν χάρις ἐστίν;), whereas Matthew uses the rhetorical double question in each case. The evangelists concur in the content of the first question that refers back to the love command. But Luke's second and third questions (Luke 6:33–34) pick up the twofold theme of the inserted unit of 6:29–30 (6:29 = "to do good" [ἀγαθοποιέω] and 6:30 = "to lend" [δανείζω]). All three questions may well have originated at the time of combination of 6:29–30 into 6:27–28, 35 in order to serve as threads binding the units together. This adaptation also explains the necessity to repeat the now remote love command in 6:35a. In spite of Luke's interest in χάρις (8x in Luke, not at all in Matt or Mark), the presence of the "Lucan" form of the question in *Did* 1:3 and the similar traditional usage of χάρις in 1 Pet 2:20 may well support the pre-Lucan formulation of the questions (so Best, "I Peter," 100; con. van Unnik, "Feindesliebe," 296; cf. *idem.* "Good Works," 99–100; Schürmann, *Lukasevangelium,* 353, n. 77).

what reward will you have? Luke also refers to reward (μισθός) in 6:35, which some have viewed to be a reminiscence of the original question in Q now found in Matt 5:46 (Schürmann, *Untersuchungen,* 115; *idem, Lukasevangelium,* 353, n. 77; Luhrmann, "Feinde," 420). Yet Luke's "your reward shall be great" parallels almost verbatim the promise of the final Beatitude in both Matthew and Luke (5:12, par. Luke 6:23), whereas Matthew's *to have a reward* (μισθὸν ἔχετε) occurs only here and in 6:1, a Matthean redactional unit introducing 6:2–18 (see Note 6:1). If a reminiscence is to be found, 5:46 containing Matthean redaction refers to the original promise now found in Luke 6:35, par. 6:23, and used later by Matthew in 6:1.

Do not the tax collectors do the same?   Matthew's use of οὐχί redactionally elsewhere (6:25, cf. Luke 12:23; 13:56, cf. Mark 6:3; 18:12, cf. Luke 15:4) further supports his redactional reworking of the Q material here. Whereas Luke refers to "sinners" (ἁμαρτωλοί, 17x cf. 5x in Matt, 6x in Mark) consistently in all three questions, Matthew's *tax collectors* refers to the group whose conduct and profession was most despised among the Jews. Only the Gentiles could be worse, and they appear in 5:47. The point of the comparison is obvious. To act in a loving manner only within a reciprocal relationship is to do no more than the *tax collectors,* who hardly offered models for Jewish behavior.

5:47.   *If you greet only your brothers.*   The second question has no parallel in Luke. Rather Luke's second question (ἀγαθοποιῆτε, 6:33) focuses on the inserted saying of nonresistance in 6:29. 1 Pet 2:20 has the same verb (ἀγαθοποιέω) with similar meaning, namely, to return good for evil or to exhibit good conduct in the face of adverse situations (van Unnik, "Good Words," 99–100). Luke also has a third question, totally absent in Matthew, that clearly refers to the pre-Lucan tradition (see Note on 5:42) in 6:30 by its use of the verb "to borrow" (δανίσητε). Since both distinctively Lucan questions refer back to 6:29–30 and since Matthew has used that material to help fill out the Antithesis of 5:38–42, these questions found in Q have lost their immediate setting in Matthew. Consequently, Matthew's second question focuses on "greeting" (ἀσπάσησθε, cf. 23:7, par. Mark 12:38). His only other use of this verb occurs in the mission situation of 10:12, cf. Luke 10:6, where the more special connotation of a blessing is involved. If that semitechnical usage of a Jewish greeting of peace were brought into the current setting, the second question would fit with the thrust of the second element in the command to pray for one's persecutors (cf. especially Luke 6:28a, εὐλογεῖτε). Therefore, the two Matthean questions would each focus on an element of the command of 5:44, the context with which Matthew is left after removing 5:39b–42, par. Luke 6:29–30. Furthermore, *brothers* offers a parallel for *neighbor* in Judaism (Str-B 1:276), though in Matthew it refers to members of the Church (Davies, *Setting,* 98; Frankemölle, *Jahwebund,* 178–85).

what more do you do?   Just as the previous question concluded with a Matthean phrase parallel to his redactional comparing of the disciples with the scribes and Pharisees (cf. 5:46 and 6:1), so this phrase (περισσόν) is reminiscent of a similar redactional comparison in 5:20 (see Note on 5:20). In both 6:1 and 5:20 "righteousness" is at stake, as indeed it is here. Not only does 5:11–12 tie in verbally with 5:44, but 5:10, growing out of 5:11–12 and 5:3 (see Note on 5:10), specifically speaks of *persecution for righteousness' sake.* These negative questions of 5:46–47 add further indirect but significant evidence for Matthew's understanding of righteousness as consisting in conduct, but conduct befitting totally new relationships. As will be seen in 5:48, the fundamental relationship is that of sonship (cf. 5:45).

The two rhetorical questions underscore the demand *to love one's enemies* and *to pray for one's persecutors* by showing that not to do so would be indicative of conduct becoming the "enemy" himself. In other words, the command of 5:44 presupposes positively that one has become a son and thus is to display conduct befitting the Father; or, negatively, that one is different from the *tax collectors* and *Gentiles* who, from a Jewish perspective, represent those that stand either by choice or birth outside God's redemptive activity.

5:48. *Be whole as your Father in heaven is whole.* Luke 6:36 differs in content and setting. Instead of concluding the unit on Love Your Enemies (Luke 6:35), Luke 6:36 calls for "mercy" (οἰκτίρμονες) to introduce the next Sermon section on Judging (6:36–42, par. Matt 7:1–5). These differences are traceable to the Matthean redaction. First, in support of Luke's priority, the adjective "merciful" (οἰκτίρμονες) and thus the context of 6:36–42, cf. Matt 7:1–5, corresponds to the fifth Beatitude in Matthew 5:7. In the latter, *merciful* (ἐλεήμονες), an Old Testament hendiadys with οἰκτίρμων, is reminiscent of the Q section of Luke 6:36–42 (see Note on 5:7; Lührmann, "Feinde," 415). Second, Matthew's insertion of τέλειος ("wholeness") into his parallel of Mark 10:21 is clear indication of his redactional activity. The rich young ruler, recognizing Jesus to be a rabbi or "teacher," an address reserved exclusively for "outsiders" in Matthew (Bornkamm, "End-expectation," 41), inquires about securing eternal life (19:16, par. Mark 10:17). After referring him to the Law including the love commandment (19:19, cf. Mark), which the young man had faithfully kept from his youth (19:18–19, par. Mark 10:19), Jesus confronted him with the necessary requirement (19:21) for eternal life (not a second stage in discipleship, con. Kretschmar, "Askese," 61), namely, *wholeness* (τέλειος). This scene correlates to Matthew's redaction of 5:19–20 in which keeping the Law was important (5:19, cf. 19:18–19) but inadequate for entrance into the Kingdom (5:20, cf. 19:20–21).

Matt 5:20 sets the demand for a "greater righteousness" as the entrance requirement for the Kingdom; 19:21 sets *wholeness* (τέλειος) as the requirement for eternal life. Therefore, δικαιοσύνη (5:20) and τέλειος (5:48), opening and closing the Antitheses, hold the key to Matthew's understanding of Jesus' demand—for some, the key to Matthew's christology (e.g., Luck, *Vollkommenheitsforderung;* Suggs, *Wisdom*).

Excursus: τέλειος in Matthew

The background of Matthew's usage of τέλειος has been variously traced to the Old Testament (e.g., Schlatter, *Matthäus,* 197; McNeile, *Matthew,* 73; Hill, *Matthew,* 131), to Qumran (e.g., Rigaux, "Révélation," 237–62; Davies, *Setting,* 209–15), and to Wisdom (e.g., Luck, *Vollkommenheitsforderung,* 28–38). The term τέλειος itself occurs rather infrequently in the LXX as the translation for two common Hebrew terms, *tmn* (Gen 6:9; Exod 12:5; Deut 18:13; 2 Sam 22:26) and *šlm* (Jud 20:26; 1 Kgs 8:61; 11:4; 15:3,14; 1 Chron 28:9). In both cases, τέλειος describes one's relationship with God, a "personal qualitative" standing before God (DuPlessis, ΤΕΛΕΙΟΣ, 95–96). The references in 1 Kings connote a "whole-hearted allegiance to the Lord" (DuPlessis, ΤΕΛΕΙΟΣ, 99). This relational dimension concurs with the synonymous terms in 2 Sam 22:21–27 (e.g., "blameless," "righteous," "loyal," "clean," "pure") and characterizes the usage of τέλειος in the other passages (except Exod 12:5). Thus the positive term *wholeness* best renders the force of τέλειός in such contexts.

In Qumran, the Hebrew *tmn,* occurring twenty-two times in 1QS alone (cf. CD 2:15; 1QM 7:5; 14:7; 1QH 1:36), almost exclusively refers to the "perfect of the way" or those who "walk perfectly," implying that one's life totally fulfills the God-revealed way of life (Delling, *TDNT* 8:73). So characteristic was this term for the community that they referred to themselves as the "House of Perfection" (1QS 8:9). "Perfection" applied only to those who lived totally according to the Essenes' teaching of the Law. The "way" and one's "walk" referred to the special understanding of the Law revealed exclusively to the community. Consequently, a strong, legal, ethical tone had become dominant in their use of *tmn*. It is in this understanding of perfection "rooted in a particular interpretation of the Law" that Davies has found the background to 5:48 (*Setting,* 212). Both Matthew and Qumran apparently called their communities to a perfect obedience of a given interpretation of the Law. The contrast lay only in their different interpretations of the Law (*Setting,* 212).

Luck has sought a slightly different context for the use of *tmn* in Qumran, namely, the Wisdom literature of the period. Using Wis 9:6, which states that one who is supposedly τέλειος but lacking Wisdom amounts to nothing, as the key passage, Luck sees τέλειος, Wisdom, and the Law to form an integral complex (*Vollkommenheitsforderung,* 30–31). He seeks further support for this view in the Qumran material (*Vollkommenheitsforderung,* 31–33). Since "perfection" in Qumran is ascribed to the one who totally does the will of God, the Law, one becomes "perfect" by doing the Law. But Wisdom plays a critical role of actually effecting τέλειος by revealing God's will and aiding one in carrying it out. Thus by the study of the Law Wisdom comes to enlighten and empower one to fulfill the Law's demands (e.g., Wis 6:12–25; 9:9–10; cf. 1QS 3:18–20; 11:3–8). Accordingly, Matt 5:48 stems from a Wisdom understanding of the Law and of Jesus as a Wisdom teacher whose teaching reveals God's will (*Vollkommenheitsforderung,* 35–38; cf. Suggs, *Wisdom,* 99–120).

The determination of whether Matthew's usage of τέλειος parallels the Old Testament, Qumran, or Wisdom remains elusive because Matthew uses the term only twice. In both contexts the term connotes *wholeness,* since a culpable insufficiency or inadequacy is underlined (5:48, cf. 5:20; 19:20). Therefore, the demand for τέλειος stands as a demand for something more, a *wholeness* nothing less than which will do. The critical question focuses on what that something more is. The answer can only come from the context, indeed, both contexts of Matthew's usage.

Most scholars, whether or not they choose the Wisdom or Qumran setting as the Matthean counterpart, appear agreed that Matthew's demand for τέλειος connotes the total keeping of the "Law" as taught by Jesus (e.g., Bornkamm, "End-expectation," 29; Barth, "Understanding," 96–103; Trilling, *Israel,* 193–95; Hasler, *Gesetz,* 22; Davies, *Setting,* 211–12; Luck, *Vollommenheitsforderung,* 20–28; Suggs, *Wisdom,* 99–127). Such an understanding, apart from the various christological starting points, implies that Matthew understood the Antitheses of 5:21–48 legally as a Messianic Torah or a final, radical interpretation of the Law which one was to carry out in order to be τέλειος. In other words, τέλειος connotes totally keeping the "Law" as taught by Jesus.

In spite of the parallels for such a Law-oriented usage of τέλειος in the Wisdom and Qumran literature, this "legal" understanding overlooks three critical contextual indications in Matthew that point in a different direction. First, such a view of τέλειος misses the function of the legal form used in the Antitheses. The radical impossibility of the Antitheses' demands that outlaw anger, lust, divorce, dishonesty, retaliation, while demanding love for the enemy, intentionally forces one beyond the limits of the Law and a morality determined by the Law. One is forced to look for a totally new starting point. Rather than an end in themselves, the Antitheses point by means of hyperbolic legal demands to the necessity of new relationships between individuals without which the demands are utopian at best. This new relationship implicit in the Antitheses' demands is nothing less than the "greater righteousness" demanded in 5:20, the "righteousness of God" (6:33) which comes as a gift from God (5:6) and from which the corresponding conduct issues (5:10, 20; 6:1). The conduct is not the means of righteousness (cf. 5:19); it is the concomitant of righteousness, the new relationship between God and humanity characteristic of the new age.

Second, such a view short-circuits Matthew's christology by reading 5:21–48 as Matthew's understanding of Jesus' fulfillment of the Law (5:17) through the latter's interpretation of it. As seen in the discussion of 5:17, Matthew's christology is not Law-related as much as promise-related. His is a fulfillment christology. Jesus came as the Messiah to fulfill the promise of God's redemptive activity in history by restoring broken relationships between himself and his creatures. This message in Matthew is the gospel of the Kingdom (see Note on 4:23). The Antitheses bear witness to the *coming to pass of all things* (5:18), the fulfillment of *the Scriptures* (5:7), by setting forth demands for conduct commensurate with the new age, the age of salvation, the age of restored relationships between God and his people and consequently among his people, as the sixth antithesis clearly states (5:44).

Third, τέλειος meaning to keep totally the Law taught by Jesus fails to account for the usage in 19:20–21, where Jesus is not depicted as a teacher or interpreter of the Law. One cannot avoid this problem by taking Jesus' demand to sell all and give to the poor as a radical interpretation of the love commandment. Selling all and giving to the poor was not intended as a means to perfection and thus eternal life but as the crossing of the barrier to discipleship, the ability to surrender all and trust only in what God was doing and would do through Jesus (cf. 6:25–34). The young man's righteousness and wealth, typical of the Pharisee, made Jesus' demand too risky. At stake was whether Jesus was more than a rabbi (διδάσκαλε), indeed, whether he was the Lord (κύριε) in whom God's sovereign rule had entered history and was at work restoring relationships between himself and his people (cf. the disciples' response in 19:27–30, par. Mark 10:28–31). Therefore, Jesus' demand in 19:20–21, as in the Antitheses, was for conduct commensurate with a new relationship between the young ruler and God. Selling his possessions and giving to the poor were indications of, not pre-conditions for, that relationship. Jesus was calling him to much more than a disciple-rabbi relationship. Rather, Jesus was summoning the young man to a relationship of total surrender and trust that would cut across the self-sufficiency of his righteousness and wealth.

In 5:48 and 19:21 τέλειος is not a call to radical obedience but to a new relationship with God. Instead of connoting legal perfection, the term connotes *wholeness* in one's relationship with God and others. To be sure, a moral element in terms of commensurate conduct is involved, as with Matthew's use of *righteousness.* But the moral ingredient is subsequent, not primary, as in Qumran. Consequently, the final demand of 5:48, like the demand in 19:21, has the same interest as the Antitheses themselves, namely, to point and to summon one to the new relationship of *wholeness* with God and with one another (cf. 5:44–47) available in view of Jesus' coming and ministry.

As noted above, the LXX usage of τέλειος carries just such a relational meaning. Should one look for a particular text that might have stood behind Matthew's usage, perhaps Deut 18:13 comes closest, since it stands within the larger context of Deuteronomic material found elsewhere in Matthew's redactional work in the Sermon (Deut 18:19–22, cf. Matt 7:15–23; Deut 19:16–21, cf. 5:38–39b). Drawn from the Old Testament usage and placed in the Q form of the saying in Luke 6:36, par. 5:48, τέλειος summarizes the call to new relationships demanded in the last Antithesis (5:43–47) as well as in all six Antitheses.

Matt 5:48 redactionally concludes what 5:20 redactionally introduced, namely, a call for a righteousness that exceeds the inadequate legal righteousness and perfection of the scribes and Pharisees. This righteousness (5:20) connotes conduct (5:21–48) befitting the new relationships (*wholeness,* 5:48) characteristic of the age of salvation.

Comments

Matt 5:20 concludes the section of 5:17–20 with the warning, "Unless your righteousness exceeds that of the scribes and Pharisees, you will not enter the Kingdom of Heaven." This warning took precedent over and qualified the matter of rank in the Kingdom (5:19) based on one's keeping of the Law. Yet at the same time the warning of 5:20 also serves as an introduction for what follows (5:21—7:12) focusing on the nature of that "greater righteousness." The immediate context consists of a series of Antitheses (5:21–48) that set forth Jesus' demand for conduct commensurate with the new relationships between individuals indicative of the fulfillment of the age of promise in Jesus' ministry (cf. 5:17–18). These Antitheses offer many questions regarding meaning, intent, applicability, and background. To approach these questions, the ensuing comments will deal separately with the "Greater Righteousness" of 5:21–48, the "Kingdom Ethics" and their implications, and finally a history of the tradition behind this complex.

A. The "Greater Righteousness"

The heart of Matt 5:21–48 consists of the six Antitheses containing a premise with the introductory formula "You have heard that God has said (to the generation of old)" and an antithesis opening with "But I say to you." Although parts of these formulas have parallels in rabbinic thought, the antithetical framework and usage in this context stand without parallel (see Notes on 5:21, 22). In this respect Jesus' demand for conduct pleasing to God stands over against that demanded in the Old Testament Law.

Each premise has a material counterpart in the Old Testament Law. But more is at stake than simply the citing of the Old Testament Law. Placed in the forms of a legal ordinance and an apodictic command, legal justice and moral justice are combined so that each premise depicts the Old Testament Law as the legal principle controlling human behavior. Whereas for Jesus' audience this legal principle was clearly the Mosaic Law, our own law today corresponds essentially with that of all six premises. Thus, the Antitheses, while addressing another time and people, are neither irrelevant nor foreign to our situation today.

Each Antithesis sets Jesus' own demand over against the Law's legal demand in the same form and context. In this manner, Jesus demonstrates the legalistic orientation of human society, especially in his day. The Law justified and condemned one on the societal level, but it also held implications for one's standing before God. To the extent that one was guiltless or right before the Law, to that extent one was right before God, since the Law was viewed as the expression of God's will for his people. Ethics had become swallowed up in the legalistic definition of one's conduct before God and others. By setting his demands in this antithetical framework, Jesus pointed out the total inadequacies of such a legalistic view of the Law and the human impossibility of his own demand when legalistically perceived.

The ultimate contrast or antithesis between the Law's legal demands and Jesus' demands seen legally lies in the different starting points. The Law was predicated on the reality of sin and evil. Jesus' absolute demands set in a legal framework predicate the absence of evil as a dominant force and the restoration of the broken relationship between God and his own as well as between individuals. This reconciliation is most succinctly expressed in the love commandment of the sixth Antithesis. Notwithstanding the occasional parallels to the introductory formulas in

Judaism, the antithetical format and the content of Jesus' demands stands without parallel in rabbinic Judaism (see Notes on 5:21, 22).

1. Anger: Matt 5:21–26

The premise (5:21) consists of an apodictic prohibition (5:21a) and a legal ordinance (5:21b) that states the consequences of one's actions. The absolute command cites the sixth commandment, "You shall not kill" (Exod 20:13, LXX). The legal ordinance, although not taken verbatim from the Old Testament, expresses the Old Testament Law's teaching that murder was not only morally wrong but legally wrong as well. Exod 21:12–14, Lev 24:17–21, and Num 35:16–17 detail the specifics for the legal verdict of guilt with the corresponding penalty, which was usually death. Matt 5:21b does not spell out the precise penalty but states that a murderer must stand trial with view to the sentence of death. Therefore, the premise sets forth the Old Testament Law against murder as perceived from a legal standpoint.

The Antithesis (5:22) counters with three statements in the form of legal ordinances. The first outlaws anger and the other two outlaw the use of invectives or name-calling. Technically, little or no difference exists among the three crimes (see Note on 5:22). Whereas anger indicates one's feelings of estrangement, the invectives merely make that feeling explicit. Furthermore, "idiot" and "fool" translate two common Aramaic expressions that were all but synonymous, as they are in English (see Note on 5:22). Any attempt to distinguish them strains at the impossible. The only difference in the three statements occurs in the legal consequences. In the first (5:22a), "anger," like murder, makes one liable to stand trial with view to the same sentence expected in the parallel of 5:21b. Calling another an "idiot" (5:22b) meant standing trial before the supreme court of the land, the Sanhedrin, and calling a person "fool" (5:22c) would lead to the sentence of eternal punishment by God at the last judgment.

Numerous attempts to soften or clarify Jesus' demand have emerged. The earliest such attempt appears in the manuscripts as the secondary qualification of the absolute prohibition of anger "without cause" in an attempt to bring the demand into line with the realities of life. Some have taken the prohibitions of the invectives at face value and avoided the actual utterance of such terms. But most contemporary approaches have sought to eliminate them in one way or another as being secondary applications of Jesus' prohibition against anger (see Note on 5:22). Not only is substantial evidence for this alternative lacking, but the elimination of 5:22bc does not make 5:21a any more manageable. All three statements belong to the same piece of cloth. Only together do they compose the pattern that expresses the intention of the Antithesis. The ascending order of judicial proceedings involved and the minor or nonexistent difference in the crimes holds the key to the meaning of this and the following Antitheses.

Setting the premise in the form of a legal ordinance and using that form to declare anger and name-calling illegal by referring them to increasing levels of judicial processes, focuses the antithesis primarily on the legal orientation of the Old Testament Law against murder. Put somewhat crassly, one's standing before God was measured in terms of one's standing before the Law. One's standing before the Law was determined by a court proceeding. Therefore, if one was guiltless before a human court of having broken the Law, one could legitimately assume that one would be guiltless before God at the last judgment, since the human court simply carried out God's Law. Using this legalistic reasoning characteristic of the day, Jesus ironically framed his demand in an ascending order of judiciaries with no significant difference in the crimes or the penalties (see Note on 5:22).

The result of this kind of framing is twofold. First, the irony of Jesus' demand countered the common understanding that one's status before God could be determined by legalistic means, since Jesus' demand defies any legalistic possibility of literally carrying out the content. Second, whereas the Law forbidding murder was predicated on the reality of broken human relationships, the consequences of which the Law sought to control, Jesus' demand presupposes unbroken relationships, relationships between individuals characterized by reconciliation and wholeness. Using the format of contemporary legal casuistry, Jesus demanded conduct commensurate with the new relationships characteristic of the day of salvation when the alienating force of sin has been overcome.

Precisely this theme of restored relationships combines the following two parables (5:23–24, 25–26) with the Antithesis. In the first (5:23–24), one's relationship to God is intimately related to one's relationship with one's "brother," even when the brother holds the grudge (see Note on 5:23). In the second (5:25–26), one has the responsibility of using the available time to make reconciliation with the "adversary" who has been wronged (5:25). Thus, while the Law set the culpable limits on the actions of estrangement, Jesus' demand outlawed the estrangement itself.

Jesus' demand simply cannot be legalistically or casuistically applied. One can focus on the specifics of name-calling and other displays of temper. But the experience of anger itself lies beyond the control of sinful human beings. Even should one gain a modicum of "self-control," one struggles with the "legitimate" instances of "righteous indignation" that qualify Jesus' own actions in cleansing the Temple and pronouncing his anathemas on the scribes and Pharisees. Yet Jesus' demand in 5:22, legalistically understood, offers no such exceptions. Rather, by using the form of a legal ordinance, Jesus called for attitudes and behavior indicative of the presence of the Kingdom—the age of salvation—as seen in restored rather than broken relationships between individuals. Consequently, anything less than the restored relationship leaves one culpable before God.

2. Lust: Matt 5:27–30

The premise (5:27) of the second Antithesis, citing the seventh commandment (Exod 20:14, LXX), consists solely of the absolute prohibition, "You shall not commit adultery." Adultery in the Old Testament meant extramarital sexual intercourse between a man and another's wife. Whereas a husband could have an affair with an unmarried woman and not be guilty of adultery, he would be so charged if the woman were married. To this extent the laws regarding adultery were culturally conditioned by the wife's status of belonging to her husband in Jewish society (see Note on 5:32). In case of adultery, both the adulterer and the adulteress, according to the Law (Lev 20:10; Deut 22:22), were to be put to death.

The antithesis (5:28), in the form of a legal ordinance, counters by outlawing even the lustful desire for another's wife. Although the premise does not contain an explicit statement of the legal ordinance, that the absolute command was understood legally becomes evident from the form and content of the antithesis. Formulated as a legal ordinance, the antithesis simply states that the consequence of lustful desire for another's wife is to have committed adultery personally (in one's "heart") with her; in other words, in such a case, one is already *guilty* of adultery.

In spite of numerous parallels from rabbinic thought about committing adultery with the eye and heart (see Note on 5:28), these teachings appear to represent largely preventive measures to protect oneself from transgressing the seventh commandment (Moore, *Judaism* 2:269). Realizing that thoughts and desires often precede actions, one could, by taking prior measures, avoid the transgression of the Law. Yet granting Montefiore's statement, ". . . No simple Rabbinic Jew who read the utterance of Jesus for the first time would find anything startling . . ." (*Synoptic Gospels* 2:63), one very significant difference emerges. Montefiore unconsciously notes this difference when he concludes with "*except* [my italics] the implication that there was any opposition between the old Law and the new" (ibid.). But precisely within the context of the antithetical format we perceive the thrust of Jesus' demand in this Antithesis.

Jesus' demand was deliberately set in antithesis to the Law. Whereas the rabbis sought to interpret the Old Testament Law in its broadest implications, including one's "eyes," "heart," and "hands," Jesus' demand counters the legal premise of the Old Testament Law itself. The rabbis saw their teaching as being inherent in the Law; Jesus saw his at least as going beyond the Law.

Legally, the Old Testament Law prohibited physical, sexual relations between a man and a woman married to another man. But Jesus countered this legalistic understanding of man-woman relationships by declaring that lustful desire for another's wife made one guilty of adultery. Much more was at stake than a redefinition of adultery or a radicalizing of the seventh commandment. Jesus' statement in antithesis to the Old Testament commandment condemned the covert desire by setting it in place of the overt act. In other words, Jesus demanded a relationship between men and women that not only outlawed the physical act of adultery but also the adulterous thought. Nothing appears in the context about a "second look" or any other casuistic softening of the demand. As in his outlawing of anger, Jesus absolutely outlawed all adulterous thoughts.

The demand incriminates without prosecution. Indeed, prosecution is no more feasible in the second Antithesis than the first. But the legal format vividly reminds us of how culpable we are. We are again faced with the human impossibility, the absurdity of meeting such a demand, since one cannot legislate thoughts or feelings. One can meet the requirements of this demand only by means of a new relationship between men and women. Whereas the Law set inviolable limits on the husband-wife relationship because of the propensity of the human desires, Jesus' demand calls for nothing less than a totally *wholesome* relationship between man and woman in which evil itself is no longer predominant.

Apart from completely new relationships between individuals, not even the most drastic actions can protect one against evil. The ineffectiveness of a stopgap approach to combatting evil finds its graphic illustration in the two hyperbolic sayings that follow (5:29–30). Focusing on the "physical" dimension, one could mutilate oneself to avoid eventual judgment. But self-mutilation has no more effect than legislating against adulterous thoughts. The root of the problem lies within one's person, one's relationship with others. Jesus' demand therefore presupposes a new starting point in man-woman relationships.

3. Divorce: Matt 5:31–32

The third Antithesis involves a topic with parallels in an isolated saying in Luke 16:18, a controversy-teaching narrative in Mark 10:2–9, 10–12, par. Matt 19:3–9, and Paul's reference to Jesus' teaching in 1 Cor 7:10–12. The antithetical format does not appear in any of these parallels except in Matthew's rearrangement of the Marcan parallel to form an antithesis between the Law and Jesus' teaching in 19:7–9, cf. Mark 10:4, 11 (see Note on 5:31). Consequently, one can safely conclude that the evangelist, using the same background from Deut 24:1 found in Mark 10:4, formed and introduced this Antithesis into its present setting by using the catch-word "adultery" (5:27–28, 31–32a).

The premise (5:31) beginning with just the core of the introductory formula—"God said"—(see Note on 5:31) sets Deut 24:1 in the form of a legal ordinance. Whereas the subject of Deut 24:1–4 dealt with the question of remarriage, especially the remarriage of a wife to her first husband, it had long since become the Old Testament legal basis for divorce in Judaism as seen in Mark 10:4, par. Matt 19:7 (see Note on 5:31). So clear were the legal implications of Deut 24:1 for the possibility of divorce that the issue of "whether" seldom arose in rabbinic discussion. Rather, the critical question in Judaism focused on the "why." In choosing Deut 24:1 for the premise, Matthew accurately reflects the legal understanding of the Old Testament Law regarding divorce.

The antithesis (5:32) doubtless drawn by Matthew from his form of the Q tradition (see Note on 5:32) consists of two legal ordinances. The first reflects two significant differences from the Q parallel in Luke 16:18 as well as the tradition in Mark 10:11. First, whereas Luke and Mark declare that the one who divorces his wife and marries another woman commits adultery, 5:31a ascribes the adultery to the divorced wife and places the responsibility for her adultery on her former husband.

This difference between Matthew and Luke corresponds to the Old

Testament Law. According to Deut 24:1–4, the bill of divorce freed the wife to remarry, an action assumed in 5:32a. Furthermore, a man within Judaism could most certainly remarry without committing adultery, since in the polygamous context a man might have more than one wife simultaneously without being guilty of adultery. In fact, by virtue of the definition of adultery, a married man could even have an affair with an unmarried woman without committing adultery. Therefore, the focus of Luke 16:18 and Mark 10:11, par. Matt 19:9, on the husband's remarriage would have sounded foreign to Jewish ears. Yet since Matthew does not alter this clause in 19:9, par. Mark 10:11, the alteration in 5:32a most likely occurred in a pre-Matthean stage of the tradition in an attempt to align the saying more closely with the Old Testament Law and Jewish customs.

The second difference between 5:32a and the parallel in Luke 16:18a and Mark 10:11 is the so-called "except-clause" that qualifies the unconditional demand in the parallels (see Excursus on 5:32 for full discussion of this clause). Matt 19:9, cf. Mark 10:11, also has an "except-clause," although formulated somewhat differently. The presence of this clause in 5:32a in contrast to Luke 16:18a and in 19:9 in contrast to Mark 10:11, plus the absence of any trace of the clause in Paul's reference in 1 Cor 7:10–12 to Jesus' teaching, strongly suggests that the "except-clause" came into the tradition at a later stage. This conclusion finds further support in the similarity of the wording in 5:32a and the underlying Hebrew phrase in Deut 24:1. In other words, the Old Testament text that served as the basis for the discussion of the legitimate grounds for divorce in rabbinic Judaism also offered the basis for the "except-clause" in 5:32a.

Since Matthew deliberately set the divorce saying in antithesis to Deut 24:1 in both 5:31 and 19:7–9, cf. Mark 10:4, 11, he could hardly have then been responsible for adding an "except-clause" based on Deut 24:1 that would have aligned the antithesis with the premise. Furthermore, the clause in 19:9, which may well have been Matthean, no longer maintains any trace of Deut 24:1 (see Note on 5:32). Consequently, the "except-clause" in 5:32 most likely originated in the strict Jewish-Christian community that had reworked the Q tradition behind 5:18, cf. Luke 16:17, and the first part of 5:32, in order to align Jesus' teaching with the Old Testament Law.

By adding the clause based on Deut 24:1, Jesus' demand no longer set aside the Old Testament Law for divorce but applied it rabbinic style in a very restricted sense. Whereas a legalistic usage of Jesus' demand in Luke and Mark absolutely denies the possibility of divorce for any reason, including adultery and incestuous marriages (cf. Acts 15:29; 1 Cor 5:1), by introducing πορνεία ("immorality") as the grounds for divorce, the "except-clause" limited the grounds more narrowly than anything known in Judaism (see Note on 5:32) but also covered the various situations that were considered unthinkable in Judaism. More important, the "except-clause" maintained Jesus' teaching within the context of the Law in contrast to Mark and Luke in which Jesus' demand sets the Law aside. Therefore, the "except-clause," like "without cause" in 5:22, represents an understanding of Jesus' demand to be a legal ordinance on divorce and offers an apologetic and/or paranetic interpretation of Jesus' demand.

For Matthew, however, the saying could hardly have represented a more rigorous interpretation of Deut 24:1. It is true that the "except-clause" has often been used casuistically as the one legitimate ground for divorce and thus interpreted as intended by the Jewish-Christian community. But this understanding overlooks the evangelist's deliberate juxtaposition of Deut 24:1 in antithesis to Jesus' demand in 5:31–32 and 19:7–9, cf. Mark 10:4, 11. In order to avoid a major inconsistency within the evangelist's own thinking, one must conclude that Matthew understood the "except-clause" in the sense that the Apostle's Decree (Acts 15:29) refers to incestuous marriages among Gentile converts (see Note on 5:32). This conclusion is supported by his introducing the clause in 19:9, cf. Mark 10:11, without the wording of Deut 24:1. In other words, the consensus of the mission and the concerns of the Church rather than the Law or an interpretation of the Law offered the basis for the one exception. In any case, Matthew's use of the "except-clause," like Paul's own contextual adaptation of Jesus' teaching in 1 Cor 7:12–15, demonstrates that Jesus' absolute demand was not taken as absolutely legally binding but could be qualified by the given situation within the Church's mission.

In spite of the modifications of the saying within the tradition, it seems clear that Matthew intended for 5:32a to declare in contrast to Deut 24:1 that a man who divorces his wife—except in the case of an incestuous marriage—is responsible for causing her to commit adultery by her remarrying. The second legal ordinance of 5:32b makes essentially the same claim by declaring the one who marries a divorced woman guilty of adultery. Therefore, 5:32 stands in contrast to Deut 24:1 on two issues. First, Deut 24:1 conveys the legal right for a man to divorce his wife and thereby free her to remarry. Second, Deut 24:1 explicitly states that she may marry more than once but cannot remarry her first husband. In other words, the husband can divorce his wife and set her free and she can legally remarry. Jesus' demand in 5:32 as well as in the parallels counters both points of the Law.

Taken at face value, the saying would appear to address the question of remarriage rather than divorce. In both 5:32a and 5:32b the focus is the adultery of the wife who remarries (5:32a) and the man who marries her (5:32b). Consequently, the divorce sayings have occasionally been used to forbid remarriage while permitting divorce. Such a literalistic and legalistic interpretation, however, distorts the underlying nature of Jesus' demand.

Matthew's antithetical setting of the sayings in 5:31–32 and 19:7–9 is clearly redactional. But this redactional antithesis between Jesus' demand and the Law corresponds with and provides the clue for the implications of Jesus' demand for marriage. The Law was God's provision through Moses for marriage because of the reality of sin in the human experience, the "hardness of heart" (Mark 10:5). Yet Jesus' demand in Mark 10:6–9 pointed back to creation when God made human beings male and female in order to become "one flesh," to share a oneness in relationship (Mark 10:6–9, par. Matt 19:4–6). In other words, Jesus countered the human experience of sin by calling a married couple to live according to God's intent for creation. Such a demand could only be possible with the overcoming of the "hard heart," an indication of the offer of a "new heart," a "heart of flesh" instead of a "heart of stone" (Ezek 36:26), characteristic of the age of salvation. In view of his ministry Jesus could then apodictically set his demand in marriage in antithesis to the provision of the Law, "What God has joined together, let not man put asunder" (Mark 10:9, par. Matt 19:6).

The divorce sayings (Matt 5:32, par. Luke 16:18; Matt 19:9, par. Mark 10:11–12) do not contradict Jesus' demand for a perfect marriage (Mark 10:8–9) by assuming divorce to be a given. The divorce sayings are but graphic illustrations of Jesus' apodictic demand in Mark 10:9. By saying that a man who divorces his wife and remarries or causes her to marry is involved in adultery, Jesus implies that the first marriage was never broken by the divorce (cf. Mark 10:9). In other words, the subsequent marriage resulted in adultery against the first marriage partner, because the wife was not free to remarry. Taken consistently, these divorce sayings deny the reality of a divorce. Jesus has thus expressed God's will for marriage through the form of a legal ordinance with divorce as the focus. The divorce sayings actually state in another way that there is no divorce in God's intended plan for creation. Therefore, the divorce sayings correspond to the absolute demand in Mark 10:9. Whereas the Law permitted divorce and remarriage, Jesus outlawed divorce.

Beginning as early as the Church's inclusion of the "except-clause," this Antithesis more than any other has been interpreted legalistically in the history of the Church. Yet the severity of this demand comes best to expression in 19:10 when the disciples respond, "It is not expedient to marry." Regardless of the fact that one could prosecute the third Antithesis more easily than the first two, this command was no less "absurd," humanly speaking, than the outlawing of anger or lust. Jesus countered the Law's legal minimum in Deut 24:1 with a demand for marriage that issued from a totally different starting point. Divorce was a God-given provision for the fallen condition of humanity (Mark 10:4–5, par. Matt 19:7–8). The Law started with the reality of broken marriages because of one's "hard heart." Yet outlawing divorce in no way guaranteed the God-intended wholeness of a marriage relationship (Mark 10:7–9). Such a relationship could only come from a "new heart" that had replaced the "old heart."

Therefore, the divorce sayings in general and 5:32 in particular represent by means of a graphic use of a legal ordinance Jesus' demand for new relationships between individuals, in this case between husband and wife, characteristic of the presence of the new age of salvation. The underlying intention of the divorce saying does not differ in the slightest from that of the other Antitheses. To the contrary, a legalistic rendering that leaves one feeling that God's demand has been met by avoiding divorce rather than experiencing the unbroken wholeness of a marriage relationship simply distorts and blunts the all-encompassing claim that the demand makes on all married individuals. This Antithesis as well as the divorce sayings must be understood in the total context of Jesus' demand and not singled out as any more or less important than his demand for relationships that excluded anger or lust. Just as the outlawing of anger demanded a whole relationship between individuals and the outlawing of lust demanded a whole relationship between man and woman, so the outlawing of divorce was a demand for a relationship of wholeness between husband and wife. These relationships are inherent to the presence of the new age.

In view of the teaching of the Church which has generally perceived the divorce sayings in a legalistic manner preventing either divorce or remarriage with the possible exception of adultery, one struggles today in order to "hear" anew first what the demand was all about and second, how one is to apply it to today's situations.

We must first realize that Jesus' prohibition of divorce was of the same cloth as his prohibition of anger, lust, the need for oaths, and the use of legal recourse to gain personal compensation. These demands were most likely directed initially against the "righteous" who felt themselves right before God because of their having met the Law's demands. By setting God's claim in this manner, Jesus demonstrated the inadequacy of such "righteousness." These "ideals" were meant neither as utopian ideals to be recognized politely but then ignored nor as a "new law" by which one was to live in order to be "righteous" or right with God. These demands, rather, express the realizable potential of restored relationships between individuals in view of the presence of the age of salvation. Such conduct can only emerge from a "new heart," from the center of one's person experiencing God's enabling power through the Gospel of God's redemptive activity in one's life. Therefore, these "demands" as part of the Gospel offer the married hope and power to live in keeping with God's desires.

The Gospel, however, is not predicated on one's performance but on one's acceptance by God in love and forgiveness. Sin remains a constant reality even in the life of the disciple, a reality that circumvents one's realizing the God-given potential of the Gospel. Consequently, as sinners with "hard hearts" God's Law on divorce still obtains. Just as Paul and the early church recognized the presence of sin in one's experience and adapted the divorce sayings accordingly, so today we must also recognize that divorce was also given by God as part of the Law to protect individuals for whom the element of sin has destroyed the marriage relationship. One must recognize that situations exist in which God's accepting forgiveness and the divorce Law offer opportunity for one to seek God's intended wholeness in another relationship.

The divorce itself is not evil; divorce itself is not a sin. The evil, the sin, is found in the broken relationship which divorce simply legally recognizes. To be divorced is no greater sin than to live in a broken relationship (cf. Mark 10:6–9). God's ultimate demand for marriage is "one flesh" or perfect wholeness in the marriage relationship. Divorce is but the public acknowledgment of the futility and failure of a given marriage relationship. Yet over against this reality of broken relationships, Jesus' demand offers hope and the wholeness of the age of salvation for the married either by transforming or forgiving one's hardness of heart.

4. Honesty: Matt 5:33–37

The premise (5:33) of the fourth Antithesis consists of two apodictically formulated commands. The first (5:33a) stems from Lev 19:12 and refers to swearing false oaths or perjury, and the second (5:33b) stems from Ps 49:14, LXX, and refers to keeping one's oaths made with God. Two different types of Jewish oaths are involved, an assertive oath (5:33a) by which one affirms or denies having done something, and a promissory oath (5:33b) by which one swears to do/use or not to do/use something (see Note on 5:33). The former has to do with one's honesty, the latter with one's faithfulness to one's word. In both cases, however, the oath formula involved the use of God's name, since the one swearing was using God as guarantor of his or her veracity or faithfulness. Yet the two oaths (5:33a, b) stand in tension with the heart of the antithesis (5:34a, 37a). Since the second (5:33b) corresponds with the promissory oaths in 5:34b–36 and since neither is integral to the thought of 5:33a and 34a, 37a (see Note on 5:33b), this material on promissory oaths (5:33b, 34b–36) represents a secondary addition that took place early in the tradition (cf. James 5:12) in an attempt to apply the Antithesis to the abused area of promissory oaths in Jewish life (cf. Matt 23:16–22). Therefore, the original premise referred to the Old Testament Law's prohibition of swearing a false oath in support of one's word (Lev 19:12) on the grounds that the false oath transgressed the second commandment (Exod 20:7) by taking God's name in vain.

The antithesis (5:34–37) also consists of multiple elements. The first (5:34a, 37a) corresponds to the assertive oaths of 5:33a and has the form of an absolute prohibition, "You shall not swear at all" (5:34a), followed by an absolute command, "Let your word be an emphatic 'yes' or 'no' " (5:37a; see Note on 5:37). The second element (5:34b–36) offers several illustrations of promissory oaths related to the context of the premise in Lev 19:12, since these were supposedly nonbinding or spurious oath formulas that avoided God's name (see Note on 5:34–36). By use of Old Testament references, these formulas were shown to be binding because of their direct involvement with God. The third element (5:37b) of the antithesis stems from the evangelist and summarizes the ultimate force of the original Antithesis (see Notes on 5:37). Removing the secondary elements on promissory oaths (5:33b, 34b–36) and the summary of 5:37b that rather complicate the Antithesis, one has left a premise (5:33a) that refers to the Old Testament Law's prohibition of false oaths to support one's word and an antithesis (5:34a, 37a) that prohibits the use of all oaths and demands that one's word be sufficient.

As in the case of the third Antithesis, the legalistic use of this Antithesis has a long history in the Church. The first traces of such usage appear in the earliest stages of the tradition when the material on promissory oaths was included within the Antithesis itself (5:33b, 34b–36, cf. 23:16–22 and James 5:12). On the basis of a strict application of 5:34a, 37a, some segments of the Church today still refuse to take an oath involving God's name. Yet by legalistically avoiding the use of oaths, like avoiding divorce, one can come to the false conclusion that Jesus' demand has been fulfilled. In actuality, the legalistic understanding of this and the other Antitheses can distort and blunt the absolute thrust of Jesus' demand. Jesus demands much more than the dispensing with the use of oaths. To forego the use of oaths in a society marked by the necessity of oaths because of the inherent dishonesty of human beings is as utopian as outlawing anger or lust.

The prohibition of oaths and the demand that simply one's word stand for itself is nothing less than to demand a relationship between individuals characterized by total honesty. This call for total honesty comes through most clearly in the tradition of James 5:12, where one's "yes" means "yes" and one's "no" means "no." Matthew has captured this different starting point when he redactionally added, "Anything more than one's word is of the Evil One" (see Note on 5:37). Therefore, Jesus' demand, set once again in the context of the Law, cuts to the heart of the human predicament. Whereas the Law assumes dishonesty to be a given and forbids swearing a false oath, Jesus forbids the use of any false word at all. Such a demand presupposes the context of total honesty in human relationships.

5. Retaliation: Matt 5:38–42

The fifth Antithesis, like the third, contains Q material found in Luke 6:29–30 without the antithetical format. The premise (5:38) consists of the abbreviated *lex talionis*, "an eye for an eye, a tooth for a tooth," that served as the basis for legal justice in the Old Testament Law. Stemming from as far back in history as the Code of Hammurabi, this common principle of justice originally offered protection for the guilty party from incommensurate retaliation on behalf of the victim. But this law also came to guarantee the victim the right to equal recompense. Without some such equitable basis for the enforcement of justice, anarchy and lawlessness would doubtless result. The longer formula appears three times in the Pentateuch (Exod 21:24a; Lev 24:20b; Deut 19:21, LXX), with Deut 19:21 being the immediate context for this Antithesis as seen by the similarity of vocabulary in 5:38, 39a (see Notes on 5:38, 39).

The actual antithesis (5:39a) is very brief, a prohibition constructed along the lines of the antithesis in 5:34a. The verb and object of "Do not seek legal vindication from one who is evil" stem from Deut 19:16–21, a context in which an evil adversary falsely accuses another in court. The *lex talionis* furnished the basis of the penalty for such action (Deut 19:21) by having the false accuser sentenced to the same penalty for the alleged crime. Since the evangelist has drawn both the premise (5:38) and the antithesis (5:39a) from Deut 19:16–21, the antithesis reflects a judicial setting in keeping with the premise. Rather than offering a general principle of "nonresistance," as has been argued at times, the antithesis specifically commands one to forego the legal right to seek judicial redress against an offending party.

Although the evangelist is responsible for both the premise (5:38) and the antithesis (5:39a)—in other words, the whole Antithesis—the stimulus for the Antithesis has its basis in the traditional saying found combined within the Love Your Enemies material of Q (cf. Luke 6:27–35, see Note on 5:39). Luke 6:29–30 depicts a robbery scene in which one is personally attacked (6:29a) and robbed of one's clothes (6:29b) and a less violent scene in which a beggar (6:30a) and a borrower (6:30b) confront one with a request. Matthew separates this material (see Note on 5:39–42) and relocates the first scene in the setting of a law court, possibly in view of the attacker's having slapped the *right* cheek, in the Q tradition (5:39b, cf. Luke 6:29a). Being struck on the right cheek meant that the offender used the back of the hand, an attack on one's person and honor in Judaism (see Note on 5:39); the normal recourse would have involved judicial retribution. Turning the other cheek, therefore, meant more than passive yielding to the offender; it meant foregoing one's right to legal recompense as now expressed in the Antithesis of 5:38, 39a and in the reworked legal suit for one's garments that follows (5:40, cf. Luke 6:29b).

With the Antithesis of 5:38, 39a and the reworked tradition of 5:39b–40, the evangelist has set Jesus' demand to forego one's legal rights to justice against the fundamental principle of the Law, namely, the principle of equal justice itself. Taken legalistically and applied universally, this demand would lead inevitably to chaos, the complete disruption of law and order, since the *lex talionis* presupposes the reality of evil in the human experience. Jesus' demand, however, set again in the context of the Old Testament Law, calls for conduct befitting a totally different starting point in human relationships. Once more the impossibility of the demand taken legalistically points behind the explicit to the implicit call for relationships in which evil has been defeated. Justice for justice's sake is no longer viewed as the basis of one's behavior but the restored relationships between individuals in which the other's interests are foremost. To this extent the fifth Antithesis anticipates the demand of the sixth.

The remaining examples of 5:41–42 bear out this focus by giving three different types of requests according to a diminishing order of personal obligation. In the first (5:41), one has the legal obligation to accompany the one demanding time and assistance for the distance of one mile. In the second (5:42a), one has the less binding, religious obligation of contributing alms to the beggar, and in the third (5:42b), one has the least binding obligation of a personal loan. Yet in each instance, the other individual's interest serves as the focal point. It is evident that the fifth Antithesis, like the previous four, ultimately calls for new relationships between individuals, relationships indicative of the presence of the Kingdom, the day of salvation and wholeness in which evil has been defeated and one's own best interests are no longer primary.

6. Love for the Enemy: Matt 5:43–48

The last Antithesis also has a parallel in the Lucan Sermon material (6:27–35). In fact, the Lucan material may betray the catalyst for the presence of the Antitheses in Matthew. The address to the audience of the Beatitudes with its *"But I say to you who hear"* (Luke 6:27a) contains the crucial verbal elements of the introductory formulas, "You have heard"/"But I say to you." Since Matthew often used catch-words as the point of contact for introducing material into the tradition, this opening of the Love Your Enemies section in the Q form of the Sermon may have led Matthew to introduce the three traditional Antitheses (5:21–26, 27–30, 33–37) that then became the basis for his constructing the other three, including the fifth and sixth from the Q material (see Comment C).

The premise (5:43) consists of a double command, the first with a verbal parallel in Lev 19:18 and the second with no direct parallel in the Scriptures. The evangelist also has inserted the love commandment from Lev 19:18 into a Marcan context (19:19, cf. Mark 10:19) in which this commandment along with some from the Decalogue is countered as inadequate for gaining eternal life (19:20) by Jesus' demand for discipleship that followed (19:21–22). Yet in 22:40 Matthew also notes that the love commandment cited by Jesus as the Great Commandment was the very "hinge" on which the "Law and the Prophets" hung (cf. 7:12).

Consequently, the evangelist distinguished between two different uses of love commandment, the one a legal norm to be fulfilled legalistically (19:19; 5:43) and the other an absolute demand expressing the new relationship between God and humanity as well as between individuals (22:40; 5:44–48).

The command to hate one's enemy in 5:43b offers the first premise that lacks a direct parallel in the Old Testament Law, for which reason many have assigned this premise to scribal interpretation of the Law (see Note on 5:43). Even the rabbinic literature, however, lacks such a direct command to hate one's enemies. The closest parallel stands in the Qumran literature where the sons of light were to hate the sons of darkness (e.g., 1QS 1:4). This apparent parallel has, consequently, conditioned the background of the Antithesis for some scholars. Yet the evidence leads to Matthean redaction for the source of the premise, and a Qumran background is most remote from Matthew's own audience.

Qumran, the rabbis, and the Old Testament do share a common theme, namely, a distinction between one's relationship to those sharing the same religious conviction about God's redemptive work in history and those not sharing that conviction (see Note on 5:43). The distinction exists in Lev 19:18, where the "neighbor" refers exclusively to a member of Israel. But even that limitation received further specification within Judaism as seen in the rabbis and Qumran. The classic illustration for the legalistic understanding of the love commandment follows Jesus' teaching on the Great Commandment when the lawyer asked, "Who is my neighbor?" (Luke 10:29). Therefore, the premise of 5:43 expresses the dual aspect of the love commandment. Whereas one was to love one's neighbor, a religious designation, the converse was also true: one was to hate one's enemy, also a religious designation. Qumran consistently drew this conclusion, as those writings indicate. Yet in 5:43 the source for Matthew's clause may have been his own desire to construct an antithetical framework for the Love Your Enemies commandment of 5:44.

As was the case in the third Antithesis, the evangelist found the material for the antithesis (5:44) at hand in the tradition. This tradition began with "love your enemies." Consequently, in order to form an antithesis consistent with the others, Matthew needed a premise that set forth the Old Testament Law in its legal context. Drawing on Lev 19:18 as legally understood with its limitations to one's "neighbor," the evangelist then added the converse in 5:43b to form a sharp antithesis to "love" ("hate") and "neighbor" ("enemy"). Therefore, the second command in the premise does not introduce a separate command implying that one can love one's neighbor without hating one's enemy or vice versa. Rather, the second half stands as epexegetic to the first describing the converse of the love command when legally limited to one's neighbor. In other words, the premise of 5:43 expresses, as do all previous premises, the Old Testament Law understood legalistically.

The antithesis (5:44) consists of two parallel commands, to love one's enemies and to pray for one's persecutors. The command to love one's enemies with its more developed form in Luke 6:27-28 represents one of the major distinctives of Jesus' teaching. It also characterizes his own ministry to the sick, sinners, and even on occasion to the Gentiles. Whereas the "enemy" in 5:43 referred collectively to those who were considered to be outsiders of God's redemptive activity, the "enemies" in 5:44, synonymous with one's persecutors, refers to the personal enmity experienced by those who have responded to God's overtures through the ministry of Jesus Messiah (see 5:10, 11-12). No longer an abstraction, God's enemy was also one's personal enemy. But one was to act as the "peacemaker," the one whose loving actions and prayer stand in the gap to bring such ones into a new relationship with God who cared for them as well as for his own.

Love, as illustrated in Luke 6:29-30, cf. Matt 5:38-42, means action that places the other's best interests rather than one's rights foremost. Prayer describes one's intercessory role on behalf of those who cannot pray, indeed, whose actions of persecution are the opposite of prayer. Such conduct can stem only from a new relationship between individuals, a relationship that is not limited to one's own kind, even religiously defined. History past and present is replete with brutal examples of religious persecution that attest to the human impossibility of such a demand. This demand, like all the others, assumes a different starting point, as seen in the positive and negative bases that follow.

First, such conduct has its roots in sonship (5:45, cf. 5:48). God as Father indiscriminately shares his goodness of creation. Since God indiscriminately shares his goodness of creation with the "good and the evil," the "righteous and unrighteous," one's corresponding actions toward the "enemy" distinguish one as a son. To act according to the will and the way of the Father is a mark of sonship. Therefore, the "peacemaker," the one who "loves the enemy," exhibits God's unlimited redemptive interest in all people. To such belongs the promise of recognition as God's sons at the judgment (5:9, 45). Second, to relate exclusively to one's own (5:46-47) does not distinguish one at all, since the worst examples of moral behavior, the "tax collectors" (5:46), and those normally considered outside the scope of God's grace (5:47), the "Gentiles," do as much. Jesus' demand calls for a behavior commensurate with a new relationship of wholeness indicative of God's redemptive activity in history.

The evangelist, therefore, concludes the final Antithesis and simultaneously all six Antitheses with a redactionally modified saying from the Q Sermon tradition (see Note on 5:48). One is to be "whole as the Father in heaven is whole" (5:48, cf. Luke 6:36). This imperative does not refer to moral perfection in the sense of "be perfect" or to a legal perfection of keeping the "whole Law" but to one's qualitative standing before God and others. The relationship of wholeness between brothers (5:21–26), brothers and sisters (5:27–30), husband and wife (5:31–32), friends and enemies (5:38–42, 43–47), lies at the very foundation of all the respective demands for specific conduct in the Antitheses. The conduct itself grows out of rather than produces the relationship. Together they comprise the "righteousness that exceeds that of the scribes and Pharisees" (5:20).

Ultimately 5:20, 48 and the intervening Antitheses are a call to wholeness in life and action between the individual and others. In 6:1–7:11 that same wholeness is displayed with reference to God. In both cases, the wholeness between the individual and God as well as between individuals corresponds to the "new heart," the "new covenant," the age of salvation and wholeness in which God has acted to reconcile and restore broken relationships between himself and his people and consequently among his people (cf. 1:21–23, 26:28). The demands of 5:21–48 are thus commensurate with Matthew's depiction of Jesus as the one who came to fulfill God's redemptive purposes announced in the prophets through his proclaiming and effecting God's sovereign rule of the new age in history (5:3–20). Matt 5:20–48 is nothing short of an ethic of the Kingdom in the full sense of that phrase.

B. "Kingdom Ethics"

How are we to understand the Antitheses today? Can we fulfill their demands? Are we expected to fulfill these commands as "entrance requirements" to the Kingdom? Do these demands belong to another, future era of redemptive history? Answers to these and related questions depend for the most part on the basic question: what was the intent of the Antitheses? The answer to this question generally revolves around two concerns: (a) a christological focus on what the Antitheses connote about Jesus' ministry and the Law, and (b) an ethical focus on the nature and intent of the imperative in the Antitheses.

From the christological perspective, some have perceived the Antitheses to be the new law given by the New Moses. For others the Antitheses represent Jesus' final interpretation of the Law or a Messianic Torah. For others, the Antitheses represent the tendency in the early church, perhaps stemming from Jesus, to radicalize the Law along the order of Qumran and similar Jewish movements. For still others Jesus represents Wisdom come to reveal the true will of the Father, a new understanding of the Law through his person and teaching. In any case, the demands of the Antitheses taken at face value in their legal framework set standards of ethical conduct that either supersede or set aside those of the Law.

Consequently, from the ethical perspective, one is left with a collection of legal commands that either were not meant to be carried out or are to be relegated as somewhat utopian demands to the more conducive framework of the future Kingdom. The most that one could expect for such drastic demands in this life would be to assign them to the brief interim anticipated between Jesus' ministry and the Kingdom whose dawning was imminently expected. In spite of numerous attempts in church history to apply some or all of the Antitheses legalistically, any such attempt today would be considered at best "unrealistic." Consequently, these demands often have the dubious status of moral ideals, goals beyond the reach of anyone but acknowledged as binding nonetheless. Apart from the implications of these conclusions for the credibility of Jesus and his ministry—should one trace them at least in part to his ministry—one must first question whether the text justifies any of these or other christological and ethical conclusions.

Ultimately, the answer to the christological and ethical questions lies with Matthew's redaction, since he was most likely responsible for the introduction, molding, preface, and conclusion of the Antitheses. Therefore, we shall look again at (1) the Matthean redaction, (2) the tradition, and (3) then seek to draw conclusions about Matthew's use of the Antitheses and (4) the Antitheses for us today.

1. Matthew's Redaction

Not only has the evangelist introduced the Antitheses into the traditional Sermon material between the Beatitudes and the Love Your Enemies section, the latter now comprising the content of the last two Antitheses, but he has prefaced the section with reworked tradition in 5:17–20, opened (5:20) and closed (5:48) the Antitheses with redactional summaries, and formed three Antitheses of his own (5:31–32, 38–42, 43–48).

By adding the Antitheses to the Sermon tradition, the evangelist employed them as evidence in his christological concern to set forth Jesus as the Messiah of the Word in Matthew 5–7. This christological motif of Jesus' authoritative word reaches its zenith in the Great Commission when the risen Lord, having received "all authority in heaven and earth," commissioned his own to disciple the world and teach them what he has commanded (28:18–20).

Matthew has developed more explicitly this same christological concern in 5:17–20 to form the preface for the Antitheses. By modifying 5:17, the evangelist declared that Jesus had come to fulfill the promise of the Scriptures regarding God's future redemptive activity in history (see Note on 5:17), and he underscored this theme in 5:18 by referring to the coming "to pass of all things" (see Note on 5:18). Furthermore, this fulfillment motif characterizes Matthew's christology throughout his Gospel and finds its most common expression in his distinctive fulfillment-citations. Therefore, the Antitheses are integrally related to Matthew's fulfillment-christology.

This interrelationship between Matthew's christology and the Antitheses also becomes apparent in the relationship between both and the Law. The Antitheses clearly deal with the question of the Law, and Matthew's redaction of 5:17–20 involves a tradition that had focused solely on the Law (see Notes on 5:17, 18, 19). Although the evangelist changed the focus of 5:17 from the Law to the Scriptures (see Note on 5:17) and qualified the Law's continuing validity by adding the christological reference to the "coming to pass of all things" (see Note on 5:18), he did not eliminate the role of the Law which he has preserved in 5:18, 19, but drastically qualified it in terms of Jesus' coming in 5:17, 18, 20. In other words, the evangelist views the Old Testament Law in terms of Jesus' coming (5:17, 18) and consequent demand for a greater righteousness than that of keeping the Law (5:20, cf. 5:19). Unfortunately, the evangelist left undeveloped the continued function of the Law in 5:18, 19, when he moved to the theme of the greater righteousness which he did develop in the Antitheses.

Along with the christological motif inherent in the evangelist's placing the Antitheses within the Sermon context and in his modification of

5:17–18 along the lines of a fulfillment christology, the corresponding ethical motif emerges in the Antitheses' redactional summary heading (5:20) and conclusion (5:48). By demanding a righteousness greater than that of the scribes and Pharisees (5:20), Matthew not only countered the inadequacy of a righteousness that concentrated on keeping the least of the commandments (cf. 5:19) but set the stage for the demands of the Antitheses that transcended and set aside the demands of the Law.

Yet the demands of the Antitheses represent much more than an intensification of the Law, a demand for a more rigorous ethical conduct. Their form and content point to attitudes, thoughts, and actions that lie beyond the limits of human capability—no alienation, no lust, perfect marriage, total honesty, foregoing of one's legal rights, and love for the enemy. Such behavior presupposes a different starting point in human relations; indeed, this behavior presupposes the absence of evil, which the Law could only seek to control. Matthew himself has captured this thrust with his own Anitheses (5:31–32, 38–39, 43–44) that actually set aside the Law whose claim was built on the assumption of the reality of evil. Therefore, the Antitheses demand attitudes and conduct in keeping with the presence of the age of salvation that Matthew's fulfillment-christology announces in Jesus' ministry. In light of God's work in Jesus Messiah, Matthew can summarize the demand of 5:20 and the Antitheses with the call to "wholeness" in one's relationship to others and to God (5:48).

We can thus summarize Matthew's redactional work accordingly. First, the Antitheses are integral to Jesus' person and ministry as the Messiah. Second, Jesus Messiah comes as the fulfillment of the Old Testament promise of God's redemptive activity in history, the Kingdom of heaven. Third, concomitant with Jesus' ministry comes (a) the establishment of a new relationship between God and his people (1:21–23; 26:28) and (b) the demand for conduct commensurate with the new relationships, a demand that at times supersedes and at times sets aside the legal demands of the Old Testament Law (e.g., 5:21–48). Fourth, present but undeveloped remains the premise that the Law continues in force as part of this age (5:18, 19). Fifth, at no point does the evangelist suggest or offer indication that Jesus comes as the New Moses with a new law, nor with a new, more radical interpretation of the Old Testament Law, nor as Wisdom incarnate (cf., however, 11:28–29). Matthew's own redactional Antitheses show that he saw a break between Jesus' demand and the Law, and his christology consistently points to Jesus' ministry in terms of the Old Testament promises for the age of salvation.

2. The Tradition

Matthew began with three traditional Antitheses (see Comment C): the first (5:21–22), second (5:27–28), and fourth (5:33–37). Each began with a characteristic formula which set Jesus' demand in antithesis to the Old Testament Law in its legal setting. In spite of partial parallels to segments of these formulas (see Notes on 5:21, 22), the form and content referring to the Law and Jesus' authoritative counter to it remains without parallel in Judaism (see Note on 5:21, 22). Therefore, one cannot take Jesus' demands out of context and compare them with sayings in Judaism, since to do so distorts the implications of each Antithesis as a whole. In these three Antitheses, Jesus set anger and invectives against the Law prohibiting murder (5:21–22), lust against the Law prohibiting adultery (5:27–28), and total honesty against the prohibition of false oaths that transgressed the second commandment (5:33–37). These demands do not simply radicalize the respective commandments; they show the Law to be a complex of apodictic commands and legal ordinances, and they stand antithetically opposed to the legal understanding of these commandments that leaves one feeling "righteous" as long as one has legally fulfilled the Law's demand.

By setting his own demands within the same legal framework, Jesus countered with commands for attitudes and conduct that demonstrate the inadequacy of the Law to measure one's standing before God and with each other. Whereas one could prosecute murder, adultery, and false oaths, the prohibition of anger, lust, and dishonesty in general surpasses the bounds of legal justice. Yet Jesus set these demands forth in this manner and context in order to show that the latter rather than the former had more to do with one's relationship to others. Since "righteousness" had come to connote one's keeping of the Law, from Jesus' perspective one's standing before God and others could no longer be measured by the Law. To that extent Jesus' demands stood in antithesis to the Law as a means or measure of one's righteousness. Jesus' demands called for relationships characteristic of the new age when God would "write the Law" on one's heart; a "new heart" would replace the "hard heart."

When one looks for an appropriate setting for such demands in Jesus' ministry, one comes first to his ministry with the "righteous." The righteous believed that their meticulous keeping of the Law would be rewarded or recognized by God at the last judgment (cf. 6:1–18) Convinced that by keeping God's Law they had met God's demand, the "righteous" failed to recognize that God was at work in Jesus' ministry calling a new people into a new relationship with himself and with others. Consequently, the controversy narratives of the Gospels reflect the tension between Jesus' ministry and the "righteous' " concern for the Law. Against such a setting, the Antitheses serve as a call to repentance, to the realization of the inadequacy of a legalistic rectitude to enter the Kingdom that Jesus was proclaiming.

3. Matthew's Use of the Antitheses

Matthew's use of the Antitheses correlates first of all with his christological interests in Matthew 5. We have already seen how the evangelist has reworked the Beatitudes in order to align them more explicitly with the promises of Isaiah, especially Isaiah 61. He then added a section on the nature and responsibility of discipleship (5:13–16) in which he applied the various symbols reserved in the Old Testament promise for Israel's role in the end times to Jesus' own disciples (5:11–12). But this christological focus becomes most explicit when Matthew reworks the tradition behind 5:17–18 in order to declare that Jesus had come to fulfill the Scriptures and that all things had come to pass in his coming. With these verses as the introduction, the stage is set for Jesus' authoritative "But I say to you" that stands over against "God has said to the generation of old" and calls us to a life lived in terms of the new age which these demands presuppose. In other words, the Antitheses bear witness to who Jesus is and, together with the previous sections of Matthew 5, belong to the "gospel of the Kingdom," the good news that God was acting in history as promised to establish his rule through Jesus Messiah.

Second, the Antitheses play an important positive and negative ethical role in Matthew. From the negative side, the antithetical format points out the fallacy of believing that a legalistic keeping of the Law qualifies one for the Kingdom (5:19–20), since the premises demand a conduct that is inadequate or wrong-headed in light of Jesus' demands. In this sense, the Antitheses stood as a warning to Jews and Jewish-Christians whose primary ethical concern was in meeting the Law's demands.

From the positive side and of greater concern for Matthew, the Antitheses summon us to a new kind of life and conduct with reference to others that makes the Law's demands redundant. Jesus' demands call for conduct stemming from a new starting point in human relations no longer dominated by sin. Such a starting point concurs with the presence of the age of salvation. Consequently, these demands, in spite of their form and content that defy a legalistic usage, were in no way understood by Matthew as merely ethical ideals or utopian idealism. The preface of 5:20, the conclusion of 5:48, and the warning of 7:21, cf. Luke 6:46, that failure to do the will of the Father precludes one from entering the Kingdom all indicate the seriousness with which the evangelist perceived these ethical demands. Yet at precisely this juncture, we find the tension that characterizes our struggle with the Antitheses. How can these demands be simultaneously conduct stemming from the *presence* of the Kingdom and still be entrance-requirements of the *future* Kingdom?

This dilemma leads to another aspect of Matthew's understanding, the one that underlies the christological and the ethical dimensions, namely, the eschatological perspective. Christology and ethics converge in the Antitheses that demand relationships and conduct commensurate with the promised presence of the Kingdom, the dawn of the age of salvation. That which was promised by the prophets Isaiah, Jeremiah, and Ezekiel for the end times has come to fulfillment in Jesus' coming and ministry. The new age of God's redemptive rule has come into history through Jesus Messiah as seen by his word (Matt 5–7) and his deeds (Matt 8–9). Therefore, the Antitheses in a real sense represent the resultant "ethics of the Kingdom."

Apart from the life-changing power of God's defeat of the enemy and the restoration of the broken and alienated relationships between himself and his people, the demands of the Antitheses simply confront us with the absurd. Yet the presence of the Kingdom as the starting point lies at the heart of Matthew's Gospel (see Note on 4:23). Thus, the attitudes and conduct demanded by the Antitheses concur with and give attestation of the presence of God's redemptive rule in human history. In other words, the greater righteousness connotes nothing less than life lived in terms of the presence of the Kingdom.

But the Kingdom of Heaven also contained a future dimension in Matthew (see Note on 5:3). The strong emphasis on the present eschatological element did not replace the future element. The fulfillment that Jesus announced and effected also anticipated a future consummation as seen in the parables of the Kingdom in Matthew 13. The final judgment represents the great divide between the sons of the Kingdom and the sons of the Evil One. The two coexist until the consummation. Indeed, the Kingdom has come in an unexpected form like a mustard seed that can be refused or discarded in contrast to its consummate form in the future that will crush its enemies. The Kingdom is present within history but will also come in the future as the chronological successor of this age. The ultimate differentiation between those within and those without the Kingdom begins now according to one's response to Jesus' person and ministry. One's response to Jesus, the life of discipleship (cf. 19:20–22; 28:18–20), includes more than an acknowledgement of this claim (cf. 7:21–23) but doing the will of the Father, bearing "good fruit" (7:16–20; 12:33–35). Therefore, the greater righteousness represents simultaneously the *product* of the presence of the Kingdom as well as the *basis* for entrance into the future consummated Kingdom.

This tension between the Kingdom present and the Kingdom future, between the fulfillment and consummation of God's promise of salvation for human history, applies not only to history but to the experience of the individual. One is faced with the claims of the Kingdom on one's life and the claims of this age. Yet the evangelist does not develop or resolve this ethical tension any more than he does the eschatological tension, precisely because the ethical tension is a concomitant of the eschatological tension between the Kingdom present within this age and the Kingdom future in the consummation. Matthew 5 depicts Jesus as announcing the good news of the Kingdom, including the inherent demand for relationships and conduct congruent with the presence of the Kingdom. One's response to Jesus' offer of the Kingdom and thus one's life lived in relation to others and to God are evidences of the presence of the Kingdom in one's life and the "entrance requirement" for the future consummation (5:20; 7:21).

Yet at no point does Matthew suggest that one's ethical behavior in itself qualifies or disqualifies one from entrance into the future Kingdom. The evangelist has not replaced a legalistic understanding of the Law of Moses with a legalistic understanding of the Law of Jesus. Rather the demand for attitudes and conduct in 5:20–48 arises out of the christological perspective of Matthew 5 that views Jesus as bringing the age of salvation with its new starting point between God and humanity as well as between individuals. The ethical imperative follows the christological indicative of the gospel of the Kingdom. One's ethical behavior indicates rather than creates one's relationship to God and to others. The latter is foundational to the former and integral to one's response to Jesus and his ministry.

In summary, therefore, for Matthew the Antitheses stand within the context of the gospel of the Kingdom by calling for attitudes and conduct commensurate with the new age that Jesus came to announce and effect.

Jesus' authoritative "But I say to you" set over against the Law and the content of his demands point christologically to his fulfillment of the Old Testament promise of God's redemptive activity in history for his people. Set in a legal format, Jesus' demands demonstrate the inadequacy of a righteousness based on keeping the Law, since the Law itself has been transcended by a demand for behavior stemming from relationships between individuals in which the Law's commands are redundant.

By contrast, the Antitheses demand conduct indicative of the presence of the Kingdom as the necessary prerequisite for entering the Kingdom in the future. Yet the Antitheses were not intended, as seen by the tension between the form of a legal ordinance and the content that could not be legislated, to become the basis of a new kind of legalism based on Jesus' teachings. Rather, in an exemplary fashion the content of the Antitheses forces one to a new starting point as the basis of human attitudes and conduct, namely, the presence of the age of salvation in which one's relationship to God and to others has been drastically altered, as reflected by one's conduct. Therefore, the question of "keeping" the Antitheses arose neither as optional nor as impossible for Matthew. The "greater righteousness" necessary for the Kingdom connoted both the relationships and the conduct of the Kingdom that come as gift and demand integral to the presence of the Kingdom in Jesus' ministry.

4. The Antitheses Today

How then are we to understand the Antitheses today? First of all, from the positive side, we must not lose sight of their primary focus in Matthew as integral to the "gospel of the Kingdom." The Antitheses call us to the realization that the new age has indeed come in the person and ministry of Jesus, since these demands bespeak the reconciling activity of God's forgiving acceptance and restoration of broken relationships between himself and his people, as well as among his people. The Antitheses represent the "ethic of the Kingdom" that has entered history and serve as the basis of the exhortation to "seek first the Kingdom and his righteousness" of 6:33. Divorced from this eschatological context of Jesus' ministry, the Antitheses become distorted ethical ideals that lie frustratingly beyond human experience.

Second, from the negative side, the form and content of the Antitheses demonstrate the inadequacy of a "righteousness" based on a legalistic observance of the "Law," whether Jewish or Christian. These demands were not given to be legalistically interpreted or applied. Just as keeping the Law left one short of God's will, so the mere keeping of the letter of the Antitheses leaves one short of the ultimate demand of the Antitheses, namely, "wholeness" in one's relationship with God and with others. One could avoid anger and still be estranged; one could avoid lust and still abuse the opposite sex; one could avoid swearing and still be dishonest; one could forego one's legal rights but still "get even." The demands for specific conduct represented examples of behavior stemming from "whole," restored relationships characteristic of the age of salvation.

Yet as part of the gospel of the Kingdom, the message of God's sovereign rule in history, the Antitheses do not depict abstract ethical ideals or utopian idealism. These demands are not goals to be worked toward. Rather, they represent conduct commensurate with and stemming from God's redemptive activity in human history. The attitudes and behavior required issue from the effect of God's work in one's life. The potential for living in this fashion stems from the power of the gospel rather than from human resolve. Put in another way, the demands call for signs—"fruit"—of the presence of God's redemptive work in one's life.

Third, the "greater righteousness" demanded as the entrance requirement for the Kingdom and set forth in the Antitheses reflects the tension inherent in a life lived in keeping with the new relationships of the presence of the Kingdom (e.g., 5:38–42) but simultaneously in an age characterized by evil and structured by Law. In other words, legalistically to forbid divorce, the use of oaths, or the principle of legal justice would lead to greater havoc and evil than the use of the Law for the purpose of controlling evil. The thrust of the Antitheses was neither to offer a new law nor to set aside the Law, neither legalism nor antinomianism, but to counter the use of the Law to justify oneself, to guarantee one's own best interest before God and others rather than living in a dependent relationship with God that freed one to seek and serve another's best interest (5:11–12, 43–47). Conduct in keeping with the new relationship between God and his own and among others that seeks to reach out and restore, to live in terms of another's best interest, may well use the Law or forego the use of the Law. One's motivation, however, is no longer self-justification or self-interest but the interest of one's neighbor or one's enemy. The evangelist does not develop this alternative use of the Law, since his primary concern focused on the abuse of the Law for one's own interest. But the nature of the Antitheses, which were neither legalistic nor antinomian in intent, leaves the alternative open, as does the positive reference to the Law in 5:18, 19.

Therefore, the Antitheses are the "entrance requirements" for the Kingdom. To the extent that one lives in terms of God's initiative on behalf of his own, one's relationships and conduct correspond to those demanded by the Antitheses. To the extent that one falls short of these demands, one stands before God aware of one's failure and inadequacy and open before him in need of his forgiving acceptance and mercy which in turn become the basis for the restored relationship of the Kingdom. Only when one ignores the demands or distorts them into a legalistic sense of achievement do the Antitheses stand as the basis of judgment, the entrance requirement unmet. God reaches to restore the sinner to "wholeness" by his forgiving acceptance and he calls the righteous to repentance by demanding that they be "whole" before God and with others. Both elements are inherent in the "gospel" of the Antitheses.

C. History of the Tradition

Although many of the issues involved in developing a history of the tradition underlying the Antitheses have been discussed in the Notes on 5:21–48, bringing the material together in summary fashion helps to delineate the patterns at work behind the evangelist's use of the tradition in Matthew 5. The diversity of opinions in recent literature cautions one to avoid expecting more than probabilities, but the probabilities, as is the case in any historical reconstruction, must rest ultimately on the assessment of the evidence from the text itself.

Perhaps the most discussed question with the widest differences of opinion focuses on the antithetical format. The viewpoints range all the way from attributing all six Antitheses to the tradition to ascribing all six to Matthew, with any combination of two to five in between (see Literary Analysis for literature). Consequently, our first task will concentrate on delineating the traditional and redactional Antitheses. Then we shall turn to a summary discussion of the tradition involved in the traditional and redactional Antitheses respectively. For the materials beyond the Antitheses proper (e.g., 5:23–26, 29–30, etc.), see the Notes pertinent to those verses.

1. Traditional or Redactional Antitheses?

A quick comparison of a synopsis of the Gospels indicates that four of the six Antitheses have parallels in part and thus belong to the early tradition (5:31–32, 33–37, 38–42, 43–48) but without the antithetical format. These four Antitheses would appear to be most suspect of being redactional.

a. Matt 5:31–32 has its closest parallel in Luke 16:18. But a similar saying appears without an antithetical setting in Mark 10:11, a teaching narrative following the related material of a controversy narrative in Mark 10:2–9. Matthew's handling of both Mark 10:11 and the Q saying behind 5:32 strongly suggests his redactional addition of the antithetical format. First, the evangelist incorporates the saying from Mark 10:11 into the controversy narrative and reworks the Marcan arrangement (19:7–9, cf. Mark 10:4–5, 11) in order to set the saying in direct antithesis to the Mosaic provision of Deut 24:1, the premise of 5:31 (see Note on 5:31). Second, using his familiar catch-word approach of combining traditions, Matthew introduces the Antithesis into the remotely related context of adultery (5:27–28), perhaps modifying the traditional verb of μοιχάομαι to the appropriate μοιχεύω of 5:27–28 (see Note on 5:32). Third, in the typically Matthean fashion of breaking traditional patterns, as well as his own (cf. 23:16), the evangelist begins the premise (5:31) with only the core (ἐρρέθη) of the introductory formula (see Note on 5:31). It seems safe, therefore, to conclude that Matthew redactionally constructed the third Antithesis from his own form of the Q saying in order to align its antithetical content with the Antitheses of 5:21–48.

b. Matt 5:38–42 contains a parallel with Luke 6:29–30 that serves as supporting material for the unparalleled heart of the Antithesis of 5:38–39a. The Antithesis proper (5:38, 39a) stems from Deut 19:16–21, as the similarity of language indicates (see Note on 5:39). This use of Deuteronomy concurs with the redactional premise of 5:31 drawn from Deut 24:1 and perhaps the redactional influence of Deut 18:13 on 5:48, cf. Luke 6:36 (see Note on 5:48). The primary evidence for Matthean redaction, however, stems from the similarity of language between the final Beatitudes of Matthew and Luke (5:11–12, par. Luke 6:22–23) and the Love Your Enemies command (5:11–12, cf. 5:44; Luke 6:22–23, cf. Luke 6:27–28). This similarity of language points to an original proximity of the two units no longer found in Matthew. Furthermore, the absence of evidence that Luke has redactionally reworked the material behind Matt 5:38–42 supports this conclusion. All indications point to a pre-evangelist combination of two separate traditions which Matthew has separated for his purposes.

First, the difference between the second person singular and plural in Luke 6:29–30 in the context of Luke 6:27–35 points to an earlier separate existence of two distinct traditions. Second, the repetition of the Love Your Enemies command in 6:35, along with the imperatives growing out of the rhetorical questions (see Note on 5:46), indicates that Luke 6:35 has been relocated from its original setting following the love command by the intervening rhetorical questions (6:32–34). Third, the subject matter of the rhetorical questions gives evidence of being added to bind the included examples of 6:29–30 into the Love Your Enemies section (see Note on 5:46). Fourth, the presence of δανίζω ("to borrow") in Luke 6:34, 35a, is reminiscent of an earlier pre-Lucan δανίζω in Luke 6:30 now found in the Matthean parallel of 5:42. Therefore, the introduction of the examples in 6:29–30 with the rhetorical questions of 6:32–34, 35a, into the context of 6:27–28, 35, must have occurred in the pre-Lucan tradition. This conclusion is supported by the fact that Matthew maintains the rhetorical questions (though reworded, see Notes on 5:46, 47) even though he has removed their original focus for his purposes in 5:38–42. The evidence thus points to a pre-Matthean and pre-Lucan block of traditions that Matthew has separated and remolded into a judicial scene (see Note on 5:39b, 40) in order to support the corresponding redactional Antithesis of 5:38–39a.

c. Matt 5:43–48 has its parallel in the same block of Sermon material found in Luke 6:27–36. In this case, the tradition (5:44, par. Luke 6:27–28) forms the antithesis but the premise stems from the evangelist's addition of Lev 19:18 as understood legally (see Note on 5:43). The key evidence supporting Matthew's redaction lies in a similar redactional modification of the Marcan tradition in 19:19–21, cf. Mark 10:19–21. Matthew not only inserted Lev 19:18 as a legal requirement (19:19, cf. Mark 10:19) but he also set the demand for "wholeness" (19:21, cf. Mark 10:21) against it as in 5:48. Furthermore, the remote similarity between Luke's "But I *say* to you who *hear*" (Luke 6:27) and the introductory formulas of the Antitheses suggest more Matthew's tendency to use catch-words as stimuli for adding material than Luke's preserving remnants of the Antitheses (see Note on 5:43).

d. Matt 5:33–37 has no parallel in the Gospel tradition but rather in the paranetic tradition of James 5:12 without the antithetical format. The clue to the background of 5:33–37 lies in the rather awkward construction of both the premise and antithesis (see Notes on 5:33, 34). The second part of the premise (5:33b) and the second element of the antithesis (5:34b–36), each dealing with promissory oaths, stand in tension with the reference to swearing false oaths (5:33a) and the prohibition of oaths (5:34a, 37a) involving assertive oaths and constituting the heart of the Antithesis (see Note on 5:33, 34). Therefore, the material on promissory oaths represents a secondary application of the material on assertive oaths to another tradition involving promissory oaths. Since the inclusion of the secondary material appears in both the premise and antithesis and since James contains both elements in his tradition, though much smoother, the combination must have taken place in the pre-Matthean tradition (see Note on 5:33b, 34–36). In other words, 5:33–37a shows no sign of Matthean redaction. To the contrary, the Matthean element of 5:37b (see Note on 5:37) corresponds with the reference to the assertive rather than the promissory oaths of 5:33a, 34a, 37a.

It is logical to conclude, therefore, that of the four Antitheses with parallels in the tradition, the three with Q material receive their antithetical format from Matthew's redaction, whereas the fourth had the antithetical format in the pre-Matthean tradition.

e. The remaining two Antitheses stand without parallels in the tradition. Textually, there are neither convincing arguments for Matthean redaction nor is there solid evidence for their traditional status. One can only draw implications contextually in support of their traditional status. First, the existence of 5:33–37 in the tradition could hardly have served as the model for the other five, located where it now is in Matthew 5. Second, Jesus' demand supersedes the Law in 5:21–22, 27–28, in a fashion similar to that of 5:33–37, whereas Jesus' demand in the other three clearly redactional Antitheses sets the Law aside. Third, a traditional background for 5:21–22, 23–28, 33–37, would explain the presence of the third in the context and format of the second, while the fifth follows the fourth in context (dishonesty; cf. false accusation by the "evil one" of Deut 19:16–21 behind 5:38–39a) and format with the sixth rounding off the material consistent in theme with the previous five. Therefore, the division of the six Antitheses into two groups according to their source appears to be the most probable explanation of their origin.

2. The Traditional Antitheses

a. Matt 5:21–26 consists of three traditional units, the Antithesis proper (5:21–22) and two parables (5:23–24, 25–26). The Antithesis proper, in spite of opinions to the contrary, most likely represents the tradition with roots in Jesus' ministry to the "righteous" who saw their standing before God based on their keeping of the Law. By setting his demand in a disproportionate series of legal ordinances, Jesus parodied such a legalistic understanding and set forth his own claim for unbroken relationships. The addition of the related parable in 5:23–24 points to a catechetical setting of the Antithesis within the early church. The cultic setting of the parable itself (cf. Matt 6:14–15, par. Mark 11:25) suggests an early combination with the Antithesis in the Jewish-Christian community. The second parable with its parallel in Luke 12:57–59, originally one of a series of crisis parables, was most likely added by the evangelist because of the comparable content (cf. διαλλάσσω of 5:24 and ἀπαλλάσσω of Luke 12:58). By introducing the material with the rather rare "be well disposed toward," the evangelist places the weight of the parable on reconciliation and aligns the parable with 5:9 ("peacemaker") and 5:38–48 (behavior towards the adversary). The differences between the Matthean and Lucan accounts most likely go back to Luke's redaction (see Note on 5:25).

b. Matt 5:27–30 consists of the Antithesis proper (5:27–28) and a hyperbolic illustration of extreme measures to avoid judgment (5:29–30). As with the first Antithesis, this one most likely goes back to Jesus' ministry to the "righteous" and focuses on the seventh commandment. The addition of 5:29–30 has a close parallel in 18:8–9, par. Mark 9:43–48, and may well stem from the pre-Matthean tradition. As did 5:23–24, this material underscored the thrust of the Antithesis by the use of radical hyperbole. One can no more outlaw lust than can one avoid evil through self-mutilation. This combination most likely reflects a catechetical setting in the early church. The evangelist does not add directly to this Antithesis, but his introduction of the third Antithesis was clearly related to the second.

c. Matt 5:33–37 consists of a complex premise and antithesis, as noted above (see also Notes on 5:33, 34–37). The primary thrust of the Antithesis, however, focused on the Old Testament Law and indirectly on the second commandment. Like the previous Antitheses, therefore, the original setting lay in Jesus' ministry to the "righteous." The focus on assertive oaths led to the application of the Antithesis to the much-abused promissory oaths (5:33b, 34b–35, cf. 23:16–22; Mark 7:11–12, par. Matt 15:5–6) in the Jewish tradition. The paranetic formulation of the material in James 5:12 may suggest a catechetical context in the early church for this combination. Either the evangelist or at some later point in the pre-Matthean tradition, 5:36, differing in form and number, was added to the list of such oaths (see Note on 5:36). Matthew, however, was clearly responsible for adding the summary statement of 5:37b by which he underscored the ultimate thrust of the original Antithesis (see Note on 5:37).

All three traditional Antitheses, then, reflect three stages in development: first, the Antithesis proper (5:21–22, 27–28, 33a, 34a–37a); then the perhaps catechetical expansion of each through combination with corresponding traditional motifs (5:21–22 [23–24], 27–28 [29–30], 33a, 34a–37 [33b, 34b–36]); and finally the further additions by the evangelist (5:21–24 [25–26], 27–30 [cf. 31–32], 33–37a [37b]).

3. The Redactional Antitheses

a. Matt 5:31–32 contains several differences from the Q parallel in Luke 16:18. The divorce saying itself was doubtlessly transmitted as an isolated saying stemming from Jesus' ministry. The original context was most likely that of the previous Antitheses as the controversy narrative in Mark 10:2–9, par. Matt 19:3–9 suggests. Matt 5:32 reflects several modifications stemming from the desire to align the saying with the Old Testament Jewish Law on divorce and adultery (5:32a, cf. Luke 16:18a, see Note on 5:32). The context for these changes may have been the early polemics with a Judaism that sought to legalistically interpret Jesus' demand and thus show its absurdity. But more likely the changes reflect the concern of the strict Jewish-Christian community to align catechetically Jesus' teaching within the parameters of the Old Testament Law, a concern underlying the reworking of the Q tradition in 5:18, cf. Luke 16:17. The redactional work of the evangelist focused on the premise and perhaps the exchange of μοιχεύω for μοιχάομαι to agree with the context of 5:27–28 (see Note on 5:32).

b. Matt 5:38–42 also contains numerous differences from the Lucan counterpart. The traditional unit of 5:39b–40, 42, par. Luke 6:29–30, consisted originally of two sayings transmitted as isolated sayings but concurring in theme with the command to love one's enemy. As noted above, these sayings were combined in the Sermon tradition of Q within the Love Your Enemies complex as illustrations of loving behavior. Matthew, apart from building the Antithesis and separating the material from the larger complex, reshaped the structure of the sayings (see Note on 5:39) and reset the first unit within the context of a judicial setting (see Note on 5:39, 40). He also added the reference to impression (5:41) to head a list of requests with a decreasing order of obligation (see Note on 5:41). The verbal differences between 5:42 and Luke 6:30b go back to Luke's account.

c. Matt 5:43–48 consists of material stemming from Jesus' ministry including the love commandment (5:44, par. Luke 6:27–28) and the promise of 5:45, par. Luke 6:35, as well as the exhortation to mercy (Luke 6:36, cf. Matt 5:48) and the rhetorical questions (5:46–47, par. Luke 6:32–34) that help combine the two traditional units of Luke 6:29–30 and 6:27–28, 35. Matthew has considerably reworked the material by abbreviating the Love Your Enemies commandment (5:44, cf. Luke 6:27–28), separating the examples of conduct to form his fifth Antithesis (5:39b–42), and reworking the rhetorical questions in view of the Love Your Enemies command itself (5:46–47). His most dramatic change appears in 5:48, cf. Luke 6:36, where he takes the opening saying from the next section of the Sermon material (Luke 6:36–42, cf. Matt 7:1–5), reworks it in terms of Deut 18:13, and places it as the summary parallel to 5:20 for the Antitheses.

By way of conclusion, after surveying the complex of the Antitheses (5:21–48) we can see that various elements stemming from Jesus' ministry, the early church tradition, and the evangelist have come together to form this section. In spite of this diversity of background and usage the final product in the Gospel stands consistent with the thrust of the material in Jesus' ministry. Confronting us with the inadequacies of legalistic "righteousness" the Antitheses call us to a life of surrender and discipleship by the one who offers God's forgiving acceptance to the sinner and restored relationships with God and others. It is precisely these emphases that characterize Jesus' earthly ministry to the sick, the sinner, and the righteous.

VII. ON DOING RIGHTEOUSNESS
Matthew 6:1–18

Translation

6 ¹Be on your guard not to perform your pious deeds before others to be seen by them. If not, you will not have a reward with your Father in heaven.

²Therefore, whenever you perform your deeds of charity, do not blow your own trumpet in the synagogues and the streets as do the hypocrites in order to be honored by others. Indeed I assure you, they have been paid in full. ³But when you perform your deeds of charity, do not let your left hand know what your right hand is doing ⁴in order that your deeds of charity might be a secret. Your Father who sees in secret will repay you.

⁵Whenever you pray do not be like the hypocrites, because they love to pray while standing in the synagogues and on the street corners in order to be seen by others. Indeed I assure you, they have been paid in full. ⁶But when you pray enter your inner room, close the door, and pray to your Father who is in secret. Your Father who sees in secret will repay you.

⁷When praying, do not prattle as the Gentiles. For they think that they will be heard by means of their many words. ⁸Therefore, do not be like them. For God your Father knows the needs you have before you ask him. ⁹Consequently, pray in this manner:

Our Father in heaven
Let your name be made holy.
¹⁰Let your Kingdom come,
Let your will be done
as in heaven so on earth.

¹¹Give us today our daily bread,
¹²And forgive us our debts
    as we have forgiven those indebted to us.
¹³Do not lead us into temptation
    but deliver us from the Evil One.
¹⁴For if you forgive others their sins, your Father in heaven will also forgive you. ¹⁵But if you do not forgive others, your Father will not forgive your sins.

¹⁶Whenever you fast, do not be sad like the hypocrites. For they disfigure their faces in order to appear to others as fasting. Indeed I assure you, they have been paid in full. ¹⁷But when you fast, anoint your head with oil and wash your face, ¹⁸lest you appear as fasting to others rather than to your Father who is in secret. Your Father who sees in secret will repay you.

Literary Analysis

Whereas Matt 5:21–48 developed the "greater righteousness" in terms of one's relationship to others, 6:1–18 turns to one's relationship before God by focusing on three acts of piety characteristic of Judaism: almsgiving, prayer, and fasting. Betz has captured the religious and instructional dimension of this section with the label "cult-didache" (Betz, "Kult-Didache," 446, n. 9).

The complex of 6:1–18 contains a *Kelal* heading (6:1), three parallel constructed admonitions (6:2–4, 5–6, 16–18), and an extended admonition on prayer including the example of the Lord's Prayer (6:7–15). The heading (6:1) sets the stage for the following admonitions by giving a general paranesis summarizing in a negative fashion the basic thrust of each admonition. Just as 5:20 introduced the Antitheses (5:21–48) with a warning calling for a "greater righteousness," so 6:1 warns against the wrong performance of "righteousness" that costs one any future reward with the Father.

The three admonitions (6:2–4, 5–6, 16–18) consist of a negative (6:2, 5, 16) and positive (6:3–4, 6, 17–18) command set in an almost verbatim parallelism. The negative statement in each unit opens in the form of an indefinite temporal clause (6:2a, 5a, 16a) referring to the specific act of piety. This is followed by a negative warning against being like the "hypocrites" whose actions are for display (6:2b, 5b, 16b). It concludes with an ἀμήν-saying expressing judgment in terms of the hypocrites' having already received full compensation (6:2c, 5c, 16c). The positive statement of each unit opens with a resumptive reference to the specific act set in either a participial (6:3a, 17a) or indefinite temporal (6:6a) construction, followed by an imperative to private action (6:3b, 6, 17b) based on the need for secrecy (6:4a, cf. 6b, 18a) and a concluding promise of God's reward (6:4b, 6c, 18b).

Matt 6:7–15 disrupts the unity of the original complex by supplementing the second admonition involving prayer. This section, called a "prayer-didache" by Jeremias (*Theology* 1:194), contains an introductory admonition (6:7–8) related in form and content to those of 6:2–6, 16–18, an example of correct praying (the Lord's Prayer [6:9–13]), and a concluding statement on forgiveness (6:14–15). The admonition is introduced by a reference to prayer in a participial construction (6:7a), followed by a negative comparison with the Gentiles whose prayers are determined by their anxiety of not being heard (6:7b). The admonition itself, however, has the form of a negative comparison (6:8a) based on God's providential knowledge (6:8b) rather than a positive counterpart, as found in the larger complex. The Lord's Prayer then follows as a positive example (6:9a, 9b–13), and the unit closes with a statement on forgiveness in the form of a sentence of holy law (6:14–15).

As to the question of source, the larger unit of 6:2–6, 16–18, stems from the evangelist's special tradition, whereas the Lord's Prayer has a related parallel in Q (Luke 11:2–4) and the statement on forgiveness has a related parallel in Mark 11:25(26). More debatable is the source of 6:1, 7–8, related to the larger question whether and to what extent the entire complex (6:1–18) was pre-Matthean (Wrege, *Überlieferungsgeschichte*, 94–97; Betz, "Kult-Didache," 450, 454–57) or redactionally introduced (6:1), modified by an introduction (6:7–8) for an insertion (6:9–13) of the Lord's Prayer and concluded by a statement on forgiveness (6:14–15, e.g., Bultmann, *Tradition*, 148, 150, 324). Of the alternatives, redaction by the evangelist appears the most probable, but only a closer look at the content and arrangement of the material can justify any conclusion about source (see Comment C for further discussion).

Notes

6.1. With this general paranesis Matthew opens the next section on "righteousness" (6:1–18). The typically Matthean vocabulary, the content drawn summarily from the traditional material that follows, and the similar function of the negative warning in 6:1, paralleling the redactional warning of 5:20, argue strongly for Matthean redaction (see Comment C, con. Wrege, *Überlieferungsgeschichte*, 97; Gerhardsson, "Opferdienst," 69; Betz, "Kult-Didache," 446). In 5:20 Matthew set the stage for the Antitheses by demanding a "righteousness" greater than that of the scribes and Pharisees in order to "enter the Kingdom"; in 6:1 the evangelist sets the stage for conduct befitting the proper relationship with God by demanding a *righteousness* performed in contrast to the manner of the *hypocrites* (cf. the *hypocrites* of Matt 23).

Be on your guard not to perform. Be on your guard (προσέχετε, the present imperative connoting constant vigilance, appears six times without parallel in Matthew (4x in Luke), three of which redactionally refer to the leaven of the scribes and Pharisees (16:6, 11, 12, cf. Mark 8:15). *To do* (ποιεῖν) used with both *righteousness* (δικαιοσύνην) and *deeds of kindness or alms* (ἐλεημοσύνην/ἔλεος) occurs elsewhere in the New Testament (1 John 2:29; 3:7, 10; Rev 22:11; cf. Acts 10:35; Heb 11:33; James 1:20) and reflects a common expression in the LXX for the Hebrew ʿśh ṣdqh.

your pious deeds. Rather than δικαιοσύνην *(righteousness)*, some manuscripts (LWZΘ et al) read ἐλεημοσύνην *(acts of mercy, alms)*, which would more closely combine 6:1 with 6:2–4. The change probably stems from the close relationship of the two terms in Judaism. One of the common terms for alms was ṣdqh, usually translated by δικαιοσύνη in the LXX, and δικαιοσύνη even occasionally translated ḥsd, usually translated by ἔλεος/ἐλεημοσύνη in the LXX (cf. Gen 19:19; 39:21; Prov 20:28; Isa 63:7). Yet the symmetry of structure shared between 6:2–4, 5–6, 16–18, and Matthew's use elsewhere of δικαιοσύνη suggest a broader reference in 6:1. As has been noted previously (see Excursus on 5:6), *righteousness* connotes conduct in keeping with the will of God, growing out of the new relationship established through Jesus' ministry between God and his own. In this context, *righteousness* refers to three specific deeds of piety or worship that reflect the nature of one's relationship with God. Therefore, whereas the "greater righteousness" of 5:20 introduced the demands for conduct corresponding to a new relationship between individuals (5:21–48), the *righteousness* of 6:1 introduces three admonitions for conduct corresponding to a new relationship between the individual and God.

before others to be seen by them. The phrase *before others* (ἔμπροσθεν τῶν ἀνθρώπων) occurs five times in Matthew (once in Luke), whereas the preposition ἔμπροσθεν appears nineteen times (2x in Mark; 9x in Luke).

To be seen (ϑεαϑῆναι) summarizes the intention of the following three religious exercises and corresponds to their being called *hypocrites* in a literal sense (see below). This same expression appears redactionally in 23:5 with reference to the scribes and Pharisees' practice of the Law. *By them* (αὐτοῖς) possibly reflects a Semitic influence on the dative of agent with the passive of verbs "to see" rather than the genitive of agency (ὑπὸ αὐτῶν; see Schlatter, *Matthäus*, 200).

if not. This elliptical protasis (εἰ δὲ μή γε) states the condition of failing to observe the warning: "If you do not guard against performing to be seen. . . ."

you will not have a reward with your Father in heaven. To have a reward (ἔχετε μισϑόν) appears only here and in 5:46 and may reflect the evangelist's own construction, drawn from a traditional context. In 5:46, the clause reminiscent of the Q promise in Luke 6:35, cf. Matt 5:45, formed part of the first rhetorical question (see Note on 5:46). In 6:1 this apodosis reflects the more technical ἀπέχειν μισϑόν of 6:2, 5, 16.

The concept of *reward* or merit lies at the heart of the entire complex of 6:1–18. It doubtless played a significant role in Judaism as it has in Christianity, even if a more subtle one (see Sanders, *Paul*, 107–47; Moore, *Judaism* 2:89–97). The roots of this teaching in Judaism, though variously expressed, lie deep in the history of Israel, including the prophetic warnings, the principles of life found in Wisdom literature, and the apocalyptic expectation of the final judgment. At the risk of oversimplification, one can summarize the doctrine of rewards and punishment implicit to this unit around three premises. First, one's reward corresponded to one's behavior in terms of the Law, or the Law as interpreted in a certain fashion. Second, the final accounting will take place at the last judgment, with God rewarding obedience and punishing transgressions of the Law. Third, since the basis of one's reward involves the doing of the Law, one could know one's standing before God in terms of one's performance of the Law. Since God's judgment would ultimately use the same standard as that used by others, namely, his Law, recognition now by others anticipates God's recognition at the final judgment.

The Gospels present Jesus with a similar interest in rewards and punishment (see Note on 5:12). Within the Sermon itself, the Beatitude of 5:11–12, par. Luke 6:22–23, promises those who suffer a *great reward;* 5:46, cf. Luke 6:35, asks whether living as do the tax collectors deserves any reward; 6:1, 2, 3, 4, 5, 16, 18 speak of *rewards* in terms of one's actions. Matt 5:45 promises sonship, and 6:19–21 exhorts one to store up treasures in heaven, while 5:19 promises status in the Kingdom based on the keeping of the commandments, and 5:20, 7:21-23, speak guardedly of entrance into the Kingdom. Add to these references in the Sermon the parables of the Talents (25:14-30) and the Laborers in the Vineyard (20:1-16), and it is evident Matthew's Gospel alone offers considerable material focusing on *rewards*.

Yet Jesus' sayings on *rewards*, wherever they are found, counter a strict merit system (cf. Note on 5:12). First, in 25:21, 23, and 19:29, par. Mark 10:29-30, the *reward* is disproportionately greater than one's efforts, so that the *reward* cannot be calculated as a wage that one earns. This facet stands out most clearly in the parable of the Laborers in the Vineyard (20:1-16), whose wages were the same despite the great disparity in hours worked. The master's response to the objections pointed to his freedom to do as he pleased with his own possessions (20:15). Second, Jesus focuses on God's goodness and freedom to act according to his own designs rather than simply on another's merits. God does remain the "Rewarder," but the basis is not one's merits. Third, this loss of basis in one's merit removes the possibility of calculating one's standing before God, since ultimately one's reward expresses God's gracious goodness. Thus, while using the language of reward and punishment current within first-century Judaism, Jesus taught that one's reward was based neither on the keeping of the Law nor on merit, but on God's goodness to his servants.

In 6:1-18, however, the concept of reward differs little on the surface from that of wages. To the contrary, the principle that reward equals payment underlies the argument of the section. Since one can receive only once a payment for services rendered, the present reward of recognition and acclaim by others preempts the future reward of recognition and acclaim by God. This principle explicit in each admonition that follows is implicit in the general warning of 6:1. One must not forget, however, that the issue at stake in 6:1-18 was not the doctrine of merit as such but the manner and style of one's worship or acts of piety.

6:2. *whenever you perform your deeds of charity.* Each of the three admonitions opens with the same indefinite temporal construction of ὅταν with the subjunctive (6:2a, 5a, 16a). *Deeds of charity* expresses the broader meaning of ἐλεημοσύνην, referring basically to an act of mercy or kindness. Generally rendered *almsgiving* in this context, one's contribution to the poor and needy in Judaism included to a lesser degree one's time and services (Moore, *Judaism* 2:162-79).

The underlying Semitic phrase (ʿśh ṣdqh/mšpṭ) reflects the religious overtones of this activity (Moore, *Judaism* 2:171). In the first expression, ṣdqh, often translated by *righteousness*, bespeaks God's vindication of his own in various ways including delivering them from evil. The second, mšpṭ, often translated by *commandment*, connotes one's responsibility of fulfilling a duty to other human beings. Furthermore, God himself protected the poor through the Law as seen, for example, in the legislation regulating harvests (e.g., Lev 19:9-10; Deut 24:20-21) and contributions to Levites, widows, and orphans (e.g., Deut 16:11, 14; 24:19-21; 26:12-13). The extent of Judaism's concern is seen in the lengthy discussion of one's relationship with the poor in the first of six major sections in the Mishnah.

In the first century, the poor and needy were cared for by public and private contributions collected and distributed on a regular basis (Str-B 4:436-58; Moore, *Judaism* 2:174-79). In addition, special festival days and synagogue services gave further occasion for making contributions. The reference to the streets and the synagogues in 6:2 suggests public gatherings where offerings were collected.

do not sound a trumpet ahead of you.   This warning appears to be a hyperbolic reference to ceremonial fanfare accompanying and announcing a significant fete (cf. Schlatter, *Matthäus,* 201) and implies a desire to draw attention to one's actions. This admonition focusing on the *how* rather than the *whether* of charitable services warns against the wrong manner of action by negatively comparing the actions of the *hypocrites.*

as the hypocrites do.   Each negative comparison mentions specifically the *hypocrites* (6:2, 5, 16). The use of the Greek term ὑποκριτής in this setting closely approximates the basic meaning of "actor" stemming from a theatrical background (Bauer, *s.v.;* Wilckens, *TDNT* 8:559-60). The *hypocrites* connotes those who display their acts of piety for show (cf. θεαθῆναι in 6:1; 6:2, 5, 16). *Hypocrite* in English implies a moral criticism of one who seeks to appear different from what one actually is. Consequently, it carries the additional connotation of pretense, fraud, or the intention to deceive. Attaching such a conscious lack of integrity to the term belongs neither here in 6:1-18 nor in the other occurrences of the term in the Gospel (cf. van Tilborg, *Leaders,* 21-24).

Matthew elsewhere singles out the scribes and Pharisees as the *hypocrites* (15:7, cf. Mark 7:6; 22:18, cf. Mark 12:15; 23:13, 15, 23, 25, 27, [28], 29). The term applies to them because their actions betray their desire to be seen and recognized by others (23:5-7, cf. 6:2, 5, 16) and because their appearance contradicts their relationship to God and others

(23:25–26, 27–28), even if unconsciously. They are indeed "actors" concerned with appearance, appearance related to a life role controlled by a concern for the details of the Law (23:2–3, 23–24, cf. 15:7). They seek to appear as "righteous," which they in fact desire and think themselves to be before God and others, by means of their obedience to the Law's demands. But in reality they stand alienated from God (6:2, 5, 16), from his redemptive activity (23:23, 29–35), and from others (23:4, 13). Although seeking to please God, they fail to recognize God's ultimate will in history (cf. 23:28, ἀνομία). Their conduct reflects a broken relationship rather than a restored relationship with God and others. This disjunction between their personal relationship with God and others and their actions stands in sharp contrast to the wholeness demanded by 5:48, the "greater righteousness" of 5:20. Indeed, *hypocrisy* is the opposite of *righteousness* for Matthew (6:1, cf. 6:2, 5, 16; see Trilling, *Israel*, 202; van Tilborg, *Leaders*, 24–26).

The portrait of the scribes and Pharisees in Matthew 23 corresponds with the use of the term *hypocrites* in 6:2, 5, 16. More than simply playing to their audience, they desire to worship God through charity, praying, and fasting. But their actions seek to gain recognition from God and others rather than stemming from a relationship of true devotion.

in order to receive the glory from others. The contrast between 5:16, where God receives the glory from others, and this statement in 6:2 could not be more pronounced. By seeking acclaim from others, the *hypocrites* falsely assume that they will have the same acclaim before God, since the standard of acceptance and judgment is the same, namely, God's will as expressed by the Law.

I assure you, they have been paid in full. The change to the second person plural in the prophetic word of judgment points to the formulaic character of ἀμὴν λέγω ὑμῖν. This concluding statement of the negative comparison, identical in all three units (6:2b, 5b, 16b), pronounces judgment. *Paid in full* (ἀπέχουσιν) is a semitechnical expression from the business world that means to have received a receipt *paid in full* (Bauer, *s.v.*). The present tense has the force of the perfect tense (BDR, 322, n. 2). Using the language of wages, the *hypocrites* have received their payment for services rendered and should expect no more. Their efforts do not extend beyond the limits of their audience. The manner and motivation of their acts of devotion reflect the broken relationship between themselves and God.

6:3. *whenever you perform your deeds of charity.* The genitive absolute (σοῦ δὲ ποιοῦντος) returns to the second singular, picks up the theme, and introduces the positive admonition for the correct manner of carrying out one's charitable services.

do not let your left hand know. In this unit, the correct approach begins with a negative command expressed in another hyperbole. Yet the force of the demand not only counters a public display of one's actions but also removes any basis for premeditated or calculated activities, since one's actions are to go unnoticed even by oneself (cf. 25:37–40). The merit motive of one's achievements is clearly excluded.

6:4. *in order that your deeds of charity be done in secret.* Two bases for the admonition now follow. The first contrasts the performance for public acclaim with that in secret. Numerous rabbinic parallels have been cited reflecting the same concern and warning against the ostentatious practice of piety (Str-B 1:391–92; Montefiore, *Rabbinic Literature,* 11–12). The presence of the warning in the Gospels as well as in Judaism suggests that acts of devotion done for show were no less foreign to first-century society than to our twentieth century.

your Father who sees in secret will reward you. This second basis for the admonition concludes all three units (6:4, 6, cf. 18). It consists of three elements. First, the reference to God as *your Father,* the only use of this particular designation (ὁ πατήρ σου) in the first three Gospels, implies a father-son relationship between God and the disciples (Kingsbury, *Matthew,* 55–56). Though rabbinic sources also use the designation of God as Father (Str-B 1:392–96; Montefiore, *Rabbinic Literature,* 113–14; Moore, *Judaism* 2:203–11), the relationship of father and son sets the ultimate difference between Jesus' demand for one's act of religious devotion and that of the rabbis. The practice of one's piety in private not only excludes the basis of merit but stems from one's relationship with God as the Father. One's conduct or "righteousness" in 6:1–18 as in 5:20–48 stems, therefore, from a new relationship between the individual and God rather than from an attempt to gain or establish that relationship. Second, God is depicted as the one who "looks on the heart," who sees *in secret* commensurate with the promise of the new relationship of Jer 31:31–34; Ezek 36:26–27. Third, God does reward his own (ἀποδώσει), although the nature and scope of the reward is not stated. The future reward, in contrast to the present reward of the *hypocrites,* points to the final judgment.

6:5. *Whenever you pray.* The second unit (6:5–6) focuses on prayer, and, apart from the second person plural verbs of 6:5, it shares a parallel construction in form and content with 6:2–4. Prayer played a major role in Jewish life (Moore, *Judaism* 2:212–36), in Temple worship, in the synagogue and other public places, and in one's personal, private life (Str-B 1:397). Certain prayers like the *Shema* and the Eighteen Benedictions were statutory and fixed as to times of the day and content (Str-B 1:397; Jeremias, "Daily," 67–72). Whereas the *Shema* was to be recited morning and evening, the Eighteen Benedictions was to be prayed morning, afternoon, and evening.

standing in the synagogues or on street corners. Standing (ἑστῶτες) in the perfect tense may connote an extended period of time *(having stood),* but the motif remains undeveloped. One normally prayed in a standing position (Str-B 1:401–2). Standing before the ark of the Law where the synagogue scrolls were stored, one led the congregation in prayer during the synagogue service (see Moore, *Judaism* 1:291–96). At the fixed times for prayer, one might well have found oneself on a *street corner* or in a public place. The reference, in any case, indicates a public setting.

in order to be obvious to others. This purpose clause (ὅπως φανῶσιν), synonymous with *to be seen by others* in 6:1, states explicitly the *hypocrites'* motivation to gain publicity and recognition for what they saw themselves to be, namely, the devout.

6:6. *But when you pray.* The change to the second person singular (cf. 6:5) and the positioning of the pronoun ahead of the temporal conjunction underscores the personal, didactic force of the admonition.

enter an inner room, close the door. The *inner room* (ταμεῖον) most likely refers to the small interior room without exterior walls or windows that was used for storage. The language of this command correlates with that of Isa 26:20, LXX, where one is exhorted to use the *inner room* for refuge.

pray to your Father who is in secret. Continuing the focus on the audience, Jesus contrasts the *synagogue* and *street corner* setting involving a public audience to the situation in which only God could be one's audience. This graphic difference in setting, recalls the true nature of prayer, namely, the personal communication between the individual and God.

your Father who sees in secret. Maintaining the contrast between public visibility of the *hypocrites* and private visibility with God, this phrase sets the stage for the contrast in *rewards*.

will reward you. The same promise as in 6:4 suggests that one's *reward* includes God's blessing at the future judgment in contrast to the recognition received already by the *hypocrites* (6:5b). The future orientation maintains the consistency of the doctrine of merit in terms of the future judgment without implying that the Father does not hear and respond in the present as well (cf. 6:25–34; 7:7–11).

6:7. This verse begins a second section on prayer (6:7–15) different in form and content from the first (6:5–6). The section consists of an introductory warning (6:7–8), a positive command based on the example of the Lord's Prayer (6:9–13), and a concluding statement on forgiveness (6:14–15). Although some have taken this "prayer-didache" to have been formed pre-Matthean (Wrege, *Überlieferungsgeschichte*, 98, n. 1; Jeremias, *Theology* 1:193–95; Betz, "Kult-Didache," 451), others have suggested that Matthew was responsible for drawing the three traditional elements together (Kilpatrick, *Origins*, 21; Schniewind, *Matthäus*, 79; Grundmann, *Matthäus*, 197). There are several indications supporting Matthew's using a theme from the Q tradition of 6:21–32, par. Luke 12:29–30, to set the stage for his insertion of the Lord's Prayer (Bultmann, *Tradition*, 133; Klostermann, *Matthäusevangelium*, 54). First, the antithetical construction of 6:7–8 shares a material parallel with 6:31–32, where a negative comparison with the Gentile's concern is followed by a reference to God's providential knowledge and care of his own. Second, much of the material corresponds lexically to the special context (βατταλογεω, πολυλογία, εἰσακούω), but ὥσπερ *(as)* is distinctively Matthean (10x, 2x in Luke), as is the use of ὁμοιόω *(to be like;* cf. 7:24, 26; 8x, 1x in Mark, 3x in Luke). Furthermore, the evangelist uses οὕτως in 5:16 and 7:12 within the Sermon to introduce imperatives. Third, the evangelist stylistically appropriates his context at the outset but breaks the pattern by not continuing the format (6:7a, cf. 2a).

do not prattle as the Gentiles. This unit opens like the others with a negative comparison (6:2, 5, 16). But this comparison differs in content as well as object. Whereas the units of 6:2–4, 5–6, 16–18 focus on the manner and motivation of the acts of devotion performed for public acclaim, 6:7 focuses on the content of one's prayers. *To prattle* has been variously traced to βατταρίζω *(to stammer)* as an onomatopoetic reference to pagan formulas (e.g., "abracadabra," Beare, "Tongues," 229; Grundmann, *Matthäus*, 198; Delling, *TDNT* 1:597) and to a hybrid verb formed from Aramaic *btlt* ("idly") and λαλέω ("to speak"), meaning to *babble* (e.g., Klostermann, *Matthäusevangelium,* 54; Bonnard, *Matthieu,* 80; Hill, *Matthew,* 134). Regardless of the derivation, this verb's specific meaning follows in the reference to πολυλογία. Furthermore, the object of comparison has shifted from the *hypocrites* to the *Gentiles.* The use of the *Gentiles* for comparison also appears within the Sermon in the tradition of 5:47 and 6:32 (cf. 18:17). Matthew's use of it in 6:7 drawn perhaps from the other traditional usages reflects the evangelist's interest in the *Gentiles* (cf. 10:18; 21:43; 24:14; 28:19).

for. . . by means of their many words. Rather than a purpose clause (cf. 6:2, 5, 16) an explanation (γάρ) follows the negative imperative. *Many words* has been variously interpreted as long prayers, verbosity (Str-B 1:403–6; Klostermann, *Matthäusevangelium,* 54–55; McNeile, *Matthew,* 76; Bonnard, *Matthieu,* 80) or the *Gentiles'* practice of using different formulas and predications, reflecting their polytheistic context (Manson, *Sayings,* 166; Grundmann, *Matthäus,* 198; Hill, *Matthew,* 134; Schweizer, *Matthew,* 146). In either case, their primary concern is to be heard by God, a concern which they seek to assuage by *many words.* Such reference to the abuse of prayer occurs in literature from the Old Testament (cf. 1 Kgs 18:26–29; Isa 1:15; cf. Sir 7:14) to Seneca's charge of "fatiguing the gods" (*Epis* 31:5) and reflects one's anxiety about being heard. This motivation from fear behind the *Gentiles'* prayers contrasts with the *hypocrites'* desire for public recognition.

6:8. *do not be like them.* Rather than the positive command as in the other units, this unit has a second negative command. The positive command follows later (6:9a) but after the contrasting basis for why one's prayers are to be different from the Gentiles.

your Father knows your needs before you ask. In contrast to the Gentiles' anxiety about being heard, this statement declares that the Father's providential knowledge includes the needs of his children. Thus the divine providence of 6:32 becomes the basis of one's assurance in prayer. With this assurance of God's knowledge of one's needs even before they are voiced, one can come to the Father with confidence in contrast to the *Gentiles.*

6:9. *Consequently, pray in this manner.* The positive command to pray, implicit in 6:8a, explicitly introduces the Lord's Prayer (6:9b–13). The *consequently* (οὖν) bridges the introduction (6:7–8) and the command to pray. The command to pray (προσεύχεσθε) may itself be reminiscent of a similar introduction in the Q tradition, since Luke 11:2 opens the Lord's Prayer with "Whenever you pray" (ὅταν προσεύχεσθε). *In this manner* (οὕτως) may also suggest that the Lord's Prayer was intended more as a model offering guidelines for one's prayer than as a statutory prayer to be repeated (Schweizer, *Matthew*, 147).

The setting for the Lord's Prayer is neither explicitly personal nor liturgical. Nothing from the larger context (6:5–6, cf. 2–4, 16–18) nor from the immediate context (6:7–8) suggests a liturgical setting, despite the apparently liturgical character of Matthew's version in comparison with Luke's (e.g., Jeremias, "Lord's Prayer," 89–90). Yet Matthew's introduction also falls considerably short of the personal command in *Did* 8:3 for one to "pray thus three times a day." The evangelist seems to have chosen to use this larger context of one's "righteousness" (6:1), an expression of one's conduct in relationship to God, to introduce the Lord's Prayer as a model for the content of one's prayer in public or private worship. The occasion, setting, and times of one's worship are assumed as givens for the disciple.

The Lord's Prayer appears in two different forms and contexts in the Gospels. Matthew's version consists of an address followed by several petitions that fall into two categories, three "you"-petitions addressing God in the second person singular and four "we"-petitions referring to the first person plural. Luke has a similar pattern with an address and five petitions, two in the second person singular and three in the first person plural. Furthermore, by comparison, Matthew has an expanded address, and Luke's third and fourth petitions have differences in wording from the Matthean parallels. As will be seen below, most have assigned the additional material including the petitions in Matthew to secondary developments within the tradition, whereas the verbal differences generally indicate priority to Matthew's account. Consequently, Luke represents the earlier form and Matthew represents the earlier wording.

In contrast to Matthew's context within the Sermon, Luke 11:1–13 includes the Lord's Prayer as part of a larger section on prayer. The complex opens with the disciples observing Jesus in prayer and then asking him to teach them to pray just as John the Baptist had taught his disciples (11:1). After giving the Lord's Prayer in response (11:2–4), the parable of the Importune Friend at Midnight (11:5–8) and a unit of sayings encouraging one to pray (11:9–13) round out the section. Luke 11:1–13 clearly comes much closer to being a "prayer-catechism" (Jeremias, "Lord's Prayer," 88) than Matt 6:7–15. Indeed, Matthew's nearly verbatim use of the tradition behind Luke 11:9–13 in 7:7–11 strongly suggests that the Lucan unit or Q underlay Matthew's tradition as well (see Note on 7:7–11).

The background of the Lord's Prayer involves an Aramaic original and a haunting similarity with at least two well-known Jewish prayers of the first century. Numerous scholars have attempted reconstructions of the original Aramaic prayer (e.g., Torrey, *Aramaic Gospels*, 309–17; Burney, *Poetry*, 112–13; K. G. Kuhn, *Achtzehngebet*, 32–33), but the lack of agreement demonstrates the difficulty and subjectivity of such a reconstruction. Though both Matthew and Luke reflect their Aramaic background, the agreement by both on the rare and much debated Greek term ἐπιούσιον (6:11, par. Luke 11:3) modifying *bread* indicates a rather firm Greek tradition as well.

The Lord's Prayer also reflects its Aramaic background in its similarity to the Aramaic *Kaddish* prayed at the end of the synagogue worship service (Moore, *Judaism* 1:306) and the content of the Eighteen Benedictions prayed three times daily (Jeremias, "Daily," 72–78). The opening petitions of the Lord's Prayer are startlingly similar to the *Kaddish*: "Magnified and hallowed be his great name in the world which he created according to his will; and may he make his kingship sovereign in your lifetime and in your days." The Eighteen Benedictions not only has material parallels with five of Matthew's seven petitions but also reflects a similar two-part construction centering on the petition for bread, similar rhyme and rhythm patterns in general, and similarity of purpose for individual use as well as worship (Kuhn, *Achtzehngebet*). These similarities between the Lord's Prayer and the two Aramaic prayers common to both public and private Jewish religious experience stem from a milieu with which the Gospels portray Jesus to be very familiar. Yet the similarities must not overshadow the dissimilarities, not least of which include the selection and arrangement of the concise petitions whose content uniquely characterize Jesus' ministry. Once again the old wineskins of Jewish language and religious life contain the new wine of Jesus' teaching, a content that ultimately bursts the old skins.

Our Father in heaven. By contrast to Matthew's address, Luke 11:2 has simply "Father" (Πάτερ). The use of *Father* as a designation for God has a long history among peoples of diverse cultures (Schrenk, *TDNT* 5:951–59). In the Old Testament, the term *Father* refers directly to God around fifteen times (Jeremias, "Abba," 11–15) but in a very distinctive manner. God is the Father of Israel alone and that by virtue of his choosing Israel to be his son, as well as his intervention in history to free and to redeem Israel (Lohmeyer, *Our Father,* 39–41; Jeremias,

"Lord's Prayer," 95). In Judaism God as *Father* becomes more common (Moore, *Judaism* 2:201–11, though many of the references are later than first century, Jeremias, "Abba," 19; McCasland, "Abba, Father," 84), but always qualified either by a phrase or a pronominal suffix such as "my"/"your"/"our" (Kittel, *Urchristentum,* 92–95; Manson, *Sayings,* 168).

This usage of *Father* for God with accompanying pronouns continues in the New Testament with its basis in Jesus' teaching in the Gospels (Lohmeyer, *Our Father,* 32–51; Jeremias, "Abba," 29–54; Schrenk, *TDNT* 5:984–89). But a significant difference emerges formally in the New Testament usage that materially qualifies all the other usages, namely, the addressing of God as *Father* without modifiers. The roots of this usage appear preserved in the Aramaic prayer formula *abba* in Rom 8:15, Gal 4:6, and in Jesus' own prayer in Mark 14:36. *Abba* comes from baby talk in Aramaic expressing the little child's words for the parents, mama/*imma* and dada/*abba* (Jeremias, "Abba," 58–59; Schrenk, *TDNT* 5:985). Yet in New Testament times *abba* had also become a general designation for *father,* even replacing at times other constructions denoting "my/his/our" or even "the Father" (Jeremias, "Abba," 58–59). This familiar address applied to God in the New Testament stands in stark contrast to the desire at that time to avoid the use of God's name. Doubtless this unparalleled usage in Judaism of *abba* to address God in prayer stems from Jesus' ministry and indicates his awareness of a distinctive relationship with God as Father (Jeremias, "Abba," 62–63; Dunn, *Jesus,* 22–26). Furthermore, *abba* probably stands behind the vocative use of Πάτερ (e.g., 11:25, par. Luke 10:21), πάτερ μου (e.g., 26:39–42), and ὁ πάτηρ (e.g., Mark 14:36; Rom 8:15; Gal 4:6). Therefore, Luke's address Πάτερ ("Father") quite probably reflects an underlying Aramaic *abba.*

Matthew's address, by contrast, looks very similar to another very common designation for God in the synagogues, especially after A.D. 70, namely, *Father in heaven* (Moore, *Judaism* 2:202–11; Str-B 1:410–11; Schrenk, *TDNT* 5:985–87). The roots clearly stem from the Old Testament understanding of God as Israel's Father, and the qualification *in heaven* distinguished between one's heavenly and earthly fathers (Str-B 1:410; Schrenk, *TDNT* 5:979–80). But the distinction becomes superfluous in the context of prayer. Therefore, the qualification came to connote the realm from which God would replace what was destroyed on earth, especially after A.D. 70.

In heaven appears with slight variations twenty times in Matthew in contrast to Mark and Luke's one usage (Mark 11:25; Luke 11:13). Yet the statistical difference itself does not justify assigning the phrase in 6:9 to Matthew's redaction. First, Mark's use of the concept in 11:25, par. Matt 6:14, in a context involving prayer, demonstrates the existence of a pre-Matthean traditional usage. Second, Matthew has very rarely introduced the phrase into Marcan tradition (once in 12:50; cf. Mark 3:35). Third, Luke never uses the qualification and apparently reworks it in 11:13, par. Matt 7:11 (cf. Note on 7:11 below), which may mean that other Q parallels may be traditional rather than redactional (5:45, cf. Luke 6:35; 5:48, cf. Luke 6:36). Fourth, Matthew's own source may also have used the phrase (e.g., 16:17). Therefore, no convincing evidence supports either a traditional (e.g., Wrege, *Überlieferungsgeschichte*, 102) or a redactional (e.g., Schulz, *Spruchquelle*, 85) source for *in heaven*.

In either case the meaning and function of the phrase remain consistent throughout the Gospel. *Father in heaven* represents more than simply a circumlocution for the name of God, since Matthew exhibits no such reluctance to refer to God in his Gospel (e.g., 26:63, cf. Mark 14:61). The phrase expresses more than a formulaic address, since the designation *Father* and the term *heaven* each connote different aspects of God's relationship to his own and to the world.

First, the personal relationship of God as *Father* to his own as *sons* stands out boldly in Matthew's use of the personal pronouns "your/ our/my Father," a qualification that prevents the phrase from becoming an abstract designation of God's remote transcendence (Schrenk, *TDNT* 5:986–87). This relationship of *Father* and *sons* has already played a role in the Sermon materials (e.g., 5:9, 16, 45, 48; 6:1, 4, 6, 14, 15, 26, 32; 7:11, 21) and stems again from Matthew's christological perspective. This perspective has a dual dimension, namely, with reference to Jesus as Son of God and seen in the phrase "my Father" and with reference to the disciples as sons of God and seen in the phrase "your Father" (Frankemölle, *Jahwebund*, 160–61; cf. Kingsbury, *Matthew*, 55–56).

While the phrase "my Father" appears once in Mark (8:38, par. Matt 16:27, Father of the Son of Man), once in Q (11:27, par. Luke 10:22), and three times in Luke alone (2:49; 22:29; 24:49), "my Father" occurs thirteen times in Matthew, over half of which are clearly redactional (7:21, cf. Luke 6:46; 10:32–33, cf. Luke 12:8–9; 12:50, cf. Mark 3:35; 20:23, cf. Mark 10:40; 26:29, cf. Mark 14:25). Such a heightened use of the phrase concurs with Matthew's primary christological focus on Jesus with the title Son of God (Kingsbury, *Matthew*, 40–83). Drawn from the tradition, "my Father" expresses the relationship with the Father whereby the Father reveals himself through the Son (Schrenk, *TDNT* 5:988–89; 16:17, cf. 15:13 and especially 11:27, par. Luke 10:22). Furthermore, as the obedient Son Jesus suffers death as the will of the Father. And through his relationship with the Father, those who follow him, doing the will of the Father (7:21; 10:32–33; 12:50; 18:35; cf. 5:45), are themselves the "sons of God." Yet the sharp distinction between "my Father" and "your Father" maintains the uniqueness of the former and the derivative character of the latter (Schrenk, *TDNT* 5:988; Grundmann, *Matthäus,* 236–42; Frankemölle, *Jahwebund,* 10–12).

While the relationship of God as Father to his children has a narrower focus on Israel in the Old Testament, "your Father" refers even more narrowly to the disciples and not humankind in Jesus' ministry (e.g., Schrenk, *TDNT* 5:988; Frankemölle, *Jahwebund,* 170–71). Matthew's interest in this designation becomes clear again from the statistics: Mark has one (11:25, par. Matt 6:14), Luke one (12:32), Q two (5:48, par. Luke 6:36; 6:32, par. Luke 12:30), but Matthew has eleven, eight of which contrast with their Synoptic parallels (5:45, cf. Luke 6:35; 6:8, cf. 6:32, par. Luke 12:30; 6:15, cf. Mark 11:25; 6:26, cf. Luke 12:24; 7:11, cf. Luke 11:13; 10:20, cf. Luke 12:12; 10:29, cf. Luke 12:6; 18:14, cf. Luke 15:7) and two in redactional verses (5:16; 6:1). In each of these passages "your Father" specifically applies to the small circle of those around Jesus, those who hear and do the will of the Father as revealed by Jesus the Son. Therefore, "your Father" grows out of Jesus' relationship with God as "my Father" (Schrenk, *TDNT* 5:988). This relationship between the Father and his sons has been fundamental for one's conduct in the Sermon materials so far (5:9, 16, 45, 48; 6:4, 6, 8; cf. use of correlate concept of "brother" in 5:22–24, 47). And this relationship that comes through Jesus the Son's unique relationship with "my Father" becomes the basis for the sons' corporate expression of *our Father* in prayer.

Second, *in heaven* (ἐν . . . οὐρανοῖς) designates the dynamic point of departure for God's redemptive activity in the world including heaven and earth (Traub, *TDNT* 5:518–19). *Heaven* does not refer to a remote residence of God but rather to the sphere from which God effects his rule and will on earth (cf. Kingdom of Heaven; see Note on 5:3). The interrelationship between God's activity in heaven and earth follows in the first three petitions for the glorying of God's name, the coming of God's sovereign rule, and the accomplishment of God's will *on earth as it is in heaven.* Indeed, the very context of 6:1–18 contrasts the recognition of one's work done here on earth with one's recognition by "your Father" at the judgment, the consummation of his "heavenly rule." In other words, *our Father in heaven* expresses the fundamental relationship between God and the "sons of the Kingdom of Heaven."

Let your name be made holy. This petition identical with Luke 11:2 is the first of three that focus primarily on God's action on his own behalf, *your name, your Kingdom,* and *your will.* The three petitions are not only formally parallel but also materially interrelated. The first sets the stage for the other two. Numerous Jewish prayers offer parallels to the first petition (Str-B 1:411–12), but the *Kaddish* actually begins in a similar fashion: "Magnified and hallowed be your great name. . . ." Such a request reflects the Old Testament promise that God would act in history "to vindicate the holiness of my great name which has been profaned among the nations" (Ezek 36:23).

Hallowed means to *make holy,* to *sanctify.* The petition requests that God's name be set apart in honor and glory to evoke respect and awe. The opposite means to profane, dishonor, bring into disrespect (e.g., Isa 48:11; 52:5; Ezek 20:9, 14, 22; 36:22–23). The subject of the verb is obviously God himself by virtue of the opening address, *Our Father.* But God's role in the action is also underscored by the use of the passive voice, the so-called divine passive used to circumlocute the direct reference to God's name. God himself promised through the prophets to act on behalf of his name (e.g., Isa 48:11; Ezek 20:9, 14, 22; 36:22; 39:27–28) by his redemptive deliverance of his own in the day of salvation (e.g., Isa 52:6; Ezek 36:22–23; 39:27–28). The aorist imperative connotes an event, an action in point of time rather than repeated action of a present tense. The Old Testament background, the Jewish prayers, and the immediate context point to the eschatological character of this petition. One prays for God's once-for-all hallowing of his name.

your name represents another way of referring to God's own person, since in Hebrew thought one's name and person were basically the same (cf. Exod 20:7, which warns about profaning God's name). To know God's name is to know God (e.g., Isa 52:6). By his name he reveals himself (Exod 3:13–14). Therefore, to hallow God's name means to acknowledge God for who He is, namely, God. To acknowledge God to be God connotes by definition something about God's person as well as one's relationship to him and his will. Honor, glory, awe, obedience belong inherently to God as God. Consequently, his name as revelation of his person is "the Holy One" (Isa 40:25; 43:15; 45:11; 47:4; 48:17; 54:5; 55:5; 57:15; 60:9, 14; Ezek 39:7).

6:10. *Let your Kingdom come.* The second petition, identical with Luke 11:2, also corresponds to the second petition of the *Kaddish:* "May He make his kingship sovereign in your lifetime, during your days, and during the lifetime of all Israel with all speed and soon." Without use of a conjunction, this request grows out of the previous one. God acts to hallow his name by establishing his sovereign rule in history. In other words, this petition requests the promised, eschatological consummation of God's redemptive reign, the coming of the Kingdom (e.g., 24:30–31, par. Mark 13:26–27; Rev 11:15–17). Once again the aorist imperative connotes a once-for-all character of the action, a point in time.

Let your will be done. This petition lacks a parallel in Luke 11:2 and most likely stems from Matthew's redaction (con. Wrege, *Überlieferungsgeschichte,* 103–104; Jeremias, "Lord's Prayer," 89–91) on the basis of the following evidence: First, the theme of the will of God occurs once in Mark (3:35, par. Matt 12:50) and once in Luke 22:42 but five times in Matthew, all but one of which are redactional (6:10, cf. Luke 11:2; 7:21, cf. Luke 6:46; 18:14, cf. Luke 15:7; 26:42, cf. Mark 14:39; 12:50, par. Mark 3:35; cf. 21:31). Second, Matthew alone of the synoptists uses the aorist passive of γίνομαι, and he has it five times as an imperative in contrast to his parallels (6:10, cf. Luke 11:2; 8:13, cf. Luke 7:10 [13:29]; 9:29, cf. Mark 10:52; 15:28, cf. Mark 7:29; 26:42, cf. Mark 14:39). Third, the additional phrase *as in heaven so on earth* also betrays Matthew's concept of *heaven* as the dynamic sphere of God's rule (cf. "Kingdom of Heaven," and 5:34; 16:2; 18:18).

The accomplishing of God's will correlates with the coming of the Kingdom and the hallowing of God's name. God's people have caused his name to be profaned among the nations (e.g., Amos 2:7; Ezek 36:22–23). Consequently, the establishment of his sovereign rule over his people who follow his will also vindicates his name (Ezek 36:24–27; Isa 29:23; 52:5–7). Matthew shows particular interest in the relationship between the Kingdom and the *will* of the Father (6:10a, b; 7:21; 21:31; 26:42). Without doing the *will* of the Father (7:21), as without the "greater righteousness" (5:20), one cannot enter the Kingdom, since each expression connotes the obedient acknowledgement of God's redemptive rule as revealed and accomplished in Jesus' own teaching and ministry (26:42). Perhaps it is not mere coincidence that each reference involves the *will* "of the Father" (6:9b, 10b; 7:21; 12:50; 18:14; 21:31; 26:42), thereby expressing conduct characteristic of sonship, namely, obedience to the Father's *will.* Therefore, the accomplishment of God's *will* takes place through his sons whose conduct expresses their relationship to the Father.

as in heaven so on earth. This phrase rounds off the third and final petition of the second person singular group. Matthew uses this combined expression eight times, twice from Q (5:18, par. Luke 16:17; 11:25, par. Luke 10:21) and once from Mark 13:31, par. Matt 24:35. In the traditional passages, *heaven and earth* connotes the created "world" whose days are numbered (5:18; 24:35). By contrast, in 6:10, cf. 16:2 and 18:18, *heaven* is the sphere of God's ultimate authority and rule from whence he effects his will and rule on *earth.* The singular (οὐρανῷ) rather than the more typically Matthean and Semitic plural (e.g., 6:9) stems from the LXX use of the singular in the phrase *heaven and earth,* with the latter perhaps attracting the plural into the singular and together they stand for the world (e.g., Ps 134:6, LXX). The function of *as* (ὡς) and *so* (καί) forms a comparison rather than a coordination, since God's rule is to be effected on *earth* as it is already in *heaven.* Again, the aorist tense expresses the once-for-all character of God's action in history, on *earth.*

6:11. *Give us this day our daily bread.* The fourth petition turns the focus of the following petitions from God *(your)* to the petitioners *(us/we)* and serves formally as the pivot for the Prayer. Beginning with the object of one's request rather than the verb, its form stands out in contrast to the other petitions on either side. The location and the prominence of the object demonstrate the centrality of this request to the Prayer. Its content involves one's material needs and has a content parallel in the ninth petition of the Eighteen Benedictions. Luke's form of the petition differs in the tense of the imperative and the adverbial modifier. The change from Matthew's aorist imperative to the more continuous action of the present tense, "give us continually" (δίδου, cf. δός) relates to the adverbial modification. Whereas Matthew has *give us today* (σήμερον), a completed action, Luke has "give us continually day after day" (τὸ καθ᾽ ἡμέραν). This change most likely stems from Luke's redaction, since he has introduced the same use of "day after day" in Mark 8:34, cf. Luke 9:23, and Mark 11:18, cf. Luke 19:47. Yet the basic intent of the respective petition remains the same, since the request pertains to God's supplying each day the needs of his children.

The most disputed part of the Lord's Prayer lies in the uncertain construction τὸν ἄρτον ἡμῶν τὸν ἐπιούσιον *(our "daily" bread). Bread* (ἄρτος) variously refers to *bread* in particular (e.g., Mark 14:22), to food in general (e.g., Luke 7:33; John 13:18), to spiritual nourishment (e.g., "bread of life," John 6:31–34), and to the eschatological banquet (e.g.,

Luke 14:15) in the Gospels. Furthermore, ἐπιούσιον has a very obscure derivation and meaning. Apart from this usage in the Gospels and the church fathers, the term appears in only one papyrus. Even the papyrus reference lacks clarity since part of the word is missing (Foerster, *TDNT* 2:590–91). But the context appears to indicate a portion or ration granted to a person.

A major part of the ambiguity behind ἐπιούσιον lies in whether it is derived ultimately (Foerster, *TDNT* 2:591–95) from ἐπί and εἶμι ("to come," "to follow") or ἐπί and εἰμί ("to be present"). In the first case, ἐπιούσιος, usually with "day" or "night" supplied or implied, refers to "the coming day," "tomorrow," or, taken absolutely, ἐπιούσιος refers to the bread of "the future." In the second case, ἐπιούσιος (ἐπί and οὖσιος) means "necessary for existence" or taking ἐπιούσιος as short for ἐπὶ (τὴν) οὖσαν (ἡμέραν), it means "for the day that is," or "for today" (Bauer, *s.v.;* BDF 123, n.1; Foerster, *TDNT* 2:593–94). Each alternative has a long history (Foerster, *TDNT* 2:595–99), but generally the opinions divide between "necessary for life" and "tomorrow's bread."

Each of these are philological possibilities but ἐπιούσιος = ἐπιέναι occurs five times in Acts (7:26; 16:11; 20:15; 21:18; 23:11) with extrabiblical Greek support, especially in Josephus (Schlatter, *Matthäus,* 211) as a temporal reference to the next day or night. This interpretation corresponds with Jerome's observation that the Gospel according to the Hebrews had *mḥr* ("tomorrow") as the Aramaic equivalent in the Lord's Prayer. The primary weakness of this view has not been its philology but its apparent inconsistency with Jesus' teaching about concern for the future (6:25–34), the mission instructions regarding one's provisions (10:9–11, cf. Mark 6:8), and dependency on God's provision when necessary rather than in advance (e.g., Foerster, *TDNT* 2:595–97). By contrast, ἐπιούσιος = ἐπεῖναι, expressing primarily an amount, either "bread necessary for living" or "today's bread," rather than time, lacks appropriate parallels except in the Syriac and some parallels in rabbinic prayers (cf. Prov 30:8; Str-B 1:420–22). As an expression, however, of the "bare minimum" of one's needs, this meaning corresponds to the Gospel's portrait elsewhere of Jesus' ministry (Foerster, *TDNT* 2:596–97).

At this stage in the evidence one can make the following statements with certainty. First, ἐπιούσιος occurs too rarely in the literature to help determine its derivation or meaning. Second, neither Matthew's nor Luke's usage offers a clue as to how it was understood in the early church, but the presence of the very rare word in both Luke and Matthew attests to its fixed place in the early Greek tradition of the Lord's Prayer.

Third, both alternatives refer to the amount of bread, a measure, the equivalent of a day's needs regardless of whether it also connotes "today's" or "tomorrow's." Fourth, both options are philological possibilities. Therefore, "daily bread" meaning that which is necessary and appropriate for a day's needs represents the most neutral translation.

Yet the evidence does seem to tip the balance in favor of ἐπιούσιος meaning "tomorrow's bread" on the basis of (a) the analagous uses of ἐπιούσια in Acts and in extrabiblical literature, (b) the usage of *mḥr* in the Gospel of Hebrews and in the Jewish short prayers, and (c) the possibly deliberate contrast between "tomorrow's bread"/"today," a contrast that is no longer apparent in Luke 11:3. The conflict between a petition for tomorrow's provision a day in advance and living by faith for God's supplying of the immediate is more apparent than real. Prayer for a day's advance does not mean less faith nor does it mean stockpiling to guarantee one's future. Rather, on the basis of one's prayer stemming from a trusting dependence, one can function free from cares and place one's priorities at God's disposal instead of pursuing one's own personal interests (6:25–34).

Therefore, *give us today our bread for tomorrow* expresses the request for God to supply our physical needs. *Bread* has the broader meaning of one's physical and material needs (cf. 6:25–35). Yet the eschatological symbol of *bread* signifying the presence of the *Kingdom* when God would act to meet the needs of his people (e.g., Isa 55:1–2; 61:1–6, cf. John 6:33–34), the aorist tense in the petition (δός) corresponding to the other petitions, and the "future" reference in *tomorrow's bread* in Jewish usage have led several to see the eschatological reference exclusively in terms of the consummation (e.g., Jeremias, "Lord's Prayer," 100–102; Lohmeyer, "Our Father," 155–57). Whereas the consummation is marked by plenty and feasting, the present setting of the following petitions, the personal "our," the teaching of 6:25–34, and Luke's modification to the present imperative (δίδου) all point to the present need for physical sustenance. The eschatological element remains inherent in the request, since Jesus' ministry introduced the new age, the age of plenty, and offered the basis for such a petition (6:25–34). When praying for one's needs now, one does so in anticipation of the "tomorrow" of the consummation.

6:12. *forgive us our debts.* Luke "has sins" (ἁμαρτίας), although the following clause in Luke indicates an earlier agreement in the wording of the petition (see below). *Debts* (τὰ ὀφειλήματα) reflects a common Aramaic metaphor for sin drawn from the commercial realm (cf. 18:21–35). The sixth petition of the Eighteen Benedictions also asks for forgiveness but without the additional clause that follows. Forgiveness of sins was to be an integral part of the day of salvation (e.g., Jer 31:34; Ezek 36:25–32; Isa 40:2; 55:6–7).

as we also have forgiven our debtors. This fifth petition, like the third, has two parts, the second part introduced by *as* (ὡς). Luke 11:4b has a variation using an explanatory clause introduced by "for" (γάρ), the intensive pronoun "we ourselves" (αὐτοί; cf. καὶ ἡμεῖς = *we also*), the present tense of the verb ("we forgive"), and the object in the participle singular (ὀφείλοντι) modified by "every" (παντί) excluding any exceptions. The content difference between the two conjunctions *as* and *for* is not great, since both clauses express actions concomitant with the petition. Luke's "for we ourselves also are forgiving" connotes continuous actions, whereas Matthew's *as we also have forgiven* maintains the force of the aorist imperative by the use of the perfect tense (ἀφήκαμεν) referring to past, completed action. The present tenses in the textual variants (cf. *Did* 8:2) doubtless reflect the tendency in Luke's tradition to take the clause as admonition for continuous action and thus avoid the possible misunderstanding latent to Matthew that God must now forgive us "because" we have already forgiven others (see Note on 6:14–15).

6:13. *And lead us not into temptation.* This petition has a verbatim parallel in Luke 11:4b and a content parallel in an evening prayer (as well as a nearly identical morning prayer that follows) of the Talmud (*Berakot* 605; Str-B 1:4): "Bring me not into sin, or into iniquity, or into temptation. And may the good inclination have sway over me and let not the evil inclination have sway over me." The Greek noun (πειρασμός) and verb (πειράζω) occur rarely in extrabiblical Greek (LSJ, *s.v.;* Seesemann, *TDNT* 6:23) and have almost exclusively a nonreligious, nonmoral sense of "testing." In the LXX, however, both terms take on a religious and moral dimension when an individual or Israel's relationship to God is put to the test.

The two classic old Testament examples of such "testing" appear in Genesis 3 and Gen 22:1–19. In Genesis 3, man and woman, created in God's image to honor, obey, and fellowship with him, when confronted by the serpent with the alternative of being "like God," chose to reject that relationship for one of autonomy. They and subsequent humanity failed the test, so to speak, with tragic spiritual and moral consequences. In Gen 22:1–19, God, who had chosen Abraham, made a special covenant with him, and given him a son of that covenant, "tests" Abraham's faith and obedience by commanding him to offer his son in sacrifice. Abraham obediently followed God's demand and passed the test, so to speak, to become the model of obedient faith in Wisdom (e.g., Sir 44:20) and rabbinic literature (Str-B 4:108) and in Heb 11:17–19.

In these two examples, we find two different agents at work as well as two different intentions behind the "testings." On the one hand, although the precise language is lacking, the "testing" in Genesis 3 connotes *temptation,* the negative intent being to mislead, to cause one to do that which is wrong, to fail through disobedience in one's relationship to God. The agent is Satan (Gen 3; cf. Job). On the other hand, "testing" in Gen 22:1 connotes more positively a *proving,* a placing of one on trial to demonstrate one's faithful obedience in relationship to God. In such cases, God initiates the action (e.g., Gen 22:1–19; Exod 15:25; 16:4; Deut 8:2; 13:3; Ps 26:2). Yet, strictly speaking, the actual usage of the language πειρασμός and πειράζω is limited to the second meaning in the Old Testament. In the Wisdom literature of the intertestamental period a third connotation of "testing" emerges. "Testings" give occasion for instruction, for edification (Sir 2:1–6; 4:17; Wis 3:5; 11:9; 12:26), and thus take on a pedagogical dimension.

The New Testament use of πειράζω and πειρασμός continues with the same diversity as found in the Old Testament and Wisdom literature. Apart from the secular meaning of testing (e.g., Acts 9:26; 16:7; 20:19, cf. 2 Cor 13:5, and Rev 2:2), the majority of the references apply to the religious and moral sphere. First, James 1:2 and 1:12 approximate the pedagogical function of πειρασμός found in the Wisdom literature, whereas, second, 1 Pet 1:6; 4:12, cf. Rev 2:10, sets the "trials" within the context of suffering as a means of "proving" or "testing" one's faith in a manner not unlike that of Abraham. Yet in both the agent is one's own evil desires (James 1:14) or the sufferings brought on by one's enemies of the faith (1 Peter).

Third, in contrast to the Old Testament usage and the intertestamental literature, the language of πειρασμός/πειράζω occurs most frequently in the New Testament as the *temptation* to evil (4:1–11, par. Luke 4:1–13; 1 Cor 7:5; 10:6–13). Jesus' own ministry opens with a *temptation* scene (cf. Heb 4:15) in which he demonstrates his faithful obedience as the Son of God to the Father's will (cf. Adam and Eve in the Garden, Mark 1:12–13; cf. Israel, God's son in the wilderness, Matt 4:1–11, par. Luke 4:1–13). Paul warns about Satan's *temptation* in 1 Cor 7:5 and implies as much in 1 Cor 10:13, while several passages leave the agent unspecified (e.g., Matt 26:41, par. Mark 14:38; Luke 8:13; 1 Tim 6:9; 2 Pet 2:9). At no point does God act as the source of "testing" or "temptation" (cf. James 1:13) as in the Old Testament and Wisdom literature. Finally, a new, eschatological moment of *temptation* appears in Rev 3:10: "The hour of trial is coming on the whole world." This reference which points to the period of great tribulation at the end of history, has its roots in Dan 12:10, LXX, and results from the culmination of the power and the desires of the forces of evil.

In spite of the variety of usages of *temptation* in the New Testament, all share a common denominator, namely, each form of testing or *temptation* places one's relationship to God in question. Whether one's faith is tested by suffering or persecution or whether one is tempted or seduced to do evil, the ultimate danger is apostasy (e.g., Luke 8:13). Jesus explicitly warned his disciples in the Olivet Discourse against such apostasy arising from the events surrounding the last days (Mark 13:19-23, par. Matt 24:21-26). Consequently, many have taken this petition as referring to the eschatological temptation to apostasy accompanying the period of great tribulation (e.g., Jeremias, "Lord's Prayer," 104-7; Bonnard, *Matthieu*, 87; Hill, *Matthew*, 139), while others have taken *temptation* in its more general usage referring to the threat to one's faith, obedience, and commitment to God growing out of one's everyday experience (e.g., Schniewind, *Matthäus*, 88; Schweizer, *Matthew*, 156). In either case, the *temptation* connotes the situation that places one's relationship to God in question.

The verb *lead us not* (μὴ εἰσένεγκῃς) uses the aorist subjunctive rather than the imperative, perhaps influenced by the negative. The meaning of *lead us not* carries the idea of bringing one somewhere. The petition, therefore, asks that God *not bring us* into the situation of *temptation*. God's role is not that of tempter but protector, a motif with various expressions in Mark 14:38, par. Matt 26:41, par. Luke 22:46; 1 Cor 10:13; 2 Pet 2:9; Rev 3:10.

The question of the relationship of this petition to James' emphatic statement—"He (God) himself tempts no one"—has frequently arisen. Some have even seen James 1:13 to be a "correction" of this petition in the Lord's Prayer (e.g., Windisch, *Katholische Briefe*, 8). Yet this conflict between James and the Lord's Prayer is more apparent than real on two counts. First, the petition does not necessarily imply that God initiates the *temptation*, only that he can avoid bringing us into the arena of *temptation*. Second, James 1:12-14 deals with πειρασμός as a *temptation,* a seduction to sin, rather than πειρασμός as a "testing" of one's faith (Mussner, *Jakobusbrief,* 86–88). The latter understanding of πειρασμός underlies the petition of the Lord's Prayer as well as the references to God's "testing" Abraham (Gen 22:1) and Israel (Exod 15:25; Deut 8:2) in the Old Testament. The ultimate source of the *temptation* appears in the following request that rounds off the petition in an antithetical parallelism.

but deliver us from the Evil One. This final petition forming the positive antithesis to the previous request is missing in Luke 11:4. Consequently, Matthew's Prayer has an additional petition at the end of each of the two sections (6:10b, 13b, cf. Luke 11:2, 4). The verb *to deliver* (ῥύομαι) expresses a rather strong intervention to rescue or to preserve someone or something from danger. This idea of deliverance also occurs in the seventh petition of the Eighteen Benedictions, "deliver us for thy name's sake." The theme of deliverance is very common in the Old Testament, especially in the Psalms. Set in the aorist imperative the verb again connotes a finality in the action requested.

the Evil One (τοῦ πονηροῦ) stems from an ambiguous Greek construction that could be taken impersonally as *evil* or personally as the *Evil One. Deliver us from evil* has a long tradition that appears supported by 2 Tim 4:18 and *Did* 10:5, where God is seen or asked to deliver one or his Church from "every evil" (παντὸς . . . πονηροῦ). Yet this abstract reference to evil (e.g., Schniewind, *Matthäus,* 88–89; Schürmann, *Gebet,* 99–102; Hill, *Matthew,* 139) belongs more at home in the Old Testament and rabbinic usage than in the New Testament (Lohmeyer, *Our Father,* 213–14). *Evil* (πονηρός) appears predicatively in the New Testament to qualify actions or words (e.g., 5:11, par. Luke 6:22; Mark 7:22; Acts 28:21; 1 Thess 5:22) but not as *evil* per se. Furthermore, the *Evil One* referring to Satan has been redactionally added by Matthew in 5:37; 13:19, cf. Mark 4:15; 13:38, as well as evil one(s) in 5:39 (cf. 5:45; 1 John 2:13, 14; 3:12; 5:18, 19) and fits the eschatological context of the defeat of Satan (Lohmeyer, *Our Father,* 210–17; Manson, *Sayings,* 170; Jeremias, "Lord's Prayer," 104–07; Schweizer, *Matthew,* 156–57).

Although our English version of the Prayer ends with a doxology, such an ending has a very weak textual basis. The familiar doxology has its verbal parallels in 1 Chron 29:11 and may have been one of several used as a response by the early church (cf. *Did* 8:3) until it became fixed with the Lord's Prayer as an appropriate summary of the petitions for the Kingdom, power, and glory of the Father.

6:14. *For if you forgive others their transgressions, your Heavenly Father will forgive you.* This and the negatively formulated verse that follows complete the inserted unit of 6:7–15. Matt 6:14 has a material parallel in Mark 11:25, with 11:26 missing in the better manuscripts. Mark's parallel also has a prayer setting in the introduction, whereas Matt 6:14 picks up the fifth petition of the Lord's Prayer (6:12). Mark's instruction has the form of a command followed by a purpose clause, a *do et des* relationship. Matthew's form has the same motif as a sentence of holy law using the principle of *lex talionis* (Käsemann, "Sentences," 77).

The content of 6:14–15, though expressed as a sentence of holy law, differs little from the content of 5:23–24, the fifth petition of 6:12, and especially the conclusion (18:35) of the parable of the unforgiving servant given in response to Peter's question about the limit of one's forgiveness (18:21–35). As the parable indicates, one's forgiving does not form the prerequisite for experiencing God's forgiveness (18:24–27; cf. use of "Father" in 6:9, 12; 6:14, 15). Rather the genuine experience of God's accepting forgiveness of one's immense "debt" (18:24–27) is to condition one's ability to forgive others (cf. "from the heart" in 18:35). One cannot presume upon the Father's grace and mercy, as these passages warn, since failure to extend forgiveness to others ultimately places one's relationship to God in jeopardy (6:15; 18:34–35). One's relationship with others indicates the extent to which one has indeed experienced God's forgiveness, one's "capacity" rather than one's "deserts" (Moule, "Forgive," 71–72). Consequently, in these passages involving the reciprocal character of forgiveness, God holds each accountable not only with reference to himself but also with reference to one's relationship with others (6:14–15; 18:34–35; cf. 5:23–24; 6:12).

6:16. *Whenever you fast.* Matt 6:16–18 resumes and concludes the material dealing with true devotion (6:1–18) that had been interrupted by the insertion of 6:7–15. *Fasting,* an integral part of Jewish religious life with a long history, consisted of public and private observances. The former, set for the entire community, included among others the three major fasts of the Day of Atonement, New Year's, and a fast for previous national calamities (on the ninth of Ab after A.D. 70). The latter, in question in 6:16–18, were observed by the individual on a voluntary basis (Str-B 4:77; Moore, *Judaism* 2:55–69, 257–66). The Pharisees, for example, fasted twice a week, Mondays and Thursdays (Moore, *Judaism* 2:260; Luke 18:12; *Did* 8:1).

The practice of fasting expressed penitence and contrition, an act of personal humiliation before God. As Moore has put it, "Fasting belongs so inseparably with affliction that 'afflicting oneself' became synonymous with fasting" (*Judaism* 2:55). In addition to demonstrating repentance, fasting also functioned as a "potent auxiliary" of prayer in Judaism (Moore, *Judaism* 2:259). Perhaps the inclusion of fasting in the context of prayer in 6:4–6, 16–18 (cf. 7–15) reflects this common association, as does the textual variant of 17:21 and Mark 9:29 (cf. also Luke 2:37; Acts 13:3; 14:23–27).

do not look sad. Fasting generally involved wearing a sacklike garment made of coarse, hairy material; sprinkling ashes over one's head; and going unbathed without anointing either one's body or head (Str-B 4:103–5). Remorse (cf. *do not look sad*) congruent with contrition and penitence marked one's appearance and demeanor (cf. 1 Kgs 21:27; Neh 9:1; Isa 58:5). In fact, one's personal appearance approximated that of mourning (cf. Gen 37:34). Consequently, the person fasting looked sad to reflect his or her remorse.

disfigure their faces. This phrase defies a word-play in English comparable to that found in 6:16, 18. Literally, the *hypocrites* make their faces *unnoticeable* (ἀφάνουσιν) in order to be *noticeable* (φανῶσιν) to others. Their primary motivation (6:16) is the same as those giving to charity (6:2) or praying publicly (6:4), namely, to be recognized as devout by others as well as by God.

6:17. *But you, when you fast.* Again the change to the second person singular and the location of the pronoun outside the temporal clause signals the strong contrast intended. This verse assumes, as did 6:16, the practice of fasting by the disciples, a practice in no way as legalistically conceived as in *Did* 8:1. There the believers were to fast twice a week but, in contrast to the *hypocrites,* on Wednesdays and Fridays. In Mark 2:18–20 the question was raised about why Jesus' disciples, unlike the Pharisees and the Baptist's disciples, failed to fast. Jesus' response, comparing the time of the bridegroom with the accompanying festivities (2:19) to the time when the bridegroom has been removed from the scene (2:20), does not rule out the disciples' or Jesus' observing the public fasts. Rather, Mark's pericope distinguishes between the disciples' personal fasting during Jesus' earthly ministry and that following his passion and resurrection (Roloff, *Kerygma,* 229–34).

anoint your head and wash your face. These instructions reflect a significant break with the manner of fasting in Judaism. Rather than symbolizing remorse and sorrow, one was to "freshen up" by *anointing one's head* with oil and *washing one's face.* Since anointing one's head and washing one's face were standard practices of everyday personal hygiene (Str-B 1:426; Bonnard, *Matthieu,* 89; Hill, *Matthew,* 141), these instructions simply suggest that one appear as "normal" rather than as conspicuously happy or attired for a feast instead of a fast (e.g., Dibelius, *Botschaft,* 123, sees the action to be deliberately misleading; Schniewind, *Matthäus,* 78, and Behm, *TDNT* 4:932, take it as an expression of eschatological joy). In keeping with the entire section of 6:1–18, the positive command warns against being conspicuous in one's act of worship.

Yet behind this difference in form lies a basic theological difference in 6:16–18 just as in 6:2–4, 5–6. By focusing on one's outward appearance through eliminating the symbols of remorse and mourning, the fast becomes an expression of one's experience of God's forgiving acceptance in Jesus' ministry. Indeed, Jesus' table fellowship by which he offered God's accepting forgiveness to the sinner (e.g., 11:19, par. Luke 7:34; Mark 2:15–17; Luke 15:1–32) and the anticipation of the Messianic banquet stand in bold contrast to the Old Testament and Jewish practice of fasting as seen in Mark 2:18–20. Consequently, the meal rather than a fast became the earmark of the early church's public worship. The good news brings joy rather than remorse (e.g., Luke 15:7, 10, 23–24; Acts 2:46).

Comments

With Matt 6:1 the focus of the "greater righteousness" changes from a series of demands for conduct corresponding to the new relationships between one another (5:21–48) to a call for conduct before God in keeping with one's relationship with the Father in heaven. One's life of devotion or one's worship is to stem from the proffered relationship with the Father rather than from a desire to perform for God and others. Since the following section consists of a complex of materials, the comments will cover the "Doing of Righteousness" (6:1–6, 16–18), the Lord's Prayer (6:7–15), and then a general history of the tradition behind the complex.

A. On Doing Righteousness: 6:1–6, 16–18

Whereas Matt 5:21–48 dealt with horizontal relationships, 6:1–18 pertains to the vertical relationship with God. Three examples of religious piety follow having to do with one's standing before God: giving of alms, prayer, and fasting. Each held a significant place in Jewish religious life of the first century. One's performance of these deeds was a personal expression of worship or religious piety, an expression of one's relationship with God.

The evangelist appropriately opens this section with a redactional summary warning in 6:1 that corresponds to the summary warning of 5:20. Just as 5:20 warned of the necessity of a "greater righteousness" by comparison with the scribes and Pharisees, so 6:1 warns against "doing righteousness" for the wrong reason by comparison with the "hypocrites" (cf. combination in Matt 23). The use of the term "righteousness" and the negative comparison with the "hypocrites" serve to bind the material of 6:2–18 to the demand for "greater righteousness" in 5:20. But simultaneously the specific content of 6:1 is drawn from and thus introduces the traditional material of 6:2–18 that follows. Therefore, 6:1 bridges 5:21–48 and 6:2–18 and sets the two sections under the theme of 5:20.

In 6:1 the evangelist combines charitable acts, prayer, and fasting under the phrase "to do righteousness." Here as elsewhere in the Sermon "righteousness" appears in a relational context. Whereas one's "greater righteousness" pertained more specifically to one's relationship with others in 5:21–48, the religious devotion inherent in almsgiving, prayer, and fasting points to one's relationship with God (cf. "your Father" in 6:1, 4, 6, 18). The "doing" of righteousness concurs with the thrust of 5:20 as preface for the demands of 5:21–48 and connotes conduct in keeping with the will of God growing out of one's new relationship with God and others established through Jesus' ministry (see Note on 5:6). Therefore, "doing righteousness" in this context refers to one's conduct, one's religious devotion, indicative of one's restored relationship with God.

As a warning summary for 6:2–18, 6:1 sets out the negative aspect common to all three admonitions that follow: to perform one's acts of piety before others for show results in one's not receiving a reward from the Father in heaven. On the surface, the wording of this warning conflicts with the command to let one's "light shine before others" in 5:16. The difference lies in the following purpose clauses. In 5:16 the ultimate goal is that God might receive the glory; in 6:1 (cf. 6:2, 5, 16) the ultimate goal is to gain personal recognition for one's actions. Here one finds the irony of false piety. An action supposedly intended to express one's devotion, one's relationship, to the Father is performed to gain the attention of others. Consequently, the issue is not public worship ("before others") but worship for publicity ("to be seen by them"). The focus is not on God but on oneself.

Since one's pious acts do not reflect nor stem from one's positive relationship to God but from one's motivation to gain recognition from others, the Father does not "reward" them. He recognizes such acts for what they are, a performance for and applauded by others. The failure to receive a reward assumes that God rewards and punishes his own. This understanding of God's response commensurate with the conduct of his own underlies all three admonitions—positively and negatively (see Note on 6:1). The positive aspect for those heeding the warning remains inplicit to the prohibition in 6:1, though it is stated explicitly in the following admonitions.

1. Charitable Deeds ("Almsgiving"): 6:2–4

The first example of religious devotion involves one's charitable deeds (6:2–4). This admonition shares a common structure with the other two. Each opens with a negative illustration of the "hypocrites' " behavior and its consequence; each concludes with a positive call for the appropriate conduct and an accompanying promise. The indefinite "whenever you . . ." that begins the three admonitions assumes that one will give, pray, and fast. The issue is not *whether* but *how* one practices religious piety and worships.

Care for the needy constituted an important part of Jewish religious life in the first century, as it had since Old Testament times. Offerings were taken and distributed on a regular basis with special occasions also set to collect contributions. The term for "charitable deeds" has "mercy" or "kindness" as its root. It means, therefore, to contribute acts of mercy or kindness for those in need.

Two hyperboles contrast two ways of giving. On the one hand, the sounding of a trumpet suggests an ostentatious display with fanfare in public ("in the synagogues and on the streets," 6:2). The meaning is obvious. Such a one performs charitable deeds in order to receive the honor accompanying such activity. The motivation of personal recognition underlying the act betrays its true character. It is simply a performance. Thus, each admonition refers to those so acting as "hypocrites" or, more literally, "actors" (see Note on 6:2). On the other hand, giving without letting the left hand know what the right hand does—a biological impossibility—removes all possibility of a calculated performance. This hyperbole not only eliminates the performance factor but also self-congratulations by implication. Such action precludes deliberation and con-notes a singleness focusing exclusively on the charitable deed without regard for another's opinion. One's charitable deed comes as a response to another's need, an act of mercy, rather than as an attempt to meet one's own need for recognition.

The respective results are as different as the nature of the conduct. In the one instance, the applause won by the performance represents the total benefit earned. Assuming that the standard of acceptance set by God and others was the same, one could read the response of others to one's actions as indicative of God's response at the judgment. But the judgment, "they have been paid in full" (6:2), declares that payment has been made and receipted (see Note on 6:2). Once paid, no further payment will be forthcoming. Rather than receiving public acclaim as a mere down payment or token of the divine acclaim at the last judgment, the recognition gained represents the full extent of one's reward.

By contrast, a genuine act of religious devotion consists in responding to another's need as an act of mercy and kindness with no concern for the applause of others or even of oneself (6:4). The Father recognizes such conduct ("sees in secret") and responds ("will reward you"). In other words, God sees the action for what it is—an expression of devotion stemming from one's relationship to the Father rather than an attempt to gain or maintain such a relationship. The reward remains unspecified but comes as an unexpected bonus and not as a calculable wage (cf. 25:31–46).

In summary, then, this admonition cautions us about using charitable activity as a means of gaining ultimate status with God while assuring us that genuine acts of mercy and kindness towards those in need are seen and will be recognized by our Father in heaven. The issue is not the difference between public and private giving. The issue is the ultimate motivation for our giving. The apparently selfless act of giving to another can become equally as self-serving when done privately as well as publicly. True piety stems from a whole relationship with God and comes as a response to God and the need of others rather than a responsibility stemming from selfish fears.

2. Prayer: 6:5–6

The second example of religious devotion, prayer, also played a promi-nent part in Jewish life. Apart from the prayers integral to public worship in the temple and synagogue, there were numerous personal prayers.

At least two, the *Shema* and the Eighteen Benedictions, apparently had prescribed times daily when one was to pray them (see Note on 6:5).

The contrast between the "hypocrites' " prayer and the prayer directed to the Father is drawn by the extremes in setting. On the one hand, the hypocrites pray in public settings ("in the synagogues, and on street corners," 6:5) in order to be seen by others. Reference apparently is made to the synagogue services and the statutory occasions for prayer that may find one in public places. Again the emphasis falls on the desire to be seen by others behind such conduct. On the other hand, one is admonished to pray to the Father in seclusion behind closed doors in the pantrylike room without windows located in the center of the house (6:6). The difference in setting between the public street corner and the closed room could hardly be more extreme. Yet the intent of the admonition was not to downgrade public prayer (cf. Jesus in 11:25; Mark 6:41; Luke 11:1) nor to elevate private prayer but to highlight the proper motivation for prayer as seen by the results.

The respective consequences (6:5, 6) are the same as in the first admonition. Prayer aimed at getting the attention of others achieves precisely that end and no more: "They have been paid in full." Although prayer inherently expresses a desire to talk with God, the primary focus of the hypocrites turns to the one praying. One is only playing a religious role for a public audience. Yet prayer offered without an audience, "in secret," is directed exclusively to God. Prayer behind closed doors, "in secret," connotes the exclusive nature of genuine prayer. The recognition by others and the response of the Father convey the difference in starting points. God as Father expresses the relationship within which prayer becomes a personal communication from the individual to God.

The second admonition also cautions us about using the devotional act of prayer to gain status with God and others. While prayer implies the intimate expression of one's thoughts and feelings to God in worship, it can easily become a device by which one displays one's piety in order to get attention. By setting prayer in a secluded place, the admonition does not condemn or prohibit public prayer but rather places the emphasis on the intimate relationship between the individual and God, the Father. Prayer is to come as a response from within the relationship, not as a responsibility to create or maintain that relationship. The promise of an unspecified future "reward" (6:6) offers assurance that the Father indeed hears and responds in keeping with his part of the relationship.

3. Fasting: 6:16–18

The third example of religious devotion involves the practice of fasting, yet another integral part of Jewish religious life. At least three fasts were national and statutory—the Day of Atonement, New Year's, and the Ninth of Ab, a fast in recognition of national calamities. Others were personal and voluntary (see Note on 6:16). The Pharisees, for example, apparently fasted twice a week (Mondays and Thursdays) indicating the ritual character of the act.

The contrast is again drawn between two forms of practicing one's piety. This time the focus falls on one's appearance. On the one hand, the "hypocrites" perform by looking sad or dismal and rendering their faces unrecognizable or "unnoticeable" (see Note on 6:16) in order to be "noticed" by others. The wearing of a coarse garment, spreading ashes on one's head, and displaying a sad look represented mourning, the grief of contrition. This external appearance during a fast expressed one's remorse and penitence that underlay the meaning of true fasting. Such an expression of remorse and contrition, however, is lacking when one aims the appearance primarily for show. The "hypocrites" are simply giving another performance for their own benefit. The individual again stands front and center. On the other hand, the admonition assumes fasting but under very different conditions. One is to look "normal," to wash one's face and oil one's hair as usual (see Note on 6:17). Obviously such a person would not appear to be fasting to anyone but God (6:18). In other words, in true fasting as an expression of contrition the focus is on God alone.

The results, identical to those of the first two admonitions, again demonstrate that the issue is not public versus private acts of devotion. The difference between true and false piety lies in the motivation.

Whereas we can more easily identify with giving and praying as a religious performance, the absence of fasting as a part of one's religious life—especially among Protestant Christianity—makes this example a bit remote. One might even ask why fasting has fallen out of vogue. Has the need for an expression of contrition ceased in view of the work of Christ? Mark 2:19, the role of the table fellowship in Jesus' ministry, and the meal in the early church suggest that fasting has been replaced by feasting (see Note on 6:17).

To suggest that the Christian's role is exclusively the celebration of a festive meal is to ignore the tension of feasting and fasting in the Christian life. On the one hand, as children of the Kingdom, forgiven and accepted into fellowship with God through Christ (cf. Jesus' offer of table fellowship to sinners as well as the eschatological meal of the early church centered around the Lord's Supper), we can celebrate in fellowship around the table. On the other hand, we are still a part of this evil age, sinners and sinful, failing to appropriate God's acceptance. Fasting, therefore, or contrition, remains an important aspect of our religious experience. Such action neither creates nor insures the relationship offered us by the Father through Christ but rather issues from the need experienced within that relationship. Fasting itself may have lost its meaning as an expression of contrition for us today. But a genuine expression of contrition in whatever form is not only valid but is a necessary part of religious devotion.

To summarize the admonitions of 6:1–6, 16–18, the evangelist has focused on conduct befitting one's relationship to God as our Father. For this reason he can refer to the three acts of devotion as "righteousness" (6:1). It is assumed that the disciple will give alms (6:2, 3), pray (6:5, 6), and fast (6:16, 17). But the motivation for such conduct sets the disciples off from the "hypocrites" who, by their pious deeds, seek to attain or maintain a right relationship with God. By equating the recognition of others with the future recognition by God, the "hypocrites" betray their primary concern for themselves through their seeking of public acclaim (6:2, 5, 16). Their ultimate attention is on themselves rather than God.

The disciples, however, begin with their relationship of Father-sons and offer their gifts to the needy, their prayers, and their contrition to the Father from within and in keeping with that relationship. True worship, true piety, comes as a response to God not as a performance. This conduct demanded of our vertical relationship (6:2–18) stands as humanly impossible as the conduct demanded of our horizontal relationships (5:21–48). Such conduct befitting the "greater righteousness" can only come from the presence of the new age and the new relationships established between us and God through the person and work of Jesus Christ or, to use Matthew's phrase, the "gospel of the Kingdom."

This section and the Antitheses of 5:21–48 warn us about the inadequacy of our "best," in this case our false spirituality or false piety. Piety performed to effect status with God and others achieves that status with only the latter. Yet this section also describes true piety as conduct directed to God from within the relationship of God as our Father. Such conduct is not optional but indicative of our experience of that relationship with God effected for us by Jesus Christ.

B. The Lord's Prayer: 6:7–15

Within the series of admonitions on doing one's righteousness we find an additional unit on prayer comprised of an introductory admonition (6:7–9a), the Lord's Prayer (6:9b–13), and a concluding statement on forgiving (6:14–15). Naturally, this unit keys off and supplements the admonition on prayer (6:4–6). The importance of the Lord's Prayer here will become even more evident when we observe its serving as the structural outline for the selection and arrangement of the material that follows in the Sermon up to 7:12 (see Literary Analysis and Notes on 6:19–7:11). In Luke the Lord's Prayer occurs in a different setting (11:1–13). Thus it appears that Matthew, using his catchword method of combining two different traditions, has inserted the Prayer with introduction and conclusion into the Sermon (see Comment C).

1. Introduction: 6:7–8

The Lord's Prayer is introduced by the related prohibitions followed by explanatory clauses (6:7–8). As with the admonitions on giving, prayer, and fasting, the prohibitions are made by comparison. Yet instead of the "hypocrites" the "Gentiles" become the negative examples. Furthermore, whereas the "hypocrites" are culpable because of their seeking public acclaim, the "Gentiles" are culpable for their "much speaking" (6:7). The positive counterpart in the introduction comes in 6:9a when we are commanded to pray in the manner of the Lord's Prayer that follows.

The contrast implicit between the prayer of the disciples and that of the Gentiles has to do with one's attitudes in coming in prayer to God. On the surface, the charge of "much speaking" appears to indict the Gentiles for their long prayers, their verbosity. The succinct form of the Lord's Prayer enhances this first impression. Yet the comparison lies along different lines. The onomatopoetic word for "prattle" (see Note on 6:7) and the reason given for praying differently (6:8) stress the Gentiles' anxiety about being heard. With a long list of deities responsible for various areas of life, the Gentile used a variety of formulas and titles to insure an audience for their prayer. Thus, they came to prayer with grave concerns about being heard.

The disciple does not need to prattle or use extensive formulas in prayer, since the Father in heaven knows one's need before one has even made it known. For this reason one was not to pray as did the Gentiles (6:8). Yet there is never any hint on the same basis that prayer might be superfluous. In the immediate context, an admonition on the manner of prayer precedes (6:5–6) and an explicit admonition to prayer follows (6:9), not to mention the encouragement to pray with which this larger section of the Sermon concludes (7:7–11, par. Luke 11:9–13). The issue is not whether prayer is necessary, since the Father already knows our needs, but how we should therefore pray—confidently. Unlike the Gentiles, whose prayers are marked by uncertainty, the disciple can pray confident of God's awareness. Therefore, the introduction to the Lord's Prayer supplements the previous admonition on prayer to the Father (6:5–6) by admonishing one to pray confidently as a son to a knowing Father (6:7–8).

2. The Address: 6:9

The Lord's Prayer, following the opening command to "pray in this manner" (6:9a), was to serve as a model for our prayers rather than as an institutionalized statutory prayer for the disciple. The latter function, however, did set in early, as seen in *Did* 8:2–3 where one is instructed to pray the Lord's Prayer (parallel to Matt 6:7–13, cf. Luke 11:2–4) three times daily. The nonstatutory function of the Lord's Prayer is most evident in the variations within the two New Testament settings. These variations indicate that the church and/or the respective evangelists did not feel slavishly bound to repeat in rote fashion the wording of the traditional Prayer. Indeed, the difference in wording meets us at the very outset in the two addresses: "Our Father in heaven" (6:9b) and "Father" (Luke 11:2).

As has been frequently noted (see Note on 6:9), Luke's simple address of "Father" most likely reflects Jesus' own practice of addressing God as Father *(abba)* and his offering the use of such an intimate expression to his disciples (cf. Rom 8:15; Gal 4:6). In contrast to the rather common practice of referring to God with the pronominal qualifiers of my/our/ your Father, the direct use of the warm, unqualified designation *abba/* "Father" connotes a unique understanding of sonship. Indeed it is precisely this understanding of the relationship between God as Father and the disciples as sons that underlies the admonitions of Matt 6:1–18 in general and the introduction of 6:8 in particular. In other words, the address "Father" *(abba)* expresses the essential nature of the relationship offered by God to his own (sons) through Jesus Messiah. Appropriately, therefore, Jesus teaches his disciples when praying to address God in this manner (Luke 11:1–2, cf. Rom 8:15; Gal 4:6, a sign of the new age as seen by the eschatological role of the Spirit).

Matthew, however, opens with the more common Jewish designation, "Our Father in heaven" (6:9). In spite of the presence of this address in first-century Judaism and the lack of definitive evidence pointing to Matthean redaction (see Note on 6:9), the phrase has more than a formulaic function for Matthew. Its two components, the reference to God as Father and to his heavenly abode, play significant roles in the first Gospel. Matthew's other uses of the personal pronouns—your/my—with Father correlates with his understanding that Jesus is the Son and the disciples are "sons" of God (e.g., 5:9, 45; cf. 5:16, 48; 6:1, 4, 6 in the Sermon). This relationship as sons of God ("your Father") derives from Jesus' ministry as the Son of God ("my Father," see Note on 6:9) who comes to reveal and do the will of the Father, the doing of which is a sign of sonship (cf. 7:21; 10:32–33; 12:50; 18:35). Yet the careful distinction drawn between Jesus' reference to God as "my Father" (e.g., 7:21; 10:32–33) and his reference to God as "your Father" (e.g., 5:45; 6:8; 6:15) maintains the distinctiveness of the former. Because of the special relationship of Jesus with the Father as the Son, he can offer sonship to those who follow him. Therefore, the address "our Father" belongs only to that group of disciples, the sons of God, and not to humanity in general (cf. the "Gentiles" of 6:7 and the "hypocrites," 6:5). It is Jesus' relationship with the Father that offers the basis for the sons' corporate address of God as "our Father" (see Note on 6:9b).

The designation "in heaven" obviously sets God as one's heavenly Father off from one's earthly father. Yet such a limitation is redundant in a prayer address. Furthermore, "heaven" does not function as a designation for some remote residence but as the dynamic point of departure for God's activity in the world (see Note on 6:9). The interrelationship between God's activity in heaven and on earth becomes clearer in the following three petitions that conclude with "on earth as it is in heaven." Whereas "our Father" expresses the warmth of the Father-child relationship, "in heaven" connotes the childlike awe for the Father whose person and power are so immense. To that extent, "our Father in heaven" includes not only the warmth and intimacy of Luke's "Father" but also the recognition of the power and person of "our Father."

3. "You"-petitions: 6:9b–10

Three petitions follow that address God directly, the so-called "you"-petitions. Luke has only the first two, the content of which parallels the *Kaddish:* "Magnified and hallowed be his great name in the world which he created according to his will; and may he make his kingship sovereign in your lifetime and in your days." This prayer concluded the synagogue worship service.

The request, "Let your name be made holy," reminds one of the Old Testament promise that God would "vindicate the holiness" of his name (Ezek 36:23). His name, indicative of his character and person, has been defiled and profaned by his own people through false oaths, idol worship, and immorality (Lev 18:21; 19:12; Amos 2:7; Isa 48:11; Ezek 36:22). Yet he has promised to act anew in history to sanctify his name, to show himself set apart by his redemptive activity as God indeed (e.g., Isa 48:11; Ezek 20:9, 14, 22; 36:23; 39:27-28). He will again be known as the "Holy One" of Israel (cf. Isa 40:25; 43:11; 45:15; Ezek 39:7).

By addressing this petition to God in the passive voice, one asks God himself to act by ultimately revealing himself in history both through his redemptive activity and through his own people. Consequently, to utter this petition is not to speak carelessly or thoughtlessly. One makes this petition as an expression of one's offering of oneself for God's service (cf. 5:16 and 6:19-24) as well as an anticipation of God's final eschatological revelation of himself as the Holy One. In other words, since the holiness of God's name is bound up with the character and conduct of his own people in the Old Testament, implicit in the request for God's final eschatological revelation of himself lies the petitioner's desire and commitment as one of his own to live toward that end (cf. 6:19-24).

The second petition, "let your Kingdom come," appearing frequently in prayers of Judaism, specified how God would make his name holy. The desire for God's sovereign rule to be established in history burned within Israel along with the concomitant hope of Israel's deliverance and the punishment of her enemies. In Jesus' ministry the nationalistic overtones subside but God's ultimate sovereignty revealed in history remains his goal and message. The future dimension of the Kingdom's consummation underlies many of the Kingdom parables as well as the future Son of Man sayings. Consequently, this petition, too, looks forward to the final consummation when God's sovereign rule will be established over all, his name sanctified, his person and character vindicated, his true identity as God revealed and recognized.

One cannot, however, pray this request as a disciple without recognizing that God has already acted to establish his sovereign rule in history through Jesus' ministry (cf. "our Father" and the "we"-petitions that follow). Such awareness adds confidence in God's future activity while simultaneously expressing one's total yielding of oneself now to God's reign and service. Whereas Israel looked longingly in their prayers for the future consummation based on the hope of the promise, the Church looked expectantly in their prayers to the future because of the present reality of God's reign in their lives (cf. 6:19–24).

The third petition, "let your will be done on earth as in heaven," stands without parallel in Luke or other Jewish prayers. On the surface, this request appears to be synonymous with the second. God's sovereign rule involves the accomplishing of his will and purposes in history. The will of God functions in such a setting as another expression for God's redemptive historical purposes. Yet the phrase "the will of God/Father" is typically Matthean (see Note on 6:10), and his usages usually reflect a greater ethical overtone—"to do the will of the Father" (e.g., 7:21, cf. 12:50, par. Mk 3:35). But the accomplishment of God's will in history, the vindication of his holy name, and the establishment of his sovereign rule occur at least in part through the actual doing of his will by his people. Consequently, Matthew shows particular interest in the Kingdom and the doing of the will of the Father (cf. 6:10; 7:21; 21:31; 26:42). This petition that God's will be done again points to the consummation when God's purposes will be accomplished among his own "on earth," in history. In this way, God's name which once was profaned by his people (Amos 2:7; Ezek 36:22) will then be vindicated, his will accomplished by the obedience of his own (Ezek 36:25–27; Isa 29:22–24). Jesus' own prayer of surrender in 26:42 prefigures the ultimate accomplishment of God's will through one's obedience. Therefore, to pray "let your will be done" does point to the future when Satan and the forces of disobedience will be totally destroyed, the wicked and enemies judged, and God rules supreme "on earth as in heaven." But one can hardly pray for God's will to be done in the future without also committing oneself to the doing of his will in the present.

The three petitions are integrally related. In many ways they find their central expression in the second—"let your Kingdom come"—since by the establishment of his sovereignty in history God reveals himself as God, the Holy One of Israel, and his purposes and will are accomplished among and by his own on earth. The future orientation of the petition towards the final consummation captures one's expectant hope and prayer. But inherent to each request for the future is the commitment of the petitioner for the present. The focus on the future does not obscure the present as seen by the "we"-petitions that follow.

4. The "We"-petitions: 6:11–13

The next set of petitions has a totally different orientation. Whereas the first three pertained to God and the future accomplishment of his redemption, the next four express the petitioner's concerns for the present. This change in perspective is not so extreme as to make the two halves of the prayer unrelated. It is only when one's primary concern focuses on God and the accomplishment of his purposes that one can then confidently bring to him one's own present needs (cf. Matt 6:33). In this way, one's own needs are kept in their proper perspective.

The fourth petition forms the pivot for the two sections of the Prayer. By its difference in form (lost in the English translation, cf. "our daily bread give us this day") and its central location, one's need for "bread" stands at the heart of the Prayer. Contrary to the tendency that set in early in church history to spiritualize this request and to depreciate one's physical, material needs, Jesus' ministry demonstrated how seriously he took one's physical needs. Whether healing the sick, feeding the multitudes, or teaching of God's provision (cf. 6:25–34; 10:9–10), he regarded one's physical needs as important. Thus, the centrality of this petition within the Prayer and its initial position in a series of personal requests should not come as a surprise.

This petition has received much attention because of the rare and ambiguous term underlying "daily." With the options being "the bread for tomorrow," "the bread necessary for life," and "the bread for today (the day that is)," the first alternative most likely comes closest to a literal rendering (see Note on 6:11). But the ultimate meaning of each is the same. One prays "give us today the bread for tomorrow" as a request that God supply the basic necessities of life (6:25–34). Although some have seen a strictly future expectation behind this request (see Note on 6:11), the following petitions and Luke's rendering of the imperative in the present and the adverb "this day" by "each day" clearly point to the present needs. The eschatological element of the Prayer, however, remains since one's prayer is based on the new relationship expressed in the address "our Father" and in the introductory setting of the Father's providential concern for his own (6:8, cf. 6:25–34). When one prays for God's Kingdom to come, one also prays for the benefits of the presence of the Kingdom as well.

The fifth petition, like the third, is somewhat expanded. Drawing on the Aramaic use of "debts" in a moral as well as commercial setting, Matthew's term is more "literal" than Luke's "sins," although the earlier "debtor" remains in Luke's second half of the petition. The English "trespasses" adds a third alternative. But the meaning of all three clearly refers to one's failure before God. Just as Jesus came to minister to one's physical needs through healing the sick and feeding the hungry, he was above all known as a "friend of sinners." His table fellowship with and acceptance of the sinner express God's offer of forgiveness and a new relationship. This petition might also be taken as exclusively future—God's merciful forgiveness at the judgment—but the force of the second part, the expansion of this theme in 6:14–15, the following petitions, and Luke's use of the present tense all suggest the present situation. One comes to the Father seeking his forgiving acceptance for one's failures, an acceptance exhibited by Jesus in his ministry. This forgiveness was to be characteristic of the New Age (e.g., Ezek 36:25–32; Isa 55:6–7).

The second half, "as we also have forgiven our debtors," begins with an explanatory "for" in Luke and conveys the continuing act of forgiving others, while Matthew's clause implies complete action. Yet the content remains basically the same. Our request for forgiveness relates directly to our own actions toward those who wrong us. This correlation between one's own forgiving action and God's response appears in 5:23–24, in 6:14–15, par. Mark 11:25(26), that immediately follows the Lord's Prayer, in 7:1–5 which develops the theme of the petition and in the parable of the Unforgiving Servant (18:23–35). The parable declares what this petition and the other passages presuppose, namely, one's experience of divine forgiveness does not result directly from our forgiving others, but a broken relationship with others does endanger one's relationship with God. At issue is not the deserving of forgiveness but the capacity to experience forgiveness as indicated by one's behavior (see Note on 6:12). The experience of God's forgiving acceptance forces us to forgive and accept others. The transforming power of the Father's love and forgiveness integral to the age of salvation stands behind the love command (5:43–48), the foregoing of retaliation (5:38–42), and the Beatitude to the merciful (5:7). Thus it would be mockery to ask God for forgiveness while harboring something against another.

The sixth petition asks for protection, "Lead us not into temptation." One of the evening prayers (see Note on 6:13) makes the same request: "Bring me not into sin, or into iniquity or into temptation. And may the good inclination have sway over me and let not the evil inclination have sway over me." In the Old Testament God "tests" Abraham (Gen 22:1–19), Israel (Exod 15:35), and the righteous man (Ps 26:2). In Mark 1:12–13 and especially Matt 4:1, the Spirit brings Jesus into the sphere of testing. Jesus himself repeatedly warns his disciples about the adversity and beguiling deception awaiting them in ministry (e.g., Matt 10:17–25, cf. Mark 13:9–13, 5–8; John 16:1–2). The nature of the temptation is dire. It is the temptation or testing that places one's ultimate relationship to God in question, namely, apostasy (see Note on 7:6). Although God permits such testing, even sets the stage at times for such testing (e.g., Mark 1:12–13), God also stands as one's protector (cf. Mark 13:20; John 17:14–15; 1 Cor 10:13). As in the evening prayer, this petition asks God for protection from doing that which would destroy one's relationship with him.

One can hardly avoid the obvious tension between this petition and James 1:2–3, "Count it all joy . . . when you meet various trials," along with James 1:13, "God . . . himself tempts no one." Yet a closer look at James 1 indicates a twofold usage of "temptation" (see Note on 6:13). On the one hand, James 1:2–3 refers to the value gained from one's faith having been proved by adversity, an attitude to be taken by one in the midst of testing (cf. 1 Pet 1:6, 4:12; Rev 2:10); on the other hand, in James 1:13 "temptation" refers to the lure of that which is inherently evil. Whereas God permits both types of temptation, the negative result of which would be the same, namely, failure of one's loyalty and obedience, James denies that God could be the agent of the latter. To put it in the language of the evening prayer, the latter temptation results when the "evil inclination" has held "sway over me" (cf. James 1:14, ". . . enticed by [one's] own desire"). To pray "Lead us not into temptation" is not to imply necessarily that God is the agent of such temptation. Rather, it is but a way of petitioning for divine protection from ultimate failure and apostasy. The following, final petition supports this understanding by expressing a similar desire in a different way. Thus the difference between James and this petition is one of perspective.

The seventh petition, "deliver us from the Evil One," stands without parallel in Luke and quite probably in tandem with the sixth. From the negative request that God not lead us into temptation, we turn to the positive petition for deliverance from the Evil One. Although our liturgical tradition has used the more impersonal "evil" (cf. 1 Tim 4:18; *Did* 10:5), a usage quite compatible with the Old Testament and rabbinic usage, the adjective "evil" does not designate "evil" per se in the New Testament (see Note on 6:13). More likely—especially if added by Matthew (cf. 5:37; 13:19 cf. Mark 4:15; 13:38)—the adjective indicates the personal Evil One in the eschatological context of Jesus' coming to defeat Satan.

Therefore, combined with the previous petitions, the seventh petition requests protection against and deliverance from the power of the Evil One to snatch away one into apostasy. This petition, along with the other "we"-petitions requests the ultimate blessings for the day of salvation to become a part of one's *present* experience. The supplying of one's physical, material needs, the forgiveness of sins, and the deliverance from the power of Satan were earmarks of Jesus' ministry. Just as he effected these blessings of the new age on others, he instructed his disciples to pray for similar realities in their own lives. Such requests for the present correspond to the "you"-petitions for the future, since the former are but explanations of the second petition, "Let your Kingdom come," by which God's name would be hallowed and his will done on earth as in heaven. In short, the Lord's Prayer expresses the theological content of Jesus' ministry.

5. The Conclusion: 6:14–15

Neither Matthew nor Luke has any further conclusion to the Lord's Prayer. The familiar doxology of "for yours is the Kingdom, power, and the glory forever, amen" goes back into early tradition but is missing in the better manuscripts. As early as *Did* 8:3 this doxology drawing on 1 Chron 29:11 appeared in conjunction with the Prayer. Since it was the custom to conclude prayers with just such doxologies, the Prayer left open several possibilities, not least of which would be the appropriately worded conclusion familiar to us. For Matthew, however, a further point needed to be made. Or more accurately, a previous point on forgiveness needed to be underscored.

Drawing on Mark 11:25(26) the evangelist returns to the subject of our forgiving and being forgiven. The importance of this subject is evident from the instructions of 5:23–24 and the parable in 18:23–35 given in answer to Peter's question about the frequency of forgiving a brother (18:21–22). The location of 6:14–15 immediately following the Lord's Prayer and within the larger context of prayer (6:4–13) corresponds to its setting in Mark 11:24 pertaining to prayer and to the admonition in 5:23–24 involving one's offering. Prayer as the most intimate expression of one's relationship with the Father can take place only within the context of integrity. One can hardly expect to have a right relationship with God while living in alienation and estrangement from others. One would then be like the Unforgiving Servant of 18:23–35. Prayer involving the vertical relationship between Father and child also involved the horizontal relationship between brothers. Consequently, these verses, materially parallel with the fifth petition, remind one of the integral nature of these two relationships.

Although one might conclude on the surface that these verses imply one's earning God's forgiveness by the act of forgiving others, these verses must be read in the context of Jesus' teaching about God's mercy and forgiveness. One's love for the enemy, foregoing of retaliation, and forgiving of another's wrong stem from God's love, mercy, and forgiveness of us, as the parable of the Unforgiving Servant implies (18:35). Forgiveness of another is not a prerequisite for divine forgiveness, as 6:14–15 might imply. But as 6:12 and 18:35 indicate, forgiveness of another is a corollary of divine forgiveness and indicates our capacity to receive and to give forgiveness. The bluntness of the Matthean formulation in 6:14–15 does warn his community and us in terms of our ultimate relationship with the Father about the serious consequences of an unforgiving posture.

C. History of the Tradition

We are clearly dealing with a complex of materials in 6:1–18. But the demarcation of tradition and redaction has been anything but clear. Some have divided the materials along thematic lines (e.g., Bultmann, *Tradition,* 148, 150, 324–25; Schweizer, *Matthew,* 138–40). Beginning with a core of tradition on acts of piety shaped by the pre-Matthean community but whose roots extend to Jesus' ministry (6:2–6, 16–18), the evangelist added a redactional preface (6:1) and expanded the unit on prayer by including the Lord's Prayer (6:9–13, par. Luke 11:2–4) with a redactional introduction (6:7–8) and a conclusion on forgiving (6:14–15) drawn from Mark 11:25. Some more recent treatments of the passage have placed the combination of materials in a pre-Matthean setting (e.g., Wrege, *Überlieferungsgeschichte,* 94–98; Betz, "Kult-Didache," 451–52; Gerhardsson, "Opferdienst," 70–71). Still a closer look might indicate that the traditional core was extremely narrow, limited to the positive admonitions of the second person singular in 6:3–4, 6, 17–18 which the evangelist expanded into the present complex.

The redactional character of 6:1 grows out of the thematic and lexical evidence. Thematically, the negative warning of 6:1 introduces the following admonitions just as the redactional warning of 5:20 introduced 5:21–48. Furthermore, the term "righteousness" combines this material under the general heading of 5:20 as the negative comparison with the "hypocrites" (6:2, 5, 16) parallels that with the "scribes and Pharisees" (5:20), and the reward motif continues almost verbatim the same motif of the previous section on Love Your Enemies (5:45–47). Lexically, the evidence could hardly be stronger, since the constituent elements are distinctively Matthean: "Beware," "righteousness," "before," "to be seen" (see Note on 6:1), and "your Father in heaven" (see Note on 6:9). Therefore, 6:1 was constructed by the evangelist drawing on motifs from previous material (5:20, 45–47) in order to serve as the theme and transition for the admonitions that follow.

This conclusion becomes even more credible if the section on almsgiving, prayer, and fasting itself bears the marks of Matthean redaction. Indeed, the variation in number from second person singular to second person plural, the lack of parallel construction within the parallel units, along with distinctive Matthean terms and usages within each unit point to the real possibility that the evangelist shaped this complex as well by reworking traditional material.

The evangelist doubtless found in the tradition three positive admonitions dealing with giving, prayer, and fasting. Each of these consistently maintains the second person singular and consistently admonishes the practice of one's piety before God in an unusual, unobtrusive manner: give alms without your left hand knowing what your right hand is doing; pray behind closed doors in your pantry; and fast with your normal, everyday look. The accompanying promise clarifies these admonitions: "Your Father who sees in secret will reward you." We have no basis for denying that the roots of these admonitions (cf. John 4:23–24) extend back into Jesus' ministry. Their preservation in the early community— especially a Jewish-Christian setting within the context of Judaism— offered a contrast to and a warning against superficial piety.

Beginning with this traditional core, the evangelist then expanded the admonitions by building the corresponding counterpart to each in the form of a negative contrast (cf. Antitheses), the content of which is now found in the heading of 6:1. These contrasts consisted of an indefinite temporal clause (all identical in syntax), a negative comparison with the "hypocrites" (varied in syntax; cf. 6:2, 5, 16), a purpose clause (identical in syntax), and a statement of judgment (identical). The evidence for this conclusion stems from thematic, stylistic, and lexical indications.

Thematically, the contrast with the scribes and Pharisees was set explicitly in 5:20 and carried through the Antitheses implicitly. The use of "hypocrites" in the contrast of 6:2–6, 16–18 corresponds to the usage elsewhere in Matthew with reference to the scribes and Pharisees (see Note on 6:2) who seek to be seen by others (6:2, cf. 23:5). Thus, this section (6:2–6, 16–18) also sets out how one "does righteousness" (6:1) to "exceed" (cf. 5:20) that of the "hypocrites" (the scribes and Pharisees—

5:20). Stylistically, the mixing of second person singulars and plurals in the comparison (6:2, cf. 6:6, 16), the consistent use of the plural in the *amen*-saying (6:2, 5, 16), the inconsistent syntax within the comparisons (cf. 6:2, 5, 16), and the difference in purpose clauses between 6:2 and 6:5, 16 all point to Matthew's lack of concern for precision within parallels.

Lexically, each comparison contains Matthean distinctives. All three refer to the "hypocrites" (see Note on 6:2) followed by a final clause introduced by the characteristic ὅπως (see Note on 5:45). The first comparison also has the preposition "before men" (ἔμπροσθεν) and the comparative ὥσπερ (see Note on 6:2) and the content of the final clause—"to be glorified by men"—stands in contrast to the Matthean construction of 5:16—that others "might glorify your Father in heaven" (see Note on 5:16). The second comparison uses "they love" (φιλοῦσιν) similar to the redactional usage in 23:6, cf. Mark 12:38, par. Luke 11:46. It also uses the verb "to be seen" (φαίνω—13x cf. 1x in Mark, 2x in Luke) in the purpose clause as does the third, along with the antonym (ἀφανίζω—3x in Matt). The remaining vocabulary corresponds to the positive admonition, except for the *amen*-sayings. Yet the *amen*-sayings simply express in formula the implicit contrast of the promise in 6:4, 6, 18. The final outcome of the performing for others rather than worshiping the Father who will reward his own could not be stated more poignantly: "They have been paid in full."

Should this evidence suffice to support Matthean redaction, one might also note that these additional elements of contrast merely set forth explicitly what lies implicit to the particular admonition. The evangelist's role in this section, as has been noted before, is not one of creator as much as explicator, a role he has frequently played in his reworking of the tradition (e.g., the Beatitudes, 5:17–20, the Antitheses). As a section, therefore, 6:1–18 represents the evangelist's shaping of traditional material to continue his demonstration of who Jesus Messiah is by means of his teaching that called for conduct (5:21—6:18) befitting the presence of the new age (5:3–12). The new relationship with others and God as the Father and the corresponding conduct (5:21–48; 6:1–18) are set in contrast with that which is inadequate (5:20; 6:1–6, 16–18) in view of Jesus' coming (5:17–18).

Why, then, one might ask, would Matthew have given the material this structure and then added the disruptive unit on the Lord's Prayer (6:7–15) rather than place the section on prayer at the end from the outset? As has been seen, Matthew exhibits little hesitancy in breaking traditional patterns as well as his own—especially when using catch-words as a basis for combining related materials. The present configuration would only indicate that the evangelist built the entire complex of 6:1–18 around a group of three traditional admonitions as he found them with prayer in the middle.

This additional unit consisting of an introductory setting for the Lord's Prayer (6:7–8), the Lord's Prayer (6:9–13), and a sentence of holy law on forgiving (6:14–15) gives evidence of Matthew's redaction throughout. The evangelist's tendency to break traditional units, his use of catch-words ("to pray" and "to forgive"—6:7, 14) to combine related materials, the lexical evidence (see Notes on 6:7–8, 14–15), and his use of the Lord's Prayer as the structural outline for the materials of 6:19—7:11 (see Literary Analysis on 6:19—7:12 below) suggest that the evangelist composed and inserted this unit here (see Bultmann, *Tradition*, 324; McNeile, *Matthew*, 75–76; Dupont, *Béatitudes* 1:161; Grundmann, *Matthäus*, 197; cf. Wrege, *Überlieferungsgeschichte*, 106, n. 3; Betz, "Kult-Didache," 451–52).

Furthermore, each part of this unit reflects redactional traits of the evangelist. The introduction begins with a negative comparison (6:7) but breaks off the pattern with the explanatory clause whose content does not imply a performance. Rather than a statement of judgment, 6:8 begins with another negative comparison and explanatory clause, and the change from the "hypocrites" to the "Gentiles" balances the material on prayer in keeping with the reference to the Gentiles in 5:47 and especially with the materially related comparison in the Q material of 6:31–32, par. Luke 12:29–30. Furthermore, the vocabulary, to an extent conditioned by the context (see Note on 6:7), also has distinctive Matthean comparisons in "as" (ὥσπερ) and "to be like" (ὁμοιόω). Finally, the verb "to ask" in 6:8 correlates with the motif in 7:7–11 to introduce and conclude the material related to the Lord's Prayer (6:7–15, 19—7:11).

The differences in the rendering of the Lord's Prayer between Matthew and Luke most likely stem from the respective redactional variations. Whereas Luke's wording and tenses (e.g., 11:3–4, cf. Matt 6:11–12) reflect later adjustments, Matthew's additional petitions and expanded address contain characteristics of the evangelist. Since these differences relate integrally to the exegesis of the passages, see the Notes on the address (6:9), the third (6:10), and the seventh petitions (6:13) for further discussion.

Finally, this unit concludes with material on forgiving, with a content parallel in Mark 11:25. All of the ingredients of 6:14–15 lie at hand in

Mark: the context for both is prayer (cf. Mark 11:24), the subject involves both one's forgiving and God's corresponding forgiveness, and the object of forgiving is trespasses or sins. Only the form is different, with Mark using "whenever" and the imperative of community ordinances, while Matthew has a positive and negative sentence of holy law. The use of the catch-word "to forgive" as a point of contact (6:13, cf. 6:14–15), the use of the ἐάν-conditional sentences (12x in contrast to traditional parallels), and the less than balanced antithetical parallelism with "trespasses" as the object of the protasis in 6:14 and the apodosis in 6:15, par. Mark 11:25, all suggest Matthew's redaction. Thematically, the emphasis placed on one's forgiving and its bearing on one's relationship to God recurs later in Matthew 18 in the discourse on discipline with the distinctive parable on the Unforgiving Servant (18:23–34) and its pointed conclusion (18:35).

In summary, 6:1–18 consists of traditional material which has been expanded, shaped, and arranged by the evangelist in order to continue his theme of the "greater righteousness" as conduct indicative of the presence of the age of salvation, the Kingdom. At the same time, catchwords brought related materials to mind on prayer and forgiving, and the additional unit on prayer (6:7–15) takes on its own special role when viewed in terms of the following groups of materials in 6:19–24, 25–34; 7:1–5, 6, 7–11, as will be seen below. The Lord's Prayer offers the structural outline for what otherwise appears to have no obvious ordering principle.

VIII. THE LIFE OF PRAYER
Matthew 6:19—7:12

Translation

6 ¹⁹Do not store for yourselves treasures on earth where moth and worm consume and where thieves break in and steal it. ²⁰Rather store your treasure in heaven where neither the moth nor worm consumes it and where thieves do not break in and steal it. ²¹For where your treasure is, there your heart will be also.

²²The eye is the lamp of the body. If, therefore, your eye is sound, then your whole body will be in light. ²³But if your eye is unsound, then your whole body will be in darkness. Therefore, if the light in you is darkness, how great is that darkness.

²⁴No one can serve two masters. For either one will hate the one master and love the other or one will be devoted to the one master and treat the other with contempt. You cannot serve God and material possessions.

²⁵Therefore I say to you, "Do not be anxiously concerned about your life, what you shall eat or drink or about what you shall wear to clothe your body. Is not your life more than food and your body more than clothes? ²⁶Look at the birds of heaven. They neither sow, reap, nor store grain. Your heavenly Father feeds them. Are you not worth more than they?

²⁷Who of you by worrying can add one hour to your life span?

²⁸Why do you worry about clothing? Observe the lilies of the field, how they grow but neither labor nor spin." ²⁹But I tell you, "Not even Solomon in all his glory was clothed as one of these. ³⁰If God clothes the grass of the field, which is here today and cast into the oven tomorrow, how much more will he clothe you, you of little faith.

³¹Therefore, do not worry saying, 'What shall we eat?' or 'What shall we drink?' or 'What shall we wear?' ³²For the Gentiles seek to gain all these things. Your Father in heaven knows that you have need of all these things. ³³Rather above all else seek his sovereign rule and righteousness and all these things will be additionally provided for you. ³⁴Therefore do not worry about tomorrow. For tomorrow will worry about itself. Sufficient for the day is the day's troubles."

7 ¹Do not judge, lest you be judged. ²For by the judgment you judge, you will be judged, and by the measure you measure, it will be measured to you. ³Why do you see the speck in your brother's eye but not notice the beam in your own eye? ⁴Or how can you say to your brother, "Permit me to remove the speck from your eye," but the beam is in your eye. ⁵Hypocrite, first remove the beam from your eye and then you will see clearly to remove the speck from your brother's eye.

⁶Do not give what is holy to dogs and do not cast your pearls before swine, lest they trample them with their feet and turning tear you to pieces.

⁷Ask and it shall be given you; seek and you shall find; knock and it shall be opened to you. ⁸For everyone who asks receives, the seeking one finds, and to the one who knocks it will be opened. ⁹What person among you will give one's son a stone when he asks for bread? ¹⁰or a snake when he asks for fish? ¹¹Therefore, if you being evil know to give good gifts to your sons, by how much more will your Father in heaven give good things to those who ask.

¹²All the things that you would want others to do to you so do yourself to them. For this is the Law and the Prophets.

Literary Analysis

Matt 6:19—7:12 consists of six apparently disjointed units of tradition (6:19-24, 25-34; 7:1-5, 6, 7-11, 12). These units neither relate directly to the "doing of righteousness" of the heading of 6:1 nor do they exhibit any visible interrelationship with each other. The evangelist or his tradition appears to have randomly gathered diverse admonitions together in order to fill out the Sermon (cf. the various headings and groupings given this material by the commentators that share little or no agreement). Yet a closer examination reveals clues based on the sources and arrangement of the tradition that point to a more than random selection of the materials. Therefore, we shall return to the question of the section's underlying literary structure after completing the form and source analysis.

Form-critically, the material falls into six units on the basis of opening statements set in the form of an apodictic prohibition (6:25; 7:1, 6), an apodictic prohibition and command (6:19–20), and an apodictic command (7:7), with the section concluding with the Golden Rule in the form of a legal ordinance (7:12). Most of this material belongs in form and content to the genre of Wisdom instruction (Bultmann, *Tradition,* 74, 75, 77, 80). Consequently, these apodictic commands and prohibitions are illustrated or elaborated by proverbial sayings (6:21, 24, 34); parabolic sayings (6:22–23; 7:3–5); rhetorical questions *a minore ad maius,* i.e., from the lesser to the greater comparisons (6:25b–30; 7:9–11); further commands and prohibitions (6:31, 33, 34); and sentences of holy law (7:2). Despite the obvious affinity in form and the apparent affinity of content of this material with Wisdom motifs, one needs to include a more careful analysis of the content before dismissing an original *Sitz im Leben* in Jesus' ministry.

Source-critically, the vast majority of this material has parallels in Luke but outside of the Lucan Sermon. The unit on priorities (6:19–24) consists of three Q traditions (6:19–21, par. Luke 12:33–34; 6:22–23, par. Luke 11:34–35; 6:24, par. Luke 16:13) and the unit on anxiety returns again to the material found in Luke 12 (6:25–33, par. Luke 12:22–32). Matt 7:1–5 picks up again for the first time since 5:43–48 the Q Sermon material (7:1–5, par. Luke 6:37–42), and 7:7–11 makes use of tradition found in conjunction with the Lord's Prayer in Luke (11:9–13) as part of Luke's "prayer-didache." The section concludes with the Golden Rule, drawn from its earlier place in the Q Sermon (7:12, par. Luke 6:31). The only non-Q material in this extensive section is the difficult saying of 7:6, and perhaps the concluding saying of 6:34, each of which may stem from Matthew's source. Consequently, this section offers almost exclusively Q tradition with only a brief segment taken from the Q Sermon. What theme, if any, stands behind the selection of this apparently diverse material?

In spite of the apparent futility in seeking an ordering principle behind these admonitions, there is evidence that the selection was both deliberate and coordinated. First, apart from the Q Sermon tradition on Judging (7:1–5, par. Luke 6:36–42) and the Golden Rule (7:12, par. Luke 6:31), the majority of the material comes basically from two blocks of Q tradition (cf. Luke 12:22–34 and 11:9–13, 34–36). Second, this Q material has a different arrangement as well as setting in Matthew. Not only does the tradition from Luke 12:22–34 occur interwoven with that of Luke 11:9–13, 34–36 in Matthew, but the two are divided into two units each and inverted in order (6:19–21, par. Luke 12:33–34; 6:22–23, par. Luke 11:34–36; 6:25–34, par. Luke 12:22–32; 7:7–11, par. Luke 11:9–13). Third, the theme of the introductory setting of the Lord's Prayer (6:7–8) verbally parallels the material of 6:32, par. Luke 12:30; and fourth, the Q material on Answered Prayer (7:7–11, par. Luke 11:9–13) stands noticeably distant from the thematically and contextually related material on prayer of 6:7–13, cf. Luke 11:1–4 (cf. Luke's "prayer-didache," 11:1–13) or 6:25–34, par. Luke 12:22–32.

Bornkamm has offered a suggestion that not only takes these data into account but also explains the organizing principle behind the section of 6:19—7:12 ("Aufbau," 424–31). According to Bornkamm's thesis, the Lord's Prayer serves as the basic structure for these traditional units that follow. Matt 6:19–24, beginning with sayings on Treasures (6:19–21, par. Luke 12:33–34), followed by the two sayings on Singleness of Purpose (6:22–23, par. Luke 11:34–36; 6:24, par. Luke 16:13), underscores the first three petitions of the Prayer that focus on God's honor and sovereign will in one's life in terms of one's ultimate priorities, "Where your heart is. . . ." The opening contrast between "treasure on earth" and "treasure in heaven" may even be an allusion to the reference to "heaven and earth" in 6:10. Matt 6:25–34, par. Luke 12:22–32, with its focus on one's anxiety over material needs, would then offer a concrete elaboration of the fourth petition concerning "bread" (6:11). Since both 6:19–21 and 6:25–34 come from the Q unit in Luke 12:22–34, the initial point of contact with 6:7–15 may well have been the similarity of theme between the redactional introduction of 6:7 and 6:32, par. Luke 12:30. The inversion of 6:19–21, par. Luke 12:33–34, and 6:25–33, par. Luke 12:22–32, would then have resulted from the alignment of this Q tradition with the order of the petitions of the Sermon.

Matt 7:1–5, par. Luke 6:37–42, on Judging, begins to make sense in its present location, since it now provides the counterpart to the fifth petition concerning forgiveness (6:12). The difficult saying on 7:6 also takes on new significance, if, as Bornkamm has suggested ("Aufbau," 428–29), this graphic warning pertains to apostasy (see Note on 7:6). Apostasy lies behind the sixth and seventh petitions concerning preservation and deliverance from temptation in 6:13. In other words, each of the admonitions following the Lord's Prayer expresses by use of other traditional sayings, mostly from Q, a practical elaboration of the respective petitions. Matt 7:7–11, par. Luke 11:9–13, would also make sense in its present location in Matthew. Rather than hanging disjointedly between the unit on Apostasy (7:6) and the final summary of the Golden Rule (7:12), this promise of Answered Prayer concludes the larger section on prayer of 6:7–15, 19—7:6 with its focus on the Lord's Prayer just as it did in Luke's "prayer-didache" (11:9–13). By redactionally introducing the Lord's Prayer with the assurance of God's knowledge of one's need "before you ask him" (6:8, cf. 6:32) the evangelist is able to conclude the section with reference to "those who ask" (7:7–11).

Not only does Bornkamm's thesis give structural design to what has often appeared to be a random collection of admonitions, but it also offers clarification and support for Matthew's redactional shaping of the entire section beginning with the redactional heading of 6:1 and concluding with the admonitions in 7:11. Beginning with material on acts of piety, Matthew modified it (6:2–6, 16–18), introduced it in terms of his own theme of "righteousness" (6:1), and inserted the related material on the Lord's Prayer with an introductory setting drawn from Q (see Note on 6:7–8) by interrupting or breaking the pattern of this traditional unit (6:2–6, 16–18) rather than rearranging it in order to bring the two units on prayer together at the end (6:5–6, 7–15). Doubtless the evangelist could add the material where he did because of the close relationship between prayer and fasting, the unit to which he returned after inserting the Lord's Prayer (6:7–15) in 6:16–18. Furthermore, Matthew had also added a brief excursus on forgiveness (6:14–15) focusing on the fifth petition (6:12) but closely related in material to the following unit (6:16–18), since fasting was a sign of remorse and repentance for one's sins. Then, having completed the material on acts of devotion (6:1–6, 16–18), Matthew brought together the remaining materials of 6:19—7:11 in terms of the Lord's Prayer and its setting before summarizing the two major units on righteousness (5:21–48; 6:1—7:11) with the Golden Rule drawn from the Q context of Love Your Enemies (7:12, par. Luke 6:31).

Notes

6:19–21. This unit consists of a commandment formulated negatively (6:19a) and positively (6:20a) with a dual basis drawn from everyday experience (6:19bc, 20bc) and a concluding gnomic saying (6:21) in the classic Wisdom form of "where"/"there" (Schulz, *Spruchquelle*, 143; Zimmerli, "Struktur," 185). The Lucan parallel (12:33a) by contrast offers a different form and content. Rather than opening with a negative command, Luke's material has two positive commands: "Sell your possessions and give alms. Provide yourselves with possessions that do not age and are inexhaustible in heaven . . ." (12:33).

This variation in the two accounts has been variously traced to separate sayings (e.g., Burney, *Poetry*, 88, 115), differing forms of the same tradition (Manson, *Sayings*, 114, 172–73; cf. Marshall, *Luke*, 531, a variation of Q), or to redactional modification by Matthew (Kilpatrick, *Origins*, 75) or Luke (Pesch, "Mt 6.19–21," 358–60). Since Luke's parallel assumes the contrast underlying 6:19, and since his paranetic introduction is Lucan in theme and style, Matt 6:19–21 appears to offer the earlier form of the sayings. This conclusion gains support from the Lucan vocabulary and wealth motif in 12:33ab (Schulz, *Spruchquelle*, 142; Pesch, "Mt 6.19–21," 358–60).

Do not store treasures renders a cognate construction, *to treasure up treasures* (θησαυρίζετε θησαυρούς). The Greek term for *treasure* may refer to the place where something is stored (e.g., 13:52) as well as the object stored (e.g., 13:44). The nature of the *treasure* involved and its treasury emerges from the kind of dangers mentioned. *On earth* sets the negative contrast with *in heaven* (6:20) as the sphere of the perishable, of fallen creation.

where moth and worm consume. The first of two bases for the prohibition set in clauses beginning with *where* points to destructive natural forces. *Moth* (σής) appears as a symbol for destruction in Isa 51:8 and Sir 42:13. James 5:2 condemns the rich for having clothes eaten by moths rather than worn by the poor. Consequently, one part of the treasure consisted of fine garments. *Worm* can only offer an approximate translation, since the Greek noun βρῶσις means "eating" (1 Cor 8:4) or "food" (John 6:27). The occasional translation "rust" (ἰός) for βρῶσις stands without parallel in extant literature and probably stems from the use of rust (ἰός) in comparable contexts involving precious metals (Sir 29:10), especially in James 5:3 where it parallels σής. In the Ep Jer 11 rust (ἰός) and βρῶσις appear together but not as a hendiadys. Furthermore, βρῶσις consistently denotes "eating" or "food" in the LXX (Gen 1:29–30, 3:6; Lev 7:14 [24]) with the exception of Mal 3:11, where it translates a Hebrew term for insect. Therefore, βρῶσις may well connote the consumption of one's treasure by an insect perhaps in the larva stage, or *worm.* As such, βρῶσις implies that the *treasure* consisted of precious cloths or stored foodstuffs. Either or both are compatible with the material on Anxiety that follows in 6:25–34 but precedes in Luke 12:22–32. *To destroy* (ἀφανίζω) renders a strong verb meaning "to cause to disappear" or "to wipe out," in colloquial English.

where thieves dig through and steal. The second basis for the prohibition points to the destructive force of evil persons, *thieves.* *Dig through* (διορύσσουσιν) expresses the method of "breaking in" by digging one's way through the earthen wall of the treasury (cf. 24:43). Simultaneously, this method of "breaking and entering" reflects the mud-brick construction of the Palestinian house. Together these two bases warn of the vanishing, transitory character of earthly treasure because of natural and human forces. Both grounds for the prohibition stem from the practical experience of everyday life.

6:20. *Rather store for yourselves treasures in heaven.* The positive antithesis maintains the verbal parallelism with 6:19. Luke 12:32b picks up the theme of heavenly treasure, which is labeled as "inexhaustible," as well as the same two bases. The theme of *treasures in heaven* has several parallels in Judaism (Str-B 1:429–31). *Pss Sol* 9:5 declares that the one "doing righteousness" (cf. 6:1) treasures up life for oneself with the Lord (cf. Tob 4:9; Sir 29:10–13; 4 Ezra 7:77; 8:33, 2 *Bar* 14:12; 24:1). Luke seems related to the latter by his introductory command to "sell one's possessions and give alms" (12:33a, cf. Tob 4:7–11). Despite thematic parallels in the ancient world, the specific contrast between earthly and heavenly without a reference to God's reward, the renouncing of security through possessions, and the combination of *treasure* and *heart* all set this material off as unique against a Jewish and Hellenistic background (Pesch, "Mt 6.18–24," 366).

Matthew does not specify the nature of the *heavenly treasure* or how one goes about *storing* it in *heaven.* The tradition focused on the contrast between *earthly* and *heavenly treasure* found in the explanatory whereclauses. In the one instance, one's *treasure* proved to be worthless because it was perishable; in the other instance one's *treasure* proved to be secure from any natural or evil destruction. *Heaven* stands as the sphere beyond the reach of evil or corruption, the sphere of God's rule where his will is done (cf. Note on 6:10).

6:21. *For where your treasure is, there your heart will be also.* This two-line saying using a *where/there* structure concluded this unit. It differs from the previous two strophes in structure (antithetical three-line strophes) and syntax (from second person plural to singular). Luke 12:34 maintains the plural in an otherwise verbatim parallel. This change in number and theme have led some to conclude that 6:21 once stood as an independent, gnomic saying (Bultmann, *Tradition*, 84; Schweizer, *Matthew*, 162). This conclusion gains further support from the apparent allusion of James 5:2–3 to only the first half of the unit with no reference to 6:21. In any event, the parallel in Luke 12:34 shows that this saying belonged together with the material contrasting *heavenly* and *earthly treasures* (6:19–20, par. Luke 12:33) in the pre-Matthean Q tradition.

The presence of this saying without parallel in Hellenistic or Jewish literature (Pesch, "Mt 6.19–21," 366) greatly qualifies the thrust of the unit in Matthew and Luke. The paranetic application of James 5:2–5 and Luke 12:33ab closely parallels materials in Judaism (e.g., Tob 4:9; *Pss Sol* 9:5). But the presence of 6:21, par. Luke 12:34, lays claim to one's allegiance, one's person, not to one's "possessions," be they earthly or heavenly. The focus turns to the *person* rather than to the *treasure*. In other words, the *treasure* represents the ultimate expression of one's *person*.

Heart expresses the familiar biblical understanding of one's total person. The *heart* represents the "control center" and stands for the ultimate direction of one's innermost desires (Schniewind, *Matthäus*, 91). Consequently, rounded off in this manner, 6:19–21 does not offer a call to better or more lasting *treasures* but rather to one's total allegiance. To have one's *treasure in heaven* means to submit oneself totally to that which is *in heaven—God's sovereign rule*. It is this motif that follows in 6:22–23, 24, 33, not to mention the parallels in 5:8, 7:21, and 12:34.

Therefore, 6:21 offers not a second basis for storing up *heavenly treasure* but the controlling motif for the entire unit. As a result, 6:21 belongs integrally with 6:19–20 stemming from Jesus' ministry (Pesch, "Mt 6.19–21," 68–69; Riesenfeld, "Schätzesammeln," 48). Even Luke's specific application to sell one's possessions and give alms stands in the shadow of 12:34. The demand for total commitment, absolute allegiance, in contrast to a better keeping of the Law or practice of religious deeds, set Jesus apart from his day. Matt 6:21 stands as an essential, interpretive corollary to 6:19–20 in Jesus' teaching. As such, it offers the new wine in the old wineskins of 6:19–20. Such a demand for action as well as attitude from one's person confronts one with the same impossibility of the Antitheses of 5:21–48. To orient one's life (6:21) towards *heaven* (6:20), the practical consequences of which are found in Luke 12:32

and James 5:2–5, comes as a gift from God, an expression of the first three petitions of the Lord's Prayer (6:9–10).

6:22. *The eye is the lamp of the body.* This statement directing the attention from the *heart* to the *eye* introduces the second unit (6:22–23) of this three-unit section (6:19–24). Offering one of the more difficult passages to interpret, the unit occurs in Luke 11:34–36 in a different context, with a different audience and ending. Although some have attributed these differences to independent traditions (e.g., Wrege, *Überlieferungsgeschichte*, 115), most commentators have assigned the saying to Q and the variations to the evangelists (see below). The original setting is lost behind the secondary settings of 6:22–23 addressed to the disciples and of Luke 11:34–36 addressed to Jesus' opponents. Structurally, 6:22–23 consists of thesis sentence (6:22a) followed by a balanced antithetical parallelism as a commentary (6:22b, 23a) with an application statement for the conclusion (6:23b). Luke 11:34–36 parallels the thesis sentence and the antithetical parallelism—though formulated differently—but concludes with a warning (11:35) and an additional statement forming a truism (11:36) without parallel in Matthew.

In what sense is the *eye the lamp of the body?* Does it reveal what is within the person or *body* (subjective genitive) so that by looking at the *eye* one sees "inside" the person? Does the eye illumine, give light, to the *body* (objective genitive)? The metaphor of lamp (λύχνος) and the comments that follow suggest that the eye functions in the latter sense as the source of light for the body. How the *eye* could be so understood physiologically or conceptually remains unstated and irrelevant to the metaphor (see Betz, "Matthew VI.22f," 46–50). The metaphor simply states that the *eye* gives the light to the body and sets the stage for the comparisons that follow in 6:22b, 23a and the theme of light in the conclusion of 6:23b.

If, therefore, your eye is sound. The following antithetical parallelism in Matthew consists of two ἐάν-conditional sentences (66x; cf. 35x in Mark and 29x in Luke) in contrast to Luke's indefinite temporal (ὅταν/ἐπάν) sentences. The *eye* as the source of light for the *body* remains the subject in both sentences. But the modifier, sound (ἁπλοῦς), comes somewhat as a surprise. Whereas the reference in 6:22–23 appears to be to the *eye* and *body* in a physical sense, ἁπλοῦς does not occur in Greek literature with the expected meaning of "healthy" (Sjoberg, "Licht," 90–91, and Amstutz, ΑΠΛΟΤΗΣ, especially 96–102). The connotation is much more ethical with the meaning of "upright," "sincere," "guileless," and even "generous" as found in the LXX (e.g., Prov 11:25) and the New Testament (James 1:5; cf. noun in 2 Cor 8:2; 9:11; Rom 12:8). Furthermore, the stress on "generosity" appears to gain support from the antithesis of an "evil eye" (πονηρός, 6:23) that connotes "stinginess," "jealousy," or "greed" in the Old Testament and Judaism and from the immediate context of storing up treasures in 6:19–21. Thus the focus of the saying changes from the physical to the ethical sphere. Where this statement has been viewed as setting the tone for the unit's call for generosity and a warning against jealousy and greed (e.g., Allen, *Matthew,* 62; Jeremias, *Parables,* 162; cf. Betz, "Matthew VI.22f," 55–56).

Two considerations rule against this understanding of the key word *sound.* First, the parallel case in Jewish literature is *good* (ἀγαθός)/*bad* (πονηρός) eye rather than *sound eye* (cf. Prov 11:25, Sjoberg, "Licht," 91; Str-B 1:431–32). Thus the underlying Hebrew or Aramaic term most likely was a form of *šlm* or *tm* (Sjoberg, "Licht," 92) rather than *tb.* Second, the context of Luke 12:33, "sell your possessions and give alms," might suggest generosity, but not the Matthean stress on treasures found in 6:19–21. This unit's emphasis corresponds, as will be seen, to that of 6:19–21 and **6:24** rather than functioning epexegetically to 6:19–21 as the expression of how one stores up heavenly treasure, namely, through generosity.

How then does *sound* (ἁπλοῦς) function? If the Greek term of Matthew and Luke renders an underlying Hebrew or Aramaic *šlm/tm* then the literal meanings would correspond. When used with reference to animals offered for sacrifice, these adjectives expressed wholeness, completeness, perfection—without defect or blemish. Understood in this way, *sound* qualifies the eye as being whole, complete, perfect, or without defect. In this derivative way, it describes the physical condition of the eye as being whole or *sound.* The focus would still be on the eye's physical condition and its implication for the body.

your whole body will be in light. The contrast is not only between the *sound* and *unsound eye* but, more important, between the effects on the *body.* Although your whole *body* can refer figuratively to one's total person, the reference here is more literal. *Sound eyes* mean that one has *light,* that is, one walks in light rather than in the darkness of *unsound eyes.* The eyes as a source of *light* (cf. *lamp* in 6:22a) illuminate the way for the *body.* Therefore, *sound/unsound eyes* corresponds to the consequent *light/darkness* of the *body* (Sjoberg, "Licht," 93–94).

6:23. *your eye is unsound.* As noted above, the modifier of the *eye* in
this antithesis does not exactly meet expectations, since the Jewish antithesis would be *good/evil eye.* The phrase *evil eye* (βόσκανος πονηρός/r⁽ʰ
⁽yn) does appear in the Old Testament and Judaism as a symbol for
jealousy, greed, and selfishness (e.g., Deut 15:9; 28:54–56; Prov 23:6;
28:22; Sir 14:10; 31:13; cf. Tob 4:7; ᵓAbot 2:9; 5:13; see Str-B 1:833–
35). This usage along with the ethical connotation of *sound* (ἁπλοῦς) as
generous has led several to interpret the *eye* figuratively as a spiritual
rather than physical organ (e.g., Allen, *Matthew,* 62; Schmid, *Matthäus,*
138) with the focal point of the contrast being the modifiers rather than
the *eye/body* relationship.

In addition to the contextual and lexical arguments to the contrary
(see 6:22), the phrase *evil eye*—though used symbolically in Judaism—
can also denote literally the physical condition of the eye as being sick
or unfit. Furthermore, if *sound* (ἁπλοῦς) renders the Hebrew/Aramaic
tm or *šlm* rather than *tb,* *unsound* (πονηρός) may render the Aramaic
bsh rather than r⁽ʰ = *evil* (Sjoberg, "Licht," 97). As such, 6:22a, b,
23a would focus literally on the physical condition of the eye and its
relationship to the body as the backdrop for the application in 6:23b.

your whole body will be in darkness. The application that follows
(6:23b) and the introductory statement (6:22a) as well indicate that the
contrast between living in *light/darkness* rather than the *sound/unsound*
eye as such predominates. The *eye* comes into play only as the source
of *light* for the *body.* If the eye is *unsound,* the *body* stumbles in the
darkness. Therefore, 6:22, 23a sets forth the relationship of the *eye* as
a source of *light* to the *body.* The *light* will vary depending on the condition of one's eyes.

if the light in you is darkness. This conditional clause begins the
application moving apparently *a minore ad maius* from the eyes as light
for the body to the inner light and inner darkness. The key, of course,
lies in the meaning of *the light* (φῶς) *in you.* One suggestion links *the
light* with the soul along the lines of Prov 20:27 (e.g., Str-B 1:432; Klostermann, *Matthäusevangelium,* 61). Another takes the reference more literally as an "inner light" that shines through a person (e.g., Jeremias,
Parables, 163, cf. *Gos Thom* 24). In the former, the point of comparison
would be between the *eye* as the *light* of the *body* and the soul as the
light of the person. In the latter, the comparison would be between
the *lamp* of the *body* and the inner *light,* a more obvious contrast. But
what is the "inner light"?

Perhaps, as Sjoberg has suggested ("Licht," 103–4), the clue lies in the broader context of *light* and *darkness,* not unlike that found in Qumran, where the "sons of light" stand over against the "sons of darkness." The kingdom of light is the realm of the spirit and truth; the kingdom of darkness is the realm of Satan and evil. Although the relationship may not be direct, such a background in Judaism may pertain at least indirectly to the light references of 5:14, 16; Luke 16:8; the references of John; the Pauline references in 2 Cor 6:14–15; 1 Thess 5:5; Rom 13:12; and 1 Pet 2:9. As such *the light in you* does not refer to a specific organ like the soul, conscience, or reason, but to the *light* concomitant with one's participation in the realm of light resulting from Jesus' coming, the *light* that overcomes the sphere of *darkness* (cf. 5:14, 16 and 4:16). This *light* has become a part of one's own person, *the light "in you."*

how great is that darkness. This apodosis concludes the Matthean application (cf. Luke 11:35, 36). By moving from the lesser implications of a *sound/unsound eye* for the *body* to the implications of the failure of the *light within you,* the dire consequences can be expressed by maintaining the metaphor—*how great is that darkness.* The *darkness* experienced by the *body* is nothing compared to that experienced by one in whom the light *within* is *darkness.*

The thrust of this unit is captured by Luke's concluding imperative: "Be careful lest the light in you be darkness" (11:35). In other words, the unit warns and exhorts one regarding the *light* as did the previous unit (6:19–20) regarding one's *treasure.* If indeed the *light within you* refers to the participation in the light of the Kingdom (5:14, 16, cf. 4:14–16), Jesus' ministry, then this unit calls one to a *sound,* (cf. ἁπλοῦς) involvement in that *light,* a call for the total commitment of one's person in discipleship. If the *eye, the lamp of the body,* is *sound* (ἁπλοῦς), then the *body* has *light.* If the *light within,* the participation in the realm of light, is *sound,* (ἁπλοῦς), then how great is the *light* for one's own person (cf. Luke 11:36, "If your whole body is full of light, having no part dark, it will be wholly bright . . ."). Therefore, the *sound "eye"* calls for one's total commitment no less than the claim, "Where your treasure is there your *'heart'* will be also" (6:21).

6:24. The impossibility of serving two masters completes this three-unit section (6:19–21, 22–23, 24), the common denominator of which remains the call for total allegiance. Luke 16:13 offers an almost verbatim Q parallel that serves as a partial application of the Wise Servant Parable (16:1–9). The initial application (16:10–12) regarding faithfulness and loyalty also made reference to *mammon* (16:11), which most likely provided the catch-word basis for the inclusion of the saying (16:13) into that context. The saying, also found in an expanded version in *Gos Thom* 47, most likely circulated originally as an isolated Q saying. Whereas the contextual relationship is verbal *(mammon)* in Luke 16:10–13, it is thematic in Matt 6:24 since one's *heart* (6:21), *eye* (6:22–23), and now *master* (6:24) all point in the same direction of the central, controlling focus of one's person. The evangelist, therefore, has apparently drawn together three units from the Q tradition (6:19–21, par. Luke 12:33–34; 6:22–23, par. Luke 11:34–36; 6:24, par. Luke 16:13) in order to set forth the personal implications of the opening petitions for God's sovereign rule in the Lord's Prayer (6:9b, 10).

The form of the saying consists of a gnomic statement (6:24a) followed by an explanation set in antithetical parallelism (6:24b) and an application (6:24c). Many have followed Bultmann's ascription of the proverbial statement (6:24a) to Jesus with the following elements as paranetic expansions (*Tradition*, 87; Schulz, *Spruchquelle*, 460). But little evidence exists supporting the "secondary" character of 6:24b, c. To the contrary, the content of the "expansions," especially the untypically Jewish reference to *mammon* (6:24c) stands not only compatible with 6:24a but with Jesus' ministry and demand in general (e.g., 6:11, cf. 6:25–34).

No one can serve two masters. Luke 16:13 opens with "no servant" (οὐδεὶς οἰκέτης) in keeping with the overall context of 16:1–13. To say that dual service is *impossible* (οὐ δύνασθε) is to speak practically in concrete fashion and not theoretically. The legal possibility even at times became a reality (e.g., Acts 16:16, 19; Jeremias, *Parables*, 194, n. 1) without mentioning the rather common experience today of holding two jobs. But the force of the saying lies in the verb *to serve* (δουλεύω) that implies total allegiance as seen in the explanation that follows (6:24b). One cannot offer total commitment to two different *masters*, since one will inevitably take precedence over the other.

for either one will hate the one and love the other. The first member of the symmetrical parallelism offers the familiar contrast between *love* (ἀγαπάω) and *hate* (μισέω). The contemporary connotation of emotions and feelings behind these verbs necessitates that we continually point to their comparative force (McNeile, *Matthew*, 85; Hill, *Matthew*, 143) in terms of one's actions and behavior (e.g., 5:43; Deut 21:15). One's actions will inevitably betray preference of one and indifference towards the other, a decision in favor of the one comes at the expense of the other. *To love* in this sense does not come as a supplement or additive to the verb *to serve.* In the Old Testament sense, *to love* is *to serve* (Bonnard, *Matthieu,* 93).

or one will attach oneself to the one and despise the other. This second member of the parallelism is somewhat awkward because *attach* does not correspond to *love* as smoothly as *despise* does to *hate.* To *attach oneself* (ἀνϑέξεται) occurs in 1 Thess 5:14 and Titus 1:9 with the meaning of "supporting" the weak in the former and "holding firmly" the sound doctrine in the latter (cf. Jer 8:2; Isa 57:13, LXX). To become *attached* also may have the more personal tone of *to be devoted to* someone (cf. Bauer, *s.v.*). McNeile has suggested an underlying Semitic play on words with *sbr* in the first and *bsr* in the second half of this phrase. In any event, the context suggests that one can ultimately maintain loyalty to only one *master.*

you cannot serve God and material possessions. This concluding clause makes the specific application, an application that fits the context of *mammon* in Luke 16:10–13. If one cannot serve two masters in general (6:24a, b), then one certainly cannot serve God and *mammon* in specific. The stress on total allegiance in 6:24 corresponding to the same theme in 6:19–21, 22–23 does not change from "One cannot serve two masters" to "You cannot serve God and mammon." The latter explicates the former, not the converse. *Mammon* from the Semitic root *m'mwn* (μαμωνᾶς) occurs in rabbinic literature with the amoral meaning of "property" or "material possessions." "Money" or "wealth" renders the term too narrowly. The term connotes in a positive manner one's posessions in general (Str-B 1:434–35). In antithetical parallelism with God, *mammon* is personified without the literary device suggesting any reference to the unfounded medieval view of a demon or deity with the the the name *Mammon* (Klostermann, *Matthäusevangelium,* 61; Schlatter, *Matthäus,* 225). Drawing a term for one's possessions in general from the everyday situation of life, this saying warns against seeking support or *attaching* oneself to *possessions* by *serving* them rather than God. At stake is not the question of having *possessions* per se. The question ultimately becomes one of loyalty. Are *material possessions* "to be served or to serve?" (Schweizer, *Matthew,* 164). This unit, completing the section pertaining to God's sovereign rule in one's life and correlating with the first three petitions of the Lord's Prayer (6:9b–10), also sets a smooth transition for the ensuing section dealing with anxiety about one's material needs (6:25–34, cf. 6:11).

6:25–34. This section drawn from the Q tradition (Luke 12:22–32, cf. 12:33–34 in Matt 6:19–21) by the evangelist moves to the theme of anxiety about one's material needs and offers the correlative to the fourth petition of the Lord's Prayer (6:11). It belongs to the category of Wisdom sayings (Bultmann, *Tradition,* 80–81; Schulz, *Spruchquelle,* 152) with a typical Wisdom format (Zimmerli, "Struktur," 181–88) of prohibition (6:25), support based on experience (6:26–32) and summary admonition (6:33). Although some have considered this section to be a composite of traditional units and secondary expansions (e.g., Bultmann, *Tradition,* 88; Klostermann, *Matthäusevangelium,* 62), the evidence supporting this conclusion (apart from 6:27) is meager at best. The Wisdom structure and the unity of theme and tone argue for the basic integrity of the section (Grundmann, *Matthäus,* 214; Schulz, *Spruchquelle,* 154). The style and content correspond to Jesus' own ministry.

6:25. *Therefore, I say to you.* The immediate context of 6:24 makes the *therefore* a logical transition to material dealing with one's physical needs. Yet the διὰ τοῦτο occurs in the tradition whose context is quite different in Luke 12:22 and may have been integral to the authoritative phrase, *I say to you.* Schulz (*Spruchquelle,* 153; cf. 57–61) attributes this phrase to the early Christian prophets who drew on similar formulas from the Old Testament prophetic tradition. Thus he ascribes this warning discourse to early Christian prophets (*Spruchquelle,* 153). But one does not need to deny either the prophetic or Wisdom character of this material in order to root it stylistically and materially in Jesus' ministry. The "But I say to you" of the Antitheses sufficiently indicates the prophetic authority inherent in Jesus' teaching (cf. 7:29).

do not be anxiously concerned. This apodictic prohibition opens the section. The verb (μεριμνάω) offers the same range of meanings as the English word *concern* (Bauer, *s.v.*). Generally expressing an attitude of mind (to *take anxious thought,* Bauer, *s.v.*; Bultmann, *TDNT* 4:589–93) μεριμνάω can also connote a *striving after* or *putting forth an effort* (Jeremias, *Parables,* 214; Bultmann, *TDNT* 4:591, n. 34). Jeremias has chosen the latter (see Bornhauser, *Bergpredigt,* 150–52, and Schlatter, *Matthäus,* 225–27) for this passage since it is interchanged with *seek* (ζητέω) in 6:31, 33, par. Luke 12:29, 31, and the argument of 6:27, par. Luke 6:25, implies an effort on one's part. Thus 6:25, 28, 31, par. Luke 12:22, 29, warns against expending one's "efforts in pursuit of food and clothing" (Jeremias, *Parables,* 215). By contrast, Dupont (*Béatitudes* 3:286–87) maintains the former, the more common meaning of *anxious thought* since for him *seek* (ζητέω) also denotes an attitude, preoccupation, or aspiration (see Note on 6:33). The one *concern* is characterized by *anxiety* (μεριμνάω), the other (ζητέω) is not (cf. ζητέω/μετεωρίζομαι) in Luke 12:29,

Béatitudes 3:286–87). Does this warning prohibit *putting forth effort* for food and clothing (Jeremias) or *anxious thought* about one's personal needs?

The answer must lie in the context. The fact that two very different conclusions have been reached based on the context suggests that both are possibilities. Certainly the following illustrations drawn from nature (6:26, 28–30, par. Luke 12:24, 27–28) and the example of 6:27, par. Luke 12:25–26, indicate the absence or futility of any effort to secure one's needs (Jeremias, *Parables,* 214–15; Bultmann, *TDNT* 4:591). But the designation *you of little faith* (6:30, par. Luke 12:28) includes the element of attitude as well as conduct. The use of μεριμνάω in 6:31, cf. Luke 6:29, also clearly connotes *anxious thought* rather than *effort:* "Do not be anxious saying, 'What shall we eat . . .?' " The element of personal *effort* inherent to μεριμνάω in 6:25–30 now appears in the supporting example (ἐπιζητέω) of the Gentiles (6:32) and sets the stage for the counter demand to *seek* (ζητέω) or *put forth effort* with no hint of anxiety in 6:33 (See Note on 6:33). Perhaps the use of μεριμνάω in the context of petitionary prayer (e.g., Phil 4:6 and 1 Pet 5:7) where one is admonished to turn one's *anxious concerns* over to God not only supports the relationship between this warning of 6:25–34 and the fourth petition (6:11) but also adds further support to the element of *anxious thought.*

In this context, the alternatives of either *anxious thought* or *putting forth effort* are too narrow. Both elements are present. Consequently, μεριμνάω connotes and the warning forbids any undue concern or crippling anxiety (an attitude) that drives one to seek security by one's own *efforts* apart from the Father (an activity). The warning neither calls for a simplistic lack of concern nor does it rule out forethought in responsible living. Rather the section's thrust is directed at looking at God, the Creator, as Provider and Sustainer rather than to one's self.

about your life . . . your body. The word for *life* (ψυχή) can also mean *soul,* but its parallel with *body* (σῶμα) and the following explication, "what you shall eat," indicate that the two terms are used in parallel rather than opposition (Schweizer, *TDNT* 7:1058; idem, *Matthew,* 164).

what you shall eat or drink . . . what you shall wear. Several manuscripts omit along with Luke 6:22 *or drink* (ἢ τί πίητε; ℵ, λ, al, lat, Syr^c, Sa^pt) but the reading corresponds with Matthew's stylistic trait of adding corresponding words (cf. 5:6 and 6:31) with the disjunctive ἤ (see Note on 5:17). Its absence from the manuscripts would result from the influence of Luke 12:22 and the lack of further reference to drinking in the immediate context (6:26–30). Food and clothing designate the basic necessities for life. Food for sustenance and clothing for warmth and protection represent the ultimate human needs. To pray for such provisions (6:11) negates the worried effort to secure them in one's own strength. The following bases illustrate this conclusion.

is not your life more than food? This rhetorical question offers by implication the counter to the apodictic prohibition. In Luke 12:22, as well as in Matt 6:27, 30, the question becomes a declarative statement introduced by "for" (γάρ). But in both sentences one must move beyond the obvious to find the intent of the comparison. To prohibit one's worrying about food and clothing needs more than a comparison between the relative value of *life* and *food* and the *body* and *clothing* for a basis. The implied motif in the comparison comes from the context. Since the illustrations pertaining to food (6:26) and clothing (6:28b–30) show God to be the one who provides these necessary items, one is to assume that God the Creator rather than the creature is the focus. In other words, arguing from the greater to the lesser, if God gives the greater, namely, *life* and *body,* then he certainly can provide the lesser, namely, *food* and *clothing.* Thus, one is not to seek anxiously to secure one's daily needs. One is to trust God, the Creator of life and body, to provide for one's needs, as illustrated by 6:26–30.

6:26. *Look at the birds of heaven.* The first basis for the warning/admonition of 6:25 deals with food and uses the *birds* as an illustration. Luke 12:24 opens with a different verb, *consider* (κατανοήσατε), and object, *ravens* (κόρακας). While the verbs are more or less synonymous and Lucan redaction may be likely (cf. 12:27; 20:23 and 4x in Acts; so Schulz, *Spruchquelle,* 149, n. 64), the difference in object is generally attributed to Matthew's sensitivities about using an unclean bird as an object of comparison (e.g., Hill, *Matthew,* 144; Schweizer, *Matthew,* 164; Marshall, *Luke,* 527). The presence, however, of the familiar Old Testament expression, *birds of heaven* (cf. Gen 1:26), in 8:20, par. Luke 9:58 and 13:32, par. Luke 13:19, par. Mark 4:32, suggests its traditional character (Schulz, *Spruchquelle,* 150).

neither sow nor reap nor store grain. This listing covers the normal cycle of producing food by planting, harvesting, and storing it. *To store grain* renders the more literal *to gather grain into barns* (συνάγουσιν εἰς ἀποθήκας). Luke 12:24, stylistically smoother, notes that the "ravens" "neither sow nor reap" and they have "neither storeroom nor barn." By drawing attention to the obvious, this listing of such activities does not intend to advocate the "idle" life style of the *birds.* To the contrary, the force of the comparison lies in the fact that human beings—also part of God's creation—do indeed *sow, reap,* and *store food.*

your Father in heaven feeds them. The point of the illustration rests on the *Father's* provision of food for the *birds.* Matthew's *Father in heaven* replaces simply *God* (cf. Luke 12:24) in the Q parallel (see Note on 6:9).

are you not worth more than they? The rhetorical question changed to a direct statement in Luke 12:24 concludes the illustration by moving *a minore ad maius* to the worth of the human individual as part of God's creation. To express the comparison differently, since God provides food for the birds who do not even take part in the process of raising, harvesting, and storing food, how much more so will he provide for his valued own who do.

6:27. *Who of you by worrying.* This supporting basis comes as an interrupting surprise between the two illustrations drawn from nature (6:26, 28b–30) with their concluding *a minore ad maius* question. Luke 12:26 has an additional conclusion preserving that comparitive motif. Consequently, most have assigned this saying to a secondary "insertion" of an isolated saying into the Q context because of the catch-word μεριμνάω (e.g., Bultmann, *Tradition,* 81; Jeremias, *Parables,* 171; Wrege, *Überlieferungsgeschichte,* 119; Schulz, *Spruchquelle,* 154; cf. Marshall, *Luke,* 527). Luke 12:25 follows verbatim with the exception of the number *one* that is missing. *Who of you* (τίς ἐξ ὑμῶν) serves as an introductory device with the rhetorical force of "Can you imagine that any of you would . . . ," since the question normally expects an emphatic answer either positively—"Everyone, of course!"—or negatively—"No one! Impossible!" (Jeremias, *Parables,* 103, 158).

can add one hour to your life span? The terms *one hour* and *life span* render Greek words that refer to a unit of measure generally of spatial length. *One hour* represents a somewhat free translation of πῆχυς, often translated "cubit," a measure of approximately eighteen inches, based on the length of one's forearm (Bauer, *s.v.*). *Life span* (ἡλικία) can also refer to stature as well as time (e.g., Luke 2:52; 19:3, cf. John 9:21). Consequently, *to add eighteen inches of height* offers an alternative translation (see Manson, *Sayings,* 113). The use, however, of both terms in temporal contexts elsewhere in Greek and the force of the present context on something highly desirable (cf. *by worrying*) support the translation *one hour of life span.* Even relatively speaking, to add even one short period to one's life span would be desirable, whereas to add a cubit or eighteen inches to one's height most likely would not be a cause for "worry."

The direction of the argument changes from 6:26, 28b–30, where the movement is from the lesser to the greater to an argument based on the total futility of accomplishing anything by anxious efforts. If one cannot add to one's life span by worrying, then one should trust the Father, the Source and Sustainer of life itself (6:25b).

6:28. *Why do you worry about clothing?* The restatement of the theme from 6:25 leads to the second illustration drawn from nature. Clothing and food not only represented commodities indicating wealth (cf. 6:19–20; Luke 12:16–21; 16:19–25; James 2:2) but also the bare essentials of life. One's cloak was an inalienable right, so to speak, under the Law (Exod 22:25–26; cf. Str-B 1:343–44) since it functioned not only as a covering but also as protection from the elements.

Observe the lilies of the field. Luke simply has "the lilies" rather than the Old Testament phrase *of the fields* (e.g., Ps 103:15, cf. 6:30, par. Luke 12:28), which offers a parallel to *of heaven* in 6:26. This phrase most likely designates in a general way the wild flowers of Palestine rather than a given species, although Bauer lists autumn crocus, Turk's cap lily, anemone, or gladiolus as possibilities.

how they grow. The plural form of this and the following two verbs has been stylistically improved to the singular with the neuter plural of *lilies* (κρίνα) in Luke 12:27. The Western text of Luke 12:27 (D, it, sy, cl) omits this verb and takes the *how* (πῶς) to form a clause with the following verbs: "How they neither spin nor weave." This reading, whether Lucan or scribal in origin, is a later smoothing of the Matthean reading. An alternative reading of αὐξάνουσαν (οὐ ξαίνουσιν = *to card wool*) discovered by Skeat in the original text of Sinaiticus ("Lilies," 211–14) fits the context of spinning cloth better. Furthermore, Brunner has recently suggested this alternative for text critical reasons ("Mt. 6.28," 251–56). But the absence of any trace in the Lucan parallel and the presence of the transposed and vague κοπιάω betrays its secondary character.

but neither labor nor spin. These verbs express the division of labor between heavy labor often in the field (κοπιάω) and the finer work done at home (νήθω). The Western variant in Luke 12:27 pairs the more natural spinning (νήθω) and weaving (ὑφαίνω), since both are involved in the process of making cloth. As with the illustration on the *birds* above, the point of this observation serves the purposes of the comparison.

The *flowers* of the *field* grow without *labor* and *spinning*. Yet they are dressed in finery surpassing even Soloman's finest because of God's provision for them (6:30). The focus is on the divine provision rather than the futility of work.

6:29. *Solomon in all his glory.* The proverbial splendor of Solomon also occurs in rabbinic sources (Str-B 1:438). See 1 Kgs 9:26—10:29 and 2 Chr 9:13–28 for a description of his fabulous wealth.

6:30. *the grass of the field.* The more general term *grass* (χόρτος) subsumes the earlier *lilies of the field* (cf. Ps 103:12) to heighten the contrast that follows. The transient character of the grass and flowers surfaces in the Old Testament (Pss 37:2; 90:5–6; 102:11; 103:15; Isa 40:6–8, cf. 1 Pet 1:24–25). Once dried, grass became an important fuel source in wood-poor Palestine.

how much more will he clothe you. The ellipsis drawn from the protasis and reasoning from the lesser to the greater assures one again that God who cares for the beauty of the *wild flowers* will care all the more for his own.

you of little faith. Although *little faith* (ὀλιγόπιστοι) occurs redactionally otherwise in Matthew (8:26; 14:31; 16:8; 17:20), this occurrence has its roots in Q (Luke 12:28) from where the evengelist may have taken his other usages (cf. Str-B 1:438–39). In Matthew's usage the term always applies to disciples and designates the weakness and not the absence of their faith (see Frankemölle, *Jahwebund*, 23–24, 152–54, con. Strecker, *Weg*, 233). In this context *you of little faith* refers to those whose loyalty is torn between placing complete trust in God as Provider for one's needs and one's own anxious endeavors to secure one's necessities for life. Therefore, *little faith* helps direct the focus of these illustrations from simply suggesting a carefree life of idleness comparable to the *birds* who do not raise their food and the *lilies* that do not work for their attire to placing unreservedly one's confident trust in the *Father* who supplies the needs of his creation. This underlying motif of 6:26–30 now becomes explicit in the summary admonition of 6:31–34.

6:31. *Therefore do not worry.* Resuming the warning of 6:25, this verse concludes (*therefore, οὖν*) the illustrations and sets the stage for the positive admonition in 6:33. Luke 12:29 omits the resumptive warning with μεριμνάω by substituting ζητέω (cf. μετεωρίζεσθε that follows) with the meaning of "consider" or "deliberate" (see Note on 6:33) and changes the questions to commands in line with the avoidance of the rhetorical questions in Matt 6:25b, 6:26, 6:30; cf. Luke 12:22, 12:24, 12:28.

What shall we wear? Instead of Matthew's *wear* (περιβάλλω) which appeared in 6:29, par. Luke 12:27, Luke 12:29 has the hapax legomenon μετεωρίζεσθε as another verb for *to be worried* (Deissner, *TDNT* 4:630–31) and no reference to clothing. The use of μεριμνάω (cf. 6:25, 27, 34), the rhetorical question format (6:25, 26, 30) and the contextually compatible reference to clothing (6:25, 29–30) suggest the priority of Matthew's material.

6:32. *For the Gentiles seek to gain.* The argument takes a different turn with a reference to the Gentiles and to the Father's providential knowledge. The previous illustrations supported the prohibition of worrying by pointing to God's provision for his creation without any anxious endeavor on the part of the *birds* or the *lilies* (6:26, 28–30). The implication was that God would most certainly, therefore, provide for his own who do grow food and do labor and, most important, are of such greater value. Now the argument portrays such anxious endeavors *to gain all these things* as *Gentile* or characteristics of those who fail to recognize God as God. The use of *Gentiles* as a negative example, perhaps based on this reference, set the stage in 6:7–8 for the Lord's Prayer (see Note on 6:7).

for your Father in heaven knows. This argument offers the positive basis set in the Father's providential knowledge, a reference which also opened the Lord's Prayer (see Note on 6:8). Just as the Father's knowledge served to encourage one to pray in 6:8–9, the Father's knowledge of one's needs in this context precludes undue concern for life's necessities *(all these things)* by trusting his provision (cf. *Give us today. . .* , 6:11). *In heaven,* missing in Luke, reflects the evangelist's redaction (see Note on 6:9).

6:33. *Rather above all else.* This introduction brings the positive counterpart (δέ) to the negative warnings of 6:25, 28, 31. Luke 12:31 underscores the contrast (12:29, μὴ ζητεῖτε/12:31, πλὴν ζητεῖτε) with the evangelist's redactional use of πλήν (cf. 6:24, 27; Dupont, *Béatitudes* 3:32–34; Schulz, *Spruchquelle,* 152). *Above all else* suggests one of two connotations for Matthew's *first* (πρῶτον) missing in Luke. Its original status depends to an extent on one's rendering of it. If the term means the *first* in a series, it would imply a secondary softening of the contrast by implying that, after seeking the Kingdom, one then could seek to satisfy one's needs

(Klostermann, *Matthäusevangelium*, 64; Schmid, *Matthäus*, 143; Dupont, *Béatitudes* 3:275-77; Wrege, *Überlieferungsgeschichte*, 122-27; Marshall, *Luke*, 530). If one takes *first* to mean *above all else* (e.g., Soiron, *Bergpredigt*, 393-94; Michaelis, *TDNT* 6:870; Riesenfeld, "Schätzesammeln," 49), then it functions to heighten the contrast between an anxious seeking of one's security and a seeking of the Kingdom. Luke's stronger adversative (πλήν) accomplishes the same effect and would make an original πρῶτον somewhat redundant (Braun, *Radikalismus* 2:76, n. 1; Schulz, *Spruchquelle*, 152).

The first alternative not only runs counter to the evangelist's stress on entering the Kingdom (e.g., 5:20; 7:21 in the Sermon) and the summons to an undivided allegiance to God's rule in the redactionally arranged unit of 6:19-24, but it also would differ from a similar passage in 23:26, cf. Luke 11:41, where Matthew again has πρῶτον with an imperative and Luke has an introductory πλήν. The force of the two statements remains the same. To clean the inside of the cup results in its outside being clean. The one (cleaning the inside) includes the other (cleaning the outside) but not the converse (cf. 23:25, par. Luke 11:39). Thus *to seek above all the Kingdom* results in the receiving of all the benefits of the Kingdom *(all these things)*. Therefore, *first* indicates an action whose priority is not one of a series but all-encompassing. The question of its source remains unanswerable and moot for our understanding of 6:33, par. Luke 12:31.

seek. This verb (ζητέω) has a range of meanings (Bauer, *s.v.*), including to "ask" (1 Cor 4:2), "look for" (Matt 28:5), "investigate" (John 8:50), "try to obtain" or "desire to possess" (Matt 26:59), and to "strive for" (Phil 2:21). Obviously the context determines the appropriate meaning. But the different nuances of *Kingdom* (βασιλεία) and *righteousness* (δικαιοσύνη), plus the contrast, with the warning against anxious striving to gain one's needs (6:25, 28, 31), makes determining the specific meaning of the verb more complex in 6:33.

If, for example, to *seek* implies an active pursuit to obtain food, drink, and clothing in 6:31, par. Luke 12:30, how does one actively pursue the obtaining of the Kingdom when defined as an exclusively eschatological entity? Or if the Kingdom stands for God's dynamic sovereign rule in the present as well as the future consummation, would not striving to live under his sovereign rule (e.g., 6:19-24, cf. 6:9-10) offer a stark antithesis to a life lived apart from God (cf. *Gentiles*, 6:31, par. Luke 12:30) in pursuit of one's daily needs? Since *seek* (ζητέω) in 6:33 stands as the counter demand to the prohibition of *worrying* (μεριμνάω) in 6:25,

28, 31, par. Luke 12:22, 25, cf. 29, the primary clue must come from the larger context instead of the ambiguous terms *Kingdom* and *righteousness*.

Jeremias, who interprets μεριμνάω in terms of ζητέω (*Parables*, 214–15), takes *seek* to connote *putting forth effort* exclusively in the service of the imminent Kingdom rather than in obtaining food and clothing (cf. Mark 6:8). Consequently, the contrast between the prohibition in 6:25, 28, 31, par. Luke 12:22, 29, lies in the different object of one's pursuit rather than in the verbs. Dupont, however, has sharply distinguished the two verbs, based among other considerations on the prohibition of μετεωρίζομαι alongside of ζητέω in Luke 12:30 (*Béatitudes* 3:286). Whereas μεριμνάω contains the negative element of anxiety, ζητέω is a more neutral concept and thus needed the additional verb μετεωρίζομαι = *to be worried* in view of the previous context of μεριμνάω. Thus, 6:33, par. Luke 12:31, commands one to be preoccupied without anxiety with the coming of the Kingdom instead of being anxiously preoccupied with one's personal needs (*Béatitudes* 3:286–87).

To render *seek* (ζητέω) as primarily an attitude of preoccupation conflicts with the use of the counterpart (μεριμνάω) in 6:25–30, par. Luke 6:22–28 and the comparisons of 6:26–30, par. Luke 12:24–28, where the point of no effort or the futility of human effort is inherent to the comparison, and it also fails to note the different usage of ζητέω between Luke 12:30, the passage crucial to Dupont's interpretation, and Luke 12:31, the passage in question. Like μεριμνάω, ζητέω can connote an activity and/or an attitude. But in 6:32, 33, an activity is predominant.

In 6:32, par. Luke 12:30, the *Gentiles* are cited in support of the prohibition in 6:31, cf. Luke 12:30, against *worrying* or having *anxious* thoughts by illustrating that those apart from God strive to obtain, put effort into gaining (ἐπιζητέω), life's necessities. Whereas 6:31 focused on the attitude (μεριμνάω, see Note on 6:25), 6:32 focused on the activity which until now (6:31, cf. Luke 6:29) had been subsumed in the verb μεριμνάω (6:25–30, par. Luke 12:28) with the stage now set through 6:31–32 for Jesus' demand that one *seek above all* or *strive for the Kingdom* (6:33, par. Luke 12:31). Therefore, in 6:32, 33 (ἐπι) ζητέω designates one's life-controlling efforts and not primarily an attitude.

In Luke 12:29, ζητέω has replaced the μεριμνάω of Matt 6:31 and has, in context, the meaning of *to deliberate* with the indirect questions that follow. Its presence here may result from a stylistic desire to align 12:29 with the verbs of 12:30, 31. Its connotation of neutral concern, an attitude rather than an effort, is balanced by and necessitates the μὴ μετεωρίζεσθε *(do not worry)* in keeping with the warning of 12:22–28. Therefore, one must determine the meaning of *seek* (ζητέω) from the larger context rather than from this distinctive usage in Luke 12:29 (con. Dupont, *Béatitudes* 3:286–87).

In summary, the command *to seek* relates directly to the Gentiles' *seeking* to obtain (ἐπιζητοῦσιν) life's necessities in 6:32, par. Luke 12:30. The admonition calls in this context for one's controlling drive, one's ultimate quest, to be the obtaining of the *Kingdom,* to *worry* (μεριμνάω) and to *seek* (ζητέω) are paired in tandem to refer to the total involvement of one's person in pursuit of a goal. Therefore, *seek* means to give oneself unreservedly to the pursuit of the Kingdom.

his Kingdom. The *textus receptus* has the *Kingdom of God* (βασιλείαν τοῦ θεοῦ) as a clarification for *his* (αὐτοῦ) here and in Luke 12:31 (Metzger, *Commentary,* 161). The antecedent of *his* is *your Father* in 6:32, par. Luke 12:30.

Popularly, seeking first the Kingdom parallels the laying up of treasures in heaven in the belief that a greater value is placed on spiritual than on material concerns. Consequently, anxious striving to obtain security through one's obtaining food and clothing paralleled trying to amass earthly treasures that one was to eschew. Related as the passages may appear, their common denominator does not consist in their distinguishing between spiritual and physical concerns. Such an understanding not only misses the point of the comparisons in 6:26–32, par. Luke 12:24–30, the promise of 6:33b, par. Luke 12:31, but, more important, distorts the meaning of *Kingdom.*

For many scholars, the *Kingdom* in this context refers to the future, apocalyptic consummation of God's rule in history (e.g., Kümmel, *Promise,* 125–26; Schmid, *Matthäus,* 143; Barth, *Understanding,* 139; Strecker, *Weg,* 155; Schneider, *Bergpredigt,* 87; Dupont, *Béatitudes* 3:293–95) whose imminence conditioned the disciples' attitude towards material needs (e.g., Jeremias, *Parables,* 215; Schulz, *Spruchquelle,* 155). The admonition to *seek the Kingdom* would then be a call to concern oneself above all with the future eschatological *Kingdom* rather than one's present need for food and clothing.

Such an interpretation often leaves vague how one was actually to concern oneself with the Kingdom. A concern that was primarily attitudinal in the form of a desire for or a preoccupation with the Kingdom rather than food and clothing would run contrary to the emphasis in the passage on one's anxious efforts. Thus *to seek the Kingdom* must involve one's endeavors. But how? Either the call meant to give one's efforts to attaining the Kingdom at the end and thus implies that the ethical concern (e.g., Schulz, *Spruchquelle*, 156–57)—which many feel that Matthew brought to the saying with his "entrance requirement" of *righteousness*—was already present in the tradition as found now in Luke 12:31. Or the command calls for the giving of one's efforts to preparing in mission (e.g., Mark 6:8, par.) for the imminent Kingdom and the accompanying age of abundance in lieu of one's efforts to obtain food and clothing now (e.g., Jeremias, *Parables*, 215).

Still another interpretation of the *Kingdom* in this passage has emerged in more recent literature (e.g., Schniewind, *Matthäus*, 95; Schweizer, *Matthew*, 166; Hill, *Matthew*, 145; Riesenfeld, "Schätzesammeln," 49). Rather than having an exclusive apocalyptic sense, *Kingdom* can also connote both a present and a future dimension to God's sovereign rule (see Note on 5:3) and remain a technical eschatological expression for God's redemptive rule in history promised his people. The good news of the Kingdom is that God has already acted now in the person and ministry of Jesus Messiah to offer his sovereign reign to his own (Bonnard, *Matthieu*, 95) and will act definitely in the future to bring his rule to its consummation at the end of history. Consequently, to *seek the Kingdom* does not have to refer exclusively to a future apocalyptic coming of the *Kingdom*.

To take the *Kingdom* in its broader sense of God's sovereign rule present and future fits the context of 6:25–33, par. Luke 12:22–31. First, the *Kingdom* as God's sovereign rule is most compatible with the passage in general. Instead of consuming one's energies in anxious pursuit of food and clothing, one is called to submit oneself to God's rule and to live in confident trust of his power to provide. If the God of creation can provide for his creation (6:26–30, par. Luke 12:22–28), how much more can the God of redemption whose reign is being revealed in history care for his own (6:32–33, par. Luke 12:30–31). Second, the presence of the Kingdom corresponds with the concluding promise of the admonition in particular (6:33b, par. Luke 6:31b). If *all these things* actually accompany the *Kingdom* now as additions (*shall be added,* see below), the *Kingdom* must also come in the present (Schniewind, *Matthäus,* 95). Therefore, to *seek the Kingdom* rather than to *anxiously pursue food and clothing* means to live one's life in total submission to and in light of God's redemptive rule in history both present and future—in other words, to live life in response to Jesus' ministry (Bonnard, *Matthieu,* 95).

and his righteousness. The pronominal modifier *his* (αὐτοῦ) stood in the tradition with *Kingdom* (see Luke 12:31). Its present location comes from the addition of *righteousness.* The difficulty arises in determining whether *his righteousness* connotes a descriptive, subjective, objective, or, as in some systematic formulations, a possessive genitive. The alternatives have generally focused on whether the Father offers righteousness (subjective genitive) or whether he is the object (objective genitive) in the sense of a *righteousness* pleasing or valid before him. Perhaps both elements lie behind the construction: a *righteousness* prescribed and made possible by the Father that was accordingly pleasing to him. Only an examination of *righteousness* as used here and elsewhere in the Sermon can delineate the precise function of *his* (cf. Dupont, *Béatitudes* 3:288–95).

This object of *seek,* missing in Luke 12:31, clearly stems from Matthew's redaction (cf. 5:6, 10, 20; 6:1 within the Sermon; see Excursus on 5:6) and has occasioned various interpretations for this context. Apart from the infrequently held "Pauline" sense of righteousness accorded one at the last judgment (e.g., Michaelis, *Matthäus* 1:211–14), two major interpretations have surfaced. First, several have taken *righteousness* with the future, eschatological sense of Kingdom as the eschatological vindication or salvation by God of his own (e.g., Schlatter, *Matthäus,* 234–35; Schniewind, *Matthäus,* 94; Hunter, *Pattern,* 81; Filson, *Matthew,* 102). The modifier *his* functions in this case as the subjective genitive. Second, a great number take *righteousness* to refer to the life lived in keeping with the will of the Father however defined (e.g., Schmid, *Matthäus,* 143; Trilling, *Israel,* 146–47; Barth, "Understanding," 130; Descamps, *Justes,* 176–79; Nötscher, "Reich," 237–41; Strecker, *Weg,* 155; Hill, *Matthew,* 145; Dupont, *Béatitudes* 3:303–304; Riesenfeld, "Schatzesammeln," 49). The redactional use elsewhere in the Sermon precludes the first alternative, since a life lived congruent with the will of the Father belongs to the concept for Matthew (see Excursus on 5:6).

At stake here as elsewhere in the Sermon is not whether *righteousness* involves human conduct in keeping with the will of God but whether that conduct issues from the enabling gift of the Father. Many see 6:33 to demand *righteousness* as conduct prerequisite for entrance into the Kingdom (cf. 5:20 and 7:21–23, e.g.; Barth, *Understanding,* 130; Strecker, *Weg,* 155; Dupont, *Béatitudes* 3:303–40). To *seek the Kingdom* is to strive for *righteousness,* namely, conduct in keeping with the Father's will (e.g., Trilling, *Israel,* 146–47; Dupont, *Béatitudes* 3:302–303). The stress lies on one's own responsibility for attaining the Kingdom by meeting the conditions.

This interpretation of 6:33, along with similar interpretations of 5:20 and the following Antitheses, as "entrance requirements" for the Kingdom (see Note on 5:20) is only half correct. Matthew does deliberately combine *righteousness* and the *Kingdom* as integrally related but not in the sense that the former opens the door for the latter. Both *righteousness* as conduct in keeping with God's will and the *Kingdom* as God's sovereign, redemptive rule come as God's offer—his gift—to his own as promised for the age of salvation through Jesus Messiah. The demand for *righteousness* is a demand for conduct stemming from new relationships that God is effecting between himself and his own as well as among his own (5:21—6:18) in Jesus' ministry through which God's sovereign rule has come. Therefore, Jesus' call for *righteousness* corresponding to the new age indicates the presence now of the new age, the Kingdom of Heaven. To *seek righteousness,* to set one's efforts in pursuit of conduct corresponding to the Father's will, is not merely the prelude or the entrance requirement of the *Kingdom.* It is the concomitant of the presence of the *Kingdom.*

By adding *righteousness* to the command to *seek the Kingdom* of the Father, the evangelist simply underscores the presence now of the *Kingdom* as God's sovereign rule (cf. Schniewind, *Matthäus,* 95; Schweizer, *Matthew,* 166; Hill, *Matthew,* 145; Descamps, *Justes,* 176–79; Riesenfeld, "Schatzesammeln," 49). Apart from the enabling gift of God's redemptive reign (the presence of the Kingdom), one could not carry out the demand (the right conduct or *righteousness*) that stems from transformed relationships between God and his own. The good news of God's fulfilling promise through Jesus' proclamation (the Beatitudes of 5:3–12) leads to a call for discipleship (5:13–16); the fulfilllment of the Scriptures in Jesus' coming (5:17–18) leads to a call for the "greater righteousness" (5:20—7:12). Only those who live in keeping with the presence of the Kingdom can hope to stand before the "Father" as "sons" when God's sovereign rule is established in the consummation (5:20; 7:21–23). But this responsibility, the "entrance requirement" for the future consummation of the Kingdom, comes as a response to God's offer of reconciliation commensurate with the new age through Jesus' ministry (cf. the Antitheses of 5:21–48 following 5:17–18).

and all these things. This reference picks up the same designation in 6:32 of food, drink, and clothing. Luke 12:31 only has the demonstrative, *these things* (ταῦτα). The focus of the passage on one's material needs for existence that opens 6:25, par. Luke 12:22, is not lost or subordinated to some "spiritual need" as this concluding promise demonstrates.

The Lord's Prayer opens with petitions for God's establishing his sovereignty in history (6:9-10; 6:19-24) but the pivot of the Prayer deals with one's "daily bread." Our needs are not eclipsed by our commitment to the Father; they are simply placed in perspective.

shall be added. This verb (προστίθημι), set in the divine passive with God as the implied subject, holds the key to much of the passage. It promises the provision of one's needs, the focus of the anxious efforts prohibited in 6:25, 28-31, par. Luke 12:22, 29, and assures one that God not only knows the needs of his own (6:32, par. Luke 12:30, cf. 6:8) but will meet those needs (7:11). Furthermore, this verb implies that the *Kingdom and his righteousness* are included as part of God's provision now.

One cannot dismiss the force of the prefix in this passage (cf. 6:27, par. Luke 12:25) as denoting *additional* benefits granted by the Father (con. Strecker, *Weg,* 155). Nor can one maintain that the verb *shall be added* corresponds to the command to *seek* as though the benefits additionally accompanied one's seeking rather than the *Kingdom and his righteousness* (see Dupont, *Béatitudes* 3:298). Even if the two verbs are correlated, they both share the same object—*the Father's Kingdom and righteousness*—the one explicitly, the other implicitly. Consequently, although the disciples are called to commit themselves and the focus of their life to God's sovereign rule and will, both that rule and the accomplishing of his will come about in the present tense as a gift from the Father.

To summarize, this passage (6:25-33, par. Luke 12:22-31) demands that the disciple's life be directed by *(seek)* the sovereign rule of the Father (the *Kingdom*) and the doing of his will *(righteousness)* rather than in anxious pursuit of obtaining one's own needs *(worry)* apart from God *(the Gentiles).* It also assures the disciples that the Father will provide not only the primary *(above all)* object of one's life but all of one's needs besides. To live life in this perspective is to acknowledge the Father as sovereign (6:9-10) and to commit one's daily needs (6:11) to his provision as the one whose sovereign rule has entered history.

6:34. *Therefore, do not worry about tomorrow.* This anticlimactic command, missing in Luke, may well be redactional to refocus on the initial prohibitions of 6:25, 28, 31 and may also relate the section to the fourth petition (6:11) with the reference to *tomorrow* (αὔριον) in contrast to the assurance of provision for *today* (σήμερον). The content of this conclusion has numerous parallels in the ancient world (Bultmann, *Tradition,*

116–17), and, taken in isolation, both bases would be depressing. Yet set in the context of 6:25–33 the disciple gains confident assurance from God's provision rather than from one's anxious endeavors. It is this faith in God's provision expressed in the fourth petition of the Lord's Prayer (6:11) that changes the pessimistic and fatalistic tone of the saying (Schniewind, *Matthäus,* 96).

7:1–5. This section on Judging corresponds to the fifth petition regarding one's being forgiven and forgiving (6:12) and also returns to the Q tradition of the Sermon (par. Luke 6:37–42) for the first time since the Love Your Enemies unit of 5:43–48 (see Literary Analyses on 6:1–18 and 6:19—7:12). In the Q Sermon material, this unit was one of three located between the Beatitudes (5:3–12, par. Luke 6:20–26) and the concluding Parable of the Builders (7:24–27, par. Luke 6:47–49), the other two being the units on Love Your Enemies (Luke 6:27–35, par. Matt 5:39–47) and Fruits (Luke 6:43–45, par. Matt 7:15–20). Furthermore, this section on Judging, as introduced by Luke 6:36 (cf. Matt 5:48), corresponds with the Beatitude to the merciful that served as a beatitudinal preface for this material in the Sermon (see Note on 5:7).

The structure again parallels that of a Wisdom complex consisting of an apodictic prohibition (7:1), bases (7:2), illustrations (7:3–4), and concluding admonition (7:5). Luke 6:37–42 follows quite closely with the exception of two prohibitions and two admonitions in pairs that may indicate the earlier form (Burney, *Poetry,* 114, 123; Schürmann, *Lukasevangelium,* 362–65; cf. Schulz, *Spruchquelle,* 146) with only one basis rather than two (6:38b, cf. Matt 7:2).

7:1. *Do not judge.* Luke 6:36 opens this section with the positive admonition to "be merciful (οἰκτίρμων) as your Father is merciful" that appropriately follows the material on Love Your Enemies (6:27–35, 36–42). Matthew, however, has reworked this admonition in order to use it as the conclusion of the Antitheses in 5:21–48 (see Note on 5:48). Therefore, the negative command corresponding to the openings of the two previous sections (6:19–24, 25–34) now opens this unit (7:1, par. Luke 6:37).

The absolute prohibition, *do not judge* (μὴ κρίνετε), contains several possible meanings because of the various uses of *to judge* in Greek as well as English. They span the scale from an aesthetic discerning to a legal act of a judiciary. Yet the broader context of the Beatitude to the merciful (5:7), the original Q context following the command to Love Your Enemies (Luke 6:27–35, 36–42), the opening admonition in

Q pointing to God's mercifulness (Luke 6:36), and Matthew's alignment of this section with the fifth petition (6:12) preclude the more technical legal sense of a legal judiciary and the more general sense of distinguishing or discriminating. *Judging,* therefore, refers to the censorious condemnation of another, an attitude accompanied by commensurate actions toward another. That action belongs to God exclusively as seen by the immediate context of the corresponding verbs set in the divine passive.

lest you be judged. Luke 6:37 has the paratactic subjunctive of strong denial (καὶ οὐ μὴ κριθῆτε). The divine passive sets the scene with reference to the final judgment and reminds one that God alone is the ultimate judge. This injunction forcefully states the instruction of 7:1–5 totally forbidding any condemnatory judgment of others. It directly relates one's actions with God's actions at the end in a manner reminiscent of 5:7, 6:12, 14–15; 18:23–35. The converse, however, does not imply that the foregoing of judging results in one's not being judged at the final judgment, only that one will not be culpable for such behavior and will indeed receive "mercy" (5:7) and "forgiveness" (6:12, 14–15, 18:35).

7:2. *For by the judgment you judge, you will be judged.* The first of two bases grows out of the language in the instruction (7:1) and corresponds in format to the basis that follows (7:2, par. Luke 6:38b). Matthew has most likely constructed this basis in lieu of his abridging the opening series of two prohibitions and two commands found in Luke 6:37b–38 (cf. 5:44, par. Luke 6:27–28; so Schürmann, *Lukasevangelium,* 362, and Wrege, *Überlieferungsgeschichte,* 125; con. Schulz, *Spruchquelle,* 146). James 5:6 may contain a reminiscence of the underlying tradition behind Luke 6:37b (cf. καταδικάζω).

On the surface, this basis appears incongruous with the absolute prohibition of judging, since it assumes a judgment (κρίμα) has taken place (e.g., Schulz, *Spruchquelle,* 147, n. 46). Yet the injunction both prohibited judging and made the connection between God's judging and one's judgment of another that parallels the connection between God's mercy and forgiveness and one's own actions (cf. 5:7; 6:12, 14–15; 18:35; Luke 6:36). In other words, one's standing before God at the final judgment (*shall be judged,* κριθήσεσθε) is directly related to one's relationship with others as illustrated by 7:2a, b. This same motif underlies the demand for a "greater righteousness" as an "entrance requirement" for the future Kingdom and the conduct of the Antitheses stemming from restored relationships between individuals, relationships in keeping with the presence of the age of salvation now. The response to others betrays whether one is protective and vindictive of one's own concerns or one has demonstrated the capacity to experience God's overture of mercy and forgiveness (see Note on 6:12). Therefore, this basis actually supports, as does the one that follows, the total prohibition of condemning others. To condemn another is not to act out of mercy and forgiveness (5:7; 6:12) and thus has no claim for same at the last judgment. Therefore, to receive mercy at the last judgment means that one appropriates God's forgiveness now and offers it to others (6:12, 14–15).

by the measure . . . it will be measured to you. This second basis (par. Luke 6:38b) appears commonly as a proverbial expression in the ancient world (cf. Str-B 1:444–46). The Mishna contains a verbal parallel in *Soṭa* 1:7, "With what measure a man metes it shall be measured to him again." Mark 4:24 has the same saying in a different context, suggesting a doublet tradition with which the evangelist may have aligned the saying (7:2, par. Mark 4:24, cf. Luke 6:38b). One might take this statement as common-sense advice to be liberal in order to receive liberally and vice versa, but the phrase signifies, as did 7:2a, the basis for not judging at all by linking one's own *measuring* with the divine *measuring* at the end (future, passive, μετρηθήσεται). Since to *measure* made one culpable, *not to measure at all* meant God's merciful acceptance at the judgment.

7:3–4. *speck . . . beam.* Two graphic examples (Str-B 1:446–47) set in hyperbole as rhetorical questions follow to illustrate the principle of 7:1–2. Luke 6:39–40 has two additional "parables" without exact parallels in Matthew (Luke 6:39, cf. 15:14 and 23:16; Luke 6:40, cf. 10:24). The first (7:3, par. Luke 6:41) compares the blindness to one's huge faults (cf. *the beam* [δοκός] *in your eye*) and one's sharp vision in spotting another's tiny defects (cf. *the speck* [κάρφος] *that is in your brother's eye*). The second (7:4, par. Luke 6:42, without the disjunctive *or*) maintains the hyperbolic expressions but moves from perception to actions and suggests that one is much more prone to judge another for something of far less consequence than one's own faults. In other words, one is not to condemn others at all (7:1) since one's own failures are so glaring and since judging another will occasion judgment rather than mercy (7:1).

7:5. *Hypocrite.* This startling address opens the concluding admonition involving an apparent two-stage process *(first . . . then)*. *Hypocrite* in the Q tradition (par. Luke 6:42) generally applies to the Jewish leaders in Matthew (see Note on 6:2) and expresses a judgment aimed at the one who appears to be something that he is not, an actor playing a role—no matter how sincerely—and receiving the acclaim of others rather than God (van Tilborg, *Leaders,* 24–25). Since the disciples are not designated *hypocrites* elsewhere in the Gospels, Jeremias has assigned the passage originally to Jesus' ministry to the Pharisees (Luke 6:39, cf. Matt 15:14 and 23:16; *Parables,* 167; see Schürmann, *Lukasevangelium,* 376, for a broader referent). At any rate, in the present context of the Sermon tradition (7:1–5, par. Luke 6:36–42) the address clearly applies to the audience of disciples, and both evangelists let it stand as a warning not unlike 24:51, cf. Luke 12:46, and the section 7:13–27 (especially 7:21–23) that follows. *To judge* another is to set oneself above another as though without sin and thus to be a *hypocrite.*

first take out . . . then . . . you will see . . . to take out. This admonition apparently prescribes the steps to resolving the dilemma of the hyperbolic examples by means of the obvious. The first step expands on the action of the second example—removing the beam from one's own eye (7:4). The second step includes the limited perception implied in the first example (7:3)—seeing clearly—and the action of the second example (7:4)—removing the speck from one's brother's eye.

But how does this concluding admonition fit with 7:1–4? Two interpretations have emerged (Bonnard, *Matthieu,* 97). On the one hand, taken in a straightforward manner, this verse demands that one deal first with the major issues in one's own life. The force of the rhetorical questions (7:3–4) shocks one into realizing one's own great failures and liability at the last judgment and leads to the seeking of forgiveness and mercy as a sinner. Only then, second, as a forgiven sinner to a sinner, can one go with the humble desire to help correct a brother whose failure, though visible, was of lesser significance than one's own. There is no basis for hypocrisy in such an approach, which parallels the practice of discipline in the early church (e.g., Matt 18:15–18; Gal 6:1–5, cf. Rom 2:1–11). In this manner, the passage itself bridges between the absolute prohibition of judging or condemning others (cf. 7:1–4) and the appropriate concern for the evil present in the lives of the members of the community (e.g., Schniewind, *Matthäus,* 98; Grundmann, *Lukas,* 153; Eichholz, *Bergpredigt,* 151–52; Schneider, *Bergpredigt,* 89, and Marshall, *Luke,* 271).

On the other hand, taken in the spirit of the hyperboles of 7:3–4 and the force of the preceding verses (7:1–4), this concluding admonition (7:5) can be interpreted as an ironic restatement of the principle—*do not judge at all* (e.g., Schürmann, *Lukasevangelium,* 149; Hill, *Matthew,*

147; Schweizer, *Matthew,* 169; Schulz, *Spruchquelle,* 149). The thrust of the verse rests on the address, *hypocrite.* Judging is totally forbidden to the disciple whose standing before God is indicated by his actions toward others (7:1–2). Having received God's forgiveness and mercy, one reflects that experience of mercy in dealing with others (5:7; 6:12; cf. 18:35). To *judge* another, therefore, betrays the presence of the *beam (hypocrite)* in one's own life, a life with no experience of mercy. Consequently, this admonition, like the command to throw the first stone in John 8:7, redirects one's attention from a false desire to correct a brother to the need for personal repentance. It was not intended to set the preconditions for correcting another (Schürmann, *Lukasevangelium,* 371).

The latter interpretation maintains harmony with the context and is probably to be preferred over the former. The force of this section on Judging does not exclude the desire or the need to aid another who is in the wrong by humbly seeking out of an awareness of one's own great failings and God's mercy to correct or discipline a brother. The passage in no way suggests that the disciple must avoid dealing with evil except in one's own life but it does not deal with that issue here (Schürmann, *Lukasevangelium,* 372, n. 183; Schweizer, *Matthew,* 169). Rather, the absolute prohibition of judging another focuses on the attention on one's relationship with others and the correspondence of one's actions with one's standing before God in line with the previous statements on mercy (5:7; Luke 6:36) and forgiveness (6:12, 14–15; 18:35). In particular, this section on Judging directly corresponds with the thrust of the fifth petition regarding forgiveness in the Lord's Prayer (6:12), just as the sections 6:19–24, 25–34 have done with the preceding petitions.

7:6. This verse, without parallel in Luke, stands alone without any apparent relationship to its immediate context. The most that can be suggested is a loose qualifying relation to the previous section on Judging. Whereas 7:1–5 totally prohibits condemning others, 7:6 sets limits where discretion and discernment are necessary (e.g., McNeile, *Matthew,* 91; Klostermann, *Matthäusevangelium,* 66; Schniewind, *Matthäus,* 98).

At the heart of this contextual dilemma lies the basic question about what the enigmatic saying meant in its original setting as well as here in 7:6. Almost all recent commentators have interpreted the saying with reference to the mission context. Yet even this context remains unclear, since *dogs* and *swine* often refer to heathen or Gentiles in Jewish literature (Str-B 1:447–50), but neither Jesus nor Matthew speaks adversely against the Gentile mission (Schmid, *Matthäus,* 146–47; Schneider, *Bergpredigt,*

91). Some have resolved this problem by assigning the original *Sitz im Leben* to the strict, Palestinian Jewish-Christian community (cf. Grundmann, *Matthäus,* 221–22; Schweizer, *Matthew,* 170; Bornkamm, "Aufbau," 429). Instead of Gentiles as the original referent, others have taken *dogs* and *swine* to point to the cynical mockers who blaspheme and degrade the gospel (e.g., Schniewind, *Matthäus,* 98; Eichholz, *Bergpredigt,* 153; cf. Schlatter, *Matthäus,* 243–44). Or perhaps the verse simply warns against an overzealous forcing of the gospel on others by illegitimate means (Schmid, *Matthäus,* 146; Schneider, *Bergpredigt,* 90). This variety of interpretations underscores the obscurity of the saying.

Even the early church reflects this diversity of interpretation. *Gos Thom* 93 applies the saying in the context of instruction to the disciples. *Did* 9:5 used it to exclude the unbaptized from sharing the Lord's Supper. And Pseudo-Clem *Recog* 3:1 applies the verse in a mission context to screen those who have "unworthy ears."

Yet, the saying must have had a more intelligible function in 7:6 for Matthew's audience. The lack of contextual coloring and redactional elaboration imply its proverbial and almost self-evident usage by the evangelist. Unfortunately, what might have been clear to his audience because of a common understanding of this saying appears lost to the reader today. Perhaps the clue lies in a totally different direction from the mission setting, which lacks any supportive basis in the immediate context of 7:6. Just as the previous units of 6:19–24, 25–34, and 7:1–5 corresponded to successive petitions of the Lord's Prayer, this saying also refers to the content of the final petitions for deliverance from temptation and the Evil One (Bornkamm, "Aufbau," 428–29). Such a starting point would also be consistent with the proverbial use of *dogs* and *swine* in 2 Pet 2:22 to refer to apostasy (cf. 2 Pet 2:20–22) and would approximate the warning of 5:13 about what happens to salt that has lost its saltiness (see Note on 5:13). Instead of the mission per se, this saying warns the disciple against apostasy, the failure to take discipleship seriously.

Do not give what is holy to dogs. Once again this unit opens with an apodictic prohibition (cf. 6:19, 25; 7:1) set in a chiastic parallelism. *What is holy* (τὸ ἅγιον) stands for food offered in sacrifice in the Old Testament (e.g., Exod 29:33; Lev 2:3; 22:10–16; Num 18:8–19; cf. Str-B 1:447), a background that the *Gos Thom* might still reflect in light of the consequence—"lest they cast it upon the dung heap" (cf. also *Did* 9:5 with reference to eating the Lord's Supper). Since, however, *sacred meat* offers a less-than-expected parallel to *pearls,* some have posited an underlying Aramaic *(qdš')*, meaning both *ring* and something *holy*, that was either mistranslated as *holy* (e.g., McNeile, *Matthew*, 91; Jeremias, "Matthaus 7:6a," 83–87) or intentionally translated *holy* as an interpretation along the lines of *Did* 9:5 (Black, *Approach*, 200–202). Furthermore, a *golden ring* would also correspond to Prov 11:22 where a woman without discretion is compared to a gold ring in a swine's snout.

Although a *gold ring* does form a better parallel with *pearls* and the theme of discretion found in Prov 11:22 seems to fit the context (cf. 7:1–5) according to most interpreters, this alternative loses its attraction on closer examination. Not only does throwing a *dog* a *gold ring* make little sense in the context of feeding animals (*pearls* are conversely to swine swill what stones are to bread, 7:9), but the theme of discretion (cf. Prov 11:22) is hardly the issue after all. Furthermore, the further reworking of the text based on a supposed Aramaic original (e.g., Jeremias, "Matthäus 7:6a," 83–87) only does greater violence to the Greek text (Bornkamm, "Aufbau," 428, n. 10). Consequently, *what is holy* most likely refers to the throwing of *sacred meat* from sacrificial animals to *dogs*.

Dogs and *swine* both function as symbols of disdain for obvious reasons, especially the ritually unclean *swine*. Numerous applications of these terms in Judaism point to Gentiles and heretics (Str-B 1:447–49). Consequently, interpreters have naturally sought a specific group as referents behind this saying—either Gentiles, or cynics hardened to the gospel. If the former, then the saying would have had its roots in a strict Jewish-Christianity opposed to a Gentile mission, a motif foreign to both Jesus and Matthew. This tradition, as that behind 5:17–19, would then have come to the evangelist from such a traditional context only to be reinterpreted by his present usage (e.g., Schweizer, *Matthew*, 170, and Bornkamm, "Aufbau," 429). Such a conclusion, however, appears unnecessary since neither *Gos Thom* 93 nor *Did* 9:5 use the saying with reference to a limited mission. Furthermore, although *dogs* and *swine* often make allegorical references to specific groups in the ancient world, this saying may have been intended as simply a vivid metaphor (cf. 2 Pet 2:22) whose source was Jesus' own ministry. Certainly, the theme of apostasy strikes a harmonious chord with other sayings in Jesus' ministry.

trample under foot . . . tear you to pieces. A chiastic pattern would mean that the *swine* do to the *pearls* (καταπατήσουσιν) what people do to salt (καταπατεῖσθαι) that has lost its value (5:13, cf. Mark 9:50 and Luke 14:35). Valued jewels are discarded like waste with less value than swine swill. The usage of this verb in such similar contexts of warning against apostasy seems hardly coincidental especially when we take into consideration the punitive use of καταπατέω in the LXX (Bertram, *TDNT* 5:941–42). *Tear you to pieces* in the chiasm would then indicate the ungrateful disdain of rabid *dogs* who turn on their "benefactor."

Set against the backdrop of the final petitions of the Lord's Prayer, this saying takes its natural place in the immediate context as one of a series of practical expositions of the Lord's Prayer. By using graphic proverbial expressions of waste and desecration, 7:6 functions as a metaphor rather than an allegory. It warns against the temptation of apostasy, of falling prey to the Evil One by forfeiting what is holy and precious, namely, one's privileged rights as a son of the Father and one's life as a disciple in the Kingdom. This warning, like those of 6:19, 25; and 7:1, can only be carried out in the spirit of prayer (Matt 6:13).

7:7–11. This unit on Answered Prayer, located between the Warning of Apostasy in 7:6 and the Golden Rule in 7:12, appears to be totally unrelated to its immediate context (e.g., McNeile, *Matthew,* 90; Schmid, *Matthäus,* 147; Hill, *Matthew,* 148). The Q parallel occurs in Luke 11:9–13, where the unit appropriately concludes the prayer-didache of 11:1–13 focusing on the Lord's Prayer. Yet taken along with the four previous units (6:19–24, 25–34; 7:1–5, 6), this admonition belongs to the Lord's Prayer complex in Matthew as well (Bornkamm, "Aufbau," 430; cf. Schniewind, *Matthäus,* 99). Whereas the other units offer a practical commentary in the petitions of the Lord's Prayer, this unit offers in context an appropriate concluding assurance of the Father's (cf. 6:8, 9, 11) answer to prayer. In fact, the key verb in this unit, *ask* (αἰτέω, 7:7, 8, 9, 10, 11) has a verbal parallel in the introduction to the Prayer (αἰτέω, 6:8), and the assurance motif that redactionally introduces the Prayer (see Notes on 6:7–8) finds its extended basis in this concluding unit. Therefore, the evangelist has redactionally bracketed the Lord's Prayer and its commentary (6:9b–15, 19—7:6) with the promise of the Father's response to the prayer of his own.

The structure of this unit follows the Wisdom pattern of statement, basis, examples, and conclusion (see Notes on 6:25–34). But the symmetry of 7:7–11 distinguishes each unit. The command consists of three lines set in synonymous parallelism (7:7). The basis follows in identical three-line parallelism (7:8). Next come the two examples (7:9–10) also set in synonymous parallelism containing two lines each, and the conclusion (7:11) moves *a fortiore* to its application.

7:7. *Ask, and it shall be given you.* In contrast to the previous units in 6:19—7:11, this one opens with a positive admonition. All three imperatives use the present tense to denote the continuous process of *asking, seeking,* and *knocking.* To *ask* (αἰτέω) occurs in the prayer context of 6:7 and often connotes a prayer of supplication (Stählin, *TDNT* 1:191–93). The future use of the divine passive in the second clause, *shall be given* (δοθήσεται), again implies that God is the subject (so 5:11) and confirms the prayer setting for *ask* here. Together the force of the imperative and promise may be interpreted as conditional in the construction with the emphasis resting on the second half: "If you ask, it shall be given you." Or, more in keeping with the larger Prayer context, the emphasis may be on the command calling one to pray with the accompanying assurance of receiving the object of one's request: "Ask, for it will be given to you." Since the basis of 7:8 underscores the element of assurance, 7:7 most likely stresses the imperative to pray (Marshall, *Luke,* 467).

The object of one's request remains unstated. Yet taken in the broader context of the Lord's Prayer and the assurance of the Father's awareness of one's needs before they are voiced (6:7, 32, cf. 7:9–11), the request doubtless covered the spectrum of the disciple's desires and needs in view of the Kingdom present and future (6:33, see Note on 7:11). The parameters of one's desires are set by the relationship of the son to the Father. This relationship recognizes him to be the Holy One of Israel whose sovereign rule is being and will be established in history as well as in the life of each of his own (6:9–15, 19—7:6). In short, the request encompasses the blessings of the new age (cf. *the good gifts,* ἀγαθά; cf. 7:11).

seek . . . knock and it shall be opened. The two imperatives reinforce the command to *ask* (Grundmann, *Matthäus,* 224). To *seek* occurs frequently in the Old Testament with God and his will as the object (e.g., Deut 4:29; Ps 105 [104]:4; Isa 65:1). Jer 29:13 (36:13, LXX) uses the same expressions of *seeking* and *finding* in the LXX: "You will seek me and find me." Furthermore, the preceding use speaks explicitly of prayer: "Then you will call upon me . . . and pray to me and I will hear you" (Jer 29:12). To *knock* (κρούω) clearly depicts one standing in front of a closed door awaiting its being opened (ἀνοιγήσεται). This command most likely functions metaphorically here for prayer as it also did at times in Judaism (Str-B 1:458–59) rather than allegorically referring to entrance into the Kingdom (cf. Jeremias, *TDNT* 3:178; Schweizer, *Matthew,* 173; Schneider, *Bergpredigt,* 94). Therefore, the metaphors of *seeking/finding* and *knocking/being opened* combine to reinforce the command to *ask* as a call for the disciple to come expectantly to the Father in prayer.

7:8. *For everyone who asks . . . seeks . . . knocks.* The basis (*for*, γάρ) for the admonition of 7:7 comes as a restatement of the imperatives in the form of substantial participles (ὁ αἰτῶν, ὁ ζητῶν, τῷ κρούοντι). In this way, the stress falls on the promises expressed in the verbs. Therefore, one is to *ask, seek,* and *knock* (7:7) because one is assured of *receiving, finding,* and *having the door opened* (7:8). *Everyone* (πᾶς) removes any qualifying limitations on the petitioner in order to be heard. Yet one must not lose sight of the larger context, where Jesus has set prayer in contrast to the *hypocrites* (6:5-6) and the *Gentiles* (6:7-8). Thus, *everyone* refers to any who recognize and accept the new relationship offered by God through Jesus Messiah to his own as the Father (6:6, 8, 9, 32-33; 7:9-11).

7:9. *Or who among you.* The verbatim parallels so far between Matt 7:7-8, par. Luke 11:9-10, give way to some divergencies in the two examples that follow. Matthew opens with the disjunctive *or* (ἤ) that may be a redactional transition (cf. Luke's δέ in 11:11) between the command of 7:7 or the basis of 7:8 and the illustrations leading to the conclusion of 7:9-11. On the function of *who among you* and the rhetorical question (cf. Luke's contextually more explicit "What father among you") as a literary device implying "No one!" (see Note on 6:27). The use of father-son examples as illustrations of God's dealing with his own was also familiar to Judaism (Bonnard, *Matthieu,* 100; Hill, *Matthew,* 148).

7:9-10. *bread . . . stone . . . fish . . . serpent.* These symmetrically constructed rhetorical questions focus on the staples of a Galilean diet— *bread* and *fish.* Therefore, the examples refer as did 6:25-34 to the basic necessities of human life, one's everyday needs (cf. 6:11, 25-33). The contrast in each case stems from the similarly appearing but worthless substitute. *Bread* had the same flat, round shape and color as a stone. *Fish* most likely referred to the eel-like fish that could be mistaken for a serpent.

Luke 11:11-12 has *fish/serpent* in common with Matthew, although the order of occurrence is different. But Luke has egg/scorpion as the second example. The relationship is no longer one of appearance but of result—that is, beneficial/harmful. While *bread* and *fish* are a natural pair and may represent the original examples, one might argue for an original three (e.g., McNeile, *Matthew*, 92) with transmissional variations accounting for the two in Matthew and Luke (Marshall, *Luke*, 469) or Lucan redaction (Schmid, *Lukas*, 215; Ott, *Gebet*, 109–12; Schulz, *Spruchquelle*, 162).

7:11. *if you being evil.* The conclusion set in the second person plural moves *a minore ad maius* from the experience of earthly fathers to the *Heavenly Father* (see Note on 6:9 for Matthew's redactional *Father in heaven* in contrast to Luke's more original "The Father will give from heaven"). Yet the comparison does not simply lie along the lines of earthly, human and heavenly, divine. Rather, if those who are *evil* can give *good gifts* (δόματα ἀγαθά) as implied in 7:9–10 *how much more* can the Heavenly Father in whom there is no evil give *good gifts* (ἀγαθά). The assumption of the *evil* or malicious character of humanity underscores the contrast between human behavior and God's actions. One's evil surfaces in comparison with the ultimate standard, namely, God himself.

good gifts. Luke has the *Holy Spirit* where Matthew has ἀγαθά. Most ascribe the difference to Luke (e.g., Schulz, *Spruchquelle*, 162; cf. Wrege, *Überlieferungsgeschichte*, 108; Grundmann, *Lukas*, 235; Marshall, *Luke*, 430). The ἀγαθά must correspond to δόματα ἀγαθά of the protasis (7:11a). At issue, however, is whether the *a fortiore* argument between the subjects *(evil fathers—Father in heaven)* extends to the objects, the gifts. The question is moot for the evangelists' usage in light of the eschatological context of the entire prayer complex of 6:5–15, 19—7:11. The present and future dimensions of the Kingdom and life lived commensurate with the Kingdom underlie the Lord's Prayer and its explication (6:7–13, 19—7:6). Thus, God's gifts of his Kingdom, with the corresponding relationships and conduct as well as personal needs, come together (6:33, par. Luke 12:31) as the eschatological benefits of the Kingdom present and future. These are the *good gifts* that the Father gives his own. To the extent that the Holy Spirit also represented one of the primary benefits of the new age, the meaning of Luke 11:13 would parallel the broader promise of 7:11.

to those who ask him. This final reference to *asking* the Father corresponds to the introductory reference to *asking* in 6:8. Therefore, this phrase rounds off the prayer complex for both Matthew and Luke and forms a bracket in Matthew around the whole section of the Lord's Prayer (6:7–15, 19—7:11).

Matt 7:11 concludes this unit on Answered Prayer (7:7–11, par. Luke

11:9–13) as well as the larger context on prayer or more precisely on how to pray (6:5–8). This question is answered by contrasting the *hypocrites* and the *Gentiles* (6:5–8) and with an example of what to pray (6:9–13), which is then explicated in terms of one's life of prayer or devotion (6:14–15, 19—7:6). This concluding unit calls one again to prayer and does so with the declaration of the Father's desire to hear and respond to one's petitions. The motivation to pray stems from and is based on one's relationship with the Father. Thus prayer as uttered by voice (6:9–13) and by life (6:14–15, 19—7:6) stands as a constituent element of life in the Kingdom, life lived in the restored relationship with the Father. The evangelist has appropriately expanded on this act of devotion (6:5–6) rather than the others (6:2–4, 16–18) in developing his theme on "doing righteousness" (6:1) as an expression of one's vertical relationship with the Father (6:1—7:11, cf. 5:21–48).

7:12. This saying, often referred to since the eighteenth century as the Golden Rule, stands at the end of this series of traditional units with no evident material connection to its immediate context. By contrast, Luke has the saying in a more natural setting as part of the Love Your Enemies complex (6:31). If, however, the apparently disparate units in 6:19—7:11 do in fact function as the practical exposition of the petitions of the Lord's Prayer and its setting, then 7:12 would form an appropriate summary for the larger section on "righteousness" beginning in 5:21 whose prologue was 5:17–20 (McNeile, *Matthew*, 93; Eichholz, *Bergpredigt*, 155).

What began with a redactional reference to Jesus' coming to fulfill the Law and the Prophets (see Note on 5:17) concludes with another redactional reference to the Law and the Prophets (Grundmann, *Matthäus*, 223). Jesus' coming fulfills the Scriptures' promise of God's acting to establish a new relationship with his own (e.g., 5:3–12, 17–18), the consequence of which involves a corresponding conduct, the "greater righteousness" (5:20), based on and growing from this new relationship in its horizontal (5:21–48) as well as its vertical dimension (6:1—7:11). Therefore, the evangelist uses the Golden Rule taken from its Q setting to conclude this larger section of the Sermon (5:17—7:12) and to set the stage for the warnings that follow (7:13–27).

The content of this saying has parallels in a broad spectrum of ancient literature in the Greek, Roman, Jewish, and Oriental world (Dihle, *Regel*, 8–12, 80–109; Jeremias, *RGG* 2:1688). One of the most commonly cited parallels comes from the Talmud where Hillel, who lived just before

Jesus, answered a query about the Law's content with "What is hateful
to you, do not do to your fellow-creature. That is the whole Law; all
else is explanation" (*b. Šabb* 31a). Numerous other parallels exist in
late Jewish literature (e.g., Tob 4:15; Sir 31(34):15; *2 Enoch* 61:1; *Ep
Arist* 207; *T Naph* 1). Although some have attributed the positive formulation to Jesus and the negative to common sense and thereby distinguished between the basic thrust of the two formulations (e.g., Schlatter,
Matthäus, 247), the positive expression also appears in *Ep Arist* 207, *T
Naph* 1, and *2 Enoch* 61:1. Furthermore, the early church preserved
the saying in its negative form in *Did* 1:2 and Acts 15:20, 28 *(v.l.)*. In
other words, it would be difficult to demonstrate that the content of
the Golden Rule in itself was unique to Jesus or the early church.

The question whether the more common negative formulation merely
expresses a common-sense principle based on a selfish motive to avoid
receiving the undesirable in return or on a more noble concern for other
remains moot for the Christian usage. Both the Western interpolations
in Acts 15:20, 28 and *Did* 1:2 use the negative formulation but based
on one's concern for others more than oneself. The variant readings of
Acts 15 occur within the Apostolic Decree forbidding Gentile behavior
detrimental to Jewish-Christian and Gentile-Christian fellowship. And
Did 1:2 uses the Golden Rule as an extension of the commandment to
love God first and then one's neighbor as oneself. In neither case does
the Rule reflect a selfish concern. These and later usages although negatively expressed concur with the positive expression found in Q.

As in *Did* 1:2, the usages in both Luke and Matthew correlate with
the love commandment. In Luke 6:31 the Rule follows the examples
of conduct illustrating love for the enemy (6:29–30) and offers a principle
for personal conduct towards others, especially one's enemies. Matthew
has reworked this traditional complex (see Notes on 5:38–42 and Comment C on 5:21–48) and set the Rule at the end of the longer section
on conduct befitting God's will (5:21—7:11). But the evangelist by removing this saying from its Love Your Enemies context in Q has not lost
sight of its connection with and basis in the love commandment, since
his summary usage in 7:12 as that of the Law and the Prophets corresponds with his redactional notation that the Law and the Prophets
hinge on the love commandment in 22:37–40. Therefore, the Golden
Rule must be seen against the background of the love commandment
as a practical expression of love for others.

therefore. The conjunction οὖν, omitted in the translation, does not
follow logically from what immediately precedes. Rather, it represents

the evangelist's conclusion to the larger section of the Sermon setting forth one's "good deeds" (5:16) as an indication of the presence of the new age (5:3–12) that has dawned through Jesus' coming (5:17–18). These "good deeds" refer, as we have seen, to the "greater righteousness" (5:21–48) and the "doing of righteousness" (6:1—7:11) as befits the sons of the Father (e.g., 5:16, 45–48; 6:1–18, 32–33; 7:7–11). After concentrating initially in the larger section of 5:17—7:11 on the new relationship between individuals to be seen in the conduct demanded in 5:21–48, the evangelist turned to the relationship between individuals and God seen in the conduct demanded in 6:1—7:11. He now returns (*therefore, οὖν*) to the former (5:21–48) by using the Golden Rule as a summary of the way one was to live in terms of the new relationship with both God and others (Grundmann, *Matthäus,* 225).

all the things. Luke 6:31 by contrast has the adverbial expression, "As you wish . . . so do," with view to the manner or quality of one's actions (cf. οὕτως καί in Matt 7:12). Matthew's *all the things* (πάντα ὅσα ἐάν) adds a quantitative dimension (Bonnard, *Matthieu,* 101). Yet this phrase may also reflect the underlying tradition, since both *Did* 1:2 and Acts 15:20, 28 *(v.l.)* also have ὅσα ἐάν. The use of πάντα as a reinforcement of the inclusive character of the statement corresponds to the evangelist's usage elsewhere (e.g., 6:33, cf. 13:46; 18:25; 28:20).

that you want others to do to you. Both Matthew and Luke share a common construction (θέλητε/θέλετε ἵνα ποιῶσιν), while *Did* 1:2 and Acts 15:20, 28 *(v.l.)* have θέλω with γίνομαι in the first half and ποιέω in the second half. The specific reference to what one "does" (ποιέω) moves from the theoretical to the actual in a statement of how one acts towards another. This positive formulation sets the standard for one's conduct in terms of one's own desires but not necessarily with the idea of attaining or obtaining one's desires from another. The exhortation does not imply manipulative behavior in its context here, in Luke 6:31, or in *Did* 1:2. The standard serves as a guide, not a goal for one's actions.

so do yourself. This use of οὕτως καί appears often in Matthew (19x in contrast to parallels; Sand, *Gesetz,* 95), but Luke also uses his "likewise" (ὁμοίως) frequently (11x; cf. 3x in Matt, 2x in Mark). Thus it is impossible to determine which was earlier.

For this is the Law and the Prophets. This conclusion is missing in Luke 6:31 and most likely stems from Matthew (cf. 22:40 and 5:17). The *Law and the Prophets* standing for the Scriptures occurs in two contexts for Matthew; the one (5:17, 11:13, par. Luke 16:16) has a fulfillment motif in terms of Jesus' coming (see Note on 5:17) and the other

(7:12; 22:40) has a normative motif (Trilling, *Israel,* 173). Yet these two moments, as we have seen, are closely related in Matthew. With Jesus' coming that fulfills the Scriptural promise of God's redemptive activity in history on behalf of his own also comes the corresponding conduct anticipated for the new age (e.g., Jer 31:31–34; Ezek 36:25–27; cf. Isa 56:1; 2:2–6, par. Mic 4:1–5). God's will comes to fruition in history as he establishes his sovereign rule, his Kingdom, through Jesus Messiah (e.g. 4:23; 5:3–12, 17–18; 8–9), but his will is also accomplished in the lives and conduct of his own (5:14–16, 21—7:11; cf. 7:16–23). This conduct itself characteristic of the new age represents a part of the fulfillment motif, the "Zion-Torah" of the age of salvation (see Note and Excursus on 5:17).

Comments

This section of apparently randomly selected units of tradition from the Q material with only one unit found in the Sermon tradition (7:1–5, par. Luke 6:35–42) has often stood in stark contrast to the other sections in Matthew's Sermon with their more obvious homogeneity (e.g., 5:3–12, 13–16, 17–20, 21–48; 6:1–18 [7–15]; 7:13–27). Yet traditional, thematic, and lexical indications present within this block of material do point to a unity not inherent within the material itself but derived from this section's relationship to the redactionally inserted unit of the Lord's Prayer (6:7–15). Rather than being contextually related to each other, four of the six units (6:19–24, 25–34; 7:1–5, 6) correspond to successive petitions in the Lord's Prayer. One rounds off this larger section on prayer as it began, with a note of assurance (7:7–11, cf. 6:7–8), and the last unit offers a summary to the entire section on the "greater righteousness" (5:21—7:11) whose prologue begins with 5:17. Therefore, one might justifiably call the section in 6:19—7:11 the Life of Prayer, since it offers a practical commentary on living according to the Lord's Prayer.

A. Your Kingdom Come: 6:19–24

The first block of material consists of three traditional units using different metaphors to make the same basic point. One's "treasure," "eye," and "master" betray one's commitment, one's priorities in life. Each metaphor illustrates graphically the fundamental alternatives confronting one in the gospel of the Kingdom. Or more precisely, each example points to the only alternative left the one who honestly prays: "Let your name be made holy; let your sovereign rule come; and let your will be done on earth as in heaven" (6:9–10). To pray that prayer, to make those petitions, is to offer oneself in total commitment to God's sovereign rule and give him and his will first claim and priority in one's life.

1. The first example contrasts storing treasure where it can be lost with storing treasure in a safe place beyond the reach of any kind of loss, namely, "in heaven" (6:19–21). But the ultimate significance of this unit lies in the final declaration that identifies the focal point of one's life ("your heart") with one's treasure and thus defines the true nature of one's treasure (6:21). One's treasure is what controls one's very person.

Matthew has taken this material from his Q tradition (cf. Luke 12:33–34), rearranged the order (cf. 6:25–34, par. Luke 12:22–32), and used it as the first of three units, each with a similar thrust. Opening with a warning (6:19) followed by an admonition with identical form and wording (6:20), the unit concludes with a declaration (6:21).

The warning prohibits one from storing treasure on earth where natural processes can destroy or human forces can steal it. The stage is set with a vivid description of how one loses treasure here on earth. The natural forces, "moths" and "worms" (see Note on 6:19), suggest a treasure of fine cloth or clothing reminiscent of Isa 58:8: "The moth will eat them like a garment, and the worm will eat them like wool" (cf. also James 5:2). The human forces, "thieves," steal the treasure by using the appropriate break-in methods for that time, by "digging through" the walls. In other words, the warning of 6:19 grows out of common, everyday experience.

The almost verbally identical admonition of 6:20 simply relocates one's treasure in heaven rather than on earth, since neither natural nor human forces can destroy it there. The function of the metaphor is clear. But one is left with the question of how one stores up treasure in heaven or, more to the point, what kind of treasure one can store now in heaven. In one sense, the admonition appears to share a clear parallel in Jewish literature. Tob 4:7, 9–10 encourages the reader to "Give alms from your possessions . . . so you will be laying up a good treasure for yourself against the day of necessity. For charity delivers from death. . . ." Luke 12:33 seems to concur by admonishing one to "sell your possessions, and give alms; provide yourselves with purses that do not grow old."

Therefore, treasure in heaven comes as the result of one's sharing of earthly treasure or wealth in favor of the poor. The natural conclusion of Luke 12:33 would be to forego amassing treasures or wealth here in lieu of helping the poor and gaining a more secure "wealth" in the life to come. The metaphor consequently appears to have a dual thrust: the foregoing of wealth in this life and the amassing of wealth for the life to come.

Yet to take the metaphor as qualitatively distinguishing between material and spiritual values or as setting off this life from the life to come is to short-circuit the metaphor. The metaphor does not end in either Matthew or Luke with the comparison between treasures stored on earth and treasures stored in heaven. Rather, the concluding statement introduced by the explanatory "for" sets a different motif as the crux. The stress is neither on the place nor on heavenly versus earthly treasure per se. The issue goes much deeper. One's treasure ultimately indicates where one's personal priorities lie: "Where your treasure is, there will your heart be also." To that extent this unit parallels the parable of the Treasure in the Field that cost its purchaser all that he had (13:44).

Therefore, the unit invites us to make a commitment, to yield ourselves ("heart"), totally to that which is not transient but is "heavenly." The primary focus then of "treasure" directs attention to one's person, the "heart" as the control center of one's life. The one whose "heart" is set on "heaven," the sphere of God's rule and sovereignty, lives out the petition, "Let your sovereign rule come . . . on earth as in heaven." The heavenly treasure does not consist exclusively in what we do but in who we are and how we live in relationship to "our Father in heaven."

2. The second example (6:22–23) compares the function of the eye for the body with one's life-controlling perspective. This traditional unit has its almost verbatim Q parallel in Luke 11:34–35 where, following the Lamp and Bushel parable (11:33, par. Matt 5:15), it serves as a warning to a growing audience (Luke 11:29). Matthew's selection of it for this context may stem from its thematic similarity to 6:19–21 where the "heart" offers a parallel to the "eye" here.

The unit opens with a statement that the "eye is the lamp for the body" (6:22a). In other words, the eye acts as the source of light for the body. This thesis is then developed by an antithetical parallelism drawing on that metaphor. First, an eye that is healthy offers light for the whole body. Second, by contrast, an unhealthy eye means that the body moves about in darkness. These conclusions drawn from everyday experience then lead to the application of the example to one's total person: "If the light in you is darkness, then how great is that darkness" (6:23b).

Some have interpreted this parable as an allegory with "sound eye," "evil eye," and "body" as figurative expressions. This tendency gains support from the rather unusual use of the Greek word behind "sound" in a physiological rather than the more commonly found ethical context (see Note on 6:22). The use of "body" to connote one's person rather than more literally one's physical body has numerous parallels. Furthermore, the "evil eye" appears within Jewish literature with reference to greed. Accordingly, this material warns against a greedy amassing of things for oneself and serves to expand on the previous example that warned against storing up treasures.

Such an interpretation, however, falters at more than one point. First, the warning of 6:19–21 centered on one's controlling interests, one's treasure identified by one's priorities in life, rather than on material goods as such. Second, the ultimate comparison in 6:22–23 lies between the "light" of the body and the "light" in you (6:21, 23b) rather than the "sound/unsound eye." The quality of one's eye comes into question only in support of the thesis that the eye is the lamp for the body. In other words, if the eye is healthy, the body has light; if the eye is not healthy, the body is in darkness. No need for any figurative meanings arises from this context. Third, even the unusual use of the adjective "sound" to refer to the eye may stem from an underlying Hebrew/Aramaic term signifying wholeness, something without defect, as in the case of a sacrificial animal (see Note on 6:22). It most certainly does not render the more expected contrast to "evil eye" with the more common "good eye" familiar to Jewish literature. Fourth, the argument moves from the lesser to the greater. If the physical eye brings light/darkness to one's physical body, the light within does even more so to one's person.

The crucial question in this passage involves the meaning of "the light in you." Is this light also to be taken literally or figuratively? Taken literally, "the light in you" might refer to the soul as it does in Prov 20:27 or one's conscience or reason. Or it might refer to an undefined inner light that shines from within a person. Yet neither of these possibilities makes sense in this context. In fact, each stands in tension within the unit itself. The first alternative would have the ultimate comparison between the eye as the external source of light and the soul, conscience, or reason as the internal. Yet the contrast does not pertain to the sources of light but to the light itself. The second alternative more accurately sets the comparison between the "lamp" of the body (6:22a) and the inner "light" (6:23b) but leaves unanswered the meaning of the inner light.

Perhaps one clue to the "light in you" lies in the broader context of Q. Just prior to this unit Luke has the parable referring to lighting a lamp and what one does with that lamp (11:33, par. Matt 5:15). Furthermore, the implication drawn from the context of Luke 11:29–36 focuses on Jesus' ministry and warns the audience to take care "lest the light in you be darkness" (11:35). Matthew has already used a similar light motif with Jesus' ministry at the outset of his Gospel in conjunction with Isa 8:27—9:1 (4:15–17), and he further developed it in 5:15–16 with reference to the disciples (see Notes on 5:15–16). The "light in you," therefore, might well connote one's participation in the "light" of Jesus' ministry. This use of the light motif finds numerous parallels in the New Testament (e.g., Luke 16:8; several Johannine references; 2 Cor 6:14–15; 1 Thess 5:5; Rom 13:12; and 1 Pet 2:9) and in Judaism, especially in Qumran where the covenanters were known as the "sons of light" (e.g., 1QS 1:9–10; 2:16; 3:13, 24–25; 1QM 1:11, 13, 14) in contrast to the "sons of darkness."

By moving from the common experience of the eye as the light for the body, this example concludes by noting how great the loss to one's person, should the inner light be dark. If the "light in you" refers to participation in the light manifested in Jesus' ministry, the Kingdom (cf. 4:15–17, 23), then this unit calls one to let that light shine to illuminate one's life. Just as the first example in 6:19–21 of the treasure expressed one's controlling interest in terms of one's "heart," this example in 6:22–23 points to the light (cf. "eye") that gives perspective to one's living. Both units call for a life lived with God at the center ("treasure in heaven") in light of his sovereign rule ("light in you") as prayed in the opening petitions of the Lord's Prayer (6:9–10).

3. The third example (6:24) moves to the impossibility of serving two masters. This unit explicitly states what is implicit in the first two. Luke 16:13 offers the almost verbatim Q parallel in the context of the parable of the Wise Servant (16:1–13). The evangelist's decision to use it in this context appears again to be thematic. One might see an underlying motif of wealth behind treasure in 6:19–21, greed ("evil eye") in 6:22–23, and mammon in 6:24. But as noted above, this theme at most remains definitely secondary—if present at all. The common motif revolves around one's commitment or one's allegiance as especially seen in this example. Perhaps the evangelist brought this third unit into play here because the number of examples in 6:19–24 would then correspond in general

with the first three petitions of the Lord's Prayer regarding the Father's activity on "earth as in heaven" (6:9–10).

The thesis sentence meets us at the outset: "No one is able to serve two masters" (6:24a). One might want to take issue with such a categorical statement, not only in view of the somewhat common experience today of holding two jobs, but also in view of the definite possibility of having two masters even in the ancient world (cf. Acts 16:16, 19). Yet the force of this saying lies behind the verb "to serve." Its usage here implies total allegiance, as the following explanation indicates.

Inevitably, one of the two masters will get priority. Serving two masters involves a collision course where choices have to be made. At such times, one must display preference in favor of one master at the expense of another, as seen in the verbs to "love the one" and to "hate the other," which is meant comparatively rather than sentimentally, although the latter is not necessarily excluded. In other words, to love and to hate simply express the obvious; to love is to serve and to hate is not to serve when the ultimate choice of conflicting interests arises.

The application comes as a parallel with the thesis sentence: "You cannot serve God and mammon." "Mammon" frequently connotes wealth or money. But such a rendering is much too narrow (see Note on 6:24). In Jewish literature it plays a positive role and generally refers to one's material possessions or personal property. Whereas most people are not wealthy and might avoid the thrust of this saying if so interpreted, few are without material possessions or personal property. But what does this application mean with reference to personal property?

We face again the situation similar to 6:19–21. There treasure stood for what one's heart was centered on, what controlled one's life. Possessions can also become the focus of one's life, one's idol to which one devotes oneself, a master controlling one's allegiance and destiny. Yet this saying does not preclude the possession of personal property (cf. 6:33, par. Luke 12:31). The question is whether one's material possessions are meant to serve or to be served. For the one living in terms of the petitions of the Prayer that God's name be made holy (cf. 5:16), that his sovereign rule be made real and that his will be accomplished on earth as in heaven, God alone is the Master and all that one has comes from him and is to be used in his service. We are free then to serve him rather than our own concerns. We are indeed free to turn to him as Father and Master for his sustenance and care (6:11, 25–34) as the next unit indicates.

B. Give Us Our Daily Bread: 6:25-34

The second half of the Lord's Prayer consists of "we"-petitions concerning one's daily sustenance, one's standing before God and others, and the danger of destroying the relationship offered to us by God (6:11-13). The one who turns to God in prayer for the coming of his sovereign rule and the doing of his divine will offers oneself in trust to God as the Father in heaven and orients one's priorities in life accordingly. With such a perspective one can pray and live dependent upon God to furnish his own the necessities of life. But what does it mean practically speaking to pray: "Give us our daily bread"? This unit of tradition in 6:25-34 drawn again from the Q material (cf. Luke 12:22-32) expands on that petition.

The unit opens with the prohibition of anxious striving for food, drink, and clothing (6:25a) followed by a rhetorical question about the relative value of one's life to food and one's body to clothing (6:25b). Support for this prohibition comes from nature (6:26, 28-30), from the human incapacity to change one's life span by anxious endeavors (6:27), and from the negative example of those who live apart from God (6:31-32). Then come the positive admonition and promise of God's abundant supply in 6:33, rounded off by a final warning in 6:34 that is missing in Luke 12:22-32.

"Worry" in this context connotes much more than simply concern or forethought. It implies an anxious endeavor to secure one's needs, as the examples that follow (6:26-32) and the contrasting admonition (6:33) indicate. This same motif occurs in Phil 4:6 and 1 Pet 5:7 in conjunction with petitionary prayer and suggests the corresponding posture of one's life through prayer. Indeed, "worry" in such a setting would simply reflect another form of laying up treasures on earth, a darkened inner light, and the serving of mammon. In other words, one of the ways we live out our prayer for God's sovereign rule and will is by turning to him as the Sustainer and Provider for his own, since such sustenance was inherent with the presence of the new age (cf. Jesus' ministry to the poor and his table-fellowship with sinners).

The support for this prohibition comes initially from God seen as the Creator. The rhetorical question in 6:25b implies that the One who gave us life and body can certainly supply food and clothing. For example, your Father in heaven feeds the "birds of heaven" who do nothing to raise their own food (6:26), and he clothes the "lilies of the field" in greater splendor than even Solomon had, even though they do nothing to produce their own clothing. By arguing from the lesser to the greater, can God the Creator not do so for his own who are of greater importance than the birds of the heavens or the lilies of the field and who obviously contribute to the raising of their own food and the producing of their own clothes by contrast? The point of comparison with the birds and lilies is not their idleness but God's sustaining provision for his creatures.

Furthermore, anxious efforts to prolong one's life span accomplish little (6:27) and worrying about what one will eat, drink, or wear has its place among the Gentiles who seek to secure such things (6:31–32). The Gentiles stand as a glaring negative example because they represent those who live apart from God as though God did not exist for them. This same use of the Gentiles in a negative comparison also immediately preceded the Lord's Prayer (6:7–8) to remind those who recognize God as their Father that the Father knows their needs before they ask (6:8, 32b). Consequently, those who call him Father can come to him with confidence that he knows the needs of his own (cf. 7:7–11).

With the comparison to the Gentiles who put forth effort to secure food, drink, and clothing in 6:31–32 comes the positive admonition to set one's own efforts in terms of the Father's "Kingdom" and his "righteousness" (6:33). This admonition, when removed from its context, can thus be easily misunderstood. In its present location, the admonition basically follows the pattern of the Lord's Prayer in which one's first petitions involve the coming of God's sovereign rule (6:9–10). The precedence of the "you"-petitions over the "we"-petitions belongs essentially to one's prayer. Only when the "we"-petitions are set in light of the "you"-petitions do they express the petitioner's commitment and trust in the work of the Father.

Jesus does not simply promise his followers that God will provide for his own because of a simplistic view of creation (6:26, 28–30). He does not look at nature and then optimistically conclude that human beings are better than birds and plants and thus have no basis for worry about what they will eat or wear. Rather, Jesus sees creation in light of the presence of the new age, the coming of God's sovereign rule into history (cf. 6:33). Only in light of the new age, the coming of the Kingdom, does Jesus assure his own that the Father in heaven will act on their behalf. Inherent with the Kingdom come the blessings of the Kingdom. Therefore, Jesus calls his disciples to set themselves for the Kingdom, to submit to God's sovereign rule now, and the blessings of the Kingdom, the physical and spiritual needs of the sons of the Kingdom, will be met.

Although the meaning of the Father's Kingdom, his righteousness, and the relationship of the two concepts to each other offers numerous alternatives, the basic question has to do with the force of "Kingdom" in this passage for the evangelist. If the Kingdom refers exclusively to the future consummation of God's rule in history, then the admonition suggests that one should seek above all to attain it in contrast to one's material needs. Accordingly, "his righteousness" might function coordinately with his "Kingdom" to refer to the vindication of his own, their deliverance and salvation from the hands of their enemies. Or "his righteousness" may be subordinate to the "Kingdom" as the means by which one attains the Kingdom through a right conduct pleasing to God (see Note on 6:33). If the Kingdom, however, is not exclusively future in this saying, then both concepts take on a different tone. The question must find its answer within the context of 6:25–34.

The theme of this traditional unit has been the anxious pursuit of one's material needs—food and clothing. Jesus warns his own against permitting such concerns to preoccupy their endeavors but rather he admonishes them to look to the Father in confidence (cf. 6:30–32) who, as Creator and Redeemer, can supply one's needs for the present (6:25b–30, 33). These concerns hardly bespeak the coming consummation. They involve the here and now of the disciple's existence. Even in the broader context, this unit accompanies the previous (6:19–21) and following units (7:1–5, 6) as one of the practical expositions of the Lord's Prayer for one's life with this one being an elaboration of the request for bread "today." Therefore, the context of 6:33 clearly pertains to one's present needs and God's supply.

With that context in mind, no sufficient reason surfaces for taking "Kingdom" as exclusively future. Indeed, the promise of 6:33b explicitly states that "all these things," referring to one's material needs in the context, will be "added," a verb that implies the receipt of more than simply one's material needs (see Note on 6:33). In other words, the object of one's actual pursuit, namely, the Father's Kingdom, is also included in God's provision now. Such an understanding also corresponds with the larger context of the petition for the Father's sovereign rule to come on earth as in heaven (6:10) and with the practical explication of how that works itself out in one's life in the previous material of 6:19–24. The Lord's Prayer involves both a personal and present as well as a future and cosmic dimension, just as does the concept of the Kingdom in Jesus' ministry (see Note on 5:3). But the former comes to center stage here in the practical explications of 6:19—7:6.

If, therefore, the pursuit of the Kingdom eventuates in one's receiving it as God's gift, we must also interpret "righteousness" accordingly. Matthew has consistently used this term in the Sermon to mean both the conduct in keeping with God's will for his own and the relationship established by God between himself and his own vertically and among his own horizontally that enables one to live in keeping with his will (see Note on 6:33 and Excursus in 5:6). In 6:33 the evangelist adds "righteousness" as a corollary with "Kingdom," since God's sovereign rule and his will are integrally related (cf. 6:10). To pursue the Kingdom is to yield to God's sovereign rule in one's life; to pursue righteousness is to live so that his will is done in one's life. Righteousness means doing the will of the Father (cf. 5:20 with 7:21). Yet Matthew sees both the presence of God's rule and the doing of the Father's will to be part of God's enabling gift to his own. These primary benefits come from the Father who "adds" to them the benefits of our material needs (6:33b).

What then does it mean to pray: "Give us our daily bread?" First, it means negatively that we do not spend our energies with debilitating anxiety attempting to secure our personal needs. Nor does it mean that we can sit idly by and irresponsibly expect God to feed and clothe us as he does the birds and flowers. Implicit in the comparison with the birds and the lilies lies not only the difference in worth between the human creature and the animal and plant world but also the inherent capacity of the human creature to sow, reap, and store as well as to labor and spin. There is nothing here to suggest that God's supply does not come through one's normal activities. Second, it means positively to live life in light of God's redemptive actions in history, to live our life under God's sovereign rule, and to do his will above all else. Living in this manner, we view all of life as a gift from God. The ability to raise food and produce clothing then takes its appropriate place in our lives. Such a perspective will not only mean living in dependence upon God but will also mean practicing appropriate stewardship with what we have as part of God's blessing.

But what about hungry Christians? Does their presence in the world imply lack of faith on their part or that God selectively answers the requests of his own? Christians suffer from famine and malnutrition as do non-Christians. What then does this explication of the fourth petition have to say to the "realities" of life?

First, we must not overlook the basic thrust of this unit. As an explication of the fourth petition, it functions primarily negatively. One does not pray "Give us our bread" and then live as though it were solely one's own responsibility. Such an attitude leads to a self-centered sense of accomplishment and ownership when successful or an anxiety-driven pursuit of security when not. Neither recognizes God's role in one's life and both are more pagan than Christian (6:31–32). Therefore, this unit addresses very practically what it means to live under God's sovereign rule in terms of our attitudes and actions regarding the necessities of life. It does not intend to assure us that we will never go hungry or in need of shelter.

Second, the question of hunger in particular or natural calamities in general relates to the nature of God's reign in history. The age of plenty that accompanies the consummation of the Kingdom belongs to the "not-yet" of the future when God will ultimately act to remove the forces of evil and supply his own with plenty. Caught between the present coming of God's sovereign reign in history and its future consummation, his own will suffer both from their enemies as well as from the forces of evil including hunger, sickness, and death. Such personal suffering and loss occur for the Christian as a part of a fallen, sinful world. Such experiences do not necessarily reflect "little faith." Yet this passage remains equally as pertinent for the person in dire need as for the person with plenty—one's priorities are to remain submissive to God's sovereign rule and obedient to his will rather than to pursue anxiously the securing of one's own necessities at the expense of the former.

Third, since God's sovereign rule and all the benefits for our material needs come from God to us, this passage suggests by implication that we can become a part of God's redemptive force in history by sharing these benefits with those who are in need. God's sovereign rule comes into history through his own. Part of the presence of the Kindgom is indeed material blessings. Therefore, we can hardly live under God's reign, receive his blessings, and not use them to help alleviate the evil of hunger and need elsewhere. Not only do we recognize that all we have comes from God, but we also recognize that sharing that with others to remove their suffering is to defeat the enemy and to "seek the Kingdom . . . on earth as in heaven." Therefore, while this passage deals primarily with the individual's relationship to God in the prayer for daily food, it also deals with the individual's relationshiop to God in terms of the needs of others. The vertical and the horizontal relationships belong together.

C. Forgive Us . . . As We Have Forgiven: 7:1–5

Matthew at this point returns to the Sermon tradition momentarily for the first time since the section on Love Your Enemies (5:44–48, par. Luke 6:27–36). He does so because this unit on Judging (7:1–5, par. Luke 6:37–42) appropriately corresponds with the fifth petition in the Lord's Prayer. This unit consists of a categorical prohibition of judging (7:1) followed by two reasons set in parallelism (7:2) and a hyperbolic example (7:3–5).

One of the first questions involves the meaning of "to judge." This word in Greek as well as English covers a broad spectrum of meanings from "discerning" to "condemning" (see Note on 7:1). The immediate context supports the latter usage. The prohibition itself has a negative result clause, "lest you be judged," that is expanded by the following bases in the future passive ("you will be judged" and "you will be measured") connoting the final judgment before God (7:2). Furthermore, this passage, as did the previous two (6:19–24, 25–34), pertains to the larger context of the Lord's Prayer. The fifth petition asks for forgiveness and also notes one's own act of forgiveness toward others (6:12). "Judging" would then be the opposite of forgiving. Therefore, judging in the immediate and larger context connotes the censorious condemnation of another.

The apparent reciprocity between one's actions and God's in dealing with one at the final judgment has appeared elsewhere in the Sermon (e.g., 5:7; 6:12, 14–15). Both the prohibition and the bases (7:1, 2) make it quite explicit here. Consequently, we might conclude that by not "judging" or "measuring" another we ourselves can avoid being judged at the final judgment. Yet the thrust of these passages does not follow a strict *do et des.* While it is valid that the one who judges another will be similarly judged, it does not follow that one can escape judgment entirely by not judging.

This reciprocity addresses our capacity to know and experience God's gracious mercy towards us rather than our deserving of same by virtue of our actions (see Note on 6:12). Luke 6:36 commands one to be merciful as the Father in heaven is merciful. One exhibits one's own genuine appropriation of God's mercy by showing such mercy toward others (e.g., Matt 18:23–35). Therefore, to stand in judgment over another means that we ourselves have yet to experience God's forgiving mercy and cannot expect to receive it at the judgment. To judge another sets ourselves over that individual as though we ourselves were not culpable. But the warning that we shall be judged by the same judgment and measured by the same measure indicates that we too are in need of mercy as the following hyperbole graphically illustrates.

Two rhetorical questions set the stage. How can anyone with a beam in the eye see well enough to notice the tiny speck in a brother's eye? Or how could one with a beam in the eye remove the speck from another's? Both questions remind us of our blindness to our own great failings and our need for mercy. This same motif lies behind the Unjust Servant in 18:23–35, whose treatment of another demonstrated his failure to experience the implications of his master's great mercy.

Yet the concluding admonition appears on the surface to set aside what has stood in 7:1–2 as a categorical prohibition of judging by giving set instructions for how to deal with another's sin. First, one is to remove the beam from one's own eye (cf. 7:4), then one can see (cf. 7:3) to remove the speck (cf. 7:4) from another's eye (see Note on 7:5). Having recognized and dealt with the major failure in one's own life, one in humility as a forgiven sinner could then come to another concerning the latter's rather minor fault.

Yet this interpretation still leaves the admonition of 7:5 in opposition to the apodictic command not to judge at all and at odds with the sayings in 5:7; 6:12, 14–15, and 18:35. By maintaining the hyperbole and the irony of the examples in 7:3–4, this admonition, like the command to cast the first stone in John 8:7, leaves us with the great sense of our own failures and need for mercy and forgiveness (6:12a). Therefore, the emphasis of 7:5 would fall on the charge, "hypocrite," the playing of the role that God alone can have by standing in judgment over another. The size of our "debt" (6:12; 18:23–34) is so great that we have no room to condemn another.

But what about church discipline, the "fruit inspection" that seems to follow from 7:15–20? Is that not judging? Is there no room for dealing with evil in a brother's life? Perhaps by distinguishing between the absolute prohibition of judging in 7:1–5 and the following statement that one can distinguish a false prophet by his fruits appears to beg the question. Yet the issues and attitudes are separate. Going to a brother in error as one who has been forgiven with a desire to help and restore him through mercy and forgiveness (cf. Gal 6:1) is quite remote from standing in condemnatory judgment over another's faults. After all, one must recognize another's "debt" or fault in order even to offer mercy and forgiveness. Consequently, not judging does not imply overlooking sin. But such "discerning" does not compare with the censorious judgment of 7:1–5. Should the offending brother, however, prove recalcitrant and the fruits indicate an opposition to God's mercy and forgiveness, then the behavior must be seen for what it is. Only God, however, can pronounce the final judgment. We must leave the door of mercy and forgiveness open even if disciplinary action has to be taken.

This unit, therefore, corresponds to the fifth petition of the Lord's Prayer where forgiving others (6:12b) stands at the extreme opposite of censorious condemnation (7:1) towards those at fault. The conclusion, with its charge of "hypocrite" reminding us of the beam in our own eye (7:5), appropriately directs us back to the petition: "Forgive us our debts" (6:12a). In this manner the evangelist adapts the Sermon tradition on Judging that began with a call for mercy towards others (Luke 6:36, cf. Matt 5:48) to fit his purposes in his section, which sets forth practically the way one lives according to the petitions of the Lord's Prayer.

D. Lead Us Not into Temptation: 7:6

The last unit, dealing with the various petitions of the Prayer, consists of a single saying that stands without parallel in Mark or Luke. Formulated as another prohibition (cf. 6:19, 25; 7:1), its meaning can hardly be missed. One simply does not waste something of value on an inappropriate and undeserving object. Yet, removed from context, this obvious point lacks a point of reference. Set against the background of the Lord's Prayer, as were the previous units, its point of reference becomes quite specific.

The metaphor could hardly depict a more graphic scene. The contrasts vividly portray objects that are sacred and precious on the one hand and animals that are common, with the swine actually ceremonially unclean, on the other. The first object, "that which is holy," most likely refers to meat dedicated for use in sacrifices (see Note on 7:6); the second, "pearls," involved precious stones whose value is self-evident. By giving sacred meat to dogs and throwing pearls as swill to swine, one obviously desecrates what is holy and valued. Furthermore, the results that follow underscore the waste when the swine merely trample the pearls underfoot and the dogs ravenously attack their feeders.

Since most interpretations have taken this saying without an immediate context—there being no obvious one in 7:1–11—the tendency has been to interpret it allegorically with reference to the Church's mission. The referents lie at hand in Judaism with both dogs and swine used symbolically for Gentiles and heretics (see Note on 7:6). If, however, this saying belongs along with the previous units to the larger context of the Lord's Prayer, then its meaning closely parallels the salt metaphor of 5:13 whose end is similar to the result in 7:6. The saying would then be a warning against apostasy and expand on the sixth and seventh petitions for deliverance from temptation and the Evil One (6:13). Rather than being an allegory, as such, the saying metaphorically expresses the great waste involved when one abandons that sacred and precious life as son or daughter of the Kingdom.

One must not take lightly the privilege of the Kingdom nor the life in it. Matthew repeatedly calls his readers and us to remember that God demands a life lived in keeping with his will, a possibility that he offers to us as part of his sovereign reign, the coming of the age of salvation. In fact, the concluding sections of the Sermon (7:13–27) pick up this very theme, just as the section on discipleship opened with it in 5:31 (see Note on 5:13). Yet by placing this saying in conjunction with the final petitions of the Lord's Prayer, the evangelist reminds his readers that even the warning against apostasy can only be carried out through a life of prayer and dependence upon the Father.

E. To Those Who Ask: 7:7–11

With this unit on Answered Prayer (7:7–11) drawn from the Q context of the Lord's Prayer (cf. Luke 11:9–13), Matthew rounds off the longer section on prayer which he developed by inserting the Lord's Prayer complex in 6:7–15 and following it with traditional elements corresponding to the respective petitions (6:19—7:6). This unit consists of a positive admonition to pray with the imperatives "ask," "seek," and "knock" (7:7) followed by the assuring promise set in identical parallelism (7:8). Then comes an illustration drawn from the experience of a father whose son has need of food (7:9–10) and applied by comparison as the conclusion (7:11).

In Luke 11:9–13 this material concludes the instruction on prayer initiated by the disciples' request that Jesus teach them how to pray. Matthew has this unit in the same location relatively speaking (6:7–15, 19—7:11). Furthermore, he has introduced the Lord's Prayer with a reference to "asking" the Father (6:8), a concept that opens this unit ("ask and it shall be given you," 7:7a) and concludes it ("to those who ask him," 7:11). In this way, the evangelist also brings to a conclusion the larger block of material on "doing righteousness" beginning in 6:1 and pertaining to one's vertical relationship with the Father. Prayer involves one's life (6:19—7:6) as well as one's words (6:9–13). Consequently, the life of prayer (6:7–15, 19—7:6) corresponds to "righteousness" as conduct lived in keeping with one's relationship to the Father.

Living a life of prayer, however, does not preclude the Father's granting one that life in answer to the earnest request of his child. The requests known to the Father before one asks (6:8) are still to be made as stressed by the three imperatives, each pertaining to prayer (see Note on 7:7). Whereas "ask" frequently expresses the petition of prayer, both "seek" and "knock" simply reinforce that command. For example, Jer 29:12–13 promises, "you will call upon me . . . and *pray* to me, and I will *hear* you. You will *seek* me and *find* me," in a context combining praying and seeking. Knocking was also used metaphorically for prayer in Judaism. Therefore, all three clauses admonish one to make request in prayer. The bases for this command in 7:8 simply turn the commands into declarations of assurance that the Father will hear and respond accordingly.

By way of supporting argument, a rhetorical question asks who would respond to his son's request for bread and fish by deceptively offering him a similar-looking but useless—indeed, harmful—counterpart in the form of a stone or serpent (7:9–10). The answer, of course, is an emphatic "No one!" Therefore, with this as the basis, the conclusion declares that if fallen human beings respond to the needs of their sons in light of the latters' request, how much more so will the Father in heaven do for those who ask him (7:11).

Removed from the context, this unit appears to give a blank check to any who have a desire. Without any apparent constraints either in terms of what is requested or who makes the request, all ("everyone who" in 7:8) may "ask," "seek," and "knock" with the promise of "receiving," "finding," and having it "opened." Yet this traditional unit has the same basic context in both Matthew and Luke. The subjects and the object are indeed qualified. Those invited to pray have a special relationship with God as their Father, as has been seen repeatedly in the larger context (6:6, 7, 14, 15, 26, 32), in the heart of the comparison and conclusion of this unit (7:9–11), and above all in the address of the Lord's Prayer (6:9).

The object of one's prayer also finds its qualification within the larger context. In 7:11 Jesus promises that the Father will give his own "good things," a term that stands in parallelism with the "good gifts" that a father gives his son (7:11a). The comparison of 7:9–12 suggests that the gifts pertain to one's material needs as 6:33 has previously promised. But this unit's role as the conclusion of the larger section on prayer invites one to pray with the promise of the Father's response to all our needs. These needs which the Father knows even before they are voiced (6:8) are set forth in the Lord's Prayer (6:9–13) and in the life lived accordingly (6:19—7:6). In other words, our requests encompass the whole of life as lived under God's sovereign rule, the life in the Kingdom.

This concluding unit on Answered Prayer assures us, therefore, that God hears our requests for a life lived in terms of the presence of the Kingdom. God will work to make his name holy, to bring his rule into effect, to accomplish his will through us as we seek "his Kingdom and righteousness." Furthermore, he will grant us the blessings of the Kingdom by meeting our daily needs, forgiving us our sins and delivering us from the Evil One. In short, the Father enables us to live life now in light of the vertical relationship established by him with his own as promised for the day of salvation.

F. The Golden Rule: 7:12

The so-called Golden Rule concludes the entire section on "righteousness" beginning with the prologue in 5:17–20. The Lucan parallel of this Q saying occurs within the Love Your Enemies material (Luke 6:31), where it finds a more natural setting. Matthew, however, has relocated it in this context and added the summary suggesting that the Rule is the constituent of the Law and the Prophets.

Although the Rule offers a practical guide for conduct between individuals and, taken from its context, often functions as the epitome of Jesus' or Christian ethics, the evangelist has a much more profound purpose behind his use of it in 7:12. Matthew has just completed a lengthy section on "doing righteousness" pertaining to one's life lived in relationship with the Father (6:1—7:11). This material followed another section on life lived in relationship to others, a section which concluded with the material on Love Your Enemies (5:44–48). Both of these sections constitute the "greater righteousness" demanded in 5:20, a conduct growing out of the restored relationships between God and his own and among his own. Furthermore, these restored relationships and the corresponding conduct come through Jesus Messiah, whose coming "fulfills" the Scriptures (5:17–18) by inaugurating the age of salvation with his gospel of the Kingdom.

In order to tie this material together, the evangelist has taken the Rule to be a succinct expression of the life one was to live in the age of salvation. First, by placing it at the end of 6:1—7:11, he sets the Rule in the immediate context of the vertical relationship between the Father and his own, a relationship that conditions one's relationship to others (e.g., 6:12, 14–15; 7:1–5, cf. 5:44–48). Second, he picks up the previous material dealing with one's horizontal relationships (5:21–48), since the Rule's content focuses on one's actions toward others. Because this Rule expresses the manner of life concomitant with the Scriptural promises for the age of salvation which Jesus' coming brought to pass (5:17–18), the Golden Rule, then, as the love commandment in 22:37–40, can be taken by Matthew to be the summary of the Law and Prophets. For him, the Golden Rule, within this context of the relationship with the Father as the determining factor for one's life (6:1—7:11; cf. the first commandment to love the Lord, 22:37–38), states the practical implications of the love commandment toward others (5:43–48; cf. the second commandment to love your neighbor as yourself, 22:39).

With this context in mind, the Rule represents much more than a common-sense rule or self-centered motivation for conduct. The primary focus of this saying is on doing for others rather than on what one will have done in return. To be sure, the Rule does occur in a broad range of ancient literature where it expresses a popular ethical principle often negatively motivated by a desire to avoid someone's retaliation. Even the positive form occurs there, suggesting one's concern for others. Yet the context of the Rule in Jesus' ministry as well as in Matthew and Luke functions within this context of conduct indicative of the age of salvation. One is called to do what is not always "natural," to go beyond the human limitations of conduct to do for another that which brings *shalom* or wholeness (e.g., 5:9, 43–48) in view of the new relationships offered to us by the Father (see Note on 5:48).

Therefore, the Golden Rule sums up the section on "righteousness," conduct in keeping with the relationships that God has established. This conduct does not merely correspond to the "intent" of the Law, the true meaning of the Mosaic Law, nor does it correspond to a new, radicalized understanding of the Law. Rather, this conduct typified by the Golden Rule and the love commandment in 22:37–40 and exemplified by the demands and prohibitions of 5:20—7:11 corresponds to the life in the new age, the life in which God has acted to establish his sovereign rule and enable his own to live accordingly. As such, the Golden Rule offers a summary of the kind of life promised in the Scriptures for the age of salvation and thus reflects the "Law and the Prophets." It is much more than a rule of thumb; it is a rule for life in the Kingdom.

IX. THE NARROW GATE
Matthew 7:13–27

Translation

7 ¹³Enter through the narrow gate.
For the gate is wide and the way is spacious that leads to destruction.
They who enter through it are many. ¹⁴For the gate is narrow and the
way is constricted that leads to life. They who find it are few.

¹⁵Be on your guard against false prophets who come to you in sheep's
clothing but are ravenous wolves inside.

¹⁶By their fruits you will recognize them. Surely, they do not gather
grapes from thorn bushes or figs from thistles, do they? ¹⁷Thus every
good tree produces good fruits, but a rotten tree produces bad fruits.
¹⁸A good tree is not able to bear bad fruits nor is a rotten tree able to
bear good fruits. ¹⁹Every tree not producing good fruit will be cut down
and cast into the fire. ²⁰Indeed, by their fruits you will recognize them.

²¹Not everyone who says to me, "Lord, Lord," will enter the Kingdom;
only the one doing the will of my Father who is in heaven. ²²Many
will say to me in that day, "Lord, Lord, did we not prophesy in your
name? Did we not cast out demons in your name? And did we not
perform many miracles in your name?" ²³Then I shall declare openly
to them, "I never knew you. Depart from me, you who do evil."

²⁴Therefore, everyone who hears these my words and does them will
be like a wise man who built his house on the rock. ²⁵The rain came
down, the torrents came, the winds blew and they beat upon that house.
It did not fall. For its foundation had been laid on the rock.

²⁶Everyone who hears these my words and does not do them will be
like a foolish man who built his house on the sand. ²⁷The rain came,

the torrents came, the winds blew and they struck against that house. It did fall. And its fall was tremendous.

Literary Analysis

This concluding section of the Sermon with its final admonitions calls the audience to hear and respond to the teaching of Jesus Messiah. Finding the core of this material in the Sermon tradition, the evangelist again has actively shaped various traditional elements to expand the underlying Sermon tradition. Whereas the form and source for most of this section seems rather obvious, the primary literary question arises over the structural relationship of the central units of 7:15–23.

As to source, all of 7:13–27 except 7:15 has a parallel in the Q tradition which appears in two contexts in Luke. The first, found in Luke 13:22–30, contains a parallel to 7:13–14, par. Luke 13:23–24, and to 7:22–23, par. Luke 13:26–27. The considerable difference in wording, setting, and context most likely stems from the redactional work of the respective evangelist as the following discussion of the sayings indicates. The second appears at the end of the Sermon where 7:16–20 parallels Luke 6:43–44, 7:21 parallels Luke 6:46, and 7:24–27 parallels Luke 6:47–49. These parallels in the Q Sermon tradition also reflect considerable redactional modification by both evangelists that accounts for their numerous differences. Although some have considered 7:15—the one saying without a Q parallel (cf. Dupont, *Béatitudes* 1:170–71)—to be an isolated logion found in M (e.g., Manson, *Sayings,* 175; guardedly, Davies, *Setting,* 199–200) or a part of a longer traditional complex underlying 7:15–23 (e.g., Krämer, "Propheten," 369–76), the wording consists of traditional motifs found elsewhere in Matthew ("false prophets," 25:11–12; inside/outside, 23:27–28; "sheep and wolves," 10:16). The wording of 7:15 then stems from the tradition, but its construction from Matthew's redaction. The evangelist thus concludes the Sermon by selecting and shaping the tradition to expand the underlying Sermon tradition as he has done throughout the Sermon.

As to forms, this complex contains an amalgam of Wisdom and prophetic sayings. The section opens with a prophetic exhortation in the Wisdom mold whose roots may well go back to Jesus' ministry (e.g., Bultmann, *Tradition,* 77, 105, 119). Luke's setting addressing a Jewish audience most certainly reflects the earlier *Sitz im Leben* in contrast to

Matthew's use with reference to the disciples. Matt 7:15 has the same form stemming from the evangelist's reference to the threat of false prophets. The heart of 7:16–20 (7:16, 18) takes the form of Wisdom sayings consisting basically of two metaphors, one regarding good and rotten trees (7:18, par. Luke 6:43) and one regarding fruit-bearing bushes (7:16, par. Luke 6:44). Both sayings could well have had an original setting in Jesus' ministry to the "righteous," with 7:16a, 20 forming a redactional inclusion, 7:17 a positive, redactional restatement of 7:18, and 7:19 a redactional insertion taken from the Baptist tradition of 3:10, par. Luke 3:9. Matthew has also reworked 7:21, cf. Luke 6:46, into an entrance-saying, and 7:22–23 has become a judgment scene. This section in particular and the Sermon in general then conclude with the parable of the Two Builders set in a symmetrical antithetical parallelism (7:24–27, cf. Luke 6:47–49).

In structure, this series of admonitions brings the Sermon to its conclusion by admonishing those who hear to respond positively to Jesus' words. The exhortations contain alternatives—the one offers life (7:14), entrance into the Kingdom (7:21b), and salvation (7:24–25); the other offers destruction (7:13b), exclusion from the Kingdom (7:21a, 23), and irreparable loss (7:26–27). Furthermore, the admonitions indicate that the response is neither easy nor popular (7:13–14), that it is easily counterfeited (7:15–23), and that it is headed for failure unless based on a firm foundation (7:24–27). These positive exhortations thus serve as warnings as well.

Within this complex, whose beginning (7:13–14) and ending (7:24–27) are clearly delineated, the question surfaces whether the middle unit involves one or two warnings. Matt 7:16–20 definitely refers to the appearance of false prophets. But 7:21–23 has been variously interpreted as, on the one hand, a further elaboration of 7:15–20 (e.g., Bonnard, *Matthieu*, 105; Bultmann, *Tradition*, 117; Eichholz, *Bergpredigt*, 157–62; Grundmann, *Matthäus*, 234; Schweizer, *Matthew*, 186–89; idem, "Observance," 224–25) or, on the other hand, as a separate warning referring to false disciples (e.g., Gaechter, *Matthäus*, 246–49; Manson, *Sayings*, 176; Schniewind, *Matthäus*, 104–105; and most recently, Hill, "Prophets," 335–48).

Apart from the numerous points of contact between 7:21–23 and 7:15–20 (see Note on 7:21–23), 7:21–23 taken as an elaboration of 7:15–20 would form a single unit on false prophets and give us a concluding section consisting of three units (7:13–14, 15–23, 24–27). The section opens with an exhortation to enter the narrow gate (7:13–14). It then moves to a warning about the real threat of being led down the wrong way by false prophets (7:15–23) whose words and deeds cloak an insidious nature that will be revealed at the final judgment. Finally, the section closes with the parable (7:24–27) that illustrates the admonition of 7:13–14 and the doing of the will of the Father in 7:21. In other words, the parable not only explicates the alternatives of 7:13–14 in terms of hearing and doing Jesus' words but also indicates how one can best guard against being misled by the false prophets. In this manner 7:15–20 becomes an integral part of the section rather than having a rather parenthetic function as would be the case given the other alternative. Matt 7:13–27, therefore, though a complex of sources and themes, comes together as a related unit rather than as a series of disparate admonitions.

Notes

7:13–14. These verses open the final section of the Sermon with an exhortation framed in an apodictic command followed by a symmetrical elaboration set in an antithetical parallelism. Luke 13:24 has a parallel saying but with striking differences in context and content. In the setting of Luke 13:23–30 the saying addresses the urgency of entering the Kingdom while there is time. Adapted to the context of 13:24–30, it refers to a "narrow door" (θύρα) rather than *gate,* makes no reference to any *way,* and lacks the antithetical parallelism of Matt 7:13–14. These differences have led some to conclude that the sayings with roots in Jesus' ministry were similar but independent (e.g., Michaelis, *TDNT* 5:71); others to trace an original saying to Jesus' ministry with Matthew and Luke each using transmissional variations of the saying (e.g., Manson, *Sayings,* 175; Wrege, *Überlieferungsgeschichte,* 135); and still others to conclude a common Q tradition reworked by Matthew (e.g., Klostermann, *Matthäusevangelium,* 29; Dupont, *Béatitudes* 1:98–100; Hoffmann, "Πάντες," 195) or Luke (e.g., Schulz, *Spruchquelle,* 309–12). The notes that follow will support the priority of the Matthean saying, leaving moot for our purposes whether Luke found the saying within its present context or himself reworked it.

Enter through the narrow gate. This straightforward command confronts the hearer with the need for a response to that which has been spoken and sets the stage for the concluding warnings against false prophets (7:15–27). But it does so in light of the Sermon's content, especially 5:17—7:12. To *enter* is to *find* life (7:14), a synonym for the Kingdom of Heaven. Thus this exhortation repeats the warning of 5:20, the preface to 5:21—7:12. Whereas the Golden Rule (7:12) itself can hardly represent the *narrow gate* (con. Bornhäuser, *Bergpredigt*, 205-207), as the encompassing conclusion to 5:17—7:11, the Golden Rule does offer an appropriate setting for 7:13-14 (cf. *Did* 1:1-2).

Luke 13:24 shares the common motif of a narrow entry way. But both the verb, "strive to enter," and the object, "the narrow door," betray secondary modifications. The former reflects a paranetic use of a hellenistic expression found in the ethical diatribe, "to strive" to do something (Hoffman, "Πάντες," 196); the latter refers to the "door" of a banquet hall or house in keeping with the setting of 13:25-30. The *gate* (πύλη), by contrast, most likely represents the city gate, perhaps even an allusion to the eschatological hope for the new Jerusalem, a symbol for the coming Kingdom. Yet the following elaborations in 7:13b, 14 show that the primary focus of the *gate* does not lie in its symbolic location but in its function as a means of entry. The question, therefore, arises: What is the *narrow gate?* One can better answer this question after examining the elaborations of 7:13b, 14.

For the gate is wide. The first of two explanatory clauses offers the contrast between the ease and space of the one and the difficulty and limitations of the other. Textually, this opening phrase poses two problems. Rather than the explanatory use of ὅτι = *for,* the Old Latin manuscripts read an exclamatory τι = *how!,* an obvious stylistic modification. The more significant problem involves the absence of *gate* in several manuscripts (ℵ* 1646 it[a,b,c,h,k,] Dia, Cl, Or Cyp Eus Aug) which has led some to view it to be a later adaptation to 7:13a drawn from 7:14. But the presence of *gate* in 7:14 also appears somewhat questionable, since it too is omitted in several mss, some of which omit it in 7:13b (113 182* 482 544 it[a,h,k,] Dia[syr] Cl Tert [Or] Cyp Ps-Cl Eus). One must either drop *gate* from both verses or read it in both. The weight of the manuscript evidence supports the reading in both. Its absence from some texts most likely resulted in part from the tension caused by the apparent inversion of the expected order *way-gate* rather than *gate-way.* One would normally expect the *way* to lead to the *gate* rather than vice versa.

the way is spacious. The figure of *wide gate* (πλατεῖα ἡ πύλη) in contrast to the *narrow gate* (στενὴ ἡ πύλη) of the opening command follows quite naturally. But the use of *spacious* (εὐρύχωρος) with *way* comes as an unusual pairing of terms, since the Greek adjective generally denotes "roominess." Although frequently translated "easy," the adjective denotes ample space appropriate to the *many* that *enter* through it (cf. 7:14). To be sure, the contrast in size also connotes the relative ease and difficulty corresponding to the respective gates and ways that make the exhortation in 7:13a necessary in the first place.

Luke 13:24 maintains the reference to entering the "narrow door" in the explanation that follows, but it has neither the antithetical parallelism nor any mention of the two ways. The contrast between the *few* (ὀλίγοι) and the *many* (πολλοί) also occurs in the broader context of Luke 13:22–24 which suggests its presence in the original saying and implies that Luke somewhat characteristically (e.g., Bultmann, *Tradition,* 92) dropped the more Semitic parallel construction. The absence of the two ways in Luke 13:24 has led several to suggest that their presence in Matt 7:13b–14 was secondary, stemming from the rather common paranetic two-ways motif of Jewish and early Christian tradition (e.g., Dupont, *Béatitudes* 1:98–100; Grundmann, *Matthäus,* 228; Hoffman, "Πάντες," 195; Jeremias, *TDNT* 6:923; Klostermann, *Matthäusevangelium,* 68; Manson, *Sayings,* 175; Wrege, *Überlieferungsgeschichte,* 133–34).

The two-ways motif has its root in the Old Testament, with occurrences in Jer 21:8; Ps 1:6; Prov 14:2. It runs through the intertestamental literature of Sir 21:10; *2 Enoch* 30:15; *T. Asher* 1:3, 5; *Aboth* 2:12–23 and is most developed in 4 Ezra 7:1–9. Its most familiar early Christian expression comes in *Did* 1:1; 2:2; 5:1 and *Barn* 18:1. Numerous rabbinic references (Str-B 1:460–62) and the "way of light" in contrast to the "way of darkness" in Qumran (e.g., 1QS 3:20–21) demonstrate the rather extensive usage of this vocabulary in Judaism and early Christianity.

Yet the widespread usage of the two-ways motif in itself does not offer sufficient basis for positing its secondary character in 7:13–14, whether it was introduced by the evangelist or had its source in the pre-Matthean tradition. One could just as easily argue that the motif in this saying goes back to Jesus' own ministry, since the usage here is neither dualistic nor essentially ethical as was the case in late Judaism and early Christianity. Luke's evidence to the contrary is hardly convincing, since its absence in 13:24 corresponds to the reworking of the saying that altered the metaphor's function from encouraging the entrance through a "narrow door" (13:24a) to warning about being shut out by a "closed door" (13:24b–25). Any reference to the two ways would be completely out of place. Furthermore, to argue that Matthew's usage corresponds to the ethical application of the motif in Judaism and the early church (e.g., Hoffman, "Πάντες," 195) is to understand Matthew's intention here and in the rest of the Sermon too narrowly and from an ethical rather than christological perspective.

But does the two-ways motif fit this context, especially since one would expect the *way* to lead more naturally to the *gate?* Just how do the *gate* and the *way* relate to each other? Jeremias takes the order to be a *hysterion-proteron,* a reversed order, caused by the combination of the two synonymous metaphors to form a double metaphor (*TDNT* 6:923, n. 14; see also Dupont, *Béatitudes* 1:100, n. 2, and Hoffman, "Πάντες," 195). If, however, the *gate* and the *way* were synonymous metaphors, there is no reason they cannot stand as synonymous, independent metaphors in this context, since their presence would underscore the point made by each antithetically parallel sentence in 7:13b, 14. One enters the *gate* (7:13a, b); one enters through the *way* (7:13b). Both metaphors are controlled by the verb *to enter* (7:13a, b). The one does not lead to the other (Michaelis, *TDNT* 5:71; Bonnard, *Matthieu,* 102; Grundmann, *Matthäus,* 230–31). This theme then simply gained further elaboration by the addition of familiar, synonymous metaphor of the *way* explaining the two alternatives.

that leads to destruction. In Jer 21:8 the Lord offers his own "the way of life and the way of death." Although the *way* specifically leads to destruction, one cannot forget that the *gate* also opens to death (cf. Matt 16:18). The parallel in 7:14 indicates that the *destruction* (ἀπώλεια) refers to the ultimate death of the final judgment. Therefore, entering the *wide gate* and the *spacious way* which ends in death sets forth the alternative to entering the *narrow gate.*

they who enter through it are many. This statement finds its material parallel in Luke 13:24 where "many seek to enter but are not able." The *wide gate and spacious way* represents the popular decision, the choice of the majority. The evangelist does not delineate who the *many* are by referring to any particular group. Their identity emerges from the warnings that follow in 7:15–27, and they stand in clear contrast to the *few* of 7:14.

7:14. *For the gate is narrow and the way is constricted.* Resuming the opening reference to the *narrow gate,* the second half of the antithetical parallelism stands in stark contrast to the first half. Just as the *wide gate* and *spacious way* connoted the relative ease with which the majority make their choice, the *narrow gate* (see Note on 7:13 for text critical considerations) and the *constricted way* suggest the difficulty for those choosing to enter. This difficulty is heightened by the final comment: *few find it.*

that leads to life. This qualifier of the *way* (cf. Jer 21:8) contrasts with *the way that leads to destruction* and thus explains the meaning of the *narrow gate.* To enter the *narrow gate* is to *find the way to life* or to enter into *life.* Yet *life* itself represents but another expression for the Kingdom (e.g., 18:8, par. Mark 9:43, 47, where used interchangeably; cf. 5:29–30 where the opposite is hellfire; 19:16–17, 23–30, par. Mark 10:17, 23–31). This saying thus corresponds to the entrance-sayings of 5:20 and 7:21, where a contrast is also made with those who will not enter (cf. 22:12 and 23:13), and serves as an appropriate introduction for the final warnings of 7:13–27.

They who find it are few. Luke has a material parallel but in the introductory question of 13:23: "Lord, will those being saved be few?" The identity of the *few* (ὀλίγοι), like that of the *many,* remains unspecified except in the larger context of 5:20—7:12, cf. 7:21–23. The smallness of the *gate* and *way* in no way implies that the number is set by the space available. Rather, it underscores the contrast with the way chosen by the majority. Only a relative few *"find the way to life."* The verb *find* (εὑρίσκοντες) stands parallel to *enter* in 7:13b. But *to find* does not merely connote the discovery of something hidden. Rather, it connotes the divine revelation of something "sought" (cf. Luke 13:24, "many seek to enter") as in 7:7, 8 (cf. 6:33, par. Luke 12:31). Therefore, to *enter the narrow gate* involves a personal decision to pursue that which God has revealed.

What, then, does it mean to *enter the narrow gate, to find the way of life?* The motif of the two ways with its ethical overtones in Judaism and the *Didache,* as well as the immediate context of 7:15–23, has led many to conclude that Matthew has "ethicized" the original saying in contrast to Luke's urgent "eschatological" exhortation to enter the Kingdom before it is too late. However, one must pause to consider the broader context in Matthew. To be sure, the evangelist has chosen to place the Q saying within the larger context of the Sermon and specifically as an introduction to the final warnings of 7:15–27. Yet the conduct demanded in 5:21—7:12 involves, as we have already seen, much more than an "ethicizing" of Jesus' ministry as found, for example, in the *Didache.*

To enter the narrow gate means to follow Jesus in discipleship, which certainly involved conduct (5:20, 21—7:12). But that conduct so frequently seen as primarily "ethical" presupposes a crucial christological-eschatological element. Whereas one cannot enter the Kingdom without the "greater righteousness" (5:20, 21—7:12), bearing "good fruits" (7:16–20) and doing the "will of the Father" (7:21–23), such conduct becomes a possibility because of the new age that has come through the person and ministry of Jesus Messiah (5:3–12, 13–16, 17–18). Through him God has revealed the presence of the Kingdom, the new relationship between God himself and his own, as well as among his own, which the *few find* (6:33; 7:7–11) as the basis for the "greater righteousness," the "good fruit," and for doing the "will of the Father." Therefore, rather than using this saying simply to call one to live ethically according to Jesus' teaching or to take courage and leave the masses behind to follow the struggling, suffering path of the mission, Matthew uses it to express a call to discipleship, to accept Jesus as the Messiah who brings the Kingdom to those who seek.

7:15. This verse opens the next unit whose limits have been much debated (see Literary Analysis). The focus turns to *false prophets* and clearly obtains through 7:20. But the identity of these *false prophets* and the grounds for the warning depend to a great degree on whether 7:21–23 further specifies the nature of the warning in 7:15 or offers yet another more general warning about the entrance requirements for the Kingdom (7:13–14). As will become evident in the Notes that follow, the former option appears to better fit the material of 7:15–23 and the overall context of 7:13–27, and reflects Matthew's particular concern about *false prophets* within his own community.

This verse stands without parallel and stems most likely from the evangelist's use of common metaphors to depict the appearance and character of the *false prophets,* a concept integral to the eschatological discourse in 24:12–23. The figure of *sheep* and *wolves* also appears in a Q saying that Matthew has placed within the mission discourse of 10:16 (par. Luke 10:3). Therefore, this saying, though redactional, consists of traditional motifs used in two of the evangelist's other discourses.

Be on your guard. This second use within the Sermon (6:1) of the somewhat characteristic Matthean verb (προσέχετε), a "Septuagintism" (Schweizer, "Observance," 224, n. 1; Sparks, "Semitisms," 134), states the warning in language used elsewhere of the "hypocrites" (6:1, cf. Matt 23), Jewish opponents (10:17), and the "leaven of the scribes and Pharisees" (16:6, cf. Mark 8:15; 16:11, 12). Such a consistent setting for this verb elsewhere adds support to the identification of the *false prophets* with Jewish adversaries in this context as well.

false prophets. In the Olivet Discourse (24:11–12) the evangelist again has a warning about *false prophets* (ψευδοπροφῆται) who will arise to deceive *many* (πολλούς, cf. 7:13b) with the following explanation that ἀνομία (cf. 7:23) will increase and "love" (ἀγάπη) will "cool" (ψυγήσεται). The verbal and thematic relationship to the context of 7:15 hardly appears to be coincidental. Yet the present tense of the verbs in 7:15 and the use of προσέχω elsewhere to warn against present dangers make the warning here much more acute than in 24:11–12, unless one were to take 7:15–23 to be a common apocalyptic reference to the end times parallel to 24:11–12 (e.g., Strecker, *Weg*, 137, n. 4). Matthew 7:15 would then refer to the future coming of *false prophets* rather than the present threat.

Such an almost formulaic usage of *false prophets,* however, does not fit the more concrete admonitions and warnings of the Sermon, especially 7:13–14, 24–27 in the immediate context. Therefore, the expected eschatological appearance of the *false prophets* in Jesus' final discourse (24:11–12) has already become a reality for Matthew's community. Certainly the widespread concern about *false prophets* in the early church (e.g., 1 Cor 12:1–3, 7; 1 John 4:2; 2 Pet 2:1; *Did* 11:7–14; Hermas, *Man* 11:7–16; Ps-Cl *Hom* 2:6–11) make this conclusion a real possibility.

If, then, the *false prophets* represented a very real threat to Matthew's church, who were the *false prophets?* The answers to this question have ranged between various representations of Judaism including the Pharisees (e.g., Lagrange, *Matthieu,* 152; Hill, "Prophets," 340–48), the Zealots (e.g., Schlatter, *Matthäus,* 252–54; Cothenet, "prophètes," 299–305) and the Essenes (e.g., Daniel, "Prophètes," 45–80) and various representatives of Christian groups including gnostic teachers (Weiss, *History* 2:759; cf. Bacon, *Studies,* 73–74), "antinomians" (e.g., Barth, "Understanding," 73–75; Hummel, *Auseinandersetzung,* 64–65), "enthusiasts" (Käsemann, "Beginnings," 83–84), and, more generally, Christian prophets whose conduct did not measure up to Jesus' demands (Schweizer, *Matthew,* 187–89; *idem,* "Observance," 224–26). The problem of identity becomes even more complex when one attempts to distinguish between the saying in Jesus' ministry and Matthew's usage (e.g., Cothenet, "prophètes," 281–308, and Krämer, "Propheten," 349–77). The answer to this question can only come from the larger context of 7:15–23.

who come to you in sheep's clothing. Although the setting suggests a literal rendering of the present tense (ἔρχονται) rather than referring to a future event, it remains unclear whether the verb implies the itinerant character of the *false prophets'* mission (e.g., Reiling, *Hermas,* 59, n. 1; cf. *Did* 11:7–14) or the less literal sense found elsewhere in Matthew, as in the LXX, of being present within or among (Bonnard, *Matthieu*, 104). The context appears to point to the latter.

The description of the *false prophets* strikes a familiar note about *sheep* and *wolves*. This rather common motif implying the designation of "flock" for the people of God, a designation with Old Testament roots and developed most fully in John 10:1–29, suggests that *sheep's clothing* bespeaks their outward "appearance" as belonging to the flock. Consequently, the *false prophets* would have been a part of the Christian community. This interpretation taking the *sheep's clothing* as purely symbolic of their deceptive appearance comes with more cogency than a more literal reference to the actual prophetic garb worn by the imposters (cf. Hill, "Prophets," 345–46; Böcher, "Schafspelzen," 405–26), especially since the normal term for sheepskin clothing was μηλωτή (e.g., Heb 11:37). It seems clear that 7:15 refers to Christian rather than Jewish *false prophets*.

but inside. The discrepancy between appearance and reality, or external and internal, underlay much of Jesus' charge against the "righteous," the "scribes and Pharisees" in Matthew, or the "hypocrites" (e.g., 6:1–18; 23; especially 23:27–28). By contrast, the integrity of the "pure in heart" was pronounced "blessed" (5:8), wholeness was demanded as the greater righteousness (5:48, cf. 5:20), and the tree was known by its fruit (7:16–20). This breakdown between what the *false prophets* appeared to be and do and what they actually were and did not do, supplies the connecting thread running through 7:16–23. Rather than appearing to be one of the flock in word and deed (7:21–22), they stand as dangerous *(be on guard)* imposters whose words and actions were used to evil ends *(ravenous wolves).*

ravenous wolves. This phrase, which occurs in Gen 49:27 with reference to Jacob's description of Benjamin, depicts the true character of the *false prophets*. Preying on the sheep, their insidious desire stems from personal greed and self-aggrandizement (cf. 7:22). This same motive of "spiritual" rather than "material" greed and self-justification appears throughout the contrast between the conduct demanded by Jesus of his disciples and that of the "scribes and Pharisees" (5:20–48) and the "hypocrites" (6:1–18). Furthermore, Matt 10:16, par. Luke 10:3, speaks of sending the disciples as "sheep in the midst of wolves," and the following material refers to Jewish persecution (10:17). Consequently, the description of the *false prophets* leaves us with an anomaly. Dressed in *sheep's clothing* implies that they belonged to the Christian community; the *inside/outside* contrast, their designation as *ravenous wolves,* as well as the consistent use in Matthew of προσέχω with reference to the "hypocrites"/"Pharisees" point to their belonging to the Jewish community that opposed the Church.

Perhaps this very anomaly holds the key to the identity of the *false prophets.* Rather than *either* a Jewish *or* a Christian group, as the choice has most often been, the *false prophets* represented *both* elements as rigorous Jewish-Christians who sought to implement the strict adherence to the Mosaic Law (Käsemann, "Beginnings," 86–87) and may have sought to impede the Gentile mission of Matthew's church as well. We have already seen that 5:17–19, 32, 33b–36; 23:2–3, etc., all reflect just such a reworking of the tradition to use dominical sayings in support of their position. Their presence and threat in the Matthean community may have been precipitated by the events surrounding the fall of Jerusalem and the need to leave the Jerusalem environs for safety in the Syrian Church.

Thus the sharp polemic against the "scribes and Pharisees"—"hypocrites" in Matthew—especially in the Sermon, may have had a dual focus. On the one hand, rooted in Jesus' ministry to the "righteous" of his day, these passages addressed the stark contrast between Pharisaic Judaism in Matthew's day and his church. The tone was one of polemics rather than mission. The synagogue was *their* synagogue (see Note on 4:23). The Jewish opponents who create hardship for the church will not enter the Kingdom (cf. 5:20); they receive the pronouncement of judgment (cf. the Woes of Matt 23) rather than salvation (cf. the Beatitudes of Matt 5). On the other hand, Matthew used this same traditional material to address the "Judaizers" within his own community, whom he also saw to be the heir of the Pharisaic fallacy—to have failed to perceive the gospel of the Kingdom with its implications for life and conduct.

Consequently, the evangelist corrected their distorted use of the tradition (see Notes on 5:17–20) and warned against the eventual result of such a *way* (cf. 7:13 and 7:21–23). They were *wolves* ("Pharisees") in *sheep's clothing* ("Christians"). Thus Matthew's community was beset by Jewish opponents from without and "Judaizing" Christians from within, a situation not all that different from what Paul's letters reflect (cf. 2 Cor 11:1—12:12).

7:16–20. The evangelist returned again to the Q tradition of the Sermon (7:16, 18, par. Luke 6:43–44) to illustrate the true nature of the *false prophets.* Using two related metaphors whose original *Sitz im Leben* may well have been in Jesus' ministry among the "righteous," Matthew inverted them (7:16, par. Luke 6:44; 7:18, par. Luke 6:43) appropriate to his context and expanded them by first developing a positive counterpart to the negatively formulated saying regarding good and bad trees (7:17, cf. 7:18, par. Luke 6:43), then by adding the judgment saying from the Baptist's preaching (7:19, cf. 3:10, par. Luke 3:9), and finally by concluding with a repetition of 7:16a in 7:20 that forms an inclusion and makes application of 7:16–19 to the false prophets of 7:15.

In many ways, Matt 12:33–35 offers the closer parallel to Luke 6:43–45. There the evangelist has reused the Q tradition in a context where Jesus has been charged by the Pharisees of exorcising in league with Satan (12:22–32). The accent clearly falls on what one *says*, as it does in Luke 6:43–45 (cf. 6:45), which betrays one's true nature. The emphasis on the "heart" as the seat of one's integrity in 6:45, par. Matt 12:34–35, was "introduced" by the Beatitude to the "pure in heart" of 5:8, a motif present in 12:34–35, par. Luke 6:43–45 but now missing in 7:16–20 (see Note on 5:8). Therefore, the relation of 7:16–20 to 5:8, like 7:1–5 to 5:7, which parallel more closely the respective Q passages in Luke's Sermon (5:8, cf. Luke 6:43–45; 5:7, cf. Luke 6:36–42), not only indicates the pre-Matthean existence of 5:7–8 along with 5:9 (cf. 5:43–48, par. Luke 6:27–35), but the earlier form of the Q Sermon material now found in Luke and reworked by Matthew in 5:48, 7:1–5, cf. Luke 6:36–42 and 7:16–20, cf. Luke 6:43–45.

7:16. *By their fruits you will recognize them.* The evangelist shifts metaphors from the animal kingdom of 7:15 (*sheep* and *wolves*) to the plant kingdom of 7:16–20 (*trees* and *bushes*). He forms this introduction to bridge to the tradition found in Luke 6:43–45 by taking the concluding element of the first metaphor having to do with good and bad trees (Luke 6:43, 44a, cf. Matt 7:17–18) and placing it at the outset of 7:16–20.

you will recognize them. The change from "to know" (γινώσκω; Luke 6:44, par. Matt 12:33) to *to recognize* (ἐπιγινώσκω) may point to a semi-technical, Matthean use of *to recognize*, since he adds it in two other significant passages. In 11:27 the verb connotes a theological recognition of the Son of Man, as it does in 17:12 with reference to Elijah. Only in the parallel of Mark 6:54, par. 14:35, does it have its more usual meaning. The use of 7:16, 20 might also connote more than a normal preception and imply a special usage as well.

The future tense could well support this distinctive use of *to recognize.*

Although it can be translated as a command or exhortation (Bonnard, *Matthieu*, 105), it most likely maintains its future force. If it had paralleled 7:15a, then the shift from the present imperative form in 7:15a (προσέχετε) to the future indicative form with the same imperative function in 7:16a, 20a (ἐπιγνώσεσθε) would seem awkward at best, particularly since both verbs stem from the evangelist's redaction.

If future in force, when would the community *recognize* the *fruits* of the *false prophets?* The final judgment offers the only logical answer. This recognition of the *fruits* or, more accurately, the true nature of the *tree* or *bush* at the judgment is supported by the addition of the judgment saying in 7:19, immediately preceding the concluding repetition of 7:16a in 7:20, and leads into the judgment scenes of 7:21–23. Therefore, *you will recognize* them points ahead to the judgment when the *fruits* obvious only to the judge will be revealed, since the words and deeds, the apparent fruit, belong to the *sheep's clothing* by which they mislead the community.

The shift from the singular *fruit* (καρπόν) of Luke 6:43–44, par. Matt 12:33, to the plural *fruits* (καρπούς) in 7:16–18, 20 adds intensity to this material. Matt 7:19, a quotation from the Baptist tradition found in 3:10, par. Luke 3:9, offers the lone exception of the singular. The *fruits* remain qualified as *good* and *evil* but undefined in what follows. Staying within the boundaries of the metaphors, the evangelist's concern is to show that one will be known by one's products just as is a tree or a bush. His concern is to underscore the fact that the *false prophets* are so because they are *wolves* at heart and not *sheep.* They do not belong to the community with which they seek to identify and doubtless consider themselves to be a part.

Surely they do not gather grapes from thorn bushes or figs from thistles, do they? Commensurate with his introduction in 7:16a, the evangelist goes directly to specific examples drawn from the tradition (Luke 6:44). The saying in Luke has the form of a declarative sentence—perhaps the later form of the saying—and a different pairing of the examples ("figs" from "thorn bushes," "grapes" from "brambles") whose meaning is identical with Matthew's pairing. The point of the saying could not be more obvious: a bush bears according to its essence; a person produces in keeping with one's nature.

7:17. *Thus every good tree produces good fruits.* The first metaphor in the Q tradition (Luke 6:43, par. Matt 7:18) now becomes the theoretical basis for the second in Matthew's inversion, even though what is logically sound may be practically absurd. Whereas a *good tree* logically and practically produces *good fruits* (καρποὺς καλούς), a *rotten tree* (σαπρὸν δένδρον) does not produce *bad* (evil) *fruits* (καρποὺς πονηρούς). The thought of the context, the *evil fruits* of *false prophets*, has clearly influenced the evangelist's reshaping of the metaphor (cf. 7:18, par. Luke 6:43, par. Matt 12:33). The shift from *rotten fruit* (καρπὸν σαπρόν) in Luke 6:43, par. Matt 12:33, to *evil fruits* (καρποὺς πονηρούς; 7:17, 18) doubtless includes a moral element mixed into the metaphor by the evangelist. In so doing, the evangelist betrays his orientation on *deeds* in 7:16–20 rather than *words* as found in Luke 6:43–45, par. Matt 12:33–34. Thus he omits here the concluding reference to the "mouth" speaking from the "abundance of the heart" in Luke 6:45, par. Matt 12:34 (con. Hill, "Prophets," 346–47). In this manner, the evangelist sets the stage for 7:21–22 that follows.

7:18. *A good tree is not able to bear evil fruits.* This negatively formulated saying (par. Luke 6:43 and Matt 12:33) opens with the redactional addition of δύναται that underscores the impossibility of a *tree* producing contrary to its nature.

7:19. This saying taken from the Baptist's proclamation (3:10, par. Luke 3:9) interrupts the thought of fruits indicating the nature of the plant. Furthermore, syntactically *fruit* in the singular here contrasts with the plural in 7:16–18, 20. Yet just such a break in the pattern often betrays the evangelist's style. Keying on the tradition referring to a *tree* not producing *good fruit* (οὐδὲ . . . δένδρον σαπρὸν ποιοῦν καρπὸν καλόν, Luke 6:43, par. Matt 7:18), Matthew inserts the parallel theme from the Baptist's tradition to pronounce the final outcome of the *false prophets* in anticipation of 7:21–23 with its judgment scene.

7:20. *by their fruits.* Returning to the introductory statement of 7:16a, Matthew uses this declaration to conclude the metaphors and apply them not only to the *fruits* of the *false prophets* but also to their true nature as *wolves* rather than *sheep*.

If, however, the recognition would first come at the judgment (see Note on 7:16a), why then the warning in 7:15a and the listing of the following "criteria" of 7:16–20? First, the warning of 7:15a becomes all the more critical, since indeed the *false prophets* look like *sheep*. If the difference were so obvious as 7:16–20 might imply, there would be no threat to the flock. Matt 7:22 indicates that their words and deeds, that could easily be misconstrued as *fruits* by the community, were only *sheep's clothing* and not *good fruits* after all. Therefore, the threat becomes most insidious and all the more dangerous. One can only *guard against* the *false prophets* by entering the *narrow gate* (7:13) or doing the *will of the Father* (7:21) as taught by Jesus, for example, in the Sermon (7:24, 26). The task of the believer is not to "shoot the wolves" or even to "disrobe" them of their sheepskins. Their task is to hear and obey the words taught by Jesus.

Second, the "criteria" of 7:16–20 illustrate the nature of the *false prophets* who attempt to *bear good fruits*—even appear to do so but, like the Pharisees and a nonbearing tree, are incapable of doing so. They are *wolves,* not *sheep; thorn bushes,* not grape vines; *thistles,* not fig trees. Therefore, the judgment falls upon them (7:23) because they not only do not produce, they cannot by their very nature. The "criteria" of 7:16–20 will become clear to the disciples when revealed by the judge *in that day* (7:23).

7:21–23. This unit has at times (e.g., Klostermann, *Matthäusevangelium,* 70; Schniewind, *Matthäus,* 104–105; Manson, *Sayings,* 176; Hill, "Prophets," 335–48; undecided, Schmid, *Matthäus,* 151–52) received separate treatments from 7:15–20 as one in a series of concluding admonitions (7:13–14, 15–20, 21–23, 24–27). This approach has in part the support of the Q Sermon tradition in which Luke 6:46, par. Matt 7:21, stands separate from 6:43–45, par. Matt 7:16–20, as the introduction (Schürmann, *Lukasevangelium,* 379–80) to the final parable (Luke 6:47–49, par. Matt 7:24–27). Furthermore, Matthew has redactionally formed an inclusion in 7:20 with 7:16a to round off 7:16–20, and he has reworked this Sermon tradition behind 7:21 by adding a judgment scene drawn from the same Q context (Luke 13:25–27) where he also found 7:13–14 (Luke 13:23–24). Consequently, 7:23 forms a conclusion to the unit of 7:21–23, and the parable of 7:24–27 now stands alone without an introduction. Thus, both tradition and redaction point to two units, 7:16–20 and 7:21–23.

But does the presence of two units imply two different subjects (e.g., "false prophets" in 7:16–20 and "charismatics" in 7:21–23, as in Hill, "Prophets," 340–48)? Hardly, since 7:16–20 itself stands as a separate traditional and redactional unit from 7:15 but clearly related to 7:15 in theme. Consequently, the ultimate question has to do with the thematic relationship of 7:21–23 to the larger (7:13–27) and narrower context (7:15–20).

In terms of the larger context of 7:13–27, 7:21–23 fits as an appropriate parallel to the admonition of 7:13–14 by indicating that the *wide gate* and *spacious way* even included those claiming Jesus as Lord and doing many marvelous deeds in his name while the *narrow gate* and *constricted way* that leads to life, the Kingdom of Heaven (7:21), meant doing the *will of my Father in heaven.* The concluding parable of 7:24–27 would then be an illustration of these alternatives. This structure, however, leaves 7:15–20 as somewhat parenthetic, a result that hardly corresponds with the deliberate redactional development of 7:13–27. If 7:21–23 was intended to be an elaboration of the more abstract metaphors in 7:16–20, then one would have an admonition in 7:13–14 followed by a warning of a serious, misleading threat in 7:15–23 and a concluding parable in 7:24–27 that illustrated the *narrow gate* of 7:13a–14 in contrast to 7:15–23 and stood as a summary of the Sermon.

In terms of the narrower context, 7:21–23 actually follows the themes of 7:15–20. It explicates the *good fruits* (7:21b) and the *evil fruits* (7:23b), specifies their true nature (7:15, *wolves,* and 7:23, doers of *evil*) in contrast to their apparent nature (7:15, *sheep's clothing,* and 7:22, *"Lord, Lord,"* and marvelous deeds), and pronounces their end (7:19) to be the final judgment (7:23). Certainly the deeds listed as done in Jesus' name—prophecy, exorcisms, miracles—belong to those gifts corresponding to one's claim to be a prophet. Therefore, 7:21–23 offers a further delineation of the *false prophets'* identity.

7:21. *Not everyone who says to me, "Lord, Lord."* Luke 6:46 has what is probably the more original saying in the form of a question: "Why do you call me, 'Lord, Lord'?" (Bultmann, *Tradition,* 116; Klostermann, *Matthäusevangelium,* 70; Grundmann, *Matthäus,* 234; Schulz, *Spruchquelle,* 427; cf. Hahn, *Titles,* 90–92). By shaping the tradition into the form of an entrance-saying, Matthew defines who will enter the Kingdom. Although assigned by some to a prophetic utterance within the early church (e.g., Trilling, *Israel,* 189; Schulz, *Spruchquelle,* 428), the saying could just as easily have come from Jesus' own ministry to those who addressed him as Master but failed to take seriously what he said (e.g., Bultmann, *Tradition,* 128, 151; Schürmann, *Lukasevangelium,* 380).

For Matthew, however, the designation of Jesus as κύριε connoted more than a term of respect like "Master" or "Rabbi," since the address κύριε only appears on the lips of the disciples (cf. Judas in 26:25, 49) or those sincerely seeking Jesus' help and willing to commit themselves unreservedly to him. Furthermore, such ones never addressed Jesus with the title of teacher or rabbi as did the outsiders (see Note on 4:23). So consistently does the evangelist hold to this that he even changed the tradition when κύριε occurred on the lips of an outsider (e.g., 8:25, cf. Mark 4:38; 17:15, cf. Mark 9:17). Therefore, the use of κύριε, κύριε here clearly implies the acceptance of the *false prophets* in and by the community. The *sheep's clothing* of the *false prophets* looked like the genuine article. Indeed, more than lip service was involved, as seen in 7:22. Yet appearances can be deceiving, since not all such *will enter the Kingdom of Heaven.*

the will of my Father in heaven. Luke 6:46 has, "What I tell you," leading to the parable in 6:47–49. We have already noted the redactional character of the phrase in Matt 6:10 (see Note on 6:10 for *my Father*) and the integral relationship of the *will of the Father* and the *Kingdom* (see Note on 6:10). For Matthew the content of the *Father's will* included Jesus' teaching (cf. 7:24, 26) as illustrated by the Sermon. Thus it consists neither of a more rigorous keeping of the Mosaic Law (cf. 5:17–48) nor of an amorphous love ethic summarized by the love commandment.

To the extent that the love commandment (22:37–40) and its practical expression in the Golden Rule (7:12) represent an expression in summary of the total conduct growing out of the new relationship between God and his own and among his own, demanded, for example, in 5:21—7:12, the love commandment also expresses in essence the *will of my Father* (cf. 24:12). The love commandment itself, however, is only representative of, rather than the total expression of, the *Father's will.* But if the *false prophets* in 7:15 were indeed rigorous Jewish-Christians, 7:21b like 5:20–48 would be directed against the distortion of Jesus' teaching found in 5:17–19 as being the *will of the Father.* They would represent the opposite extreme of the so-called "Christian antinomians."

Inherent to *my Father's will* was the christological basis of Jesus Messiah, the fulfillment of the Old Testament promise for the day of salvation (e.g., 5:3–12; 5:17–18), that brought about a different orientation to the Mosaic Law. Therefore, any "prophecy" that attempted to apply rigorously the Mosaic Law failed at precisely the same point where the Pharisees broke with Jesus' ministry, namely, at the implications of his coming for the old order, the Law in Judaism. Put another way, those seeking to live and to influence others to live under the "Sinai Torah," the Law of Moses legalistically understood, had not accepted Jesus Messiah and the accompanying "Zion Torah" whose basis was the presence in history of the new age with its message of salvation and reconciliation between God and his own. They had ultimately failed to hear the "gospel of the Kingdom," which offered a new basis and power for conduct, "righteousness," as seen in 5:21—7:12 (see Note on 5:18). Therefore, the doing of the *Father's will* was an eschatological event (cf. 6:10) of the Kingdom present that had directly to do with one's entrance into the Kingdom future (5:20; 7:21).

7:22. *Many will say to me in that day.* The Q parallel to this and the following saying is found in Luke 13:26–27, the same context of 7:13–14, par. Luke 13:23–24. But Matthew and Luke diverge considerably from each other in wording and in audience. Whereas Luke has Jesus addressing a Jewish audience with the need for decision, Matthew applies these sayings (cf. 7:13–14 also) to a Christian audience. Like the Q material behind 7:13–14, the *Sitz im Leben* in Jesus' ministry of 7:22–23 seems closer to that found in Luke than in Matthew. Yet because of the similarity between the rigorous Jewish-Christians threatening the Matthean community and the Pharisees, Matthew could take over the tradition and apply it accordingly.

The *many* (πολλοί) may allude to the *many false prophets* (πολλοὶ ψευδο-προφῆται) found in 24:11 and would offer a confirming support for the relation of 7:21–23 to 7:15. The phrase *in that day* sets the judgment scene of 7:22–23. Its roots in the Old Testament (e.g., Isa 2:11, 17; Zech 14:6) point to the final judgment (Mark 13:32). The same setting is implicit in Luke 13:25–26 behind the figure of the closed door.

Lord, Lord, in your name. The address here in 7:22 does not differ that much from the same address in 7:21, since both entailed a common christological perspective of Jesus as Lord (see Note on 7:21). Only the setting differs. The one addressed as *Lord in that day* stands as the exalted *Lord* in judgment. The recognition now of Jesus as *Lord* (7:21) adds to the evangelist's point that the recognition expressed "correctly" in the terms, *"Lord, Lord,"* both within the community (7:21) and at the judgment (7:22), does not necessarily indicate one's own identity. Furthermore, ministry by invocation and in the power of Jesus' *name* belongs to the *sheep's clothing* that leads to one's acceptance in and by the community but not by the Lord (7:23).

prophesied, cast out demons, and performed many miracles. Luke 13:26, which may come closer to the original *Sitz im Leben* (as in Hill, "Prophets," 336, cf. Schweizer, "Observance," 225–26), makes reference to personal contact with Jesus' earthly ministry—"eating and drinking" in his presence and his "teaching" in their "streets"—as the basis for entrance. Matthew's listing of deeds done in Jesus' name appropriate

to a "prophetic" ministry has led several commentators, most notably
Käsemann, to identify this group as "enthusiasts" or "charismatics"
(e.g., Käsemann, "Beginnings," 83–84; Hoffmann, "Πάντες," 200; Hill,
"Prophets," 336–37, 340–41). Yet at issue for Matthew was not charismatic activity as such (e.g., Trilling, "Amt," 34–38; Schweizer, "Observance," 226; Hill, "Prophets," 332–33, 336–37; con. Käsemann,
"Beginnings," 82–107), since the evangelist clearly supported such ministry in 10:7–8. Rather, these activities, accomplished in Jesus' name, were
cited because they were to serve as the basis for the *false prophets'* defense
before the judge. Indeed, the very use of such deeds, like the use of
"Lord, Lord," implies their validity.

It was not the use of *"Lord, Lord"* nor the marvelous deeds done
under the invocation of Jesus' *name* per se that brought about the judgment on them but what the listing of these deeds signified about the
true nature of their supposedly Christian ministry. Working in Jesus'
name and in his power actually became a basis for their own personal
power and honor *(have we not done . . .).* The *false prophets* appeal to
such deeds for legitimation and validation of their ministry. Their attitude
and conduct regarding Jesus' coming and the Law, however, bespoke
their true nature, as fruit is indicative of the nature of a tree (7:16–20,
23b). This disparity between appearance and reality, between their appearing to be ministers of Jesus Messiah *(sheep's clothing)* but in reality
seeking their own self-centered power and honor *(ravenous wolves)* by
using his name and person and thus insuring acceptance not only among
the flock but at the judgment, corresponded to the Pharisees' use of
the Law which led to the related charge of "hypocrites" (e.g., 6:1–18,
23). Such conduct Matthew calls ἀνομία (e.g., 7:23; 24:12).

7:23. *I shall declare openly to them.* The use of *to declare openly*
(ὁμολογέω) in a judgment setting occurs again in Q in the much-discussed
Son of Man saying (10:32, par. Luke 12:8). The adaptation of this material
to Luke's context carries through in the phrase, "But he will say, 'I
tell you . . .' " (καὶ ἐρεῖ λέγων ὑμῖν, Luke 13:27).

I never knew you. Luke 13:27 has the contextually influenced, "I
do not know where you come from," whereas Matthew has the ban-
formula found in rabbinic usage (Str-B 1:429; 4:293). In spite of their
address of recognition—*"Lord, Lord"*—and their use of his *name* in
their work thus laying claim to identification with Jesus Messiah, the
exalted Lord as judge will deny having ever known them. They are
not of his flock, sheep though they appear to be; they are wolves at

heart which the good shepherd can recognize. The judge passes judgment in the words of Ps 6:9, LXX.

depart from me. Luke 13:27 has the LXX wording of Ps 6:9 (ἀπόστητε ἀπ' ἐμοῦ) in contrast to Matthew's sole use of ἀποχωρεῖτε in his Gospel (cf. Luke 9:39; 20:20 v.l.). The change may have stemmed from Luke's preference for ἀφίστημι (4x in Luke, 6x in Acts compared to none in Matthew, Mark; Hoffman, "Πάντες," 202). The meaning remains the same in either case, since the judgment involves dismissal, separation, exclusion from the Kingdom. The judgment of 7:19 is now carried out.

you who do evil. Matthew parallels verbatim Ps 6:9, LXX. His use of ἀνομία, often translated literally as "lawlessness" (cf. Luke 13:27, ἀδικία), has led to the identification of the *false prophets* as "antinomians" (e.g., Barth, "Understanding," 73-75, 159-64; Hummel, *Auseinandersetzung,*" 64-65). Such a conclusion, however, ignores the evidence that the term ἀνομία lacks a "strictly legal overtone" anywhere else in the New Testament (Davies, *Setting,* 203).

That "legal overtone" certainly does not obtain in Matthew's other uses of the term in 13:41; 23:28; and 24:12 (Hill, "Prophets," 337-38). In 23:28 one finds the term used with reference to the Pharisees in a context quite similar to the present context. Described as "whitewashed tombs," the Pharisees have the external appearance of δίκαιοι, the "righteous," which contrasts starkly with their internal nature—full of hypocrisy and ἀνομία. In the interpretation of the parable of the Tares (13:36-43), the tares include those who do ἀνομία, who will be cast into the lake of fire at the judgment (13:41-42), although until the harvest they will grow, planted by the Devil (13:39), together with the wheat. Finally, the ἀνομία resulting from the influence of the "many false prophets" will cause "love to grow cold," an obvious contrast to Jesus' demands as found in 5:21-48. Therefore, "lawlessness" not only fails to identify the work of the *false prophets* as antinomians but inadequately translates ἀνομία too narrowly in the sense of the Law.

The situation really does not improve much by exchanging Jesus' interpretation of the Law for the Law of Moses and thus defining "lawlessness" accordingly (e.g., Schweizer, *Matthew,* 189; Grundmann, *Matthäus,* 235; Hoffmann, "Πάντες," 203; Hill, "Prophets," 312). To be sure, working ἀνομία stands antithetically to doing *the will of my Father.* But we have seen that *the will of the Father* connotes more than ethical conduct for Matthew (see Note on 7:21). As with *righteousness* (see Note on 5:6) so with *the will of my Father,* the concepts contain *both* an ethical and an eschatological element. The fallacy common to both the Pharisees

(23:28) and the false prophets lay in their failure to recognize the significance of Jesus Messiah as the fulfillment of the Old Testament promise for the day of salvation (5:17–18). Nor did they see in his coming that attitudes and conduct had a new starting point other than the Mosaic Law (e.g., 5:20–48) which they insisted was fundamental to one's relationship with God.

The appearance of the *false prophets* as Christian, claiming Jesus as Lord and working in his name, made their position all the more insidious but no less vulnerable to the judgment (7:21,23, cf. Woes of Matt 23). Precisely this dichotomy between appearance *(sheep)* and reality *(wolves)*, between claiming Jesus as Lord and insisting on a rigorous observance of the old order, underlies the metaphors of 7:16–20. Therefore, ἀνομία connotes more than a lawlessness, however one may define the "Law." It actually included a rigorous conduct whose basis in the Mosaic Law stood antithetically to the person and work of Jesus Messiah, especially as depicted in his teaching of the Sermon. Yet perhaps a touch of irony does exist in that those concerned about keeping the letter of the Law (the Pharisees in 23:28 and the false prophets in 7:15, cf. tradition underlying 5:18–19) should be condemned for ἀνομία at the judgment.

7:24–27. The Sermon ends in a fashion common to Jewish discourse— with a parable. This ending was already present in the pre-evangelists' Sermon tradition. The parable consists of two antithetical parts (hardly a double parable, as in Jeremias, *Parables,* 90; Manson, *Sayings,* 91) whose parallelism is better preserved in Matthew and sacrificed for Greek style in Luke (Manson, *Sayings,* 61). Yet both evangelists have made serveral redactional modifications (Schulz, *Spruchquelle,* 312–13).

7:24. *Everyone who hears.* Luke 6:47 opens with "Everyone who comes to me and hears," which refers to the Lucan setting of the Sermon in 6:17, "They came to hear him . . . ," and helps bracket the Sermon material. Matthew opens with the adverbial conjunction οὖν, which draws the conclusion with view to all that has been said beginning with 5:3. In both instances the evangelists were simply underscoring the parable's function as an exhortation for the hearers to take the Sermon seriously.

these my words and does them. Matthew leaves no doubt about which words by adding the demonstrative, *these* (τούτους; cf. 7:26), that refers to Jesus' teaching in 5:3—7:27. Both evangelists, and thus the tradition, specify the words as Jesus' words (μου), a statement that lays claim to personal authority extending beyond that of the rabbis, even beyond that of the prophets, in light of the content of 5:3—7:27 (cf. 7:28–29). The contrast comes out best in comparison with a similar parable attributed to Rabbi Elisha ben Abuya, ca. A.D. 120, that specified the knowing and doing of the *Torah* as providing a firm foundation against the floods (Str-B 1:469–70). *And does them* also stands in both Matthew and Luke (cf. James 1:22–25), indicating that Jesus' words pertained to one's life and not just to one's mind or "understanding." *To hear and do the words* of Jesus meant to do *the will of the Father* (7:21), to exhibit the greater righteousness (5:20), and to hear and live according to the gospel of the Kingdom (4:23), since these words revealed the accomplishment of God's will in history, the coming of the Kingdom in the ministry of Jesus Messiah (Matt 5–9).

will be like a wise man. Luke 6:48–49 has neither the adjective *wise* (φρόνιμος) nor *foolish* (μωρός). The Q tradition has the adjective φρόνιμος in 24:45, par. Luke 12:42, but Matt 10:16 uses the modifier in a context somewhat reminiscent of 7:15: "I send you out as sheep in the midst of wolves; so be *wise* as serpents and innocent as doves." Furthermore, both *wise* and *foolish* occur four times in the parable of the Ten Virgins (25:1–13) whose conclusion has a material parallel in Luke 13:26–28, the Lucan context for the Q material found in 7:13–14, 22–23. Therefore, Matthew might well have taken these appropriate adjectives from the larger traditional context behind 7:13–23 and inserted them into this concluding parable. To be *wise* in 25:1–13 as here means to "grasp the eschatological situation" (Jeremias' quotation of H. Preisker, *TLZ* 74 [1949]:89 in *Parables* 46, n. 83, 194) by responding in complete surrender and obedience to Jesus (Jeremias, *Parables,* 194–95).

built his house on the rock. Luke 6:48 has a more elaborate description, including excavation, which would hardly have been necessary in Palestine. The *rock* stands as the solid base for the foundation in both accounts. This same metaphor appears with reference to the Church in Matt 16:18, cf. 1 Cor 3:10–11.

7:25. *The rain came down, the torrents came, the winds blew.* Matthew's description of the fall rains and accompanying storms graphically tells of a Palestinian situation where heavy rainstorms bring torrential flooding from the mountains into the wadis. Luke 6:48, by contrast, uses a genitive absolute to express "high water" or "flooding" (πλημμύρης δὲ γενομένης) as found when a river overflows its banks.

and beat upon the house. It did not fall. Luke expressed in more detail the same effect of the flood upon the house.

For its foundation had been laid on the rock. This basis for the house's survival once again returns to the solid foundation, whereas Luke's "Because it had been well built" dilutes the point of the parable.

7:26. *does not do these my words will be like a foolish man.* This part of the parable parallels the first almost verbatim, but set in antithesis to same. The issue focuses on the *doing* or *not doing* of Jesus' *words,* since both the *wise* and *foolish hear* his *words* of the Sermon. This warning, along with the tone of the Sermon in, for example, 5:13, 20; 6:1; 7:13, implies that the audience of *disciples* or Matthew's community (see Notes on 5:1–2 and Comment C, chap. 2) needed reminding of the demands of discipleship. This need has surfaced especially since the persecution from those outside the community (e.g., 5:10–12, cf. 5:13) as well as the threat of false prophets from within the community (7:15–23) could lead to apostasy (e.g., 5:13; 6:13; 7:6).

house upon the sand. Luke 6:49 has "without a foundation." The contrast between a *rock* foundation and one built on *sand* needs no further elaboration.

7:27. The description of the storm parallels almost verbatim that of 7:25. Only the verb *to strike* (προσέκοψαν) differs, although the meaning remains the same. The result, of course, was that the *house fell. Its fall was tremendous* expresses the irreparable nature of the destruction, a note of finality.

This parable of the Two Builders, therefore, offers the concluding admonition parallel to 7:13a that summoned the audience of the Sermon to carry out in their own life and experience Jesus' message of the Sermon. To fail to do so is to choose the way of destruction (7:13b) so vividly illustrated in 7:27. In view of the larger context, the storm most likely refers to the final judgment, although one questions if the "second Deluge" appropriately describes its symbol (cf. Jeremias, *Parables,* 169–70).

Comments

This section of 7:13–27 concludes the Sermon with a series of admonitions that can be separated into three units (7:13–14, 15–23, 24–27).

Each, however, relates to the content of Jesus' teaching in the preceding sections and confronts the reader/hearer with the alternative of responding positively or negatively and the corresponding result. As has been the case in most of the other Sermon sections, the evangelist has selected and modified traditional materials and concepts in order to expand on the underlying Sermon tradition (see Literary Analysis). Matt 7:13-14 opens with an exhortation to enter the narrow gate, an exhortation that gains its explanation through the parable of the Two Builders in 7:24-27. Between these two admonitions to the disciples or the community of believers, the evangelist has placed a warning against the danger of false prophets that threatened to mislead the believers from the narrow gate of doing Jesus' words (7:15-23). By concluding the Sermon in this manner, Matthew underscored the interrelated christological and ethical dimensions of the Sermon and applied the Sermon directly to his community's needs.

A. The Narrow Gate: 7:13-14

The first admonition to "enter the narrow gate" (7:13a), followed by an elaboration set in antithetical parallelism (7:13b-14), has a thematic parallel in Luke 13:23-24 whose content and context are quite different. Matthew most likely has the earlier form, while Luke has the earlier setting in Jesus' ministry in which he addressed a Jewish audience with the call to repentance. Matt 7:13 within the context of the Sermon addresses the disciples or believers. Therefore, the summons comes as an exhortation rather than an initial invitation. It reminds the disciples that Jesus' ministry demanded an active response that by virtue of its very nature was not a once-for-all decision. The exigencies of life, the alternative of another easier and more popular way, the advice and instructions of others ("false prophets," 7:15-23) continually threatened the believer's response to Jesus.

The "narrow gate" uses the symbol of a city gate with a possible allusion to the eschatological Jerusalem that stood for the consummation of the Kingdom. Luke's use of the "door" to the banquet hall (13:24-25) has the same eschatological reference to the coming Kingdom or the messianic banquet. Matt 7:14 elaborates by supplementing the "narrow gate" with the "constricted way" that "leads to life," a synonym for the Kingdom. Therefore, to "enter the narrow gate" meant to enter into salvation, the Kingdom of Heaven. The "narrow gate" itself and the "constricted way" each connote Jesus' teaching as found in 5:3—7:12. This implicit reference becomes explicit when the evangelist modifies the concluding parable to refer to "these my words," the doing of which means to build on a firm foundation (7:24, cf. 7:26).

By contrast, 7:13b offers the alternative of the easier, more popular way. Described as a "wide gate" and a "spacious way," the size most likely refers to the ease of entry and the space commensurate to the "many" who enter this way. It remains unclear whether the contrast in size also implies a degree of difficulty in recognizing the two ways. Whereas the "wide gate" and "spacious way" stood obvious for all to see, the "narrow gate" and "constricted way," however, were "found" (7:14). Whereas the verb "to find" might support the discovery of the more difficult way, "to find" also connotes God's revelation to those who "seek" in 7:7–8, a prayer motif drawn from the Old Testament (see Note on 7:7). Jesus stands as the signpost for those who recognize or "find" him as such. "Many" pass by him and the way; "few" find him and the way.

The results of entering the wide gate and spacious way, though popular and easy at this point in life, are disastrous. The way leads to ultimate destruction. Again the final parable graphically illustrates this alternative with the description of the house built on the sand by the one who does not do Jesus' words (7:26). When the storms come, the house is utterly and irreparably destroyed. "Its fall was tremendous" (7:27).

In contrast to the use of the "two ways" in early Christian literature with specific instruction for the way of life (e.g., *Did* 1:1—6:3), in Judaism where the obedience to the Law was primary (Str-B 1:460–62), or in Qumran where the two ways distinguished the sons of light from the sons of darkness (e.g., 1QS 3:20), the two ways of 7:13–14 parallel the two gates that bespeak entrance into rather than a process or journey that qualifies one for entrance. Neither way (7:13, 14) leads to or from the gate. The two metaphors parallel each other as synonyms. Therefore, the exhortation does not call the disciple to a qualifying standard of ethics as such but to a life of discipleship to Jesus Messiah and the corresponding conduct that ensues from surrendering oneself to him and God's sovereign will that he came to proclaim and effect. In this way, one comes to experience the greater righteousness, the reconciled relationship between God and his own and among his own that becomes the basis for conduct according to these new relationships, and to do the will of the Father on earth as it is in heaven. To live in such a manner is to enter the Kingdom, to have and experience life—even when this unpopular way is fraught with difficulties, detours, suffering, and rejection by the "many."

B. Wolves in Sheep's Clothing: Matt 7:15-23

The evangelist next turned to a warning against false prophets who threatened to deceive and mislead the disciples. This unit consists of at least three traditional units (7:16-20, 21, 22-23) brought together by the evangelist under a heading (7:15) that consists of traditional motifs. The danger of false prophets appears in Jesus' final discourse (24:11-12) and a reference to sheep and wolves in his mission discourse (10:16). Combining these motifs, the evangelist set this warning at the outset of the Q Sermon tradition on bearing fruit (7:16-20, cf. Luke 6:43-45, par. Matt 12:33-35), which he then explicated by the use of 7:21, par. Luke 6:46, the introduction for the final parable in the Q Sermon (cf. Luke 6:46-49), and 7:22-23, drawn from another Q context (cf. Luke 13:25-27, cf. Matt 7:13-14, par. Luke 13:23-24).

Matt 7:15 opens with the same warning found in 6:1 regarding the "hypocrites" (cf. Matt 23). "Be on your guard" also refers to the Jewish opponents in the mission discourse (10:17) and the "leaven" of the scribes and Pharisees in 16:6, 11, 12. From such a consistent usage of this warning, we may gain a clue to the identity of the "false prophets" who threatened the community. But the description of them as "ravenous wolves" in "sheep's clothing" also indicates their presence and acceptance among the "flock" as believers. Indeed, their words and deeds as noted in 7:22 would appear to bear out their profession. Therefore, we can identify them as professing believers who performed marvelous deeds in Jesus' name but who represented a rigorous Jewish-Christianity that stressed the strict adherence to the Mosaic Law (see Notes on 5:17-19).

The evangelist found his community threatened by a group not at all unlike the "Judaizers" who threatened the Pauline churches. Their appeal to the Jesus tradition (e.g., 5:17-19; 23:1-4, etc.) for support only made their danger the more insidious. Matthew's manner of dealing with the problem stands in contrast to Paul's. While the latter dealt with this problem christologically in terms of the death and resurrection of Jesus Christ, Matthew confronted these false prophets christologically in terms of Jesus' earthly ministry as the One who came to fulfill the Old Testament promise of the new age with its corresponding implications for the life and conduct of the believer. This christological theme has run throughout the Sermon from the Beatitudes through the Golden Rule. The "false prophets" threatened to replace the "gospel of the Kingdom" with a christology in which a major component doubtless appeared more rabbinic, perhaps not unlike the Teacher of Righteousness of Qumran. Matthew, like Paul, found such a perspective, in spite of its pretense, to stand under the anathema of preaching "another gospel."

In 7:16–20 the evangelist brought together and modified the first of three traditional units to explicate the true nature of the false prophets and their eventual demise. These sayings in the Sermon tradition belonged to the third major section forming the heart of the Sermon ("Love Your Enemies," Luke 6:27–35, cf. Matt 5:38–48; "Judging Others," Luke 6:36–42, cf. Matt 5:48, 7:1–5; "Integrity of Person," Luke 6:43–45, cf. Matt 7:16–20) which the additional Beatitudes of 5:7–9 had introduced. In the pre-Matthean tradition, the Beatitude to the "pure in heart" corresponded to this section calling for personal integrity by pointing out that fruit indicated the nature of the tree. The correspondence extended to the specific reference to the "heart" in the tradition (Luke 6:45, par. Matt 12:34) which Matthew has omitted in the reworking of the material for his purposes here in 7:16–20 (see Note on 5:8).

Although the evangelist applied this tradition to the false prophets, he did not do so in order to give his community objective criteria by which to identify the false prophets. He opened and concluded this unit (7:16a, 20) by stating that the community *will* recognize the false prophets by their fruits, a recognition that lay in the future at the final judgment when the trees not bearing good fruit would be cut down and cast into the fire (7:19) or when those whose words and deeds invoked Jesus' name were exposed as imposters (7:21–23). Consequently, these sayings were arranged and developed by the evangelist to illustrate that the false prophets' true nature made impossible the production of good fruit (7:16b–18). As "ravenous wolves" (7:15), "thorn bushes," "thistles," and "rotten trees," their nature would ultimately betray them, appearances notwithstanding. At the judgment the appearances to the contrary would be revealed for what they were and the dichotomy of personal profession and allegiance would spell their doom (7:19, 22–23).

Consequently, the evangelist concluded this unit with a judgment scene (7:22–23) drawn from Q (cf. Luke 13:25–27). According to 7:22, cf. Luke 13:26, the "false prophets" even appealed to their works undertaken in Jesus' name. Not only did they confess him to be Lord, they invoked his name and power in a ministry that included prophecy, exorcisms, and many miracles. These deeds in themselves represented the continuation of Jesus' earthly ministry that he had shared with his disciples (cf. 10:1) and thus could serve as the basis for their defense before the judge. In this case, however, such deeds helped constitute the "sheep's clothing" which enabled the "ravenous wolves" to identify with the other "sheep."

Jesus' piercing words, "Depart from me; I never knew you," indicate that even those deeds that accompanied their words were not the "good fruits" that identified their true nature. Rather, their produce was "bad fruits," not "doing the will of the Father," ἀνομία = evil. The word ἀνομία literally means "lawlessness," the failure to keep the Law. But such a rendering fits neither the "false prophets" nor any other use of the term in the New Testament. Rather, it connotes a fundamental failure to recognize and do God's will that shows itself in the breakdown of relationships between individuals. In 24:11-12, as a result of the influence of false prophets, ἀνομία increases, and ἀγάπη, conduct that befits the new relationships that God has established through Jesus Messiah (5:43-48; 7:12; 22:37-40), grows cold. Such "bad fruits" indicate the true nature of the false prophets—"ravenous wolves," "thorn bushes," "thistles," "rotten trees"—whose end is destruction (7:19, 21, 23).

Although some have found a contradiction between 7:15-23 and the prohibition of judging in 7:1-5—indeed, some have even taken 7:15-23 as the grounds for "fruit inspection," a thinly veiled form of judging—the evangelist intended for this unit to serve solely as a warning for the believers. The effect of the false prophets on the community may well become evident in the breakdown of the relationships that God offers his own through Jesus Messiah (24:11-12). But Matthew offers no encouragement for the community to expose or judge the false prophets, a task that belonged to the Lord when he comes in judgment. Even the "objective" evidence that will be used against them, their "bad fruits," comes to light only at the last judgment.

Therefore, by warning the believers to be on guard, the evangelist calls the community to their only defense against such insidious threats, namely, a faithful allegiance to the person and ministry of Jesus Messiah. One's sure defense meant entering the "narrow gate" (7:13), doing the "will of the Father" (7:21b), and hearing and doing "these my words" (7:24, 26). For the evangelist, the person and ministry of Jesus Messiah was fundamental to his demands for corresponding conduct in the lives of his disciples. Thus Matthew has presented a portrait of Jesus Messiah by his selection and modification of the tradition, a portrait which, as we have seen, closely corresponded to Jesus' earthly ministry. The root of the issue for the evangelist lay in one's relationship to Jesus Messiah. Thus the final judgment comes in the judge's sentence: "I never knew you."

What relevance, if any, does this first-century warning against false prophets have for us today? To be sure, we do not find rigorous Jewish-Christians insisting on a strict adherence to the Mosaic Law. Yet the warning still has its valid place in the Church. Remembering that the "false prophet" gives every indication of belonging to the community of believers by not only claiming Jesus as Lord—using the correct language—but also performing marvelous deeds in Jesus' name—giving evidence of Christian ministry, such "false prophets" bring their threat from within the community.

The "false prophet" of today, as in Matthew's community, distorts the "gospel of the Kingdom" through a faulty christology that leads to a faulty basis for conduct and attitudes. In other words, failure to recognize the presence of the new age, the coming of the Kingdom, within history in Jesus' ministry leads to insistence on conduct whose motivation lies in the individual's concern about qualifying for the Kingdom, by fulfilling the "Law's" demands—however "Law" may be defined in this case. This is just the opposite of a life lived on the basis of the good news of reconciliation offered us by God through Jesus Christ.

Our task, however, is not to defrock the "false prophets" or even to repudiate them directly. As with Matt 7:15–23, the ultimate verdict comes from the Judge. We are called to enter the narrow gate, to hear and do the words of Jesus, and thus to do the will of the Father. The task, like that of the evangelist, is to proclaim with clarity the "gospel of the Kingdom" that calls one to a response of discipleship to Jesus Messiah. The "good news" itself offers the best counter to the message of "false prophets."

C. The Two Builders: Matt 7:24–27

The evangelist returns once again to the Sermon tradition for this concluding parable of the wise and foolish builders (7:24–27, par. Luke 6:47–49). The Sermon tradition began with a series of Beatitudes; then came three major sections dealing respectively with love for one's enemies, judging one another, and fruits as indication of integrity; finally the parable brought the Sermon to its conclusion. Luke's parallel lacks the sharp antithetical parallelism of Matthew's construction because of stylistic modifications, but Matthew, too, has made his own redactional adjustments.

The major point of the parable consists in "doing" or "not doing

Jesus' words" (7:24, 26, par. Luke 6:47, 49). Both evangelists make clear that the "words" in question refer to the Sermon. Luke resumes the language of his setting, "Everyone who comes to me" (6:47, cf. 6:17), whereas Matthew adds the demonstrative pronoun, "these," to "my words" (6:24, 26). One's positive response to Jesus' teaching in the Sermon is then compared to a man who builds with or without a firm foundation. The ultimate outcome of the respective house when inundated demonstrates the value of having a firm foundation.

For Matthew, the one who builds his house on the "rock" is "wise" (7:24); the one who builds on the "sand" is "foolish" (7:26). Both designations appear in the parable of the Ten Virgins in the Olivet Discourse (25:1–13, cf. Luke 13:26–28), with the "wise" having taken the situation seriously and the "foolish" having come poorly prepared. The eschatological context of the latter parable parallels that of 7:24–27, as seen in the alternatives of 7:13–14, 21, 23. Thus, while the autumn storms characteristic of Palestinian geography provide the ultimate test of the house's foundation, the ultimate test of the "wise" and "foolish" builder comes at the judgment.

In other words, this parable offers a parallel to 7:13–14. In some ways, it explains the alternatives of the two ways. To enter the "narrow gate" and "constricted way" (7:13a, 14) means to "do Jesus' words." To enter the "wide gate" and the "spacious way" (7:13b) means "not to do Jesus' words." But what does it mean "to do Jesus' words"? The answer to this question takes us back to the theological function of the Sermon in Matthew. For those who view Matthew to be presenting Jesus as the New Moses with a New Law or those who view Matthew to be presenting Jesus as the interpreter of the Law, "to do these my words" means to obey scrupulously Jesus' demands as found in the Sermon. The emphasis falls on a radical ethical obedience that would correspond to Matthew's role as a representative of an "incipient Christian rabbinate." Eschatology has been swallowed up by ethics in the Matthean Sermon.

Yet we have found the Sermon to play another, more fundamental role for Matthew. To be sure, the accent on conduct begins with 5:13 and runs through the concluding parable. Terms and phrases like "good deeds" (5:16), the "greater righteousness" (5:20), "doing righteousness" (6:1), "doing the will of my Father" (7:21), and "doing these my words" (7:24–26) along with the commands and prohibitions of 5:21—7:12 all point to conduct toward others and/or God. But under this emphasis on conduct lies a more basic concern for christology. Not only does

Matthew 5–7 combine with Matthew 8–9 to depict Jesus as the Messiah who brings the promised age of salvation into history through his preaching, teaching, and healing (4:23–25), but the Matthean emphasis throughout the Sermon underscroes Jesus' person and ministry as the fulfillment of the Old Testament promises. The evangelist opened the Beatitudes by aligning them with Isaiah 61 and followed by giving the disciples the promised role of Israel in 5:13–16. The implicit christology in Jesus' proclamation of the Beatitudes becomes explicit christology in 5:17–18, which set the theological background for the demands summarized by 5:20 that follow in 5:21—7:12.

The conduct demanded represents neither a radicalizing of the Mosaic Law nor the streamlining of the complex Mosaic Law by use of the love commandment but a call for conduct that corresponds to the new relationship that God now offers to his own as seen in the coming of the Kingdom. The Sermon did not announce an "interim ethic"; it announced the "Kingdom ethic," the very content of which bore witness to the presence of the Kingdom in Jesus Messiah. Discipleship involved more than a legalistic obedience to the Law of Moses or even the "law" of Jesus; it also involved a totally different attitude and focus of one's life in terms of Jesus Messiah and what he came to accomplish.

Therefore, to "hear and do these my words" meant to respond to Jesus Messiah by yielding one's life in total surrender to God through him and to live commensurate with his teachings whose focal point was God and others rather than oneself. One's life ultimately indicated one's relationship to Jesus Messiah (7:13–27, especially 7:21–23) not because Jesus established a new ethic per se but because he established a new basis for ethics through the new, promised relationship between God and his own and among his own that enabled one to live accordingly. The "gospel of the Kingdom" proclaimed christologically-eschatologically that the Kingdom of Heaven had entered history through Jesus Messiah and through him its final consummation would culminate history. It also proclaimed ecclesiologically-ethically that a people were being called out, a new people of God, whose identity was found in the life of discipleship lived in keeping with the presence of the age of salvation that would enable one to pass the final judgment that all must face and to enter the consummated Kingdom (e.g., 5:20; 7:13–14, 21, 24–25).

X. EPILOGUE
Matthew 7:28-29

Translation

7 ²⁸When Jesus finished these words, the crowds were astounded at his teaching. ²⁹For he was teaching them as one who had authority, and not as did their scribes.

Literary Analysis

Matthew redactionally concludes the Sermon with a brief summary composed of two elements drawn from two separate sources. First, he used, "When Jesus finished these words," a statement occurring at the end of all five of his discourse sections (7:28; 11:1; 13:53; 19:1; 26:1). Each summary opens exactly the same with "When Jesus finished" (see Note on 7:28) and closes with "these words" (7:28; 19:1; 26:1), "these parables" appropriate to the Parable Discourse (13:53), and the contextually related "instructing his disciples" after the Mission Discourse (11:1). The roots of this summary may well stem from the Q tradition underlying the Sermon's conclusion now found in Luke 7:1, "When Jesus completed all his sayings," which Matthew then reworked into his own formula (see Note on 7:28).

Second, Matthew has taken almost verbatim the second half of a Marcan summary from 1:21–22 to complete his own summary in 7:28b, 29. The Marcan summary followed Jesus' calling of his first disciples (1:16–20, par. Matt 4:18–22). At that point, Matthew breaks with Mark's outline. He omits the exorcism of 1:23–28 and the reference to Jesus'

414

departure from Capernaum in 1:35–38 before turning to Mark 1:39 in his summary of 4:23 that helps set the background for the Sermon in 4:23—5:2 (see Notes on 4:23). Two other episodes from Mark 1:23–28 appear in the miracle setting of Matthew 8–9 (1:29–31, 32–34, par. Matt 8:14–15, 16–17). In 7:28b–29 the evangelist returns to the Marcan summary in 1:21–22 for the crowds' initial response to Jesus' ministry, since the Sermon presents Jesus' first public discourse in Matthew and the response found at the opening of Jesus' ministry in Mark 1:22 relates thematically to the Matthean counterpart in 5:3—7:27.

Matthew's formulaic summary of 7:28a has played a significant role in the discussion of the structure and interpretation of the First Gospel. Most notable, of course, has been the work of Benjamin Bacon *(Studies)* who viewed these formulae as dividing the Gospel into five sections behind which he saw a pentateuchal motif. Numerous other commentators have followed suit in dividing the Gospel into five parts, even when avoiding Bacon's pentateuchal motif (e.g., Schlatter, *Matthäus,* 125–28; Kilpatrick, *Origins,* 107–108, 135–36; Stendahl, *School,* 21–27; Bonnard, *Matthieu,* 110; Gaechter, *Matthäus,* 16–17; Hill, *Matthew,* 44–48; Grundmann, *Matthäus,* 50). Yet this division has not gone unchallenged, particularly in the more recent studies (e.g., Stonehouse, *Witness,* 130–31; Schniewind, *Matthäus,* 23–25; Schmauch, "Komposition," 64–87; Green, "Structure," 47–59; and most recently, Kingsbury, *Matthew,* 1–7).

Does the formulaic summary offer the structural framework of the Gospel? The answer involves theological as well as literary aspects. Theologically, Davies *(Setting,* 14–108) has demonstrated the lack of convincing literary and theological evidence supporting Bacon's pentateuchal thesis with Jesus as the New Moses. Stendahl *(School,* 20–29) took issue with Kilpatrick's ecclesiological focus on the Gospel as a liturgical document and suggested that it had a didactic function along the lines of the Didache and the Manual of Discipline of Qumran. Whether "catechetical," "apologetic," "didactic," or a "book," Kingsbury *(Matthew,* 5) has correctly noted that such designations stress to the extreme the paranetic element and fail to do justice to the evangelist's own phrase for the contents of his work, the "gospel of the Kingdom." Furthermore, Kingsbury, developing Stonehouse's observation of a different structure in Matthew, has offered another theological and literary structure (1:1—4:17; 4:18—16:20; 16:21—28:20) that bears the weight of the evangelist's literary and theological intentions (see Chap. 2, Comment A).

Literarily, these formulae leave much to be desired as the structural basis of the Gospel. First, the fivefold division leaves dangling as preamble and epilogue two very integral parts of the Gospel, the infancy and passion narratives (Davies, *Setting*, 25; Green, "Structure," 49; Kingsbury, *Matthew*, 4). Secondly, the primary function of each summary is to conclude a given discourse section as seen in the phrases "these words" (7:28; 19:1; 26:1), "these parables" (13:53), and "instructing his twelve disciples" (11:1), and to serve as a transition to what follows as seen in the syntax. Each formula, a dependent temporal clause, sets the stage for the main verb which, with the exception of 7:28, involved Jesus' departure for other activities. Kingsbury has summarized the function of these formulae as multiple: (a) they provide the literary conclusion for a discourse section rather than the literary structure for the Gospel, (b) they focus attention on Jesus Messiah by underscoring what he has said and set the stage for what he is about to do, and (c) they signal historical movement integral to Matthew's concept of salvation history (*Matthew*, 7).

Notes

7:28. *When Jesus finished.* This phrase renders the Semiticism behind the more literally translated, "And it came to pass when Jesus had finished . . ." (καὶ ἐγένετο ὅτε ἐτέλεσεν ὁ Ἰησοῦς). Luke 7:1 has a content parallel in better Greek style (Ἐπειδὴ ἐπλήρωσεν). The presence of this conclusion in Luke 7:1 and the following Lucan pericope of the Centurion in 7:2–10, par. Matt 8:5–13, strongly suggest that a similar conclusion had terminated the Q Sermon (Grundmann, *Matthäus*, 244; Schürmann, *Lukasevangelium*, 391, 396). Matthew has inserted two Marcan passages into the Q tradition (7:28b–29, par. Mark 1:22; 8:1–4, par. Mark 1:40–45).

Matthew may well reflect the earlier form of the conclusion which Luke has stylistically improved. But Luke most likely has the earlier verb to "complete" (πληρόω), a verb that has a much too technical "fulfillment" connotation for Matthew, especially when used with reference to the spoken word (see Note on 5:17). Consequently, the evangelist exchanged the theologically pregnant *to fulfill* for *to finish* (τελέω) with its more neutral meaning and used the verb to express its basic meaning in this context of bringing the discourse material to an end.

The object of this verb, *these words*, (τοὺς λόγους τούτους), also differs from Luke's "all his sayings" (πάντα τὰ ῥήματα αὐτοῦ). Whether Matthew's phrase, which picks up the same phrase of 7:24, 26, or Luke's, which statistically appears more frequently in Luke-Acts (19x in Luke, 12x in Acts; cf. 5x in Matt, 2x in Mark), occurred in the tradition lies beyond our control, since Luke demonstrates no redactional bias either way. Matthew does use ῥῆμα on occasion but usually referring to a word or statement (e.g., 12:36; 26:75; 27:14). The similar use of ῥῆμα to refer to a longer discourse in Acts 2:14; 5:20; 10:22, 44 may tip the scale in favor of Matthew's having the more original phrase. In either case, the clause not only terminates the Sermon in 7:28 but becomes a formulaic summary used by the evangelist to conclude the discourse materials in 11:1; 13:53; 19:1 and 26:1.

the crowds were astounded by his teaching. Matthew takes the main clause almost verbatim from Mark 1:22. He had broken with the Marcan order after the call of the first disciple in 4:18–22, par. Mark 1:16–20. In 4:23 the evangelist skipped to the Marcan summary in 1:39 to help shape the background for 5:1—9:35, and he returned to that context in 8:1–4, par. Mark 1:40–45. Matthew omits the intervening Marcan material of 1:23–28 except for the miracles of 1:29–31, 32–34, taken over in 8:14–15, 16–17. In this way the evangelist sets the Sermon within the Marcan tradition.

One of the two divergencies from Mark occurs in Matthew's addition of *the crowds* (οἱ ὄχλοι). This subject resumes a previous reference to *the crowds* in the setting of 4:25 and 5:1 (see Notes on 4:25 and 5:1) and includes them in the wider audience of the Sermon. In 5:2, *the disciples came* to Jesus and he *taught* them, but now at the end of the Sermon *the crowds* are singled out with no further reference to *the disciples*. In 8:1, after descending the mountain *great crowds* will again *follow* (see Note on 4:25) Jesus, as they did in 4:25 (see Note on 4:25), and set the stage for the miracles of Matthew 8–9. Thus Jesus' teaching (Matt 5–7) and miracles (8–9) take place with *the crowds* as witness. Just as they are present at the end of this discourse in 7:28, they express their amazement at the end of Matthew 8–9 in 9:33 and become the object of Jesus' compassion (9:36) in anticipation of the Mission Discourse in Matthew 10. Yet they remain observers for Matthew, a part of the landscape for Jesus' ministry. Their response sets Jesus off as someone distinct from normal, everyday experiences without their actually recognizing him to be Jesus Messiah or addressing him as "Lord," a role reserved for those of faith (see Notes on 4:25—5:1).

In this context, the *crowds'* response to Jesus' *teaching* (διδαχῇ) connotes more than surprise; they were overwhelmed. Their astonishment approaches shock. Furthermore, the use of the imperfect tense suggests the ongoing state of their response.

7:29. *For he was teaching . . . authority.* This statement expresses the basis for the *crowds'* response. By introducing the so-called "Sermon" with the verb to *teach* (see Note on 5:2) and by concluding the Sermon with specific reference to Jesus' *teaching* in noun (7:28b) and verb (7:29) drawn from the Marcan tradition, Matthew clearly expresses his perception of 5:3—7:27 as being *teaching.* To that extent the "Sermon" on the Mount represents a misnomer.

Yet *teaching* and *preaching* belonged closely related for the first evangelist. One cannot use the dogmatic categories of "gospel" for the one and "law" for the other nor can one use the exegetical categories of "kerygma" for the one and "paranesis" for the other. Such distinctions have little basis in Matthew's usage of *teaching* and *preaching* (see Note on 4:23). To be sure, *preaching* connoted for Matthew the special "heralding" or "proclamation" of the coming Kingdom by the Baptist (3:1), by Jesus (4:17, 23; 9:35), and by the disciples (10:7; 16:13; 24:14). But *teaching* also involved the "gospel of the Kingdom." Those who had the "eyes" and "ears" of faith could "see" and "understand" from his actions and teaching who he was, namely, the one through whom the Kingdom has come into history. Consequently, those who "understood" in faith addressed him as "Lord," while those who did not "hear" addressed him as "teacher" in keeping with the formal similarity between Jesus and the rabbis of his day.

In 5:3—7:27 Jesus never used the familiar prophetic formula of "Thus saith the Lord," did not simply stay with general proverbial platitudes as found in Wisdom teaching, made no reference to the tradition or the Law in a fashion typical of the scribes; rather, he taught *as one who had authority.* The *crowds* recognized the difference in style based on the content of his *teaching.* This recognition, limited though it was to shock, supported Matthew's portrait of Jesus Messiah whose *words* revealed him to be unique (cf. his *deeds* in 9:33). The "ear" of faith enabled one to acknowledge him as Lord and recognize his *authority* as that given by the Father to announce the fulfillment of the Father's promises and the presence of the Kingdom. Therefore, for the disciples also 5:3—7:27 can be called the "Sermon" on the Mount in that it presents Jesus as the Messiah whose declarations and demands set forth the gospel of the Kingdom.

not as. . . . their scribes. The second divergence from Mark 1:22 comes with the addition of *their* (αὐτῶν). This pronoun maintains the distance between the Jews and Matthew's community (see Note on 4:23) and also identifies the *crowds* with those on the outside rather than with the believers. The comparison between Jesus and the *scribes* lay at hand in the formal nature of Jesus' ministry. While appearing to be like the *scribes,* Jesus stood in stark contrast in his content and method. Thus Matthew concluded the Sermon with his christological concern by referring to Jesus' person, at least by implication through the *crowds'* response. The evangelist does the same at the end of the miracles of Matthew 8–9 by means of the *crowds'* response in 9:33.

Comments

With the summary of 7:28–29, the evangelist brings the Sermon to its close. Yet this brief unit provides more than a formal conclusion to the discourse. Composed of a formulaic summary (7:21a), redactionally placed at the end of each larger discourse section (7:28; 11:1; 13:53; 19:1; 26:1), and a part of a Marcan summary (7:28b–29, par. Mark 1:22). this unit with its numerous redactional elements makes its own statement. This statement, like that in 9:33 at the conclusion of the series of miracles, betrays the evangelist's ultimate concern in both Matthew 5–7 and Matthew 8–9 to be christological rather than ecclesiological or paranetic. This christological motif provided the setting for the Sermon in 4:23–25, ran consistently throughout the Sermon, and now concludes the Sermon.

Somewhat surprisingly, the evangelist chose to make this statement through the "crowds" response rather than the disciples' confession. He accomplished this first by his redactional selection of Mark 1:22 to form the main clause of the summary. In each of the other formulaic summaries, the main clause involved Jesus' next activity expressed by a verb denoting his departure (11:1; 13:53; 19:1; 26:1). The use of Mark 1:22 shifts the attention to "the crowds." Second, by redactionally adding "the crowds" to the Marcan tradition (cf. Mark 1:21–22), the evangelist has reintroduced "the crowds" into the Sermon context, after having taken leave from them in 5:1 to focus the Sermon on the disciples (5:1–2).

Why does Matthew go to such lengths to introduce "the crowds" who represent neither Jesus' opponents, the "scribes and Pharisees," nor his followers, those who call him "Lord"? Perhaps the answer lies in the Sermon's dual audience. Matt 5:3—7:27 clearly addresses the disciples, those who have responded in faith to Jesus' ministry, the announcement of salvation (5:3–12), their role as God's people (5:13–16), Jesus as the fulfillment of the Old Testament promise (5:17–18), and the demand for conduct corresponding to the presence of the Kingdom (5:20—7:27). This message, the Sermon, comes both as reassurance and as warning for the disciples. Christology and ecclesiology, kerygma and paranesis intertwine in the redemptive historical perspective of the Kingdom present in Jesus' ministry and the anticipation of the Kingdom future at the consummation. For those who "hear" with the "ear" of faith and "understand," that is, respond accordingly, Matt 5:3—7:27 proclaims the "gospel of the Kingdom."

Yet "the crowds" furnish the background of the Sermon. They focus the attention on Jesus (4:25—5:1) in response to his teaching (7:28–29) and his miracles (9:33). But their response is that of confused curiosity rather than faith. They register shock (7:28) and bewilderment (9:33) at Jesus' teaching and ministry. The evangelist removes all doubt about their ultimate relationship to Jesus with his redactional insertion of the possessive pronoun "their" with the noun "scribes." It was "their" synagogues where Jesus had opened his ministry in 4:23. Yet if they stand in contrast to the disciples or believers, they also stand in contrast to the "scribes and Pharisees" in Matthew 5–9 who take issue with Jesus' ministry (e.g., 9:3–8; 33–34, cf. 5:20; 6:1–18). Therefore, as we noted in 4:25, "the crowds" appear to function along the lines of a Greek chorus. They express the reactions of a somewhat neutral observer in contrast to the positive response of the believers and the negative response of the "scribes and Pharisees."

But "the crowds" also seem to play more than a literary role of stage setting through transitional observations. One might see them as representing the focus of the Church's mission by symbolizing the masses who are "open" to the gospel of the Kingdom. Matt 9:36 sets the background for the Mission Discourse by describing Jesus' compassion for them in their bewilderment that reminded him of "sheep without a shepherd." Yet we cannot ignore the fact that the crowds never respond in faith to either Jesus' or his disciples' ministry. On the contrary, the religious rulers orchestrate their call for Jesus' ultimate rejection in 27:20.

Perhaps "the crowds" play a somewhat subdued apologetic role for Matthew. As "neutral" observers, their response to Jesus' ministry carries its own weight. They recognized that he was different, his teaching was different, his attitude towards others was different. He left them shocked, amazed, grateful, and finally disappointed and angry. By noting their reaction, Matthew demonstrates his own christological concern to depict Jesus as the Messiah, the one who confounded human understanding based on the observable. Therefore, even the neutral observers recognized that Jesus was unique. To those who had been given to understand the "mystery of the Kingdom," he was the Messiah. To those who found him a threat to their own religious security and their "righteousness," he was a mortal enemy. Any way one approaches the subject, one has to confront the reality of Jesus' person and ministry.

Therefore, "the crowds," "the disciples," and "the scribes and Pharisees" all play distinctive roles in the Gospel. Their response composes part of the evangelist's portrait of Jesus Messiah. To be sure, each group also has its significance for Matthew's community. The historical counterpart to the "disciples" was doubtless the believers in Matthew's Community. The historical counterpart to the "scribes and Pharisees" was doubtless the Jewish religious leaders who continued to make life difficult for Matthew's community and perhaps also the rigorous Jewish-Christians whose life and teaching approached that of the "scribes and Pharisees." A historical counterpart for "the crowds" may have been those in response to the mission who showed curiosity and interest but lacked the commitment of discipleship. The evangelist's primary interest, however, in each of these groups stems from how they bore witness respectively in the context of Jesus' earthly ministry to Jesus Messiah. The gospel of the Kingdom centers on Jesus Messiah.

BIBLIOGRAPHY OF WORKS CITED

The abbreviations of journals and series in this bibliography correspond to the listing in the "Instructions for Contributors" in the *Journal of Biblical Literature* 95 (1976):339–46. Abbreviations from that listing that are used here, as well as abbreviations for journals and series not carried in the *JBL* article, are identified below.

AnBib	Analecta biblica
ATANT	Abhandlungen zur Theologie des Alten und Neuen Testaments
ATD	Das Alte Testament Deutsch
ATLA	American Theological Library Association
BEvT	Beiträge zur evangelischen Theologie
BHT	Beiträge zur historischen Theologie
Bib	*Biblica*
BibLeb	*Bibel und Leben*
BJRL	*Bulletin of the John Rylands University Library of Manchester*
BKAT	Biblischer Kommentar: Altes Testament
BR	*Biblical Research*
BWANT	Beiträge zur Wissenschaft vom Alten und Neuen Testament
BZ	*Biblische Zeitschrift*
BZNW	Beihefte zur *ZNW*
CH	*Church History*
CNT	Commentaire du Nouveau Testament
EBib	Études bibliques
EvT	Evangelische Theologie
ExpTim	*Expository Times*
FRLANT	Forschungen zur Religion und Literatur des Alten und Neuen Testaments
FTS	Frankfurter theologische Studien
HKAT	Handkommentar zum Alten Testament
HNT	Handbuch zum Neuen Testament
HNTC	Harper's New Testament Commentaries
HTKNT	Herders theologischer Kommentar zum Neuen Testament
HTR	*Harvard Theological Review*
ICC	International Critical Commentary
IEJ	*Israel Exploration Journal*
JBL	*Journal of Biblical Literature*
JQR	*Jewish Quarterly Review*
JTS	*Journal of Theological Studies*
LUÅ	Lunds universitets årsskrift
MeyerK	H. A. W. Meyer, Kritisch-exegetischer Kommentar über das Neue Testament
MTS	Marburg theologische Studien
NCB	New Century Bible

NICNT   New International Commentary on the New Testament
NIGNTC   New International Greek New Testament Commentary
NovT   *Novum Testamentum*
NovTSup   Novum Testamentum, Supplements
NTA   *New Testament Abstracts*
NTD   Das Neue Testament Deutsch
NTS   *New Testament Studies*
RB   *Revue biblique*
RHLR   *Revues d'histoire et de littérature religieuses*
RNT   Regensburger Neues Testament
RQ   *Römische Quartalschrift für christliche Altertumskunde und Kirchengeschichte*
SANT   Studien zum Alten und Neuen Testament
SBLMS   Society of Biblical Literature Monograph Series
SBM   Stuttgarter biblische Monographien
SBT   Studies in Biblical Theology
SE   *Studia Evangelica I, II, III*
SEA   *Svensk exegetisk årsbok*
SNTSMS   Society for New Testament Studies Monograph Series
SNTU   Studien zum Neuen Testament und seiner Umwelt
ST   *Studia theologica*
TEH   Theologische Existenz Heute
THKNT   Theologischer Handkommentar zum Neuen Testament
TS   *Theological Studies*
TSK   *Theologische Studien und Kritiken*
TZ   *Theologische Zeitschrift*
WMANT   Wissenschaftliche Monographien zum Alten und Neuen Testament
WUNT   Wissenschaftliche Untersuchungen zum Neuen Testament
ZAW   *Zeitschrift für die alttestamentliche Wissenschaft*
ZKG   *Zeitschrift für Kirchengeschichte*
ZKT   *Zeitschrift für katholische Theologie*
ZNW   *Zeitschrift für die neutestamentliche Wissenschaft*
ZST   *Zeitschrift für systematische Theologie*
ZTK   *Zeitschrift für Theologie und Kirche*

Agouridès, S. "La Tradition des Béatitudes chez Matthieu et Luc," in *Mélanges B. Rigaux*. Edd. A. Descamps and A. de Halleux. Gembloux: Duculot, 1970. 9–27.

Allen, W. C. *A Critical and Exegetical Commentary on the Gospel According to S. Matthew*. ICC. Edinburgh: Clark, 1912.

Amstutz, J. ΑΠΛΟΤΗΣ: *Eine Begriffsgeschichtliche Studie zum jüdisch-christlichen Griechisch*. Bonn: Hanstein, 1968.

Arens, E. *The Ηλθον-Sayings in the Synoptic Tradition: A Historico-critical Investigation*. Göttingen: Vandenhoeck und Ruprecht, 1976.

Augsburger, M. S. *The Expanded Life: The Sermon on the Mount for Today*. New York: Abingdon, 1972.

Bacher, W. *Die exegetische Terminologie der jüdischen Traditionsliteratur*. 2 vols. Leipzig: Hinrichs, 1899, 1905.

Bacon, B. W. *Studies in Matthew*. London: Constable, 1930.

Baltensweiler, H. *Die Ehe im Neuen Testament*. ATANT 52. Zurich: Zwingli, 1967.

———. "Die Ehebruchsklausel bei Matthaus." *TZ* 15 (1959): 340–56.

Banks, R. *Jesus and the Law in the Synoptic Tradition*. NTSMS 28. Cambridge: University Press, 1975.

Barth, G. "Matthew's Understanding of the Law," in *Tradition and Interpretation in Matthew*. Philadelphia: Westminster, 1963.

Bauer, W. *A Greek-English Lexicon of the New Testament and Other Early Christian Literature*. 4th rev. and aug. ed. Trans. W. F. Arndt and F. W. Gingrich. Chicago: University of Chicago Press, 1952.

Beare, F. W. "Speaking with Tongues: A Critical Survey of the NT Evidence." *JBL* 83 (1964): 229–46.

Benoit, P. "Remarques sur les sommaires des Actes," in *Mélanges Goguel. Aux Sources de la tradition chrétienne.* Paris: Delachaux et Niestlé, 1950. 1–10.

Berger, K. *Die Amen-Worte Jesu.* BZNW 39. Berlin: de Gruyter, 1970.

———. *Die Gesetzesauslegung Jesu.* WMANT 40. Neukirchen: Neukirchener Verlag, 1972.

———. "Zu den sogenannten Sätzen des heiligen Rechts." *NTS* 17 (1970–71): 10–40.

Berner, U. *Die Bergpredigt: Rezeption und Auslegung im 20. Jahrhundert.* Göttingen: Vandenhoeck und Ruprecht, 1979.

Best, E. "Matthew V. 3." *NTS* 7 (1960–61): 255–58.

———. "1 Peter and the Gospel Tradition.: *NTS* 16 (1969–70): 95–113.

Betz, H. D. "Eine judenchristliche Kult-Didache im Matthäus 6:1–18," in *Jesus Christus in Historie und Theologie: Festschrift für H. Conzelmann.* Ed. G. Strecker. Tübingen: Mohr, 1975. 445–457.

———. "Matthew vi. 22 f and Ancient Greek Theories of Vision," in *Text and Interpretation: Studies in the New Testament Presented to Matthew Black.* Edd. E. Best and R. McL. Wilson. Cambridge: University Press, 1979. 43–56.

Black, M. *An Aramaic Approach to the Gospels.* 3rd ed. Oxford: Clarendon, 1967.

Blass, F., Debrunner, A., and Funk, R. *A Greek Grammar of the New Testament and other Early Christian Literature.* Chicago: University Press, 1961.

Blass, F., Debrunner, A., and Rehkopf, F. *Grammatik des neuentestamentlichen Griechisch.* 15th ed. Göttingen: Vandenhoeck und Ruprecht, 1979.

Böcher, O. "Wolfe in Schafspelzen: Zum religionsgeschichtlichen Hintergrund vom Matth. 7, 15." *TZ* 24 (1968): 405–26.

Boice, J. *The Sermon on the Mount.* Grand Rapids: Eerdmans, 1972.

Bonhoeffer, D. *The Cost of Discipleship.* London: SCM, 1959.

Bonnard, P. *L'Evangile selon Saint Matthieu.* CNT 1, 2nd ed. Neuchatel: Delachaux et Niestlé, 1970.

Bornhäuser, K. *Die Bergpredigt.* Gütersloh: Bertelsmann, 1927.

Bornkamm, G. "Der Aufbau der Bergpredigt." *NTS* 24 (1977–78): 419–32.

———. "End-Expectation and Church in Matthew," in *Tradition and Interpretation* in Matthew. Philadelphia: Westminster, 1963.

———. "Der Lohngedanke im Neuen Testament," in *Studien zu Antike und Christentum: Gesammelte Aufsatze.* Vol. 2. Munich: Kaiser, 1959.

Branscomb, B. H. *Jesus and the Law of Moses.* New York: R. R. Smith, 1930.

Braun, H. *Spätjüdisch-häretischer und frühchristlicher Radikalismus: Jesus von Nazareth und die Qumran Sekte.* 2 vols. BHT 24. Tübingen: Mohr, 1957.

Broer, I. "Die Antithesen und der Evangelist Matthäus: Versuch eine alte These zu revidieren." *BZ* 19 (1975): 50–63.

Brown, F., Driver, S. R., and Briggs, C. A. *A Hebrew and English Lexicon of the Old Testament.* Oxford: Clarendon, 1953.

Brown, R. E. *The Birth of the Messiah.* Garden City: Doubleday, 1977.

Bruce, F. F. *The Acts of the Apostles.* Grand Rapids: Eerdmans, 1960.

Brun, L. *Segen und Fluch im Urchristentum.* Oslo: Dybwad, 1932.

Brunner, K. "Textkritisches zu Mt 6, 28." *ZKT* 100 (1978): 251–56.

Bultmann, R. *The History of the Synoptic Tradition.* Oxford: Blackwell, 1963.

Burchard, C. "The Theme of the Sermon on the Mount," in *Essays on the Love Commandment.* Ed. R. Fuller. Philadelphia: Fortress, 1978.

Burney, C. F. *The Poetry of Our Lord.* Oxford: Clarendon, 1925.

Butler, D. *The Originality of St. Matthew.* Cambridge: University Press, 1951.

Cadbury, H. J. "The Summaries of Acts," in *The Beginnings of Christianity.* 5 vols. Edd. J. Foakes-Jackson and K. Lake. London: Macmillan, 1938. 5:392–402.

Carlston, C. "The Things that Defile (Mark 7:14 and the Law in Matthew and Mark)." *NTS* 15 (1968–69): 75–96.

Catchpole, D. R. "The Synoptic Divorce Material as a Traditio-Historical Problem.'" *BJRL* 57 (1974): 92–127.

Conzelmann, H. *Die Apostelgeschichte.* HNT 7. Tübingen: Mohr, 1963.

Cothenet, E. "Les prophètes chrétiens dans l'Évangile selon saint Matthieu," in *L'Évangile selon Matthieu: Rédaction et Théologie.* Gembloux: Duculot, 1972.

Cross, F. M. *The Ancient Library of Qumran and Modern Biblical Studies.* 2nd ed. New York: Doubleday, 1961.

Dalman, G. *Jesus-Jeschua: Studies in the Gospels.* New York: KTAV, reprint 1971.
——. *Orte und Wege Jesu.* 3rd ed. Gütersloh: Mohn, 1924.
——. *Die Worte Jesu.* 2nd ed. Leipzig: Hinrichs, 1930.
Danby, H. *The Mishnah.* Oxford: University Press, 1933.
Daniel, C. " 'Faux Prophètes': surnom des Esseniens dans le Sermon sur la Montagne." *RQ* 7 (1969–71):45–79.
Daube, D. *The New Testament and Rabbinic Judaism.* London: Athlone, 1956.
Davies, W. D. "Matthew 5:17, 18," in *Christian Origins and Judaism.* Philadelphia: Westminster, 1962. 30–66.
——. *The Setting of the Sermon on the Mount.* Cambridge: University Press, 1964.
Degenhardt, H. J. *Lukas Evangelist der Armen: Besitz und Besitzverzicht in den lukanischen Schriften.* Stuttgart: Katholische Bibelwerk, 1965.
Delling, G. "Das Logion Mk x.11 (und seine Abwandlungen) im Neuen Testament." *NovT* 1 (1956):263–74.
Descamps, A. *Les Justes et la Justice dans les évangiles et le christianisme primitif hormis la doctrine proprement paulinienne.* Gembloux: Duculot, 1950.
Dibelius, F. "Zwei Worte Jesu." *ZNW* 11 (1910):188–92.
Dibelius, M. *The Sermon on the Mount.* New York: Scribner's, 1940 = "Die Bergpredigt," in *Botschaft und Geschichte.* 2 vols. Ed. G. Bornkamm. Tübingen: Mohr, 1953. 1:79–174.
——. *From Tradition to Gospel.* London: Nicholson and Watson, 1934.
Dibelius, M. and H. Greeven. *James.* Philadelphia: Fortress, 1976.
Dietzfelbinger, C. *Die Antithesen der Bergpredigt.* TEH 186. Munich: Kaiser, 1975.
Dihle, A. *Die Goldene Regel: Eine Einführung in die Geschichte der antiken und frühchristlicher Vulgärethik.* Göttingen: Vandenhoeck und Ruprecht, 1962.
Dodd, C. H. "The Beatitudes: A Form Critical Study," in *More New Testament Studies.* Grand Rapids: Eerdmans, 1968.
Dunn, J. D. G. *Jesus and the Spirit.* Philadelphia: Westminster, 1975.
Du Plessis, P. J. ΤΕΛΕΙΟΣ: *The Idea of Perfection in the New Testament.* Kampen: Theologische Akademie, 1959.
Dupont, J. *Les Béatitudes: Le problème littéraire. Les deux versions du Sermon sur la Montagne et des Béatitudes.* Vol. 1. 2nd ed. Bruges: Abbaye de Saint-André, 1958.
——. *Les Béatitudes: La Bonne Nouvelle.* Vol. 2. Paris: Gabalda et Cie, 1969.
——. *Les Béatitudes: Les Évangelistes.* Vol. 3. Paris: Gabalda et Cie, 1973.
Egger, W. *Frohbotschaft und Lehre: Die Sammelberichte der Worten Jesu im Markusevangelium.* FTS 19. Frankfurt: Knecht, 1976.
Eichholz, G. *Auslegung der Bergpredigt.* Neukirchen: Neukirchener Verlag, 1965.
Fiebig, P. *Jesu Bergpredigt.* FRLANT 20. Göttingen: Vandenhoeck und Ruprecht, 1924.
Filson, F. "Broken Patterns in the Gospel of Matthew." *JBL* 75 (1956):227–31.
——. *The Gospel According to St. Matthew.* HNTC. New York: Harper and Row, 1974.
Fitzmeyer, J. "The Matthean Divorce Texts and Some New Palestinian Evidence." *TS* 37 (1976):197–226.
Flender, H. *Heil und Geschichte in der Theologie Lukas.* BEvT 41. Munich: Kaiser, 1965.
Flusser, D. "Blessed are the Poor in Spirit." *IEJ* 10 (1960):1–13.
Frankemölle, H. *Jahwebund und Kirche Christi.* NTA 10. Munster: Aschendorff, 1974.
——. "Die Makarismen (Mt 5:1–12; Lk 6:20–25). Motive und Umfang der redactionellen Komposition." *BZ* 15 (1971):52–75.
Fridrichsen, H. "*Excepta fornicationis causa.*" *SEÅ* 9 (1944):54–58.
Furnish, V. P. *The Love Command in the New Testament.* Nashville: Abingdon, 1972.
Gaechter, P. *Das Matthäus Evangelium.* Innsbruck: Tyrolia, 1962.
George, A. "La 'Form' des Béatitudes jusqu'à Jésus," in *Mélanges bibliques redigés en l'honneur de André Robert.* Paris: Bloud et Gay, 1957. 398–403.
Gerhardsson, B. "Geistiger Opferdienst nach Matth 6:1–6, 16–21," in *Neues Testament und Geschichte: O. Cullmann zum 70. Geburtstag.* Zürich: Theologischer Verlag, 1972. 69–77.
——. *The Testing of God's Son (Matt 4:1–11 and Par): An Analysis of an Early Christian Midrash.* Lund: Gleerup, 1966.
Gese, H. "Das Gesetz," in *Zur biblischen Theologie.* Munich: Kaiser, 1977. 55–84.
Goppelt, L. *Die Bergpredigt und die Wirklichkeit dieser Welt.* CH 96. Stuttgart: Calwer, 1968.
——. *Der erste Petrusbrief.* MeyerK 12, 1. Göttingen: Vandenhoeck und Ruprecht, 1978.
Green, H. B. "The Structure of St. Matthew's Gospel." *SE* IV (= *TU* 102). Berlin: Akademie, 1968. 4:47–59.
Greeven, H. "Die Ehe nach dem Neuen Testament." *NTS* 15 (1968–69):365–88.
Grundmann, W. *Das Evangelium nach Lukas.* THKNT 3. 2nd ed. Berlin: Evangelische Verlaganstalt, 1961.

———. *Das Evangelium nach Matthäus.* THKNT 1. Berlin: Evangelische Verlaganstalt, 1968.

Guelich, R. "The Antitheses of Matthew V. 21–48: Traditional and/or Redactional?" *NTS* 22 (1976–77):444–57.

———. "The Matthean Beatitudes: 'Entrance-Requirements' or Eschatological Blessings?" *JBL* 95 (1976):415–34.

———. "Mt 5²²: Its Meaning and Integrity." *ZNW* 64 (1973):39–52.

Gundry, R. "Verba Christi in I Peter: Their Implications concerning the Authorship of I Peter and the Authenticity of the Gospel Tradition." *NTS* 13 (1966/67):336–50.

Gunkel, K. *Die Psalmen.* HKAT 2:2. 4th ed. Göttingen: Vandenhoeck und Ruprecht, 1926.

Hahn, F. *The Titles of Jesus in Christology.* London: Lutterworth, 1969.

Hare, D. *The Theme of Jewish Persecution of Christians in the Gospel According to St. Matthew.* SNTSMS 6. Cambridge: University Press, 1967.

Haenchen, E. *The Acts of the Apostles.* Philadelphia: Westminster, 1971.

Hammerton-Kelly, R. G. "Attitudes to the Law in Matthew's Gospel: A Discussion of Matthew 5:18." *BR* 17 (1972):19–32.

Harnack, A. von. *The Sayings of Jesus.* Translated by J. R. Wilkinson. London: Williams & Norgate, 1908.

Hasler, V. *Amen. Redaktionsgeschichtliche Untersuchungen zur Einführungsformel der Herrenworte "Wahrlich Ich sage euch."* Zurich: Gotthelf, 1969.

———. *Gesetz und Evangelium in der alten Kirche bis Origenes: Eine auslegungsgeschichtliche Untersuchung.* Zurich: Gotthelf, 1953.

Herrmann, W. *Ethik.* Tübingen: Mohr, 1901.

Herrmann, W., and Harnack, A. von. *Essays on the Social Gospel.* London: Williams and Norgate, 1907.

Hill, D. "False Prophets and Charismatics: Structure and Interpretation in Matthew 7, 15–23." *Bib* 57 (1976):327–48.

Hill, D. *The Gospel of Matthew.* NCB. Greenwood: Attic, 1975.

Hoffmann, P. "Auslegung der Bergpredigt." *BibLeb* 10 (1969):57–69, 111–22, 175–89, 264–75; 11 (1970):89–104.

———. "πάντες ἐργάται ἀδικίας." *ZNW* 58 (1967):188–214.

Honeyman, A. M. "Matthew V. 18 and the Validity of the Law." *NTS* 1 (1954–55):141–42.

Howard, V. *Das Ego Jesu in den synoptischen Evangelien.* MTS 14. Marburg: Elwert, 1975.

Huber, H. *Die Bergpredigt.* Göttingen: Vandenhoeck und Ruprecht, 1932.

Hübner, H. *Das Gesetz in der synoptischen Tradition.* Witten: Luther, 1973.

Hummel, R. *Die Auseinandersetzung zwischen Kirche und Judentum in Matthäusevangelium.* BEvT 33. Munchen: Kaiser, 1963.

Hunter, A. M. *A Pattern for Life: An Exposition of the Sermon on the Mount.* 2nd ed. of *Design for Life.* Philadelphia: Westminster, 1965.

The Interpreter's Dictionary of the Bible. Ed. G. Buttrick. 4 vols. Nashville: Abingdon, 1962.

Janzen, W. "'Ašrê in the Old Testament." *HTR* 58 (1965):215–26.

Jeremias, J. "Abba," in *The Prayers of Jesus.* SBT 6. Naperville: Allenson, 1967, 11–66.

———. "Daily Prayer in the Life of Jesus and the Primitive Church," in *The Prayers of Jesus,* 66–81.

———. *Jesus' Promise to the Nations.* Naperville: Allenson, 1958.

———. "Kennzeichen der ipsissima vox Jesu," in *Abba: Studien zur neutestamentlichen Theologie und Geschichte.* Göttingen: Vandenhoeck und Ruprecht, 1966. 145–52.

———. "Die Lampe unter dem Scheffel," in *Abba,* 99–102.

———. " 'Lass deine Gabe' (Matt 5:23 f.)," in *Abba,* 103–07.

———. "The Lord's Prayer in Light of Recent Research," in *The Prayers of Jesus,* 82–107.

———. "Matthäus 7:6a," in *Abba,* 83–87.

———. *New Testament Theology.* 1 vol. New York: Scribner's, 1971.

———. *The Parables of Jesus.* 2nd ed. New York: Scribner's, 1963.

———. *The Sermon on the Mount.* Philadelphia: Fortress, 1963.

———. "Zum Problem des Ur-Markus," in *Abba,* 87–90.

Käsemann, E. "The Beginnings of Christian Theology," in *New Testament Questions of Today.* London: SCM, 1969. 82–107.

———. "Sentences of Holy Law in the New Testament," in *New Testament Questions of Today,* 66–81.

Keck, L. "The Poor among the Saints in the New Testament." *ZNW* 56 (1965):100–29.

Keller, C. "Les 'Béatitudines' de l'Ancien Testament," in *Hommage à W. Vischer.* Montpellier: Cause, Graille, Castelnau, 1960. 88–100.

Kiefer, R. "Weisheit und Segen als Grundmotive der Seligpreisungen bei Matthaus und Lukas," in *Theologie aus dem Norden.* Ed. A. Fuchs. SNTU. Linz: Fuchs, 1976. 2:29–43.

Kilpatrick, G. D. *The Origins of the Gospel According to St. Matthew.* Oxford: Clarendon, 1946.

Kingsbury, J. D. *Matthew: Structure, Christology, Kingdom.* Philadelphia: Fortress, 1975.

Kissinger, W. S. *The Sermon on the Mount: A History of Interpretation and Bibliography.* ATLA 3. Metuchen: Scarecrow, 1975.

Kittel, G. "Die Bergpredigt und die Ethik des Judentums." *ZST* 2 (1924–25):555–94.

———. *Die Religionsgeschichte und das Urchristentum.* Gütersloh: Bertelsmann, 1932.

———. and Friedrich, G. *Theological Dictionary of the New Testament.* 10 vols. Grand Rapids: Eerdmans, 1964–76.

Köhler, K. "Zu Matthew 5:22." *ZNW* 19 (1919):91–94.

Klostermann, E. *Das Matthäusevangelium.* HNT. 4th ed. Tübingen: Mohr, 1971.

Koch, K. *The Growth of Biblical Tradition.* New York: Scribner's, 1969.

Krämer, M. "Hütet euch vor den falschen Propheten: Eine uberlieferungsgeschichtliche Untersuchung zu Mt 7, 15–23/Lk 6, 43–46/Mt 12, 33–37." *Bib* 57 (1976):349–77.

Kraus, H.-J. *Psalmen.* 2 vols. BKAT 15. 4th ed. Neukirchen: Neukirchener Verlag, 1973.

Kretschmar, G. "Ein Beitrag zur Frage nach dem Ursprung frühchristlicher Askese." *ZTK* 61 (1964):27–67.

Kretzer, A. *Die Herrschaft des Himmels und die Söhne des Reiches.* SBM 10. Echter: KBW, 1971.

Kümmel, W. G. "Jesus und die jüdische Traditionsgedanke." *ZNW* 33 (1934):105–30.

———. *Promise and Fulfillment: The Eschatological Message of Jesus.* SBT 23. London: SCM, 1961.

Kuhn, K. G. *Achtzehngebet und Vaterunser und der Rheim.* WUNT 1. Tübingen: Mohr, 1950.

Kutch, E. "Eure Rede aber sei ja ja, nei nein," *EvT* 20 (1960):206–18.

Ladd, G. *The New Testament and Criticism.* Grand Rapids: Eerdmans, 1967.

———. *The Presence of the Future.* Grand Rapids: Eerdmans, 1974.

Lagrange, M. *L'évangile selon Saint Matthieu.* EBib 4. Paris: Gabalda, 1923.

Lane, W. *Commentary on the Gospel of Mark.* NICNT. Grand Rapids: Eerdmans, 1974.

Légasse, S. "Les pauvres en espirit et les 'volontaires' de Qumran." *NTS* 8 (1961–62):336–45.

Lidell, H. G., Scott, R., and Jones, H. S., eds. *A Greek-English Lexicon.* Oxford: Clarendon, 1940.

Lieberman, S. *Greek in Jewish Palestine.* New York: Jewish Theological Seminary, 1942.

Lipinski, E. "Macarismes et psaumes de congratulation." *RB* 75 (1968):321–67.

Ljungman, H. *Das Gesetz Erfüllen: Matth. 5:17 ff. und 3:15 Untersucht.* Lund: Gleerup, 1954.

Lloyd-Jones, D. M. *Studies in the Sermon on the Mount.* 2 vols. Grand Rapids: Eerdmans, 1959–60.

Lohmeyer, E. *Das Evangelium des Matthäus.* MeyerK. Göttingen: Vandenhoeck und Ruprecht, 1962.

———. *"Our Father": An Introduction to the Lord's Prayer.* New York: Harper and Row, 1965.

Lohse, E. "Aber ich sage euch," in *Der Ruf Jesu und die Antwort der Gemeinde: Festschrift für J. Jeremias zum 70. Geburtstag.* Ed. E. Lohse. Göttingen: Vandenhoeck und Ruprecht, 1970. 189–203.

Loisy, A. *Les Evangiles synoptiques.* 2 vols. Ceffonds: Près Montier-en-der, 1907.

———. "Le Discours sur la Montagne." *RHLR* 8 (1903):97–132.

Luck, U. *Die Vollkommenheitsforderung der Bergpredigt.* TEH 150. Munich: Kaiser, 1968.

Lührmann, H. D. "Liebet euere Feinde (Lk 6, 27–36/Mt 5, 39–48)." *ZTK* 69 (1972):412–38.

———. *Die Redaktion der Logienquelle.* Neukirchen: Neukirchener Verlag, 1969.

Luz, U. "Die Erfüllung des Gesetzes bei Matthaus." *ZTK* 75 (1978):398–435.

Manson, T. W. *The Sayings of Jesus.* London: SCM, 1957.

Marshall, I. H. *The Gospel of Luke.* NIGNTC. Grand Rapids: Eerdmans, 1978.

———. "The Meaning of Reconciliation," in *The Unity and Diversity of New Testament Theology: Festschrift for G. Ladd.* Ed. R. A. Guelich. Grand Rapids, Eerdmans, 1978. 117–32.

Marxsen, W. *Mark the Evangelist.* Nashville: Abingdon, 1969.

Meier, J. P. *Law and History in Matthew's Gospel: A Redactional Study of Mt. 5:17–48.* AnBib 71. Rome: Biblical Institute Press, 1976.

Metzger, B. M. *A Textual Commentary on the Greek New Testament.* London: United Bible Societies, 1971.

Michaelis, W. *Das Evangelium nach Matthaus.* 2 vols. Zurich: Zwingli, 1948–49.

Montefiore, C. G. *Rabbinic Literature and Gospel Teachings.* New York: KTAV, 1970.

———. *The Synoptic Gospels.* 2 vols. 2nd ed. New York: KTAV, 1968.

Moore, G. F. *Judaism in the First Centuries of the Christian Era: The Age of the Tannaim.* 3 vols. Cambridge: Harvard University Press, 1954.

Moule, C. F. D. "'. . . As we forgive . . .': a Note on the Distinction between Deserts and Capacity in the Understanding of Forgiveness," in *Donum Gentilium: New Testament Studies in Honour of David Daube.* Edd. C. K. Barrett, E. Bammel and W. D. Davies. Oxford: Clarendon, 1978. 68–77.

———. "Fulfilment-Words in the New Testament: Use and Abuse." *NTS* 14 (1967–68):293–320.

———. "Uncomfortable Words: The Angry Word: Mt 5:21 f." *ExpTim* 81 (1969):10–13.

Mowinckel, S. *The Psalms in Israel's Worship.* 2 vols. Oxford: Blackwells, 1962.

Mussner, J. *Der Jakobusbrief.* HTKNT 13. Freiburg: Herder, 1964.

McArthur, H. K. *Understanding the Sermon on the Mount.* New York: Harpers, 1960.

McCasland, S. V. "Abba Father." *JBL* 72 (1953):79–91.

McConnell, R. S. *Law and Prophecy: The Authority and Use of the Old Testament in the Gospel of St. Matthew.* Basel: F. Reinhardt, 1969.

McNeile, A. H. *The Gospel According to St. Matthew.* London: Macmillan, 1915.

Nissen, A. *Gott und der Nächste im antiken Judentum.* WUNT 15. Tübingen: Mohr, 1974.

Nötscher, F. "Das Reich (Gottes) und seine Gerechtigkeit (Mt vi 33 vgl Lc xii 31). *Bib* 31 (1950):237–41.

Ott. W. *Gebet und Heil. Die Bedeutung der Gebetsparänese in der lukanischen Theologie.* SANT 12. Munich: Kösel, 1965.

Pedersen, J. *Israel: Its Life and Culture.* 2 vols. London: Oxford University Press, 1926–40.

Percy, E. *Die Botschaft Jesu: Eine traditionskritische und exegetische Untersuchung.* LUÅ n.s. 49. Lund: Gleerup, 1953.

Perrin, N. *The Kingdom of God in the Teaching of Jesus.* Philadelphia: Westminster, 1963.

Pesch, R. *Das Markusevangelium.* 2 vols. HTKNT 2. Freiburg: Herder, 1977.

Pesch, W. "Zur Exegese von Mt 6:19–21 und Lk 12:33–34." *Bib* 40 (1960):356–78.

Rad, G. von. *Das fünfte Buch Mose Deuteronomium.* ATD. 2nd ed. Göttingen: Vandenhoeck und Ruprecht, 1968.

———. "Die Stadt auf dem Berge." *EvT* 8 (1948–49):439–47.

Reiling, J. *Hermas and Christian Prophecy.* NovTSup 37. Leiden: Brill, 1973.

Religion in Geschichte und Gegenwart. 3rd ed. 6 vols. Ed. K. Galling. Tübingen: Mohr, 1957–62.

Riesenfeld, H. "Vom Schatzsammeln und Sorgen—ein Thema urchristlicher Paranese, zu Mt. VI, 19–34," in *Neotestamentlica et patristica. Eine Freundesgabe, O. Cullmann zu seinem 60. Geburtstag überreicht.* Leiden: Brill, 1962. 47–58.

Rigaux, B. "Révélation des Mystères et Perfection à Qumran et dans le Nouveau Testament." *NTS* 4 (1957–58):237–62.

Roloff, J. *Das Kerygma und der irdische Jesus.* Göttingen: Vandenhoeck und Ruprecht, 1970.

Rothfuchs, W. *Die Erfüllungszitate des Matthäus-Evangeliums.* BWANT 89. Stuttgart: Kohlhammer, 1969.

Sand, A. *Das Gesetz und die Propheten: Untersuchung zur Theologie des Evangeliums nach Matthäus.* Regensburg: Pustet, 1974.

Sanders, E. P. *Paul and Palestinian Judaism: A Comparison of Patterns of Religion.* Philadelphia: Fortress, 1977.

Schaller, B. "Ehescheidung und Wiederheirat in der synoptischen Tradition," in *Der Ruf Jesu und die Antwort der Gemeinde: Festschrift für J. Jeremias zum 70. Geburtstag.* Ed. E. Lohse. Göttingen: Vandenhoeck und Ruprecht, 1970. 226–46.

Schechter, S. "Some Rabbinic Parallels to the New Testament." *JQR* 12 (1900):415–33.

Schlatter, A. *Der Evangelist Matthäus.* Stuttgart: Calwer, 1948.

Schmauch, W. "Die Komposition des Matthäus-Evangeliums in ihrer Bedeutung für seine Interpretation," in . . . *zu achten aufs Wort: Ausgewählte Arbeiten.* Ed. W. C. Schmauch. Göttingen: Vandenhoeck und Ruprecht, 1967. 64–87.

Schmid, J. *Das Evangelium nach Lukas.* RNT 3. 4th ed. Regensburg: Pustet, 1960.

———. *Das Evangelium nach Matthäus.* RNT 1. Regensburg: Pustet, 1965.

Schmidt, H. "Grüsse und Glückwünsche im Psalter." *TSK* 103 (1931):141–50.

Schnackenburg, R. "Die Ehe nach dem Neuen Testament," in *Schriften zum Neuen Testament.* Munich: Kösel, 1971.

———. *God's Rule and Kingdom.* New York: Herder and Herder, 1963.

———. "Ihr seid das Salz der Erde, das Licht der Welt. Zu Matthäus 5, 13–16," in *Mélanges Eugène Tisserant.* Vatican City: Biblioteca Apostolica Vaticana, 1964. 365–87.

Schneider, G. *Botschaft der Bergpredigt.* Aschaffenberg: Pattloch, 1969.

Schniewind, J. *Das Evangelium nach Matthäus.* NTD 2. Göttingen: Vandenhoeck und Ruprecht, 1964.

Schoeps, H.-J. "Die jüdischen Prophetenmorde," in *Aus frühchristlicher Zeit: Religionsgeschichtliche Untersuchungen.* Tübingen: Mohr, 1950. 126–43.

Schubert, K. "The Sermon on the Mount and the Qumran Texts," in *The Scrolls and the New Testament.* Ed. K. Stendahl. London: SCM, 1957.

Schulz, S. *Q: Die Spruchquelle der Evangelisten.* Zurich: Theologischer Verlag, 1972.

Schürmann, H. *Das Gebet des Herrn.* Freiburg: Herder, 1958.

———. *Das Lukasevangelium.* HTKNT 3, 1. Freiburg: Herder, 1969.

———. *Traditionsgeschichtliche Untersuchungen den synoptischen Evangelien.* Düsseldorf: Patmos, 1968.

Schweitzer, A. *The Mystery of the Kingdom of God.* New York: Dodd and Mead, 1914.

Schweizer, E. "Formgeschichtliches zu den Seligpreisungen." *NTS* 19 (1972–73):121–26.

———. *The Good News According to Matthew.* Atlanta: John Knox, 1975.

———. "Matth. 5, 17–20—Anmerkungen zum Gesetzesverständnis des Matthäus," in *Neotestamentica.* Zurich: Zwingli, 1963. 393–406.

———. "Noch einmal Mt 5, 17–20," in *Das Wort und die Wörter. Festschrift G. Friedrich.* Stuttgart: Kohlhammer, 1973. 69–73.

———. "Observance of the Law and Charismatic Activity in Matthew." *NTS* 16 (1969–70):213–30.

Seitz, O. J. F. "Love Your Enemies; the Historical Setting of Matthew V:43f; Luke VI:27f." *NTS* 16 (1969–70):39–54.

Selwyn, E. G. *The First Epistle of St. Peter.* London: Macmillan, 1969.

Sjoberg, E. "Das Licht in dir. Zu Deutung vom Matth. 6,22f Par." *ST* 5 (1951):89–105.

Skeat, T. C. "The Lilies of the Field." *ZNW* 37 (1938):211–14.

Smith, M. "Mt. 5:43: 'Hate thy Enemy.'" *HTR* 45 (1952):71–73.

———. *Tannaitic Parallels to the Gospels.* SBLMS 6. Philadelphia: Society of Biblical Literature, 1961.

Soiron, T. *Die Bergpredigt Jesu. Formgeschichtliche, exegetische und theologische Erklärung.* Freiburg: Herder, 1941.

Sparks, H. F. D. "The Semitisms of St Luke's Gospel." *JTS* 44 (1943):129–38.

Staab, K. "Die Unauflösigkeit der Ehe und die Ehebruchklauseln," in *Festschrift für E. Eichmann.* Paderborn: Schöningh, 1940. 435–52.

Stählin, G. "Zum Gebrauch von Beteuerungsformeln im Neuen Testament." *NovT* 5 (1962):115–43.

Stange, C. "Zur Ethik der Bergpredigt." *ZST* 2 (1924–25):37–74.

Staudinger, J. *Die Bergpredigt.* Vienna: Herder, 1957.

Steck, O. H. *Israel und das gewaltsame Geschick der Propheten: Untersuchungen zur Überlieferung des deuteronomistischen Geschichtsbildes im Alten Testament, Spätjudentum und Urchristentum.* WMANT 23. Neukirchen: Neukirchener Verlag, 1967.

Stendahl, K. "Hate, Non-Retaliation, and Love. 1 QS X, 17–20 and Romans 12:19–21." *HTR* 55 (1962):343–55.

Stonehouse, N. B. *The Witness of Matthew and Mark to Christ.* Grand Rapids: Eerdmans, 1944.

Strack, H. L., and Billerbeck, P. *Kommentar zum Neuen Testament aus Talmud und Midrasch.* 6 vols. Munich: Beck, 1926–61.

Strecker, G. "Die Antithesen der Bergpredigt. (Mt 5,21–48 par)." *ZNW* 69 (1978):37–72.

———. "Die Makarismen der Bergpredigt." *NTS* 17 (1970–71):255–75.

———. *Der Weg der Gerechtigkeit.* 2nd ed. Göttingen: Vandenhoeck und Ruprecht, 1966.

Streeter, B. H. *The Four Gospels: A Study of Origins.* London: Macmillan, 1926.

Strobel, A. "Der Berg der Offenbarung (Mt 28:16; Apg 1:12)," in *Verborum Veritas, Festschrift für G. Stählin.* Wuppertal: Brockhaus, 1970.

Stuhlmacher, P. *Historical Criticism and Theological Interpretation of Scripture.* Philadelphia: Fortress, 1977.

———. *Das paulinische Evangelium.* FRLANT 95. Göttingen: Vandenhoeck und Ruprecht, 1968.

———. "Zum Thema: Biblische Theologie des Neuen Testaments," in *Biblische Theologie Heute.* Ed. K. Haacker. Neukirchen: Neukirchener Verlag, 1977. 25–60.

Suggs, M. J. "The Antitheses as Redactional Products," in *Essays on the Love Commandment.* Ed. R. Fuller. Philadelphia: Fortress, 1978. 93–107.

———. *Wisdom, Christology and Law in Matthew's Gospel.* Cambridge: Harvard, 1970.

Suhl, A. "Der Davidssohn im Matthäus-Evangelium." *ZNW* 59 (1968):57–81.

Sutcliff, E. F. "Hatred at Qumran." *RQ* 7 (1960):345–56.

Taylor, V. *The Gospel According to St. Mark.* 2nd ed. New York: St. Martin's, 1966.

Torrey, C. C. *The Translations Made from the Original Aramaic Gospels.* New York: Macmillan, 1912.

Trilling, W. *Das Wahre Israel: Studien zur Theologie des Matthäus-Evangeliums.* 3rd ed. Munich: Kösel, 1964.

van Tilborg, S. *The Jewish Leaders in Matthew.* Leiden: Brill, 1972.

van Unnik, W. C. "A Classical Parallel to I Peter 2:14 and 20." *NTS* 2 (1955–56):198–202.

———. "Die Motivierung der Feindesliebe in Lk 6:32–35." *NovT* 8 (1966):284–300.

———. "The Teaching of Good Works in 1 Peter." *NTS* 1 (1954–55):92–110.

Waitz, H. "Das Problem der sogenannten Aposteldekrets." *ZKG* 55 (1956):227–63.

Walter, N. "Die Bearbeitung der Seligpreisungen durch Matthäus." *SE* IV (= *TU* 102). Berlin: Akademie, 1968. 4:246–58.

Weise, M. "Mt 5[21] f.—ein Zeugnis sakraler Rechtssprechung in der Urgemeinde." *ZNW* 49 (1958):116–23.

Weiss, J. *The History of Primitive Christianity.* 2 vols. Ed. F. C. Grant. New York: Wilson-Erickson, 1937.

Wildberger, H. "Die 'Sektenrolle' im Toten Meer." *EvT* 13 (1953):25–43.

Windisch, H. "Friedensbringer—Gottessöhn."*ZNW* 24 (1925):240–60.

———. *The Meaning of the Sermon on the Mount.* Philadelphia: Westminster, 1951.

Wrege, H. T. *Die Überlieferungsgeschichte der Bergpredigt.* WUNT 9. Tübingen: Mohr, 1968.

Zahn, T. *Das Evangelium des Matthäus.* 2nd ed. Leipzig: Deichert, 1905.

Zimmerli, W. "Die Seligpreisungen der Bergpredigt und das Alte Testament," in *Donum Gentilicium: New Testament Studies in Honour of David Daube.* Edd. C. K. Barrett, E. Bammel and W. D. Davies. Oxford: Clarendon, 1978. 8–26.

———. "Zur Struktur der altestamentlichen Weisheit." *ZAW* 10 (1933):177–204.

SCRIPTURE INDEX

AUTHOR INDEX